Cashtown
York
Gettysburg
V   N   I   A
NSBORO GAP
Frederick
Monocacy
A
R
Y
Baltimore
Susquehanna R.
PP. 92
NEW
JERSEY
DELAWARE
Delaware
Bay
ll's Bluff
Arlington
Ft. Stevens
Washington
Alexandria
Run
Centreville
L
A
Annapolis
Manassas Junction
Patuxent R.
Chesapeake Bay
N
Fredericksburg
Potomac R.
m Church
Rappahannock R.
D
North Anna
Mattaponi R.
N   I   A
ellow Tavern
Mechanicsville
Gaines' Mill
Cold Harbor
Pamunkey R.
Richmond
Pines   Savage's Sta.
Glendale
Malvern Hill
Bermuda Hundred
Charles City
ff
ity Point
Harrison's Landing
Williamsburg
York R.
Ft.
Stedman
Yorktown
Petersburg
James R.
Atlantic Ocean
Fortress Monroe
Hampton Roads
MONITOR VS MERRIMAC
MARCH 9, 1862
Norfolk
Miles
0   10   20   30

Jefferson Davis: Confederate President

This portrait in oils of Jefferson Davis was painted by Daniel Huntington in 1874, nine years after the War Between the States. It was commissioned by the War Department and hung with portraits of other former United States Secretaries of War. It is now in the Pentagon and is here reproduced by permission of the Department of the Army.

JEFFERSON DAVIS

CONFEDERATE PRESIDENT

———◈———

BY HUDSON STRODE

———◈———

Harcourt, Brace and Company

NEW YORK

Hudson Strode established himself as a Southern historian with the publication in 1955 of his best-selling *Jefferson Davis: American Patriot,* the first volume of his brilliant portrait of the President of the Confederacy. In this present volume, he again demonstrates his remarkable ability to put the spark of life into one of the most fascinating figures in American history.

Dr. Strode is Prewitt Semmes, Jr. Professor of English at the University of Alabama, where he has lectured for many years on Shakespeare and conducted his famous class in creative writing, from which have emerged a number of promising young writers. He is also widely known for his authoritative interpretations of foreign countries, hailed by critics as unexcelled in their field.

For
THÉRÈSE

"It behooves every man who values liberty of conscience for himself, to resist invasions of it in the case of others."

    —THOMAS JEFFERSON *in a letter*
     to Benjamin Rush, 1803

"History, when the case is fully understood, will do justice to the men who have most suffered from hasty judgment and unjust censure."

    —JEFFERSON DAVIS *in a letter of*
     March 13, 1862

CONTENTS

INTRODUCTION

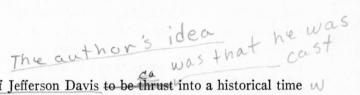

The author's idea was that he was cast

IT WAS the fate of Jefferson Davis to be thrust into a historical time
woefully out of joint and to be chosen to try to set it right for his side.

If Froissart is right, the most profitable thing in the world for the
understanding of human life is history; so the biography of a man who
played an important role in a particular period of history should be
enlightening. For this better understanding, I have combined the state-
craft and the military operations of a struggling new nation under
mighty handicaps with intimate glimpses of its leader's everyday life.
I have endeavored—however far I may have missed the mark—to devise what Ortega y Gasset calls "a unity of dramatic dynamism between the two elements, the I [of Jefferson Davis] and the world,
which make his life." In other words, I have sought to create that
sense of immediacy which gives impact to exciting events. Though I
describe the times in which Jefferson Davis lived, the emphasis is
on the man himself, what he sees, thinks, and feels, while history is
occurring.

Probing into the mind and heart of Jefferson Davis these past seven
years, I have come up with ideas at variance with the clichés long
accepted by a large portion of the public. These stereotyped judgments
had their origin in his Southern as well as his Northern foes; they
have been hardened into acceptance by the thoughtless repetitions of
decades. Shelby Foote discovered the same thing in his years of research for *The Civil War*. "I have never in my life been so amazed
at anything as at the results of my research on Davis," he wrote me.
"All my reading life I have heard things told as fact, and printed as
such by reputable historians, which I now find were invented from

the whole cloth. It is as if a gigantic conspiracy had been formed for the purpose of misrepresenting Davis so as to hide his true nature from the world."

Again and again I have found that controversies in which Jefferson Davis was involved have been completely misrepresented, though all the evidence is there to be read by anyone willing to take the trouble. The stale accusation that he "meddled" with his generals cannot be sustained by reading the *Official Records* or Dunbar Rowland's ten-volume collection of personal and official letters. Davis was the victim of vituperative fabrications by inimical editors and a few disappointed generals. These fabrications have seeped down the years into the minds of students on both sides of Mason and Dixon's line.

Though Jefferson Davis is still a controversial figure, there is virtually no disagreement today as to whether or not he was the one best fitted for the position of President of the Confederacy. As Professor Kenneth Stampp of the University of California declared in 1955: "Those who contend that the South made a mistake by elevating Davis to the Presidency of the Confederacy have not yet come up with a man who would have done a better job in that difficult position." Even North Carolina's acid Robert Winston wrote in 1930: "Undoubtedly Davis was fitted for the job—no one better. Rhett, Yancey, Cobb, Toombs —these were of small calibre; they could not have stood up against the world for four devastating years and taken punishment." With remarkable insight and fairness, the Boston historian Charles Francis Adams, grandson of John Quincy and son of the eminent wartime Minister to England, affirmed: "No fatal mistakes either of administration or strategy were made which can be fairly laid to his account. He did the best possible with the means that he had at his command."

In dealing with a period in which political stresses were at a maximum and war was raging on far-flung fields, the technical problems have been considerable. Because it is essential for the subject of a biography to be a dramatic projection, the selection of material used has continually posed questions.

When James Boswell finally confronted the mass of primary material he had gathered on Dr. Johnson, he was so overwhelmed that tears would stream uncontrollably in public. In the light of the voluminous material on Jefferson Davis, it is not hard to understand Boswell's emotional reaction. When I began writing this biography in June, 1951, I intended to make a one-volume study. But after initial researches from Colorado Springs to Washington, from New York to New Orleans, I found such a plethora of worthwhile data that two volumes seemed advisable. As I proceeded with the second volume, I realized that for an adequate portrait of Jefferson Davis and his times I needed three volumes. In this decision I had the moral backing of three experts in their fields: Dr. Allan Nevins, Mr. Bruce Catton, and the late Professor Frank Owsley. So I end this present volume in January, 1864. The third volume will take Jefferson Davis through the last fifteen months of the war and to his death in 1889.

As Mr. Catton frankly adds "The Story of the Union Side of the Civil War" to his title *This Hallowed Ground,* I present the struggle for Southern independence from the South's point of view.

In 1860, Horace Greeley wrote of Jefferson Davis as belonging "to a higher grade of public men." The Confederate President could never be swerved from the theme that conscience and moral law should govern all his political decisions. Once, in the United States Senate he had said impulsively, "What my heart tells me is right, nothing can prevail upon me not to do." Not the weight of the entire body politic could cause him to go against his honest conviction.

Good sense, however, was fundamental in Davis's make-up. This good sense revealed itself in his judgment, his taste, and in a rare acumen in practical affairs. Yet this good sense was interwoven with an extraordinary sensitivity, which held within itself the defects of its quality. His faults most often stressed are "pride" and "over-sensitivity." His pride was of a kind that belonged to heroes of Greek tragedy; Greeley wrote understandingly that Davis's "occasional unintentional arrogance revealed his consciousness of great commanding power." His sensitivity had its counterpart in his deep humanity—his compassion for all sufferings of the body and distresses of the mind. At times he was suffused with an unnamable sorrow, something beyond that caused by events, tragic or shoddy.

While he lacked the ruthlessness that generally dominates revolutionary leaders, Davis possessed real military gifts and had a remarkable insight into problems of strategy. General Lee told Burton Harrison that Davis was "the best military adviser he had ever consulted."

Strangely, one of the most persistent misconceptions about Jefferson Davis is his "coldness," which has been reiterated in countless monographs and tomes. Though he sometimes seemed to be distant and self-enclosed, he was really the warmest of men and such a friend as anyone would be fortunate to encounter in a lifelong search.

It is surprising to discover how many prominent men, by their own written testimony, "loved him as they never loved another man on earth." The burly Texan John Reagan wrote thus after fifty years in national public life. L. Q. C. Lamar, who became a Justice of the United States Supreme Court, declared, "I love and honor our Chief above all men." Not only scores of Southerners, but numerous Northerners, like General George W. Jones of Iowa, expressed their devotion to the man Jefferson Davis in unabashed superlatives.

Born with a temperament distinctly aristocratic, despite his modest origin, Jefferson Davis was the kind of aristocrat the common man intuitively likes and trusts. He had the charm to attract and the gift to give courage to the discouraged. The North admitted his "power to stimulate a mood for high deeds."

Believing with Heraclitus that "wisdom consists of saying what is true," Davis faced his fellow men of every kind with "the same look of dignified respect and sincerity, without a suggestion of premeditated caution." But he could detect sham quickly, and it was difficult for him to conceal his contempt for it. While courteous, he could not make himself charming to men in whom he detected dishonesty or hypocrisy. Self-seeking persons felt his silent disapproval; they hated him for making them esteem themselves less, and longed for his fall.

What has struck me perhaps more forcibly than anything else in my delving into facts is the struggle Davis had with difficult personalities among his compatriots. Dealing with certain ambitious, malicious, or misguided Southerners, both civil and military, consumed as much of his vital energy as fighting off the invading battalions from the North.

Though Davis lacked a certain political fluidity, he was aware that planned action needs constant modification. A firm adherent of the Constitution and State Rights, he believed in adjustment to changing circumstance. As he wrote Governor Zebulon Vance of North Carolina on July 14, 1863, "The officers of this Government have always been instructed to insist upon a rigid construction of the laws *only* where it appeared necessary."

Patience was not a quality inherent in Jefferson Davis; it came from years of cultivating self-control. When in pain, he was sometimes impatient, and, on occasions, irritable. His intense "holding in," how-

ever, could bring on agonizing neuralgic attacks. When in such discomfort from inflamed nerves that he could hardly sit still during
an interview, he strove to preserve an inner calm that gave him surpassing power and strength.

Davis was not ambitious in the accepted sense of the word. He felt
no necessity to extend his ego. In the political arena he had had almost
every high office thrust upon him. He accepted the appointment as
Secretary of War by Franklin Pierce with great reluctance. When he
left the United States Senate in January, 1861, he had earned a reputation unsurpassed by any contemporary then alive (Webster, Clay,
and Calhoun were dead). Davis certainly did not covet the Presidency
of the Confederacy. He took it only because the South, demanding
a man of vision and force whom it could trust, would have no one
else. As he ascended this new eminence to fame, he frankly prayed
for the support and guidance of a higher power.

Except for the ineffable consolation of a clear conscience, Jefferson
Davis was not to breathe freely for years to come. Beyond three days
of recuperation at an anonymous farm near Richmond in the late
summer of 1861, the President took no vacation during the war. And
never for one day was there a cessation of the stupendous problems
he had to face, nor the pestering daily annoyances of human experience. It is remarkable how he could walk in and out of the crashing
discords of the hour, and, through them all, maintain his spiritual
integrity.

As President of the Confederacy, Davis was continually torn between military and political needs. It was impossible for him to concentrate the armies as much as he desired, for each state was fervently
intent on protecting itself. Few could see, as he could, their country
as a whole. The average Southerner saw his state or his district; he
rarely pictured necessities several hundred miles from home. In almost
every phase of essential civil activity, as well as of war-making, there
was a glaring want of manpower in the Confederacy. As one soldier
complained, "The plagued Yankees have such an ability and habit
of outnumbering us."

In considering Jefferson Davis's abilities almost a century after
the War for Southern Independence, it might be remembered that
George Washington assumed his Presidential duties when his victorious little nation was at peace and he himself the land's supreme
hero. Yet the Father of His Country was subjected to such vicious
attacks that he cried out, "I would rather be in my grave than in

the Presidency." To Thomas Jefferson, he wrote: "Every act of my administration is tortured in such exaggerated and indecent terms as could scarcely be applied to Nero, to a notorious defaulter, or to a common pickpocket."

Abraham Lincoln inherited a government that had enjoyed established order for fourscore years and that possessed four times the white population of the Confederacy, together with an army, a navy, a merchant marine, arsenals, and manufactories representing an estimated fifty to one hundred times the industrial power of the South. It was far easier to be chief executive of a powerful country with a flag respected around the globe than to create a brand-new nation with few resources except cotton and courage.

When Jefferson Davis became President of the Confederacy, the infant republic had an appalling lack of arms and equipment, "not a powder mill, not a ship or a shipyard." In a paper read before the Massachusetts Historical Society in February, 1924, General Morris Schaff declared, "How he met this helpless chaotic state of affairs is a matter of history and the wonder of the world." "The armies he put in the field," the Union veteran said, "the great odds they had to meet and the victories they won, the four years he held the South loyal to its Cause amid the sorest trials, tell the story of his sagacity, energy, and inspiring, indomitable will."

While it is no part of this work to present a contrasting study of the character of Mr. Lincoln, as the chief antagonist on the Northern side, I touch upon him as Mr. Davis thought of him and read about him in the foreign press. To give weight to the impressions, I quote from Northern authorities such as the noted historian James Ford Rhodes and Lincoln's scholarly biographer Professor J. G. Randall, and from diarists like Gideon Welles, his Secretary of the Navy. In his assumption of a dictatorial role, I am aware that Mr. Lincoln believed the end justified the means—that at all cost the Union should be saved. In presenting the Southern point of view, I am not unmindful of the Northern feeling that the Union was everlasting because of changes in opinion that time had brought, even though on a historical, constitutional basis, the South was more accurate in interpretation.

That the War for Southern Independence was merely a struggle of the rich planters to keep their slaves is believed by few thinking persons today. In 1863, a British observer, Lieutenant Colonel Fremantle of the Coldstream Guards, discovered that "the natives [the poor farmers] were red-hot in favor of fighting for their independence to the last." When some uncomprehending Federal officer asked a ragged Confederate prisoner, obviously no slaveowner, why on earth *he* was fighting, the fellow looked him coolly in the eye and answered for the South with devastating simplicity: "Because y'all are down here."

As the war's centenary approaches, Southerners may need to be reminded that one reason why they can take such pride in their heritage is because Jefferson Davis was chosen President of the Confederacy. Senator John Daniel of Virginia put the whole matter simply when he said in 1890: "Had a man less sober-minded and less strong than Davis been in his place, the Confederacy would not only have gone down in material ruin—it would have been buried in disgrace."

Like the Greeks, Davis regarded honorable defeat as only less glorious than victory. To give up while there was the possibility of success would not only have been treasonous, but would have ended the struggle without honor. After her husband's death, Varina Davis wrote hopefully in her *Memoir:* "Posterity is the just and generous judge to whom Confederates look to write his honored name high on the shining lists of brave, self-sacrificing heroes."

When Colonel Crafts J. Wright, an admiring Union officer, was vigorously attempting to correct falsifications about the former President, Mr. Davis wrote him in 1877: "Truth *is* eternal, but as you indicate, it requires advocates and defenders." Since Robert E. Lee, the Confederate soldier, has been accepted as a national hero, one can hope that by the war centenary's end in 1965 all Americans may come to appreciate the true caliber of Jefferson Davis, the President. As John Keats declared, "A Man ought to have the Fame he deserves."

HUDSON STRODE

Cherokee Road
Tuscaloosa, Alabama
May 30, 1959

Jefferson Davis: Confederate President

CHAPTER I

A NEW NATION IS MADE
AS WAR LOOMS

A SLENDER MAN with fair hair turning gray walked to a window in his apartment in Montgomery's Exchange Hotel and glanced thoughtfully down upon the iron fountain flecked with gilt in the rising sun. Women and boys, white and colored, were filling pails with sparkling artesian water. In the early-morning light the figures made variegated changing patterns, like a kaleidoscope, as they departed by five different streets radiating, starlike, from the large open space that was too lopsided to be called either a plaza or a square. The broadest of the streets led up along a gentle incline east to Alabama's white-domed capitol set on green terraces, where just a fortnight ago the man had been inaugurated President of the newborn Confederacy.

Now Jefferson Davis had had only fourteen days in which to get a brand-new nation functioning before Abraham Lincoln was sworn in as President of the United States. He had been under a ceaseless strain of decisions, each more or less final in itself. With teeming problems pressing upon his brain, he had not slept well. On this fourth day of March, 1861, he was particularly concerned with what Mr. Lincoln would say in regard to peace or war between the North and the South.

Since Lincoln's election in November, Jefferson Davis, and the world as well, had been waiting for some pronouncement from the President-elect. Except to possibly a few close political friends, Lincoln had remained noncommittal in Springfield, giving out nothing to the press. His silence had raised great expectations of some profound pronouncements as soon as he started his tour to Washington. By coincidence, each man began his famous trip into history on February 11, the day

3

after Davis received news that the Confederacy's chief office had been thrust upon him and the day before Lincoln's fifty-second birthday.

In the hope of divining Lincoln's intent, Davis had followed, through the papers, his rival's progress and had carefully noted reports of his speeches. But from his speech in Cincinnati on February 12 until his arrival in Washington, the President-elect had said nothing one could hold to with any assurance. "The crisis," Lincoln declared pleasantly, "is all artificial." He enjoined his countrymen to keep cool, because nothing was going wrong. North and South would have to wait for the inaugural address to know—if one ever could know— what Mr. Lincoln really had in mind.

Davis was in almost total ignorance of the character of the Illinoisan. He read in the papers and heard people continually referring to the contrast between his own arrival to cheering crowds in Montgomery and Lincoln's stealthy entrance into Washington with only two heavily armed companions. According to all accounts, because Maryland was seething with secessionist sentiment the President-elect had been persuaded to make a secret journey from Harrisburg to Washington. Rumors had circulated that Lincoln would be assassinated as he passed through Baltimore from one railway station to the other. It had also been whispered that his special train would be derailed and hurtled down an embankment, where "a Baltimore barber and his gang" would finish him off. Old General Winfield Scott, greatly excited, had sent word to William H. Seward, who was to be Secretary of State, that Lincoln must change his travel schedule.

Lincoln placed his safety and his movements in the hands of a former Scottish barrelmaker named E. J. Allen, who, as Allan Pinkerton, was now a detective. Leaving his wife and official party in Harrisburg, Lincoln was whisked back by way of Philadelphia in a single-coach train, in which he and Ward Lamon, his law associate in Springfield, were the only passengers. In Philadelphia they were met by Pinkerton and driven across town to the P.W.&B. station. In the shadowy night, according to the friendly New York *Times,* the President-elect, disguised in a Scotch plaid cap, a bunchy muffler, and a very long military cloak,[1] was put aboard the sleeping car in the guise of an invalid.

Around six o'clock, when the train huffed into the Washington station, the conductor was surprised to see the rangy sick man, now re-

[1] The Scotch cap was later discredited as an invention of the reporter, but the incognito was never denied.

markably recovered, descend the car steps in "a slouch hat, a shawl, and a short overcoat." He walked off into the waiting room between his two wary-eyed protectors, Lamon and Pinkerton, whose coats bulged with concealed weapons.

Only one person, Senator Elihu Washburn of Illinois, was at the station to meet the incoming President of the United States. Apparently no one else in the station recognized the man who was to be acclaimed one of history's greats.

At Willard's Hotel, Senator Seward, who had barely missed being President himself, waited to welcome him. After a speculating glance, with perhaps a spicule of malice at his successful rival's embarrassment, he suavely felicitated Mr. Lincoln on his safe journey through disaffected Maryland.

To Davis, Lincoln's furtive entrance into Washington seemed as unnecessary as it must have been embarrassing. He had completely discounted rumors of any attempt in Baltimore to assassinate the Republican President, despite the threats. But the behavior of Marylanders the next afternoon, when the Presidential train did arrive— like *Hamlet* without Hamlet—made Davis hopeful that Maryland would soon join the Confederacy. The papers carried exciting stories, and Howell Cobb, President of the Provisional Congress, showed Davis a letter from I. K. Bowen stating that an estimated 10,000 persons were at the Baltimore station "to show their colors." "The moment the train arrived," he wrote, "supposing Lincoln was aboard, the most terrific cheers ever heard were sent up, three for the Southern Confederacy, three for 'gallant Jeff Davis,' and three groans for 'The Rail Splitter.'" "Had Lincoln been there," Bowen declared, "contrary to my preconceived opinions, he would have met with trouble."

During the interval between Mr. Lincoln's arrival at Washington and this fourth of March, when he would leave his hotel in a carriage with James Buchanan to be sworn in as President, Davis had often wished he could penetrate the enigma of this odd-looking man from Illinois, who had been born only a hundred miles from his own birthplace in Kentucky and some eight months later. He felt that, in a large measure, out of the convolutions of that one brain the destinies of both the Union and the Confederacy would be given direction. But Davis heard that Seward confidently expected to rule. And according to all the information he had received, Seward was now believing that the only possible policy was appeasement. The new Secretary of State was said to regret bitterly his famous "irrepressible conflict" phrase and to be willing to do everything in his might to nullify his own prediction. The London *Times* spoke of him as one whom "the convulsions of the country have terrified into moderation . . . terrified by the complete fulfilment of his own prophecy." Davis pondered the significant question: How powerful would Seward be in the new Administration?

In the weekend that preceded this Monday, March 4, a grim tension was evidenced throughout the South, in the Confederate Congress, in the hotel lobbies, and at women's gatherings. What would Mr. Lincoln's inaugural address bode? On Sunday the tenseness was felt even in the churches, where men and women made their private prayers for peace. President Davis had attended service at St. John's Episcopal Church, occupying the pew that had been specially marked for his family's use. The people who saw him took courage from his outward serenity. In his eyes there was an expression of fearless candor. Even the wiliest of churchgoing politicians might discern something incorruptible in him, a quality that could not be assailed or circumvented.

That Sunday night, on the eve of Lincoln's inauguration, while the Confederate capital, Montgomery, remained in suspenseful waiting, Washington was astir. Wild rumors echoing Baltimore circulated. Many men had sent their women and children from the city that afternoon to avoid no one knew what. All night, orderlies dashed about; "guard details were marching to all points of danger." Because of a whisper that the Capitol would be blown up, police searched in "sewers and secret places" for explosives. There was undoubted resentment to Mr. Lincoln's being inaugurated, as numerous prominent Southerners still in the United States capital reported. A private wire had been rigged to bring news from Washington directly to the Confederate Executive Offices in the plain brick building diagonally across the square from President Davis's hotel suite.

The fourth of March dawned clear in Washington, as it did in Montgomery; but up North the day turned bleak and disagreeable, with a blustery wind.

As telegraphic items were received, the apprehension Davis felt over the regime of a sectional Chief Executive, elected by a political party that made little secret of its active enmity to the South, was not mitigated by accounts of Lincoln's unprecedented "military" inauguration. In Washington, armed troops were "ostentatiously thrust everywhere upon the public attention." On roof tops along Pennsylvania

Avenue squads of sharpshooters were half concealed. A Northern gentleman, author of *The Diary of a Public Man* (reputedly Samuel Ward, brother of Julia Ward Howe), later confessed that he never felt such a sense of shame and mortification for his own country as he felt that day "in entering the Capitol through hedges of Marines armed to the teeth."

At a distance from the Capitol, old General Winfield Scott and older General John C. Wool were stationed in command of their respective flying batteries—the batteries whose guns had roared through the Mexican War and made possible the acquisition of California and the Southwest. Several Southern observers commented on the coincidence of those same cannon being set to protect Abraham Lincoln, who, during his one term in Congress, had so fulminated against the war that an indignant Illinois citizenry had refused to elect him to another term.

Virginia's Roger Pryor, who kept his seat in Congress until Mr. Lincoln's inauguration, felt that "on that mournful day a shadow and a fear hung over everything" and that no one was more oppressed by the gloom than the President himself. Everyone, from outgoing President Buchanan to the armed guard, seemed ill at ease. "In his uncontrollable agitation," old Chief Justice Roger B. Taney, who had sworn in eight former Presidents, now trembled at coming events and could hardly enunciate.

Mr. Lincoln was "pale and obviously nervous"; some alarmist friends had warned him that he might be shot while he spoke. The committee on arrangements had not made things comfortable for him; instead of a solid lectern, only a small rickety table had been provided. When the rangy man rose to read his address and took off his black stovepipe hat, there was not enough room for it on the table top. His longtime political enemy Stephen A. Douglas, who had made his way through the tight throng to the front row close beside the President, solved the difficulty by reaching forward, taking the hat, and accommodating it on his knees throughout the ceremony.

The crowd before the stand was not so large as had been expected. Though well behaved, it manifested little enthusiasm. Mr. Lincoln's midwestern voice, however, carried well above the wind, and he read with feeling and earnestness. As the laid-by sheets of his address began to ruffle with the gusts, he used his gold-headed California cane for a paperweight. All went quietly until suddenly a loud snap was followed by a crash, with "something like a struggle on the ground." Mr. Lincoln looked up, startled, as was everyone else. But it was only a broken tree bough, on which a venturesome spectator had crawled out too far and had sustained a hurtless tumble.

With keenest attention, Jefferson Davis studied the text of the inaugural address when it came in by special wire. He did not know that when Mr. Lincoln had submitted to his chosen Secretary of State the draft so carefully prepared in Springfield, Seward had urged him to delete the two last sentences, which he considered "too warlike," and then had suggested closing with "some words of affection . . . of calm and cheerful confidence." Lincoln had therefore scratched through the lines "You can forbear the assault upon it [the United States Government]; I can not shrink from the defense of it. With you, and not with me, is the solemn question of 'Shall it be peace, or a sword?'" Davis did not suspect that it was his onetime friend Seward who wrote the substitute famous last paragraph which, reworded by Lincoln, read: "We are not enemies, but friends. . . . Though passion may have strained, it must not break our bonds of affection. The mystic chords of memory, stretching from every battlefield, and patriot grave, to every living heart and hearthstone, all over this broad land, will yet swell the chorus of the Union, when again touched, as surely they will be, by the better angels of our nature."

At one other point in his address, Lincoln attempted to soothe the South: "I have no purpose, directly or indirectly, to interfere with the institution of slavery in the States where it exists. I believe I have no lawful right to do so, and I have no inclination to do so."

But he derided any constitutional right of secession. "I shall take care," he declared, ". . . that the laws of the Union be faithfully executed in all the States. . . . The power confided to me will be used to hold . . . the property and places belonging to the Government, and to collect the duties and imposts; *but beyond what may be necessary for these objects, there will be no invasion.*"

The last clause stood out in Davis's mind italicized as a sinister threat. Lincoln would not cause bloodshed *if* the Confederate States would permit Federal troops to reoccupy the Southern forts and to collect duties for the United States Treasury at customhouses in Confederate ports! Only two forts of importance to the South were still occupied by Federal garrisons: Sumter at Charleston and Pickens at Pensacola. For several weeks now, Federal tariffs had ceased to be collected in the seceded States, though feeble attempts had been made from ships stationed off Charleston Harbor. United States courts no longer held session in the Cotton States. Of all the Federal institutions, only the Post Office still continued to function and do business in its accustomed way.

Clear in Davis's memory were the often-quoted words Lincoln had uttered with conviction in 1848: "Any people whatever have the right to abolish the existing government, and form a new one that suits them better. This is a most valuable, a sacred right." Apparently now that he was in the top executive office, the new President had different ideas about the rights of the governed to choose their government.

Louis Wigfall, South Carolina-born Senator from Texas, dashed off a telegram to Governor Francis Pickens of South Carolina: "Inaugural means war. . . . There is strong ground for belief that reinforcements will be speedily sent [to Fort Sumter]. Be vigilant." The warning was relayed to Jefferson Davis.

When the Inaugural Ball was in progress in Washington that night, with Democrat Stephen Douglas escorting Mrs. Lincoln, who wore a bright blue gown, certain Southerners met in conference and sent a telegram to Montgomery. "We all agreed that it was Lincoln's purpose at once to attempt the collection of revenue, to enforce and hold Sumter and Pickens, and to retake the other places. He is a man of will and firmness. His cabinet will yield to him with alacrity." This judgment on Lincoln's character, which Davis remarked with sharp interest, was penetratingly shrewd, because the vast majority in the North seemed to believe that the new President would be managed by his Cabinet and that policy would largely be dictated by the more experienced Seward.

In the days that immediately followed, Davis noted that the two most important New York papers agreed on Lincoln's threat of coercion. He was deeply disappointed that Horace Greeley had had such a change of heart since his recent famous dictum that one section of the nation could not be pinned to the other by bayonets. Lincoln had sagely granted to the powerful *Tribune* the liberty to speak as the organ of the new administration, and now Greeley admired Lincoln's strength in threatening coercion, and declared the address was "right." The New York *Herald* agreed on the coercive threat, but it did not admire the speech. It affirmed, however, "the inaugural is not a crude performance—it abounds in traits of craft and cunning." The editor professed to discern "marks of indecision, and yet of strong coercive proclivities."

In the local Montgomery *Daily Advertiser,* President Davis read that its Washington correspondent found the inauguration peculiarly depressing. The Southern partisan noted "a lack of all manifestation of applause," [2] and claimed that "the anxious air of everyone, save the Abolitionists, gave the whole affair more the mourning appearance of a funeral than that of a joyful ceremonial."

In the same issue, Davis read a flattering editorial about himself: "All military movements should be under the [Confederate] President, and we are blessed by Providence with such a President that every Southern soldier may freely trust his honor and his country's safety in his hands. . . . Mr. Lincoln and the *Tribune* affect to believe that we are not in earnest. Mr. Davis' force will convince them of the contrary, and then we will have peace. In preparedness for war lies our safety, and we know, and the world will soon know, that the right man is in the right place, and that with our Hero President at the head of our Confederacy, we are invincible."

The Confederate President noted that the Border States, whose future actions would affect the very crux of the matter, seemed bewildered as to Mr. Lincoln's meaning, but were darkly suspicious. The *Enquirer* of Richmond, where the Virginia Convention was now in session debating secession, spoke of "the cool, unimpassioned, deliberate language of the fanatic." "The question 'Where shall Virginia go?'" it declared, "is answered by Mr. Lincoln. She must go *to war*."

The influential Baltimore *Sun* claimed that Lincoln's Inaugural "assumes despotic authority, and intimates the design to exercise that authority to any extent of war and bloodshed. If it means what it says, it is the knell and requiem of the Union and the death of hope." From Knoxville, in the pro-Union part of Tennessee, came a March 5 dispatch declaring: "President Lincoln's Inaugural is universally condemned, and, if reported correctly, will induce Tennessee to fight him to the bitter end."

As Jefferson Davis perused newspaper opinions, he unhappily reflected that it was all coming about much as he had expected, and for which dread exigency he had begun preparing immediately on taking office. He saw that the confidence of his Secretary of War, Leroy Pope Walker, who had jocosely agreed to wipe up with his handkerchief all the blood spilled because of secession, was considerably dashed. And Robert Barnwell Rhett's *Mercury*, which had insisted that the North would never initiate coercion, now gravely announced: "It is our wisest policy to accept the Inaugural as a declaration of war."

[2] Carl Sandburg speaks of "a slight ripple of applause."

One significant bit of information that none of the papers knew was that the very morning after the inauguration, before he had had one peaceful day in office, President Lincoln had been handed a disturbing dispatch from Major Robert Anderson. The commander of Fort Sumter reported that the Confederates were preparing batteries "to invest the fort" and that his food supplies were running out. Though he had a good supply of salt meat, bread could last only twenty-eight days, and other commodities, like beans, rice, and sugar, from eight to forty days.

Without knowledge of the immediate crisis facing Lincoln, because of the implied threats in his inaugural address, on Wednesday, March 6, the Confederate Congress took the precaution of authorizing President Davis, if necessary, to call out 100,000 volunteers to serve for twelve months, "to repel invasion, maintain the rightful possession of the Confederate States, and to secure public tranquility and independence against threatened assault."

T. C. De Leon was the first eyewitness to arrive from Washington after Mr. Lincoln's inauguration. The young man, who had known the Davises in the capital, had been asked by the Confederate Peace Commissioners to carry to Mr. Davis "their report of the inauguration and its effects."

Before presenting himself to the President, De Leon watched Mr. Davis enter the Exchange dining room to take his evening meal. He saw some of the more recent arrivals stare "with respectful curiosity" as the President moved to a place beside General Samuel Cooper, whom he had made his army's Adjutant General when the Northern-born West Pointer had resigned that same position in the United States Army. "Absently, but not discourteously," Davis acknowledged the general salutations and immediately began an absorbing conversation with Cooper, "leaving his supper untouched."

De Leon finally sent a card over to announce his arrival with the documents from the Peace Commissioners, whom the President had sent to Washington to arrange an amiable separation. After supper, Davis eagerly received him in his private parlor and began glancing through the wordy report. But shortly he threw the pages aside and began questioning the young man specifically. The Confederate President was interested in Mr. Lincoln's personal behavior; several times he asked if he had showed uneasiness. De Leon poured out what he had observed, and flavored his report with bits of Washington gossip.

and a few other extreme Southern radicals—the Constitution was regarded as "a model of wise, temperate and liberal statesmanship." Its indubitable intention was to perpetuate the fundamental principles of the Constitution of the United States. The peace-desiring New York *Herald's* judgment on the Confederate Constitution was very pleasing to Davis: "The new Constitution is the Constitution of the United States with various modifications and some very important and desirable improvements. We are free to say that the invaluable reforms enumerated should be adopted by the United States with or without a reunion of the seceded States, and as soon as possible. But why not accept them with the propositions of the Confederate States on slavery as a basis of reunion?"

On the evening of March 11, the Alabama Convention in a body called on the President. He received them in the public parlor of the Exchange with Vice-President Stephens, members of the Cabinet, and Alabama's Governor A. B. Moore. Judge W. M. Brooks, President of the Convention, made a flattering little speech, and Davis "responded eloquently," counseling firmness and "union among ourselves in defense of the position we have assumed before the world." Davis's emphasis on "union among ourselves" was a foretaste of four years' pleading with ambitious politicians and jealous generals to minimize personal interest for the good of the Confederacy.

Five days later, the three commissioners Davis had chosen to send to Europe, Dudley Mann, Pierre Rost, and William Yancey, received their instructions from Secretary of State Robert Toombs. They were to make clear the absolute constitutional right of the South to withdraw from the Union, and to emphasize the importance of trade with the Confederacy. They were to hint that if war were permitted to be launched against the Cotton States, the all-important commodity, cotton, would be cut off from British mills. Because slavery might be a stumbling block to recognition, since European repugnance to that institution was general, the commissioners were to touch the subject lightly, and call special attention to the provision in the Confederate Constitution that prohibited slave trade.

In sending William Yancey, a radical proslavery advocate, to England, many conservatives were of the opinion that the President had blundered. The eloquent agitator, they said, was hardly the person to impress Old World chancelleries. Though he had declined to be Attorney General, Yancey's claim to some reward could not be ignored, and he was, moreover, able, impressive-looking, and very persuasive.

As chairman of the Committee on Foreign Affairs, Robert Rhett had advocated a guarantee of twenty years of free trade as an exchange for recognition. To be freed from Northern domination, Rhett was willing to mortgage the South to Europe for twenty years. Perhaps Rhett's idea was good. But to Davis such a promise smacked of economic vassalage. Like a majority of Congressmen, he favored a very moderate tariff for purposes of needful revenue. Besides, Davis anticipated eventual establishment of all sorts of manufactories in the South, which he had been urging, unheeded, for a decade. If the all-important question of sovereignty recognition could be settled first, the President felt there would be little difficulty in agreeing on commercial treaties.

At the last hour, Rhett advised Yancey to resign from the diplomatic mission, because his power to treat was curtailed. Though Yancey did not resign, he departed in uncertain temper, carrying a handsome gold-headed cane, which admiring Montgomery ladies had presented to him, along with a bouquet of camellias.

For all his inspiring words, which stirred the Southern people to patriotic devotion and confidence, the President knew that early recognition by England and France was of prime importance to his success in building a nation. George Washington had had the great good fortune to receive the flaming support of the young democratic idealist Lafayette, who persuaded France to back his personal intervention. And the Colonies had had abroad a brilliant emissary in that homely prince of ambassadors Benjamin Franklin. Without France's timely intervention, the American Revolution would most probably have collapsed, in which case George Washington would not have immortal fame as the savior-father of his country.

Davis, who admired British culture, understood that the majority of the English were sympathetic with the Anglo-Saxon South rather than with the North, now infiltrated with many breeds of Continental emigrants. England was drawn to the South by some similarity of temperament, particularly in the resemblances to her own squirearchy, and she rejoiced for economic reasons in the Confederacy's leaning to free trade. Davis knew from history, however, that Her Majesty's Government was never moved by mere quixotic impulses, but was impelled largely by material and political motives. He did not believe that Britain would actually intervene to the point of armed assistance. But recognition of the Confederate States he did expect, and he hoped for it very soon.

In the game of diplomacy with England, Davis was aware that the

South held something that looked like an ace of trumps: raw cotton. The largest industry of the world's leading industrial nation was textile manufacture, and England got from the South approximately 80 per cent of her cotton supply. In 1860, her cotton business amounted to some £80,000,000; an estimated 4,500,000 people were dependent on the industry.

In January, 1861, *De Bow's Review* had declared that England was convinced she would be ruined if the South's cotton could not reach her. For almost a decade the idea had been waxing that cotton planting put the South in a commanding position. The famous slogan "Cotton is King" had originated in 1855, when David Christy, living in Cincinnati, published a little book called *Cotton Is King; or Slavery in the Light of Political Economy*. The phrase caught the imagination of Southerners and was repeated everywhere until finally it approached an incantation that produced a kind of hypnosis.

In the Senate in 1858, Davis had heard Senator James A. Hammond of South Carolina defy the North to make war on cotton, alias the South. "Without firing a gun," Hammond declared, "should they make war on us we could bring the whole world to our feet." "What would happen," he asked, "if the South refused to plant cotton for three years? England would topple headlong and carry the whole civilized world with her, save the South. No, you dare not make war on cotton. Cotton is king!"

The British economists themselves, in articles and charts, helped to fix in the minds of politicians and planters a belief in the sovereign power of cotton. The Northern mills, too, were dependent on Southern cotton, consuming in 1860 some 360,000,000 pounds, about a fourth that used in British industry.[3]

Though Jefferson Davis himself was never committed to an all-out advocacy of the King Cotton theory, he had a mass of evidence to make him believe in cotton as a mighty factor in foreign diplomacy. In the spring of 1861 "the belief in the power of cotton to force European intervention was almost universal." All Southern Governors supported the idea, as did most of the press, the majority of legislators,

[3] As Frank Owsley points out in his detailed *King Cotton Diplomacy*, Southern leaders did not accept the King Cotton theory until they had carefully considered the importance of cotton to England, France, and the Northern States. In 1859, he says, the South's exports, of which cotton was overwhelmingly foremost, amounted to $198,489,351, out of a total of $278,392,080 for the whole United States. The South was thus responsible for the bulk of America's medium of international trade, though the North profited through both intermediary wholesale trade and the lucrative shipping.

and the planters themselves. Davis's conservative good friends South Carolina's Robert Barnwell and R. M. T. Hunter, Virginia's leader in Montgomery, both advocated keeping cotton at home, regardless of the strength or lack of strength of any blockade the Federals might institute.

In truth, however, in February, 1861, comparatively few bales lay in Southern warehouses; most of the previous fall's crop had been disposed of. Of the total 1860-61 crop officially reported at 3,849,000 bales, more than three million had already been sent abroad and to the North. The new crop had not been planted. Besides, the South had no ships of her own in which to transport cotton. England was not inclined to send her vessels to fetch the commodity; for currently her factories had more than an adequate supply, and the price of cotton cloth was in a slump.

At the first Cabinet meeting, according to Secretary of War Walker, Attorney General Benjamin suggested shipping all available cotton to England as a bank to be used in purchasing supplies and defense materials. But Walker himself was loudest in pooh-poohing the idea of actual armed conflict. Had not Horace Greeley himself, the Abolitionist and strong Unionist, denied the authority of the Federal Government to coerce the States? By April, however, Benjamin had become a champion of the King Cotton diplomacy and expressed himself in strong terms to foreign correspondents and observers.

In his *Memminger,* Bishop Capers answered Joseph E. Johnston's charge in 1874 that the financial policy of the Confederacy failed because of the Administration's lack of forethought. To Johnston's absurd assertion that "it would have been easy" (from March to the blockade of May) "to ship and convert into money four or five million bales of cotton," Capers declared the General's accusation of administrative failure "resolves itself in a fleet of phantom ships loaded with phantom cotton."

The subject of cotton was thoroughly discussed by the Cabinet. Though doubting the full magic potentialities claimed for the white gold, the President agreed with the decision of his Cabinet and the will of the vast majority. Anyhow, the disposition of cotton was related to the Department of Finance, and finance had never been a speciality of Jefferson Davis. He would have to let the financial policy of his government be largely directed by men more experienced in business than himself.

Although he had desired Robert Toombs, a successful man of affairs, for his Secretary of the Treasury, he had been persuaded to give the post to Charleston's C. G. Memminger, who bore a high reputation as a banker and whose integrity was unimpeachable. At first, though it started with a bare cupboard, the Confederacy had little difficulty about finances. In response to Memminger's call for an immediate first loan of five million dollars, subscribers answered with bids of eight million, all at par or above. The credit of the Confederate Government was good, so strong, in fact, that treasury notes could be exchanged for gold; no serious decline was to occur until December. Because the Provisional Congress was not inclined to vote a special defense tax, Memminger later had to resort to the expediency of fiat money, which simply meant that paper currency was made legal tender by fiat or law. It was not backed by gold or silver, and not necessarily redeemable in the coin of the realm.

The fiat method of raising funds was a rather surprising one coming from Memminger, who was a most conservative banker. But if the Confederacy were recognized by England and France, as President Davis expected, the paper accepted in faith would be good. If the Confederacy had secured her independence, the fiat expediency would have succeeded.

The President had daily informal conferences with one or two of his Cabinet members as well as regular meetings. In three of his Cabinet, Davis felt confidence: Judah P. Benjamin, the Attorney General, later Secretary of War and of State; Stephen R. Mallory, the Secretary of the Navy; John H. Reagan, the Postmaster General. Benjamin's subtle brilliance was founded on solid knowledge and cultivated scholarship. Mallory, who had been chairman of the Committee on Naval Affairs in the United States Senate, knew as much about ships as any man in the South. Reagan, the hulking Texan, who reminded some of an ox-team driver, was unswervingly loyal to the President, though they often disagreed. These three were to remain in the Cabinet until the dissolution of the Confederacy in 1865.

Memminger, the successful Charleston banker, Davis respected, though he could never feel close to him. As the first Secretary of State, Robert Toombs chafed over having little to do while waiting to hear from the Confederate Commission in Europe. The ways and manners of Toombs were somewhat too flamboyant and imperious for Davis; and now people were saying that Bob Toombs would never get over not being chosen President. Davis liked the willing Leroy Pope

Walker, whom the Alabamians Yancey and Clement Clay had urged upon him, but he was not adequate for the position of Secretary of War. So, with his broad military knowledge, the President, as Commander in Chief, would form the military policy. And, as William E. Dodd has written, "the President very properly threw himself into the details of the War Department as completely as if he himself had been the Secretary of it." Though telegrams and important orders for supplies or reinforcements and troop movements would pass through his hands, Davis was tactfully careful that orders were sent out in Walker's name.

While Jefferson Davis was driving with all his powers at establishing a new nation, he and his wife were living in two rooms in the noisy, crowded Exchange Hotel. The three children had been left temporarily with Mrs. Davis's mother in New Orleans.

From a sprawling town of 8,000, Montgomery's population had swelled to twice that number in a fortnight. Besides politicians seeking sinecures, it held a goodly proportion of the Cotton States' foremost politicians, as well as officers recently resigned from the United States Army, and eager youths bent on enlisting. Accommodations were extremely hard to obtain. The smaller hostelries, as well as the Exchange, were jam-packed. Even the meanest boardinghouses were doing more than capacity business. Many of the leading families were taking hand-picked paying guests. A few first-rate boardinghouses, like Mrs. Cleveland's, catered only to gentlemen who had been distinguished in Washington: Vice-President Alexander Stephens, Attorney General Judah P. Benjamin, and Secretary of State Robert Toombs gave her patronage.

Though the President was forced to decline almost all social invitations because of the pressure of work, his Cabinet officers and certain members of the Provisional Congress were wined and dined by Montgomery's fifty best families. Davis would take an occasional hour off in the late afternoon to ride horseback about the pleasant riverside town set in groves of oak, hickory, pine, and magnolia.

Jefferson Davis, who never cared greatly for cities, found the little Confederate capital quite agreeable. Strategically located on the broad Alabama River that flowed to the Gulf, the town, incorporated in 1819, was in 1861 one of the most affluent cotton centers of the deep South. After Andrew Jackson had won the decisive victory over the Creek Indians at Horseshoe Bend in 1814, well-to-do young planters from Virginia and the Carolinas had come into Alabama, bringing with them

cultural amenities, as well as slaves. Many had settled in Montgomery County, which lay in the center of the Black Belt, that irregu-
lar band of rich black soil, about a hundred miles in width, stretching
from the Atlantic to the Mississippi River. As quality attracts quality,
high-toned South Carolinians and Virginians, who came in the '40's
and '50's, found many of their kind already settled in the county.

Planters had built tall white town houses, and many of their sons
had become well to do from law practice, banking, and commerce.
Though the general tone of society was provincial, ingrained family
tradition and pride in good living were obvious. Davis had hoped
that the executive mansion that had been chosen would suit his wife,
who had so relished diplomatic society in Washington. While the place
was not even faintly comparable to the White House in Washington, it
was, as Mrs. Davis deemed it, "a gentleman's residence." Conveniently located at the corner of Bibb and Lee Streets,[4] it was only a
short walk from the Exchange Hotel and the Executive Offices. It was
a large two-story white house with green shutters. An ornamental white
iron fence surrounded a small green lawn. On the ground floor, two
parlors and a spacious dining room were on the left of the reception
hall; the three rooms on the right included a library and two master
bedrooms. Behind the dining room, Varina Davis was pleased to find
commodious serving pantries for large-scale entertaining. Beyond
the detached kitchen lay a vegetable garden and extensive stables,
which would stall the mounts used by various Cabinet members, as
well as Mr. Davis's saddle horse and Mrs. Davis's carriage horses.
Since the place was to be rented furnished—at $5,000 a year—the
President's lady made notes of the extras in the way of silver, china,
and linen she should fetch from Brierfield, the Davises' home in Mississippi, while the house was being redecorated.

The balmy weather of Jefferson Davis's inauguration day continued
into mid-March. Flowers bloomed in every Montgomery garden. The
ladies kept the Davis suite filled with fragrant narcissuses, Roman
hyacinths, and japonicas. In the hotel parlors, Mrs. Davis received
callers continually. Among the visitors were warm friends from Washington, like Mary Chesnut, whose husband, James Chesnut, Jr., recent
United States Senator from South Carolina, was now a special adviser

[4] In 1920 the house was moved to Washington Street, across from the Capitol, and is
now a museum known as The First White House of the Confederacy, furnished with
many authentic Davis pieces and personal effects of the President.

to the President. "She met me with open arms," Mrs. Chesnut wrote. "We did not allude to anything by which we are surrounded. We eschewed politics." But the hotel lobby, jammed night and day with office seekers, was a pandemonium of gesticulating politicians.

With a statesman's skill, in a few short weeks Jefferson Davis, according to an admiring editor, had "moulded the revolutionary party into a model government." Both civil and military departments had been set in operation with remarkable rapidity. The captured Federal forts were put in order. Depots for medicines and soldier's clothing, as well as ordnance, were established. The gilded youth of the aristocracy were going cheerfully into volunteer ranks, side by side with hillbillies, demonstrating that this was not a rich man's struggle, but a stand for independence.

A traveler from Tennessee reported in Nashville that farmers were acceding to the plea to reduce cotton acreage and plant cereals and other foodstuffs. Planters made donations of provisions for encampments. Banks offered loans in large amounts. The presidents of all Southern railroads came in convention to Montgomery and offered Jefferson Davis the use of their lines for transporting troops at half-fare, taking Confederate bonds in payment. Montgomery churches were kept open every day; women from the town and the county gathered in them to sew on rough uniforms, while their colored maids, clustered on the porches or under shade trees, plied their needles at the same tasks as their mistresses, pausing sometimes to drink a dipperful of iced lemonade or to note new units of recruits marching to martial music.

At the end of March, harmony and enthusiastic good will seemed to pervade the seven seceded states. A New Orleans paper reported that a District of Davis, like the District of Columbia, would be created as soon as the permanent Confederate capital was selected. In Charleston, a purchased vessel, readied for defense, was rechristened the *Lady Davis* in compliment to the President's wife. The people, De Leon wrote, were perfectly content to think that the government was in the hollow of Mr. Davis's hand.

Even from northern latitudes, Davis received scattered tokens of esteem. The Bangor (Maine) *Union* excoriated its rival, the *Whig,* for urging that the official vote by which the trustees of Bowdoin College had conferred an honorary degree on "traitor Jefferson Davis" should be expunged from the records. Championing the Confederate President in ringing affirmatives on April 3, the indignant *Union* declared:

No language can express the loathing that every brave and honourable man must feel for those contemptible and sneaking cowards who could for a moment entertain or recommend such an idea. . . . What more dastardly act than to creep within the sacred precincts of a college to stab the character of a man whose character is unblemished before the world.

Jefferson Davis a traitor! What statesman in the whole history of America has lived a purer or more upright life than he? Apply to the survivors of Buena Vista, and ask them is Jefferson Davis a traitor? . . .

Bowdoin College never more justly bestowed a degree than that conferred upon him; and it will be a long day before her trustees will become so bigoted, as to strike from their roll of honor the brightest name upon it.

The President was touched that he still had such admiring Northern friends. He recalled that summer of 1855 among the hospitable people of Maine, where he and Varina had been "accepted" with such heart-warming courtesy.

On the whole, one month after his own inauguration, Jefferson Davis began to feel a bit more easy about the Lincoln Administration. With keenly realistic eye, however, he saw ponderous difficulties before him. But, he reflected, if war *could* be averted during Lincoln's term, then the Confederacy was a fixed fact and might look to a future of worthy achievement and renown. Most observers from Washington insisted that Seward "was in the ascendancy" and that everyone thought him "the friend of peace." Though from experience Davis knew that the adroit Seward was not to be trusted too far, he believed that his former friend would never favor warlike aggression.

The Confederate President was deeply gratified when the North's Number One Democrat boldly took the stand for peace. On March 25, Stephen A. Douglas proposed in the Senate "withdrawal of the garrisons from all forts within the limit of the States which had seceded, except those of remote Key West and Dry Tortugas, needful to the United States for coaling stations." He argued that Charleston was entitled to Sumter and Pensacola to Fort Pickens, unless the Washington Government intended to reduce the seceding states to subjection. "We cannot deny," he said, "that there is a Southern Confederacy *de facto,* in existence, with its capital at Montgomery. We may regret it. *I* regret it most profoundly, but I cannot deny the truth of the fact, painful and mortifying as it is. . . . I proclaim boldly the policy of those with whom I act. We are for peace." Thus the powerful Douglas, who could in no sense be suspected of sympathy with secession, spoke out vigorously against war, and at the same time he virtually "recognized" the Confederacy.

With the head of the Northern Democratic party and "Mr. Republican" Seward himself opposing coercion, Davis felt the radicals might have a hard time influencing President Lincoln to risk a fratricidal war, unless he himself was so inclined.

CHAPTER II

"VACILLATION AND DOUBLE-DEALING JUGGLERY"

THE WARM SPRING of 1861 in Alabama had brought unprecedented early fruition. On March 21, the Montgomery *Daily Mail* reported that Mrs. Janney had discovered the first ripe strawberry of the season. Soon Mr. Davis was receiving boxes of the luscious berries, which turned his thoughts to maturing fruits and vegetables at Brierfield. There was little time for nostalgia, however, for trouble from an unlikely source came almost simultaneously with the first strawberries. The President was dismayed at the lack of political tact exhibited by his Vice-President. In a rabble-rousing address at Savannah on March 20, Stephens had burst forth on the subject of Negro slavery, which Davis had been careful not to mention in his Inaugural. Stephens said:

> Many governments have been founded upon the principle of the subordination and serfdom of certain classes of the *same* race; such were, and are in violation of the laws of nature. Our system commits no such violation of nature's laws. With us, all of the white race, however high or low, rich or poor, are equal in the eye of the law. Not so with the negro. Subordination is his place. He, by nature, or by the curse against Cain, is fitted for that condition which he occupies in our system. . . . Our new government is founded on the opposite idea of the equality of races. Its foundations are laid, its corner-stone rests upon the great truth, that the negro is not equal to the white man.

To Davis's amazement, Stephens bypassed the all-important constitutional guarantee of State Rights and emphasized the institution of slavery. Could anything, he wondered, have been more calculated to damage the Confederate cause both in the North and abroad than his Vice-President's unfortunate speech? Abolitionists instantly seized

24

upon Stephens's sentiments with cries of outrage and began demanding drastic measures by the Lincoln administration. Jefferson Davis's efforts to promulgate the fact that State sovereignty was the paramount issue of secession, which he devoutly believed to the end of his life, were now discounted by Stephens's foolish and inopportune words.

Many Northern papers, which had been fairly quiescent about the South's withdrawal, even accepting the fact, now turned a glare of bad publicity on Stephens as spokesman for the whole region. Though calm voices like that of England's *Quarterly Review* might point out the absurdity of fixing the phrase of a single speaker expressing an individual view upon some millions of people, "the great majority of whom had nothing to do with slavery," temperate words were lost in a whirlwind of condemnation. Alexander Stephens's ill-advised speech helped launch the Sumter relief ships that were to start the war. But the Savannah harangue was by no means the worst trouble his Vice-President was to cause Jefferson Davis.

Stephens did not return to Montgomery from Savannah, but retired to his plantation at Crawfordsville, Georgia, to await events or the summons of the President. It had not occurred to Stephens that he was being indiscreet. He had evidence galore, he felt, that numerous Northerners believed as he did. For instance, William Tecumseh Sherman, West Pointer from Ohio, who had headed a boys' military school in Louisiana, "thought slavery a necessary institution." In December of 1859, when Abolitionist denunciations were rampant, Sherman had declared, "I would not, if I could, abolish or modify slavery." [1]

As a testimony of the good relations between the Negroes and the white people in the South, President Davis was pleased to receive a letter from a colored man written one week after Stephens's unfortunate Savannah speech. Dated March 27, it came from Bowman Seals, of Clayton, in Barbour County, a former slave who had been emancipated for meritorious conduct. Under the Alabama Guardian Act of 1853-54, he had chosen his former owner for his guardian.

To His Excellency the President of the Confederate States:
The undersigned, Bowman Seals, a free man of color, residing in the said county begs to offer his services in whatever capacity that may be deemed of most value in resisting the enemy now threatening to invade the country. My guardian D. M. Seals, Esqr., of this place approves of this offer. . . . I know enough of Yankees and of their treatment of the starving blacks

[1] W. E. Woodward, in *A New American History*, points up the opinions of numerous Federal officers regarding the Negro and slavery.

among them to understand that their war upon the South is prompted by no love of us, but only by envy and hatred, and by an intermeddling and domineering spirit. And I know, too, that if they were to succeed, instead of benefitting any race or individual here, they would only bring disorder and ruin upon all. . . . I am accustomed to the use of firearms and have been regarded as a good marksman; am a practical mechanic, and ready and willing to work or fight against enemies threatening with such evils the land where I have been brought up and protected. . . . I presume not to ask any office or emolument, but only that your Excellency . . . shall assign me some duty that may make me serviceable in its defense.

The President might have questioned the authenticity of such a letter, since some of the phrasing seemed beyond a former slave's capacity. Yet he had only to recall how well the Montgomery brothers, slaves on his brother Joseph's plantation, expressed themselves in writing; one of them Joseph had trained from a teen-age boy to act as his private secretary. And even if Mr. Seals had helped the colored man with the letter, the sentiments expressed reflected the attitude of many Southern Negroes toward "Yankees." [2]

Stephens's Savannah speech was particularly disturbing to the President, for he was already discouraged by the official reception of the Peace Commissioners he had sent to Washington a few days after his inauguration. While A. B. Roman, Martin J. Crawford, and John Forsyth had been royally welcomed by what remained of fashionable society, they had not been received by the Lincoln Administration. Davis had fully expected Lincoln or Seward to be willing to discuss matters in dispute "with dignity and honor" around a conference table.

But days passed, and the Commissioners were ignored, for President Lincoln took the position that the seceded states were not out of the Union. Finally, through the mediation of Justice Samuel Nelson and Justice John A. Campbell of the Supreme Court, the Secretary of State said he was prepared to talk with the Confederate emissaries "indirectly" through the Judges. So the Confederate President ordered that proper form and ceremony be waived and that they confer with an intermediary. Seward was most courteous and reassuring. His government had only peaceful intentions, he insisted; Fort Sumter would certainly be evacuated.

[2] Whatever response the President made to Bowman Seals's offer of services has not come to light, but the freedman's letter was printed in the Clayton (Alabama) *Banner* of April 18, 1861, and quoted in a Master's thesis, *The Free Negro in Alabama, 1819 to 1861,* by Lewy Dorman in 1916 at the University of Alabama.

On March 9, the *National Republican* had announced that the garrison would be withdrawn from Fort Sumter. This information may have been put out as a "feeler," for Lincoln made note that it "agitated the Republicans to opposition." But the commissioners informed the Montgomery Government that despite the views of the "stiff-backed" new President, they found Northern public sentiment inclined strongly to peace, even at the price of final separation.

Justice Nelson, a New Yorker, visited three Cabinet members—Seward, Salmon P. Chase, and Edward Bates—to dissuade them from adopting any policy of coercion. He had carefully examined the laws of the United States, he said, and, after consulting Chief Justice Taney, he had concluded that coercion could not be effected by the Executive Department without very serious violations of the Constitution and the United States statutes.

Justice Campbell, an Alabamian, asked the Secretary of State what he should write President Davis about Sumter and Fort Pickens. Seward authorized Campbell to say that before the letter reached Mr. Davis he would learn that the order for the evacuation of Sumter had been made. He said that no change would be made in the status of Fort Pickens, which was already bound by an armistice arranged under Buchanan. The assurance, which Campbell gave the commissioners orally in Washington, was sent by mail to the Confederate President.

Having been promised by Seward that the Federal Government would order the evacuation of Sumter within a few days after March 15, Davis had his Secretary of War forward the news to Brigadier General P. G. T. Beauregard, whom he had put in charge of the coastal defenses at Charleston. A West Point graduate, Beauregard had served as an engineer on General Scott's staff during the war with Mexico. Late in 1860, he had been appointed superintendent of the United States Military Academy, but because he openly declared his intention of following Louisiana if she seceded, his transfer was ordered five days after he assumed his duties. In January he had resigned from the Federal Army; and, on February 10, he had promptly sent Davis congratulations on his being chosen President, asking, at the same time, for a commission in the Confederate Army. His brother-in-law, John Slidell, and other prominent Louisiana politicians had recommended him for a brigadier.

Six days after Davis's inauguration, Major Beauregard had arrived in Montgomery, where he was warmly received by the President. Decidedly Latin in type, Beauregard was a handsome man, with olive complexion, black hair, and heavy-lidded eyes in which "intense fires of ambition were banked." His expression was both impassive and keen. Exuding an air of uncommon self-confidence, Beauregard's bearing had more than a soupçon of the imperious. Napoleon was his idol.

In a conference that lasted far into the night, the President had asked Beauregard to take command at Charleston and strengthen the batteries surrounding Fort Sumter. The next morning he sent him a commission of Brigadier General. In a glowing state of mind, Beauregard had reached Charleston on March 3 and assumed command of the volunteers in Charleston the day of Lincoln's inauguration.

Davis found Beauregard's reports of work progress good. But five days after Seward's promise, when no evacuation had taken place, Beauregard reported to Montgomery that instead of preparing to depart, Major Robert Anderson, his former instructor in artillery, appeared to be strengthening Fort Sumter's defenses. Confronted with this relayed intelligence, Judge Campbell again approached Seward, whom he found "buoyant and sanguine in his reassurances." Seward spoke with confidence of his ability to carry through his peaceful policy. And he promised that if Lincoln and his Cabinet should institute any change in plan in regard to Sumter, Campbell and the commissoners would be straightway informed.

Naturally Davis could not fathom the secret courses in Washington, but he knew there was division of opinion, which apparently lay strongly on the side of peace. According to his Secretary of the Navy, Gideon Welles, Mr. Lincoln was at first averse to offensive measures and desired to avoid them. He had asked General Scott to prepare a statement about Fort Sumter. "Scott was decidedly opposed," wrote Mr. Welles, "to any attempt to relieve Major Anderson. The Navy, he was confident, could not do it, and an army of at least 20,000 men would be necessary to effect it. We had no such army, and the government could not collect and arm one before the garrison would starve." But Montgomery Blair "warned the President that the abandonment of Sumter would be justly considered by the people, by the world, by history, as treason to the country." On the other hand, Mr. Lincoln was aware that a repulsed attempt would bring ridicule on his Administration similar to *The Star of the West* incident under President Buchanan. If he sent an expedition, it would have to be a strong one.

General Scott had already written out an order to Major Anderson, which he hoped the President would let him send.

You will, after communicating your purpose to His Excellency, the Governor of So. Carolina, engage suitable water transportation & peacefully evacuate Fort Sumter . . . [and] with your entire command embark for New York.[3]

But Lincoln withheld the order. Dissatisfied with Scott's opinion, he sent Gustavus Vasa Fox, a Massachusetts textile agent who had formerly been a naval officer, at Fox's suggestion to Charleston to judge the probability of successfully reinforcing Sumter.

On the pledge that he had come on pacific purposes, Fox was permitted by Governor Pickens to visit the fortress on March 21. President Davis was duly informed. At Sumter, without taking Major Anderson into his confidence, Fox made notes and secretly matured his own plans of supplying and reinforcing the island. When he returned to Washington, he enthusiastically expounded his scheme to Lincoln. Fox was eager to lead the venture. The President sent him secretly to New York to begin exploratory preparations for a relief expedition.

A few days after Fox's "pacific" visit, Davis learned from Governor Pickens that Lincoln had also sent to Charleston, as his confidential agent, his Springfield friend Ward Lamon. Lamon informed the Governor that he "had come to try to arrange for a removal of the garrison." On March 25, Pickens let this second emissary go to Sumter, presumably to tell Anderson to prepare for removal. On his return, Lamon asked the Governor if a war vessel might remove the Federal troops. Pickens replied that no war vessel could be permitted in the harbor on any terms. Lamon then said he believed Major Anderson would prefer an ordinary steamer. He hoped to return in a few days to remove the garrison.

The two visits by Lincoln's personal emissaries and the word of his Secretary of State seemed on the surface to evidence good intentions. Yet Davis was disquieted by the delay in evacuating; fifteen days had passed since Seward's original assurance that the troops would be withdrawn.

Lamon reported to the disappointed President Lincoln that the sole Union sympathizer in all of Charleston was old Judge James Louis Petigru, who had insisted from the first that secession would lead to

[3] The order may be found in *The Lincoln Papers,* edited by David Mearns (Vol. II, p. 476), which were made public only in 1948.

disaster. He also reported that Major Anderson strongly favored evacuation. Of all the high-ups in Lincoln's immediate political family, only the aggressive Montgomery Blair and the ambitious Gustavus Fox seemed stanch advocates of holding and strengthening the Charleston fort.

In Lincoln's first Cabinet poll, on March 16, both Secretary of War Simon Cameron and Secretary of the Navy Welles joined Seward in advising against a relief expedition. Secretary of the Interior Caleb B. Smith and Attorney General Bates also agreed that such a move would be unwise. In his note, Seward wrote: "Suppose the expedition successful, we have then a garrison in Fort Sumter that can defy assault for six months. What is it to do then? Is it to make war by opening its batteries and attempting to demolish the defenses of the Carolinians? . . . I would not initiate war to regain a useless and unnecessary position on the soil of the seceding States."

Welles asked in his memorandum: "By sending, or attempting to send provisions into Sumter, will not war be precipitated? It may be impossible to escape it under any course of policy that may be pursued, but I am not prepared to advise a course that would provoke hostilities." Chase gave half-hearted approbation to the idea, if the President were sure it would not inaugurate civil war. "If," he wrote, "the attempt will so inflame civil war as to involve an immediate necessity for the enlistment of armies and the expenditure of millions, I cannot advise it in the existing circumstances of the country and in the present condition of the national finances." [4] Only the Postmaster General, Montgomery Blair, voted in an unequivocal affirmative. Such a move, he avowed, would demonstrate firmness in the new administration.

After a state dinner on March 28, Lincoln asked his Cabinet to remain. He had just been advised by General Scott, he said, that Fort Pickens should be evacuated as well as Sumter. Montgomery Blair burst out in indignant denunciation. The President scheduled a Cabinet meeting for the next day. According to W. E. Smith, in *Blair Family*, when old Francis P. Blair, Sr., called at the White House next day, the President said he did not know whether or not he would withdraw Anderson's garrison. The imperious Blair admonished him sternly,

---

[4] J. G. Randall, in *The Civil War and Reconstruction*, says that Chase was really in favor of letting the lower states go in peace. In 1862, Chase wrote: "It is true that, prior to the attack on Fort Sumter, I shared a quite general opinion that it would be better to allow the seven States to try the experiment of a separate existence rather than incur the evils of a bloody war."

declaring that evacuation would be treason and would forfeit public confidence. His son, Montgomery, went to the Cabinet meeting prepared to hand in his resignation if Lincoln decided to abandon Sumter.

Again President Lincoln put the question of Fort Sumter to the Cabinet members. The answers, according to Dr. Randall, were "substantially the same," except that Welles shifted his position and was willing "to concur in the sending of provisions and reinforcements." Seward was still vehemently opposed.

Lincoln now had Blair, Welles, and (reservedly) Chase agreeing with him on the plan he had discussed with Fox, which the Captain was already implementing at the New York Navy Yard. Without majority Cabinet support, Mr. Lincoln made his decision, and penned the fateful order that was to cause the most bitter tragedy the American people have ever suffered.

To the Secretary of the Navy he handed this directive: "I desire that an expedition, to move by sea, be got ready to sail as early as the 6th of April next, the whole according to memorandum attached, and that you coöperate with the Secretary of War for that object." The memorandum designated specifically the warships *Pocahontas* and *Pawnee* and a revenue cutter, and specified that three hundred seamen and two hundred other men should be gathered at New York with all necessary equipment.

The South Carolinians were expecting a peaceful evacuation almost immediately after Lamon's visit. Mrs. Caroline Gilman of Charleston was so sure the crisis was over that she got a military pass to visit her summer place on Sullivan's Island and took a gardener down to arrange her flower beds. But the Charleston *Courier,* dubious at the delay, burst out: "It is time this game of procrastination and vacillation and doubledealing jugglery were stopped."

On April 1, Jefferson Davis observed that the Montgomery oaks were budded; the dogwood was at the height of bloom, and the air balmy with full-fledged spring. According to the *Daily Advertiser,* "a lovely sunny week" followed. So it was, with nature; but rarely was a calendar week more supercharged with tensions, in both Montgomery and Washington.

On that same first day of April, in a fantastic attempt to forestall an armed conflict, Secretary of State Seward laid an extraordinary document on Mr. Lincoln's desk. It was entitled "Some Thoughts for a President's Consideration." First, he chided the Chief Executive, who had declared that his "policy was to have no policy," for not making some declaration of policy. "We are at the end of a month's administration," Seward charged, "and yet without a policy, either domestic or foreign." Then he complained that the need to meet "applications for patronage" had taken precedence over "more grave matters." Once more he urged the termination of the occupation of Fort Sumter. And in a most radical proposal calculated to bring the seceded states back into the Union, he suggested that Lincoln should convene Congress and declare war against Spain or France "if satisfactory explanations are not received" for their meddling in Mexico and Santo Domingo. Seward felt that it was worth the drastic expedient of instigating a foreign war to unite the states and avoid "the irrepressible conflict" he had regrettably prognosticated. The Secretary of State suggested that if Lincoln would not direct a policy, he himself would not be averse to assuming such responsibility.

Mr. Lincoln, politely but firmly, wrote his overbold Secretary that whatever must be done, he himself must do it.

While Lincoln played a dilatory game concerning Fort Sumter, a general rumor of unprecedented activities in the New York Navy Yard was spreading. President Davis had his Secretary of War send instructions to General Beauregard to be prepared to meet a hostile force at any hour.

Davis had been keenly following the debates in the Virginia Convention, which was then considering secession. On April 4, to his sore disappointment, sentiment was 89 to 45 not to withdraw. The mountainous western counties were almost totally for the Union. But happily for Davis and less happily for Lincoln, the convention remained in session to await future events.

Those Virginia delegates in favor of Southern independence were saddened, because they believed that without the Border States to support it the Confederacy would be summarily crushed. Few, however, doubted that if hostilities actually began, Virginia would side with the South. Some ardent Virginia secessionists determined to bring "a popular pressure" on "the slow Montgomery government" to assault Sumter without further delay.

Fearing that the Sumter expedition, which was about ready to set forth, might cause Virginians to change their votes, President Lincoln conferred with Colonel John Baldwin, pro-Union leader of the Virginia Convention. According to reported testimony, Lincoln made a conditional suggestion to withdraw the Sumter garrison. "If you will go back to Richmond," Lincoln is credited with saying, "and get the Union majority to adjourn and go home without passing the ordinance of secession . . . I will take the responsibility of evacuating Sumter. . . . A State for a fort is no bad business." [5]

In his own account of the interview, however, Baldwin wrote that the President lamented the fact that the interview had come too late, but refused to credit Baldwin's prediction: "I tell you before God and man that if there is a gun fired at Sumter war is inevitable."

In that delightful first week of April, Jefferson Davis, burdened with a terrible sense of responsibility, could not rest. His appetite was gone, and Varina, who had returned to Brierfield, was not there to tempt him with the few palatable dishes the hotel could prepare. Contradictory rumors came thicker than telegrams.

On April 5, a Washington dispatch to the Montgomery *Daily Mail* announced: "The frigate *Powhatan* goes to sea tomorrow morning, fully equipped and provisioned, and will probably take three companies of troops. The impression at the Navy Yard is that Forts Sumter and Pickens are both to be *relieved*."

As the patience of the frustrated peace commissioners ran out, Judge Campbell wrote Seward a strong letter demanding to know whether the assurances of evacuation so often given were well- or ill-founded. On April 7, Seward answered in writing: "Faith as to Sumter fully kept. Wait and see." When the message was relayed to Jefferson Davis, he may have taken a modicum of hope from the cryptic words; but, still distrusting Seward, he was wary.

The very next day, a mysterious, unsigned telegram arrived in Charleston informing Governor Pickens that an immediate attempt would be made to relieve Sumter. It was supposedly sent by a newspaperman named James Harvey,[6] whom Seward was later to recommend as Minister to Portugal. That same evening, Robert Chew of the State Department called in person on Governor Pickens and read to him and General Beauregard a message that he said came from President Lincoln.

Pickens and Beauregard listened gravely as Chew read aloud the brief notification: "I am directed by the President of the United States

[5] The quotation appears in *Annual Report,* American Historical Association, 1915, p. 211. Baldwin's testimony of February 10, 1866, appears in House Reports, No. 30, of 39 Congress, first session.

[6] Harvey had sent previous telegrams to personal friends in Charleston assuring them Sumter would be evacuated.

to notify you to expect an attempt will be made to supply Fort Sumter with provisions only; and that if such an attempt be not resisted, no effort to throw in men, arms, or ammunition will be made, without further notice, or in case of an attack upon the fort."

The full instructions to Chew, dated April 6, may be read in the *Official Records:*

Sir—You will proceed directly to Charleston, South Carolina; and if, on your arrival there, the flag of the United States shall be flying over Fort Sumter, and the fort shall not have been attacked, you will procure an interview with Gov. Pickens and read him as follows: [Here was inserted the exact message Chew read aloud.]

After you shall have read this to Governor Pickens, deliver him the copy of it herein inclosed, and retain this letter yourself.

But if, on your arrival at Charleston, you shall ascertain that Fort Sumter shall have been already evacuated, or surrendered, by the United States force; or shall have been attacked by an opposing force, you will seek no interview with Gov. Pickens, but return here forthwith.

Before Chew reached Charleston, the relief expedition was on its way, and Seward's famous message, "Faith as to Sumter fully kept," had been relayed to the Confederate President. Did Mr. Seward half expect that Sumter would already have been evacuated?

The arrival of the expedition might have been expected shortly after the delivery of Lincoln's message, which would have given Beauregard little opportunity to get instructions from the Confederate Government. But President Davis had already advised him to be on the alert for a conflict, and his forces stood in readiness. In addition, because of cross-purposes within Lincoln's Cabinet, created by Seward's manipulations, and due to a severe storm at sea, the arrival of the Federal vessels was delayed.

As to the size of the so-called "relief" expedition, the historian James Ford Rhodes wrote: "Fox had arranged that it should consist of the war-ships *Powhatan, Pawnee, Pocahontas,* and *Harriet Lane*; the steam-tugs, *Uncle Ben, Yankee,* and *Freeborn*; and with the merchant ship *Baltic,* with two hundred men and the necessary supplies on board." It was altogether a formidable little armada that was to enter Charleston Harbor. The total number of men and cannon has been variously estimated, with figures running as high as two thousand men and sixty-odd guns, but according to the Federals' own statement, the relief expeditions consisted of "eight vessels, carrying twenty-six guns and about fourteen hundred men."

CHAPTER III

AWESOME DECISIONS AND SUMTER'S FALL

JEFFERSON DAVIS had reason for his conviction that the weight of Northern civilian opinion was mightily opposed to any move on Mr. Lincoln's part that would start a war. However, Martin Crawford had telegraphed Confederate Secretary of State Toombs that in the opinion of the Confederate Peace Commissioners Lincoln "did not have the courage to give the order of evacuation," because it might lose him popularity in the North. They believed that he was shifting responsibility to Major Anderson "by suffering him to be starved out."

Davis did not know that the Commander of Fort Sumter himself earnestly urged the Washington Government not to instigate coercive measures. Major Anderson had told Captain Fox that the fort could not be successfully supplied; and Mr. Lincoln's personal agent, Ward Lamon, had led Anderson to believe that the idea of "relief" had been abandoned. But on April 7, a communication from the War Department quite shattered Anderson's hope for peace. It was the first written word he had had from the Lincoln Government since the inauguration a month previous. General Scott had not been permitted to send his order of withdrawal. Neither President Lincoln nor his Secretary of War had written Anderson a line. He had been left in ignorance, and deceived. Now Cameron informed him that the ships were on the way. "You will therefore hold out, if possible," he wrote, "till the arrival of the expedition." Then came two buck-passing paragraphs:

It is not, however, the intention of the President to subject your command to any danger or hardship beyond what, in your judgment, would be usual

35

in military life; and he has entire confidence that you will act as becomes a patriot and soldier, under all circumstances.

Whenever, if at all, in your judgment, to save yourself and command, a capitulation becomes a necessity, you are authorized to make it.

The next day Major Anderson wrote a distressed letter to the Adjutant General, Colonel Lorenzo Thomas.

Colonel: . . . I had the honor to receive, by yesterday's mail, the letter of the honorable Secretary of War, dated April 4, and confess that what he there states surprises me very greatly. . . . I trust that this matter will be at once put in a correct light, as a movement made now, when the South has been erroneously informed that none such would be attempted, would produce most disastrous results throughout our country.

It is, of course, now too late for me to give any advice in reference to the proposed scheme of Captain Fox. I fear that its result can not fail to be disastrous to all concerned. Even with his boat at our walls, the loss of life (as I think I mentioned to Mr. Fox) in unloading her will more than pay for the good to be accomplished by the expedition. . . .

We have not oil enough to keep a light in the lantern for one night. The boats will have to, therefore, rely at night entirely upon other marks. I ought to have been informed that this expedition was to come. Colonel Lamon's remark convinced me that the idea, merely hinted at to me by Captain Fox, would not be carried out.

We shall strive to do our duty, though I frankly say that my heart is not in this war, which I see is to be thus commenced. That God will still avert it, and cause us to resort to pacific means to maintain our rights, is my ardent prayer.[1]

Beauregard intercepted the dispatch and sent it to Jefferson Davis. As the President read the manly, frank, and moving letter, he saw that his old friend Bob Anderson was absolved from any suspicion of complicity. Though the language was restrained, Anderson was obviously shocked at the deceit which had been practiced on him, a Union officer, as well as on the Confederate Government. Anguish of soul was revealed between the lines. The words "I frankly say that my heart is not in this war, which I see is to be thus commenced" were of peculiar significance. Robert Anderson placed the blame of starting the war squarely on the Lincoln Administration.

On April 8, Beauregard received a useless, warning telegram from Judge Crawford: "We were reassured yesterday that the status of

[1] The letter, which is recorded in *Official Records,* Series 1, Vol. I, p. 294, has a postscript from Anderson asking Colonel Thomas to destroy it. Apparently, Anderson considered it too damning to the Administration.

Sumter would not be changed without previous notice to Governor Pickens, but we have no faith in them. The war policy prevails in the Cabinet at this time." This dispatch was also relayed to Montgomery.

As President Davis knew, the Confederate Commissioners in Washington were pressing Seward for "a definite disposition" to their note of March 12, delivered several weeks past. While Federal warships and transports plowed the Atlantic on their way to Charleston, Seward coolly wrote that he must decline official intercourse with the Commissioners, for he did not admit or assume that the states they represented had withdrawn from the Union.

On April 9, the frustrated Peace Commissioners composed their final note to the Lincoln Administration, accusing it of trickery. In the copy sent to him, President Davis read:

Your refusal to entertain these overtures for a peaceful solution, the active naval and military preparations, and the formal notice . . . that the President intends to provision Fort Sumter by forcible means, if necessary . . . can only be received by the world as a declaration of war. . . . For the President of the United States knows that Fort Sumter cannot be provisioned without the effusion of blood. . . .

The undersigned are not aware of any Constitutional power in the President of the United States to levy war, without the consent of Congress, upon a foreign People, much less upon any portion of the People of the United States. . . .

Whatever may be the result, impartial history will record the innocence of the Government of the Confederate States, and place the responsibility of the blood and mourning that may ensue upon those who have denied the great fundamental doctrine of American liberty, that "Governments derive their just powers from the consent of the governed," and who have set naval and land armaments in motion to subject the people of one portion of this land to the will of another portion.

The Commissioners' last dispatch to the Confederate Government, dated April 10, merely reported something they had read in a New York paper: "The *Tribune* of today declares the main object of the expedition to be the relief of Sumter, and that a force will be landed which will overcome all opposition."

On that same day, the rival New York *Herald*, which, as Carl Sandburg noted, spoke for "a variety of powerful interests," daringly declared: "Our only hope now against civil war of an indefinite duration seems to lie in the overthrow of the demoralizing, disorganizing and destructive sectional party, of which 'honest Abe Lincoln' is the pliant instrument."

Throughout the Confederacy, from city sidewalks to crossroad stores, tautness was evident in eyes and voices. "Why doesn't Jeff Davis act?" men asked each other. "Why doesn't he take Sumter before the Yankees get there?"

Davis knew well how the people felt. But he could not tell them that however much he questioned Seward's manipulations, he must gamble on Seward's good intentions. To strike a blow too soon would be a fatal error. The President was pleased to read in the Montgomery *Daily Mail* of April 9 a defense of his caution and a tribute of confidence. It was a personal letter to the editor from New Orleans, which he published because he deemed it "a just and noble tribute to the Southern President."

You may rest assured that he (Pres. Davis) will prove himself fully equal to the responsible position he occupies.

He has done more than conquer an empire; he is complete master of himself, and will meet every obstacle in the path of the Confederacy with a cool and unclouded judgment—not with the impetuosity of a soldier, but with the higher courage of a commander. . . .

The greatest of all victories is a bloodless one, and if it is possible to achieve it, our Commander-in-Chief will do it. . . .

Keep cool . . . and be assured that the policy of Jeff. Davis will soon vindicate itself. . . . The honor of our young Republic is safe in his hands.

Because of raging rumors of war, coolness was not a recognizable quality in the new republic. In Montgomery, great excitement prevailed. On the tenth, Leroy Walker could hardly get in and out of his War Department office for the turbulent throng of anxious visitors. "All seem to concur," reported the Montgomery *Daily Mail,* "that 'war is inevitable', and they are 'ready, willing and awaiting' the firing of the first gun; and, with their muskets and knapsacks, are ready, at a moment's warning, to march in defense of their country's right and honor."

Letters and telegrams from persons important and obscure came pouring into President Davis's office. On April 10, he received an imperative telegram from his old friend Senator Louis Wigfall, now in Charleston.

No one now doubts that Lincoln intends War. The delay on his part is only to complete his preparations. All here is ready on our side. Our delay therefore is to his advantage, and our disadvantage. Let us take Fort Sumter, before we have to fight the fleet and the Fort. General Beauregard will not act without your order. Let me suggest to you to send the order to him to begin the attack as soon as he is ready. Virginia is excited by the preparations, and a bold stroke on our side will complete her purposes. Policy and prudence are urgent upon us to begin at once. . . .

While President Davis was counseling cool patience, the Charleston *Courier* of April 10 publicly sounded a war cry: "Let the strife begin —we have no fear of the issue." That day impetuous Roger Pryor, the Virginian who had resigned his seat in Congress after Lincoln's inauguration, arrived in Charleston to stir up excitement. In an impassioned speech before a large street crowd, the aristocratic young firebrand urged the Confederate forces "to strike a blow." "I will tell your Governor what will put Virginia in the Southern Confederacy in less than an hour by Shrewsbury's clock. *Strike a blow!*"

That same April 10, Beauregard telegraphed the Secretary of War that Lincoln would definitely try to reinforce Sumter immediately. President Davis summoned his Cabinet. A grave discussion was under way when Secretary of State Toombs arrived late. He was handed Beauregard's telegram, which he read standing. Scowling, he said darkly: "The firing upon the fort will inaugurate a civil war greater than any the world has yet seen; and I do not feel competent to advise you." Toombs was too agitated to sit. He walked the floor, eyes on the carpet, hands clasped tight behind his back. While the discussion proceeded at the table, the Secretary of State continued his moody pacing. At last, he halted, whirled around, and cried out: "At this time, to fire is suicide. It will lose us every friend at the North. You will wantonly strike a hornet's nest. Legions now quiet will swarm out and sting us to death!" [2] But he confessed he had no helpful solution to offer.

Jefferson Davis regarded the situation from every angle, weighed the risks each way. To him and to the general Southern mind, as Professor Randall wrote, "Lincoln's plan to relieve Sumter seemed a threat, a challenge, and a breach of faith." Like Toombs, Davis clearly saw the advantage to the side that caused the other to fire the first shot. If, however, to avoid firing first, he tamely allowed the fort to be supplied and strengthened, the effectiveness of Charleston both strategically and commercially would be lost and, worse, the integrity of the Confederacy would be so traduced that dissolution might result. Yet if he reduced the fort flying the American flag, the Federal Gov-

---

[2] Whether Toombs made precisely this Cassandra speech is not certain; but Ulrich Phillips follows Pleasant A. Stovall in quoting the lines. Rembert Patrick discredits the story.

ernment would have its excuse for launching a war of subjugation. The cards seemed stacked to Mr. Lincoln's advantage.

All of Davis's Cabinet, except possibly Bob Toombs, agreed that the Charleston defenses must not be caught in a crossfire between Fort Sumter and Federal warships. The President heard his advisers out. Then he decided to sleep over the matter. He postponed a reply to Beauregard until the next day.

Precious little sleep the President got that night. Of all the decisions in his public life, the one he now faced was perhaps the most momentous. The destiny of millions was involved. The prolonged horrors of fratricidal warfare, infinitely more dreadful than fighting foes of alien blood, rose up before him. He earnestly prayed for Divine guidance.

The next morning, supported by the majority of his Cabinet, but with Toombs not voting, the President asked Beauregard to demand evacuation of Fort Sumter, and if the ultimatum should be refused, to reduce it.

On the afternoon of April 11, under a flag of truce, Beauregard's aides, Colonel James Chesnut, Jr., and Captain Stephen D. Lee, set out in a small boat and conveyed the ultimatum. Deeply perturbed, Major Anderson debated with himself. Because of the recent letter from his government, he decided that he could not in honor comply. As he handed his formal reply to Chesnut, he remarked sadly, with a resigned smile, "I will await the first shot." Then he added, as if casually: "If you do not batter us to pieces we will be starved out in a few days." Along with the result of the visit, Beauregard communicated to Montgomery Anderson's significant last remark.

When President Davis received the report, he understood the miserable quandary of his old friend Bob Anderson, as clearly as he saw through Lincoln's maneuver to make the South shoot. Knowing that the fort must not be reinforced and that time was running out, he yet made one last effort to avoid war. He had Secretary of War Walker telegraph Beauregard.

We do not desire needlessly to bombard Fort Sumter. If Major Anderson will state the time . . . at which he will evacuate, and agree that in the meantime he will not use his guns against us unless ours should be employed against Fort Sumter, we will abstain from opening fire. You are thus to avoid the effusion of blood. If this or its equivalent be refused, reduce the fort as your judgement decides to be the most practicable.

The eyes of the entire nation were fixed, like those of Jefferson Davis, on that little sea-girt mass of rock and sand surmounted by pentagonal works of red brick in Charleston Harbor. News editors were on the alert for the message that would mean evacuation or reduction, peace or war. In Washington, William Howard Russell, brilliant correspondent for the London *Times,* packed his bags for Charleston.

Anderson's refusal to withdraw had passed by word of mouth until every Charlestonian knew that the powder keg was about to explode. The tension was such that the nerves of some cried out for the cannon's roar, while others shuddered with apprehension. But of one thing they were all determined: armed ships of an alien nation must not be allowed in Charleston waters.

Rumors circulated that the Confederate batteries would open fire at eight o'clock that evening, April 11. The Federal fleet was hourly expected. Thousands gathered on Charleston's esplanade and peered steadily into the darkness toward Sumter and Fort Johnson. But across the water nothing whatever broke the utter stillness. When the clock in St. Michael's tower struck eleven, all but the most determined watchers began plodding home to catch some sleep. None knew that at some time after nine o'clock General Beauregard had received that second temporizing message from Montgomery.

At that very hour of eleven, Beauregard prepared another communication conveying the substance of the Secretary of War's directive. "If," he wrote Major Anderson, "you will state the time at which you will evacuate Fort Sumter we will abstain from opening fire upon you." Then he sent Colonel Chesnut, Captain Lee, and Lieutenant Colonel A. R. Chisholm, all three South Carolinians, with full authorization to enter into an agreement with Anderson. This time that fiery young Virginian Roger Pryor, so eager to strike a blow, accompanied the emissaries.

The missive was presented. Anderson held a midnight conference with his top officers. His second in command, Major Abner Doubleday, a New Yorker, who later achieved fame as the "father" of baseball, urged defiance of the Rebels. At length, Anderson retired to a private Gethsemane in his room. Few good men were ever faced with such a soul-searching decision. A dutiful soldier and a loyal Unionist, Anderson was also a Kentuckian, and married to a Georgian; he loved the Southern people. If he had not misguidedly moved from Moultrie to Sumter on that fateful Christmas night, "to prevent an effusion of blood," he would not be in his present miserable dilemma! If to avoid a war between the states he now agreed to evacuation before the garrison's last slab of salt pork was gone, Anderson knew he would be branded as a traitor. The alternative might eventually involve a whole sea of blood, and right now his men would be facing personal destruction.

After painful, almost unbearable, deliberation, at half past two in the morning of April 12, Robert Anderson took up his pen to compose a formal reply. "I will," he wrote, "if provided with the proper and necessary means of transportation evacuate Fort Sumter by noon of the 15th instant, and I will not in the meantime open my fire upon your forces unless compelled to do so by some hostile act against this fort or the flag of my Government by the forces under your command . . ."

Anderson paused. If he had stopped there, the course of American history might have been different. The moment was pregnant with destiny. But the Major felt impelled to add a restrictive clause. He wrote on: "should I not receive prior to that time controlling instructions from my Government or additional supplies."

When the ink was dry, the communication was handed to Colonel Chesnut, who read it with mounting hope until he came to the proviso. For half an hour he and the other emissaries deliberated. The conditions Anderson imposed could not be accepted. The relief expedition was overdue off the Charleston coast. Though they did not know it, the *Harriet Lane* had already arrived at the rendezvous, and at 3:00 A.M. Captain Fox, on the *Baltic*, communicated with her commander.[3] Beauregard's aides reckoned much as did William T. Sherman: "If Major Anderson can hold out till relieved and supported by steam frigates, South Carolina will find herself unable to control her commerce." Instead of returning to present the case to General Beauregard, who might just possibly have deemed it expedient to ask further instructions from President Davis, Chesnut requested paper and pen. He addressed to Major Anderson a single sentence of colossal import. "By authority of Brigadier General Beauregard, commanding the provisional forces of the Confederate States, we have the honor to notify you that he will open the fire of his batteries on Fort Sumter in one hour from this time." The time recorded was: "3:20 A.M."

Major Anderson accepted the decision ruefully. As the Confederates took their courteous leave, they saw that he was deeply moved. Ander-

---

[3] The *Pawnee* was sighted at 6:00 A.M. The *Pocahontas*, another man-of-war, steamed up the following day. The tugs *Yankee* and *Uncle Ben* had been blown from their course by a severe storm: one had sought refuge at Wilmington, the other near Savannah.

son did them the honor of accompanying them down to their little boat and seeing them into it. In brotherly farewell he pressed their hands, one after another. As the Confederates pulled away, the Kentuckian called out softly, "If we never meet in this world again, God grant that we may meet in the next."

Exhausted from staring out toward Sumter, Mrs. Chesnut had finally gone to bed after midnight. She could not close her eyes: her husband was somewhere out on the dark water between rival trained guns. The previous afternoon she had bewailed in her diary: "Why did that green goose Anderson go into Fort Sumter? Now they have intercepted a letter from him urging them to let him surrender. He paints the horrors likely to ensue if they will not. He ought to have thought of all that before he put his head in the hole."

Mary Chesnut lay sleepless, knowing that "if Anderson does not accept terms at four, the orders are, he shall be fired upon." When the bells of St. Michael's began to chime the hour of four, she held her breath. A deep silence enveloped the night. She began to breathe normally, and closed her eyes in blessed relief. Half an hour passed in stillness. Then came an ominous boom. She sprang out of bed, and on her "knees prostrate" she prayed as she had never prayed before.

At half past four on that morning of April 12, the first shot was fired from Fort Johnson. The distinction of sending the first shell had been offered to Roger Pryor, but the ardent young man could not bring himself to do it. So the doubtful honor went to venerable, white-locked Edmund Ruffin, noted Virginia agriculturist and for thirty years editor of the authoritative *Farmer's Register*. He had been more eager than Pryor to put his Old Dominion into the Confederacy. The militant Ruffin, who was passionately interested in the South's betterment, was "highly gratified by the compliment and delighted to perform the service."[4]

The signal gun from Fort Johnson set the other batteries to firing. The prolonged prologue was over. America's tragedy had begun.

In the first faint streak of dawn that Friday morning, the roar of distant guns and the flash of flame arching across the black water electrified the straggling watchers on Charleston's Battery. And as cannon after cannon boomed at two-minute intervals from the different forts and floating batteries, the crowds increased. Houses disgorged their

[4] On receiving news of Lee's surrender at Appomattox four years later, Ruffin shot again: he put a pistol to his head and blew his brains out.

people. Flat roofs, piazzas, balconies, and widow's-walks became thronged. Men, still arranging their outer clothing, rushed to the sea front, followed shortly by their womenfolk. No festival ever brought more girls to the promenade; most of them had sweethearts, husbands, sons, brothers, or fathers among Beauregard's forces.

For a couple of hours, the citizens were relieved and somewhat incredulous that no answering shots came from the guns of Sumter. Then, at seven o'clock, when watchers were stealing away to snatch some breakfast, the Stars and Stripes was run up above Sumter. Anderson's cannoneers began pouring iron hail on Fort Moultrie, on Stevens's battery, and on the floating batteries. Detonations jarred the ears of spectators, and the smell of saltpeter bit at their nostrils. As the smoke blew across the harbor, the eastern sky turned dark with lowering rain clouds.

In Montgomery, President Davis, sleepless, awaited Anderson's answer. Before breakfast, he had his Secretary of War telegraph Beauregard to ask specifically what the Major's reply was to his proposition contained in last night's dispatch. The General sent back seven words. Walker brought the telegram to the President. Davis read the remarkable understatement: "He would not consent. I write today."

Whatever pain the laconic message brought to his heart, Jefferson Davis received it with his usual outward calm. He had hoped with all his soul that conflict might be prevented. Extremely reluctant to fire on Sumter, he had yet been unceasingly aware that "the purpose of his office was the defense of the Confederate States at every point." Even Horace Greeley, with his intense partisan feeling, was to admit that "whether the bombardment and reduction of Fort Sumter shall or shall not be justified by posterity, it is clear that the Confederacy had no alternative but its own dissolution."

As a soldier, aware of the strength of the opposing batteries, Davis could envision what might be taking place. If the Northern warships had arrived to join in the fight, the Confederates would be having a stiff battle. In any case, he knew Bob Anderson for a brave officer who would not easily surrender under fire; the Sumter garrison might be annihilated. Davis had often told provincial Southerners, in so many words, that "only fools doubted the courage of the Yankees."

In Charleston a leaden drizzle began to dull the scene for spectators, as flaming shot "roofed the sky," pouring into Sumter and onto Confederate batteries. All day long the people, aghast, thought they were witnessing a holocaust. On the roof tops, some women sobbed with hysteria, while others prayed with all their might.

In Montgomery, on that night of April 12, according to the *Daily Mail*, "at a late hour, 1000 persons or more, with a band of music," gathered in front of the Exchange Hotel to serenade the President. Mr. Davis, deep in affliction of spirit at the shooting in progress in Charleston, appreciated the demonstration of affection, but he could not rouse himself to face his admirers. He asked his Secretary of War, who lived in the hotel, to make his excuses. Leroy Walker appeared on the balcony and explained that the President had been so closely confined by his arduous duties that he greatly needed repose. Then he himself made "a brief, stirring, patriotic speech" and told the President's well-wishers that four of Sumter's big guns had already been silenced by Beauregard's batteries. The President heard the loud cheering, followed by more music in his honor. When at last the crowd departed, he felt assured of one thing: the South was valiantly determined to resist invasion, whatever the odds.

In Charleston, the April weather turned unseasonably cold that historic night. As harsh winds drove the rain, the firing gradually relaxed. Then watchers saw a crescent moon break through the clouds and hang clear for a few minutes; they took it for a good omen. And in the early morning, as the sun burst forth in the refreshed atmosphere, witnesses, passing St. Phillip's churchyard, where John C. Calhoun lay buried, saw a gamecock fly to the top of the great man's tomb, flap his wings and crow, as if in victory.

"From four to six-thirty a.m., the enemy's fire was very spirited," wrote Major Abner Doubleday in *Reminiscences of Fort Sumter*. Nineteen Confederate batteries, encircling four sides of Sumter's pentagon, hammered away. Balls and shells from ten-inch columbiads poured into the fort. At seven, when a fresh rainstorm came on for an hour, there was a lull in Beauregard's cannonading. Then as the batteries renewed the bombardment with full force, the officers' quarters of Sumter caught fire from an incendiary shell. When that fire was put out, a mortar shell lodged in the roof, and flames burst out anew. By eleven o'clock, in Doubleday's words, "the conflagration was terrible and disastrous." The magazine holding three hundred barrels of powder was in danger of explosion. The men were almost suffocated; some crawled on the ground, holding wet handkerchiefs over their mouths. "The roaring and crackling of the flames, the dense masses of whirling smoke, the bursting of the enemy's shells and our own exploding in the burning rooms, the sound of masonry falling in every direction, made the fort a pandemonium."

Shots from Sumter came so infrequently now that, at each futile blast, Confederate soldiers would leap up on their parapets and cheer the game Yankees, who were taking such hellish punishment. They mocked and hooted the Federal ships that did not come in to Anderson's rescue, but were bobbing idly about on the choppy water beyond the reef.

The soldiers viewing them did not know, any more than did Jefferson Davis in Montgomery, that frustrated Captain Fox on the *Baltic* was longing desperately to get into the fight, particularly since he was the master originator of the expedition, and expected fame. But Captain S. C. Rowan, commander of the warship *Pawnee*, absolutely refused to venture in with the *Baltic*. Rowan stood firm on his orders, which he told Fox "required him to remain ten miles east of the light and wait the *Powhatan*." "I am not going in there," he declared, "to inaugurate civil war." Naturally, neither the Confederates at Charleston nor the President in Montgomery suspected that Seward's counter-maneuver had rendered impotent the "relief" squadron by depriving it of its flagship, the *Powhatan,* which carried the orders as well as the launches and the sailors to man them.

Shortly before one o'clock, the Sumter flagstaff was shot in two. Former Senator Wigfall, seeing the Stars and Stripes go down in the dense smoke, and eager to stop the imagined carnage in the garrison, took it upon himself to secure surrender. Commanding two terrified Negroes to be his oarsmen, the huge, fierce-eyed "stormy petrel" leaped into a rowboat, fixed his linen handkerchief to the point of his sword and thrust it aloft. While cannon balls flew over his head, he was rowed to Sumter. Oddly, no one from the garrison saw the strange spectacle of Wigfall's approach or noted him clambering up a rocky ledge. A gunner was flabbergasted to behold a flushed human face appear beside his cannon's mouth in an embrasure. Squeezing through the opening, the self-appointed emissary demanded to be taken to Major Anderson.

Wigfall, who had not been in contact with Beauregard for thirty hours, offered Anderson generous terms of surrender. Believing Wigfall had authority, the Major accepted them, requesting to be allowed to salute his flag on departing. Wigfall agreed. Across the water, the amazed Beauregard, who had just seen the American flag run up again on an improvised flagpole, now beheld it brought down and a white one hoisted.

Later that afternoon, Secretary of War Walker took President Davis a telegram from General Beauregard. "We take possession of Fort Sumter tomorrow morning. I allow him the privilege of saluting his flag. No one killed on our side."

When further information reached Montgomery that not a single Union man had been killed by Confederate fire, it seemed to Davis like a special dispensation of Providence. In wiring congratulations to Beauregard, Davis indicated no hint of triumph. Half of his message attested to his concern for the defeated Federals. His magnanimity of spirit was inherent in his simple words: "Thanks for your achievement and for your courtesy to the garrison of Sumter. If occasion offers, tender my friendly remembrance to Major Anderson."

The next day, April 14, the people in Montgomery were satisfied and elated. The President read in the *Daily Advertiser* an editorial entitled "Glory Enough For One Day." "The intelligence that Fort Sumter surrendered to the Confederate forces yesterday sent a thrill of joy to the heart of every true friend of the South. The face of every Southern man was brighter, his step lighter, and his bearing prouder, than it had been before."

On that Sunday morning, the exhausted Sumter garrison stood at attention as salutes to their flag were fired. On the last and fiftieth round, a cannon burst. A private was killed and five others wounded. The first serious casualty occurred after the battle was over.

Beauregard courteously stayed away from Sumter until his former instructor in artillery had departed. When the ship bearing the defeated garrison passed Cummings' Point, the Confederates lined up respectfully with heads uncovered. Anderson had defended Fort Sumter for thirty-four grueling hours, "until," as he reported officially, "the quarters were entirely burned, the main gates destroyed by fire, the gorge walls seriously injured, the magazine surrounded by flames." He sailed off to a hero's reward. A few Northern papers, however, condemned his surrender as treachery. Had his men suffered annihilation and martyrdom, the Lincoln Government might have had a clearer conscience for beginning a war.

When Anderson's steamer passed out of sight, General Beauregard and Governor Pickens took possession of the wrecked fort. As the flags of South Carolina and the Confederacy were run up, boatloads of excursionists set out from Charleston. The South went into jubilation. Northern papers were emblazoned with flaming headlines. Though their editors could not cry out that American blood had been spilled, they burst into tirades about the insult to the flag.

CHAPTER IV

LINCOLN CALLS FOR
TROOPS

DURING the terrific strain of the Sumter reduction on Saturday, President Davis looked up from his desk to find the Secretary of War glumly holding a telegraphic dispatch from Braxton Bragg, commander of the Confederate forces at Pensacola. "Re-enforcements thrown into Fort Pickens last night by small boats from the outside. The movement could not even be seen from our side, but was discovered by a small boat reconnoitering." Walker had cause to look stricken. "The Yankees," he said, "have violated their agreement."

Davis received the news quietly; but it was a serious blow. The reinforcement of Pickens, which commanded the harbor of Pensacola, made the seaport useless to the Confederacy.

Davis did not know that Seward had advocated the strengthening of more remote Fort Pickens, because *there,* the Secretary of State had argued cogently, "the psychology of the situation was quite different from that of Charleston." Seward did not believe war would necessarily result from any encounter at Pickens. He had urged President Lincoln to show firmness by reinforcing Pickens, and to avoid war by evacuating Sumter.

An armistice in regard to Pickens had been in effect since the end of January. The day Florida seceded, January 10, the Federal commander at Pensacola had imitated Major Anderson and moved his garrison from Fort Barrancas on the mainland to Fort Pickens on Santa Rosa Island. Confederate volunteers had then promptly taken over Fort Barrancas and the Navy Yard. On January 24, the warship *Brooklyn* had been sent to Fort Pickens with men, artillery, military stores, and provisions. But Stephen Mallory, then Senator from Florida, and some other Southerners made a truce with President Buchanan in which the Administration agreed "not to disembark the troops from the Brooklyn," and the Confederate commander promised not to attack the fort. The Cabinet and General Scott approved the agreement, which permitted the landing of the provisions but not one armed man.

Despite the agreement in effect, just eight days after his inauguration, Lincoln had General Scott send an order to seize the first favorable opportunity to get the soldiers from the *Brooklyn* into the fort. Either the order did not reach Captain Henry Adams, commander of Federal naval forces, until March 31 or he chose to ignore it until that date.

Adams, who held the initial papers constituting the agreement, was perturbed at the new directive. He refused to comply without further instruction. On April 1, he sent a special messenger to Washington with a protesting letter and a copy of General Scott's questionable order.

In a belt strapped under his shirt, Naval Lieutenant Washington Gwathmey brought the documents to Secretary of the Navy Welles. Adams reminded the Lincoln Administration that "he was operating under an armistice which both are faithfully observing." As recently as March 30, General Bragg had reassured him the conditions would not be violated by the Confederates. He himself was concerned over "the fearful responsibility of an act which seems to render civil war inevitable." When Welles took the letter to Lincoln, the President decided to disregard the agreement, without informing the Confederates. The Secretary of the Navy then prepared an unequivocal order for Captain Adams to put the soldiers into the fort. But Lieutenant Gwathmey refused to take back such an answer; he was resigning from the United States Navy immediately, he said, to join the Confederate forces.

Welles chose Lieutenant John L. Worden for the job, instructed him to memorize the dispatch, and then destroy it. On arrival at Pensacola on the afternoon of April 11, Worden secured an interview with General Bragg. His simulated sincerity so impressed the Confederate commander that he gave the officer permission to take his "verbal message of a pacific nature" to Captain Adams. The next morning Worden made a copy of the memorized message and delivered it to the dismayed Commander. That afternoon he took the cars and sped from Pensacola.

About the time the message was being delivered, General Bragg received a telegram from Secretary Walker ordering him to intercept Worden's dispatches. But Bragg had already fallen into the same trap as had South Carolina's Governor with Gustavus Fox. He wired Montgomery: "Mr. Worden had communicated with fleet before your dispatch received. Alarm guns have just fired at Fort Pickens. I fear the news is received and it will be reenforced before morning. It cannot be prevented. . . ."[1]

That night the artillery company from the warship was slipped into the fort.[2] In the hullabaloo let loose by events at Sumter, the Pickens gesture that Seward had believed might make up to the Republican radicals for a peaceful Sumter evacuation was hardly noticed.

President Davis remarked wryly to Secretary Walker that the 8,000 Confederates at Pensacola could have taken Fort Pickens if "mere considerations of military advantage had been consulted." Though he had been aware of the dissatisfaction of some "ardent advocates of more active measures," he had been scrupulously careful not to make any move that might initiate war. "It may be that *they* were right," he subsequently wrote, "and that we who counselled delay and forbearance were wrong. Certainly, if we could have foreseen the perfidy that was practised our advice would have been different."[3]

Jefferson Davis thereafter looked upon "the enemy" as not to be trusted. Reviewing the Sumter affair, and, incidentally, that of Pickens, he wrote:

The history of the negotiations with the Federal Government is the narration of a protracted course of fraud and prevarication practised by Mr. Lincoln's administration. Every pledge made was broken, and every assurance of good faith was followed by an act of perfidy. The remonstrances, the patient and reiterated attempts of the South Carolina and Confederate Commissioners to open negotiations had been met by evasion and prevarication. It was evident that no confidence could be placed in any pledge

---

[1] Worden got off on the train before Bragg knew of his return from Pickens. He was arrested in Montgomery, but because nothing could be proved he was released. Later, at the Battle of Hampton Roads, March 9, 1862, it was Worden who commanded the *Monitor*.

[2] Captain David Porter on "Seward's" *Powhatan* arrived at Pensacola five days after the deed was accomplished. So cleverly camouflaged was the warship that even those who knew her well were baffled when she steamed up flying British colors.

[3] After reinforcement, Fort Pickens held a garrison of 992 soldiers and had six months' supplies, while the four warships standing by had an aggregate of 1,025 men, with six hundred more men en route on the *Minnesota*. The figures are taken from Captain M. C. Meigs's report to Chief Engineer Joseph G. Totten as reprinted in *Official Records*. Throughout the war, Fort Pickens flew the United States flag.

or promise of the Federal Government. Yet no resistance other than that of pacific protest and appeals for an equitable settlement was made until . . . it was known that a hostile fleet was on the way to support and enforce it.

The forbearance of the Confederate Government in the circumstances is held up as unexampled in history. It was carried to the verge of disregard of the safety of the people who had entrusted to that Government the duty of their defence.

To have waited further strengthening of the enemy by land and vessel forces, with hostile purpose, now declared, for the sake of having them "fire the first gun," would have been as unwise as it would be to hesitate to strike down an assailant who levels a deadly weapon at one's heart until he has actually fired. He who makes the assault is not necessarily he who strikes the first blow or fires the first gun.

To Jefferson Davis, Seward's behavior seemed only to point to arrant duplicity. But Seward, naturally, could not tell the Confederate commissioners of Lincoln's decision to send a relief force to Sumter, lest the Confederates immediately reduce the fort and stir up such Northern antagonism as could not be appeased. And besides, until the very last hour, Seward hoped that he could dissuade Lincoln from actually giving the order for the Sumter expedition to move. He had reason for his hope. The historian James Ford Rhodes maintains that while Lincoln had virtually decided on April 4 to send it, he reserved in his mind "the privilege of countermanding it or changing its destination should he hear that his former order touching Pickens had been executed." If Fort Pickens had been successfully reinforced before April 5, would Mr. Lincoln have let the Sumter expedition sail?

According to Secretary Welles's diary, "Military preparations were made, and a squadron was promptly fitted out by the Navy Department within a week of the executive order to cooperate with the military. But the whole plan and arrangement were defeated. At the moment of sailing, the expedition was deprived of its commander and flagship without the knowledge of the Secretary of Navy. . . . The *Powhatan,* with boats, supplies, and men destined for Sumter had been sent . . . without naval orders or record, under a secret and useless mission to Pensacola, by the Secretary of State." When the Sumter squadron finally arrived at the rendezvous, it was "destitute of a naval commander, flagship, and instructions."

On April 6, after the *Powhatan* had sailed, with a substitute commander chosen by Seward, the Secretary of the Navy discovered something amiss. Welles burst into the President's office in a blazing, accusing fury. Lincoln looked up from his desk and, seeing the extraordinary expression of Welles's face, asked defensively, "What have I done wrong?" Welles handed him two papers with the President's undeniable signature. Lincoln said he must have signed the orders without reading them—"for he had not time, and if he could not trust the Secretary of State, he knew not whom he could trust."

President Lincoln had originally given his approval to Welles's instructions to Captain Samuel Mercer as commander of the *Powhatan*, the flagship which would carry the orders. At the last hour, in the President's name, Seward sent a contrary secret order to Captain Andrew H. Foote of the New York Navy Yard that Lieutenant David D. Porter should take command of the *Powhatan*. Porter was to proceed, not to Sumter, but to Fort Pickens.

It turned out that Seward had worked secretly with Captain Montgomery Meigs, an army engineer, whom Jefferson Davis as Secretary of War had put in charge of the Capitol's reconstruction work. He wanted Meigs to lead the military expedition to Fort Pickens, which would include the soldiers on the *Powhatan* and those in readiness on the battleships anchored near Santa Rosa Island. On April 1, together they prepared the new orders for the President's signature, which Seward *did* secure.

Meigs wrote in his diary: "I was by [the] President made responsible and told not to let even the Secretary of the Navy know that this expedition was going on."[4] Lieutenant David Porter was handed confidential orders signed by Lincoln, one of which he presented to Foote. The latter order read:

Sir: You will fit out the *Powhatan* without delay. Lieutenant Porter will relieve Captain Mercer in command of her. She is bound on secret service, and you will under no circumstances communicate to the Navy Department the fact that she is being fitted out.

Abraham Lincoln

At Welles's insistent demand, the President asked his Secretary of State to telegraph and countermand his order to Porter. Seward remonstrated; but with the accusing eyes of Welles upon him, Lincoln became "imperative." Reluctantly, Seward dispatched a telegram to the naval authorities in New York: "Give the Powhatan to Captain Mercer. Seward." He cannily sent it in his own name and not that of the President.

At 3:00 P.M., when the *Powhatan* was out of sight, the bewildered

[4] Montgomery C. Meigs's diary, March 29-April 8, 1861, appeared in *American Historical Review*, Vol. XXVI, 1920-21.

Captain Foote of the Navy Yard chartered a steamer to chase the warship. It was overtaken just as it reached the open sea. The message was delivered. But Porter, having in hand orders with President Lincoln's undoubted signature, refused to relinquish command. "I received my orders from the President," he said, "and shall proceed and execute them." The *Powhatan* steamed off for remote Pensacola.

Apparently the wily Secretary of State had outfoxed Gustavus Fox and everybody else who was willing to start a war. Seward's real backstage maneuvering in Washington was not suspected by Jefferson Davis in Montgomery. All that he knew was that a fleet of armed ships had sailed for Charleston, and Seward had seemingly deluded Justice Campbell.

Having deprived the expedition of its flagship and instructions, Seward may have felt he had averted war, for it was the next day that he wrote "Faith as to Sumter fully kept. Wait and see." And because he had promised that if there was a change in attitude about evacuation he would notify Charleston, he had sent Chew to Charleston to carry out the letter of that promise.

It was all a complicated maze of deceptions, but Seward's audacious craft was practiced in the best possible cause, the cause of peace. Jefferson Davis little dreamed how desperately Seward schemed behind the scenes to avoid armed conflict. When subsequent events turned out as they did, Seward undoubtedly hoped the Republicans would never know the full extent of his manipulations. Though he could not bear the idea of disunion, to him a real war between the states was almost too horrible to contemplate. He was convinced that conciliatory policies would woo the South back into the Union.

Was Abraham Lincoln a party to Seward's daring move for the sake of peace? Seward had indubitably secured Lincoln's signature not only to that changed secret order concerning the *Powhatan,* but to other orders pertaining thereto. Dr. Randall, the most scholarly of Lincoln's admiring biographers, believed that Lincoln did not read the Porter order before he signed it. But such carelessness seems hardly likely in the canny Lincoln, who was keenly aware of Seward's cunning.

Gustavus Fox wrote his wife: "Mr. Seward got up this Pensacola expedition and the President signed the orders in ignorance and unknown to the Department. The President offers every apology possible." But on May 11, 1861, when the nation was bristling with armed men, President Lincoln himself assumed responsibility for the secret change in orders, which most historians attribute to the "bungling" or

"meddling" or "madness" of Seward, claiming that Lincoln did not
know what he signed. The letter, as it appears in *Official Records,
Navy* (Series I, Vol. IV, p. 239), seems conclusive:

Lieutenant D. D. Porter was placed in command of the Steamer *Powhatan*
and Captain Samuel Mercer was detached therefrom by my special order,
and neither of them is responsible for any apparent or real irregularity on
their part in connection with that vessel. . . .

Abraham Lincoln

Did Mr. Lincoln, at the very brink of war, agree with his Secretary
of State and attempt to draw back? By merely launching the supply
fleet he would have shown firmness and satisfied the Blairs and the
radicals. If through some switch in orders, for which his Secretary of
State was willing to take the blame, the expedition did not enter the
harbor, could the President himself be censured? If Anderson withdrew his forces "to avoid starvation," who could blame the President
for that?

Many persons will agree with Professor Randall that what one finds
hardest to reconcile with the evidence is the supposition that "all the
while the President was planning a war-provoking maneuver." Yet
Randall points up the weight of influence of those strategic persons
or groups who urged Lincoln to evacuate Sumter: General Scott and
other leaders of the army; that influential and adroit Republican
Thurlow Weed; leading Democrats and Unionists like Stephen Douglas and Andrew Johnson. The Border States were overwhelmingly in
favor of withdrawal. Even some of the extreme antislavery radicals
favored withdrawal.

On one thing almost everyone, North and South, seemed to concur:
reinforcing Sumter meant armed conflict. President Davis had made
it clear that it was his duty to protect the Confederacy at every point.
He could not let armed alien ships enter Charleston Harbor, and, since
the Confederate States had assumed the position of an independent
nation, no foreign power "should retain a strong fortress commanding
one of their important harbors."

"In a sense of frustration," one can ask with Professor Randall,
"Why did not Mr. Lincoln follow all the weight of advice for evacuation and peace?" The direct issue of war or peace was up to him to decide. Lincoln might have considered, as Jefferson Davis pointed out,
that the ultimate question for history would be: "Who offered the first
aggression, who first indicated the purpose of hostility?"

*

On that Sunday of the Federal garrison's departure from Sumter, President Davis attended the morning prayer service at St. John's and heard the young Northern-born rector pray for the President of the Confederate States, as was being done now in all the Episcopal churches throughout the new nation. Naturally unaware of certain facts and subtleties concerned with Seward's manipulations, Davis had need to relieve his packed heart of bitterness as well as to give thanks for the miracle of deliverance without bloodshed and to pray for peace.

Though the Confederate President felt no elation of triumph himself, all Sunday afternoon and evening he was receiving reports of the South's glowing reaction to the Sumter victory. Charleston churches held special thanksgiving services to which the unregenerate as well as the faithful flocked. In the Catholic Cathedral, *Te Deums* were sung with swelling voices. At St. Michael's the Episcopal rector solemnly told his congregation that "this signal and bloodless victory was due to the infinite mercy of God, who interposed His hand in behalf of our righteous cause."

From the Atlantic Coast to the plains of western Texas the South manifested joy. Dispatches proclaimed that Southerners were willing to endure any sacrifices to be free of "the oppressive, insulting North." "No more to pay duties to enrich New England industrialists at Southern expense," an editor exulted, "and to pour tax money into Washington's treasury!" Many Southerners felt, as Dr. E. Merton Coulter put it, "A new nation would give the South a chance to profit from its own wealth and prevent the North from siphoning away an estimated $100,000,000 annually." A mighty hope surged through the Confederate States.

Since no Union soldier had been killed by Confederate shot, Jefferson Davis may have had a flashing vision that the newborn nation could yet achieve a peaceful fruition. "Firing on the flag" of the *Star of the West* in January had been more or less accepted by the North as an accompaniment of secession. No hint of war followed. As William Russell was shortly to write the London *Times,* "It is absurd to assert . . . that the sudden outburst when Fort Sumter was fired upon was caused by the insult to the flag. Why, the flag had been fired on long before Sumter was attacked . . . it had been torn down from the United States arsenals and forts all over the South. . . . Secession was an accomplished fact months before Lincoln came into office. . . . The North was perfectly quiescent. . . . New York was then engaged in discussing States' Rights and in reading articles to prove that the New Government would be traitors if they endeavored to reinforce the Federal forts."

Through that Sunday night of April 14, while Southerners celebrated and Northerners gathered in indignation meetings, men of good will on both sides prayed that a war between brothers might be avoided. The next day, April 15, the verdict ran hotly over the nation's telegraph wires. President Lincoln had called for 75,000 volunteers.

Lincoln's actual call for troops stunned a large part of the North as well as the South. To Jefferson Davis it was a sickening blow, and something of a surprise, since the United States Congress was not in session. Davis, who knew the Constitution of the United States by heart, was quite aware of President Lincoln's usurpation of power. The Constitution clearly read: "The Congress shall have power to provide for calling forth the militia to execute the laws of the Union, suppress insurrections, and repel invasions." No such power was vested in the Chief Executive. In his proclamation, Lincoln dug back to an idea of the 1787 Federal Convention. He declared "the laws of the United States are opposed and the execution thereof obstructed . . . by combinations too powerful to be suppressed by the ordinary course of judicial proceeding." He commanded "the combinations aforesaid to disperse."

As Davis ironically said to his Cabinet: "It can but surprise anyone in the least degree conversant with the history of the Union, to find States referred to as 'persons composing combinations' and that the sovereign creators of the Federal Government, the States of the Union, should be commanded by their agent to disperse."

In America's greatest crisis, Davis noted that Lincoln had no desire for the help of Congress, either immediately or for the next eighty days; he had asked Congress to convene in extraordinary session "at 12 o'clock noon, on Thursday, the fourth of July next." Apparently Mr. Lincoln did not want the constituted lawmakers to interfere with an assumption of authority he did not legally possess. To Davis, it seemed an indication of Lincoln's determination to rule as long as possible as a dictator.

Jefferson Davis himself was not troubled by the question that has worried subsequent generations. "The question," as Dr. Coulter put it, "is whether Lincoln was a marplot and bungler or a cunning villain and provocateur; whether he stumbled into war at Sumter or whether he planned it." Did Mr. Lincoln get caught "in his own web of confusion," as some historians suggest? Did he blunder into a war he did not want? Without knowledge that Lincoln had said privately just after his election, "If the tug has to come, better now than later," Davis believed the President of the United States had deliberately maneuvered a war. Later, Lincoln's own devoted private secretaries, John G. Nicolay and John Hay, seemed to agree with Davis's view. In Dr. Robert McElroy's opinion, these collaborative biographers put the responsibility on President Lincoln "by arguing that his aim in the Fort Sumter Expedition was to tempt the Confederates to fire upon the flag, and then become the aggressors in a conflict which he felt to be inevitable."

In dealing with the Confederacy, Lincoln had to contend with a united people. Since he did not have a united North behind him, he felt that his main chance for unifying his people lay in "showing firmness" by asserting national authority in the harbor of Charleston.

After his call for volunteers, President Lincoln sent a consoling, if cryptic, letter to the disappointed Captain Fox on his failure to supply Sumter. "You and I," he wrote, "both anticipated the course of the country would be advanced by making the attempt to provision Fort Sumter, even if it should fail, and it is no small consolation now to feel that our anticipation is justified by the result."[5] The immediate result was a political victory for Lincoln himself, to be followed by the loss of four more States to the Confederacy. Jefferson Davis regarded Lincoln's call for troops much as did the London *Times,* which was to exclaim: "What a spectacle is here! A government going to war for no principle, for no object, save that of aggrandizement."

All the morning of April 16, President Davis was closeted with his Cabinet. That afternoon he issued a proclamation asking for 32,000 of the 100,000 volunteers Congress had already authorized in case the North became coercive. This number was all the government currently had arms for.

The hope of those Southerners who had entertained a lingering belief that they might again become members of the Union perished with Lincoln's warlike act, which made the fracture complete. Even the most wishful were convinced that reunion was now an impossibility. Despite all arguments and warnings, Mr. Lincoln had apparently little understanding of the Southern temper if he thought the Confederacy was bluffing. The Montgomery *Evening Mail* bespoke the gen-

---

[5] Lincoln's letter is significantly quoted in both Samuel W. Crawford's *Genesis of the Civil War* and Avery O. Craven's *The Coming of the Civil War.*

eral attitude when it declared: "To advocate a political reunion with the North is to advocate the basest kind of treason." Jefferson Davis saw eager volunteers pouring into the Southern capital by railway cars and in farm wagons, on thoroughbreds and on mules. And many a rural fellow, with his "hunting piece" across his shoulder, arrived afoot.

CHAPTER V

LEE'S CHOICE

WILLIAM HOWARD RUSSELL, correspondent of the London *Times,* had set out from Washington for Charleston just as reduction of Sumter got under way. Two days later, he saw Confederate flags flying all over North Carolina, which was still in the Union. As the train passed, "men, women and children, of all colours, whooped and yelled vehemently," and at each stop the engineer would holler, "Hurrah for Jeff Davis!" Nowhere along the route could Russell discern a sign of the affection for the Union that Seward had assured him "underlay the Secession proclivities."

In Charleston, Russell noted the streets were "crowded with lanky lads, clanking spurs, and sabres, with awkward squads marching to and fro, with drummers beating calls, and ruffles, and points of war, around them groups of grinning negroes delighted with the glare and glitter, a holiday, and a new idea for them—secession flags waving out of all the windows." He wrote in his diary: "The streets of Charleston present some such aspect as those of Paris in the last revolution. Crowds of armed men singing and promenading the streets, the battle blood running through their veins—that hot oxygen which is called 'the flush of victory' on the cheek. . . . Sumter has set them distraught; never such a victory. It is a bloodless Waterloo."

Russell visited the half-demolished fort, met General Beauregard, Governor Pickens, the Wigfalls, the Chesnuts, almost everybody of importance, and many rich young privates from aristocratic families. "With all his faults and provincialism," he observed, "your true Carolinian is as charming and fascinating a being as one ever encountered."

While Russell was observing in Charleston, Jefferson Davis's attention was riveted on Virginia. Had Roger Pryor been right? The day after Lincoln's clarion call, a body of responsible Richmond citizens organized a Spontaneous People's Convention to spur immediate action. Though a grandson of Patrick Henry cautioned moderation, he was followed by a flood of impassioned speeches demanding withdrawal.

On April 17, the Virginia Convention adopted an Ordinance of Secession—by a final vote of 103 to 46—to be made binding when approved by the people.[1] "The announcement," noted Mrs. Pryor, who was in Richmond, "was followed by a thrilling moment of silence, succeeded by tears of gladness and deafening shouts of applause. Old ex-President Tyler made a stirring address: 'Generations yet unborn,' he avouched, 'would bless those who had the high privilege of participation in the present struggle.' " Thousands of Richmonders, "frantic with delight," marched to the capitol, while the Fayette Artillery triumphantly fired a hundred-gun salute. "As if by magic," wrote another eyewitness, "a new flag, the symbol of the Southern Confederacy, appeared on the Capitol, appeared on all the hills of Richmond, in the windows of houses, in the hands of passengers on the street."

On the seventeenth, in Montgomery, when summer was daily expected, wintry weather unseasonably gripped the town. The President had to get out his overcoat. In the Executive Offices, fires were blazing when he arrived. In the afternoon came the warming news of Virginia's secession. Davis's spirits rose immeasurably. Nothing could add such prestige and moral strength to the infant nation as the addition of Virginia. Mr. Lincoln's call for troops had presented the Confederacy with the "Mother of States," which had bred four of the first five Presidents —Washington, Jefferson, Madison, Monroe—together with John Marshall and a host of other distinguished names. As cannon salutes honored the glad tidings in Montgomery, the townsfolk responded with delirious shouts.

The Confederate President was hardly prepared for the exultant enthusiasm Virginia's citizens manifested. In Petersburg, he learned, three hundred free Negroes promptly offered their services "either to fight under white officers or to ditch and dig." In answer to a Northern friend's question, "What will the Union men of Virginia do now?," John J. Baldwin, Union leader of the Convention, replied: "We have no Union men in Virginia now; those who were 'union' men will stand

[1] The negative vote came largely from representatives of the rugged western counties.

to their guns and make a fight which will stand out on the page of history."[2]

Although the plebiscite to make secession legal was not scheduled until late May, President Davis lost no time in sending Alexander Stephens to Richmond to seek an offensive and defensive alliance with Virginia. The Vice-President left Montgomery on April 19.

The very next day, Virginia's Colonel Robert E. Lee, to whom General Scott had just offered the command of all the Union forces to be brought into the field, tendered his resignation. From his estate, Arlington, across the Potomac and in sight of the Capitol, Lee wrote to Virginia-born Scott. He explained that his resignation would have been presented at once, "but for the struggle it has caused me to separate myself from service to which I have devoted the best years of my life, and all the ability I possessed. . . . Save in defense of my native state," he ended his letter, "I desire never again to draw my sword."

Jefferson Davis was profoundly gratified by Lee's rejection of the gift of the Federal high command. But he had expected his resignation, though he understood what special sacrifices were involved, among them the likely loss of Arlington, his wife's beloved and valuable inheritance. To his intimates, Davis remarked: "Anyone who knew Lee could have foretold what his choice would be."

For the Confederacy, it was a glorious decision. Robert E. Lee had not waited until the Ordinance of Secession had been submitted to the people of Virginia; he had resigned when offered the leadership of coercing the South. Davis had an excellent answer to the North's charge that Lee acted from ambition when he left the service of the United States. "With a small part of Lee's knowledge of the relative amount of material possessed by the North and the South," he wrote, "anyone must have seen that the chances of war were against us. . . . Alone he rode forth, his guiding star being Duty, and offered his sword to Virginia."

The Virginia Convention promptly made Lee head of the Council of War and conferred on him the commission of Major General. The same day that he reached Richmond, a taciturn teacher of mathematics, with rough-hewn features and a dark rust-colored beard, arrived with a corps of cadets from the Virginia Military Institute. Thirty-

[2] Baldwin overstated the case. The people of mountainous northwestern Virginia, whose economic interests were largely dependent on the Ohio River, remained loyal to the Union.

seven-year-old Thomas J. Jackson had resigned his professorship at Lexington; and, now appearing in an old Mexican War uniform, he offered his West Point training and his fighting arm to Virginia's defense. Lee sent him to command at strategic Harpers Ferry.

On invitation, General Lee came to call on Jefferson Davis's emissary, Vice-President Stephens, at the Ballard Hotel. Lee desired an immediate alliance between Virginia and the Confederacy. Generously, he declared he was entirely willing to put his services and those of Virginia's officers under the Confederate Government and "be ruled by it."

On April 24, former President John Tyler, head of the Virginia committee, and Vice-President Stephens signed a temporary "convention" placing Virginia's military forces "under the chief control and direction of the President of the Confederate States." General Lee straightway began preparing his state's defenses and readying volunteers for effective service.

On his return to Montgomery, Stephens, who had resented making the journey to Richmond and "thought little enough of Lee anyhow," gave Jefferson Davis a rhapsodic account of his capitulation to the man's qualities. "He stood there, fresh and ruddy as a David from the sheepfold in the prime of his manly beauty. . . . I had before me the most manly man and entire gentleman I ever saw." While Lee sat in Stephens's room at the Ballard, the Vice-President became convinced "that his seeming modesty was genuine, that this worth, which his compatriots believed, was real, that his character was utterly unselfish." Stephens confessed that when he took Lee's hand in parting that night he had feelings of "almost reverence."

The following week, President Davis received reports that General Lee was working with driving energy against May 5, the date Mr. Lincoln had set for "the dispersion" of the secessionists. Patriotism so flowered in Virginia that the recruiting stations could hardly handle the volunteers, and for lack of arms Lee had to send home youths under eighteen. Among the few like the realistic Jefferson Davis, R. E. Lee predicted a prolonged conflict. A week after he had set about preparing defenses, he wrote his wife: "The war may last ten years."

Lee had a tremendous task, as Davis understood, for Richmond, only a hundred miles from Washington, might be threatened at three particular points, each more than a hundred and fifty miles from the other: from the Peninsula and Fortress Monroe, which remained in Union hands; from Harpers Ferry, in northwestern Virginia; and from

Manassas Junction, about thirty miles south of Washington. No direct railway connections linked one region with another, and the state's country roads certainly could not be called good.

Although Virginia's pro-Union Governor John Letcher rebukingly wrote President Lincoln, "You have chosen to inaugurate civil war," he had exasperated importunate Virginians weeks before by refusing to send state troops to capture Fortress Monroe, the Norfolk Navy Yard, and Harpers Ferry, when almost all the other strongholds below Mason and Dixon's line were changing hands.

Now, following the Virginia Convention's vote for secession, the Federal commander of the Harpers Ferry arsenal acted with celerity. He applied the torch to the buildings, and evacuated, leaving a state of destruction, including the complete ruination of 15,000 stands of arms. The shipyard at Norfolk was abandoned by Union forces to the accompaniment of another devastating fire, which destroyed valuable engines and a vast amount of machinery. Besides, the Federals burned their large ship *Pennsylvania*, and sank six others, including the frigate *Merrimac*, later to be salvaged by the Confederates and, as a rearmed ironclad, named the *Virginia*.

Jefferson Davis was impressed on hearing of Colonel Thomas Jackson's first bold action at Harpers Ferry. Jackson had temporarily cut the Baltimore & Ohio Railroad line, which connected the West with Washington, and "diverted" a quantity of sorely needed rolling stock to other lines in Virginia.

President Davis had constant assurances that the Southerners would not shrink from the sacrifices they would be called upon to make for independence. Men of every economic and social category were determined to defend their homes. Aside from endearing old Judge Petigru in Charleston, there seemed to be only two outstanding men in the South eager to use their influence for the Union. One was Davis's enemy Senator Andrew Johnson of Tennessee, who hated all planters and aristocrats. The other was his admirer of younger days, aging Sam Houston, who decried the folly of believing in the ultimate success of the seceded states. But Houston was renounced wholesale by his once idolizing Texans. He was deposed as governor, and saw his own beloved son put on a Confederate uniform. Senator Johnson was badly mauled at Lynchburg by angry Virginians while passing from Washington to his home in eastern Tennessee. In the cars, "the enemy of Southern ways" had his nose pulled literally and viciously. Only the passengers saved him from being ignominiously dragged out to the platform where, according to the papers, a "large crowd groaned him and offered him every indignity he deserved."

With intense interest, Jefferson Davis watched every dispatch and comment on the reactions of the Border States. If, he reflected, the upper South from Maryland through Missouri would join the lower South, this more even balance in the opposing line-ups might forestall war. The bitter replies of Border State Governors to Lincoln's call for volunteers were more than reassuring. In an outburst of indignation, Governor John W. Ellis of North Carolina informed the President of the United States that he would furnish no troops and would not be a party "to this wicked violation of the laws of the country, and to this war upon the liberties of a free people." He put teeth into his refusal by seizing the arsenal at Fayetteville and three Federal forts within the state's boundaries.

Tennessee's Governor, Isham G. Harris, advised Lincoln that he would not furnish one man for the purposes of coercion, "but 50,000, if necessary, for the defense of our rights, and those of our Southern brothers." Henry M. Rector, Governor of Arkansas, showed his resentment by adding insult: "The people of this Commonwealth are freemen, not slaves, and will defend to the last extremity, their honor, lives and property against Northern mendacity and usurpation." He promptly possessed the United States military stores at Napoleon, Arkansas.

Jefferson Davis had expected considerable caution on the part of Kentucky, Missouri, and Maryland, which directly bordered antislavery states. He knew that a choice would be hard to make, because if the likely war came, their soil might logically become the chief battlegrounds.

Governor Beriah Magoffin of Kentucky wrote Lincoln rather sharply: "I say, emphatically, Kentucky will furnish no troops for the wicked purpose of subduing her sister Southern States." Missouri's Governor, Claiborne F. Jackson, who openly advocated secession, sent Lincoln the most stinging rebuke of all: "Your requisition is illegal, unconstitutional, revolutionary, inhuman, diabolical, and cannot be complied with."

Davis was particularly concerned about Maryland, for that strategic state was regarded somewhat as the South's outpost. Though the Eastern Shore people and those in Baltimore were Southern in sentiment, the western counties were largely pro-Union. So Maryland's Governor Thomas H. Hicks assumed a neutral role. On April 18, he issued a proclamation urging the citizens to preserve peace, and assured them that no troops would be sent out of Maryland, "unless in defense of the national capital," which stood on soil that had been ceded by Maryland.

The next day, however, when the Sixth Massachusetts Volunteers arrived at the railroad station in Baltimore, an angry mob disputed their passage through the city to a connecting train. Baltimoreans attacked the soldiers with paving stones picked up in a street that was under construction. The surprised young men in uniform started firing without orders. Some determined citizens wrenched muskets from the volunteers and turned their weapons against them. The city militia was called out to restore order. Four soldiers and nine Baltimoreans lay dead. More than a hundred persons were wounded, some seriously.[3] Guarded by the police, those soldiers who had fought their way through the city took the Southern Railroad for Washington. But, by the Governor's orders, the rear portion of the regiment was sent back to Maryland's northern border.

Mayor George William Brown of Baltimore dispatched three gentlemen by express train to President Lincoln "to explain fully the fearful condition of affairs in this city." In his protesting note, he said: "The people are exasperated to the highest degree by the passage of troops, and the citizens are universally decided in the opinion that no more should be ordered to come. . . . It is my solemn duty to inform you that it is not possible for more soldiers to pass through Baltimore unless they fight their way at every step."

The next day, Maryland citizens began burning their railroad bridges. The President of the Pennsylvania Central Railroad wrote a frantic letter to Secretary of War Cameron that "the Baltimoreans and Marylanders have destroyed the whole of the bridges on the Northern Central. This seems to have been a mere spite action and must convince the Government that those loyal to the Government are in vast minority."

That same day, however, as Jefferson Davis learned, Major General Benjamin F. Butler, in command of the Third Massachusetts Volunteer Militia, seized the capital, Annapolis, as well as the Elk Ridge Railroad. On April 27, directed by President Lincoln, General Scott announced the suspension of the writ of habeas corpus in Maryland, to the utter astonishment of Chief Justice Taney, who declared "he

[3] Rhodes says 362 suffered wounds; Nicolay and Hay put the number at 118.

could not find a shred of legality for the act." A few days later, Butler took possession of Relay House, the railway junction nine miles from Baltimore. As quickly as possible, to prevent the secession of Maryland, which would put Washington within the Confederacy's borders, Lincoln strengthened key points with Federal troops. Then Butler began clamping in jail prominent citizens of Confederate sympathies, including members of the State Legislature. Almost before the state knew what was happening, she found herself in the grip of military occupation. Thousands of Marylanders began refugeeing to Virginia.

On April 27, President Lincoln issued a second proclamation of blockade. Lincoln's act was a violation of the Constitution: he had no right to declare a blockade of ports in states that he claimed were still in the Union; and, if out of the Union, a blockade was an act of war, which only Congress could decree. Jefferson Davis hoped this blockading move would spur England's quick recognition of the Confederacy. In the meantime, as a counterstroke to the paper blockade, he issued a proclamation offering letters of marque and reprisal to any private vessel that would arm herself and, while under the Confederate flag, attack Federal shipping.

CHAPTER VI

"THE HEART AND BRAINS OF
THE GOVERNMENT" AT HOME
AND AT OFFICE

THOUGH Jefferson Davis had been without his wife's comforting ministrations during the Sumter engagement, she had returned on the Sunday Major Anderson was allowed to depart with salutes to his flag. When the President's Lady arrived on the river boat *King,* she herself was honored with a salute of seven guns. The President met her and the children at the landing and drove them straightway to the Presidential mansion, which had been redecorated according to her wishes during her absence. Soon she was directing the unpacking of barrels and crates from Brierfield: silver and china, special linens, lamps, pictures, a few favorite books. Varina had brought a couple of her good colored servants from the plantation, and in New Orleans she had hired a French chef for the official entertaining. She had also had several dresses made for herself and for Margaret Howell, her "pale, pretty, svelte, and witty" young sister, who was to stay with the Davises, as she had in Washington.

To be settled in a commodious house with his affectionate family about him was the best possible medicine for the overworked President, who had undergone heart-gripping trials the past fortnight. The unpalatable meals at the Exchange, which everybody damned, were hard on the toughest man's digestion. Now Varina was here to see that her uncomplaining husband got the simple, well-prepared food he needed. The cook from Brierfield knew exactly how he liked his corn bread, and three times a day, regardless of what tempting dishes the chef might prepare. Davis had often remarked that his Winnie's talent for making people comfortable amounted almost to genius, and that she was at her best when people were troubled in body or mind. It was cheering now to feel her expansive warmth, to have someone to talk to intimately, to "let down" before. He liked to see the three children playing about the fenced-in garden when he left for his office in the morning and eagerly awaiting his return in the late evening. Next to a sea voyage, Jefferson Davis found the companionship of his children the best prescription for taking his mind off the burdens and irritations of official business. The youngsters' delight in his presence rarely failed to give him temporary relief from care.

Entertaining, the President conceded, was part of a chief executive's job, and he greeted his good fortune in having a wife schooled in social graces. Not only was Varina an instinctive hostess, but she had been through the diplomatic mill in Washington, had seen the game played, had herself enjoyed a leading role. A thoroughbred, with a sense of humor but without frivolity, Varina knew how to turn on charm. A born conversationalist, she was what was known in the South as "excellent company." Trained by her old Massachusetts tutor, Judge George Winchester, and by her husband, she could talk men's talk with the best of them. Davis knew that his wife possessed political acumen as well as sound knowledge, though he often had to caution her about the sharpness of her repartee, which sometimes made enemies.

In that critical April, though the President was too pressed to accept invitations, the Davises gave several small dinners in their new home. Sometimes Mr. Davis would relax completely and be in top form. "He was exceedingly appreciative of wit," Mary Sidney Lanier commented, "and at his own parties he was much given to telling amusing anecdotes, which he did admirably well. The President would have the guests in a complete state of merriment without a show of a smile on his face, which added to our convulsed state."

When Mrs. Davis gave her first general reception, her husband was too busy at the last hour to receive with her. She was very disappointed, but she induced him to notice the arrangements of hundreds of cultivated roses sent in, according to Southern custom, by friends. The six downstairs rooms and the reception hall were aglow with pink, red, and yellow roses, and the banisters of the staircase were entwined with white Cherokee roses that grew wild in the countryside. For the occasion, Varina wore a gown designed by Olympe of New Orleans. It was a smart and elegant creation of heavy white silk with a fine hair stripe of black and scattered pink rosebuds woven into the material.[1] Though Varina's girlish slimness was gone now at thirty-five, and her figure verged on the matronly, the added weight, her husband thought, enhanced her natural regal bearing. His First Lady was indubitably a handsome and distinguished-looking woman, and the President had reason to be proud of her.

As he kissed her good-by, he knew that she would carry off the reception in fine style without him. And he was convinced that she had too much plain sense to have her head turned because people were calling her "Queen Varina" behind her back—some in admiration and some in jealousy, with a soupçon of mockery.

The success of Mrs. Davis's first reception, however, was somewhat marred by "vague, dismal news." "Men from Washington," Mary Chesnut wrote, rushed in "with white lips crying 'Danger. Danger!'" Several harped on the vast superiority of the enemy's men and resources. Vice-President Stephens was in a particularly gloomy mood. Mrs. Chesnut gave him a friendly rebuke for being obsessed "with fears of the future instead of exultation at the success at Sumter and the withdrawal of Virginia." She called him "half-hearted," and accused him of looking back. "The women," she declared stoutly, "had no intention of becoming pillars of salt."

No matter how disturbed the President himself might be, he almost never showed discouragement in public. But on one occasion, the beautiful Mrs. Fitzpatrick, who had poked him with her parasol after his inauguration, resented his telling her candidly that the Confederacy had to prepare for a long war and "perhaps unmerciful reverses at first." Mrs. Chesnut, however, invariably found him good company. After one of the Davises' intimate dinners, she wrote in her diary: "Dined at the President's and never had a pleasanter day. He is as witty as he is wise. He was very agreeable; took me in to dinner. The talk was of Washington; nothing of our present difficulties."

As the Chief Executive was often unable to attend scheduled social affairs at the last minute, so he was unpredictable about bringing home unexpected dinner guests. One day, to his wife's near consternation, he brought, without warning, sixteen gentlemen for a two o'clock dinner. Mrs. Davis sent servants galloping on horseback to this place and

[1] Intimate details in this section were given by Mrs. Davis to her close friend Mrs. Caroline Phelan Beale in New York in 1906. Original manuscript notes are in possession of the author.

that for special supplies, and before long had ready "a very creditable dinner." This particular day, as it turned out, the President's mind was so preoccupied with critical matters that he hardly spoke, and his wife had to muster her resources to keep the entire company entertained.

Davis was somewhat concerned when the carriage his wife had selected in New Orleans finally arrived by river boat. It was a very handsome affair indeed, and costly. But Varina, who had far more worldly sense than her husband, felt that no commonplace vehicle should transport the President or his Lady on public thoroughfares. She had ordered it, however, before Mr. Lincoln's call for troops. According to the newspapers, the equipage was of great distinction, in fact, "the most splendid piece of workmanship" ever received by Messrs. R. Marsh, Denham and Co. of New Orleans from their manufactory in New Jersey. A French *calèche* in design, the vehicle was upholstered in "rich mazarine blue silk rep and had handsome mountings of princess metal." "The *calèche*," declared the New Orleans *Picayune,* "cannot fail to be greatly admired at Montgomery, and would be remarked anywhere—in Hyde Park or the Bois de Boulogne." Though it was called "the President's carriage," only on the rarest occasions did Mr. Davis himself ever ride in it. He walked to his office; and for diversion, he rode horseback. With his military bearing and simple tastes, he found a spirited mount far more congenial than luxurious carriage cushions.

As April 29 approached, the date President Davis had set for a special "self-defense session" of the Confederate Congress, dignitaries and hopeful hangers-on began arriving by every train. The James Chesnuts returned on the cars from Charleston with Robert Barnwell, South Carolina's revered citizen, whom the President had wanted for his Secretary of State. The Wigfalls arrived and were house guests of the Davises. Wigfall, according to Mrs. Chesnut, was "black with rage" at Anderson's account of the fall of Sumter given to the Northern papers. "Catch me risking my life to save him again," Wigfall sputtered. "He might have been man enough to tell those New Yorkers the truth, however unpalatable to them a good word for us might have been. We did behave well to him. The only men of his killed, he killed himself, as they killed themselves, firing a salute to their old striped flag."

Davis often winced at the irreverent way Wigfall spoke of things.

And perhaps Bob Anderson had been misquoted. Charleston had certainly been generous to him; up to the last six weeks of his stay, it had supplied him with delicacies, besides showing him every courtesy. Now this good man, who had caused the original trouble by moving on his own hook from Moultrie to Sumter, was being sent to Kentucky by Mr. Lincoln to restrain the state from joining the Confederacy. But Davis was unceasingly grateful to Wigfall for his unauthorized act, which probably saved Anderson's life as well as the lives of other Federal soldiers.

The friendship of Davis and Wigfall seemed odd to their mutual friends. Few personalities could have been more markedly different. About the only traits they had in common were patriotic devotion and a kind of genius for extemporary eloquence. Wigfall had been feared by Congressional opponents in debate for the bitterness of his sarcasm. He could damnify and enrage with acid taunts, and frighten by his fierce readiness for a fight with fists or weapons. Physically, the contrast between the men was extraordinary: Wigfall was powerfully built, while Davis was rather ascetically slender. In literary encaustic, William Russell limned a most vivid portrait of Louis Wigfall:

"His face was not one to be forgotten—a straight broad brow, from which the hair rose up like vegetation on a riverbank, beetling black brows—a mouth coarse and grim, yet full of power, a square jaw—a thick argumentative nose—a new growth of scrubbly beard and moustache—these were relieved by eyes of wonderful depth and light, such as I never saw before but in the head of a wild beast. If you look some day . . . into the eyes of a Bengal Tiger . . . you will form some notion of the expression I mean."

Davis and Wigfall so complemented each other that the very differences may have bred the attraction between them. But such a friendship could hardly be harmonious forever. When, however, Congress convened on April 29, Wigfall was in complete accord with the President, as was virtually the entire Southern body politic, except for a handful of chronic malcontents like Charleston's R. B. Rhett.

In his address to Congress, Jefferson Davis pronounced Mr. Lincoln's call for volunteers "a plain declaration of war, which I am not at liberty to disregard, because of my knowledge that under the Constitution of the United States the President is usurping a power granted exclusively to Congress." Nineteen thousand Confederate troops, he said, were now in the field protecting the various Southern forts, while 16,000 more were on their way to Virginia's defense. After a summary of the internal affairs of the government and the necessity for raising funds to defray the expenses of maintaining independence, he closed his message with words intended especially for Northern ears:

We protest solemnly in the face of mankind, that we desire peace at any sacrifice, save that of honor. In independence we seek no conquest, no aggrandizement, no concession of any kind from the States with which we have lately been confederated. All we ask is to be let alone—that those who never held power over us shall not now attempt our subjugation by arms. This we will, we must, resist to the direst extremity. The moment that this pretension is abandoned, the sword will drop from our grasp, and we shall be ready to enter into treaties of amnesty and commerce that cannot but be mutually beneficial. So long as this pretension is maintained, with a firm reliance on that Divine Power which covers with its protection the just cause, we must continue to struggle for our inherent right to freedom, independence, and self government.

Davis's message pleased Congress, and in accordance with his desires, it promptly passed acts authorizing the President to use the whole land and naval force to meet the necessities of defense, and to issue letters of marque to armed private vessels, which, in the emergency, he had already done. He was empowered to make a loan of fifty million dollars in bonds and notes. An act was passed to provide revenue from imports.

This first Confederate Provisional Congress was made up of good material, and its members worked harmoniously with the President. "It is certain," one correspondent wrote, "that Mr. Davis is the heart and brains of the Government and his popularity with the people is, at this time, unbounded."

After spending a fortnight in and about Charleston, visiting plantations and being entertained with traditional Southern hospitality, William Russell started for the Confederate capital to meet President Davis. Like Mr. Lincoln's confidant, Ward Lamon, the Londoner had met only one Unionist in all South Carolina: pleasant, witty Judge Petigru, "the sole specimen of the genus," affectionately tolerated because of his rarity. Across Georgia, Russell beheld the Stars and Bars flying from pine tops as well as at road stations, and heard continual lusty cheers for Jeff Davis. At Macon he saw Georgia volunteers flocking into the cars to go to Virginia's defense. At another railway junction he was joined by General Beauregard, who was on his way to report to the President. The Creole was in top spirits, but tired of the speechmaking clamored for at every stop—"the price of a hero," he sighed.

In Montgomery, where Russell had to sleep at the jampacked Exchange with six in a room, he happily fell into the hands of the supercharged Louis Wigfall, whom he had earlier met in Charleston and who was now a kind of aide to the President. Wigfall undertook to be his guide and sponsor.

Russell was particularly eager to meet Jefferson Davis. Seward had told him Davis was the only man with "the brain, the courage and the dexterity" to bring the "Secession plot" to a successful issue. Russell had already discovered that "all persons in the Southern States spoke of Davis with admiration."

Russell, accustomed to the grand chancelleries and imposing formalities of European courts, was unprepared for the democratic plainness of the corner brick building sometimes called "Jeff Davis's State Department." On the second floor, the door on which was written "The President" stood open. Wigfall walked in directly and returned, announcing "The President will be glad to see you; walk in, sir." Mr. Davis was engaged with four gentlemen, who were making him offers of aid. Thanking his visitors "in the name of the Government," the President shook hands with each and bowed them out. Then turning to the correspondent, he said with a smile, "Mr. Russell, I am glad to welcome you here, though I fear your appearance is a symptom that our affairs are not quite prosperous."

He invited his caller to sit close to his own chair at his office table, and then proceeded to talk of the Crimean War, to which, as Secretary of War, he had sent three observers, among them young George B. McClellan. He spoke of the deserved fame of Russell for the brilliance of his reports on the Crimean campaigns. He asked questions about Sevastopol and the siege of Lucknow.

While they conversed, Russell noted the simplicity of Mr. Davis's clothes: "a rustic suit of slate-colored stuff, with a plain black silk handkerchief about his neck." "I had an opportunity of observing the President very closely," he wrote in his diary that night. "He did not impress me as favorably as I had expected, though he is certainly a very different looking man from Mr. Lincoln. He is like a gentleman."

With the strain of past months, Davis had grown quite thin, and Russell found "the jaws too hollow to be handsome." "The lips are thin, flexible and curved," he wrote, "the chin square, well-defined, and the eyes deep set, large and full—one seems nearly blind, and is

partly covered with a film, owing to excruciating attacks of neuralgia."
Though the expression of the face was somewhat careworn, "no trace
of anything but the utmost confidence and greatest decision could be
detected in his conversation."

In the course of their agreeable talk, Russell asked the President
for some sort of passport or protection in case he fell into the hands of
a guerrilla leader when he journeyed northward. Davis smilingly reassured him: "Sir, you are among civilized, intelligent people, who
understand your position and appreciate your character. We do not
seek the sympathy of England by unworthy means; for we respect
ourselves, and we are glad to invite the scrutiny of men into our acts.
As for our motives, we meet the eye of Heaven." There was nothing
self-righteous or sententious in the tone; the President was merely
stating his absolute conviction in the justice of the Southern cause.

Russell was surprised that during the entire conversation the President made no allusion whatever to the authorities in Washington. But
Davis wanted to know if Europe supposed there was really going to
be war? Russell replied that the public did not think there would be
actual hostilities. "And yet you see," Davis said quietly, "we are
driven to take up arms for the defense of our rights and liberties."

Noting the immense mass of papers on the table, Russell rose and
made his bow. The President accompanied him to the door. Giving him
his hand, he said graciously, "As long as you may stay among us you
shall receive every facility it is in our power to afford you, and I shall
always be glad to see you."

Outside, Wigfall was waiting to introduce Russell to various Cabinet members. When he was taken into the room marked "Secretary of
War," Russell found General Beauregard closeted with Leroy Walker.
They were both in fine humor, for unreleased news had just been received that Arkansas and Tennessee had joined the Confederacy that
day, May 6. Beauregard was "measuring off miles of country with
his compass, as if he were dividing empires." "Is it not too bad," he
said, looking up at Russell, "these Yankees will not let us go our own
way, and keep their cursed Union to themselves?" Russell reflected:
"Mr. Seward could not have been more wrong. There was no love in
the South for the Union now."

The Secretary of War made little impression on the correspondent,
except for his tobacco chewing and his utter confidence in the Confederacy's speedy success. But Judah P. Benjamin, the short, stout,
"olive-coloured," bright-eyed, Jewish Attorney General, impressed

him forcibly. Russell found him "the most open, frank and cordial of all the Confederates he had met," and brilliant as well. Benjamin seemed to have firm faith that Britain's cotton interests would bring her to recognize the Confederate Government. "All this coyness about acknowledging a slave power," he said affably, "will come right at last. . . . We are quite easy in our minds on this point at present."

Benjamin was convinced that English authorities on law would advise the Federal Administration that the blockade of Southern ports was illegal so long as the President claimed them to be ports of the United States. "At present," he said assuredly, "their paper blockade does no harm; the season for shipping cotton is over. But in October next, when the Mississippi is floating cotton and all our wharves are full, it is inevitable that the Yankees must come to trouble with this attempt to coerce us."

Though the President himself had not mentioned cotton, Russell informed the *Times* that the people in Montgomery "firmly believe that the war will not last a year. They believe in the irresistible power of Cotton to force England to intervene." He had found the same thing in Charleston: "The doctrine of 'cotton is king'—to them is a lively, all powerful faith without distracting heresies or schisms."

On his way to Mrs. Davis's reception that afternoon, Russell passed a company of volunteer artillerymen going to the station to entrain for Virginia. The band was playing "Dixie," and "crowds of whites and blacks of both sexes" followed, cheering vociferously.

When Russell was presented "in the 'demi-jour' of a moderately-sized parlor," Mrs. Davis was surrounded by a few ladies and gentlemen with whom "she seemed to be a great favorite." The Britisher found her a "comely, sprightly woman . . . of good figure and manners, well-dressed, lady-like and clever." Though he knew she had exerted considerable social influence in Washington and was now being compared to Queen Victoria, he noted no affectation whatever. Mrs. Davis received him cordially with frank graciousness. She told him that she had just heard that some Northern paper had offered a reward for "the head of the arch rebel Jeff Davis." With a flash of anger in her dark eyes, she said she believed they were quite capable of such acts. When Russell made his adieus, Mrs. Davis invited him to come some evening when her husband would be at home.

Two days later, as Russell was departing by river boat for Mobile, he received an invitation to dine with the President. He was much chagrined at being obliged to decline. But he felt he had to complete his Southern tour speedily, for he feared mail communication with the North would soon be suspended and the blockade might cut off communications by sea.

Among Russell's last diary entries from Montgomery was an observation like a summational opinion of his few weeks in the divided land: "The North thinks that they can coerce the South and I am not prepared to say they are right or wrong; but I am convinced that the South can only be forced back by such a conquest as that which laid Poland prostrate at the feet of Russia."

CHAPTER VII

LAST WEEKS IN MONTGOMERY

THE PRESIDENT'S authorization by Congress to use the naval force was highly ironic at the time, because there was nothing in the South that could be called a navy. But the Secretary of the Navy was by no means idle. Davis had chosen the best equipped man in the Confederacy for the job. In the United States Senate, Stephen R. Mallory had headed the Committee on Naval Affairs. He was clear-sighted and practical, with a sharp eye for details. And, in addition, he possessed imagination, invention, and a high degree of initiative. Mallory and Davis were continually in conference and generally in cordial agreement.

On May 9, after perfecting their plans, the President instructed the Secretary of the Navy to send James Dunwody Bulloch of Georgia[1] to England to purchase or build six steam-propelled vessels to be prepared, if necessity arose, to prey on United States commerce. The next day, on Mallory's recommendation, Congress appropriated a million dollars for Bulloch's mission and voted an additional two millions for the purchase or construction of two ironclads either in England or France. Naval Lieutenant James H. North was forthwith commissioned to proceed to Europe to obtain the ironclads.

Mallory and Davis agreed that the possession of an iron-armored ship was a matter of prime necessity. "Such a vessel at this time," Mallory optimistically told Congress, "could traverse the entire coast of the United States, prevent all blockades, and encounter, with a fair prospect of success, their entire navy."

---

[1] Bulloch, uncle of Theodore Roosevelt and great-uncle of Eleanor Roosevelt, wrote the comprehensive, two-volume *Secret Service of the Confederate States in Europe*, published in London in 1883.

Correspondents soon began speaking of the length to which the Congress would go to please Jefferson Davis. Often when a bill was not framed to his liking, he would return it with suggestions for corrections and emendations. At this second assemblage of the Confederate Congress, it was still believed that the entire Government was "in the hollow of the President's hand" and that whatever measures the Chief Executive recommended were good for the young republic. "Congress," De Leon observed, "remained a formal body to pass bills and ratify acts, the inspiration for which derived from the clearest and coolest brain in the South."

However, there was one important matter in which the President had not got his way: the period of enlistment. During February, the belief had prevailed in the South that there would be no war, or, if there were, that it would last only a brief time. The first bill that had passed Congress provided for accepting troops for sixty days. The President, divining more accurately the temper of the Federal Government and foreseeing the probability of a long and bitter struggle, had called in Francis Bartow, Chairman of the Committee on Military Affairs, and urged him to persuade Congress to adopt a bill specifying three-year enlistments. But Bartow had insisted that he would do well if he could persuade the legislators to extend the period to twelve months. On February 28, 1861, this new bill had become a law, authorizing the President to receive volunteers "for not less than twelve months, unless sooner discharged."

On May 17, the newly arrived war clerk, John Beauchamp Jones, pro-Southern newspaper editor who had fled Philadelphia, was presented to the President. Jones, who was to become the most indefatigable diarist of the period, straightway set down his first impression of Jefferson Davis in his journal.

He was overwhelmed with papers and retained a number in his left hand, probably of more importance than the rest. He received me with urbanity, and while he read the papers I had given him, as I had never seen him before, I endeavored to scrutinize his features. . . . His stature is tall, nearly six feet, his frame is very slight and seemingly frail, but when he throws back his shoulders he is as straight as an Indian chief. The features of his face are distinctly marked with character, and no one gazing at his profile would doubt for a moment that he beheld more than an ordinary man. His face is handsome, and on his thin lip often basks a pleasant smile.

About the time Jones was presented, Davis had just finished steering through Congress the measures for a complete military establishment, which had been complicated by the time element involved in the transfer of soldiers and facilities from state to Confederate Government control.

While this complicated business was being implemented, Virginia's Joseph E. Johnston arrived in Montgomery to get some new assignment in the Confederate Army. Against his wife's desire, he had resigned his commission as Quartermaster General in the United States Army a few days after Lee had been made Commander in Chief of Virginia's military and naval forces. Lee had promptly given him the rank of Major General, and put him to instructing the troops assembling at Richmond. But within a fortnight, Johnston was flabbergasted when the Virginia Government reduced him to Brigadier General, on the ground that only one man, Lee, should hold the higher rank. As soon as he recovered from the shock, he went to Montgomery to put his case directly to the Confederate President.

Davis knew that, while Johnston was valuable as a soldier, he was at the same time extremely ambitious and touchy about his personal dignity. Though as cadet mates at West Point they had been mere acquaintances, in Washington during the past year their high-spirited wives had been intimate friends. Johnston had been brought there for special assignments by Secretary of War John B. Floyd, his cousin by marriage. And in July, 1860, Floyd had named him Quartermaster General.[2] There was some Congressional opposition and criticism from officers who outranked Johnston, but Senator Jefferson Davis, as chairman of the Committee on Military Affairs, had helped to get the appointment confirmed.

Now, in Montgomery, Davis saw that the slightly built Johnston carried his fifty-four years and his five feet eight inches as erect and proud as in their cadet days at West Point, when he had something of a gamecock swagger to his walk. His hair had grayed and was receding from his forehead, but his side whiskers and a well-groomed tuft of beard gave his gravely handsome face distinction. Calm, deliberate, low-voiced, Johnston had a certain magnetism. Though one of his friends considered him "critical, controversial and irritable by nature," he had the gift of winning subordinates. Aloof in manner, he was yet an adroit politician in furthering his own position.

[2] Lee, who had outranked Johnston in the field, was according to Douglas Southall Freeman, "stung" by what he considered Floyd's preferment of Johnston. Lee wrote his son Custis that Johnston "has been advanced beyond anyone in the army and it has thrown more discredit than ever on the system of favoritism and making brevets."

Davis gathered that Johnston, who could not bear "to be beaten even in a game of billiards," was unhappy about having to take commands in Virginia from his classmate Robert E. Lee, and that he desired some high commission in the Confederate service. But since there was no higher rank than Brigadier in the Confederate Army at this time, he would have to content himself with that. Johnston's old friend Adjutant General Samuel Cooper and the President finally decided to put him in command at Harpers Ferry, where Lee had already sent Colonel Thomas J. Jackson.

Davis regarded Harpers Ferry as a most strategic spot for protecting Virginia. It lay where the Shenandoah River flowed into the Potomac and where the Baltimore & Ohio Railroad, which connected the West with Washington, crossed the Potomac. Davis and Lee both placed great value upon the retention of the command of the Shenandoah Valley and the position at Harpers Ferry. An evacuation, Davis emphasized, "would interrupt our communications with Maryland, and injure our cause in that State."

The President little suspected then what he would have to deal with in Joseph Johnston. Within three weeks of receiving a commission in the Confederate Army, Johnston was to be at open variance with both President Davis and General Lee as to how the war should be conducted.

While Johnston was in Montgomery, the President had under consideration a pressing invitation from the Virginia Convention to make Richmond the capital of the Confederacy. Davis was doubtful about the prudence of such a move. From a military standpoint, he reasoned that putting the capital so close to the Federal lines had serious disadvantages. If the Union forces were to concentrate on attacking Richmond, they would be conveniently close to their base of supply, whereas Montgomery was a thousand miles from Washington. On the other hand, he saw an advantage to his government and himself as Commander in Chief in being close to the field of operations. And he fully realized the prestige of having the Confederate capital in the state of Washington and Jefferson. Besides, Virginia deserved special reward, for, with eyes open and courage high, she had offered herself as a potential sacrifice on the battlegrounds.

In Montgomery, Virginia's R. M. T. Hunter was an impressive lobbyist for the removal of the capital to Richmond. Hunter, whose college mates nicknamed him "Run Mad Tom," from his intials, had been United States Senator from 1847 to 1861 and twice Speaker of the

House. He could talk well on English literature and he had remarkable political sway over large assemblies. His great ambition had been to be President of the United States. He would have relished the honor of being the first Confederate President. Now, with four inches of fat on his ribs, Hunter looked rather "tumbled-up" in the Montgomery heat; "his hair invariably needed brushing, his waistcoat, pulling down." A joke circulated that every time he beheld the tombstones of the Montgomery marble yards on his way up to Capitol Hill, he would groan in agony and predict that he would sicken and die in Montgomery.

The poor food, the crowding, and the lack of comfort at the Exchange Hotel and the lesser inns proved weighty allies to Hunter's persuasive lobbying. Mary Chesnut prophesied that "the uncomfortable hotels here will at last move the Congress." Even though it meant arduous repacking and unpacking, Varina Davis was an advocate for Richmond, which was five times the size of Montgomery.

It had been rumored that the President would veto the removal; but when Congress adjourned on May 21, it was scheduled to meet again on July 20 at the new Confederate capital in Virginia.

In mid-May, President Davis, accompanied by Secretary of the Navy Mallory, took the cars for Pensacola. It was whispered in Montgomery that everything was in readiness for an attack on Pickens. Some military men said the fort could be taken. Toombs said it ought to be taken. The President preferred to look for himself, to confer, to decide.

By the time the President had reached General Bragg's headquarters, he doubted a successful outcome. The Federal fleet was in sight. The *Powhatan,* "stumpy, thick-set, powerful," was prominent among the ships, repainted again like her old self and flying the Stars and Stripes. Through glasses, Davis could see how heavily she was armed, with "ten-inch Dahlgrens and an eleven-inch pivot gun, with rifled field pieces and howitzers on the sponsons." Like the flagship *Sabine* and the other vessels standing by, the *Powhatan* was ready for action. The fort itself was formidable. Though General Braxton Bragg commanded 8,000 men and had diligently thrown up earthworks, strengthened his batteries, and made his mainland position so strong that he did not think his guns could be silenced, he knew that he could not take Pickens without tremendous loss of life.

Bragg was anything but prepossessing in appearance. He was gaunt and somewhat cadaverous-looking. Despite his West Point training, the North Carolinian stooped badly. His hair and stubbly beard were grizzled. His bushy black eyebrows, which met in a tuft at the bridge of his nose, gave him a forbidding expression. But his piercing black eyes were bright and quick to note anything out of order. A victim of nervous dyspepsia, he also was subject to migraine headaches. His acerbity of manner alienated many who might have been his friends, but he always showed the greatest esteem for Jefferson Davis. While Davis had never found Bragg personally attractive or congenial, he valued his proved qualities as an organizer and a disciplinarian.

General Bragg now invited his old comrade in arms at Buena Vista to review the troops. As Jefferson Davis rode forth with Secretary Mallory, the General, and his staff, he saw drawn up on the gleaming white beach line upon line of well-trained volunteer organizations. The variegated uniforms, sun-glinting muskets, and waving banners made a colorful display. In the rear, to the north, the piney woods formed a dark background; between the trees and the beach stood neat rows of white tents laid out in company streets by regiments. The stretch of blue-green water was broken by Santa Rosa Island, above which Pickens reared grimly. On the parapet a Union band was playing "The Star-Spangled Banner."

As the President rode down the Confederate lines, the Yanks stopped playing out of curiosity. And as he passed along the volunteer regiments, a model of horsemanship, the Confederate regimental bands struck up, and the soldiers, throwing off constraint, cheered with their mightiest voice. In the testimony of an eyewitness, "the wildest huzzas —not even restrained by the presence of their 'incarnate discipline' [Braxton Bragg]—told how firm a hold Mr. Davis had taken upon the hearts of the army."

The President was particularly impressed by "the perfect state of drill and efficiency" of six hundred swarthy Zouaves from the slums of New Orleans. With their baggy scarlet trousers, white gaiters, blue shirts cut low, and heavily braided jackets flung cavalierly off the shoulder, they were a picturesque, if unclean, lot. Sunburned darker than Arabs, with brutish or cunning expressions, muscular, agile, inured to gutter hardship, living by their wits or their light fingers, they were tough, resourceful, and chock-full of endurance.[3]

The Zouaves were a striking contrast to the South Carolina boys

[3] The fastidious T. C. De Leon was fascinated by these Zouaves. These details are taken largely from his sprightly book *Four Years in Rebel Capitals*.

in their silver-trimmed gray, and to the Georgia "crackers" in their butternut brown. The lawless lot of Zouaves obeyed their young, middle-class officers, who gave commands in French, and who, in cases of flagrant insubordination, had little hesitancy in putting a bullet through an offender's anatomy or cracking his skull with a revolver butt. Bragg did not interfere with the Zouave officers' original methods of discipline.

That night, while the soldiers speculated on whether the President's visit might mean scaling ladders and a midnight assault on Pickens, Davis held a lengthy conference. He agreed with Bragg and Mallory that no attempt to take the fort should be made in the immediate future. Even if the operation were successful, it might well cost the lives of more than a thousand men, who were urgently needed in Virginia. The President asked Bragg to send to Lee at once as many troops as he could conveniently spare. Then he and Mallory returned to Montgomery.

As information filtered through the camp that some regiments would straightway proceed to Virginia, lusty cheers arose. The soldiers, bored with drilling, were eager for action. The Zouaves were among those chosen to go to Virginia.

On the way to Montgomery next day, at a "breakfast stop," while the officers were eating in the station, the Zouaves uncoupled their coach and stole the rest of the train. At dirk's point, the engineer was forced to proceed to the capital. The red-fezzed hellions aimed to have a high old time, and let off three months' pent-up steam before the officers could catch them.

Montgomery was shortly treated to memorable excitement. Grinning Zouaves tore into saloons, scattered customers, filled themselves with liquor. Some burst open grocery stores to get more grog. In shops they appropriated any trifle that took their fancy. A few pantalooned knaves, looking like illustrations from *Arabian Nights,* entered private homes and scared the daylights out of the womenfolk. Up and down the streets groups of Zouaves lurched drunkenly, roaring out "Zouzou," their favorite song.

Officials in the Executive Offices stopped work to stare from their windows. As blacks and whites alike scampered from the streets, a Georgia regiment was ordered to fix bayonets and hold the wild ones at bay. The crisis was at its height when the relief engine and coach came screeching into the station bearing the abandoned officers, who began jumping off before the train halted.

Into the roaring street mob and into the pandemonium of shops flew the young officers, yelling commands, swearing in gutter French, and felling recalcitrant thugs with pistol butts. When, on command of a short teen-aged lieutenant, a gigantic sergeant hesitated in dropping his booty, the youth leaped for his throat with one hand and cracked him over the temple with his revolver. The habit of obeying officers who meted out rough punishment asserted itself through the alcoholic maze. Within half an hour, the rounded-up battalion, minus nine unconscious ones, was docilely mustered on Main Street. For Montgomery, the spree of the Zouaves was the last big excitement in its brief reign as the Confederate capital.

After the President's return to Montgomery from Pensacola, Mrs. Wigfall brought him a perceptive letter, which she had received from a friend in Providence. The Rhode Island-born lady had lived in the South until her widowhood, when she had returned with her children to her Northern home. Davis read with special interest:

We are always delighted to hear from you—and indeed your letters and Louis's are the only comfort we have in this Yankee land surrounded by people who have no sympathy with us, and who only open their lips to revile the South and utter blood-thirsty threats. This morning an amiable lady wishes she had Jeff Davis in front of a big cannon. . . . We have now sufficient proof of how much stronger hate is than love of country. Where was the patriotism of Massachusetts when the country was at war with the English in 1812? I lived then at the South, and was ashamed of my countrymen who refused to assist in the war. . . . Now they are subscribing millions, and urging every man to go and fight their own countrymen. It is not patriotism; it is hatred to the South, and woe is me, that I must live here among such people. God grant you success. It is a righteous war and all the bloodshed will be upon the souls of those who brought it on. . . .

I think, however, that you at the South are wrong to undervalue the courage and resources of the Northern States. They are no doubt less accustomed to the use of firearms—there are very few who know how to ride, and they are less fiery in their impulses. They are less disposed to fight, but they are not cowardly where their interests are concerned; and will *fight for their money*. Where their property is at stake they will not hesitate to risk their lives.[4]

---

[4] This letter in its entirety appears with other Wigfall letters in a most interesting book by Wigfall's daughter, Loulie, Mrs. D. Giraud Wright: *A Southern Girl in '61, the War-Time Memories of a Confederate Senator's Daughter.*

The Rhode Island lady was right, the President agreed, in saying New Englanders had plenty of courage, and doubtless they would fight for what they believed their financial interests. Another friend in Montgomery had recently received a mourning letter from her Southern brother, now successfully established in business in Chicago. While deploring the awful state of impending strife and admitting that the Southern States had an undoubted constitutional right to secede, he declared: "We need you in our economy, and we shall have to fight you in self-defense, for our own preservation."

The day before Congress adjourned, President Davis received both good news and disappointing news. North Carolina unanimously passed an ordinance of secession. The Confederacy now had eleven states. But on that same May 20, because there was not a sufficient majority of Confederate sympathizers in Kentucky to overbalance those who wanted to remain in the Union, pro-Southern Governor Magoffin issued a neutrality proclamation and warned both sides against sending troops into the state. Davis had heard that Lincoln was particularly apprehensive about his native state and that he had remarked drolly that he *hoped* God was on his side, but that he absolutely *had* to have Kentucky. Davis, too, felt keenly the need for Kentucky; he believed that if Kentucky left the Union, the North might give up the war.

After Governor Magoffin declared for neutrality, the Confederate War Department set up recruiting stations along the border of Tennessee for the induction of Kentuckians who desired to join the Confederate Army. Among these were three of Mrs. Lincoln's brothers, all four of her brothers-in-law, and several cousins.[5] Kentucky was painfully divided. Brothers parted to go to opposite camps. One of John J. Crittenden's sons, George B., became an officer in the Confederate Army; another, Thomas L., held a commission in the Union Army. In one wide street in Louisville, Union volunteers were seen marching up one side, while Confederates marched down the other. President Lincoln had made Robert Anderson a Brigadier General and stationed him in Indiana, across the Ohio River, with a command that "on paper" embraced Kentucky. Two of Anderson's brothers-in-law put on Confederate uniforms.

[5] Only one of Mrs. Lincoln's brothers was pro-Union. But he did not fight, and died in 1862.

Events in Missouri were more discouraging to President Davis than those in Kentucky. Though Governor Jackson was ardently pro-Confederate, secession in that state had been at least temporarily defeated, largely by the strategy of Francis Blair, Jr. Even before Mr. Lincoln's inauguration, Blair had managed to get the war materials in St. Louis' Federal arsenal moved across the river to Illinois. And he had rounded up several thousand of the city's antislavery Germans and started them drilling in their club halls. Despite the high irregularity of the act, Captain Nathaniel Lyon, new commander of the Federal arsenal, began swearing them into United States service.

Fiery, red-bearded little Lyon worked fast against the return from Washington of General William S. Harney, who commanded the Federal Department of the West. Jefferson Davis had served with the old Indian fighter Harney in the wilds of Wisconsin, and recalled that he had been one of the few officers who had no interest in cards or gambling, but made gardening his diversion. A thoroughly loyal Union man, Harney yet believed in respecting the law of the land. Before being summoned to Washington at Blair's secret request, Harney had entered into a compact of peaceful neutrality with state authorities.

During Harney's absence, in early May, when Governor Jackson assembled some militia in annual encampment on the outskirts of St. Louis, Blair sent Captain Lyon, heavily veiled, sunbonneted, and reputedly dressed in Mrs. Blair's blind mother's clothes, to spy on the maneuvers. Driving through the camp in an old buggy, with a basket of eggs concealing loaded revolvers, Lyon observed and made plans. On May 10, the combative Captain led several thousand troops, largely composed of Germans, out to Camp Jackson. At gun point he seized seven hundred militiamen, appropriated 1,200 muskets, some twenty-five kegs of powder, and whatever else he wanted. As he started off to the arsenal with his prisoners, angry citizens tried to bar the way, brandishing sticks, throwing stones, and cursing the "damned Dutch." Soldiers began firing into the crowd. Twenty-eight persons, including some women, were killed outright and many were seriously wounded.

The Camp Jackson "massacre" created a mighty indignation throughout Missouri. A local civil war seemed imminent. When General Harney returned, he attempted pacification. Ordering the German companies out of St. Louis, he sought to make a truce with the state authorities. In the meantime, the Missouri Legislature had met, expressed condemnation, and passed bills for organization of militia.

Former Governor Sterling Price, Virginia-born Mexican War veteran, was made Commander in Chief of the state militia. Enormously popular, and known as a "Union man" who had voted against secession, Price was so outraged at the tactics of Lyon and Blair and the extreme Unionists that he became a devout secessionist.

On May 21, Price entered into a kind of cease-fire compact with the trustworthy General Harney. Both the Federal and the state forces would endeavor to prevent bloodshed and protect property of all citizens. Excitement was allayed temporarily. But Lyon and Blair were by no means satisfied. Both men wrote strong letters to powerful sources in Washington. In answer, Captain Lyon received a commission as Brigadier General, and Blair was instructed to remove General Harney if he saw fit. Before the month was out, Harney was transferred from the Missouri area and Lyon assumed his command. The Missouri situation was again critical, and President Davis feared another Maryland.

On May 24, the day after Virginia's voters approved secession, General Scott promptly moved Federal troops across the Potomac, occupied the town of Alexandria and the neighboring heights of Arlington. As if in revenge, because Lee would not lead the fight against the South, Scott turned Mrs. Lee's ancestral home, Arlington, into army headquarters. The estate, which had come to Mary Custis Lee from George Washington's stepson, was looked upon as having a certain sanctity by Virginians. They never forgave native-son Winfield Scott for his action. As one newspaper said, the whole South regarded the invasion of Lee's estate and Virginia's "sacred earth" as a "pollution."

General Lee, anticipating Scott's move, had written his wife some days before: "I grieve at the necessity that drives you from your home. . . . When I reflect upon the calamity impending over the country, my own sorrow sinks into insignificance." On the twenty-fifth, Robert E. Lee was transferred, with all the Virginia troops, to the Confederate States Army.

That same day, President Davis learned of a little flare-up at Harpers Ferry, which Joseph Johnston did not reach until May 23. Colonel Thomas J. Jackson declined at first to recognize Johnston's authority, although he was seventeen years Jackson's senior in age and service. "Until I receive further instructions from Governor Letcher or General Lee," the grim-faced Jackson said, "I do not feel at liberty to transfer my command to another." But he finally surrendered command when Johnston produced a paper with an endorsement referring to him as "commanding officer at Harpers Ferry."

Because it seemed evident that the North might soon launch an all-out attack on Virginia, Davis now decided to leave for Richmond as soon as the archives could be packed. The captious Charleston *Mercury* paid him a surprisingly generous tribute: "As to the object of the President's hastening to Virginia, we are convinced that it is the success of our cause which has attracted him. His presence will infuse additional life and vigor among the troops. Finding him willing to run any personal risk, they will emulate his example and defeat the hordes of Abolitionists Lincoln has arrayed against us."

But two days before the scheduled departure on May 27, the unremitting labor and anxiety of the last three months finally prostrated the President. War Clerk Jones noted in his diary, "He came down with a chill"; adding, "he works incessantly, sick or well." The weather had become intensely hot, and Mrs. Davis did not believe her husband able to travel. Apprehensively, she had watched him wear himself down.

In a letter to ailing Clement Clay in Huntsville, on May 10, Varina had written of her husband's working too hard. "He comes home to eat his meals, but always eats under a protest against the time occupied. 'Oft in the stilly night,' he is forced to come home for there is no one to help to work. Sometimes the Cabinet 'sans Scotch cap' depart surreptitiously one at a time. To make a long story short he overworks himself and all the rest of mankind."

Later, she wrote in her *Memoir*, "He left for his office before nine and came home exhausted, and silent, if no guests were there. But," she continued, "he was so gentle and patient that Pierce Butler, a houseguest at one time, asked me jestingly, behind his back, of course, if the President was always a combination of angel and seer like that."

In his present feverish debility, his physician said he should not make the trip. Jefferson Davis's will, however, made him rise and dress himself in time for the train scheduled to depart at eight on Sunday evening. When his anxious wife saw him leave Montgomery, "it was upon his bed." Since there were no sleeping cars at that time in the South, a bed had been set up for him at one end of a private coach. The President departed, accompanied by his body servant, Secretary of State Toombs, Louis Wigfall, and Mrs. Wigfall. Varina, with the children, would follow at her convenience after packing and closing up the house.

Aboard the train, the President went immediately to bed, or, rather, reclined, after removing his coat, neckerchief, and shoes. Because of his indisposition, precautions had been made to keep the journey as quiet as possible. But the news leaked out, and everywhere along the way, at all hours, eager people gathered, hoping to catch a glimpse of their leader.

At Atlanta, Augusta, and Wilmington, crowds filled the stations, cheering and calling for the President. Feeling constrained to respond, Davis would rouse himself and make brief speeches. At some of the smaller places, while he slept the sleep of the exhausted, a certain number of importunate citizens were permitted to tiptoe through the car and take a look at his careworn face. At Goldsboro, North Carolina, when the train stopped for midday dinner, the President went with the others into the hotel dining room. He was instantly surrounded by the town's prettiest girls in ruffled organdies, who wreathed him with garlands and fanned him while he ate. North Carolinians knew Mr. Davis only slightly. But when they saw him and heard him, they had "an instantaneous enthusiasm for him." According to the press, his fine presence, his austere handsomeness, and his beautiful speaking voice stirred them strangely. As Mrs. Wigfall wrote her daughter, it was "a glorious demonstration" all along the way. "The President was everywhere rapturously received."

"It was a terribly fatiguing trip," Mrs. Wigfall added. "The whole country, as we came through, was like a military camp. The cars were crowded with troops, and all as jubilant, as if they were going to a frolic, instead of a fight."

On this second stage of his journey into tragic history, while he lay with eyes closed, Jefferson Davis must have reflected somewhat in the vein of James Ford Rhodes's thinking three decades later. "Had the North thoroughly understood the problem," Rhodes wrote in his *History of the United States,* "had it known that the people of the Cotton States were practically unanimous; that the action of Virginia, North Carolina, and Tennessee was backed by a large and generous majority, it might have refused to undertake the seemingly unachievable task."

CHAPTER VIII

"THE MANTLE OF WASHINGTON
FALLS GRACEFULLY"

ON THE MORNING of May 29, when the President's train emerged from a cut through a bluff, Jefferson Davis could, from the spindly James River bridge, see Richmond spread out like a panorama. Its green amphitheatric hills were dotted with white houses and punctuated by pleasing church spires. In its early summer flowering, Richmond was picturesque. Far below, he observed the shallow current foaming over rocks and gliding around the little islands to navigable water some three miles from Hollywood Cemetery. As he looked down on this beautiful burial ground, where President James Monroe slept among the illustrious dead, Davis had no thought that evergreen Hollywood was destined to be his own final resting place.

When the train pulled into the station, the President was greeted by a salute of fifteen guns. A deputation, headed by Virginia's Governor Letcher and the Mayor of Richmond, welcomed him and conducted him through cheering crowds to the Spotswood Hotel, located at the corner of Main and Eighth Streets. The hostelry's doorways, windows, and halls were adorned with Confederate flags. His suite, the best in the hotel, was garnished with flowers.

From the hotel balcony, President Davis made a brief, fitting speech, and withdrew. Then Mississippi's young L. Q. C. Lamar excited the radiant street crowd. "Thank God!" he cried. "We have a country at last, to live for, to pray for, and, if necessary, to die for."

Commenting upon the enthusiasm aroused all along the way by the Confederate President, the Richmond *Daily Enquirer* declared: "The mantle of Washington falls gracefully upon his shoulders. Never were a people more enraptured with their Chief Magistrate than ours are with President Davis."

In fact, the entire Virginia press welcomed Mr. Davis to the Old Dominion with glowing warmth. His character and his ability were extolled. Emphasis was laid upon the remarkable advantage of having a Chief Executive who was both a statesman and a man of military education and experience. Davis's superior mental vigor, his mastery of detail, his thoroughness, and his personal charm were all specifically praised. Difficult-to-please Virginia could not have been more delighted with any man who was not a native son.

Hardly before the President had time to relax from the fatiguing journey, he attended a crushing reception in his honor. At half past five, accompanied by a cortege on horseback, he rode to the New Fair Grounds, where an assemblage of ladies and gentlemen mingled with the troops encamped there. When he left his saddle, he was all but overwhelmed by the pressure of a crowd eager to shake his hand. In his first speech to soldiers on Virginia soil, he addressed them as "My Friends and Fellow-Citizens":

I look upon you as the last best hope of liberty. . . . Upon your strong right arm depends the success of your country. In asserting the birthright to which you were born you are to remember that life and blood are nothing as compared with the immense interests you have at stake. . . . I know there beats in the breast of Southern sons a determination never to surrender—a determination never to go home but to tell a tale of honor. . . . The country relies upon you. Upon you rest the hopes of our people; and I have only to say, my friends, that to the last breath of my life, I am wholly yours.

With a sincerity that could not be simulated, Jefferson Davis made them know that he was now absolutely dedicated to the cause of independence. Here was a man to believe in, to follow with confidence, as volunteers had done at Monterey and Buena Vista. The cheering was tremendous.

The Executive Offices had been set up in the Customs House, a short walk from the Spotswood. The President's room was on the third floor, at the head of the stairs as one entered from Bank Street. Close by, the plain halls of the vast Mechanics Institute were being partitioned into offices for the various departments of government. Hammering and sawing made a din by night and day.

Both the Customs House and Mechanics Hall faced on Capitol Square, a large sloping greensward area with winding walks under shade trees, all enclosed by an iron fence. The state capitol, with its Grecian columns, occupied a center elevation. In the capitol the President admired Jean-Antoine Houdon's marble statue of Washington, which Benjamin Franklin had commissioned in Paris in 1785. And on the walk leading from the capitol to St. Paul's Episcopal Church, he saw Thomas Crawford's dramatic equestrian Washington in bronze, which the sculptor had been making during Davis's last years in the U.S. Senate.

Capitol Square was a favorite rendezvous for colored nurses in charge of children, and the President found it pleasant to see youngsters in high spirits tumbling over the green lawns. Impressed as he was with the classic simplicity of the capitol and of St. Paul's, he knew that the most valuable structure in Richmond was the slate-roofed Tredegar Iron Works, belching smoke down by the foaming river. The only rolling mill of any size in the entire South and the only foundry capable of casting cannon, Tredegar might prove more important to Southern independence than any governmental agency.

Immediately, the President's burdens began to increase. Some Northern papers were already clamoring "On to Richmond!" Federal troops were daily pouring into Washington, D.C., only a hundred miles from the Confederate capital.[1] Herds of beef cattle to feed them grazed on the lawns of the Smithsonian Institution while awaiting slaughter. A stout defense of Virginia had to be speeded, the new republic put into mature routine, and persistent, unqualified office seekers disposed of with tact.

Happily, in Richmond Jefferson Davis found able hands to help him with the infant government. And the same feeling that animated Virginia's women in the Revolutionary War possessed them now. Everywhere women were at work, making clothing and even tents and cartridges. Davis was told that "the ladies were as determined to fight as the men," and, half jokingly, that there was scarcely a house on Main Street where they had not collected a "heap of rocks" and other missiles, which they intended throwing upon the heads of Yankees should they venture into Richmond. "If the women," wrote Catherine Cooper Hopley, a British subject in the city, "did not positively shoulder their muskets and set out for camp, they nevertheless took no mean share in

[1] Professor W. E. Dodd wrote in his biography of Jefferson Davis that "More than 100,000 soldiers, including volunteers, had been put in motion by the North when Davis reached his capital" (p. 245). But, of course, a large majority of the Northern troops were volunteers.

the common cause, using all their influence and eloquence in urging upon sons and brothers to 'resist aggression'." But the President did not find Virginia's ardent men needing a prod; they were enlisting with enthusiastic promptitude, after giving their young sisters and sweethearts practice lessons in the use of pistols to defend themselves while they were away.

General Lee had not been in Richmond to welcome President Davis. He had gone to Manassas Junction to inspect conditions. He had not found them to his liking. Only about 6,000 men were concentrated there; the officer in command, General M. L. Bonham of South Carolina, did not seem sufficiently experienced to handle that strategic danger spot. An hour after his return to the capital, Lee was closeted with the President to give him a survey of the state of affairs at Manassas and a report of all that he himself had done since May 1.

Davis was delighted to find his long-time friend in prime physical condition; at fifty-four, Lee was easily the handsomest and most impressive-looking officer in the Army. The President commiserated with him on the loss of Arlington. Lee bore the misfortune with philosophic stoicism, but he was grieved at his wife's inconsolable sorrow. Yet Mary Lee, as Davis had heard, had been a secessionist before her husband, and she invariably spoke of the Confederate cause as "glorious." Now Mrs. Lee and the daughters were refugee guests in various country houses of friends. The President had asked Custis Lee, the eldest son, whose Number One record at West Point had surpassed his father's Number Two, to be one of his aides. The second son, W. H. F. Lee, called Fitzhugh, Fitz, or, generally, Rooney, a strapping, vital fellow, six foot four, was already a cavalry captain. The third, Rob, Jr., a university student at Charlottesville, was chafing to enter the service.

Lee, the titular Commander in Chief of Virginia forces, explained that he had organized and sent into various fields some 30,000 men, including those the President had dispatched from the Cotton States. John Bankhead Magruder, who had been a plebe when Davis was graduated from West Point and who was nicknamed "Prince John" because of his elegance, was preparing a defensive line in the Peninsula from Yorktown up to Williamsburg. Lee said that Manassas, the railway junction near the little stream called Bull Run, only thirty miles from Washington, should be strengthened immediately. Davis fully agreed, and the two of them decided that Beauregard was the man to send to meet invasion at Manassas.

The President felt that no one could have done a better job of organization and arrangement than Lee had. It was heartening to have a man of Lee's caliber as his adviser. In Montgomery, he had sometimes felt more or less alone with his devouring multiplicity of cares; now Lee could take much of the War Department's burden off his shoulders, and at this critical time Lee's special knowledge of conditions in Virginia was indispensable. An energetic worker, unsparing of himself, devoid of conceit, blessed with humility, a specimen of mankind framed to inspire—that was how Davis regarded Robert E. Lee.

"The life of Davis," as Dodd has written, "now merges to a considerable extent with that of Robert E. Lee." Lee appreciated Davis's understanding of military matters, which was sound, for his viewpoint in war was essentially that of the professional soldier. And Lee was to find in Davis a discerning and consoling champion, who never lost faith in him, no matter what failures were chalked against him or what sarcastic scorn the press meted out. This esteem of Jefferson Davis, wrote Freeman, was one of Lee's greatest assets. The two men were in remarkable accord from the first, and they were to agree on virtually everything throughout the war.

The last day of May, 1861, had marked the end of the United States Post Office in the Confederacy. On June 1, Southern postmasters could no longer accept letters bearing United States stamps. Shortly after taking office as Postmaster General, John Reagan had sent a secret agent to Washington, who enticed several high postal officials to join the Confederacy and bring along their "forms, contracts, and needful postal information." His chief difficulty now was lack of Confederate stamps. Until engravers and equipment were secured from abroad, postmasters would have to send letters unstamped on the payment of the proper fee.[2]

After being lionized in Richmond society for a couple of days, General Beauregard took command at Manassas. Immediately, he demanded 10,000 reinforcements. Although there was no visible sign of imminent invasion, he threatened retreat if they did not arrive soon. And straightway he raised a clamor against the Commissary Department, headed by Colonel Lucius B. Northrop, who, he claimed, was not sending the food required.

[2] The first crudely lithographed Confederate stamps—of five-cent denomination in green, bearing the likeness of Jefferson Davis—were made by a Richmond firm and appeared on October 16, 1861.

Northrop was to become a prime target for general criticism. This South Carolinian, who had entered West Point in Jefferson Davis's last year, was prevented by a wound from doing regimental duty. He had seen service in the United States commissariat. Besides his acquired special knowledge, Northrop possessed, in Davis's opinion, "strong practical sense and incorruptible integrity."

On Monday, June 3, 1861, Jefferson Davis became fifty-three years old. He was feeling quite fit. At the height of his popularity, he was, according to the press, indubitably the first name in the South. Three special events marked his birthday: news of the death of Stephen A. Douglas; the raising of the Confederate flag on the *Sumter* by Raphael Semmes at New Orleans; and the first Federal victory, at Philippi, in the mountains of western Virginia.

In mid-career, at only forty-eight, the North's great Democrat was suddenly dead, his ambition unfulfilled. Mary Chesnut casually recorded in her diary: "Judge Stephen A. Douglas, the little giant, is dead; one of those killed by the war no doubt; trouble of mind."

Did the death of Douglas augur ill or good for the Confederacy? Davis reflected on how courageously and eloquently Douglas had striven in the Senate to stem the tide of war, how he had pleaded with the Lincoln Administration to evacuate Sumter and Pickens. But when Lincoln called for troops, Douglas was the first Democrat to offer his patriotic support. Recently, he had been touring the North to whip up fighting spirit among the antiwar Democrats; reports said he had been drinking excessively to whip up his own enthusiasm. Under the strain, the powerfully built Douglas collapsed. Now, only seven weeks after President Lincoln's war call, he was dead. It was indeed a blow to the Northern Democratic party; there was no one with his impellent personality or political caliber to assume leadership.

Yet, Davis recalled, it was Douglas who had persuaded him and President Franklin Pierce, against their better judgment, to support the opening of the Kansas-Nebraska Territory, which inadvertently stirred up bloody local clashes and pointed the way to war. And it could be reasoned that Douglas's uncompromising ambition had split the Democratic party and brought about the election of the Republican Lincoln, which in turn had touched off a chain of secession ordinances. Yet the removal from the scene of the Republican's foremost political opponent could hardly be good for the Confederacy. Douglas might have proved helpful to the South, which he understood better than most Northerners, since he had been happily married to two Southern women successively. And, above all others, he had possessed the strength and brilliance effective to fight vengeful radicals like Edwin M. Stanton, Charles Sumner, and Thaddeus Stevens.

On June 3, at New Orleans, Raphael Semmes, who was to become the Confederacy's most noted naval commander, and his officers messed on board the transformed *Sumter* for the first time. Semmes had taken an old packet boat, "full of upper cabins and other top-hamper, as unlike a ship of war as possible," dismantled her, and reconstructed the first Confederate vessel for preying upon Federal commerce in retaliation for Mr. Lincoln's blockade.

That same third of June, at Philippi, an insignificant village, Union troops surprised and drove out a small Confederate force. This very minor skirmish gave the North its first "victory" for the papers.

But by no means did the majority of Americans on either side of the Mason and Dixon Line feel that actual war was inevitable. A former West Pointer from Ohio, William Tecumseh Sherman, who had resigned as Superintendent of the Louisiana Military Academy in December, was mildly surprised at being summoned to Washington. Now vice-president of the St. Louis Street Railway Company, which provided horse-car transportation, he wrote the company president, David Hartley Armstrong, a casual business memorandum dated June 7, 1861.

I have just received a dispatch from Washington calling me thither immediately. I am going downtown and may be will meet you, but should I miss you I leave this letter for you. We have on hand oats for say 8 days. Hay plenty at lower stables—and any day it can be bought at upper stables. I may be back in about a week. At all events I will write from Washington immediately what they want with me.

I wish you would look in occasionally and if anything occurs I will be obliged if you would apply the remedy and I will stand by it when I get back.

Everything is working smoothly and I think will continue to.

> Your friend
> W. T. Sherman[3]

Sherman did not return to his job in a week or ever. After some days, Armstrong received word that he had accepted a commission as Colonel of the Thirteenth United States Infantry. Events moved

---

[3] David Hartley Armstrong, who was pro-Southern, was later United States Senator from Missouri. This holograph letter from Sherman is owned by his grandson, Brigadier General Donald Armstrong, Washington, D.C., who showed the author the original letter and had it photostated for him.

swiftly. In July he was commanding the third brigade at the battle of Bull Run.

On the June 7 that Sherman wrote of oats and hay for the draft horses, the Confederate War Department was agitated to hear from General Joseph Johnston that he purposed to abandon Harpers Ferry. He had been in command there less than a fortnight. Lee promptly reiterated by telegram the great value the President put on the place and reminded Johnston that the loss of the strategic stronghold would be a blow to public morale and would injure the Confederate cause in Maryland.

"Notwithstanding this determination of the Executive," Johnston coolly wrote in his *Narrative of Military Operations* (pp. 20-21), "I resolved not to continue to occupy the place." Word had come to Johnston that aging General Robert Patterson, a sixty-nine-year-old veteran of the War of 1812, had begun moving down with a Federal force from Chambersburg, Pennsylvania. Though Johnston had only some 8,000 active troops at Harpers Ferry, Colonel Thomas Jackson felt that the Confederates could easily hold the fort against the larger Union army. Agreeing with Jackson were other subordinates destined for fame: Edmund Kirby Smith, A. P. Hill, J. E. B. Stuart, and Colonel W. N. Pendleton, Episcopal Rector of Lexington and a West Pointer who remembered his artillery training.

But Johnston hesitated to withdraw only because he wanted the War Department to take the responsibility of ordering him to do so. There was marked asperity in the exchange of letters between Adjutant General Cooper and himself. When Johnston heard a local rumor that another Federal army was moving toward Romney, a town sixty miles west, he sent his quartermaster stores thirty-five miles away to Winchester. Then on June 15, the disgruntled troops, who were eager to fight "Yankees," moved out of Harpers Ferry after destroying the Potomac bridges and wrecking railway facilities and public buildings that might aid the Federals.

As it turned out, Patterson had already given up plans of an offensive and sent some of his troops back to General Winfield Scott, who feared an attack on Washington. Jackson was utterly disgusted with Johnston. All Richmond felt consternation at the withdrawal. Jefferson Davis kept his thoughts to himself.

The first significant clash between Northern and Southern troops came on June 10, around a country church called Big Bethel, thirteen miles below Yorktown on the Peninsula. Some 1,400 Confederates under the general command of John Magruder, but led by North Carolina's D. H. Hill, tangled with seven Federal regiments belonging to General Ben Butler's command at Fort Monroe. The Federals, numbering close to 4,000, were driven back with nearly one hundred casualties.[4] The Confederates suffered eleven.

Magruder enthusiastically proclaimed the action as being as decisive as any in the Mexican War. The Richmond *Dispatch* went absurdly further, declaring Big Bethel one of the most extraordinary victories in the annals of war. Hill was extolled as extravagantly as "Prince John," and he, in turn, lavished praise on others, particularly on Major George Wythe Randolph, a grandson of Thomas Jefferson, who had commanded the guns.

Though this victory boosted Confederate morale, already romantically high, Davis knew the danger and foolishness of regarding the fight at Bethel as indubitable evidence of Southerners' superiority in combat. To both the President and General Lee, the Bethel engagement was chiefly important in pointing out the pressing need of building up the eastern defenses of Richmond. Potent assistance was soon given Magruder, and lines of earthworks were thrown up at strategic spots before Yorktown and Williamsburg. Largely because of this engineering work ordered in June, 1861, Richmond was to be saved from the onslaught of McClellan in the spring of 1862.

In revenge for the defeat at Bethel, squads of Ben Butler's men made depredations on the lower part of the Peninsula, particularly in the county of Gloucester. Crops were wantonly destroyed, furniture spoiled, some houses burned down. Bonds and private papers found in desks or in wall safes were torn to bits. Many valuables were carried off by Federal soldiers and sent as souvenirs to Northern relatives. Scores of slaves were stolen and reported as fugitives. General Butler termed the Negroes brought into his camp "contrabands of war," and made them work harder for rations than they had worked on the plantations.

On June 17, one week after the hullabaloo over Big Bethel, President Davis rewarded Colonel Magruder with a commission of brigadier general. At the same time, ten other colonels were raised to the rank of brigadier. Among these were three of Joe Johnston's command at Winchester: Thomas J. Jackson of Virginia, E. Kirby Smith of Florida, and Barnard E. Bee of South Carolina. It was well that Johnston had

---

[4] D. H. Hill claimed three hundred Federal casualties. Douglas Freeman said seventy-seven was nearer correct.

such able lieutenants, for a really formidable force of 20,000 was now being collected by General Patterson to drive the Confederates up the Shenandoah Valley.

Mrs. Chesnut reported in her diary that Richmond had been "horrified" at Johnston's retreating from Harpers Ferry and blamed it on "that slow-coach" Secretary of War Walker for not giving him enough ammunition. In this criticism of Walker, which was general, the usually astute Mrs. Chesnut was unjust. Walker had done everything in his power to get ammunition from the various states. With grave misgivings, President Davis had found that instead of pooling resources of troops, ammunition, and equipment in the hands of the Confederate Government, individual states, carrying out the letter of the State Rights doctrine, withheld for local defense soldiers and arms needed in general service. Some Governors even insisted upon retaining certain rights over their forces in the Confederate Army, including the appointment of officers.

This keeping of troops and material within states was caused partly by the apprehension of a slave insurrection. While, in truth, this fear was ever present and there was a definite need for "home guards," it was exaggerated as an excuse for withholding troops and arms. Davis often had a tough struggle to get possession of soldiers and equipment. In theory, the individual states had transferred to the Confederate Government the material captured at United States forts and arsenals, but in reality most Governors retained a large proportion of the arms.

As early as March, 1861, on requesting arms, Secretary of War Walker had received a communication from Alabama's Governor A. B. Moore saying that he believed the arms "should be retained by the State to enable her to meet any emergency and protect and defend her citizens." [5]

The President was pledged to defend the Confederacy at all points, and, because of the intense State Rights feeling, it was inevitable that military policy necessitated what is often criticized as "dispersion."

---

[5] On July 4, 1861, while Federal General Irvin McDowell was massing forces at Arlington for the conquest of Virginia, Governor Moore felt he could not release 3,000 men called by the Confederate Government. On the other hand, he equipped six regiments and 2,500 more emergency troops to defend the Alabama coast, which was in no danger. Even in his own state, President Davis met reluctance. On July 17, a few days before the Battle of Manassas, Governor John J. Pettus of Mississippi was to telegraph the Secretary of War that he had no power under state law to arm regiments that had just been raised at Iuka, Mississippi.

In Virginia, Governor Letcher was not at all pleased at having to relinquish some of his power to the Confederate Government. Davis's problems with the State of Virginia are innocently revealed in the diary of Betty, daughter of the famous oceanographer Matthew Fontaine Maury: "He [father] is rather blue. . . . The President has made it understood that now Virginia is given up to him and is one of the Confederate States, all commissions and appointments given by her are null and void. . . . There is great jealousy between the Virginia and the Confederate forces."

The little victory at Big Bethel was soon more than offset by a substantial Confederate defeat in western Virginia. Lee had been so concerned by conditions in that region that he had sent his adjutant, Brigadier General R. S. Garnett, to take charge. Complaining of an inadequate force, Garnett had left Richmond prophetically murmuring to friends, "They have sent me to my death."

Western Virginia was extremely difficult territory, not only because of its steep mountains, but because some of its pro-Union people acted as spies and false guides. But soon Garnett was writing optimistically that he held "the gates to Northwest Virginia and hoped at the proper hour to swoop down on the twice as numerous Federal forces."

However, in late June, Major General George Brinton McClellan entered Virginia from Ohio, with approximately 20,000 men. In May, McClellan had resigned his position as President of the Ohio and Mississippi Railroad, with headquarters in Cincinnati, to accept a high commission in the Union Army. He had been put in command of everything along the Ohio border, and now, leading twenty-seven regiments, he was about to strike at the Confederate forces on Rich Mountain.

The news gave President Davis considerable concern. The thirty-four-year-old McClellan had been a onetime favorite lieutenant of his. When Davis was Secretary of War, he had discerned the young man's superior qualities and had sent him as an observer to the Crimean War, in which capacity he had proved extremely able. Davis liked this cultured Philadelphian, who was an adept in several languages and a first-rate executive, besides being a good soldier. He believed that with his intelligence, vigor, and qualities of leadership, McClellan had the makings of a great commanding officer. Of all the Federal officers, Davis would undoubtedly have preferred to have him on the Confederate side.

On July 11, in a skillful flank movement executed by the Dutch-descended Brigadier General William S. Rosecrans, McClellan's second in command, the Confederates were routed, and General Garnett was killed in a maze of mountain laurel. Although the Confederates lost only seven hundred men, killed, wounded, or taken prisoner, McClellan's telegraphic dispatches presented the event as a military maneuver of peculiar brilliance. Though he himself was not even present at the engagement, McClellan had planned it, and the Northern press lauded him as if the battle had been equal to a second Austerlitz. McClellan possessed a gift for self-advertising as well as a natural ability to rouse the highest enthusiasm in his men. He caught the public's imagination immediately and became the idol of the North.

With the arrival of the President, Richmond had really become the capital of the Confederacy. The normally quiet city of less than 40,000 soon became gorged with office seekers, concessionaries, camp followers, hangers-on. The presence of the Government had brought a mighty influx of persons from other states, not only green recruits, but anxious relatives who wanted last glimpses of their loved ones before they went into battle. Hotels stayed packed. The homes of gentry in reduced circumstances began offering boarding accommodations. Soldiers from the suburban camps strayed through the streets, seeking amusement. Privates with proper letters of introduction knocked at the best doors and were welcomed as honored guests.

Trains from the west and the south daily unloaded men in varieties of uniforms. On the crowded streets, the Georgians' butternut jackets and homespun grays were good foils for the scarlet pantaloons of the New Orleans Zouaves and the blue-and-orange outfits of the Maryland Zouaves. Smartly tailored officers from South Carolina made a striking contrast to Texan cavalrymen with their long hair, jingling spurs, and peaked saddles, and to western mountaineers in bearskin shirts and fringed leggings.

A large house at the corner of Clay and Twelfth Streets had been bought by patriotic citizens, subscribing to a forty-thousand-dollar fund, as a present from the city to the President. He declined to accept it as a gift, though he was pleased to take it for his home upon condition that the municipality receive rent from the Confederate Government. Built by Dr. John Brockenbrough in 1818 and known as the Brockenbrough House, it was a handsome, three-story building of a rather severe style. Its ceilings were high; its carved mantels were of

Carrara marble. The apartments for entertaining were in the rear and *en suite,* with a parlor between the drawing room and dining room. Wide French windows opened on a sixty-seven-foot-long piazza, "noble with towering columns." This veranda gave on a garden sloping in terraces, abounding in apple, pear, and cherry trees as well as flower beds.

From the upper windows, Jefferson Davis could see into Henrico County, with its orchards and small farms. Nearer, were tree-shaded suburban homes. To the southeast, he saw the James far below, meandering toward Drewry's Bluff. On the second floor, he selected the rooms for his private office and bedchamber. While the house was being redecorated and furnished, the President's family were to be the city's guests at the Spotswood.

When Mrs. Davis arrived with the children and servants and her sister Margaret Howell, the President was at the station to meet his wife in a carriage and four presented for their use by the City Council until their own carriage arrived. Mrs. Wigfall wrote her daughter that the people of Richmond seemed "disposed to do all they can to show their joy at the exchange from Montgomery."

Varina Davis was delighted to find in Richmond many old friends, like the Harrisons of Brandon and her "dear Lydia," wife of General Joseph E. Johnston. In her first introductions to Virginia's ladies, Mrs. Davis was impressed by the simplicity and sincerity of their manners, their soft beauty, and "the absence of the gloze acquired by association in the merely 'fashionable society.'" Though they received her graciously enough, she noted a certain reserve. It was, she thought, something like the wary manner of English county folk to strangers when first introduced, no matter how impeccably.

Some days after reaching Richmond, President Davis had appointed June 13 as a day of fasting and prayer throughout the Confederacy. The South's newspapers urged due observance, with suspension of all business activities. The nation responded in commendable spirit, and from the pulpits ministers exhorted self-denial and resolution. The church collections of the day went to support of the Army.

The President himself rarely failed to attend Sunday-morning services at St. Paul's. But not even divine worship kept him from his duties. During June he would go to the Executive Offices before or after church. The third Sunday, before church time, while War Clerk Jones was working alone in his office, the President "approached lightly" and stood behind his chair waiting for him to look up. "At length," Jones wrote, "I turned my head and beheld the President not three feet from me. He smiled, and said he was looking for a certain letter referred by him to the Secretary of War. . . . We then proceeded into the Secretary's office in search of it. The Secretary's habit was to take the papers from his table, and after marking on them with his pencil the disposition he wished made of them, he threw helter-skelter into a large arm-chair. This chair now contained half a bushel; and the President and I set to work in quest of the letter. We removed them one by one; and as we progressed, he said with an impatient smile, 'It is always sure to be the last one.' And so it proved. Having found it, he departed immediately; and soon after I saw him on his way to church."

Orderly in the extreme himself, Jefferson Davis found it hard to see the lack of order in his Secretary of War's office. But he never took Leroy Walker to task. He knew the high-strung man was not well; Walker had tried too hard and overworked himself. But he seemed to lack administrative ability, and he did not know how to "economize his time." He had as much difficulty in making decisions as in keeping his papers straight. One day, when his nerves were on edge, Walker said, with a sigh, to Jones: "No *gentleman* can be fit for office." And Walker, despite his tobacco chewing, was a gentleman; his wife was a beauty and the best-dressed woman in the capital. Personally, Davis liked Walker, whose patriotism was unsurpassed; he regretted that he had little instinct for military affairs.

Davis knew he had made a mistake in acceding to the urging of Yancey and Clement Clay to give the Alabamian the post. But, blessedly, now he had Lee close at hand to advise him. Lee, like himself, took a hearty interest in the details of war. In the late afternoons, the two would be seen, splendid figures on horseback, riding out together to the encampment in West End, where the volunteers were drilled from morning to night.

After the middle of June, Mrs. Davis began holding small receptions at the Spotswood. Occasionally her husband would attend. At one of them the President sat for almost an hour in a tête-à-tête with Mary Chesnut, whose sprightly talk he keenly relished. But this day he was not very consoling to her. He was of the same mind he had been in, in Montgomery: it would be a long war, and the South would endure many bitter experiences before it was over. He laughed at the Southerners' faith in their own prowess. "We are like the British," he said; "we think every Southerner equal to three Yankees." "After his experience of the fighting qualities of Southerners in Mexico," Mary Chesnut wrote in her diary, "Mr. Davis believes that we will do all that can be done by pluck and muscle, endurance and dogged courage, dash and red-hot patriotism, and yet his tone was not sanguine. There was a sad refrain running through it all."

Mrs. Chesnut did not know the sad refrain was in some measure due to fresh concern over Missouri. General Lyon was threatening to disarm all pro-Confederate citizens and put arms in the hands of pro-Union men. In a called conference, Governor Jackson and General Price had again offered neutrality. They would disband their militia and keep out Confederate armies if Blair and Lyon would disband their Federal troops, euphemistically called "Home Guards." Lyon scorned the peaceful overtures. He would see every citizen dead before he would concede that the State of Missouri could put any conditions upon the Federal Government.

Gathering his many thousand well-armed troops, including "the damned Dutch," Lyon started a military march on the capital, Jefferson City. The surprised Governor fled to the northwest, and General Price, who had gone recruiting in the western part of the state, soon joined him at Booneville. Lyon and Blair had destroyed the idea of peaceful neutrality. Governor Jackson now issued a call for 50,000 volunteers "to protect control of domestic affairs." Price took command in the field. Secession was not openly mentioned, however much it was thought on. Missouri was still a huge question mark.

Davis longed to be able to send substantial troops to assist Missouri's Governor and Sterling Price, but he had none to spare. With the continued concentration of Federal forces in and about Washington, Virginia was in grave danger.

The Confederate President was naturally anxious about the tack that would be taken when Mr. Lincoln's eighty days of personal rule ended on July 4. Northern comments upon Lincoln's interim use of power left no doubt, as Dr. McElroy has written, "that many Unionists wished that a less autocratic, less lawless leader, had been chosen." In his address to the convened Congress, Lincoln reserved a special bitterness for Virginia. "The people of Virginia," he declared, "have thus allowed this insurrection to make its nest within her borders; and this government has no choice left but to deal with it, where it finds it."

Almost immediately after Lincoln's address, reports reached the

Confederate President that the invasion of Virginia might be expected at any time. General McDowell, with headquarters in Arlington, was energetically whipping into shape a great army of green volunteers with the help of 1,800 regulars. General Patterson was a constant threat to Joseph E. Johnston's position at Winchester.

Two days after the United States Congress convened, Davis was confronted with a most serious situation. A privateer, the *Savannah*, had been captured by a Federal warship, its crew put in irons and taken to New York charged with "piracy and treason." According to Lincoln's interpretation of the war as a "mere domestic insurrection," they faced execution.

Davis acted with celerity and resolution. On July 6 he sent a stiff demand that the men from the *Savannah* be treated as prisoners of war, and not as traitors or pirates. In "strong ink" he wrote the President of the United States:

It is the desire of this Government so to conduct the war now existing as to mitigate its horrors as far as may be possible, and, with this intent, its treatment of prisoners captured by its forces has been marked by the greatest humanity and leniency, consistent with public obligations. . . . Painful as will be the necessity, this Government will deal out to the prisoners held by it the same treatment and the same fate as shall be experienced by those captured on the *Savannah*. And if driven to the terrible necessity of retaliation by your execution of any of its officers or crew, retaliation will be extended as far as shall be requisite to secure the abandonment of a practice unknown to the warfare of civilized men, and so barbarous as to disgrace the nation which shall be guilty of inaugurating it.

He sent Colonel Richard Taylor, son of Zachary, to carry the message personally to Lincoln. The President declined to see him. General Scott, however, assured Taylor that Davis's stern dispatch had been placed in Lincoln's hands. The sailors of the *Savannah* were not executed. Davis's unequivocal stand resulted in an exchange of prisoners and the recognition that men captured on privateers would be treated not as pirates but as prisoners of war. The Southern press rang with exalted expressions of admiration for the firmness of the leader.

With the Federal Army preparing to advance on Richmond, President Davis now conferred with General Lee and Adjutant General Cooper for entire afternoons. Preparations for meeting the invasion at Manassas took up the major portion of their conferences. The question of supplying arms and munitions of war was the pressing consideration, for their lack was alarming. The problem of transportation for reinforcements and supplies was disturbing in the extreme. On July 10, Davis wrote to General Johnston at Winchester:

> Your letter found me trying by every method to hasten re-enforcements to you, but small as our force is, the want of transportation does not allow me to send such as we have except at a rate which makes me heart-sick. . . . Everybody disappoints me in their answers to my requisitions for troops, and the last hope of a large force of militia coming to your aid seems doomed to add another to past disappointments.
>
> I know you will do whatever is possible, and that you will only follow the dictates of your own good judgment and true patriotism. The anxiety of the reckless and the short-sighted policy of the selfish may urge you to fight when your judgment decided otherwise. The responsibility is great. I have tried for a week to get off and join you, but have not been able to do so, without having arrangements for procuring and forwarding troops to be delayed if not deranged. . . .
>
> May God bless and direct you in this critical hour of our national existence.
> Your friend,
>
> Jefferson Davis

Three days later, in answer to another pressing communication from Johnston, the President, while himself "weary and heart-sick" because of his lack of arms to supply troops, sent the General a warm, solicitous letter phrased to bolster his morale and forestall a retreat.

> I realize the difficulty to which you refer of a retreat, and feel that it would expose Virginia to temporary, if not permanent, disintegration. . . . I have therefore resorted to a call for the militia in all the counties north of James River from the Alleghany to the Atlantic. If they come with promptitude and spirit and the sixteen regiments which I hope for from the cotton States should arrive in time, we may yet drive the invaders from Virginia and teach our insolent foe some lessons which will incline him to seek for a speedy peace. I need not assure you that my confidence and interest in you both as an officer and as a friend cause me to turn constantly to your position with deepest solicitude. . . .

These two letters of July 10 and July 13 from Davis to Johnston, which may be found in *Official Records*, Series II, Volume I, pages 973-974 and 976-977 respectively, reveal the President's courtesy and "careful handling" in dealing with the commander of the Army of the Valley.

By July 10, Beauregard's force at Manassas had been strengthened to nearly 18,000 men. His official dispatches now revealed him as subject to fluctuating opinions. After he had got some of his brigades in position north of Bull Run, at the news of McDowell's imminent advance, Beauregard's feet turned cold. He wrote pleadingly to Louis Wigfall to get the President to send him help. Davis read the letter with some astonishment. At one moment Beauregard spoke despairingly of "sacrificing so many valuable lives without the least prospect of success"; and, in the next, he exclaimed, "Oh, that I had the genius of Napoleon to be more worthy of our cause! . . . If I could only get the enemy to attack me, I would stake my reputation on the handsomest victory that could be hoped for."

This letter of conflicting moods was followed by one to the President revealing a confusion of plan and tinged with misgivings about being able to hold his position. Then, on July 13, his spirits somersaulted. He was no longer concerned with fears and doubts about defense. He was inspired with an exciting idea for an offensive movement. He sent Colonel Chesnut to Richmond to present his scheme orally.

On the fourteenth, when Chesnut arrived, the President immediately received him. That evening he called for General Lee and General Cooper to meet with Chesnut and him in his hotel parlor. The three listened in amazement to Chesnut expounding from notes Beauregard's grandiose plan to take Washington and end the war. The President was to order Johnston to join Beauregard with 20,000 of his troops, leaving 5,000 to protect the head of the Shenandoah Valley. (Davis, Cooper, and Lee knew that Johnston had only 11,000 men altogether, and surely Beauregard knew this too.) The combined forces would then strike and crush McDowell's 40,000 troops. Johnston would return to Winchester with his 20,000 plus 10,000 lent by Beauregard to destroy the Federals under Patterson. Then Johnston would send enough troops to rout the enemy from western Virginia. When the victorious Confederates rejoined Johnston, he was to invade Maryland and march on Washington's rear, while Beauregard would attack it from the south. "With 35,000 men properly handled," Beauregard argued, "I have not the least doubt that we could annihilate 50,000 of the enemy." [6]

The three sagacious old soldiers in Richmond saw only too clearly the eager Creole's miscalculations and blind assumptions. In his own mind Beauregard had figured out the Federal moves and points of attack and assumed that the enemy would accommodate him by mov-

[6] In writing enthusiastically of this proposed strategy to General Johnston, Beauregard proclaimed, "I think this whole campaign could be completed brilliantly in from fifteen to twenty-five days."

ing according to his conception. The Confederate forces, inferior numerically and in equipment, without modern artillery or adequate transportation facilities, lacked the mobility Beauregard imagined. Davis and Lee were uneasy not only at Beauregard's want of technical reality, but by his seeming implication that he would manage the forces of his superior, General Johnston.

Colonel Chesnut, who was in the conference all evening, annoyed his wife by refusing to divulge any details. He tried to satisfy her by telling her "how sensible and soldierly this handsome General Lee is." "Lee's military sagacity was also his theme," she wrote in her diary, adding, "Of course the President dominated the party, as well by his weight of brain as by his position."

In rejecting Beauregard's plan for an immediate attack, the President replied tactfully and "moderately." He did not even point up his doubt that an army with little artillery, inadequate ammunition, and weak transportation facilities might encounter difficulty in storming Washington. But he did suggest that it would be "brief and fruitless" to retake Alexandria if Beauregard's "rear was not covered."

The cool, intellectual standard by which Jefferson Davis weighed men was aided, as a friend expressed it, by "an intuitional flash that made his judgment remarkably keen in most cases." For all Beauregard's abilities and paradeful dash, Davis began to question his qualifications for top command. Besides, he disapproved of Beauregard's extravagant loose talk, of his boastful contempt for the North, of his quoted assertion that the South could win even if her arms were no more than "flintlocks and pitchforks."

With Lee's and Cooper's help, the President now devised a more feasible defense for Manassas, by which Johnston was to join Beauregard at the psychological hour before McDowell's attack. If Johnston gave up his western position too soon, the Union army under Patterson might sweep up the Shenandoah Valley from Winchester. To the discretion of the President was left the timing of Johnston's move. While Lee now gave his energetic attention to throwing up stouter defenses around Richmond, Davis struggled to build up the forces at Manassas, where he expected the Federals to strike with all their might.

By mid-July, General Scott had amassed around Alexandria the largest force in America's history—an army of 40,000 men, supported by modern artillery reckoned as the best in the world and more than the Confederacy could yet field from its entire eleven states. But the Commanding General of this Army of the Potomac, Irvin McDowell, did not feel that his troops were ready for invasion. The Northern press and the politicians, however, were impatient for action. "On to Richmond!" was a persistent ringing chorus in the General's ear. Under great pressure, McDowell reluctantly made ready to advance.

On July 16, President Davis received a secret dispatch that General McDowell had begun to move his men south from Washington with three days' rations in their haversacks. The news was not unexpected, for, a few days earlier, a woman courier had arrived at an outpost of Beauregard's forces with information that the advance was planned for the middle of the month. The courier was a pretty black-haired Maryland girl named Betty Duval, who had slipped out of Washington across the Chain Bridge, dressed in country calico and sunbonnet. Once past the Federal lines at Alexandria, she had secured a horse from friends, changed to riding habit, and galloped to General Milledge L. Bonham's headquarters at Fairfax Court House, from which he commanded a picket outpost of 3,000 men. Betty had said she had an urgent message for General Beauregard, which Bonham had promised to send to Manassas posthaste. She had then let down her dark cascade of hair and extracted a package no larger than a silver dollar, sewn up in black silk. The message, in simple cypher, had been dispatched to Beauregard, who had rushed it to the President. Davis promptly alerted Johnston in Winchester that the time was about ripe for moving to Beauregard's aid.

The message, Davis knew, came from an impeccable source: a distinguished Washington widow and an avowed Confederate sympathizer, who yet retained prominent Northern friends, including Secretary of State Seward. The lady had been born Rose O'Neil, of a Maryland planter family, and she had married the aristocratic Robert Greenhow, Virginia attorney and scholar. Her sister was the wife of Dolly Madison's nephew, James Madison Cutts, while her namesake niece, Rose Adèle, had married Stephen A. Douglas.

Davis remembered well the beautiful Mrs. Greenhow, with her fine olive skin and flashing eyes. Her good looks and graceful figure were matched by wit and a bluestocking's mind. She had had considerable influence with President Buchanan and had been admired by Lord

Francis Napier, the British Ambassador. Rose Greenhow was extremely attractive to men: Senator Henry Wilson, Abolitionist from Massachusetts, was rumored to be deeply in love with her. Her modest salon was the most popular in the capital; young men in government posts constantly danced attendance. Rose ironically attributed her enormous vogue to the fact that "the refinement and grace which had once constituted the charm of Washington life had departed." The new women, she openly observed, "were not of a class to shed much lustre on the Republican Court." Mrs. Greenhow, Davis reflected, was an intelligent woman, hard to fool; any secret information she secured would be genuine.

Colonel Thomas Jordan, Beauregard's chief of staff, who was Mrs. Greenhow's chief espionage contact below the lines, had sent George Donellan in disguise to Washington for more specific information. He had presented himself at the Greenhow house with a card on which Jordan had written two words in code: "Trust Bearer." Donellan returned with the news that McDowell would begin his advance on July 16 via Fairfax Court House and Centreville.

On July 17, while the President was preparing his message for the opening of Congress on the twentieth, he received a dispatch from Beauregard, the tone of which suggested the General's agitation.

The enemy has assailed my outposts in heavy force. I have fallen back on the line of Bull Run and will make a stand at Mitchell's Ford. If his force is overwhelming I shall retire to the Rappahannock Railroad Bridge, saving my command for defense there and future operations. Please inform Johnston of this, via Staunton, and also Holmes. Send forward any re-enforcements at the earliest possible instant and by every possible means.

Davis had Adjutant General Cooper telegraph Johnston at Winchester to move at once to Beauregard's aid.

General Beauregard is attacked. To strike the enemy a decisive blow, a junction of all your effective force will be needed. If practicable, make the movement, sending your sick and baggage to Culpepper Court-House, either by railroad or by Warrenton. In all the arrangements exercise your discretion.

The President began ordering all available troops to be rushed to Manassas. He telegraphed Beauregard:

We are making all efforts to reinforce you. We cannot send today, but afterwards they will go regularly, daily, railroad permitting, Hampton's Legion, McRae's regiment, and two battalions, Mississippi and Alabama, under orders.

The next day he dispatched another reassuring telegram:

McRae's regiment, N.C. goes to you this evening. Barkdale's Mississippi Regt. goes to you from Lynchburg. Hampton's Legion and others will go as soon as possible. I have tried to join you, but remain to serve you here as most useful for the time.

According to Colonel A. R. Chisholm, volunteer aide-de-camp, when Beauregard got news on July 17 of Johnston's coming, instead of rejoicing, he dramatically flung the telegram aside, crying "Too late, too late! McDowell will be upon me tomorrow with his whole force and we shall have to sell our lives as dearly as possible."

But his confidence returned in a few hours, for a Federal advance guard that attacked the Confederate position under Bonham at Blackburn's Ford was driven back in confusion. Beauregard dashed on horseback to observe. He saw the Federals retreat. In his long, detailed official report, a now-jubilant Beauregard blew up the engagement to make it seem that "heavy masses" retired in "utter rout." Bonham did take twenty Union prisoners, who were sent straightway to Richmond. To the matériel-hungry Confederacy, the capture of 175 stands of arms and "a large quantity of accoutrements" was accounted cause for rejoicing, and the papers made a minor victory out of the skirmish.

On the morning of July 20, when the whole of Richmond was in a hubbub over the expected clash at Manassas, the President, as he was dressing to appear before the convening Congress, received a communication from General Johnston demanding to know his official status and rank in relation to Beauregard.

Aware of Johnston's self-esteem, equaled only perhaps by that of Gustave Beauregard himself, Davis took careful thought as he framed a reply. These two officers, who guarded their *amour-propre* with the jealousy of prima donnas, were to share a divided command. Harmony between them at this most critical juncture was an essential to success. The President sent Johnston this tactful telegraphic answer:

You are a General in the Confederate Army possessed of the power attaching to that rank.
You will know how to make use of the exact knowledge of Brig. Genl. Beauregard, as well of the ground as of the troops and preparation available for the success of the object in which you cooperate. The zeal of both assures me of harmonious action.

The President did not casually choose the words "cooperate" and "harmonious." Perturbed by Johnston's telegram about his rank on the eve of battle, Davis became anxious lest some serious complication or misunderstanding between the two officers might arise. So he determined to go to the battlefield on Saturday after he had delivered his scheduled message to Congress.

Though in two letters to Richmond General Johnston had expressed doubts about his power to retire from before the superior Federal force under Patterson, who was only twenty-five miles away, he masked his withdrawal skillfully. According to his friend and biographer Colonel Bradley T. Johnson, who was with him at Manassas, Joseph Johnston, who had never seen volunteers march or fight before this July of 1861, was convinced "that they were utterly incapable yet awhile of accomplishing anything with their legs." "President Davis, on the contrary," the author pointed out, "had not seen the army of the Shenandoah march, but he had seen the First Mississippi regiment, with him as colonel, march and fight at Monterey and Buena." He could have added that Davis set inestimable value on the Southern volunteer if inspiringly led and directed, and this Thomas J. Jackson was to do triumphantly.

While battle lines were being formed on both sides of Bull Run, the President addressed the Confederate Congress on the State of the Nation. Preserving an impeccably cool and collected demeanor, he mentioned briefly the "perfidy" of the Federal Government in regard to deceptions concerning evacuation of Sumter and the scrapping of the Fort Pickens armistice. Pointing out what he called Lincoln's "ingenious sophistry," he said that now Lincoln had "abandoned all further disguise and proposes to make this contest 'a short and decisive one' " by having placed at the control of the United States Government at least 400,000 men and $400,000,000. This, Davis declared, was an avowal in the eyes of civilized man that the United States had abandoned the "absurd pretense of being engaged in dispersing rioters." He emphasized that the Federal Government had recognized the separate existence of the Confederacy "by the interdiction, embargo, and blockade" of all commerce between them not only by sea, but by land.

Davis charged the Lincoln Administration with deliberately attempting to deceive the Northern people into believing that the purpose of the Confederacy was conquest, rather than peace. He spoke of "the cool and deliberate malignity" which makes special war on "the sick, including women and children, by carefully devised measures to prevent their obtaining the medicines necessary for their use." "The sacred claims of humanity," he said solemnly, "are outraged in cold blood by a government and people that pretend a continuance of fraternal connections."

But against retaliation, the Confederate President took an emphatic stand. "All these outrages must remain unavenged," he declared, "save by the universal reprobation of mankind. . . . They admit of no retaliation. The humanity of our people would shrink instinctively from the bare idea of waging a like war upon the sick, the women, and the children of the enemy."

He spoke critically of President Lincoln's "trampling on all principles of constitutional liberty," of suspending the writ of habeas corpus, and of delegating that power to military commanders.

Davis closed, however, on a note of high optimism. He was happy to be able to say that at the end of five months from the forming of the Confederacy, "not a single hostile fort presses the soil" of any of the original seven seceding states.[7] He reported that the grain crop was the most abundant in the South's history. He expected subscriptions to proposed government loans based on cotton to exceed fifty million dollars.

In the last paragraph, he spoke with stirring eloquence: "To speak of subjugating such a people, so united and determined, is to speak a language incomprehensive to them. . . . Whether this war shall last one, or three, or five years, is a problem they leave to be solved by the enemy alone; it will last till the enemy shall have withdrawn from their borders—till their political rights, their altars, and their homes are free from invasion. Then, and then only, will they rest from this struggle to enjoy in peace the blessings which with the favor of Providence they have secured by the aid of their own strong hearts and sturdy arms."

To deafening applause, and in the assurance that the nation was heart and soul with him, Jefferson Davis retired. He walked the short distance to his hotel and began to get ready to take the train for Manassas.

[7] Fort Pickens was on an island in the Gulf of Mexico.

CHAPTER IX

DAVIS GOES TO THE BATTLE
AT MANASSAS

THE PRESIDENT was detained in Richmond, however, through Saturday and could not leave until Sunday morning. On that very day his eldest brother, Joseph, was arriving with all his family for his first visit to the Confederate capital. The President lamented the fact that he could not be present to welcome the man who had been father-mentor to him.

Turning affairs in Richmond over to General Lee and leaving all unforeseen contingencies to be dealt with at his discretion, Davis traveled as lightly as possible by a single-coach special train. He took with him only one aide, his nephew Colonel Joseph R. Davis, son of his sister Lucinda. He did not want to be encumbered with a staff. Louis Wigfall was extremely miffed because he, too, had not been asked to go, and he never quite forgave the President.

The morning had broken with extraordinary heat, and the temperature mounted. According to A. H. Garland, Congressman from Arkansas, that July 21 in Richmond was "the hottest, closest and most sultry day" he had ever seen. The iron frame of the railway coach made the temperature within it almost unbearable.

As the train approached Manassas Junction, Jefferson Davis noticed a great cloud of dust to the west of the railroad. For a moment he feared that Beauregard was retreating to the Rappahannock River as his second line of defense. But the dust came from supply wagons being sent to the rear for security. Minutes later, the two Davises heard the sound of firing and knew that a general engagement was in process. On reaching the junction, five miles from Bull Run, the train was surrounded by excited men who had fled the scene of battle. They were voluble with tales of Confederate defeat.

Singling out a calm-faced, gray-haired soldier, the President asked for a lucid account. It was not encouraging. The man believed the Confederate line was broken and the battle lost. The President inquired about the Commanding Generals. The man said that they were still on the field when he left it.

The conductor refused to take the train farther. The President insisted the train must proceed, since he could not get a horse until he reached headquarters, and in the terrific heat he could not walk to the battlefield. And there was no time for walking; the disorganized troops had to be rallied quickly. The excited crowd about the station, fearing the President's capture, sided with the frightened conductor. He was finally persuaded, and agreed to detach the coach and run the President some distance forward in the locomotive. So Davis and his nephew climbed up into the cab and rode toward the battlefield.

At headquarters, they found Beauregard's Adjutant General, Jordan, who emphasized both the danger and the impropriety of the President exposing himself. But he provided horses and pointed out the route.

As the Davises proceeded, demoralized stragglers became more numerous. They warned of the hazards ahead and begged the President to go back. Joe Davis also advised against proceeding. "But," insisted the President, "this is not the time to go back. We must go forward." Wounded men, lying helpless under trees, cheered Jeff Davis as he went on. One incapacitated stripling being painfully borne on the shoulders of a comrade to the rear took off his cap and waved it cheerfully at the Chief. Coming upon some exhausted troops stretched out beside a captured Federal cannon, the President heard the word passed, "It's Jeff Davis!" The men on the ground roused. One mortally wounded boy raised himself on his elbow, took off his cap, threw it into the air, crying "Hurrah for Jeff Davis!" and sank back dead.

As the President advanced, "the battle rolled westward and lost its fury." All along the way, retreating stragglers, seeing the President riding forward, began returning to the fray, though the dust swirled up from the bone-dry fields and the panting men were obviously suffering from thirst.

When the President reached Joseph Johnston, on a hill commanding a wide view, the General told him the Confederates had won the battle. The Federals were now retreating toward Centreville. Johnston said he had sent orders to General Bonham at Mitchell's Ford to cut them off. Jeb Stuart was charging with his small cavalry command from the left.

Davis left Johnston and rode farther west. He was joined by a small band of horsemen led by Captain John Lay, who insisted that the President was too near the enemy to proceed without escort. His good friend James Chesnut, who had been dashing about all day sending regiments to this place and that, rode up and joined the party. Shortly, they approached a column of infantry that turned out to be Federals. When the men in blue broke, Lay's force gave chase.[1] "This," in Davis's words, "was the last of the enemy's forces maintaining their organization, and showing a disposition to dispute the possession of the field of battle." Davis and his companions rode on, remarking the line of fugitive flight. "Here was a musket, there a cartridge-box, there a blanket or overcoat, a haversack, as if the runner had stripped himself of all impediments to speed. . . . The signs of an utter rout of the enemy were unmistakable."

As the sun set behind the blue-hazed mountains, Davis reached the extreme left of the Confederate lines and greeted Kirby Smith's troops, whose fortunate arrival had averted impending disaster. The exhausted men, who had had to double-quick five miles from the station to reach the firing line, said they had chased the enemy until they disappeared to the northeast, in the direction of Washington. Almost immediately on reaching the enemy's line, General Smith had been dangerously wounded: a Minié ball had grazed his upper spinal column, torn the neck muscles, and passed out near the collarbone. He had given the command to his senior colonel, Arnold Elzey of Maryland.

According to eyewitness Private W. W. Goldsborough of the First Maryland Infantry, when President Davis rode up to Colonel Elzey, his countenance was "beaming with excitement and enthusiasm." "*General* Elzey," he said, extending his hand, "you are the Blücher of the day."

The President saw night closing in on the exhausted, bloodstained men, who had no shelter but the trees and who had eaten nothing for eighteen hours. But noting that their position was well adapted for pursuing the fleeing foe, he made brief, inspiring addresses along the lines, begging the men to stay where they were. He promised to send

[1] Mrs. Chesnut recorded in her diary that her husband continued the chase with Lay's men until midnight, when a torrential rain halted them.

food and supplies as quickly as possible. Night soon fell, and the President rode back in the dark to headquarters. Though there was a moon, it was obscured by clouds.

When Davis arrived, he congratulated General Johnston with fervent warmth. He asked that food be sent immediately to Kirby Smith's ravenous men. A quantity of ham and hard bread was dispatched. Beauregard had not yet returned. Not conceiving the extent of the Federal defeat, he was moving the tired brigades from the left to the right to resist an expected counterattack.

While official facts were being compiled, Davis sent a telegram to his wife at the Spotswood Hotel.

We have won a glorious though dear-bought victory. Night closed on the enemy in full flight and closely pursued.

Attorney General Benjamin got the news from Mrs. Davis immediately and walked over to the Executive Offices, where the Cabinet was assembled. He repeated from memory the exact words and let the press correspondents have the message.

While Richmond went into a delirium of joy, the President, in conference with the two top generals, discovered that the assumption that had caused him to wire the two words "closely pursued" was not entirely justified. After Beauregard's return at about ten o'clock, and after more information from the field had come in, Davis sent a more restrained "official" telegram to Adjutant General Cooper.

Night has closed upon a hard-fought field. Our forces were victorious. The enemy were routed, and precipitately fled, abandoning a large amount of arms, knapsacks, and baggage. The ground was strewn for miles with those killed, and the farm-houses and ground around were filled with the wounded. Pursuit was continued along several routes towards Leesburg and Centreville, until darkness covered the fugitives. We have captured many field batteries and stands of arms, and one of the United States flags. Many prisoners have been taken. Too high praise can not be bestowed, whether for the skill of the principal officers, or the gallantry of all our troops. . . .[2]

That Sunday night at headquarters, Jefferson Davis got a clearer picture of the battle activities. He learned that Brigadier General Thomas J. Jackson had arrived with the first troops at noon Saturday,

[2] Both of the telegrams Davis sent on the night of victory appear as quoted in *Official Records,* Series I, Vol. II, pp. 986-987. Though the longer one is addressed to General Cooper, there is no indication that the earlier short one was sent to Mrs. Davis. But both War Clerk Jones and Mrs. Davis in her *Memoir* are authorities that she was the recipient, and the Richmond papers so stated.

followed shortly by General Johnston, who said he expected the rest to reach Manassas that same night. The Commanding General had been somewhat surprised that Beauregard had concentrated so many troops on the right, four full brigades, compared to one in the center and two on the left.

But being very tired, General Johnston told the younger man to prepare the combat order while he caught a little sleep. At half past four on Sunday morning, Beauregard handed him the battle plan, which called for an immediate attack on McDowell at Centreville. But it had to be discarded, because, soon after 5:00 A.M., Federals began firing on the Confederate left. As General Jubal Early wrote: "The battle which General Beauregard planned was never fought, because the enemy did not move as he expected him to move."

From the Confederate standpoint, many things went wrong. General Richard S. Ewell had been alerted to be ready to advance on Centreville, but not until 8:30 did someone remember to send him the order to move. Then the courier could not find Ewell. At 10:30 it was too late for him to lead an offensive; so Beauregard ordered him to move south of Bull Run.

On a commanding hill, half a mile behind Mitchell's Ford, Johnston and Beauregard took a position where they could view the battlefield diorama-fashion. As the enemy's modern guns roared like thunder, the valley before them swirled with smoke and dust. When the battle to the left became more furious, Johnston told Beauregard to send immediately all possible troops to that area. Johnston, soon followed by Beauregard, rode four miles to the scene and observed from another rise. He saw the critical situation that had developed, for McDowell had about 17,000 men across the stream on the south side of Stone Bridge. The Federal commander had extended his line toward the southwest until it resembled a crescent. At noon the Union troops were dislodging the Confederates, pushing them back disastrously. Beauregard, who had mistakenly believed that McDowell would strike at his right, had put his major strength in the wrong place. Realizing his almost fatal error, he bravely attempted to inspire the weakhearted with eloquent words and daring personal exposure on the field. But many Confederates, believing they were being slaughtered by the Northern forces, continued to maneuver themselves to the rear. Those who fell back to Henry Hill were half dazed by the Federal onslaught.

General Barnard Bee's men, who caught the brunt of the battle, were giving way under the enemy's mighty thrusts. He was forced to give orders to retire. His soldiers, though losing cohesion, fought as they fell back, turning now and then, staying the enemy. Bee shouted to Jackson, "General, they are driving us back." "Sir, give them the bayonet," Jackson yelled encouragingly.

A little later, after a desperate effort to rally his hard-pressed forces, Bee expected Jackson to move down to his relief. But Jackson, having a good tactical position on Henry Hill, though bullets whizzed about him, stood motionless where he was. As Bee saw his own men dropping all around him, he audibly denounced Jackson "in a passionate expression of anger" for "standing there like a stone wall" and allowing Bee's regiment to be sacrificed.[3] A few moments after giving vent to his emotion in a phrase that was to immortalize Jackson, the gallant Bee fell, mortally wounded. Bee's brother-in-law and aide-de-camp, James Hill, who was with him when he fell and at his deathbed, declared that Bee, in his excitement and despair, condemned Jackson for refusing to move to his aid. Johnston's chief of staff, Major T. G. Rhett, who reached Bee after his fall and was with him when he died, also gave the bitter version of Bee's cry.

No one has ever attributed an unworthy motive to Jackson, for he was unflinchingly brave, but he was ever known to do what he thought best from a military point of view, regardless of whom it helped or hurt. Whatever the true circumstances, the epithet "Stonewall" would not have stuck in history if it had not accorded with the intrepid Jackson's fixity of purpose and undaunted courage.

Jackson, who had been painfully wounded in the hand early in the day, withstood the new pressure of the enemy's attack, as Johnston and Beauregard galloped onto the field. Johnston, seizing the standard of a disintegrating Alabama regiment, offered to lead them. Beauregard sprang from his horse and shouted to the troops, "I have come here to die with you!" Finally, battlelines were more or less re-established, but the situation was desperate. At this point Beauregard had less than 7,000 infantry and artillerists engaged and only thirteen cannon. The Federals caught the idea that they had already won the day, and the news of victory went to the rear guard. Telegraph wires

[3] The phrasing above is Colonel John Haskell's in his unpublished "Memoirs." Haskell knew both Bee and Jackson, and said he told the true story only "to show how things can be distorted afterwards." The Richmond correspondent of the Charleston *Mercury* was the first to report the "Stonewall" incident, three days after the fight, and in his version, which history has chosen to accept as orthodox, he had South Carolina's hero, Bee, speak in admiration, adding the words: "Let us determine to die here, and we will conquer. Follow me." Freeman reports Haskell's account in an appendix to *R. E. Lee.*

carried it north. At noon, official Washington was already exulting, and President Lincoln arranged to take an afternoon carriage drive.

The truth was that the Confederates were whipped, but their officers did not know it. The Southerners had been flanked by numbers that seemed overwhelming. Beauregard now begged Johnston to retire and let him manage the battle. He said the Commanding General should be safe where he could survey the whole field and send reinforcements. At first, the astounded Johnston refused to leave. Then he retired a mile and a half and began ordering more troops from the right to save the left.

Beauregard dashed courageously along the lines, rallying the confused men, trying to get them into positions to meet the next attack. With pithy eloquence he flattered and exhorted. When the bearer of South Carolina's Palmetto flag was felled, Beauregard asked to carry it himself. When his horse was shot from under him, he quickly mounted another. "With eyes flaming, his countenance blazing with enthusiasm, he pointed his sword at the enemy" and urged the men forward.

From one o'clock to three the Federals and the Confederates contended for Henry Hill. First one side had it, then the other. Old Mrs. Judith Henry, bedridden, dying of a mortal disease, was relieved of her misery when a shell burst in her bedroom. She became the first civilian killed in the war. Not far away, Colonel Francis Bartow, Georgia's "most promising spirit," was shot through the heart.

When Beauregard saw an approaching column about a mile to the southwest, he feared Patterson's troops had arrived from Charles Town and Harpers Ferry. "At that moment," he later confessed, "my heart failed me." But a breeze shook out the folds of the flag, and he saw the Confederate colors. Brigadier General Kirby Smith and his men had finally arrived and were coming on the double-quick.

Smith's forces had been delayed because they had had to wait for a day and a half at Piedmont for transportation on the overworked line. The exhausted trainmen had been compelled to get some sleep. The troops had got aboard the cars only at two o'clock that morning. It was one o'clock in the afternoon when they reached Manassas Junction, where word from Johnston awaited them to push forward with all possible dispatch. Throwing off their knapsacks, they had struck out across the country in the direction of the artillery smoke. Though nearly prostrated by the terrible July heat and their own dust, they covered the four miles rapidly. Within a mile of the battlefield, wagons coming at headlong speed blocked the road. Scores of fugitives urged them back. "All is lost!" they cried. "The army is in full retreat. Go back or you'll be cut to pieces."

Colonel Elzey of Maryland, second in command, gave the order "Forward!" "Pay no attention to cowards and skulkers," he cried. "Charge!"

With one wild, deafening yell, amidst a hail of bullets, the Confederates charged. Kirby Smith was wounded in the first charge, and Elzey assumed full command with skill and daring. At the first sound of the Marylanders' Rebel yell, the high-pitched, triumphant screech was taken up by Southerners all along the front, and they, too, started rushing forward. "Yell like furies," Jackson commanded his men as they bore down on the Federals. The amazed enemy were driven pell-mell from their strong position and pursued through a thicket. Other troops, under Jubal Early, having made a rapid swing around from the Confederates' right, joined Elzey's brigade for the final blows against McDowell's extreme right flank.

About the same time, the Federals lost the Griffin and Rickett batteries, just after they had been moved into strategic position on Henry Hill. By a fatal error, Captain Charles Griffin mistook the advancing Thirty-third Virginia, who were still wearing their old-time blue uniforms, for Federals. He held his fire until the Confederates had approached to pistol range and leveled their muskets. In the instant that he realized his mistake and opened his mouth to give the order that would have annihilated the Confederates with canister, the Southerners' murderous volley virtually wiped out the Federal artillerists.

The Confederates quickly seized the guns and turned them on the flabbergasted supporting regiments, who had just witnessed the table-turning. The Union infantrymen fired one or two volleys, then turned and fled down the hill. The tough New York Fire Zouaves, who had sworn to hang Jeff Davis's scalp in the Capitol, led the getaway. James B. Ricketts, seriously wounded, was taken prisoner.[4] A Confederate named Allan Green stumbled over an abandoned portmanteau containing a supply of clean shirts. Slipping behind a tree, he stripped off his own sweat-drenched shirt, put on a fresh Yankee one, and returned eagerly to the fray. But the fighting was all but over.

Just when McDowell had thought he would clinch the victory, Fed-

---

[4] Ricketts's wife was permitted to visit her husband in prison and nurse him. Several Richmond ladies called on her and extended social courtesies as well as sympathy.

eral commands got mixed and organization broke down, partly because he could not keep in touch with brigade commanders in the woods. According to Lloyd Lewis, General McDowell was suffering from an acute bowel complaint caused by eating tainted canned fruit the night before, which made horseback riding so unbearable that he had to dash about the field in a carriage. When McDowell saw that Henry Hill was definitely lost and that Kirby Smith's forces had routed his right, he ordered retreat. Jefferson Davis had arrived in time to see the backs of the fleeing Federals.

CHAPTER X

FANTASTIC ROUT

IN THE HEADQUARTERS tent near midnight on July 21, President Davis sat at a table with Colonel Thomas Jordan, Beauregard's chief of staff, opposite him, and Beauregard and Johnston facing each other. When he had finished writing his victory dispatch to General Cooper, someone brought out cigars. After some moments of relaxation from the terrible strain of the day, the President asked pointedly, "What troops are pursuing the enemy?"

The Generals looked at each other. "None," one of them replied.

Davis could not veil his surprise. Jordan spoke up and said that a report had come from one of Johnston's captains that he had been as far as Centreville and had seen the Federal Army completely routed and in full flight toward Washington.

The President inquired which brigade had suffered the least fatigue during the day. General Bonham's was mentioned; it had been stationed at the far right, where Beauregard had mistakenly figured the main attack would come. The President suggested that Bonham be ordered in pursuit at once. Both Generals remained silent. Finally, Colonel Jordan asked the President if he himself would dictate the order. Mr. Davis at once dictated an order for immediate pursuit.[1]

[1] Jordan wrote from 63 Broadway, New York, on April 18, 1878, "Mr. Davis with much animation asserted the necessity for an urgent pursuit that night by Bonham, who, with his own brigade and that of Longstreet, was in close proximity to Centreville at that moment. . . . This was the only instance during Mr. Davis's stay at Manassas in which he exercised any voice as to the movement of the troops. . . . His bearing towards the generals was eminently proper; and I repeat he certainly expressed no opposition to a forward movement, nor did he display the least disposition to interfere by opinion or authority touching what the Confederate forces should or should not do."
"General Johnston," Jordan added, "was decidedly averse to an immediate offensive, and

After he had finished, Johnston protested, "The men are too tired to go on their own legs and there is no adequate transportation for them." Beauregard spoke of formidable defenses at Alexandria, which he was deceived in thinking existed.

When someone recalled that the captain who had reported the rout had a reputation for romantic exaggeration, the President, considering the hazards of a night march and the Generals' reluctance, modified his order; "immediate pursuit" was changed to read instead: "to be commenced at dawn." After he had reworded the order, Colonel Jordan said to him, from across the table, "If you will send the order, sir, as you first dictated it, the enemy won't stop till he gets into the Potomac."

General Thomas J. Jackson, a mile or so away, was perhaps even more sanguine than Colonel Jordan or the President. "Give me ten thousand fresh troops," he is reported to have said earlier that night, "and I would be in Washington tomorrow." But the word "fresh" was a poser, for there were hardly 2,000 fresh troops to be had at that hour.

The President went to sleep believing that Bonham would lead a full-scale pursuit at dawn. Before day broke, he was awakened by a downpour of terrific violence, and feared the chase would be impeded. But he did not dream that Beauregard had scrapped the order with the President's signature and substituted one of his own, "Special Orders 140," which did little more than call for a reconnaissance in force and the collection of abandoned supplies, to be sent in wagons down to headquarters.[2]

At early breakfast, with a warm smile, the President handed Beauregard a note, which he had composed before he retired: "Appreciating your services in the battle of Manassas and on several occasions during the existing war, as affording the highest evidence of your skill as a commander, your gallantry as a soldier, and your zeal as a patriot, you are appointed to be General in the army of the Confederate States of America. . . ." In less than five months, Davis had elevated the Creole officer from a major to a full general.

emphatically discountenanced it as impracticable." Jordan was no friend of Jefferson Davis, but very close to Beauregard. On April 24, 1878, Beauregard forwarded Jordan's letter to Davis and wrote: "The account given herewith by General Jordan of what occurred there respecting further pursuit that night agrees with my own recollection." Letters and comments on this subject are to be found in Jefferson Davis's *Rise and Fall of the Confederate Government*. The original letters are in Confederate Memorial Hall, New Orleans.

[2] After the war, General Bonham sent to Davis Beauregard's original order. It is quoted in full in *The Rise and Fall of the Confederate Government*, p. 309.

In another tent, while the rain poured dismally, Jackson sat ruminating on the victory and nursing his wounded left hand. Perhaps to ease his vague discontent at the lack of orders to move forward, Jackson took up a pen and wrote a characteristic note in formal, businesslike phrases to the Presbyterian minister at Lexington. He did not mention the Confederate success.

My dear Pastor—

In my tent last night, after a fatiguing day's service, I remembered that I failed to send you my contributions to our colored Sunday School. Enclosed you will find my check to that object, which please acknowledge at your earliest convenience, and oblige

Yours faithfully

T. J. Jackson

When first light came, Bonham's men were roused and, despite the downpour, moved forward. The night before, Colonel Jeb Stuart's cavalry had chased retreating Federals twelve miles beyond Manassas. They had captured so many prisoners along the way—sending them back under guard to the infantry—that he "hardly had a squad left" when he encamped after midnight on Sudley's farm. Nearby Sudley, a church used as a hospital by the enemy contained about three hundred wounded, "the majority mortally," according to Stuart's report in *Official Records*. As he advanced next morning, Stuart found the evidences of disorder so extraordinary that he could hardly believe his eyes. He moved warily, suspecting a trap. The roads were lined with sutlers' wagons, guns, and abandoned carriages containing baskets with leftover, choice picnic fare. Prime muskets littered the ground, along with blue jackets, knapsacks, hats, and caps scattered helter-skelter. One lucky Confederate trooper picked up twenty golden double eagles dropped, one by one, at intervals on a woodland path. At Fairfax Court House the yard was filled with brand-new wall tents; the building itself was heaped with clothing and sundry supplies.

By Monday afternoon, while bewildered Federal volunteers were still arriving in Washington in abject disorganization, President Davis and his Generals received exciting reports of the rout. It was more complete and demoralizing than Davis had imagined. But both Johnston and Beauregard were still opposed to a forward movement. After being hailed triumphantly for the victory of Manassas, they seemed to dread risking a rebuff, despite the optimism of Stuart, James Longstreet, Jackson, and the President of the Confederacy. Johnston continued to plead the weariness of his men, and now the water-soaked ground did render the movement of wagons and cannon extremely difficult.

Had Davis himself been in command of the troops, however, it is probable that the hero of Buena Vista would have gone on to Washington. He understood the magic of morale. He knew, as did Joseph Johnston's biographer Bradley T. Johnson, that when an army overcomes or routs the enemy, "the courage, the enthusiasm, the high spirit, the *morale* which the beaten army looses is attracted to and absorbed by the victorious army." Since normally a pursuing army should be more capable of supreme effort than a retreating one, Davis believed that victors could march farther, fight harder, and exist on scantier rations than losers. "But General Johnston," confessed his admiring biographer, "did not know the enormous force of morale in men, the prodigious power of enthusiasm." In any case, Johnston assumed full responsibility for the delay and lack of action after the First Battle of Manassas, and to the end of his life he continued to be satisfied with the wisdom of his contention that the Army was not prepared for an offensive movement.

If the Confederate troops had marched on, they would have found much that they lacked laid out for them: guns and ammunition, shining new rifles, shoes, baskets of bread, and quarters of beef hanging invitingly from tree branches above smoldering embers.

By approaching Washington via White's Ford, the Southern troops could have avoided Federal gunboats down the Potomac. There were indications that the Government would have fled at the Confederates' approach. If Washington had been occupied, pro-South Maryland would doubtless have been "liberated" from the Federal domain and seceded; in which case both Kentucky and Missouri would have joined the Confederacy. With Southern forces holding Washington, recognition in Europe would most likely have been forthcoming. And with the strong antiwar element in the North daring to make itself voluble, a peace giving the South independence might have been made. So, at least, many thoughtful persons have argued. Whether the Confederates could have held Washington is highly doubtful. Yet, if the violent rain had not come so providentially for the North, Davis might have urged the gamble.

And how would the citizens of the District of Columbia have reacted to the coming of Confederates? A significant answer was given by Colonel William Tecumseh Sherman shortly before he marched off to Bull Run as one of McDowell's twelve brigade commanders. As

quoted in Lewis's biography, Sherman declared sharply to a group of
fatuous Congressmen: "The sentiment of the people of Washington is
such that they would cut the throats of our wounded and on the sidewalks with table knives, if our army should meet with disaster in their
neighborhood." While the Washingtonians were not as violent as
Sherman's own fiery disposition led him to suggest, the majority would
undoubtedly have rejoiced in helping to speed the parting Republicans
beyond their gates.

The victory at Bull Run, though decisive and important in both
its moral and its physical effects, had been dearly bought. On Monday,
the Confederates estimated that their casualties in dead and wounded
had passed 1,500. President Davis grieved in particular over two
deaths: that of General Barnard Bee, who had given Jackson his death-
less sobriquet of "Stonewall," and that of Colonel Francis Bartow,
his first Chairman of the Committee on Military Affairs.

Davis was told that as Bartow fell, he had called out with his dying
breath, "They have killed me, boys, but don't give it up!" His last
words contrasted sharply with those of a dismayed Union lad who expired on the field demanding to know "Christ! What is this all about?"
To some, those two cries from the heart symbolized the different attitudes of Confederate and Federal soldier. The Southerner was fighting for independence and in defense of his home from an invading foe,
as his ancestors had done in 1776.

In the afternoon, President Davis rode about with a guide to visit
the wounded in the temporary hospitals. A mortally hurt South Carolina youth touched his heart by cavalierly quoting an old Latin line, "It
is sweet to die for such a cause." Because of disorganization of the
troops, it was dusk before Davis was able to find a young kinsman of
his, Private Edward Anderson, whom he had heard was wounded. The
boy had died only minutes before he arrived at his cot. Someone told
him that when ambulance men had come to carry Anderson off the
field, the boy had pointed, though in agony from pain and thirst, to a
less severely wounded soldier nearby and said, "Take him. He may
recover. I can't."

When Davis returned to headquarters, his heart heavy with the
sense of suffering, he found quantities of retrieved booty. He noted
the disparity between the old-fashioned muskets of the Southern
soldiers and the Northerners' new-model rifles. The differences in
artillery were even more marked, not only in the number of guns that

had been engaged, but in type. Captain W. N. Pendleton, the Episcopal minister whose battery was manned principally by young communicants of his Lexington church, had fought valiantly with light smooth-bore guns against the enemy's long-range rifled cannon. The spoils of victory were a bounteous windfall to the scantily supplied Confederacy, which now added to its military stores twenty-six wagons, sixty-four sturdy artillery horses, a field of tents, quantities of clothing, and a supply of food, cooked and uncooked.

That evening of July 22, President Davis learned more details of the fantastic rout. As the Union forces broke, they had fallen back toward a creek called Cub Run, a mile beyond Bull Run. On the high rolling meadows between the two streams, sight-seers from Washington had spread themselves in groups as at a *fête champêtre*. United States Senators and small politicians mingled with knots of newspaper correspondents, including Henry Raymond of the New York *Times* and William Russell of the London *Times*. Private citizens of Washington had come in their own carriages. A few adventurous ladies were there with opera glasses, and some prostitutes of both first and second category in filmy summer frocks. Mathew Brady, the famous photographer, was taking pictures, his black-curtained wagon full of equipment for developing plates.

The crowd had had an exciting day watching the columns move into battle, listening to the close-range thunder of cannon, and indulging in all the spectator-sport sensations of a game hunt. Around two o'clock, an officer had galloped up, waving his cap and shouting, "We've whipped 'em at all points. They are retreating as fast as they can and we are after them." The picnickers had cheered wildly. "Congressmen shook hands with each other and cried out 'Bully for us! Bravo. Didn't I tell you so?'" Or so William Russell was to report to London and Jefferson Davis was to read some weeks later.

At the news of victory, Russell rode on horseback three miles nearer to the battle. And then, when the dust of the road became so thick that he could hardly breathe, he encountered returning wagons with men in uniform running beside them. "Turn back!" they cried with vehement gestures. "Turn back! We are whipped." Drivers of ammunition carts going toward the battle endeavored to turn their horses about on the narrow road. Men swore; horses plunged and kicked. "The heat, the uproar and the dust were beyond description," Russell wrote, "and these were augmented when some cavalry soldiers, flourishing sabres and preceded by an officer, who cried out 'make way there—make way for the General,' attempted to force a covered wagon, in which was seated a man with a bloody handkerchief round his head, through the press."

When, around half past four, the holidaymakers on the green hills beheld the Union Army in undoubted retreat, they rapidly harnessed their horses and drove lickety-split to the Cub Run bridge. As the mass of soldiers approached the bridge, an artillery shot struck a team and wagon in the center of the bridge. In a few minutes, a traffic jam blocked that narrow exit. Congressmen's landaus, army wagons, horses pulling mounted cannon, ambulances bearing wounded, re-treating men on foot—all piled up against each other. Orders were shouted; no one paid attention. As men yelled "The Rebels are com-ing," fluttery female screams rent the air. Panic seized the mob. When the broken wagon and wounded horses were finally got off the bridge and the vehicles got in motion, the panic increased. Congressmen were as eager to get to the Potomac as the begrimed volunteers. Wheels of vehicles became interlocked. Riderless horses trampled men who had stumbled. The swirling dust half strangled the fugitives. With the road choked, the mass exodus spread a hundred yards to right and left, into fields and woods. A few officers courageously attempted to form a resistant body of troops, but the men thrust them aside. A daring American newspaper correspondent grabbed up a flung-away flag, hoisted it, and patriotically called out for men to rally. He was virtually stampeded, as thousands of soldiers ran by. Some frantic chaps cut the harness of horses drawing carts and carriages, and rode off on them bareback, leaving the stranded cursing. A bunch of un-conscionable Zouaves from New York dragged the protesting, pleading wounded from an ambulance and drove off in it themselves.

William Russell, who had been robbed of his gig, now realized he was lucky to be on a horse. Seeing no necessity for the furious rush, the Britisher pleaded with the men to stop and make a stand. When they ignored him, he tried to shame them to some display of bravery. A huge fellow by Russell's side, who was shouting "Run! Run!" as loud as he could, seemed to delight in creating alarm. "What on earth are you running for?" Russell demanded sternly in his British ac-cent. "What are you afraid of?" The soldier, taken aback, stopped, and eyed the Britisher disdainfully. "I'm not afraid of you," he said, and, raising his revolver, deliberately aimed and pulled the trigger.

Luckily, it did not go off. Russell spurred his horse and quickly lost himself in the crowd. "There was nothing left for it," he wrote, "but to go with the current one could not stem."

The distraught mass surged on, every man for himself, ignoring the pleas of the wounded and those who fell out from exhaustion. At Centreville, the exhausted General McDowell made an effort to halt the fugitives, but the contagion of panic possessed them.

"The ground," Russell noted, "was now covered with arms, clothing of all kinds, accoutrements thrown off and left to be trampled in the dust under the hoofs of men and horses. The runaways ran alongside the wagons, striving to force themselves in among the occupants, who resisted tooth and nail. The drivers spurred, and whipped, and urged the horses to the utmost of their bent. I felt an inclination to laugh, which was overcome by disgust, and by that vague sense of something extraordinary taking place which is experienced when a man sees a number of people acting as if driven by some unknown terror."

When the sun set, Washington was still some eighteen miles before him. The moon lighted the road, and, as his tired nag trotted toward the capital, he meditated on the account he was to write for the *Times*.[3] Not until the men were in sight of Washington did the mass hysteria begin to subside. But they wanted to put the river between them and the imagined pursuit of the Rebels. At Alexandria there was such a rush of troops onto the decks of the riverboats that they came near sinking. By midnight Russell reached his rooms. Immediately he dropped into an exhausted sleep.

About six, he woke. Rain was beating with "a dull thudding sound against the leads" outside his window. But, louder than all, he heard a strange noise, "as if of the tread of men, a confused tramp and splashing, and a murmuring of voices." From his window Russell saw a steady stream of drenched soldiers, pouring irregularly, "without a semblance of order," up Pennsylvania Avenue toward the Capitol: "New Yorkers, Michiganers, Rhode Islanders, Massachusetters, Minnesotians, mingled pell-mell together." Many were minus knapsacks, crossbelts, and firelocks. Some wore no shoes; a few were covered with blankets.

While the rain poured and the tramp of feet went on, the corre-

[3] Russell's story of the rout of Bull Run became such a famous piece of journalism that he was given the sobriquet "Bull Run"; even after he was knighted, he was still spoken of as "Bull Run" Russell.

spondent began writing his report. Now and then he lifted his eyes from the paper and gazed upon "the beaten, footsore, spongy-looking soldiers, officers and all the debris of the army filing through the mud and the rain, and forming in crowds in front of the spirit-stores."

Later in the day, after some investigations, he wrote: "General Scott is quite overwhelmed by the affair, and is unable to stir. General Mc-Dowell has not yet arrived. The Secretary of War knows not what to do, Mr. Lincoln is equally helpless, and Mr. Seward, who retains some calmness, is, notwithstanding his military rank and militia experience, without resource or expedient."

That night some gentlemen called on the *Times* correspondent, bringing more news, confirming his impressions of the magnitude of the disaster. "With the army disorganized, Washington rendered almost untenable," they declared that many thought the contest was over. "The inmates of the White House are in a state of utmost trepidation," Russell commented, "and Mr. Lincoln, who sat in the telegraph operator's room with General Scott and Mr. Seward, listening to the dispatches as they arrived from the scene of action, left it in their despair when the fatal words tripped from the needle, and the defeat was clearly revealed to him. . . . Why Beauregard does not come I know not, nor can I well guess."

There was some similar thought in the mind of Jefferson Davis. After supper on the night of the twenty-second, he called another conference with Johnston and Beauregard to see if they had changed their minds about a march on Washington. But they both agreed on their inability to cross the Potomac. When Davis suggested an advance to the south side of the river to push the invaders from Virginia soil, Beauregard still insisted that at Arlington Heights they would encounter strong fortifications occupied by garrisons not infected by the panic of the defeated forces. Johnston said the Confederates had no sappers or miners, and lacked adequate excavating tools. Beauregard described "wide deep ditches, with palisades, which would prevent the escalade of the works." [4]

In the face of his Generals' objections, President Davis did not use his authority as Commander in Chief to press the issue. Anyhow, the Confederacy was more or less committed to a defensive war. The conservative General Lee stood out at this time for defensive war only,

[4] Instead of impregnable strongholds hedging Washington, which Beauregard had feared, General McClellan, on arrival to assume command a few days later, declared that he found only some "hasty entrenchments and a few detached works . . . in no sense, any general defensive line."

as did Attorney General Benjamin. And, of course, invasion of the national capital at the outset *might* lose valuable friends in the North and really "stir up a hornet's nest." So the President returned to Richmond, as he wrote, "to employ all the power of my office to increase the strength of the army, whether in offensive-defensive or purely defensive operations on the renewal of invasion."

Loudest in denunciations of the flight from Bull Run were the very Northern politicians whose blocking carriages had helped create the stampede. In sentences as vivid as those in William Russell's brilliant report to the *Times,* a humiliated Congressman from Ohio, A. G. Riddle, wrote:

There was never anything like it for causeless, sheer, absolute, absurd cowardice, or rather panic, on this miserable earth before. . . . The further they ran, the more frightened they grew, and although we moved on as rapidly as we could, the fugitives passed us by scores. We tried to tell them there was no danger, called on them to stop, implored them to stand. We called them cowards. . . . Put out our heavy revolvers and threatened to shoot them, but all in vain . . . a cruel, crazy, mad, hopeless panic possessed them. The heat was awful although now about six; the men were exhausted —their mouths gaped, their lips cracked and blackened with the powder of cartridges they had bitten off in the battle, their eyes starting in frenzy; no mortal ever saw such a mass of ghastly wretches.

The whole North was stunned by the rout. An estimated one-fourth, however, believing in the rightness of the Southern cause and desiring peace above everything, may have found some secret gratification in the defeat. The Northern public had been led to believe that with one decisive blow the Federals would wipe out all rebellious opposition in the South. Only now was Mr. Seward willing to believe that the South was serious about wanting independence. Mr. Lincoln realized that something was started that would require all the country's resources to finish.

Senator Wilson from Massachusetts, who was rumored to have brought his dancing pumps with him so that he might be ready for the victory ball in Richmond, was among the first dignitaries to reach safety in Washington. Congressman Alfred Ely of New York was less fortunate. Beaten out of a ride, he hid behind a tree, only to be captured by a Confederate sergeant named Mullins. Ely got the scare of his life when he was haled, along with a Federal private and an escaped slave, before a Confederate officer loaded with celebrating liquor. "Whip the negro and send him back to his master," the angry Captain ordered. "Shoot the two Yankees." But the officer was not taken seriously, and Ely was sent as a prisoner of war to Richmond, where he was to remain until Christmas.[5] They joked in Virginia that "the Yankee Congress man came down to see the fun, came out for wool and got shorn."

One Northerner, confessedly as frightened as ashamed, was a Pennsylvania Democrat and Abolitionist named Edwin McMasters Stanton, who openly blamed what he called the "national disgrace" on the "imbecility of the Lincoln Administration." On July 26, Stanton wrote former President Buchanan: "The capture of Washington seems now to be inevitable; during the whole of Monday and Tuesday [July 22 and 23] it might have been taken without resistance."

Unfortunate General McDowell, who had planned his attack well, did not merit the censure heaped upon him by the very ones who had forced him to fight before he was ready. He refrained from any attempt to lay blame on others. But he was deeply disturbed to see Washington "full of drunken men in uniform" and his army so demoralized that "its officers and men were leaving their camps at will." The Confederates would have found almost all the positions that commanded the capital open for their occupation.

"Poor McDowell," wrote Russell to the London *Times,* "has been swiftly punished for his defeat. . . . As soon as the disaster was ascertained beyond doubt, the President telegraphed to General McClellan to come and take command of the army." With manly resignation, General McDowell accepted his removal from command.

Beauregard had been as lucky as McDowell was unlucky. Manassas had been very nearly lost. A little more will to fight on the Federals' part might have resulted in disaster for the South. Beauregard's success had come, according to his biographer T. Harry Williams, "without his having done much to bring it about and even despite grave errors on his part." [6]

Now General Beauregard had reached his zenith. The easy victory at Sumter and the desperately fought one at Bull Run had catapulted him to romantic fame. After July 21, 1861, however, he was not to know refulgent success.

According to Frank Alfriend, onetime editor of the *Southern Lit-*

[5] President Davis personally sent Ely some white blankets for his comfort when cold weather came.

[6] Beauregard, as Williams says, in *P. G. T. Beauregard, Napoleon in Gray,* failed to get his specific battle plans accepted by the Davis Administration "because they were nearly always unsound; and sometimes . . . almost fantastic."

erary Messenger and Jefferson Davis's first biographer, the President left the victorious Army "with a heart elastic with hope, at what he considered the certainty of even more glorious and valuable achievement." But his heart was constricted, too, with the remembrance of the dead young men who had gone to fight for independence so full of *élan*. And now on the train with him returning to Richmond were the bodies of General Bee and Colonel Bartow, who were to lie in state in the capitol. It was something like his triumphant return to New Orleans after the battle of Buena Vista with the body of his boyhood comrade Henry Clay, Jr., in a pine box.

When the train reached Gordonsville, the Twelfth Mississippi Regiment under Colonel Richard Griffith was lined up to greet the President. He addressed them as "Fellow Mississippians" and told them how much he grieved for the relatives of those killed on both sides. As a parting word, he impressed upon the regiment that they should always be kind to their prisoners. "Fight the enemy with all the power that God has given you, and when he surrenders, remember, as Southern gentlemen, to treat the captured with courtesy and kindness." [7]

That Tuesday evening at the Richmond station, an eager crowd awaited the President. When the cheers subsided, he addressed them briefly:

Fellow-citizens of the Confederate States:
I rejoice with you, this evening, in those better and happier feelings which we all experience, as compared with the anxiety of three days ago. Your little army—derided for its want of arms—derided for its lack of all the essential material of war—has met the grand army of the enemy, routed it at every point, and it now flies, in inglorious retreat, before our victorious columns. We have taught them a lesson in their invasion of the sacred soil of Virginia. We have taught them that the grand old mother of Washington still nurtures a band of heroes; and a yet bloodier and far more fatal lesson awaits them, unless they speedily acknowledge that freedom to which you were born.

Within the Spotswood, to welcome the President, were Cabinet members and top-ranking military men. After embracing his wife and the three children, he greeted his septuagenarian brother Joseph, his sister-in-law Eliza, Joseph's nearly grown-up grandchildren, Lise and Charles Mitchell, old family servants from Hurricane, various kin,

---

[7] The record of this little impromptu speech was sent to Mrs. Davis at Beauvoir on December 3, 1891, by William L. Allen, a member of the Twelfth Mississippi. The letter is in Confederate Memorial Hall, New Orleans.

along with Mrs. Joe Johnston and Mrs. Chesnut. Unspoken pride
glowed on the distinguished face of Joseph Davis. He had not seen his
youngest brother since that February day that Jeff had set off in a
plantation rowboat, with a colored lad at the oars, to start for his inauguration in Montgomery. With his countenance now illumined by the
flush of victory, Jefferson looked to Joseph like an ideal President of a
republic.

Before the President had time to freshen up, a huge crowd in the
street began calling for him. When Jefferson Davis stepped through
the floor-to-ceiling window onto the little balcony, Joseph watched the
reactions of the people. The blaze of gas light from the façade windows
and the sheen of the risen moon illuminated the scene like a stage set;
Joseph's old farsighted eyes could take in details. A deep hush fell
over the crowd as the President began to address them, "with thrilling
effect," according to Frank Alfriend, who was also watching the
crowd's reaction. "Mr. Davis recounted some of the incidents of the
battle, which he declared to be a decisive victory . . . and counseled
moderation and forbearance in victory, with unrelaxed preparations
for future trials. He spoke of the honored dead and words of consolation to the wounded who had reaped a glory beyond the scars they
wore." And toward the close of his impromptu speech he uttered an
injunction that was to become famous: "Never be haughty to the humble, or humble to the haughty."

Joseph beheld the citizens listening with breathless attention to his
brother's words. "Old men leaning on staves stood up erect." Irreverent urchins were motionless and wide-eyed. Color came back into the
pale faces of anxious women, and their tears dried.[8]

An hour after his address, when the President was in the privacy
of his rooms, surrounded only by his family, rain began to fall in torrents just as the first ambulance train from Manassas arrived. In
the driving storm, relatives and friends watched at the station, their
straining faces lit by the fitful glow of lanterns. As the stretchers were
removed and watchers saw the young men maimed and bloodstained,
their hair matted, their teeth clenched against agony, many broke
down and sobbed aloud.

The Southern casualties at Manassas were soon known to be greater
than had been estimated on Monday afternoon. Altogether they totaled
just under 1,900, of whom almost five hundred were killed. The Fed-

[8] This account is vouched for by another eyewitness, T. C. De Leon.

eral casualties approxmiated 1,500 dead and wounded, and 1,460 lost as prisoners.[9]

In the days immediately following, as more ambulance trains with multilated burdens arrived, the women of Richmond took on roles as nurses in the improvised hospitals. Some brought wounded strangers into their own spare rooms to care for them. They little dreamed then their services were to be required for four harrowing years.

Jefferson Davis was deeply grateful to the Richmond women, who offered to serve long hours as volunteer nurses. "The exception," his wife told him, "was a woman who did not nurse at some hospital." Many who could not nurse carried baskets of delicacies to the hospitals and denuded their summer gardens of flowers for the wounded. Mrs. George Wythe Randolph, born an Adams in Natchez, was insisting that the flowers as well as available medicines should be "divided equally between the sick Confederates and the sick Federal prisoners." According to the Englishwoman Catherine Hopley, at this early stage of the conflict Northern prisoners claimed that "if they had known how kind Southerners were, they could not have been induced to enlist in a war against them."

Constance Cary, in *Recollections Grave and Gay,* wrote of her aristocratic mother's devotion in tending the wounded: "Sleeping on a soldier's bunk, rising at dawn, laboring till midnight, my mother faced death and suffering with the stout spirit that was a rock of refuge to all around her. Her record, in short, was that of a thousand other saintly women during that terrible strife. How many dying eyes looked wistfully into hers; how many anguished hands clung to hers during operations or upon death-beds!"

As gentlewomen became familiar with the agony and the stench of makeshift hospitals, so impressionable youths learned to face the grim realities of battle. A young man named W. E. Winn of the Eleventh Alabama wrote his sister in Demopolis from "Bull's Run" on August 7, 1861: ". . . It is astonishing how soon a man gets accustomed to the horrors of such a scene. I, who at first disliked to look at a dead body, could go through a field on which 4 to 5 hundred lay and take an interest at that. I knew our troops had charged bayonets several times and I wanted to see whether the enemy stood the charge." Young Winn had picked his way among the moldering, still-unburied Union dead to note which ones had bayonet wounds.

[9] The historian Rhodes put the total Union casualties at 2,896, the Confederate at 1,897; thus making one less than 1,000 in the South's favor.

CHAPTER XI

AFTER THE VICTORY, TROUBLES
MULTIPLY

IN THE SPOTSWOOD dining room, the President's table swelled to plantation proportions. Besides his immediate family of five, there were the Chesnuts and the young Joe Davises, old Joseph Davis and his wife, Joseph's grandson, granddaughter, and son-in-law, Dr. Charles Mitchell, two youthful relations of Eliza Davis, and "darling Cousin Helen Keary, who had come to put herself under Uncle Jeff's protection" while her captain husband was fighting.[1] It was hardly the time for a family reunion, but that was what the family-loving President found thrust upon him, though he had virtually no time to be with his relatives except at meals.

The third morning after his return, the President met Mary Chesnut in the corridor. Taking her by both hands, he said eagerly, "Have you breakfasted? Come in and breakfast with me." Alas, she had already eaten. Then, laughing and pressing his left hand to his breast, he said in French, "I am disappointed, with all my heart." Mrs. Chesnut recorded in her diary: "Things must be on a pleasanter footing. When he jokes it is a good sign." But she was distressed that Wigfall had turned cool to the President.

On the night of July 26, Mrs. Davis had a select party in her hotel drawing room, the last before the family moved into the refurnished Executive Mansion. The new Secretary of State, R. M. T. Hunter, was a guest, and Senator Robert Barnwell, to whom Davis had originally offered the post. Mrs. Chesnut pronounced the affair "brilliant,"

[1] Lise Mitchell's "Journal," which is now in the Manuscript Room of the University of North Carolina Library, gives intimate glimpses of Jefferson Davis in July, 1861. Helen Keary was a daughter of Jefferson Davis's brother Samuel.

and found Mrs. Davis "in great form." Outside in the street, a crowd gathered and began calling for the President. He went out on the balcony to speak to them. "He is an old war horse," Mrs. Chesnut wrote affectionately, "and scents the battle from afar."

Colonel Chesnut also spoke. While he was giving the populace thrilling descriptions of the Manassas victory, his wife demanded of the company within: "Then why do we not go on to Washington?" Someone answered, "You mean why *did* they not. The time has passed, the opportunity is lost." "Silence!" commanded Robert Barnwell. Hunter smiled obliquely at her, "Don't ask awkward questions."

To her diary, Mrs. Chesnut commented: "Everybody said at first, 'Pshaw! There will be no war!' Those who foresaw evil were called ravens, ill-foreboders. Now the same sanguine people all cry 'The war is over!' . . . But the safe and circumspect say very little, but that little shows they think the war barely begun."

The President's schedule was as crowded as in the critical days preceding the battle. He was in continual conferences with Generals Lee and Cooper, Secretary of the Navy Mallory, and the new Secretary of State. The first Secretary of State, Robert Toombs, had chosen to send in his resignation on July 19, the day before Congress convened and just as the battle at Manassas was about to begin. Toombs had not waited to see whether England would recognize the Confederacy if the advancing Federal forces were defeated. Since there was so little yet in the way of diplomatic correspondence, he had chafed at having nothing to do. And he could still hardly reconcile himself to playing a lesser part instead of being President. His enormous energies and ambition made him desire the laureled field of battle. In view of his age and his overweight, Mrs. Toombs despaired of her husband's being able to endure the rigors of camp.

Though aware of Toombs's military deficiencies, President Davis felt the Georgian was too powerful in his state for his wishes not to be respected, and, despite the family protests, he commissioned him a Brigadier General. However, he gave just as few high commissions to politicians as possible, for he feared their actual performance on the field might cause mischief. In this respect Davis differed sharply from Lincoln, who gave commissions to politicians right and left, and particularly to Democratic opponents, as he cannily said, "to keep them from fighting me with their mouths."

Davis had persuaded Toombs to stay in office several more days until Virginia's Hunter was familiarized with the work. Then the fat

Georgian donned his handsome new uniform. But his first chosen appearance as a soldier was not auspicious. At a celebration at the Fair Ground, the President was to present a Lone Star flag to the Texans. Mrs. Wigfall, accompanied by Mrs. Chesnut, bore the banner out to the parade grounds in her open carriage, preceded by Mrs. Davis's landau drawn by "spanking bays." The President, with Colonel Chesnut, Custis Lee, and some other aides, dashed by on horseback and took their positions. Chesnut then rode over and received the flag from Mrs. Wigfall, and bore it aloft to Mr. Davis. Hat off, the President presented it with a patriotic speech to the Texans, commanded for the day by Senator Wigfall. After replying, Wigfall maneuvered his compatriots briskly all over the field in the ninety-plus temperature. In the midst of the mustering and marching, while flags flew, bands played, and guns boomed, Robert Toombs made his entry on the parade ground.

President Davis saw what Mrs. Chesnut recorded:

That bold Brigadier, the Georgia General Toombs, charging about too recklessly, got thrown. His horse dragged him up to the wheels of our carriage. For a moment it was frightful. Down there among the horses hoofs was his face turned up to us purple with rage. His foot was still in the stirrup, and he had not let go the bridle. The horse was prancing over him, rearing and plunging, and everybody hemming him in. We . . . expecting him to be killed before our very faces. However, he soon got it all straight, and though awfully tousled and tumbled, dusty, rumpled and flushed, with redder face and wilder hair than ever, he rode off gallantly, having to our admiration remounted the recalcitrant charger.

With misgivings, President Davis received the confirmed news that George B. McClellan had been put in command of the Northern forces. He could think of no better choice for a vigorous organizer and administrator. In the meantime, Johnston and Beauregard seemed indifferent to taking advantage of the Federals' demoralization. General Cooper had dispatched a trainload of fresh soldiers and further supplies, which arrived at Manassas two days after the battle, to add to the captured Federal guns, ammunition, wagons, and luxuries like "fifty-two barrels of white sugar."

The mercurial Beauregard, who had proposed to dash up and take Washington ten days before Manassas, when McDowell's men were undefeated and their spirits high, had changed his mind. With Federal forces routed and their morale now at an abysmal low, with the Confederates rich with reinforcements, newly acquired matériel, and food stores, Beauregard was not eager to advance even to the Potomac. Frank Alfriend, editor of the *Southern Literary Messenger,* who knew President Davis well, wrote: "He was far from approving the inaction which followed Manassas. He confidently expected a different use of the victory." Dr. McElroy, in 1937, maintained that military experts have generally held the opinion "that a prompt and vigorous pursuit, such as Davis had ordered, might have done much towards ending the war."

The President was not at ease in his mind about Joseph Johnston either. The General certainly knew logistics; he was personally brave, and highly esteemed by his soldiers. But for all his ambition, there was an odd timidity and indecision about him that disturbed Davis. Johnston had begun his services with the Confederacy by withdrawing from Harpers Ferry and Maryland Heights, a move against which "Stonewall" Jackson strongly protested. Davis knew the story that went the rounds about Johnston on a bird shoot with Wade Hampton, Hamilton Boykin, and some others. "Everybody liked him," Boykin said. "But as to hunting he made a dead failure. He was a capital shot, but with Colonel Johnston, the bird flew too high or too low, the dogs were too far or too near. Things never did suit him exactly. He was too fussy, too hard to please, too cautious, too much afraid to miss and risk his fine reputation for a crack shot." While Wade and Boykin plunged through mud and water, briers and bushes, shooting happy-go-lucky, right and left, Johnston did not shoot at all. "The exactly right time and place never came." [2]

"Unless his ways are changed," the word came to Davis, "Johnston will never fight a battle if he can avoid it. An accomplished soldier, he is too particular."

Davis wondered if Johnston would ever find everything to his satisfaction. How could everything be satisfactory when the enemy had such enormous advantages in men and weapons? For the morale of the Confederacy, Davis could not let it be guessed how grateful he was for every single bullet picked up on the battlefield.

The Chief Executive could for the time being, however, sup and sleep better. By the victory of Manassas, the South had been rescued from the peril that had threatened it for weeks. Now the Confederacy was obviously capable of fighting for its independence with vigor,

[2] In *A Diary from Dixie,* one of the sources of the above story, Mrs. Chesnut quotes Boykin as saying that Joe Johnston was like his brother Sid, who "never in his life made up his mind that everything was so exactly right that the time to act had come!"

however poorly equipped. But the President reminded the South that the incredible Federal rout might have its value for all, "because of the lessons it contained as to the uncertainties of war and the mortification that usually follows vain boasting."

One of the President's first acts after the Manassas victory was to arrange for a special messenger to go immediately to London with new instructions to Major Caleb Huse, who had been sent by the Ordnance Bureau of the War Department to procure artillery, rifles, and munitions. Davis had a shoemaker sew the order between layers of one of the messenger's boot soles. The order read in part:

You will disregard all former instructions and act in accordance with your own judgment governing yourself by the condition of affairs as shown by the newspapers or other sources of information and send forward supplies as rapidly and as securely as possible. . . . You will not allow yourself to be governed by the political agents of the Government, but act upon your own responsibility.

As Huse was to write in 1889, "No better language could have been used to excite a young officer to do his utmost."

On the Sunday following Bull Run, the churches of the South were crowded with worshipers come to offer thanks for the Confederacy's deliverance from the enemy. At St. Paul's in Richmond, the lessons and psalms were selected to suit the occasion, "the whole tenor of the worship comprised in the words 'Give God the glory'." The President occupied the pew set aside for him halfway down on the right. As he came down the aisle with his family, he could not help but notice the bandaged heads and sling-supported arms of the wounded, who had personal as well as patriotic reasons for offering thanks. The eyes of the parishioners naturally turned quietly to where he sat. Among those present at that service on July 28 was Catherine Cooper Hopley, a British subject, who set down her impression of Jefferson Davis in *Life in the South; From the Commencement of the War.*

For the first time I had an opportunity, irresistible in spite of time and place, of seeing and observing the new President of the Southern Confederacy. Character is stamped upon every feature. A broad, full, prominent forehead, nose somewhat aquiline, lips thin, firm and delicate. There is an expression of gentleness, kindness and benevolence, but withal a touch of sadness with the least shadow of bitterness melting into sorrow. But there is plenty of resolution and dignity combined with conscientiousness, and you feel that words from those lips would not fall light and powerless. . . . Frequently he shared his book with his young son by his side, quietly pointing to direct the eye, or guide him in the chants.

Jefferson Davis glanced at the pew designated for Robert E. Lee. Wounded soldiers were occupying it. The President and his wife were perhaps the only persons present who knew why General Lee, a most faithful churchgoer, was not present. That morning he took the train for Staunton in western Virginia "to perform his first field duty for the Confederacy." Lee's departure from Richmond was inconspicuous. He traveled with two military aides, Colonel D. C. Washington, inheritor of Mount Vernon, and Captain Walter Taylor, and two colored servants. Their saddle horses were on the same train in a boxcar.

According to Lee's biographer Burke Davis, the President "had consented to allow him to go there in hopes of winning imperilled mountain counties." General W. W. Loring, who had succeeded to the command of the slain General Garnett's forces, had bogged down in inaction. His morale needed bolstering. And the two political Generals appointed by Lee, former Governor Henry A. Wise of Virginia and former United States Secretary of War John B. Floyd, each holding small separate commands, were quarreling over strategic positions and tactics.

Davis and Lee both thought that perhaps all the Confederate forces in the area might be combined to strike a decisive blow at General Rosecrans. The President hoped that by his military skill and influence over men, Lee would be able to retrieve the recent losses in the region. Lee bore no written instructions. The President gave him carte blanche to use his discretion. He was to co-ordinate forces and smooth out rivalries. "The duty to which he was assigned," Davis later wrote, "was certainly not attractive by the glory to be gained or the ease to be enjoyed. But Lee's wishes were ever subordinate to what was believed to be the public interest."

Fortune seemed to scowl on this venture from the outset. After Lee left Staunton, where the railroad line ended, to proceed by horseback to Monterey, in highland country, it began to rain. And it rained more or less some portion of every day for three months. Letters to his wife and children rarely failed to mention the rain. "Rain, rain, rain," he wrote. "It rains all the time, literally. There has not been sunshine enough since my arrival to dry my clothes. . . . It is raining now. Has been all day, last night, day before, and day before that too, etc., etc." From Custis Lee, aide to the President, Davis heard indirectly of the ordeal of rain, mud, and fog that the General and his men were under-going.

Only four days after Lee had left Richmond, a letter from General Wise, dated August 1, arrived, in which he explained his recent retreats in the Kanawha Valley. The last paragraph caused the President grave misgivings.

The Kanawha Valley is wholly disaffected and traitorous. It was gone from Charleston down to Point Pleasant before I got there. . . . The militia are nothing for warlike uses here. They are worthless who are true, and there is no telling who is true. You cannot persuade these people that Virginia can or will ever reconquer the northwest, and they are submitting, subdued, and debased. I have fallen back not a minute too soon . . . we have worked and scouted far and wide and fought well, and marched all the shoes and clothes off our bodies, and find our old arms do not stand service. I implore for some (one thousand) stand of good arms, percussion muskets, sabers, pistols, tents, blankets, shoes, rifles, and powder.[3]

Everything in the letter, the President deemed discouraging. He had been told in June, "Oh, let General Wise once appear among them and the contemptible rascals will flock to him like wild pigeons." Though Richmond had had great faith in the popular former Governor's power to encourage enlistments, he had won small support in the Kanawha Valley. The region did too profitable a business with Cincinnati, down the Ohio River; the pork packers of Cincinnati preferred Kanawha salt to any other salt. In Kanawha County, Davis knew, eleven saltworks were in operation, making an aggregate of 1,500,000 bushels of salt a year. The Confederacy needed that salt, as well as the products of five cannel coal factories, which together could produce daily some 5,000 gallons of crude oil from bituminous coal. Besides, there were valuable deposits of niter, essential for making gunpowder, and even a little gold and silver in the region. It was important to hold the Kanawha Valley for its resources alone. If anyone, Davis reflected, could inspire the people of western Virginia with Confederate fealty it was Robert Lee.

At Monterey, ten miles east of the Allegheny's principal ridge, Lee found Brigadier General Henry R. Jackson, who commanded that part of the front. It was this cultured Georgian, Yale graduate, judge, and former United States Minister to Austria, who had pressed Lee to come to western Virginia and take direct command.

[3] The full, long letter from Wise, which appears on pp. 1011-1012 of *Official Records,* Series II, Vol. I, ends that closely printed volume.

Lee found the Confederate situation in western Virginia more demoralized than he had suspected. The soldiers were in a sad plight; measles and fever had brought down hundreds, and hospital facilities were wretched. When Lee reached General Loring's headquarters, he got a chilly reception. Unlike Jackson, Loring did not desire supervision. Loring, a precise man, was timorous about advancing on the enemy until he had quantities of supplies stored at headquarters. To Lee, as well as to Loring's staff and General Jackson, it was obvious that a speedy movement against the enemy was necessary. But Lee could not even succeed in drawing Loring into a frank discussion of the situation. So he went on to Valley Mountain without any positive information about the timing of Loring's probable advance. The other officers regarded Lee as too gentle and too modest in dealing with the obstinate Brigadier. The quality of diplomatic consideration that made Lee beloved was sometimes a drawback when forceful, explicit orders were necessary.

In the pouring rain on windy mountain trails, with a small staff, including his strapping son Rooney, a cavalry Major, Lee did some personal scouting. He learned that the Union forces in the Cheat Mountain area were supremely confident; exaggerated estimates of the Federal strength ran from 12,000 to 30,000.

As mud became deeper and mountain roads steep and treacherous, Confederate mules died in harness pulling wagons loaded with flour barrels. "Circumstances beyond human control," Lee wrote Richmond, delayed the battle he was eager to begin. Davis, aware of the difficulties, had General Cooper send Lee understanding and sympathetic letters. But the President desired his confidential adviser to come to the capital as soon as possible "after he had made the west secure."

Davis's troubles were multiplying. Beauregard was one of his chief worries. Before the week after Manassas was out, the General had written to his friend Congressman Porcher Miles of South Carolina that the fruits of victory were lost: Washington should have been occupied; Maryland, liberated. "From all accounts," he exclaimed, "Washington could have been taken up to the 24 instant, by twenty thousand men! Only think of the brilliant results we have lost by the two causes [food and transportation] referred to!" The blame for his failure to advance on Washington he laid on the Administration and particularly on Commissary General Northrop, who, he said, would not furnish him with proper food; and he charged the Quartermaster Department with not providing transport wagons. Having read that all Washington wondered why Beauregard did not come, he was intent on shifting the blame from himself.

To Congress, assembled in secret session, Miles read aloud Beauregard's complaints. The President was asked if it were true there was insufficient food in the Manassas area. Davis, astounded at Beauregard's twisting of the facts, swallowed his indignation, and coolly replied that the Commissary Department was functioning quite as well as might be expected. The doings at the secret session leaked to the press, as Beauregard had hoped. Shortly, the President was being openly criticized for holding Beauregard back, with the implication in some circles that he was jealous of the General's popularity.

Colonel Jordan, Beauregard's chief of staff, complained to Chesnut that Beauregard was "not properly seconded." Of course, Colonel Chesnut well knew the truth of what had occurred that night after the Bull Run rout, how the President had urged pursuit, how Beauregard had seemed quite as opposed as Johnston to any further forward movement.

Mrs. Chesnut caustically commented in her diary: "To think that any mortal general (even though he had sprung up in a month or so from Captain of Artillery to General) could be so puffed up with vanity, so blinded by a false sense of his own consequence, as to intimate that men would sacrifice their country, injure themselves, and ruin their families to spite the aforesaid general. Conceit and self-love can never reach a higher point than that! They give you to understand Mr. Davis does not like Beauregard. . . . They say that rather than let Beauregard make a good showing, Mr. President—who would be hanged, at the very least, if things go wrong—will cripple the army."

The President, who already had enough burdens to floor a superman, was now confronted with the worst of liabilities: disloyalty and calumny. Beauregard had a few powerful friends in the halls of Congress, as well as in editors' chairs. The Confederate Congress, which had apparently been heart and soul with Davis up to Miles's reading of the Beauregard letter, began to reveal spots of antagonism. As Davis told his wife, "Any man who has been in high public office is naturally bound to have acquired some enemies." When she wanted him to reveal the facts, he said that, for the health and harmony of the Confederacy, he was not in a position to defend himself openly. On August 4, the President did write Beauregard a restrained letter, taking care not to face him with his deceitful implications.

Some excitement has been created by your letters. The Quartermaster and the Commissary Generals both feel that they have been unjustly arraigned. As for myself, I can only say that I have endeavored to anticipate wants, and any failure which has occurred from imperfect knowledge might have been best avoided by timely requisitions and estimates. I think you are unjust to yourself in putting your failure to pursue the enemy to Washington to the account of short supplies of subsistence and transportation. . . . You will not fail to remember that, so far from knowing that the enemy was routed, a large part of forces was moved by you in the night of the 21st to repel a supposed attack upon our right, and the next day's operations did not fully reveal what has since been reported of the enemy's panic. Enough was done for glory, and the measure of duty was full. Let us rather show the untaught that their desires are unreasonable than, by dwelling on possibilities, recently developed, give form and substance to the criticisms, always easy to those who judge after the event.

With sincere esteem I am your friend,

Jefferson Davis

The first week of August, a committee of townswomen announced that everything in the Executive Mansion was in place; the President's family could move in. For weeks, the committee had worked to select furniture, draperies, and ornaments that would be worthy of such a house. The Davises were touched that so much care for details had been expended. The President was surprised to find a rich, cream-colored carpet laid in his own private sitting room, though he wondered how it would fare when he received booted officers from the field.

After a fortnight at the Spotswood, Joseph Davis and his entourage left for a short visit with Joseph's second-born daughter, Caroline Leonard, at Norfolk. On their return to Richmond, Joseph suggested that his family stay again at the Spotswood. Varina was not at all averse to such an arrangement; she already had her hands full, managing her own sizable household in a large house, where, although hardly settled, she was expected to entertain informally every evening. But Jefferson said firmly that unless his brother stayed at the Executive Mansion, he would move to the hotel with him. He wanted to assure Joseph of his unflagging devotion, particularly since Varina had often quarreled with him. Besides, he enjoyed his brother's conversation, and, furthermore, the distinguished-looking Joseph could act as host when the President was too busy or too tired to see guests in the evening.

Southern gentlemen in that hospitable age rarely had much conception of a wife's trials and responsibilities. But simple Eliza Davis, writing to a distant niece on August 10, gave some indication of Varina's problems as well as an intimate sketch of the President, oppressed as he was by mounting problems and feeling the return of his old bête noire, facial neuralgia.

I long to be at home, as for health all places seem alike. My cough is just the same. Varina has two servants sick and Fannie's maid is down. Kitty [Eliza's maid] is complaining. I wish I had a healthy servant.

Varina receives every evening; sometimes the parlors are filled with strange gentlemen and a few ladies. I go to my room generally early. Your Uncle [Joseph] likes to see and talk to the people. He is very well. Mary and Lise seem to like this place. Varina is very polite to them. . . . The housekeeping *is* a trouble. One cannot get suitable servants, everything double price. The children do not see, as I do, the worry or they would wish to leave.

Last night Brother Jeff was quite unwell. He is better today. I never saw a person so sadly changed. He rarely smiles, and has not spoken to me except at table to hand something, although I sit next him. He looks as thin as Sister Lucinda and very much like her. His hair is cut close. He has so many callers he cannot take his meals in peace. Varina is at times cheerful and then again depressed. . . .[4]

Eliza's description of her brother-in-law shows him as not always making an effort in the bosom of the family to hide his worry. And it may be noted that while it was the fashion for men to wear their hair long, with beards of various trims, Jefferson Davis was then wearing his hair short. Varina's hours of depression were perhaps due in part to the fact that she was expecting a baby—her fifth—in December.

The President's grave mood in private was caused not only by foreseeing the criticism a high officer like Beauregard, aided by inimical newspapers, could bring upon the Administration, but by his anxiety over European recognition of the Confederacy. In London, William Yancey, excited by the good news of Bull Run, had straightway approached Lord John Russell and again pleaded the case for recognition, suggesting at the same time that England might raise the blockade to obtain cotton. All the South was expecting some significant reaction from Britain that would aid the Confederacy's cause.

[4] This letter was furnished the author by Joseph Davis's great-granddaughter, Mrs. Mary Lucy O'Kelley of Pass Christian, Mississippi.

The crying need for war materials was never absent from Davis's mind. The pro-Confederate volunteers in Missouri had few arms except squirrel rifles and shotguns. Though General Sterling Price possessed "an extraordinary power to secure the personal attachment of his troops," he had only a few cannon, no shells, and very few solid shot, but he made the best of rude devices: "Trace-chains, iron rods, hard pebbles and smooth stones were substituted for shot."

On August 6, the President persuaded Congress to appropriate one million dollars to aid the people of Missouri "in their efforts to maintain Constitutional liberty." Four days later, at Wilson's Creek, Nathaniel Lyon's Union troops met with a stinging defeat. The little red-bearded leader, who had been largely responsible for preventing Missouri's secession, fought gamely until he tumbled off his second horse with a bullet hole near his heart. The news of victory reached Richmond the day after Eliza wrote her letter.

For the President, another happy event of the week, besides the success in Missouri, was the apparent reconciliation with Louis Wigfall, who had bitterly resented not being taken to Manassas. The Wigfalls dined at the Davises on the twelfth, and the Wigfall girls spent the night in the White House.

In the meantime, Lise Mitchell and the other young house guests were enjoying themselves, particularly at Aunt Varina's evening receptions, where numerous youths in uniform called, some of them Mississippi boys Lise had known. Jefferson Davis liked to have gay young people about. He had been devoted to his great-niece since she was a tiny tot, and he realized how much this social fling meant to her after months of remote plantation life with aging grandparents.

But the President was really not well. He had been forcing himself to go to his office despite recurrent blinding attacks of neuralgia. Yet, in the midst of his pain, he was continually answering letters from General Joseph Johnston, touching on such items as twelve-pound howitzers, which the Chief of Ordnance, Josiah Gorgas, was making at the rate of six per week. On August 16, Davis learned that 4,800 of Johnston's immediate command of 18,178 at Manassas were sick—with measles, malaria, and typhoid. Many had just wandered off home without leave, having decided that there was little more to fear from the "Bull Running Yankees." That day the President's temperature rose, and his physician insisted on taking him to a farm in the country.

Far from relaxing his efforts after the Manassas victory, as ignorant or biased critics have charged, Jefferson Davis, even in illness, never ceased to be concerned about the welfare of the Army. His doctor could induce him to remain in the country but three days. On his return to Richmond, he wrote Johnston (August 20):

Frequent complaints have been made to me of improper food for the well and a want of care for the sick. I most respectfully invite your attention to both these subjects and hope that abuses may be promptly corrected. Is it not practicable to construct bake ovens at or near Manassas, that good bread may be supplied to the troops?

The main complaint is of bad bread, and inattention to the sick. I have repelled grumblers; but the clamor has increased in specifications until I deemed it proper to obtain the facts from you. Captains and Colonels, instead of correcting evils by personal attention, seem to have been the sources of no small part of the impressions received and circulated.

On August 23, the President received with Mrs. Davis at her reception. He spent some time talking to Mary Chesnut, who was leaving with her husband for South Carolina at the end of the Congressional session. He told her that in the meantime she must make her husband ride with him every afternoon. But in a day or two the President's physician ordered him to bed.

At the end of August, a supercharged situation created by John Charles Frémont in Missouri added to the President's anxiety. This daring adventurer, who had headed explorative expeditions across the Far West in the 1840's, and earned his sobriquet, "The Pathfinder," had been sent, on the recommendation of the Blair clan, to St. Louis as Commander of the Western Department. The first Presidential candidate of the Republican party and a onetime army officer who had been dismissed from service for insubordination, Frémont was no more to be bound by rules than by the winds. The new Major General straightway declared martial law in Missouri and announced that everyone north of the line of the Union Army caught with arms would be court-martialed, and shot if found guilty. An avowed Abolitionist, the Savannah-born Frémont threatened to confiscate all the property, including slaves, of those who had taken up arms against the Federal forces.

President Davis, like President Lincoln, learned of the Frémont proclamation through the newspapers. Both were upset. Davis dreaded a repetition of the tyranny in Maryland. Lincoln feared a disastrous effect on Kentucky. On September 2, Lincoln wrote and asked Frémont to countermand or modify his unauthorized order. "Should you shoot a man, according to the proclamation," he said, "the Confederates would very certainly shoot our best men in their hands in retaliation; and so, man for man, indefinitely. . . . The confiscation of property, and the liberating of slaves of traitorous owners, will alarm our Southern Union friends, and turn them against us—perhaps ruin our rather fair prospect for Kentucky." In a confidential letter to his friend Senator Orville H. Browning of Illinois, President Lincoln wrote that the Kentucky Legislature, which was in session, would not budge until Frémont's proclamation was modified. "I think to lose Kentucky is nearly the same as to lose the whole game," he said. "Kentucky gone, we cannot hold Missouri, nor as I think Maryland. These all against us, and the job on our hands is too large for us. We would as well consent to separation at once, including the surrender of this capital." [5]

In the meantime, Frémont had offended the Blair clan by jailing Frank, Jr., and airing his opinion that the youngest Blair was "unscrupulous, as well as a confirmed alcoholic." Lincoln sent Montgomery Blair to St. Louis to investigate Frémont's conduct and cast an eye on the group of sychophantic grafters that surrounded him. While the Federals were feuding among themselves and the Abolitionists were stoutly supporting Frémont, General Price was preparing to meet the next attack. Jefferson Davis considered what the Confederacy could do to help a state still in the Union.

[5] The letter, which appears in Nicolay and Hay, *Lincoln*, Vol. IV, p. 422, is dated September 22.

CHAPTER XII

THE DIFFERENCE BETWEEN
JOHNSTON AND JOHNSTON

IN THE FIRST week of September, the President was seriously ill. Mrs. Davis received Cabinet officers and callers and made quick decisions as to who, if any, should be taken to his room. Many in Richmond shook their heads grimly. Mrs. Chesnut's plain-spoken friend Brewster bewailed: "The President is ill, and our affairs in the hands of noodles. All the generals away with the armies, nobody here." But although some Northern papers were reporting Jefferson Davis as dying and others as dead, he managed to write a few "essential" letters. On September 5, he answered General Johnston, who was requesting half of 20,000 soldiers that he mistakenly believed to be at Richmond. Patiently, the sick President explained the Confederacy's grave lacks.

You have again been deceived as to our forces here. We never have had one fourth of that number. . . . We have been disappointed in our efforts to get arms. Had you arms to supply the 10,000 men you want, they could soon be had.

Lee is still in the mountains of Va. The rains have retarded his march, or I think he would have beaten the enemy in that quarter. . . .

To permit the enemy to gain a success over any portion of the Army of the Potomac would be a sad disaster, and I have done all that was possible to strengthen you. . . .

My means are short of the wants of each division of the wide frontier I am laboring to protect. One ship load of small arms would enable me to answer all demands, but vainly have I hoped and waited. . . .

May God protect and guide you.

> Your friend,
> Jeffn. Davis

In early September, Beauregard at length forwarded his report of the Blackburn's Ford skirmish of July 18. It turned out to be an elaborate document of almost 4,000 words. (In *Official Records*, it takes up seven closely printed pages.) Some newspapers praised it extravagantly as "a model for all future dispatches." The President could not help but smile at the *Examiner*'s dissenting opinion of September 6: "One of our contemporaries says that Gen. Beauregard writes like Caesar. Did Caesar ever occupy all that space with accounts of a battle in which fifteen men[1] were killed? Some fifty officers were mentioned for compliment in this report, and four private citizens. At any rate, it is feared that the value of official compliment will be cheapened."

On September 8, the President again wrote to Johnston, who was now making vague overtures about an attack on Washington and persistently demanding reinforcements. "We have no second line of defense," the President pointed out, "and cannot now provide one. The cause of the Confederacy is staked upon your army, and the natural impatience of the soldier must be curbed by the devotion of the patriot. . . . Had I the requisite arms, the argument would soon be changed. Missouri and Kentucky demand our attention and the Southern coast needs additional defense. It is true that a successful advance across the Potomac would relieve other places, but if not successful, ruin would befall us."

With the Confederacy's lack of arms, an advance was out of the question. Davis was unwilling to tear away all his defenses at other strategic spots in order to chance defeating McClellan's swelling forces. Besides, he knew that the various state governors, who were continually asking help for their special needs, would raise a terrific clamor against any such drastic move.

The improvement of Jefferson Davis's health was speeded by the arrival of his boyhood idol and admired friend, Albert Sidney Johnston from California. In the fall of 1860, General Scott had summoned Johnston to Washington and put him in command of the Department of the Pacific. Before sailing from New York for San Francisco with his wife, Johnston had manumitted his body servant, Randolph, who thereafter was employed on wages and who followed his master devotedly until the General's untimely death at Shiloh. On April 10, 1861, just before Sumter was reduced, Johnston, foreseeing a conflict, had

---

[1] Perhaps more than thrice that number were slain. Beauregard speaks of "sixty-four corpses picked up on the field."

resigned his Federal commission and gone to Los Angeles, as a private citizen on matters of family concern. In June, warned by his son, William Preston, that he might be arrested if he returned by water to New York, Johnston had set out across the continent on horseback for Richmond. In the terrific heat of the summer solstice, he had plunged into the desert and disappeared. Orders for his arrest were dispatched from Washington. Davis heard that bets were laid as to whether or not he would escape capture.

Under a burning sun, with scanty rations and a scarcity of water that made death ever imminent, Sidney Johnston endured extraordinary hardships. Once, he had to go seventy miles without any water for his horse. But on this "pilgrimage of patriotism," his optimism, courage, and power of endurance never flagged. Sidney Johnston "ran the gauntlet" and took the rigors of the journey as stoutheartedly as he might have done the day he was graduated from West Point.

The telegraph had finally announced Johnston's arrival in New Orleans. In Richmond, the President eagerly awaited him. On the morning of September 6, as Davis lay in bed, with the door of his upstairs room open because of the heat, he heard a man's step in the hall below. Sitting up, with a start, he exclaimed, "That's Sidney Johnston's step! Bring him up!"

Davis received his old friend with inexpressible joy. Fifty-eight and greying, Johnston was still a magnificent specimen of manhood: tall, athletic, deep-chested, broad-shouldered, bronzed by the sun. Instead of being haggard from his grueling trip, he looked remarkably fit. His good qualities of heart and mind illuminated his countenance. Poised and assured, without a tinge of conceit or self-seeking, he told Davis he had come to accept whatever service was commanded of him. Deputations from Memphis and other cities had already been to Richmond asking that Johnston be assigned to command in the West. And Johnston's West Point roommate, Bishop Leonidas Polk, now a Confederate Major General, had urgently made the same request in person and by letter.

Only two days before, on September 4, General Polk, disregarding Kentucky's neutrality, had sent troops to occupy and fortify strategic Columbus, a little town high on the Mississippi River bluffs. By this move, Polk thwarted General Ulysses S. Grant's intention to bring gunboats down the river from Cairo and halted work on Union fortifications across the water at Belmont, Missouri. Grant had retaliated by immediately occupying Paducah on the Ohio in Kentucky. The President knew that the situation in the West would soon be critical.

When Davis asked Johnston if he would serve in the West, Johnston said, "Certainly, in what capacity?" "As commander of the Department of Tennessee and Arkansas," Davis replied, adding that western Mississippi and Kentucky would be included. Then he told Johnston that he had already made him a full general, standing second in rank after Adjutant General Cooper. His recommendation to Congress, presented on August 31, had just been approved.

The President inquired about conditions in California. Johnston told him that, after his resignation, numbers had flocked to him for advice as to what Californians should do in this national crisis. He had one reply for all: "If you sympathize with either side, and feel the call of duty to take part in a sectional war, go home, and fight *there* if necessary. But *here* there should be peace. Strife here would be civil war —not North against South—but neighbor against neighbor; and no one can imagine the horrors that would ensue."

At intervals for three days, the two friends conversed on military and personal affairs, as Davis later wrote, "with the freedom and confidence belonging to the close friendship which had existed between us for many years." Varina Davis remarked that she had rarely seen her husband so happy since he had taken office. To a man as sensitive as Jefferson Davis was to approval and affection, the appearance of Sidney Johnston, radiating complete confidence in him as well as devoted loyalty, was like a revivifying tonic.

Davis unburdened his heart and spoke frankly of his problems, the worst of which was the fact that no arms of any amount from Europe had yet been received. However, Caleb Huse reported that he had a number of manufactories at work abroad, and Bulloch wrote that ships for the Confederacy *were* being built. Critics were now crying that inasmuch as the Confederates did not follow up the victory at Manassas, it was "worse than a barren one," because the Federal rout stimulated the Abolitionists to renewed effort. The United States Congress had authorized the raising and organizing of 500,000 men, while the South had no weapons for some of its regiments.

Davis had been depressed not only by the lack of war materials, but by Beauregard's strange behavior. He was disappointed, too, that circumstances had so far made it impossible for Lee to accomplish anything in western Virginia.

If Sidney Johnston were not so badly needed in the field, the President would have made him Secretary of War, and thus relieved himself of a tremendous strain. For Walker was resigning; the pressure of office had been too taxing on him.

Leaving Jefferson Davis with lifted heart, Johnston set off for Tennessee to organize an army and make the most of woefully inadequate supplies. After his departure, Davis remarked to his wife, "I hope and expect that I have others who will prove Generals, but I know I have *one,* and that is Sidney Johnston."

Another visitor whom the President received during his convalescence was Eugenia Phillips, the beautiful wife of Philip Phillips, Jewish attorney and former Congressman from Alabama. She had been recently released from prison in Washington, and she told Mr. Davis some of her experiences as a volunteer secret agent of the Confederacy. Shortly after the victory of Manassas, she had been arrested as a spy. While soldiers were searching every room in her house and turning her dresses inside out looking for treasonable papers, her Irish cook had craftily burned her private letters in the kitchen range. Mrs. Phillips, whom the Davises had known as a social favorite in the capital, said she was put in a filthy attic prison room in "surroundings appalling." She told Mr. Davis that her frantic husband interceded with General McClellan and begged the powerful lawyer Edwin McMasters Stanton to use his influence with President Lincoln for her release. When Phillips thanked Stanton for his help, the future Secretary of War said, "Yes, Phillips, you may well call it a favor as none but yourself could have tempted me into that den of infamy," and he pointed to the White House.

General McClellan released her from prison, saying he did not want to make war on women. And General Scott finally gave permission for the Phillips family to leave for the South. They had sacrificed all their household goods, "not even the wrappings of newspapers were allowed." "But," Eugenia Phillips wrote triumphantly in her memoir, "this did not prevent some very loyal Federal officers providing me with traitor notes for Jeff Davis." [2]

The day after reaching Richmond, Mrs. Phillips had unsewn the notes from the linings in her corsets, and now she presented them to

[2] Eugenia Phillips's memoir of her war experiences, which is in typescript in the Library of Congress, is one of the most vivid and terrible accounts of the unhappy period.

the grateful President. A few days later, after a series of entertainments by their old Washington friends, the Phillipses left to make their new home in New Orleans, where Eugenia was to get into serious trouble.

The President shortly received another pressing letter from General Joe Johnston, who suspected that Beauregard at Fairfax Court House was assuming too much power. With most considerate care, the President attempted to reassure him:

You are not mistaken in your construction of my letters having been written to you as the comdg. Genl. I have, however, sometimes had to repel the idea that there was a want of cooperation between yourself and the second-in-command, or a want of recognition of your position as the senior and comdg. Genl. of all the forces serving at or near to the field of your late brilliant achievements.

General Joe was not wrong in his surmise that Beauregard was acting as if his were a separate command, without relation to the Commanding General, a few miles south at Manassas. Jefferson Davis had to use all the tact he could summon to remind Beauregard that he was second in command. Vital energy that the President needed for the administration of the Confederacy was drained by his effort to keep harmony between these two officers who fatefully held the prime strategic positions of keeping the enemy from Richmond.

On August 31, the President had submitted for confirmation the names and order of rank of the five officers who, under the act of May 16, he now made full generals. He had weighed carefully the qualities, achievements, and relative ages of the five men. Since Lee was in fact a few weeks older than Joseph Johnston, the order of rank of the top five Generals accorded with their respective ages. Heading the list was Adjutant General Samuel Cooper, who had held the same position in the United States Army. Cooper's commission was dated May 16, 1861. The others followed in this order:

Albert Sidney Johnston, to rank May 30, 1861

Robert E. Lee, to rank June 14, 1861

J. E. Johnston, to rank July 4, 1861

P. G. T. Beauregard, to rank July 21, 1861.

Congress confirmed the nominations without a protest.

When Joseph Johnston got the news on September 10, he was enraged. It was impossible for him to understand how Lee, or any of the others, for that matter, should be ranked above him. Had he not been United States Quartermaster General for a few months in 1860? In vehement protest, Johnston sent the President a furious letter of some 1,800 words.

Expressing his "surprise and mortification," Johnston claimed that the ranking violated both law and justice. In his sincere opinion, he himself should have stood Number One. He spoke reverently of his sword, which he had inherited from his father, disregarding the fact that Lee had inherited his sword from that magnificent fighter General "Light-Horse Harry" Lee. The Government, he charged recklessly, "seeks to tarnish my fair name as soldier and as man." He went further: "I now and here declare my claim, that not withstanding these nominations by the President and their confirmation by Congress I still rightfully hold the rank of first General in the Armies of the Southern Confederacies."

For two days, Johnston laid the extravagantly phrased letter aside to cool before sending it. Then, as he later wrote in his *Narrative,* he mailed it without making a change.

With astonishment and mounting indignation, Jefferson Davis read the letter. It was not only bad-tempered, but an insulting reflection on him personally. Though fully aware of Johnston's touchiness, Davis could not have expected such an outburst. Yet he may have had some disturbing doubt because of Johnston's apparent jealousy of Lee; for, eight days after Manassas, Johnston had coolly informed Adjutant General Cooper that he could not regard orders from General Lee, titular commander in Virginia, because they were "illegal."

While McElroy claimed that Johnston was always "imperious and unfriendly to Davis," Douglas Freeman had the opinion that "at the outset Johnston's manner had been friendly." As revealed in Davis's dispatches and letters to Johnston, quoted in the *Official Records* and in Dunbar Rowland's *Jefferson Davis, Constitutionalist,* the President treated him with the greatest consideration and a very special tact. This one time, however, Davis did not write a lengthy letter, explaining point by point, as was too often his wont. On September 14, he answered Johnston with sharp brevity:

Sir: I have just received and read your letter of the 12th instant. Its language is, as you say, unusual; its arguments and statements utterly one-sided, and its insinuations as unfounded as they are unbecoming.

It would have been more prudent if Mr. Davis had waited a couple of days to reply and not let his own exasperation and indignation show so patently. Johnston was more grievously offended. And from this time forward, the President was to find Joseph Johnston the most difficult and troublesome officer to deal with in the entire Army. Resentment against Davis burned in his breast like sulphur throughout the war and to the end of his days. Many of Johnston's numerous friends turned cold to the President and began sniping at him maliciously. Virginia was shortly divided by a whispering, partisan controversy, which involved two of her distinguished sons.[3]

The majority favored Lee, but Johnston's adherents had powerful social and political influence. John M. Daniel and Edward A. Pollard, editors of the *Examiner* and friends of Johnston, led the anti-Davis, anti-Lee faction. Unfortunately for the Administration, they were the two most talented writers among the Richmond journalists. Black-bearded, thirty-six-year-old Daniel, "chronic critic of almost everything and everybody," except Joe Johnston, John B. Floyd, and the right of secession, was a misanthrope of virulent passions. Pollard was as unscrupulous as he was gifted. Davis's refusal to make these *Examiner* editors his confidants had so alienated them that their early laudation turned to rancor before he had been six weeks in Richmond. Now they made it their aim to discredit the President and undermine his prestige.[4]

Robert Barnwell had declared to Mrs. Chesnut that the influence of his cousin's Charleston *Mercury* had begun "this opposition to Jeff Davis before he had time to do wrong." Daniel's *Examiner,* however, went beyond Rhett's *Mercury* in seeking to damage the Administration. Because of its sprightly style and devastating sarcasm, the *Examiner* was avidly read by the soldiers in camp. As the two papers con-

[3] In a letter to Judge James Lyons, personal friend of both Davis and Johnston, Davis was to write, as late as August 30, 1878, that the complaint of his giving Lee a higher rank than Johnston was quite absurd. "Of the two, General Lee had the higher rank in the cavalry of the United States; had the higher rank in the Army of Virginia, from which they came to join the Confederate Army, and was named first when both were nominated to the Congress for commissions as Brigadier-General of the Confederacy. It is true General Johnston, as Quartermaster-General of the United States had the *staff* commission as Brigadier-General. It is equally true that he was prohibited by virtue of that commission from assuming command of troops."

[4] During the four years in Richmond, President Davis never met Pollard. After his malicious so-called *Life of Jefferson Davis* appeared in 1869, Davis wrote to Thomas C. Reynolds from Memphis on January 15, 1870, commenting on a notice of Pollard by the editor of the St. Louis *Republican.* "I never knew the creature personally," he wrote, "and only heard of him as a malignant who kept out of service by the exemption which covered an associate Editor. So his false statements in regard to me individually may have the palliation of ignorance." The letter, which is owned by the New-York Historical Society, is quoted in full in Rowland, Vol. VII, p. 59.

tinued to sow seeds of discontent, they indirectly proved potent allies of the enemy.

Varina Davis was much upset at "the carping and fault-finding" to which the President was subjected. But when Davis's advisers were to urge that anti-Administration papers be restrained, he would not hear of it. As a democrat, he believed in maintaining complete freedom of the press. Many others believed that in time of war he was carrying democratic ideals too far in not clamping down on papers stirring up doubt and disloyalty.

Despite the opposition of some newspapers and politicians, the President had been remarkably successful in handling his Congress. Bills for the complete embargo on cotton were wont to die in committee or never come to a vote because of the influence of the President, who thought it would be poor diplomacy to enact a law placing an embargo upon cotton. Though the press, state legislatures, and prominent public men were urging the Administration to take over all the cotton in the South, Davis held out for unrestricted intercourse with friendly nations.

On September 13, the British Consul in Charleston wrote Lord Russell that the Confederate Congress had left Richmond without passing the dreaded embargo act. But, as he pointed out, an act of Congress was not really necessary, because "an embargo in actuality was really the will of the people."

CHAPTER XIII

BEAUREGARD ROWS WITH THE
SECRETARY OF WAR

THE FATIGUED and disenchanted Leroy Pope Walker officially resigned as Secretary of War on September 16. The President replaced him with Attorney General Judah P. Benjamin, ad interim, since Congress was not in session. Though an attorney, like Walker, Benjamin had considerably more aptitude for military affairs. He possessed a quick, incisive mind. Order was inherent in him, and he worked with effective dispatch. He enjoyed excellent health. Nothing seemed to fluster or frighten him. Criticism made no apparent dent in his impervious armor of smiling amiability.

Davis was criticized for appointing a Jew to the most important position in his Cabinet. There had been slight murmurings in March when he had made Benjamin the first Jew ever to hold a Cabinet position in America. Now some suspicious people raised the old scandal about his being dismissed from Yale, when a teen-age youth, because money and valuables belonging to other students were found in his trunk. Davis, of course, ignored the mutterings. He knew Benjamin's value both to the Confederacy and to him personally. And for once in many weeks, the captious Richmond *Examiner* agreed with the President. On September 19, it spoke of Benjamin as "a man of most varied ability, who has never failed to master any business he undertook and whose wonderful capacity for work will qualify him for grappling with the herculean labours of the office."

Benjamin, who was well to do, always managed to live in certain style, surrounded by creature comforts. In Richmond, he had rented a gentleman's three-story residence at Nine West Main Street.[1] Here he

[1] The house was only a few doors from the more imposing Glasgow home at One West Main, where the distinguished novelist Ellen Glasgow was born and died. Her

maintained bachelor quarters with his brother-in-law, Jules St. Martin, Congressman Duncan Kenner from Louisiana, and two other friends. (His frivolous, unfaithful wife, whom he adored, had resided in Paris for many years.) The house was about a mile from the Executive Offices, and the portly Benjamin enjoyed the clarifying exercise of walking to work. He entertained well, and he kept a guest room for visiting friends, among whom was Colonel Richard Taylor, son of Zachary, who had a plantation in Louisiana. The President found it relaxing and stimulating to dine occasionally at Judah Benjamin's, where the atmosphere was cheerful and the cigars and wines of prime quality.

As soon as the new Secretary took up his duties, the War Department was invigorated. Davis found that Benjamin could dispatch more business in an hour than many men could accomplish in a day. And he liked his charming manners, his methodical habits, his attention to his duties. For the public morale, Benjamin beamed with confidence, though when he took office the needed supplies for war had been depleted and the expected arms from abroad had not arrived.

The President and his Secretary of War had respect for the intellectual qualities of each other. Benjamin was certainly no "yes man," though the judgments of the two were generally in accord. When Davis did not agree and Benjamin was overruled, the latter never sulked, but smiled blandly. Though the tempers of the two men had once clashed in the United States Senate in 1858, and Benjamin had challenged Davis to a duel, they had become good friends. The cultivated Jew, who refused to bemoan a failure or be upwrought at calumny, was a soothing asset to the President, who could still be upset by unjust criticism. In the few extant letters of Benjamin from England after the war, he almost invariably spoke of Jefferson Davis as his "noble and beloved friend."

When Benjamin stepped up to the position of Secretary of War, Thomas Bragg of North Carolina became Attorney General. Bragg, who had served his state as Governor and United States Senator, had believed that political differences between the sections could be settled within the Union. But when Lincoln called for troops from North Carolina to coerce the seceded states, Bragg wholeheartedly supported the Confederacy. His appointment to the Cabinet was approved throughout the South. Davis appreciated Bragg's logical mind and his

---

father was an official at the Tredegar Iron Works. The Glasgow house still stands, though the house Benjamin lived in was long ago razed for commercial purposes.

"unpretentious dignity." They worked together in complete harmony until Bragg resigned for unexplained personal reasons in March, 1862, asking not to be renominated in the permanent Government. But he and Davis remained the best of friends, and he was to render both the President and the Confederacy more influential service in North Carolina than he could have within the Cabinet.

On September 18, only two days after Benjamin assumed office, Jefferson Davis received an imperative telegram from General Albert Sidney Johnston: "Thirty thousand stand of arms are a necessity to my command. I beg you to order them, or as many as can be got, to be instantly procured and sent with dispatch." Such requests, and particularly one from a close friend, pained the President because of his inability to comply. Benjamin regretfully telegraphed that he had only 2,500 rifles available, but that he was sending 1,500 to Johnston "leaving one thousand for arming several regiments now encamped in Richmond and who have been awaiting their arms for several months. . . . We have not an engineer to send you." [2]

In the meantime, President Davis learned that a big fight was shaping up near Lexington, Missouri. General Frémont, to get back into the Federal Administration's good graces, purposed to achieve a smashing, decisive victory. Davis had ordered the onetime Texas ranger General Ben McCulloch to cross the Arkansas border with Confederate troops and aid General Price in resisting the assault. Beginning on September 18, fierce combat waged for three days. Price had bales of hemp soaked in water and ranged in a line for breastworks. When rolled before his advancing men, they formed "a moving rampart which was proof against shot." As the hempen breastworks inched toward the entrenched Federals, Price's small artillery kept up an effective fire. Finally, in the afternoon of September 20, the Federals surrendered, and the Missouri state forces took possession of Lexington. But the success was short-lived; the Federals augmented their troops to an estimated 70,000, and Price, unable to contend against such a force, finally withdrew to the southwestern part of the state.

President Davis had another special problem. William Yancey, discouraged by the official attitude of England toward the Confederacy's commissioners, had sent in his resignation. After the spectacular Bull

[2] Fully one-half of Sidney Johnston's troops remained unarmed during the fall of 1861. By the end of November, the enemy's force opposing Johnston numbered nearly 50,000. Johnston's, depleted by disease, numbered about 22,000.

Run rout, Yancey had written to Lord Russell and again stated the Confederate case. While he did not press for immediate recognition, he endeavored to combat the antislavery sentiment in England by emphasizing that slavery was no issue in the struggle. "It was from no fear that the slaves would be liberated that secession took place," he wrote. "The very party in power has proposed to guarantee slavery forever in the States if the South would but remain in the Union." But the strong point in his letter was the repeated invitation for England to raise the blockade to assure cotton for its mills.

On August 24, Russell had replied that England must wait "until the fortunes of arms or the more peaceful mode of negotiation shall have more clearly determined the respective positions of the two belligerents."

Disheartened by the Foreign Secretary's note, Yancey decided to resign his commission. His health was not good, and he resented being snubbed by the British Cabinet, to whom the United States Minister, Charles Francis Adams, had given strong hints that his Government would take it in very bad part if England had any official relations with the Confederate agents.

Jefferson Davis felt that Lincoln had made one of the wisest moves of his career when, on Seward's advice, he had sent Charles Francis Adams as Minister to England. This son of John Quincy was a gentleman of uncommon cultivation, who had enjoyed exceptional advantages of travel and education. He had character and an adroit mind. In the House of Representatives, he had struggled to avoid war. Though, as Professor Randall wrote, he had been depressed at the nomination of Lincoln, "whom he never fully admired," Adams had accepted the appointment, and he was to prove as valuable to the United States as any Federal general.

When Adams had arrived in the late spring of 1861, he had found the atmosphere markedly unfriendly to the United States. His son and secretary, Henry, wrote, "America can expect no sympathy or assistance in Europe from any government. They all hate us and fear us." The press, like the upper classes, was predominantly and often eloquently pro-Southern. The urbane Mr. Adams played his hand with extraordinary skill. Although Russell had informally received the Southern commissioners twice in early May, after Adams's arrival he declined to grant them interviews and requested that they put further communications in writing.

President Davis accepted Yancey's resignation on September 23.

He and Secretary of State Hunter had already conferred about the choice of a man to take his place. They decided it would be better to have a permanent representative at the court of England, of France, and of Spain than to have the commissioners visiting the various capitals at intervals. So Hunter wrote to Dudley Mann, dissolving the commission and asking him to proceed to Brussels and establish his headquarters there. Pierre Adolphe Rost was to go to Madrid. Two new representatives would be stationed in London and Paris.

As the Confederacy's representative to England, Jefferson Davis needed a man who could offset the diplomacy of the brilliant Charles Francis Adams. Virginia's James Murray Mason seemed to him a good choice. He was the grandson of the distinguished George Mason of Gunston Hall, who had been a member of the Constitutional Convention of 1788 and the author of Virginia's "Declaration of Rights." The Mason family in Virginia, like the Davises in Mississippi, were known for the more or less "ideal" conditions of their slaves. At the end of the eighteenth century, George Mason had opposed the extension of slavery to the new states to be formed in the Southwest and the Northwest, for the remarkable reason that "vulgar new people were unworthy of so sacred a right as that of holding slaves."

James Murray Mason had served as United States Senator from 1847 to 1861, a period that coincided with Jefferson Davis's years in Washington. Everyone who knew Mr. Mason attested to his fine qualities. The London *Times*'s Russell thought the English would like him: "a fine old English gentleman—but for tobacco." Mary Chesnut was among those whose first reaction to the news of Mason's appointment was astonishment. "My wildest imagination will not picture Mr. Mason as a diplomat," she wrote. "He will say 'chaw' for chew, and he will call himself 'Jeems.' Over here, whatever a Mason does is right in his own eyes. He is above the law." But later, after a small evening party, Mrs. Chesnut recorded in her diary: "We all agree that we adored Mr. Mason." "In the first place," she declared, "he has a noble presence. He is really a handsome man, a manly old Virginian, straightforward, brave, clever, the beau-ideal of an independent, high-spirited FFV. If the English value a genuine man they will have it." And so it was to prove, socially, if not politically.

As a representative to treat with the wily Napoleon III, President Davis selected John Slidell, New York-born citizen of New Orleans, who had served eight years as United States Senator from Louisiana. White-haired, urbane, subtle, and aggressive, Slidell, who spoke good

French, was noted for his shrewdness and his political manipulations. An intimate friend of Judah P. Benjamin, he was married to a sister of General Beauregard's wife. He and his Creole lady welcomed the idea of a year or so in Paris. Both Slidell and Mason accepted the commissions and arranged their affairs in order to sail secretly for Europe early in November.

In the meantime, Yancey, who had made an agreeable impression in upper-class British society, stayed on in London awaiting his successor and influencing opinion for the Confederate cause. He was ably supported in his efforts by William S. Lindsey, a powerful radical member of Parliament and the largest shipowner in Britain.

A fortnight after Benjamin was installed in office, President Davis prepared to join Generals Johnston and Beauregard in a conference at Fairfax Court House. During August and September, the Confederate outposts were at Munson's Hill, only six and a half miles from Washington; with field glasses President Lincoln could behold the Stars and Bars.[3] The Confederates, with their batteries on the south shore of the lower Potomac, had blockaded the river so that commerce could not reach Washington by water. McClellan was not yet ready to fight. He was working with fierce energy to organize a mighty army that would end the war quickly. The North trusted him implicitly. People said he was going to march to Richmond when he was good and ready and not when Horace Greeley told him to.

"Young Mac," so Jefferson Davis heard, rode the streets of Washington as if a glory were upon him. He heard, too, that his onetime young friend paid scant deference to Davis's old enemy General Winfield Scott and that he even snubbed the good-natured Mr. Lincoln. But seemingly McClellan had the co-operation of everyone from the President and General Scott down to the least volunteer. His officers were devoted to him. The men spoke of him affectionately as "Our George." From the public came letter after letter calling upon McClellan to save the country, hinting at the Presidency or a dictatorship. "He had," as Rhodes later wrote, "the sway of a monarch."

The last day of September, President Davis went to Fairfax Court House to consider the advisability of an offensive before winter set in. Johnston and Beauregard received him with civility. He spent Octo-

---

[3] At the end of September, as thousands of volunteers poured daily into Washington, Johnston deemed the position at Munson's Hill too hazardous and withdrew to safer ground.

ber 1 riding about the camps, observing. He was disappointed and surprised to find that, despite frequent reinforcements, the effective strength of the Army was little greater than on July 21. So many men were sick; so many had died. Some were on lawful leave. Others had just wandered off home. He was concerned about these stragglers. They had heard that certain members of Congress, and notably Vice-President Stephens, contended that soldiers should be permitted "to go home and attend to their private affairs while there were no active operations, and surely they would return whenever there was to be a battle."

The President heard complaints of the soldiers; the wish most generally expressed was that they be in regiments of their own home states. He noted that "Mississippi troops were scattered as if the State was unknown."

The evening of his first day in camp, Davis called a council of war, which Gustavus Woodson Smith, third in command, was invited to join. A towering Kentuckian, Smith had been graduated from West Point in 1842. He had resigned as Street Commissioner of New York City only in September, when he felt convinced that a majority in Kentucky favored the Confederacy. The President had commissioned him a Major General; the appointment seemed to please everyone, including Joe Johnston and Robert Toombs.

Now, when McClellan had ringed Washington with fortifications and inspired a greatly augmented army with soldierly morale, the Confederate commanders professed an eagerness to launch an offensive. Davis thought their chances of success were only fractional compared to the situation immediately after Bull Run. Yet he realized that the Confederates were perhaps in a better position to fight now than they would be in the spring after the demoralizing inaction of winter.

The newly arrived, aggressive Smith, a man "always determined to impress," seemed to lead the discussion. He said to the President: "Can you not, sir, by stripping other points to the least they will bear, and even risking defeat at all points, put us in condition to move forward? Success here at this time saves everything."

Jefferson Davis pondered. He considered not only the appalling lack of arms, but the score of strategic spots that would be endangered and most likely lost if he ordered such a stripping as Smith suggested. Each Governor felt that his state must be protected from invasion as much as Virginia. Lamenting pleas came to Davis from the West for supplies that would enable patriotic men to defend their homes. Private arms of citizens had proved a sad delusion, and there was no means yet of providing ammunition. General Albert Sidney Johnston had only a small proportion of the war materials he vitally needed in Tennessee and Kentucky.

Davis asked Smith for his estimate of men necessary for an offensive. "Fifty thousand effective, seasoned soldiers." Johnston and Beauregard both thought that 60,000 would be necessary, and they mentioned requirements of "large additional transportation facilities and munitions." The supplies on hand, they maintained, were inadequate for an active campaign in the enemy's country "even with our present force."

Smith, who had been in uniform scarcely a fortnight, continued to unfold his scheme. He wanted to cross the upper Potomac, occupy Baltimore, liberate Maryland, cut off communications with Washington, force the Federal Government to abandon the Capital and whip McClellan's army if it came out in open country against the Confederates.

Jefferson Davis heard him out attentively. It was a bold plan and one by no means a stranger to his own cogitations. But McClellan was in command of at least 150,000 men, whom he was putting through rigorous training. Even if Davis could give Johnston the minimum 60,000 he said he needed, the Confederacy lacked the armaments to fight against such odds.

With deep regret, the President declared that the want of war materials made a big-scale offensive impossible. The Confederates would have to remain on the defensive until arms arrived from abroad. This defensive policy was not a mere policy; it was at this time an absolute necessity.

The next day, the President took time to send a few reassuring lines to Varina. He was careful not to reveal the extent of his discouragement that so little had been accomplished in improving the strength of Johnston's army.

I am quite well though yesterday I rode many miles visiting the encampments. Today if the weather permits I shall resume my labors and tomorrow hope to return. Hourly I think of you & the children and seem to hear my dear baby complaining as he did the evening before I left you.

There was a misunderstanding as to the selection of a house for me, but Genl. Beauregard met me and took me to his Qrs. where I remain.

The condition of things here is not as good as I expected, and the position has nothing except its comfort to recommend it. Kiss the children for me, give my love to all the family and take to yourself Benjamin's portion.

Stonewall Jackson wrote his wife, Mary Anna, of the President's visit. He had not heard he was coming, and was surprised to see him drive up in an ambulance "with men cheering him along the way." The next day, he watched Mr. Davis review the troops. "His voice and manners are very mild," observed Jackson to his wife. "I saw no exhibition of that fire which I had supposed him to possess."

On his return to Richmond, Davis was greeted with bad news. His wife and Mrs. Joe Johnston had been overturned in their carriage. Lydia's arm was broken. Varina had escaped with some bad bruises. But since her baby was due in December, Davis was seriously concerned.

Days before the President went to Fairfax Court House, the Southern papers had been telling their readers that an early engagement might be expected. The ladies of the town were as impatient as the soldiers for action, and "were almost disposed to go themselves and take Washington." Jefferson Davis knew of the public's anticipation, and he regretted disappointing them. But he could not explain himself without disclosing the Confederacy's glaring lacks.

Though enemies charged him with relaxing his military efforts after "the council of war," the condition and morale of the troops were rarely out of the President's mind. On October 16, he wrote Beauregard on the necessity of reorganizing the Army.[4] The letter was written in the tone of one baring deeply felt thoughts to a sympathetic friend. Beauregard had observed the rule of keeping the Louisiana troops together, and Davis urged him to do likewise with other troops, reorganizing them as much as possible according to their state origins. This was what he had learned the soldiers most desired.

I have thought often upon the questions of reorganization and it has seemed to me . . . it was desirable to combine the troops . . . with as little delay as practicable. They will be stimulated to extraordinary effort when so organized, in that the fame of their State will be in their keeping. . . . In the hour of sickness and the tedium of waiting for Spring, men from the same region will best console and relieve each other. The maintenance of our cause rests on the sentiments of the people; letters from the camp complaining of inequality and harshness in the treatment of the men have already dulled the enthusiasm which filled our ranks with men, who by birth, fortune, education, and social position were the equals of any officer in the land. . . .

[4] The original letter in Jefferson Davis's handwriting is in the possession of Charles Dobbins, Washington, D.C.

Then Davis presented the picture of a commander that expressed an ideal close to his heart.

The General being the remote commander of the individuals; charged with the care, the direction, the preservation of the men . . . has time to visit hospitals, to enquire into supplies . . . and the men come to regard him, when so habitually seen, as the friend of the individual; but they also know him in another capacity, and then removed, as it were placed on a pedestal, he seems the power that moves and controls the mass. This is not an ideal, but a sketch of Taylor when General of the Little Army, many of whom would no sooner have questioned his decisions or have shrunk from him in the hour of danger than if he had been their father.

It could hardly have occurred to Davis that, on the witness of his own men, this might have been a sketch of himself as a Colonel in Mexico as well as of General Zachary Taylor.

On October 19, the day after receiving this constructive, diplomatic letter, Beauregard withdrew his forces from Fairfax Court House to Centreville without even informing the President of his move. Almost simultaneously, Beauregard demanded of the War Department innovations like a special chief of ordnance for his own corps and a "rocket battery company." The astute Benjamin, who had dubious regard for Beauregard's judgment, questioned his going over General Johnston's head. He politely informed him that he was overstepping his authority. In fury, the Creole replied directly to the President, and spoke contemptuously of Benjamin as "the functionary at his desk," who wrote him lectures on law "while the enemy is mustering in our front."

On October 20, in answer to an insistent telegram and a feverish letter, Davis, with inordinate patience, wrote Beauregard a long letter: "I reply," he said in one place, "that your rank being of the highest grade known to our service, is equal to any command. Your inquiry must therefore be whether there be a distinction between an army, and a *corps d'armee;* there is none in the law of our army organization. . . ."

Davis then took occasion to speak of a matter about which he had received countless protests:

Complaints are made to me of shocking neglect of the sick who are sent down in the trains; such as being put in burden cars which have been used to transport horses or provisions and into which the sick are thrust without previously cleansing the cars, and there left without water, food, or attention. These representations have been spread among the people, and served to chill the ardor which has filled our ranks with the best men in the land.

If such things have occurred, surely others than the R.R. companies must share the responsibility.

Your dispatch, I perceive, is dated at Centreville, and otherwise the news has reached me that you had retired from Fairfax C.H. The enemy may attempt to achieve something before the meeting of Congress. In this view, I had contemplated an intrenched line which would compensate for our want of numbers, and would be glad to have your conclusions upon that point.

That very same October 20, Beauregard wrote again, begging Davis's protection from "these ill-timed, unaccountable annoyances" of Benjamin, ironically disregarding the time-consuming annoyance his self-absorption was causing the President. Davis wrote another soothing letter to the angry General, gently reminding him that victory could only be achieved "by disregarding self and having zeal for the common cause."

To make explicit the Administration's stand on command, orders were sent from Richmond on October 22 announcing that the Department of Northern Virginia was established, with Joseph E. Johnston in command. There were to be three districts: the Potomac, commanded by General Beauregard; the Valley District, commanded by Major General T. J. Jackson; the Aquia District, commanded by Major General T. H. Holmes.

Beauregard was bitterly resentful of the new arrangement, which so obviously marked Johnston as his superior. A few days later, he made appointments of officers, which, the Secretary of War informed him, only the President had the legal right to do. Now Beauregard appealed to Adjutant General Cooper, saying he resented the implication that he was a usurper. However, he stated boldly that he would not hesitate to assume responsibility and leave it to those in authority and to the country to decide whether he was right or wrong in his conduct.

The President made a last effort to placate the self-assertive General, and at the same time to induce him to understand that he could not act in disregard of Congressional enactments. He ended with an appeal: "Now, my dear sir, let me entreat you to dismiss this small matter from your mind; in the hostile masses before you, you have a subject more worthy of your contemplation. The country needs all of your mind and heart. . . . My prayers always attend you; and with confidence, I turn to you in the hour of peril."

Thoroughly disgusted with Beauregard's limitless self-esteem, Benjamin marveled at the President's enduring patience.

CHAPTER XIV

BALL'S BLUFF AND LEE'S
"MORTIFICATION"

PRESIDENT LINCOLN, too, was having his troubles. McClellan continued to train troops while the North cried out for victories and paid out money, as Secretary of the Treasury Chase estimated, at the rate of $1,750,000 a day. "Little Mac" had assembled by mid-October an army of approximately 160,000 men.[1] The total force under Joseph E. Johnston's command was about 40,000.

Northern politicians had become extremely impatient with McClellan. Three months had passed without a move. Though Mr. Lincoln had no notion of rushing McClellan, who he claimed was currently far more important to the nation than himself, he was continually visiting him. William Russell wrote vividly of Lincoln's zeal at this time. One October night when the *Times* correspondent called on McClellan at his "usual time of return home," he was told by the orderly that the General had gone to bed tired and would see no one, not even President Lincoln, who had been sent away only ten minutes before. "This poor President," wrote Russell. "He is to be pitied: surrounded by such scenes, and trying with all his might to understand strategy, naval warfare, big guns, the movement of troops, interior and exterior lines, and all the technical details of the arts of slaying. He runs from one house to another, armed with plans, reports, recommendations, sometimes good-humoured, never angry, occasionally dejected and always a little fussy."

Among Lincoln's intimate friends who knew of his ardent desire

[1] According to McClellan's own figures, as quoted by Rhodes, the aggregate strength of the Army of the Potomac on October 27 was 163,318. At the same time, Rhodes wrote, Johnston's "total effective" force was 41,000.

171

for a battle was Senator Edward D. Baker from Oregon, his "dear Ned," for whom he had named his second son. Baker was now a Colonel, serving under Brigadier General Charles P. Stone, who had charge of protecting Washington. On October 21, 1861, Baker made a bold, if inexpert, effort to cheer his friend.

On that date, as Jefferson Davis learned the following day, Colonel Baker led his troops in flatboats and rowboats across the upper Potomac at Ball's Bluff, Virginia, some thirty miles northwest of Washington, to a landing not far from Leesburg, where a small Confederate force was concentrated.

When a Federal unit was thrown over the river at Edward's Ferry, the Thirteenth Mississippi fell upon its men with gusto. As another Federal brigade under Baker scaled the banks at Ball's Bluff, Colonel Nathan Evans, affectionately known as "Shanks," sent the Seventeenth and Eighteenth Mississippi to beat them back. The Confederates attacked with such impetuous fury that the Federals were dazed. Colonel Baker, who had unskillfully led his men, fell, shot through the heart. At his death, panic seized his troops. They tumbled headlong down the bluff, crowding into the boats in such numbers that some sank. Many soldiers were drowned. Several hundred who could not reach the boats surrendered. The Federal casualties in killed, wounded, and captured, amounted to about nine hundred.[2] Among the seriously wounded was a youthful Massachusetts Lieutenant named Oliver Wendell Holmes.

Though the North claimed that the Confederates greatly outnumbered the Union forces, Jefferson Davis heard from his War Department that "the loss of the enemy, prisoners included, exceeded the number of Confederate troops in action."

Measured by other battles, the Federal casualties were small, but the little disaster caused profound discouragement throughout the North. No one was more depressed than Mr. Lincoln. The shock and grief of war had struck home. The President was inconsolable over the death of his friend Baker, and, as William Russell wrote, "walked up and down his room for hours lamenting the loss."

In the eyes of the Republican Congress, the fiasco was particularly depressing because it marked the first real clash since the Bull Run rout. Although Baker's own rashness had been partly responsible for the debacle, since he had exceeded his instructions in making "a re-

[2] Bruce Catton gives the number of casualties as 900. Randall makes the total 921. McClellan, in *McClellan's Own Story*, reports only 680.

connaissance in force," General Stone was made the scapegoat. Stone was already in bad repute with the Abolitionist Congressmen because he insisted that fugitive slaves who came into his camp should be returned to their owners, according to the law of the land. Charged vaguely and fantastically with conspiring with Confederates, he was subsequently imprisoned for a hundred and eighty-nine days and refused the trial he pleaded for.[3]

Jefferson Davis was proud of the Mississippi boys, who had fought with as much ardor as had his own Mississippi volunteers at Buena Vista. But he was shocked at the treatment of Stone, a West Pointer of an excellent Massachusetts family. Here, Davis reflected, was a flagrant case of defamation of character and atrocious injustice to appease wrought-up emotions. The crime against Stone may have reminded him of something William Russell had written the London *Times* in August. One month after Bull Run, a general officer had said to the correspondent: "Do you know, in this country, if you get enough people to start a lie about any man, he would be ruined, if the Evangelists came forward to swear the story was false. There are thousands of people who believe that McDowell, who never tasted anything stronger than a watermelon in his life, was helplessly drunk at Bull Run."

During October, President Davis was acutely worried about the situation in Kentucky. A letter he received from former Vice-President John C. Breckinridge, who continued to hold his seat in the United States Senate, was peculiarly disturbing.

In the House of Representatives it was declared that the South should be reduced to "abject submission," or their institutions be overthrown. In the Senate it was said that, if necessary, the South should be depopulated and repeopled from the North; and an eminent Senator expressed a desire that the President should be made dictator. This was superfluous, since they had already clothed him with dictatorial powers. In the midst of these proceedings, no plea for the Constitution is listened to in the North; here and there a few heroic voices are feebly heard protesting against the progress of despotism, but, for the most part, beyond the military lines, mobs and anarchy rule the hour.

Look now at the condition of Kentucky. . . . Look at the position of our

---

[3] Stone was never brought to trial, and not until February, 1863, was he allowed to see a copy of the absurd charges against him. Though restored to command, with apologies, his usefulness as an officer was hampered by the scandal. In 1864, a broken man, he left the country and entered the service of the Khedive of Egypt.

State under the rule of our new protectors. They have suppressed the freedom of speech and of the press. They seize people by military force upon mere suspicion and impose on them oaths unknown to the laws. Other citizens they imprison without warrant, and carry them out of the State, so that the writ of *habeas corpus* cannot reach them. . . .

Hundreds of citizens, old and young, venerable magistrates whose lives have been distinguished by the love of the people have been compelled to fly from their homes and families to escape imprisonment and exile at the hands of Northern and German troops, under the orders of Mr. Lincoln and his military subordinates. While yet holding an important political trust, confided by Kentucky, I was compelled to leave my home and family, or suffer imprisonment and exile.

Breckinridge wrote specifically of the treatment of former Governor, former United States Congressman Charles S. Morehead, who "without indictment, without warrant, without accusation, but on the order of President Lincoln, was seized at midnight, in his own house, and led through the streets of Louisville . . . with his hands crossed and pinioned before him . . . and now lies a prisoner in a fortress in New York Harbor, a thousand miles away." "The case," Breckenridge declared, "meets every element in the definition of despotism. If it should occur in England it would be righted, or it would overturn the British empire."

With heavy heart, Jefferson Davis finished reading the long letter from the man who had run for President on the Democratic split ticket against Mr. Lincoln. Such, he remarked sadly, was neutrality in Kentucky. What could he do? He did not want the state of his birth turned into a bloody field of civil strife, as Missouri had been. Besides, he had no arms to send the Confederate sympathizers, whose committees continually begged for armed assistance. It looked as if Mr. Lincoln was going to get Kentucky by whatever expedient was necessary.

Jefferson Davis, whose father had fought for independence from Britain, was continually struck by the bitter irony of the North's determination to suppress a proud people, to deny the Southern States their right to freedom according to constitutional pledge. He felt much as did a dismayed British observer, who wrote: "One can but wonder that a people so full of admiration for liberty, a liberty which had hitherto been the boast of the American Republic, should now be prosecuting . . . a war to quench that very freedom and independence for which in their own case they fought so hard and long."

Davis often wondered how his old friend Robert Anderson could stand the unhappy role he had been thrust into. Though Anderson still determined to try to keep Kentucky in the Union, his heart was no more in recruiting troops to fight Southerners than it was in the sending of "relief" ships to Sumter, against which he had manfully protested. His health soon gave way. Reporting that he could not longer endure "the mental torture," at his own request Anderson was relieved of his command.[4] He went to New York to live, and resigned from the Federal Army in 1863.

William T. Sherman was sent to replace him. In conference with Secretary of War Cameron in Louisville, the fidgety, high-strung General insisted that 200,000 men would be needed in the West for effective offense. Cameron thought the request "insane," and frankly said so. The Northern papers shortly made such a to-do about Sherman's mind being affected that he was removed from command of the Department of Cumberland and given a subordinate position.

President Lincoln was having more trouble in Missouri than in Kentucky. On October 24, he wrote out an order removing Frémont from command in that state. Investigators declared that the Pathfinder was "incompetent, wasteful, extravagant, and under the influence of fraudulent contract manipulators." But Lincoln was viciously criticized by the Abolitionists, who looked upon Frémont as their champion. In Cincinnati, where there was a large German population, papers reported that sober citizens pulled the President's portrait from their walls and trampled on it. Determinedly, Lincoln had sought to keep the slavery issue out of the war. None of his Cabinet was pushing him in that respect. Four other Republican leaders, however, were stanchly advocating abolition: Senators Charles Sumner of Massachusetts, Ben Wade of Ohio, and Zachariah Chandler of Michigan; and, grimmest of all, Representative Thaddeus Stevens of Pennsylvania.

Coincidentally with the removal of Frémont, Governor Jackson assembled at Neosho, in southwestern Missouri, a rump legislature, which passed an ordinance of secession on October 31. Though the action had come too late to mean much, the Confederacy could add a twelfth star to her banner. And President Davis was gratified by the moral aspect of Missouri's belated action, which he hoped might have some influence on the Northern peace party. Though fear of reprisals kept Northern peace advocates largely under cover, the Confederate Government had countless ways of knowing of their sympathetic in-

---

[4] The material in *Official Records*, Series IV, Vol. I, pp. 254, 296-297, is particularly revealing of Anderson's distressing position. As soon as the war drew to a close, Anderson went abroad. He died in Nice, France, in 1871.

terest. "The people would hail the return of peace with rapturous joy," wrote the Cincinnati *Enquirer*'s editor, Washington McLean, to Secretary of the Treasury Chase. "I assure you that nine-tenths of the Democrats are at heart bitterly opposed to the war."

Jefferson Davis had been encouraged by something more promising than Missouri's gesture of secession. In a speech at Newcastle, the British Foreign Secretary, Lord Russell, had assured his hearers that the American civil war did not turn on the question of slavery or on the conflict between free trade and protection. One party, he declared, was contending "for empire, and the other for independence." A separation, he believed, was "the only logical and permanent settlement of the controversy." [5]

The French Foreign Minister, on October 26, indicated France's willingness to recognize the Confederate States if England would join her. And on the thirtieth, Henri Mercier, French Minister to the United States, tried to persuade Lord Richard B. P. Lyons, the British Minister, to use his influence, for recognition. If England would merely recognize the Confederacy as a nation, Jefferson Davis felt that a prolonged and terrible struggle might be averted.

Things were not going well with General Lee in western Virginia. On October 24, just three days after the Confederate victory at Ball's Bluff, the inhabitants of the western counties voted to detach themselves from the old Dominion and establish the free state of West Virginia.

Though aware of serious obstacles in Lee's path, Davis had had such strong belief in him that he expected success when Lee wrote that the active campaign to clear Federal troops from Cheat Mountain would begin about September 8. Richmond papers had reported that Lee's battle plan had been received by the War Department and that it was "brilliant." But nothing of importance had happened.

The cruel terrain over which Lee's troops marched became almost impassable. Cannon had to be abandoned. Such torrents gushed down mountainsides that the soldiers claimed they could not lie down at night for fear of being drowned. A freezing cold enveloped the mountain, but the men were forbidden to light fires, which would alert the enemy. Lee himself wore all his winter clothes and his overcoat, and

---

[5] Russell's speech was quoted in the London *Times* of October 16. In an editorial of September 19, the *Times* had written: "The watchword of the South is 'Independence', of the North 'Union', and in these two war-cries the real issue is contained."

still could not get warm. He wrote his wife that he suffered keenly for the greater miseries of the men.

The morning of the planned attack came thick with fog, but through fieldglasses Lee could see the unsuspecting Federal camp. Everything was in readiness. But the signal volleys from Colonel Albert Rust, who had expressly asked to lead the attack, did not come. Hours passed. A desultory firing from another sector alerted the enemy. Shortly, confusion ensued. Lee himself ran into a Federal outpost and barely escaped with his life. The whole day passed without a word from Rust as to why the attack on the mountain crest had not been initiated. Rust had turned fearful because some captured Union pickets vastly magnified the enemy's strength. Instead of attacking as prearranged or when he heard the first firing, Rust kept silent in the woods, feeling proud of saving his men from disaster. He claimed he had not understood that his firing was to be a signal for the general attack and that it should therefore be opened, whether it would be effective or not. His timorous action probably cost a Confederate victory.

On September 17, Lee wrote of his "regret and mortification" at the untoward events that caused his well-planned campaign to fail. When the news of Lee's failure to rout the Federals reached Richmond, the *Dispatch* of September 26 chided him with the reminder that "in mountain warfare, the learning of books and of the strategists is of little value."

Lee's attempt to gain the northern end of the mountain defenses having ended fruitlessly, he moved south toward the Kanawha Valley, where the feuding Confederate Generals Henry Wise and John B. Floyd were opposing the Union forces commanded by General Rosecrans. There was no agreement between the two former Governors of Virginia on strategic site or anything else; they had been continually bombarding the War Department at Richmond with complaints of each other's bad judgment. And now, acting independently of each other, they were encamped some distance apart.

On September 21, Lee arrived at Floyd's camp. He found little order, no real organization in either Floyd's or Wise's command. Nobody seemed to know where anything was; no one understood his duty; officers seemed as ignorant as men. Lee indulged in some mild scolding of lesser officers, and the Confederates braced themselves to meet the attack of General Rosecrans, who shortly drew up in sight of the combined Confederate forces.

For a week, Lee waited on the alert. Then he informed General Floyd

that he had begun to fear the enemy would not attack. "We shall therefore have to attack him," he said. On the night between October 5
and 6, Confederate pickets heard the rumbling of artillery and supply
wagons and passed the word, "Here they come."

When day broke, however, a strange silence pervaded the mountains.
After facing Lee's entrenched camp for a week, Rosecrans had decided
against a fight and slipped away. The Confederates had delayed too
long. The reduced condition of artillery horses and the well nigh impassable roads made large-scale pursuit inadvisable.

Though General Lee stayed on in western Virginia for another fortnight, the continual rains chilled initiative. The weather became so
bitter that he and Captain Taylor slept together under their combined
blankets. On the twentieth, Lee ordered Floyd to withdraw to a position less vulnerable. The country Lee had been sent to save was now
left, with all its natural resources, to the Federals.

"Carrying the heavy weight of defeat," Lee returned to Richmond
on October 31 to report to the President. He was well aware of the
people's loss of faith in him. Davis had been shocked and pained at the
derisive newspaper epithets: "too tender for blood," "a showy presence," "a parlor and parade general," and, most stinging of all,
"Granny Lee." He received Lee warmly and commented admiringly
on the handsome white beard he had grown in the mountains. He let
the General know immediately that his confidence in his "ability, zeal,
and fidelity rested on a foundation not to be shaken" by the depre-
ciatory criticism of "the carpet knights who make campaigns on assumed hypotheses."

With his characteristic self-abnegation, Lee did not attempt to defend himself. He would not present an official report of their affair
on Cheat Mountain. Only in confidence did he tell the President that
if his plans and orders had been carried out, the result might well have
been victory. In secret, Lee confessed the difficulty he had had with
stubborn or careless officers. "He was unwilling," Davis later wrote,
"to offend anyone who was wearing a sword or striking blows for the
Confederacy." This too-great respect for the feelings of others was a
flaw in Lee's character that was to cause him trouble in future crises.

To get General Lee away from the critical atmosphere of Richmond,
particularly from the derisive stares and cutting comments of Joseph
Johnston's partisans, President Davis decided to send him at once to
Charleston to take charge of the coastal defenses of South Carolina

and Georgia. Besides being a trained engineer, Lee was considered by Davis the best-equipped man in the Confederacy for the job.

Seemingly expecting a demotion, Lee asked just what his authority would be. The President, surprised, reminded him that he was a General of the Confederate forces, standing third in rank, and that naturally he would be in full command of the region.

On November 6, Lee took the train for Charleston. As a parting thrust, the merciless *Examiner* wished Lee Godspeed, with the sneering hope that he would "prove more successful with the spade than he had with the sword." As Douglas Freeman wrote, "Lee's first campaign might have been his last, but for the faith President Davis had in him."

On the first of November, five days before Lee left Richmond, President Lincoln had shown his faith in George McClellan by appointing him General in Chief of the Union Armies to succeed infirm, aged Winfield Scott. McClellan still retained personal command of the Army of the Potomac. When Lincoln wondered solicitously if he had put too great a burden on one pair of shoulders, Little Mac responded confidently, "I can do it all."

CHAPTER XV

DRAMATIC ARREST AT SEA

AS ELECTION DAY for the President of the Confederacy, November 6, approached, Jefferson Davis could have wished more than ever to be serving his country in the field, free from political responsibility and annoying intrigues. His wife always regarded his acceptance of the Presidency as his supreme sacrifice for the Confederacy.

Beauregard had created a new disturbance in his official report of the Battle of Manassas, which had reached the War Department only on October 17, though the 9,000-word document was dated August 26. President Davis first heard of it on October 29, when a Richmond newspaper reporter wrote that he had "been favored" with a synopsis of part of it, which purported to come direct from Manassas. In that synopsis, Beauregard claimed that he had been overruled by Davis in his plan for battle with the enemy south of the Potomac and for the capture of Baltimore and Washington. His claim, which had nothing whatever to do with the required battle report, was calculated to give the impression that if Beauregard's design had been followed, the result would have been spectacular. The publication of the synopsis just a few days before the scheduled Presidential election under the permanent Constitution accorded with anti-Administration press hints that Davis had purposely kept the Army inactive since Manassas for political reasons.

Some clerk at the War Department had neglected to forward Beauregard's report to the President. When Davis got it now, he was amazed and indignant. He wrote Beauregard: "With much surprise I found that newspaper statements were sustained by the text of your report. I was surprised because if we did differ in opinion as to

180

measures and purposes of contemplated campaigns, such fact could have no appropriate place in a report of a battle; further because it seemed to be an attempt to exalt yourself at my expense."

The President was astounded a few days later to read in the Richmond *Whig* a letter from Beauregard addressed to the editors but obviously intended for the whole Confederacy. It was extravagantly headed: "Centreville, Va., Within hearing of the Enemy's Guns, Nov. 3, 1861." Beauregard professed to regret publication of the synopsis and hoped his friends would not be concerned at the slanders being created about him. With a grandiloquent flourish he proclaimed, "If certain minds cannot understand the difference between *patriotism,* the highest civic virtue, and *office-seeking,* the lowest civic occupation, I pity them from the bottom of my heart. . . . I am not, and never expect or desire to be, a candidate for any civic office in the gift of the people or of the Executive."

On the eve of the election, Beauregard seemed to be announcing his refusal to be drafted as President. Because of the theatricality and the vain assumptions of his *Whig* letter, he lost prestige, and disgusted even some of his good friends.

On November 6, for the first time, the Southern people chose their President in accordance with their permanent Confederate Constitution. The mode of election was the same as that used in the United States. But there was only one candidate. And, as the historian Rhodes wrote, "One voice went up from all the States that Davis should be chosen." While there was undoubtedly an anti-Davis faction, the tone of the press bore out what William Russell had written to Senator Sumner on September 5: "The Confederates believe in no other man."

Despite rumblings against Alexander Stephens for Vice-President because he was suspected of still being a Unionist at heart, he was the Vice-Presidential candidate. Though Jefferson Davis took no pleasure in having Stephens for a running mate, he expressed no objections. When the electors from the various states met, a unanimous vote was returned. Jefferson Davis was scheduled to be President of the Confederacy for the six years following February 22, 1862.

The day after Davis's election, as a coincidental celebration, his college mate General Leonidas Polk defeated General U. S. Grant at Belmont, Missouri, across the river from Columbus, Kentucky. Grant was driven to his gunboats and back up the river to Cairo. But for his intelligent, sure-footed horse, that slid down a cliff and negotiated a single gangplank on to the last gunboat pulling away, the General might have lost his life or been captured. According to a lively account in *Battles and Leaders,* Grant "fled the field, virtually abandoning one of his regiments, leaving his dead and wounded, a large preponderance of prisoners, a stand of his colors, one thousand stand of arms, and the caissons of his battery in the hands of the Confederates."

A few days later, as Davis was informed, Grant and Polk, with staff officers, met under a flag of truce to discuss exchange of prisoners. At the simple luncheon provided by the Confederates, one of the Federal Colonels raised his glass to toast "George Washington, the Father of his Country!" With a bright twinkle in his eyes, the fighting Bishop quickly added, "And the first Rebel!" Caught in their trap, the Union officers smiled sheepishly, and drank the amended toast.

President Davis was glad that he had another victory like that at Belmont to mention along with Bethel, Manassas, Ball's Bluff, Wilson's Creek, and Lexington in his forthcoming message to Congress. But that same November 7, the date of the Belmont victory, a Federal flotilla of warships silenced the guns of the two forts that guarded Port Royal, South Carolina, the finest harbor between Charleston and Savannah. In the afternoon, General Lee arrived by special train just in time to order the helpless garrisons to withdraw from their island positions to escape capture or destruction.

When Congress convened on November 18, President Davis's address was phrased to inspire confidence and hope in the people. Putting the very best construction on dubious affairs, he could yet speak without exaggeration of the year's abundant yield of agriculture. And he emphasized an innovation in the Southern way of life: "The necessities of the times have called into existence new branches of manufactures and given a fresh impulse to the activities of those heretofore in operation."

At the end of his speech, he touched on the winter privations of English cotton-factory workers, which the British press prognosticated feelingly. "While the war which is waged to take from us the right of self-government can never attain that end," he declared, "it remains to be seen how far it may work a revolution in the industrial system of the world, which may carry suffering to other lands, as well as our own. In the meantime we shall continue this struggle in humble dependence upon Providence. . . . For the rest we shall depend upon ourselves. Liberty is always won where there exists the unconquerable will to be free."

That same day, although the northern part of Kentucky swarmed with Union troops, delegates from sixty-five counties in a rump meeting passed a secession ordinance. So, before the momentous year of 1861 closed, the Confederate flag claimed thirteen stars. Though, in fact, Missouri and Kentucky remained divided in loyalties, having the number of the original colonies was regarded as a happy omen.

Two days after Jefferson Davis's election, there occurred a dramatic event that almost brought Britain to war against the United States. Some days before, a little boat called the *Theodora*, bearing the new Confederate commissioners to Europe, had secretly slipped out of Charleston Harbor through the Federal blockade and landed in Havana. There Mason and Slidell had taken passage on the *Trent*, a British Royal Mail Packet. In the Bahama Channel, around noon of the eighth, the vessel was suddenly challenged by a United States warship, the *San Jacinto*, which fired across her bow, following this with a shell that burst just in front of her. The outraged British captain stopped his vessel. Junior officers with armed marines from the *San Jacinto* rowed over to the *Trent*. They said they had orders to arrest Mason and Slidell.

Mrs. Slidell, who was on board with her daughter, preparing to make their temporary home in Paris, asked who the *San Jacinto*'s commander was. When told it was Charles Wilkes, whom she had met socially in Washington, she exclaimed with a scornful little smile, "He is playing into our hands!" The commissioners, with their private secretaries, were forcibly removed from the *Trent* in defiance of the warning protests of the British captain and the Royal Navy agent, Commander Williams. As they were rowed away, Slidell called to his wife that they would assuredly meet in Paris in sixty days.

When Jefferson Davis received the news in Richmond several days later, he was indignant at the arrest of his emissaries. At the same time, a hope welled in his breast that the event might at least bring speedy recognition abroad. Davis was aware that Britain would interpret the action of Captain Wilkes as an insult to her flag. In formally announcing the seizure to Congress, he said, "The United States have thus claimed a general jurisdiction over the high seas, and entering a British ship, sailing under its country's flag, have violated the rights of embassy, for the most part held sacred even amongst barbarians, by seizing our ministers while under the protection and within the dominions of a neutral nation. . . . Had they been malefactors and citizens of the United States, they could not have been arrested on a British ship or on British soil, unless under the express provisions of a treaty according to the forms therein provided for the extradition of criminals."

The entire Confederacy was thrown into a state of excitement almost as intense as that which raged during the Sumter engagement. There was, as the perceptive Britisher Catherine Hopley noted, one significant difference: Sumter "was the signal for war to *commence —this* raised hopes of its being brought to a *conclusion.*" "For the time nothing else was thought of and talked of but this 'unaccountable act'," she wrote in her journal. "Whenever a guest arrived it was the first topic to be discussed; and the gentlemen stood rubbing their hands with glee to think that the 'growl of the British Lion' would now be heard to frighten the 'raving Yankees' into submission."

When the *Trent* finally reached England and the detailed news came out, British citizens were as excited as the Southerners. Commander Williams declared that marines with pointed bayonets had rushed at Miss Slidell, who clung to her father, and that he had thrown himself before the screaming young lady. London editorial writers abandoned their boasted restraint and loosed tirades against the United States. The *Morning Chronicle* declared: "Abraham Lincoln . . . has proved himself a feeble, confused and little-minded mediocrity. Mr. Seward, the firebrand at his elbow, is exerting himself to provoke a quarrel with all Europe." The sedate London *Times* went further and condemned "Yankees" wholesale. Captain Wilkes was called "the ideal Yankee." "Swagger and ferocity, built on a foundation of vulgarity and cowardice, these are his characteristics, and these are the most prominent marks by which his countrymen, generally speaking, are known all over the world."[1]

William Yancey, still in London awaiting the arrival of his successor, read the papers with gleeful optimism, and sent cuttings from them to Richmond. The scent of war was unmistakable in the autumn fog. British transports were readied; 8,000 crack troops sailed for Canada.

In the meantime, the North was cock-a-hoop jubilant over the Confederate agents' capture and their imprisonment in a Boston harbor fort. Captain Wilkes, who had made the arrest, received extravagant plaudits from the United States Government as well as from the public. The House of Representatives honored him with a vote of thanks. He was paraded along New York's Broadway to a City Hall recep-

[1] These two excerpts from contemporary London dailies are quoted in Carl Sandburg's *Abraham Lincoln* to show the animosity engendered in England.

tion. He was feted in Boston. "There is a storm of exultation sweeping over the land," William Russell reported on November 18. "Wilkes is the hero of the hour." Yet Charles Francis Adams, the wise Minister to Great Britain, was convinced that Wilkes had done wrong; he told Her Majesty's Government that he was sure his own Government was not responsible for the high-handed act.

To Jefferson Davis, reading of the North's triumphant demonstrations, "the outrage was the more marked, because the United States had been foremost in resisting the right of 'visit and search' and had made it the cause of the War of 1812 with Britain." He pondered: What would England do if the United States did not back down? How could she avoid making some move that would benefit the Confederacy's cause? For the rest of November and far into December, little else was thought of or talked of in the South but the *Trent* affair and the Yankees' dilemma.

On November 25, when the papers reported that a driving snowstorm had struck Washington, Davis was relieved. He felt that McClellan would surely not attack before spring. By then, the Confederacy would undoubtedly have some arms with which to meet the offensive. When McClellan was stricken with typhoid early in December, Davis knew that the Republican Administration must give up any attempt to take Richmond in 1861.

From the fifth to the tenth of December, while tension over the *Trent* affair continued to grip both South and North, Richmond had five days of surprisingly warm weather, with clearest moonlight. Log fires and fur pieces were discarded. At night, Jefferson Davis could sit on his long veranda with Varina, who hardly found a shawl necessary, although she was expecting her baby any day. These were hours of respite, of tender reminiscences, mingled with some apprehension of the imminent family event and nostalgia for the privacy of their remote plantation.

On December 16, at a ball given in Washington by M. de Lisboa, William Russell found Seward in fine humor. Cavalierly, he declared, "If Great Britain forces war on the United States, we will wrap the world in flames! No power so remote that she will not feel the fire of our battle and be burned by our conflagration." Russell was believing that the Secretary of State really intended to show fight, but a guest who overheard the conversation told him it was "all bugaboo talk." "When Seward talks that way," he said, "he means to break down. He is most dangerous and obstinate when he pretends to agree a good deal with you."

That same night of December 16, when Seward was threatening to inflame the world, Varina Davis gave birth to her fourth boy child. Despite her carriage accident in October, which had been a constant source of concern to her husband, she did not have a difficult time. Davis could never forget her near-death at the birth of Jeff, Jr.; and he still believed that Seward's kindness in sending his sleigh with Varina's nurse through the unprecedented snowdrifts of January, 1855, may have saved her life. The President was pleased to have the baby named William Howell for his ingratiating, ne'er-do-well, Northern-born father-in-law, of whom he was really fond.

Varina was relieved to have the birth over before Christmas, which in the hospitable South was a season of continuous merrymaking in the homes. And she decided she must silence the unjust criticisms of the *Examiner* by giving some large affairs as soon as she was strong again. Social life at the Executive Mansion had of necessity been greatly curtailed in September, by both the President's illness and his absorption in pressing business; and, because of her accident in October and the approaching confinement, her physician had insisted that she conserve her strength. Though all Richmond had known of her *enceinte* condition, the *Examiner*'s editors slurringly laid the blame for the lack of entertaining, first, on the toploftiness of the "satrap" Davises, and later, taking the tack that Washington critics had about Mrs. Lincoln, suggested that Mrs. Davis was parsimonious and that the President was "hoarding his salary."

After the birth of the baby, the President was in a sanguine state of mind. No critical situation presented itself urgently on any of the war fronts. Joseph Johnston's soldiers were settled for the winter in tents or rude log huts with mud chimneys. Camp epidemics had subsided. Scores of small manufactories had sprung up throughout the Confederacy, not only for supplying materials of war, like the powder factory at Nashville, but rude paper mills and factories for making cotton cloth, caps, and furniture. The agrarian Southerners, who had bought their merchandise from the North, were daily learning to be more resourceful. Country people near the camps were induced to collect and tan the cowhides lying about the fields, which were in turn sent to the new shoe factories that made rough boots for the soldiers.

The cotton crop of 1861, needed by British mills, had been gathered and stored on a voluntary unofficial embargo basis, awaiting England's recognition. Unless the Confederate captives Slidell and Mason were released very soon, England might actually declare war. All the foreign diplomats in Washington, as William Russell wrote, believed the prisoners would not be given up. It was rumored that President Lincoln said he would "rather die" than give them up. If he did not, the British Minister, Lord Lyons, was prepared to retire with his legation to Halifax.

With climactic news daily expected from England, the hopeful people broke into cheers whenever Jefferson Davis appeared on the street. He made a gallant figure on his thoroughbred from Brierfield; some admirer declared that "he rode with a military air and bearing not equalled by any of his generals."

In the week before Christmas, the President could give some devoted attention to his two little boys and the only girl. They were all affectionate children, handsome little Joe, not yet three, most especially so. He would get "occasions of tenderness" while playing, and run up and put his dirty little hands on either side of his father's face to kiss him. Maggie, a highly intelligent child, considerate and gentle, would sit for hours silently in her father's office when he worked at home, blissfully happy just to be in his presence. Six-year-old Jeff, Jr., though not so bright as his sister, was, in his frank mother's words, "beaming, blustering, blooming, burly and blundering; the repository of many hopes, promising but little definite yet." None of the children hesitated to come into the drawing room if there was company, and at the dinner table little Joe was accustomed to crawl up into his father's lap during dessert.

On this Christmas Eve, Jefferson Davis could lay aside his cares. Varina was up and buoyant, his children clustered about him, gifts and loving wishes arrived from admiring strangers and long-time friends. When Joe came to say his usual night prayer at his father's knee, the President had his own special petition in this season designated for good will among men. He could wish devoutly that England's imminent action might somehow lead to peace and assure the South's independence.

Christmas Day in the Davis household began, according to custom, with eggnog being passed around and the giving of presents to the Negro servants in response to their cries of "Chrismas gif'." After attending a morning service at St. Paul's, the Davises received callers all afternoon. Through the happy exchanges of pleasantries, however, an underburden of watchful waiting gripped at the President's consciousness, for it was reported that a messenger from Her Majesty's Government had arrived in Washington with a stern dispatch from

Lord Russell demanding the immediate release of the Confederate commissioners and their secretaries.

On December 27, against all the predictions, Mr. Lincoln decided to yield. Seward sent an archly courteous reply to the British Minister, Lord Lyons:

The four persons in question are now held in military custody at Fort Warren, in the State of Massachusetts. They will be cheerfully liberated. Your lordship will please indicate a time and place for receiving them.

With the news of the United States's capitulation to Britain, the protesting rage of many red-hot Northern patriots was explosive. Giving in to England's demands was a "pretty bitter pill to swallow," Mr. Lincoln admitted to Horace Porter. J. B. Jones noted scornfully in his diary: "Seward has cowered before the roar of the British Lion. . . . Now we must depend upon our own strong arms and stout hearts for defense." A pall fell upon the South. "It was little to be expected," Jefferson Davis remarked, "after such explicit commendation of the act, that the United States government would accede to the demand."

Instead of helping the South, the *Trent* affair had actually redounded to the North's benefit; for England, anticipating her own probable war needs, had held up the shipping of arms, blankets, and shoes sold to the Confederacy.

After the high-flaming hope of the pre-Christmas season, the fateful year of 1861 sputtered out in a mist of gloom for the Confederacy. As gold and silver disappeared from circulation, inflation mounted alarmingly; prices had doubled in six months. The Southern railways could not maintain their schedules; continual breakdowns occurred due to lack of repair materials. The Federal blockade was closing in on Southern ports; incoming or outgoing shipping was risky business. There was a scarcity of almost everything. Many items once considered necessities were not to be had at any cost.

When Congressman Ely, captured at Bull Run, was released from prison the day before Christmas, he smiled at the crude brown paper on which his passport was written. War Clerk Jones assured him that Southern manufacture was in the process of improvement; the blockade, he maintained, might ultimately work to the mercantile North's disadvantage. Ely pleasantly replied that he had no doubt "the South would rise to the dignity of *white* paper."

The power of King Cotton had certainly not proved absolute in 1861. England was apparently prepared to let her cotton-factory workers wrestle with starvation rather than break the blockade or recognize the Confederacy. "Did we not read," wrote Catherine Hopley, "of our English poor being limited in their labours on account of the probability of reduced importations of cotton? While the so-called *slaves* were fattening on good food, and parading to their Sunday meetings in an astonishing display of flounces, feathers, and shirt collars, were not the legislators of my own honoured England experimentalizing on how little it was possible for a man to live upon?"

When the year ended at midnight on December 31, the Richmond *Whig* pronounced it "the most eventful of the present century." In the life of Jefferson Davis, it had certainly been the most fateful. The job of being President, which he had sought to avoid, partly because of the miseries he had seen it bring upon his good friend Franklin Pierce in peacetime, had already proved in wartime far more taxing than he could have dreamed. His tribulations, however, were to be magnified in the first half of '62. Glowing expectations were to end in ashen disappointments; criticism and calumny were to be heaped upon him.

Nevertheless, as Davis now reflected, the year of 1861 had had its bright aspects as well as its distresses. Though as yet unrecognized by European powers, the Confederacy stood intact. The quick subjugation President Lincoln had expected was far from realized. The vast Army of the Potomac was no nearer Richmond than it had been in May. In the majority of battles, the ill-equipped Confederates had been victors. No hint of the servile insurrection hoped for by some Abolitionists had arisen; in general, the Negroes seemed as stoutly "anti-Yankee" as their masters.

On the first day of January, a resplendent sun shone on Richmond. The springlike morning was almost as balmy as it had been on Mr. Davis's inauguration day in Montgomery. The President and his Lady held a New Year's reception that began at eleven o'clock. For four hours, Jefferson Davis, handsome and imposing, though extremely thin, stood at the door of the main drawing room, greeting a continuous stream of callers, giving them each a smile and a cordial handclasp. Cabinet ministers, army officers, distinguished citizens, with their ladies, and the general public circulated, while the Armory Band made the Executive Mansion resound with music.

For all his disappointment in the year-end turn of events, Davis would face 1862 with an outward show of indomitable confidence. As to courage, that quality was so engrained in the fiber of his being that he had only to open his lips to stir the people to a determination to endure against incalculable odds.

CHAPTER XVI

"YOU REMEMBER THE MAN"

THOUGH the Davises themselves could not entertain until Christmas, that whole winter of 1861-62 in Richmond was socially gay. The ebullient Virginia Clay punned, "For a few months, we revelled in canvas-backs and green-backs, undisturbed by forewarnings of coming draw-backs." "The three hundred," as she termed those in top society, feasted on ducks from Chesapeake Bay, on prime oysters and terrapin. When Senator Clement Clay and she left Huntsville, Alabama for the capital, her ginger-colored maid, Emily, packed her evening gowns and jewels, despite her protest that they were going to war and to nurse the sick, not to dress and dance. But Emily had been right. Though Richmond women did their full share of nursing, sewing, and knitting, Virginia Clay found that heroes on leave had to be entertained and diverted.

A quantity of Southerners who had figured brightly in Washington society only yesterday were gathered in Richmond, and "unmeasured hospitality" was the order of the season. While the President lived with what Mrs. Clay called "an admirable disdain of display," Mrs. Davis was again "at home" almost every evening after Christmas. Only tea and wafers were served, but guests were assured of a warm welcome and a pleasant visit. If they came early enough, they might meet the President, who would remain downstairs for an hour of relaxation before beginning official labors that lasted far into the night. At these informal "evenings," Mr. Davis said little, but let his wife and her sister, Margaret Howell, lead the conversation. Margaret was almost as witty and engaging a conversationalist as Varina. The President, like everyone else, appreciated her spontaneous bons mots and epigrams "that went from court to camp."

At Mrs. Davis's fortnightly "levées," the President usually received with her. But he rarely appeared at social functions outside his own house. However, he dined occasionally at the homes of two of his Cabinet: Judah Benjamin and Stephen Mallory, the advisers with whom he had the most business to discuss. Mallory was famous for his punches and juleps; his Spanish wife was skilled in the Creole cuisine. The Secretary of the Navy could appear heavy and dullish to those who did not interest him, but to some "his wit was as sudden and brilliant as sheet-lightning," and he had a "power of summing up, when he chose to exert it, both events and people, in a most amusing manner." His adroit flattery to ladies added to his popularity.

Benjamin made himself agreeable to the tiresome as well as the attractive. Never effusive, he breathed an air of placid bonhomie. Whatever the opinion then of his conduct of war or foreign affairs, he was a recognized success in society and his "soft, purring presence" was quite as pleasing to the debutante set as to their elders.

Two other houses, besides Benjamin's and Mallory's, to which the President sometimes went were, in a sense, social adjuncts to the Executive Mansion. One, directly across the street from the Confederate White House, was that of Senator Thomas J. Semmes of Louisiana, cousin of the Navy's daring Raphael Semmes. His beautiful and talented wife, Eulalie Knox of Montgomery, took some of the burden of official entertaining off Mrs. Davis and would house distinguished foreign guests who turned up on business or out of curiosity. According to the New Orleans *Picayune*, the Semmeses were so lavish in their hospitality that in one year of the war they spent $30,000.

Another house that Jefferson Davis particularly favored was that of Senator Semmes's sister, Cora, and her husband, Colonel Joseph C. Ives, engineer aide-de-camp on the President's staff. In the years just prior to the war, the Iveses were reputed to be the most popular young couple in Washington, and there Jefferson Davis had known them. Handsome, Northern-born Ives was a West Pointer who had been a cadet at the Academy when Robert E. Lee was Superintendent. He had resigned from the United States Army because of his Southern sympathies, and Lee had promptly put him on his staff in Richmond. Then the President had commanded his services and found him to be highly efficient as well as personally charming. In the Iveses' Richmond home, a series of long "colonial parlors" made the house ideal for large-scale entertaining; and Mrs. Ives, who was an accomplished harpist, gave frequent musicals and introduced "charade" parties for charity.

Two other notable hostesses were Mrs. Robert Stanard, a widow, and Mrs. George Wythe Randolph, whose husband was to succeed Benjamin as Secretary of War. Mrs. Stanard, an exotic beauty with both brains and wealth, made a specialty of "teas," at which broiled chicken and hot muffins were served. Though she was bounteous in her hospitality to vacationing soldiers, Mrs. Stanard attracted the intellectuals and maintained something that resembled a *salon*, where Judah Benjamin was a frequent guest and would give dramatic readings. Mrs. Randolph, nee Adams of Natchez, had inherited a fortune from her first husband. Her money and her wit, together with Randolph's prestige as a grandson of Thomas Jefferson, made her house outstanding in Richmond society.

Though with many persons Jefferson Davis had the reputation of being somewhat austere in society, others found him completely engaging, "easy to approach and patient of woes of subordinates." At a stag affair attended by all the officers of state, a representative of the Charleston *Daily Courier* set down a vivid impression of Mr. Davis as gracious host. After the presentations, the President moved freely among his guests making pleasantries, exchanging reminiscences. "You look, you listen, and you talk," reported the *Courier*. "Magnetized by one of the most irresistible smiles in the world, charmed with his language, and yet, involuntarily drawn into the expression of your own sentiments, you soon forget that you are talking with the President of the Southern Union, and remember the man."

Social life in Richmond came to a brief halt on January 18 with the sudden death of former President John Tyler. Out of respect, all scheduled social events were postponed. Taken ill at his Richmond hotel, he died with a firm expectancy of the South's ultimate victory and independence. Jefferson Davis, a long-time personal friend, was grieved. He would miss Tyler's potent support in the incoming new Congress. He could speak in heartfelt eulogy of the former President, who was given the most impressive Southern funeral since that of John C. Calhoun and was buried in Hollywood Cemetery close to former President James Monroe. For Davis, Tyler's death marked the beginning of a siege of troubles that crowded the weeks preceding his inauguration.

In England, the effect of Lincoln's surrender of the Confederate envoys was quite remarkable. Anti-United States talk ceased abruptly. On New Year's Day, Mason and Slidell had been quietly delivered to the British ship *Rinaldo* at Provincetown, Massachusetts. By the time the envoys reached London, in late January, the dramatic incident seemed to have disappeared from the British public mind. For the immediate present, hopes of recognition vanished. Davis realized sharply that for some time yet the South would have to fight out in sweat and blood the bitter, unequal struggle.

When the hope of British intervention flickered out, Secretary of State Hunter asked to be relieved of his office. He determined to stand for the Senate. Sanguine about the South's ultimate success, the ambitious Hunter aspired to succeed Davis as President of the Confederacy in 1868. He feared his chances of election might be damaged if he remained too closely attached to the present Administration. Davis was reluctant to have Hunter leave the Cabinet. He liked him personally;[1] his work had been good; his reports and instructions to agents abroad, cogent, clear, well-constructed. Yet, foreseeing from the complexion of the newly elected Congress that trouble would be brewing, Davis believed that Hunter might prove more valuable to the Administration as a leader in the Senate. And this was so. Hunter did support the Davis policies until late in 1864, when he opposed the use of Negro troops.

The story later concocted by Pollard of the *Examiner* that Hunter resigned on the spur of the moment after Davis had allegedly rebuked him sharply at a Cabinet meeting had no foundation in fact whatever. Hunter's resignation had been planned[2] and discussed with the President. The *Examiner* itself, on January 8, 1862, came out against Hunter's election to the Senate. An editorial questioned "his claim to greatness" and charged that selfish ambition caused him to seek a place in the Senate. Though the paper used its influence to try to defeat him, on January 23, Hunter won by a huge majority, 140 to 24 votes. He continued to hold his office as Secretary of State until February 18, four days before the inauguration.

In Washington, too, there was a Cabinet change. Simon Cameron was removed as Lincoln's Secretary of War in January. Charged with wanton extravagance in his Department and suspected of graft on government contracts, Cameron was censured in the House. Though personal corruption was never proved, President Lincoln dismissed

[1] William Preston Johnston on January 9, 1878, wrote to Jefferson Davis: "I knew Hunter was regarded as being in perfect accord with you. I have always heard you speak of him kindly—even affectionately."

[2] Rembert W. Patrick, in his objective study of *Jefferson Davis and His Cabinet* (pp. 98-99), is enlightening on Hunter's planned resignation.

him rather curtly from his Cabinet, but softened the blow somewhat by nominating him Minister to Russia.

Davis was surprised when Lincoln appointed his own most caustic critic, Edwin McMasters Stanton, to succeed Cameron. Apparently Lincoln was not indignant that Stanton spoke openly of "the painful imbicility of Lincoln" and frequently referred to him as "the original gorilla." William Russell of the *Times* regarded Stanton with distaste: "He is excessively vain, and aspires to be considered a rude, rough, vigorous Oliver Cromwell sort of man, mistaking some of the disagreeable attributes and the accidents of the external husk of the Great Protector for the brain and head of a statesman and a soldier." Davis had no esteem for Stanton, whom he regarded as cold and unscrupulous, but he knew that Stanton was a shrewd lawyer and a man of driving energy. As a Democrat, Stanton had been a flattering admirer of President Buchanan, who had appointed him Attorney General toward the end of his regime. Stanton, who had voted for John C. Breckinridge for President, was to become the South's most relentless enemy.

Stanton had so flattered McClellan, that sincere "Little Mac" approved of his appointment as War Secretary. As soon as he was in office, Stanton began to undermine the Commanding General. On January 27, 1862, spurred by Stanton, President Lincoln impatiently issued War Order No. 1, commanding General McClellan to advance on or before February 22, the date scheduled for Jefferson Davis's inauguration. But McClellan ignored the order. Happily for the South, he was not ready to advance.

The last day in January, Jefferson Davis faced a crisis that shook the State of Virginia: "Stonewall" Jackson was offended at Secretary of War Benjamin and sent in his resignation.

These were the facts as the President heard them. In Winchester, General Jackson, heading the Army of the Valley, had celebrated New Year's Day by setting out in terrible weather to capture Romney, thirty-five miles to the northwest, where 5,000 Federals were assembled. Impeded by sleet, snow, and ice-caked roads, the movement was painfully slow. Halfway to Romney, Jackson was irritated to read of his secret plans in a Baltimore paper. On the fourteenth, the Confederates occupied the little town, from which the Federals had escaped scot-free. Jackson now proposed to take Grafton, seventy-five miles farther to the west. But his troops, some of them without overcoats in the bitter cold, grumbled so at the winter hardships that he gave up the idea. Leaving General Loring in disagreeable winter quarters in isolated Romney, Jackson returned to Winchester. The men, exposed to the dreadful weather without proper food or clothing, called "Old Jack" crazy, and, as Frank Vandiver wrote, "began to lose faith in their general."

By advancing, Jackson had placed on the alert defensive 18,000 Federals under General Stone across the upper Potomac. But Secretary of War Benjamin received a letter signed by eleven of Loring's officers asking that Romney be abandoned; the place was strategically unimportant and the men were suffering such discomforts that they threatened not to re-enlist when their term was up. Loring sent a copy of the petition by General William B. Talliaferro, who was going on leave to Richmond, to be delivered in person to the President. Davis surveyed a map of the region and was convinced that Jackson had made a mistake. Sympathizing with the officers and the men, he called Benjamin in conference. He suggested that General Johnston's opinion should first be sought. Johnston himself had feared (as shown by his correspondence with the War Department) that Jackson had "scattered his forces quite too far for safety." Johnston informed Benjamin that he was sending his acting Inspector General to examine the situation. But the Secretary of War did not wait for the report. He telegraphed Jackson: "Our news indicates that a movement is being made to cut off General Loring's command. Order him back to Winchester immediately."

Though Jackson complied, he smoldered with rage. On January 31, he wrote Benjamin: "With such interference in my command I cannot expect to be of much service in the field; and accordingly respectfully request to be ordered to report for duty to the superintendent of the Virginia Military Institute at Lexington. . . . Should this application not be granted, I respectfully request that the President will accept my resignation from the Army."

Davis and Benjamin were both extremely upset. Joseph Johnston wrote in a most conciliatory tone to the angry General. Numerous important persons, including Governor Letcher, begged Jackson to withdraw his resignation, which would be "a calamity to the country and the cause." State Comptroller Jonathan Bennett, good friend of Jackson, declared that the order of "Mr. Benjamin, the Jew," was "a most remarkable specimen of indiscretion, lack of judgement, and disregard of the courtesies." Claiming that it had met with almost universal condemnation, he urged Jackson to remain in the service, because his name alone was "worth ten thousand men." Jackson was pacified, and, most fortunately, remained in service. Benjamin unhappily acquired new enemies, and Jackson felt less kindly to the President.

Early in February, when the Confederates surrendered Roanoke Island, North Carolina, to a Federal fleet and 12,000 soldiers under General Ambrose E. Burnside, Benjamin came in for more criticism. He was not to blame. General Henry Wise, who had proved intractable in the Kanawha Valley, was in command of 3,000 men at Roanoke. He had repeatedly called for help from General Benjamin Huger, commander at Norfolk, with whom he was not on the best terms. Though, at Benjamin's order, Huger sent Wise powder from his own small store, he would not endanger strategic Norfolk by releasing troops. When Burnside attacked on February 8, General Wise, ill with pleurisy, had to be carried to safety in a blanket. His popular and gallant young son, Captain Jennings Wise, was killed, cheering on his men against the overwhelming numbers. A much-publicized funeral at St. James Church aroused all Richmond; the grieving father would not be comforted, and privately arraigned Huger and Benjamin for the "murder" of his son as well as for the defeat.

Benjamin consulted with the President as to whether it was better for the country that he submit to unmerited censure or reveal to a Congressional committee the Army's poverty and run the risk that the stark facts become known to the enemy. In the public interest, Davis advised Benjamin to submit to censure, just as he himself had done when blamed erroneously for not advancing on Washington after Manassas.

Almost simultaneous with the loss of Roanoke Island, the President received distressing news from the West. Just across the southern border of Kentucky the Confederates had erected two forts only twelve miles apart to protect the state of Tennessee: Fort Henry on the Tennessee River and Fort Donelson on the Cumberland. At the end of January, the high command in Washington had ordered Ulysses S. Grant to advance from Paducah, Kentucky, supported by gunboats, and to invest first one fort, then the other.

In January, some Congressional Representatives of the Mississippi Valley had requested that General Beauregard be transferred to the West, where a crisis was shaping. President Davis was quite willing, and so was Beauregard, who was chaffing at being under Joseph Johnston. Many of Beauregard's friends, like Roger Pryor, thought he would have more chance for glory in the West. The General left Virginia on February 2, and met Albert Sidney Johnston, his new superior, for the first time at Bowling Green, Kentucky, on the evening of the fourth. Two days later, General Grant captured Fort Henry.

Fort Henry on the east bank of the Tennessee was poorly located, weakly garrisoned. By the time Grant arrived, some of the batteries were under water from the rising river. The commander, Brigadier General Lloyd Tilghman, seeing he had no chance of saving the fort, sent all but a few artillerists to join the forces at Donelson. Keeping the enemy at bay until the escape of some 2,500 men was effected, he surrendered the fort on February 6. The Tennessee River was open now for Federal gunboats to steam southward to the northwest corner of Alabama.

The news was not only disturbing to President Davis, but caused dismay to Albert Sidney Johnston, who commanded the West and whose headquarters had been at Bowling Green, Kentucky, since October. Johnston, poorly equipped, with hardly a third of the men the public thought he possessed, had to guard against two formidable armies: General Don Carlos Buell's, at Louisville, and Grant's, which now started moving against Donelson. Johnston determined to fight for Nashville at Donelson, and gave 16,000 of his force to the fort's defense, keeping only 14,000 at Bowling Green to oppose Buell. His judgment was good, but he was unfortunate in having inept top generals at Donelson: former Secretary of War Floyd and Gideon Pillow, a Mexican War veteran.

After Grant had taken Fort Henry, he wired General Henry W. Halleck that he would destroy Fort Donelson on the eighth. But he did not reach Donelson, twelve miles away, until the twelfth. The Federal gunboats were at first so thoroughly repulsed that the Confederates thought they had won a victory.

Then reinforcements arrived to swell Grant's army to 27,000. On the night of the fourteenth, a blizzard blew down out of the northwest, making life a hell for both armies. On the fifteenth, with gunboats pouring shot into the fort from the river and Grant's forces attacking from the land side, the Confederates decided to cut their way out. In a bloody fight in the new-fallen snow, the Confederates drove back the Union infantry, got control of the Nashville road, and had a clear chance to escape. Then Floyd and Pillow floundered, lost sense of reality, and in confusion withdrew back into the fort. By nightfall, Union troops had regained the road to Nashville.

At midnight, the top Confederate officers held a dismal council of war, to which they invited Colonel Nathan Bedford Forrest. The Cavalry commander had scouted and found another road by which the men might escape. But it was partially submerged in freezing backwater. Simon Bolivar Buckner, third in command, opposed attempt to retreat by this road, claiming, as did the physicians, that three-fourths of the men might be lost from wading waist-deep in icy water. One remaining way of escape was by two small steamers that had arrived that afternoon from Nashville. These boats could save a portion of the Army. Floyd, fearing his former position as Secretary of War under Buchanan would be his undoing if captured by Union troops, decided to escape by the boats. Pillow was willing to surrender the garrison, but not himself. So the two senior officers turned the command over to Buckner. Floyd got some 1,500 of his Virginians away by the steamers, while Pillow used a skiff to reach the opposite bank. The hard-bitten Forrest, to whom surrender was anathema, took his five hundred men off down the submerged road. Some infantrymen and artillerymen who were willing to risk pneumonia and death from exposure joined Forrest as he rode away into eventual fame.

After the escapees were gone, Buckner wrote his onetime fellow-cadet Grant asking for terms. He expected moderate dealing, for they had been friends at West Point, and eight years before, in New York, when Grant was down and out, Buckner had given him the money to go home. Grant's reply, however, was a curt "unconditional surrender," which became his noted nickname. Though Buckner regarded the terms "as ungenerous and unchivalrous," when morning came, to avoid sacrificing so many lives, he ran down the Stars and Bars. U. S. Grant had now amended his tarnished record in the Army. He had won a decisive victory, and was deservedly made a Major General.

The disastrous news of Donelson's fall shook the Confederacy. Jefferson Davis was greatly dispirited. It was, so far, the South's worst defeat. Some 12,000 Confederates were taken prisoner. Kentucky seemed irretrievably lost. The way to Nashville was open for Union troops. Two hostile armies were now converging on Sidney Johnston, who had swiftly moved his remaining forces from Bowling Green to Nashville.

Johnston knew his small army could never hold the city against both Grant and Buell. When the citizens learned they were to be abandoned, consternation and despair, grief and wrath seized them. Some prepared to flee; some began to loot army supplies, which General Floyd was loading on cars for removal. A witness wrote of "the wild terror and agony of a population which believed that it was about to suffer every extremity of brutality and violence." The people of Tennessee and the Southwest realized for the first time the grim and deadly nature of the struggle.

In Richmond President Davis received frantic telegrams from persons of importance and people of no importance, calling on him for help. A former member of the United States Congress, in whose very house Johnston was making his temporary headquarters, telegraphed:

Nothing but your presence here can save Tennessee. General Johnston's army is demoralized. Your presence will reassure it, and will save Tennessee. Nothing else can. For God's sake, come!

In his prepared inaugural address, to be delivered a few days hence, President Davis had to make changes. To follow the proud line "We have maintained the war by our unaided exertions," he was now constrained to write: "After a series of successes and victories, we have recently met with serious disasters."

At the calamitous turn of events and the howls of criticism against Sidney Johnston and the Administration, Davis, to relieve his packed heart, began a letter to his intimate friend and factor, J. U. Payne of New Orleans. Payne was one of the very few persons to whom he could ever bare personal griefs.

My dear Jacob—

Dearest friend, I wish you to console me in a most trying hour. I have the most vexing problems surmounting the most vicious you and I ever twinly put down. I forbear to tell you of my utmost, my desire to see the South win, but in every standpoint . . .

Davis wrote on for ten more lines, but did not finish the letter, and the fragment was never mailed.[2] Perhaps he felt he was going too far even with the understanding Payne in revealing his anguish.

In the depth of his depression, four days before his inauguration,

[2] The unfinished letter is in the possession of Matt Tom Green of New Orleans, who inherited it from his grandmother Betty, who became a serving maid and beloved foster daughter in the Davis household at Beauvoir in the late 1880's. Betty was a nurse at Jefferson Davis's bedside when he died at the home of J. U. Payne in 1889. The last ten lines of the letter are indecipherable because of water damage suffered in the 1915 hurricane.

Jefferson Davis received a surprising letter from Dr. Charles Minne-gerode, Rector of St. Paul's. Excusing himself from trespassing on his time, the clergyman said he felt that the President's whole course had impressed upon the public both in America and in Europe his belief that the Confederacy's destinies were in the hands of God. "Oh, Mr. President," he wrote, "if immediately upon taking the oath you would yield to the spontaneous out-bursting of your heart, and—raising your hands to heaven—ask in the sight of all the people, for God's grace and blessing upon you and the country, it would send a thrill through the whole land, and from every state and every Southern home would ascend a loud 'Amen.' "

Davis pondered on the minister's suggestion and its implications. Religious feelings had been stirring within him more and more. On January 10, War Clerk Jones had recorded in his diary that it was rumored the President intended joining the church, adding, "All his messages and proclamations indicate that he is looking to a mightier power than England for assistance." Davis hoped he could sincerely follow the minister's suggestion.

CHAPTER XVII

JEFFERSON DAVIS ENTERS
"HIS MARTYRDOM"

WASHINGTON'S BIRTHDAY, the day of Jefferson Davis's inauguration, dawned ominously with forbidding clouds. At ten o'clock, the hard patter of winter rain resounded throughout the city. Mrs. Davis saw her husband come in from an early visit to his office, go into his bedroom, and close the door. An hour later, as the time approached for the inaugural ceremonies to begin, she went to his room and found him "on his knees in earnest prayer." "For the divine support I need so sorely," he explained, as he rose. Soon afterward, he left for the capitol, where assembled Congressmen and dignitaries were waiting to receive him in the Hall of Representatives.

When Mrs. Davis took her seat in the carriage sent to take her to Capitol Square, and the coachman started driving at funereal pace, she was dumfounded to see walking on either side of her coach four Negroes in black suits and grotesque white cotton gloves. They marched with melodramatic solemnity, their facial expressions fixed with unbroken gloom. Calling impatiently to the coachman to stop, she demanded to know what this lugubrious performance meant. The crestfallen driver, who had made the arrangements, explained: "This, madam, is the way we always does in Richmond at funerals and sich-like."

While Mrs. Davis confessed that evening that she almost regretted having to order "the pall-bearers" away because they were so proud of their dignified stations, the macabre incident gave her quite a turn. As she proceeded, the heavens opened up, and the rain came down in sheets. When she reached Capitol Square, the street gutters were like little swollen rivers. A great concourse of people was gathered, but their faces were obliterated by a mass of black umbrellas.

With R. M. T. Hunter, as President of the Senate, by his side, Mr. Davis led the procession out of the east door of the capitol to an awning-covered stand erected near the equestrian statue of George Washington. A prolonged cheering was followed by a portentous hush when the damp Right Reverend Bishop John Johns offered up prayer.

"In the heaviest burst of the storm," wrote De Leon, "Mr. Davis took the oath of office, and there was something in his mien . . . that, for the moment raised him high above party spite and personal prejudice. An involuntary murmur of admiration, not loud but heart-deep, broke from the crowds who thronged the drenched walks, and every foot of space on the roof, windows, and steps of the Capitol. As it died, Mr. Davis spoke to the people."

"A million men, it is estimated," he said, "are now standing in hostile array, and waging war along a frontier of thousands of miles. . . . The tide for the moment is against us, but the final result in our favor is never doubtful. We have had our trials and difficulties. That we are to escape them in the future is not to be hoped. It was to be expected when we entered upon this war, that it would expose our people to sacrifices and cost them much; both of money and blood.

"But the picture has its lights as well as its shadows. This great strife has awakened in the people the highest emotions and qualities of the human soul. . . . It was, perhaps, in the ordination of Providence that we were taught the value of our liberties by the price we pay for them."

Coming to the close of his address, and remembering Dr. Minnegerode's request, Jefferson Davis lifted his eyes, stretched out hands toward heaven, and said in deep reverence: "With humble gratitude and adoration, acknowledging the Providence which has so visibly protected the Confederacy during its brief but eventful career, to Thee, O God, I trustingly commit myself, and prayerfully invoke Thy blessing on my country and its cause."

The crowd was audibly moved. Mrs. Davis was so affected that she could remain no longer. As she saw her husband, pale, thin, noble, "dedicating himself to the service of the Confederacy, evidently forgetful of everything but his sacred oath," he seemed to her "a willing victim, going to his funeral pyre." Murmuring some excuse to those near her, she slipped away, regained her carriage, and was driven quickly home.

Judge James D. Halyburton, a nephew of Mrs. Washington, tendered the oath of office. Hunter proclaimed Jefferson Davis President of the Confederate States of America for a term of six years.

"A low wordless shout went up, wrenched from the people's inmost nature that told of a dogged resolution to stand by Jefferson Davis, to achieve a common end." The beautiful Constance Cary, observing from a window, distinctly heard cries of "God bless our President!" She saw the listeners disperse in an awed silence, as if they had been attending a religious service of peculiar solemnity. Relentlessly, the rain poured on.

When evening came, it was still raining. Jones, of the War Office, feared the dismal weather would cause "a paucity of guests" at the President's reception. But the crowd came and filled the ample rooms. Jones found Mr. Davis "calm" and Mrs. Davis "in spirits." In retrospect, however, Varina Davis made a comment on the inauguration that marked the event incisively, like a deep-cut epitaph: "Thus my husband entered his martyrdom."

One minor happening of the gloomy inauguration day turned out to be peculiarly auspicious. In the afternoon, young Colonel L. Q. C. Lamar, intimate friend of the Davis family, called to pay his respects. The President mentioned his urgent need for a private secretary; Captain Joselyn was resigning to enter the Army. With a flash of inspiration, Lamar, who understood Mr. Davis's disposition and requirements, told him that he knew the ideal man. He had just received a letter from Burton Norvelle Harrison, then teaching mathematics at the University of Mississippi while he studied law. Though he was the chief support of his widowed mother, the fall of Donelson had determined Harrison to volunteer, and he wanted to enlist either under Lamar or with the elite Washington Artillery of New Orleans. Harrison would not be twenty-four until July 12, but Lamar was confident he would make an excellent secretary.

Mr. Davis asked a few pertinent questions. Lamar told him that Harrison had made a splendid record at Yale, where he was Phi Beta Kappa, a member of Skull and Bones, an editor of the *Yale Literary Magazine,* and a leader in student activities and social life. He wrote well, and was versed in Greek and Latin. Like the President, he was no provincial: he had about as many friends in the North as in the South. While spending vacations with relatives in Maryland, he had been a favorite in the home of the Carys, where he introduced the stirring Yale air "Lauriger Horatius," to which Jennie Cary was inspired to fit the words of James Randall's "Maryland! My Maryland!," the most popular war song of the camps. Young Harrison was athletic, good-looking, immaculate in dress, and possessed the grace to please.

Despite his youth, Harrison's qualities sounded right to Jefferson Davis. Making one of his assured, quick decisions, he accepted him without consultation. That very evening, Lamar sent Harrison a telegram: "You are Private Secretary to the President. Come on at once." When Harrison arrived, the President knew that he had the right man. Harrison was immediately drawn to Mr. Davis, and soon found that he had "few equals in the art of discourse." From the first, their relations, both official and personal, were warm and intimate. As the months of trials lengthened, Harrison's admiration for Jefferson Davis became devotion, and he became indispensable to his chief.[1]

Three days after the inauguration, the President sent his Message to Congress. Formally recording that the Tennessee forts and Roanoke Island were in the hands of the enemy, he pointed out that the resources of the War Department under the volunteer system were too uncertain for permanent reliance. Volunteer regiments were scattered from Chesapeake Bay to western Missouri, from Columbus, Kentucky, to Galveston, Texas, and the one-year terms of enlistments were running out. Though he did not specifically urge an immediate conscript law, he planted the idea firmly in the mind of the Congress.

Davis had no confidence in a provisional army that was formed for twelve months' service. As he had foreseen, "the fatal effects of the short term, combined with painful deficiency of supplies were felt before the end of the year." In the phrasing of Benjamin, "while the North was vigorously engaged in preparing for an overwhelming descent upon Richmond, the Confederate army was falling to pieces." In order to induce soldiers already under arms to re-enlist, the Administration had been driven to the dangerous expedient of granting them furloughs to go from Virginia to their homes in the far South. If McClellan had suspected the actual want of manpower and supplies, he could have marched his mighty force through Virginia with small resistance. But through the gross miscalculations of Secret Service-man Allan Pinkerton, who had conducted President-elect Lincoln to

---

[1] The Burton Harrison Papers and Letters in the Library of Congress are invaluable in their revelations of the character and temperament of Jefferson Davis.

Washington, McClellan was greatly deceived as to the Confederate strength.

Though Southern Congressmen were reluctant to pass measures unpalatable to voters, the imminent danger of being bereft of a protecting army, because of the return home of the first contingents of twelve-month volunteers, drove Congress to consider an act of conscription.

The coming of severe Confederate reverses just as the new Congress assembled was most untimely for the President. The defeats gave his enemies occasion to voice bold criticism of the Administration and to maneuver subtle backstage intrigue. "The idol of the people," up to a fortnight past, Davis now found many arrayed against him. The first consideration of many politicians was their standing with constituents back home. They were to support bills they knew to be detrimental to the Confederacy's success, trusting in Jefferson Davis to veto them for the public good and thereby elevate their personal popularity at the expense of the President.[2]

"Thus," as Shelby Foote wrote, "in dignified silence he shouldered the blame for men who called him obstinate and argumentative and did their worst to swell the chorus of abuse." "If ever a people determined to bridle their Executive," declared Professor Dodd, "the Southerners did so in their choice of civil representatives during the war." That first Congress under the permanent Constitution, in Dodd's opinion, "contained all the elements of discord and disagreement it was possible to assemble under one roof in the South at this time."

James Lyons, foremost Richmond lawyer and prominent member of this first Congress, had a low opinion of that legislative body. "In justice to President Davis," he later wrote, "I must say that there never was . . . a body of men less fitted for the task which they had undertaken than the first Congress. . . . Jealousy, selfish ambition and consequent discord prevailed from the commencement, and in a month after I took my seat in it, I would have resigned but for the dissuasion of my wife, who was devoted to the cause, and said that my resignation would be misunderstood and regarded as disaffection."

Davis was quite aware that it was the fate of executives in time of war to suffer criticism, denigration, and sometimes malicious libel from those who desired to be regarded as more sagacious than the man at

---

[2] Almost forty times during the Confederacy's life, Davis exercised his veto—generally to the relief of Congress—and in every case but one, Congress sustained the veto.

the helm. Unjust attacks, however, only made his resolution the stronger. He remained firm, as was his custom, in such cases, and outwardly took little note of the cries of "autocrat." Every evening he tried to remember "not to let the sun go down on his wrath."

Georgia's opposition to the President was, peculiarly, represented by Alexander Stephens. The unfriendly attitude of the Vice-President since the November election had been most disconcerting to Davis. He had tried to ignore it and to discount rumors of Stephens's jealousy and lack of loyalty. But the disaffection was so marked that Georgia's T. R. R. Cobb wrote his wife on January 12, 1862: "Stephens is openly opposing the administration and trying to build up an opposition party." It was unpleasant, to say the least, to Jefferson Davis to have his Vice-President determinedly, if not always openly, acting as an opponent and finding flaws in the measures he advocated.

One of the most galling foes of the President in the new Congress was his long-time enemy Henry S. Foote. This former Governor of Mississippi, who had removed to California after being repudiated by his native state's Legislature, had recently come to live in Tennessee. By clever political manipulations and raffish demagoguery, he had got himself elected Representative. Posing as a friend of the Davis Administration, he had defeated a candidate who was angry with the President. In Richmond, on the surface, relations between Davis and Foote were cordial when they met. Davis often inquired after the welfare of Lieutenant Henry Foote, Jr., and extended the young man "many kind services," which both the father and the son appreciated. But in Congress, Foote began to oppose the bills that the President favored. His first blow at Davis was to demand an investigation of Secretary of War Benjamin and the War Department.

At a dinner party in Richmond, which included the Speaker of the House James Orr, General Joseph E. Johnston, Representative Foote, and some twenty other Congressmen, the subject of Benjamin's "official misconduct" was brought up. Johnston, who loathed Benjamin, expressed the opinion that he did not think it possible for the Confederacy to succeed with him as Secretary of War. Foote repeated Johnston's views in Congress, and this marked the end of Benjamin's War Department portfolio.

Benjamin, however, was pleased to seize the opportunity to defend his work. He had a clear view of the Confederacy's problems, and he would be leaving the affairs of the War Department in improved condition. Giving Congress a lucid account of his activities, he could report extraordinary progress. He boldly praised the work of unpopular Commissary General Northrop in his difficult task, though admitting a deficiency of certain articles because of the slowdown of foreign commerce. The Government armories at Richmond and Fayetteville, North Carolina, he said, were now turning out 1,500 rifles and muskets a month, the supply being limited only by the lack of skilled labor. Contracts for 66,500 muskets and rifles and large numbers of sabers and pistols were in process of being filled. Powder mills, arsenals, foundries, and workshops had been established. Though only 15,000 stands of arms from abroad had yet arrived, six times that number were expected within the next two months. In his last report, Benjamin showed an increase of 125 regiments since he had taken office in September.

With his cool assurance, easy manner, and smiling optimism, Benjamin made an admirable impression. But Davis saw that there was too much worked-up opposition to his continuation as War Secretary. For three weeks, however, because of his reluctance to relinquish Benjamin's services, the President delayed presenting his Cabinet selections under the permanent Constitution. Finally, on March 17, he sent Congress his new nominations. "In the teeth of all criticism," Davis resolutely put the name of Judah P. Benjamin at the head of the list—as Secretary of State.

The next day, despite cries of resentment, Congress confirmed his nominations. Virginia's George Wythe Randolph became Secretary of War. Former Supreme Court Justice John A. Campbell, who had been the intermediary between Seward and the Confederate Peace Commission, was made Assistant Secretary of War, a position he held until the Confederacy's end.

Since the State Department occupied the same upper floor as the President's office, Benjamin's desk was now only about a hundred feet from that of Davis. Hardly a day was to pass in which the new Secretary of State did not call upon his chief. Foote's attack had brought them even closer together. But the appointment of Benjamin to a higher office "sealed the opposition in their hatred" of Jefferson Davis. And soon the various malcontents, disappointed office seekers, and disgruntled army officers joined the inimical editors and the Joseph Johnston clique in a campaign of criticism of the President.

It pained Davis to realize that he had to use as much energy against malicious or ignorant critics within the Confederacy as against the destructive might of the Federals. Perhaps nothing could better reveal what he had to face from his own people than a letter to Circuit Judge W. M. Brooks of Marion, Alabama, who had been President of the Alabama Secession Convention. On February 25, Brooks had sent him a weighty epistle summing up reputed accusations against the President's management of national affairs. With remarkable restraint, Mr. Davis replied to Brooks, thanking him for his "friendly remembrance and for the confidence his frankness evinced." Passages from his letter point up the contradictory unreasonableness of some Southerners.

I acknowledge the error of my attempt to defend all the frontier, seaboard and inland; but will say in justification that if we had received the arms and munitions which we had good reason to expect, that the attempt would have been successful and the battlefields would have been on the enemy's soil.

You seem to have fallen into the not uncommon mistake of supposing that I have chosen to carry on the war upon a "purely defensive" system. The advantage of selecting the time and place of attack was too apparent to have been overlooked, but the means might have been wanting. Without military stores, without the workshops to create them, without the power to import them, necessity, not choice, has compelled us to occupy strong positions and everywhere to confront the enemy without reserves.

The country has supposed our armies more numerous than they were and our munitions of war more extensive than they have been. I have borne reproach in silence because to reply by an exact statement of facts would have exposed our weakness to the enemy. History, when the case is fully understood, will do justice to the men who have most suffered from hasty judgment and unjust censure. Military critics will not say to me as you do "your experiment is a failure," but rather wonder at the disproportion between the means and the results.

You inform me that "the highest and most reputable authors" say that I "have not had a cabinet council for more than four months." I read your letter to a member and ex-member of my cabinet to-day; they were surprised at the extravagance of the falsehood, and did not believe that so much as a week had at any time occurred without a cabinet consultation. . . . Your own estimate of me, I hope, assured you that I would not, as stated, treat the "Secretary of War" as a "mere clerk;" and if you know Mr. Benjamin you must realize the impossibility of his submitting to degrading at the hands of any one. The opposition here complain that I cling too closely to my cabinet, not, as in your section, that they are disregarded. . . .

Against the unfounded story that I keep the Generals of the army in leading strings may be set the frequent complaint that I do not arraign them for what is regarded their failures or misdeeds, and do not respond to the popular clamor by displacing commanders upon irresponsible statements. . . .

The grossest ignorance of the law and the facts can alone excuse the statement as to the illtreatment of Genl. Price by me. His letters do not permit me to believe that he is a party to any such complaint. If as you inform me it is "credibly said" that I "have scarcely a friend and not a defender in Congress or in the army," yet for the sake of our country and its cause I must hope it is falsely so said, as otherwise our fate must be confided to a multitude of hypocrites.

It would be easy to justify the appointments which have been made of Brig. Genls. . . . suffice it to say that I have endeavored to avoid bad selections by relying on military rather than political recommendations. . . . When everything is at stake and the united power of the South alone can save us, it is sad to know that men can deal in such paltry complaints and tax their ingenuity to slander because they are offended in not getting office. . . .

The effect of such assaults, so far as they succeed in destroying the confidence of the people in the administration of their Government, must be to diminish our chances of triumph over the enemy, and practically do us more harm than if twice the number of men I can suppose to be engaged in such work were to desert to the standard of Lincoln. . . .

Accept my thanks for the kindness which you have manifested in defending me when so closely surrounded by evil reports. . . .

Very respectfully, your friend,
Jefferson Davis

Only at the end of this clear answer to Brooks's numerous charges did Davis let a slight touch of sarcasm creep in. It would have been well if this explanation to the Alabamian had been multicopied and kept on hand for complaining men in the other states, for unjust criticism and remarkable fabrications were to increase with the days of the Confederacy.

CHAPTER XVIII

THE CLASH OF IRONCLADS

IN THE INTERIM between the fall of Forts Henry and Donelson, Joseph E. Johnston had surprised the President by inviting him to visit the Army of the Potomac. On February 14, Davis had replied that he would visit the Army as soon as other engagements would permit, "although I cannot realize your complimentary assurance that great good to the Army will result from it."

Three days after the Donelson disaster, fearing its unhappy psychological effect on the easily discouraged General Johnston, the President wrote him: "Events have cast on our arms and hopes the gloomiest shadows, and at such time we must show redoubled energy and resolution."

On February 20, in some trepidation, Johnston had come to Richmond to confer with the President and his Cabinet as to the advisability of withdrawing from the Manassas line. The General insisted that his position was unsafe and that it might be turned whenever the enemy chose to advance. Though Johnston's opinion had the backing of some of his officers, including Jubal Early, Davis and the Cabinet could not see justification for great alarm.

In the event that further developments should make retreat necessary, the President advised the General to consider the best position to which he should retire and charged him above all to save his armaments and supplies. In later years, in writing of the conference, Johnston said that "though without getting orders," he understood that the Army was expected to fall back as soon as practicable. Following Johnston's version, historians, without searching into the matter, have occasionally stated that Johnston was *ordered* back, which is quite contrary to the truth.

After Johnston's visit, apprehension had been growing in Richmond that he might abandon the northern frontier of Virginia. In consternation, Governor Letcher prepared for the draft of able-bodied Virginians to reinforce Johnston and prevent his withdrawal. On February 28, the President specifically cautioned Johnston about saving war material if he should withdraw. "The heavy guns at Manassas," he wrote, ". . . would necessarily be abandoned in any hasty retreat. . . . I need not urge on your consideration the value to our country of arms and munitions of war: you know the difficulty with which we have obtained our small supply; that, to furnish heavy artillery to the advanced posts, we have exhausted the supplies here which were designed for the armament of the city defenses. Whatever can be, should be done to avoid the loss of these guns. . . ."

Then, in an effort to hearten him, the President continued: "I rely upon your special knowledge and high ability to effect whatever is practicable in this our hour of need. Recent disasters have depressed the weak, and are depriving us of the aid of the wavering. Traitors show the tendencies heretofore concealed, and the selfish grow clamorous for local and personal interests. At such an hour, the wisdom of the trained and the steadiness of the brave possess a double value. The military paradox that impossibilities must be rendered possible, had never better occasion for its application."

In the serious pressure of the time, in the wake of recent disasters, and with portents of further calamities, Davis sent for General Lee. On March 2, he telegraphed him at Savannah: "If circumstances will, in your judgment, warrant your leaving, I wish to see you here with the least delay."

The President was not exactly sure how he could best use Lee's services, but he felt impelled to have his counsel. With celerity, General Lee made his arrangements and arrived in Richmond on March 6. The two had a long conference. The General's mission on the southeastern coast had been well accomplished, and he had returned to Richmond reconfirmed in his conviction of the value of field fortifications and protecting earthworks, which were to prove indispensable in the capital's defense. The President considered making Lee his Secretary of War, but he foresaw that Lee's command on the battlefield might soon be necessary. For the next few days, while Davis awaited the turn of events, Lee had no direct authority. But his presence was an inexpressible solace to the harried President.

They talked together and rode out to the camps together. Like Lee, always interested in horseflesh, Davis admired his friend's new mount. It was a handsome young gray horse, which the General had fancied in western Virginia and had bought when its owner's command had joined Lee in South Carolina. The horse was named Greenbrier, the General said, but it had so much endurance and was such a "fine traveller" that he was changing its name to Traveller.

The day of Lee's return to the capital, the President again wrote Johnston, urging him to so mobilize his army that when he was required to move, "it may be without public loss."

By authority of an act of Congress passed in secret session on March 1, 1862, President Davis proclaimed martial law in Richmond. The capital had been overrun with adventurers, chiselers, and gamblers, and it was the center of a Union spy ring. Brigadier General John H. Winder, a Marylander and former Major in the United States Army, was made Provost Marshal. He became a virtual military commander of the city and its suburbs. Political prisoners were incarcerated in Castle Thunder, along with pickpockets and deserters. Order was restored. The night streets became safe. At first, the law-abiding citizens were vastly relieved. Then malcontents began to complain of tyrannical abuses, and worked up such a sentiment against martial law that Congress modified Winder's powers.

As the President began to feel content about the peace and order in Richmond, bad news came from the West. To establish some harmony between the Confederate forces in Missouri and Arkansas under the individualistic Generals Sterling Price and Ben McCulloch, Davis had put Major General Earl Van Dorn in command of the region. Van Dorn was a West Point cavalryman of brilliant promise. But, unhappily, as a clash between the Federals and the Confederates became imminent, Van Dorn was suffering from a fever. The Federals were entrenched near Elkhorn Tavern in front of Pea Ridge, Arkansas. Daring as he was, the ailing Van Dorn would not attack breastworks; for his men had marched fifty miles and were now without rations. So, in the night of March 7, he took half his troops, Price's men, around to the north of Pea Ridge to attack the Federals from the rear. Delayed by obstructions in the road and the blackness of night, the Confederates were three hours late in getting to their surprise position. The fighting was furious, and soon Van Dorn thought he had won a victory. But having had no sleep and no food for twenty-four hours, his soldiers' strength evaporated. Then came news that General McCulloch, attacking from the south, had been shot through the heart. Mc-Culloch's Rangers were so stunned by the death of their leader that hundreds just wandered away.

Then Franz Sigel, the German immigrant Brigadier, reinforced the Federal commander, Samuel R. Curtis. After fierce fighting on the eighth, the Confederates were driven from the field. Van Dorn, who lost about 1,000 men in killed and wounded, regarded the matter as only a temporary setback. He informed the War Office that he had been "foiled in his intention." As he started boldly for St. Louis, he got orders to join Sidney Johnston in northern Mississippi. Neither side was aware that the Battle of Elkhorn Tavern, or Pea Ridge, had been decisive as far as Missouri was concerned. The excitement caused by the *Virginia-Merrimac* on the Atlantic seaboard immediately caught the nation's attention.

Jefferson Davis's attention had been shifting back and forth from Sidney Johnston's operations in the West to Joseph Johnston's uneasy stay around Manassas and to important maritime construction at Norfolk. From the beginning, Davis was aware that of all the manifold advantages possessed over the South by the North, the Navy was perhaps the first, the main, and the decisive. Without her ships, the United States could not possibly prevent the successful establishment of the Confederacy. When the war began, the Navy and Merchant Marine of the United States were in an efficient state, and they were soon vastly augmented and improved. At the outbreak of the war, the Federal Navy had forty-two ships, 555 guns, and 7,600 sailors; by the end of 1861, the new totals amounted to 264 ships, 2,557 guns, and 22,000 sailors. Since the Confederacy had small naval force, the Federals might be able to blockade the coasts and perhaps capture, one after another, the Southern ports. With her river gunboats, the North had already begun to slash into Southern territory and gain interior strongholds. By her Navy, the North could transport soldiers and supplies where land passage would be hazardous if not impossible.[1]

In Montgomery, Secretary of the Navy Mallory had believed in the value of possessing an iron-armored ship. He and the President knew that after the success of "floating batteries" in the Crimean

---

[1] Such ideas about the supreme importance of the Federal Navy appeared in an article in the Lowell (Massachusetts) *Weekly Sun,* June 5, 1886. The author, B. J. Williams, pointed out that but for the Navy, Grant's army would have been lost at Shiloh, and, but for it, McClellan's on the Peninsula "was lost to a man, and the independence of the Confederacy established."

War, France had constructed several ironclad warships, and England, in competition, had started constructing her own. Though Mallory had sent Lieutenant James H. North to Europe in May, 1861, to purchase an ironclad, North had found neither France nor England willing to part with one, even for millions of dollars. While so far both North and Bulloch had been frustrated in their efforts to contract for the building of an ironclad, Mallory was doing his utmost to construct his own.

As early as July, 1861, he had ordered the raising in Norfolk Harbor of the United States steam frigate *Merrimac*, which the Federals had partially burned and scuttled. With the brilliant assistance of Lieutenant John M. Brooke, Mallory experimented with plans to convert the hulk into an ironclad. The *Merrimac* was cut down to her berth deck and provided with a slantwise superstructure and walls of oak twenty-four inches thick, sheathed in four-inch iron plates. Ten guns were housed amidship.

President Davis and Mallory were often in conference about the reconstruction and its progress. They had heard that a strange new kind of ironclad, designed by a noted Swedish-born inventor, John Ericsson, was being secretly constructed by the North,[2] and they were eager to get the Confederacy's ironclad afloat first. After the New Year, 1862, Mallory set five hundred men to work on the *Merrimac*. Not satisfied with the reports from the officer in command at the Norfolk Navy Yard, he sent Naval Captain Sidney Smith Lee, brother of Robert E., instructions to work every available man at top bent and make full use of night shifts, despite Lee's objection to the danger of fire.

To deceive the enemy, Norfolk newspapers were instructed to report adversely on the *Merrimac*'s condition, to give out that she was useless and the reconstructive work wasted. The unknowing public began derisive criticism of Mallory's project. In truth, naval subordinates did try to convince Mallory that the ship could never be seaworthy or powered to navigate the ocean. But the Secretary had visions of the *Merrimac* "steaming to attack New York," or so Mallory wrote on March 7 to Commodore Franklin Buchanan, the ship's commander, who had been the first head of the United States Naval Academy at Annapolis.

[2] The yard where it was built was really a private one at Greenpoint, Long Island, owned by Thomas F. Rowland. An interesting account of the construction is given in *Life of John Ericsson* by Colonel William Conant Church, pp. 254-279.

That same day, President Davis was apprised that the *Merrimac,* rechristened the *Virginia,* but generally to be known in history by her original name, might start on her trial trip on the morrow. With keen anticipation, Davis awaited the outcome.

Near noon on Saturday, March 8, the *Merrimac,* accompanied by tenders, steamed into Hampton Roads. A Northern blockading squadron, including the *Minnesota,* the *St. Lawrence,* and the *Roanoke* lay at Fortress Monroe, and the *Congress* and the *Cumberland* at neighboring Newport News. As the strange, ugly vessel approached the latter point, Federal guns discharged their broadsides and shore batteries opened fire. Cannon balls crashing against metal made a terrific clangor but bounced back from the iron plates as if they had been made of India rubber. The *Merrimac* steered straight for the *Cumberland* and began felling men with every shot. At top speed, she rammed the sloop of war, knocking a hole in her the size of a barn door. Then she backed away, and as water surged into the wounded ship, she continued a merciless fire until the helpless *Cumberland* sank.

The *Merrimac* then turned on the *Congress,* whose fifty guns proved powerless to save her. In an effort to escape destruction, the *Congress* ran aground. The *Merrimac* relentlessly attacked, and the hot shot set her blazing to her extinction. As the Confederate ship made away to destroy the *Minnesota,* the tide was ebbing, so the pilot advised withdrawing the *Merrimac* to deeper waters.

The victor made for Sewell's Point to await dawn next day to complete annihilation of the Federal fleet. Her officers took stock. Her hull had proved impenetrable. But on the debit side, because of her wheezing old engines, her best speed was little more than five knots an hour, and her great draft of twenty-three feet made her navigable only in deep channels.

As the blazing *Congress* lit up the night for miles around Hampton Roads, the consternated Federal seamen and the soldiers at Fortress Monroe saw the presage of doom. When the triumphant news of the *Merrimac's* invincibility reached Richmond, Jefferson Davis and his advisers were stirred as they had been by nothing since Manassas. Mallory saw himself vindicated and the blockade effectively broken. If the rest of the Federal ships in Hampton Roads were destroyed, the North might soon make overtures of peace. With the morning papers, the whole Confederacy was in a state of jubilation.

Early that Sunday of March 9, President Lincoln's Cabinet rushed to a conference. The new Secretary of War, Edwin Stanton, was in panic. "The *Merrimac* will change the whole character of the war," he prophesied. "She will destroy *seriatim* every naval vessel; she will lay all the cities on the seaboard under contribution." Apprehensively looking out a window toward the Potomac, Stanton declared that a cannon ball from the *Merrimac* might very likely crash into the room before the Cabinet adjourned. Even the usually buoyant Mr. Seward, as Gideon Welles wrote, was "overwhelmed with the intelligence" and "greatly depressed." A flotilla of canal boats loaded with stone was ordered sent down the river to be sunk and obstruct the channel the instant the *Merrimac* hove in sight.

That bright Sunday morning, while Richmond rejoiced and praised the Lord for Mallory's ironclad, which would sweep the Union ships from the seas, President Davis felt that Fortune's turning point might really be at hand. The *Merrimac* steamed back to Hampton Roads to complete the destruction, with Lieutenant Catesby Jones in active command because Commodore Buchanan had been slightly wounded the day before. Jones was amazed to find an extraordinary object blocking his path. Beside the *Minnesota,* in a protective position, and hardly a foot above the water, sat an iron "cheese-box on a raft." Some thought it looked like a "tin-can on a shingle." The North's first ironclad, the *Monitor,* had with dramatic coincidence arrived in the night. As the *Merrimac*'s surprised commander opened fire on the *Minnesota,* the *Monitor,* commanded by Lieutenant John L. Worden, steered directly for her with guns blazing from a revolving gun turret, its most revolutionary feature.

For four hours, the big ship and the little ship[3] kept up a close artillery duel. But the projectiles of neither could pierce the other's armor. When the *Merrimac* attempted to ram the *Monitor,* the smaller ship slipped out of her reach. Once, when she bunted her, Catesby Jones and a handful of his men, armed to the teeth, made ready to board the enemy craft as in pirate days; but the gap was immediately too wide for leaping.

Shortly after noon, a shell from the *Merrimac* struck the sighthole of the forward side of the *Monitor*'s pilothouse and exploded, stunning the commander, Lieutenant Worden, and blinding him with powder. The *Monitor* withdrew. Thinking the enemy had given up the struggle, the *Merrimac* steamed back to Norfolk.

[3] The *Merrimac*'s 3,500 tonnage was reckoned almost four times that of the *Monitor*'s 900.

For one single day, the Confederate ironclad had been monarch of the seas. Providentially for the North and ironically for the South, the *Monitor* had been completed in the very nick of time, though the Union's top naval men had scoffed at its possibilities and tried to hinder its construction. Now the power of the *Merrimac* was disputed and neutralized. From a tactical standpoint, the *Monitor-Merrimac* engagement was a drawn battle, but, since it made obsolete the navies of the world, it made naval history.

Federal blockading strategy, which yesterday seemed doomed, had been retrieved. The relief in the North was as monumental as the disappointment in the South was abysmal. Fate appeared set to continue a cat-and-mouse game with the Confederacy's expectations. To Jefferson Davis, the most striking example yet of a glorious flare of Confederate hope and its swift extinction had been exemplified on the memorable days of March 8 and 9. The reconstructed *Merrimac* had almost won the independence of the South. Now again the great odds lay with the North. And the deadly struggle for Richmond was about to begin.

From Fairfax Court House, which he had just occupied, McClellan wrote Stanton on March 11 that the *Monitor* justified the course he had in mind to transport his troops to the Peninsula to begin an assault on Richmond from the east. Yet, in a sense, the *Monitor* was to prove a will-o'-the-wisp that would lead "Little Mac" to flounder in the dank Chickahominy swamps. Holding at bay the dread *Merrimac*, the *Monitor*, to be sure, prevented her from making havoc among McClellan's four hundred transports and supply ships, which he began moving down the Potomac to Fortress Monroe. But the *Merrimac* remained, nevertheless, a monster threat at the mouth of the James. The *Monitor* did not care to risk another open battle, and now had to play a strictly defensive game, for if she were lost before other Northern ironclads could be built, the *Merrimac* might yet obliterate the Federal blockade.

Twice the *Merrimac* emerged from anchorage at Sewell's Point and sought battle with the *Monitor* guarding the mass of Federal ships, but each time, because of her superior mobility, the *Monitor* escaped contact. And the *Merrimac* did not dare remain long away from her guardianship of the Norfolk Navy Yard, where the Confederacy was feverishly constructing gunboats. For eight weeks, the two ironclads doggedly stalemated each other. But the *Merrimac*'s presence would make it impossible for the Federal Navy to carry McClellan's troops up the James and outflank General Johnston's defensive line. So Mallory's ironclad was to play an important role in saving Richmond in the spring of 1862.

The material-rich Union soon announced that a whole fleet of ironclads was to be built. President Davis and Secretary Mallory were more eager than ever to have Bulloch and North obtain ironclads from Europe. The Confederate agents were doing all they could. But it was not until May 20 that North obtained a contract with James and George Thompson of Glasgow to build an ironclad. It was to be called the "Thompson ram." Its specifications were larger than the two Laird rams combined, which Bulloch contracted for in England in July.

Rumors reached Richmond on March 10, the day after the *Merrimac*'s stalemate, that General Joseph Johnston was on the point of retreating. In the hope of halting such a movement, President Davis telegraphed him: "Further assurance given me this day that you shall be promptly and adequately re-enforced, so as to enable you to maintain your position and resume first policy [to carry the war across the Potomac] when the roads will permit."

A few days later, the President, while out riding, was astounded to meet some of Johnston's artillery virtually in the suburbs of Richmond. Bradley T. Johnson, in his biography of General Joe, unequivocably states that Johnston "withdrew his army from before McClellan without the knowledge of his superior officer." It was not until March 15 that President Davis received official notice that Johnston was in full retreat. The letter, dated March 13, stated that he had evacuated Centreville and Manassas. With his entire army in retrograde movement, he now asked the President's advice about choosing a new position.

In reply, Davis wrote Johnston that before his March 13 letter was received he was as much in the dark as to Johnston's "purposes, conditions and necessities" as at the time of their conversation on the subject in Richmond.

It is true I have had many and alarming reports of great destruction of ammunition, camp-equipage and provisions, indicating precipitate retreat; but having heard of no cause for such a sudden movement, I was at a loss to believe it.

I have not the requisite topographical knowledge for the selection of your new position.

The question of throwing troops into Richmond is contingent upon reverses in the West and Southeast. The immediate necessity for such a move-ment is not anticipated.

Neither the President nor the Secretary of War could see justifica-tion for the fierce haste of Johnston's withdrawal, which involved the loss of millions of dollars' worth of essential armaments and supplies. Eyewitnesses described the woeful sight of big guns abandoned, and the heady smell of burning tons of salted meat and a thousand brand-new saddles. McClellan was not even intending to make a direct at-tack on Manassas; he was already prepared to embark the Army of the Potomac on transports bound for Fort Monroe.

From London, on December 16, 1880, Judah P. Benjamin wrote Davis of his clear remembrance of that March, 1862, in Richmond.

I remember perfectly well the profound feeling of surprise and distrust excited by his [Johnston's] announcement of the peril to which he con-ceived his army to be exposed, whereas nothing had come to our knowledge from any quarter indicating the existence of such peril. I also remember the indignation and alarm caused by the precipitation of a retreat (apparently without necessity), involving the loss or destruction of the supplies and munitions which it cost us such infinite pains to accumulate, and above all the acknowledgment that he was too ignorant of the topography of the Country to take responsibility for selecting the position to which it was ex-pedient to retire. I am positively certain that any statement that the with-drawal was ordered by you or that instructions emanated from you rendering withdrawal necessary is entirely erroneous, as no one was more chagrined than you were at the news of what was occurring.

At the time, in March, 1862, the usually imperturbable Benjamin was furiously resentful of Johnston's loss of scarce war materials. Davis's confidence in Johnston's judgment was severely shaken. In the crisis, he made a bold decision, which proved inspired. At his order, Adjutant General Cooper sent this dispatch: "General Robert E. Lee is assigned to duty at the seat of Government, and, under the direction of the President, is charged with the conduct of military operations in the armies of the Confederacy."

Davis had expected to be criticized for putting Lee at the head of the Army, for, as his aide Colonel Preston Johnston wrote, "General Lee was at the time under the shadow of legislative disfavor and popu-lar opposition, and supported by the almost unaided hand of the Presi-dent." Lee had one other stout supporter in another of the President's aides-de-camp, Colonel Ives. When an artillerist doubted Lee's "au-dacity," Ives replied with fervor: "If there is one man, in either army who is head and shoulders above every other man in audacity, it is General Lee. His name might be Audacity. He will take more chances and take them quicker than any other general in this country, North or South; and you will live to see it, too." [4]

Since Lee's autumn failure in western Virginia, not a word in his praise had appeared in a Richmond paper until February 18. Then the *Dispatch,* which sometimes spoke for the Administration, had said in an editorial: "We venture to say the time will yet come when his superior abilities will be vindicated, both to his own renown and the glory of his country."

The announcement of Lee's "promotion" created outraged resentment in certain circles and particularly among Joseph Johnston's admirers. The *Examiner* wrote sneeringly, "Evacuating Lee, who has never yet risked a single battle with the invader, is Commanding General." But Davis's judgment was dramatically vindicated before midsummer, when Lee glorified himself and his country.

---

[4] Ives's words were spoken to artillerist E. P. Alexander, and are quoted from pages 110-111 in Alexander's *Military Memoirs of a Confederate*. They appear frequently in biographies of Lee.

CHAPTER XIX

"THE TEST OF MERIT" AND A CHURCH NAMED SHILOH

WITH THE LOSS of Nashville, following the Donelson disaster, a deputation of Tennessee Congressmen waited on the President. With but one exception, they asked him to put some more capable officer in command. Davis listened to them politely, and then said with unshakeable conviction, "Gentlemen, if Sidney Johnston is not a general, the Confederacy has none to give you."

On March 11, a Congressional committee, with Foote as chairman, found the reports of Brigadier Generals Floyd and Pillow unsatisfactory as to their conduct at Donelson. President Davis thereupon asked General Johnston to relieve the Generals of their commands until further orders. That same day he received from Atlanta a telegraphic appeal from a member of the Confederate Congress who had gone home to investigate conditions in Georgia.

The people now look to you as their deliverer and imploringly call upon you to come to the field of our late disasters and assume command, as you promised in a speech to take the field whenever it should become necessary. That necessity is now upon us. Such a step would be worth a hundred thousand soldiers throughout the Confederacy. Can you hesitate? . . . Save us while it is yet time.

While defending Sidney Johnston to the best of his ability against the criticism of reckless journalists and excited citizens, the President wrote the General on March 12 asking him for more specific information, which would make his defense more telling. He sent the private letter by special messenger. Because of the intimacy of the friendship between them, Davis felt he could write frankly of the charges. "Such representations," he said, "with the sad forebodings naturally belonging to them, have been painful to me and injurious to us both; but, worse than this, they have undermined public confidence, and damaged our cause. A full development of the truth is necessary for future success. I respect the generosity which has kept you silent, but would impress upon you that the question is not personal but public in its nature; that you and I might be content to suffer, but neither of us can willingly permit detriment to the country." He signed himself, "With the confidence and regard of many years, I am truly your friend, Jefferson Davis."

Johnston finally replied in a long letter dated March 18 from Decatur, Alabama. He sent Captain T. M. Jack to deliver the letter in person.[1] Jack did not reach Richmond until March 26, just eleven days before Shiloh.

"Arriving at Richmond," Jack wrote of the incident, "I was at once shown into the office of Mr. Davis and presented to him. I had never before met the President of the Confederacy. He received me with courtesy, even with kindness, asking me at once, 'How is your general, my friend General Johnston?' There was an earnestness in the question which could not be misunderstood. Replying briefly, I handed him my dispatches which he was in the act of opening, when an officer entered the room, to whom the President presented me as General Lee. . . . There was something fascinating in his presence. His manner struck me as dignified, graceful and easy. He seated himself by my side at the window, and engaged me in conversation about the movements of our Western army, while the President read, in silence, the dispatches. . . .

"Listening to the pleasing tones of the General's voice, I watched at the same time, with eager interest, the countenance of the President, as he read the clear, strong and frank expression of his old friend and comrade. . . . There was softness then in his face; and as his eye was raised from the paper, there seemed a tenderness in its expression, bordering on tears, surprising and pleasing at that critical juncture in the civil and military leader of a people in arms."

Davis was moved as he read Sidney Johnston's soldierly explanations, full of facts and "breathing sentiments of a noble spirit." [2]

---

[1] William Preston Johnston in his biography of his father says that the letter was really begun on March 17 and not finished until March 22. Jack's account of the scene in the President's office is taken from a letter to W. P. Johnston, which appears in the biography on pages 521-522.

[2] The sections of the letter dealing with detailed military operations are omitted, but may be found in full in *Official Records* and in *The Life of General Albert Sidney Johnston* by W. P. Johnston.

My dear General:

. . . I anticipated all that you tell as to the censures which the fall of Fort Donelson drew upon me, and the attacks to which you might be subjected; but it was impossible for me to gather the facts for a detailed report, or spare time which was required to extricate the remainder of my troops and save the large accumulation of stores and provisions, after that disheartening disaster. . . .

The blow was most disastrous, and almost without remedy. I therefore in my first report remained silent. This silence you were kind enough to attribute to my generosity. . . .

I observed silence, as it seemed to me to be the best way to serve the cause and the country. The facts were not fully known, discontent prevailed, and criticism or condemnation was more likely to augment than cure the evil. I refrained, well knowing that heavy censures would fall upon me, but convinced that it was better to endure them for the present, and defer to a more propitious time an investigation of the conduct of the generals; for, in the mean time, their services were required, and their influence was useful.

I have thus recurred to the motives by which I have been governed, from a deep personal sense of the friendship and confidence you have always shown me, and from the conviction that they have not been withdrawn from me in adversity. . . .

You mention that you intend to visit the field of operations here. I hope soon to see you, for your presence would encourage my troops, inspire the people, and augment the army. To me personally it would give the greatest gratification. Merely a soldier myself, and having no acquaintance with the statesmen or leaders of the South, I cannot touch springs familiar to you. Were you to assume command, it would afford me the most unfeigned pleasure, and every energy would be exerted to help you to victory, and the country to independence. Were you to decline, still your presence alone would be of inestimable advantage. . . .

The test of merit in my profession with the people is success. It is a hard rule, but I think it right. Your friend,

A. S. Johnston

How characteristic of the ever-generous Sidney Johnston! Davis reflected, as he gently laid the letter by. And the people, not counting the odds, had no other test but success for a wartime President.

Taking up his pen, he began to compose an answer for Captain Jack to deliver.

My confidence in you has never wavered, and I hope the public will soon give me credit for judgment rather than continue to arraign me for obstinacy.

You have done wonderfully well, and now I breathe easier in the assurance that you will be able to make a junction of your two armies. . . . If you can meet the enemy moving from the Tennessee before it can make a

junction with that advancing from Nashville, the future will be brighter. . . .
May God bless you is the sincere prayer of your friend, Jefferson Davis.

When Captain Jack delivered the President's letter to Johnston at his new headquarters at Corinth, Mississippi, the General asked, in "a playful way," "How did the President receive you?" "As the aide-de-camp of his friend," Jack responded in the same spirit.

Johnston read the letter and took special note of the tactical suggestion. That was just what he hoped to do: fight Grant before Buell could join him. Appreciating the prayer for God's blessing, he did not dream that he was looking on Jefferson Davis's signature for the last time.

When General McClellan began landing 108,000 men at Fortress Monroe, Confederate General Magruder, occupying the lower end of the Peninsula, had only about 8,000 men to oppose him. Four thousand reinforcements were rushed to his aid. When it was definitely established that McClellan's main army was on the Peninsula, President Davis directed General Johnston to proceed there and examine conditions. After a day's inspection of Magruder's defensive line, Johnston came to Richmond with the bleak recommendation that the Peninsula be abandoned and a defensive line near Richmond be taken. The President could not concur in this plan. The entrenchments from Yorktown up to Williamsburg were good. Near Yorktown, where the Peninsula was only three miles wide, a small force might make an excellent barrier against a massive army. Davis called a council with General Lee and the new Secretary of War, Randolph, who had taken office on March 24. At Johnston's request, his friends Generals Longstreet and Gustavus Smith were also invited. Johnston presented his plan: to withdraw Magruder's forces from the Peninsula and Huger's from Norfolk, which was to be abandoned, bring up troops from Georgia and South Carolina, and unite them all with his Army of Northern Virginia.

Randolph was emphatically opposed to giving up Norfolk, which commanded the entrance to the James River. Its navy yard was the South's best hope for constructing gunboats essential for the defense of harbors and inland waterways. The President was quite in accord with his War Secretary's view. Lee, whom Davis found "unusually sagacious in penetrating the enemy's designs," insisted that the narrow Peninsula offered special advantages in resisting a numerically superior assailant. Having just come from Savannah and Charleston, Lee objected, too, to exposing those cities to probable capture. Smith, as expected, supported Johnston's plan completely, and Longstreet, partially. At the end of the discussion, which had lasted all afternoon and past midnight, the President announced his decision: McClellan should be resisted on the Peninsula and Norfolk held as long as possible. Johnston was asked to make a junction with Magruder's meager force. Though he objected, he did not request to be relieved of his command. He returned to his army, nursing his own counsel and keeping his plans to himself.

On April 1, McClellan had completed the arduous landing and disposition of his great army. Four days later, the siege of Yorktown began. On April 6, President Lincoln peremptorily ordered McClellan "to break the enemy's line from Yorktown to the Warwick River at once." The General wrote his wife, "The President very cooly telegraphed me yesterday that I had better break the enemy's lines at once. I was much tempted to reply that he had better come and do it himself."

In the meantime, the eyes of endangered Richmond were drawn to southwest Tennessee, where a brilliant spotlight of history shone upon an insignificant backwoods church called Shiloh, twenty miles north of Corinth, Mississippi.

On March 25, 1862, General Albert Sidney Johnston arrived at Corinth, a vitally important junction, where the east-west Memphis and Charleston Railway crossed the north-south Mobile and Ohio. There he joined forces with those under Beauregard, his second in command, including Polk's troops from evacuated Columbus and Bragg's 10,000 recently arrived from Pensacola. Grant had reached the river town Savannah in west Tennessee eight days earlier with 40,000 men and had placed five divisions in camp at Pittsburg Landing, nine miles up the river, to the south, nearer Corinth.

Because Grant felt certain that the Confederates could not have recovered from the demoralizing withdrawal from Bowling Green, he was confident Johnston would undertake no aggressive movement. So he had dug no entrenchments, though specifically ordered to do so by General Halleck, commander of the Department of the West. He expected Johnston to settle at Corinth and await the combined attack of his army and Don Carlos Buell's. But Johnston would not act according to Grant's calculations; he purposed to give battle on Saturday, April 5, before Buell's army could arrive.

In the early morning of April 3, preliminary orders were given to hold the troops in readiness to move at a moment's notice, with a five days' supply of cooked rations in their haversacks. That afternoon, President Davis received a dispatch from Sidney Johnston, sent as he started north out of Corinth:

General Buell in motion 30,000 strong, rapidly from Columbia to Savannah. Mitchell behind him with 10,000. Confederate forces—40,000—ordered forward to offer battle near Pittsburg. . . . Beauregard second in command, Polk the left, Bragg the centre, Hardee the right wing, Breckinridge in reserve. Hope engagement before Buell can form junction.

That same particular hope animated Davis, as he had written Johnston a week before. He reflected that the General at least had good corps commanders and that Bragg had brought disciplined troops from Pensacola, which should make up somewhat for the odds against their inadequate arms and equipment. Altogether, Johnston and Beauregard had only 40,000 arms of any kind. Few of the heterogeneous mob that had been recently organized into an army had been in battle, and only their enthusiasm could make up for their lack of training. The country dirt roads toward Pittsburg were narrow, and at two o'clock of the first morning, as the men lay on their arms in the woods, a heavy rain began to fall. They had difficulty in keeping their powder dry. Drenched, they trudged off at daylight. In the deep mud, the commands were impeded and got in each other's way. General Polk was delayed because written orders he had expected did not reach him.

The Confederates covered the twenty miles on foot in two days and were before the enemy by midafternoon of April 5. But Johnston knew it was too late to start a battle. Rain, mud, and the rawness of the troops had been delaying obstacles that caused almost a day to be lost. Some of General William J. Hardee's exuberant recruits had made such a noise whooping at scurrying rabbits and one wild deer, and testing their powder in the damp air, that Beauregard wanted to call off the attack. He told Bragg and Polk that he was very disappointed at the delay in getting the troops into position. To succeed, he said, the attack had to be a surprise. Now with all this clamor of movement, the Federal outposts, only two miles away, were bound to be aware of the Confederates presence. "The army," he declared, "will have to return to Corinth."

When General Johnston walked up, Beauregard, whose nerves seemed to be on edge, repeated his reasons for giving up the attack. He ended by exclaiming, "Now they will be entrenched up to the eyes!" Johnston calmly tried to reassure him. Then, with a resolution not to be gainsaid, he turned to the other officers who had gathered, and said, simply: "Gentlemen, we shall attack at daylight tomorrow." Walking away to end the informal council of war, he said in a ringing voice, "I would fight them if they were a million." It was precisely what Jefferson Davis, wakeful with suspense in Richmond, might have expected Sidney Johnston to say.

On that Saturday night, with Johnston's army in battle readiness less than two miles from Sherman's brigade, the Union troops slept peacefully in comfortable tents around the log chapel of Shiloh. Grant telegraphed Halleck in St. Louis: "The main force of the enemy is at Corinth. . . . I have scarcely the faintest idea of an attack (general one) being made upon us, but will be prepared should such a thing take place."

Again the Southern troops stretched out in the open. But now the night was calm and clear. A silvery starlight filtered down through budding tree boughs upon the reclining figures. An hour before dawn, while an eerie white mist hovered close to the ground the forest was stirring with muted preparations for imminent conflict. Then the sun rose in splendor, dispelling the vapors and bathing the scene in a dazzling gold light. An officer remarked on the auspicious "sun of Austerlitz," and the phrase coursed among the more literate like a password. The morning air was fresh, invigorating. Sidney Johnston felt an exultant joy surge through him. The confidence inspired by his magnetic presence stirred those who came in sight of him. As he and his staff were drinking coffee about the campfire, the moody Beauregard alone seemed dubious. Once more Johnston tried to cheer him. Beauregard, who complained of a throat infection, was to be left at headquarters to direct in the rear, particularly the reserves under General John C. Breckinridge. Again Beauregard urged return to Corinth. Just then, firing in front indicated the attack had commenced. Hardee's skirmish line had encountered Federals. Johnston asked the group to note the time. It was fourteen minutes past five. "The battle has opened, gentlemen," he said. "It is too late to change our dispositions."

Mounting his thoroughbred bay, Fire-eater, he turned for a last encouraging word to his staff and the officers nearby. Looking the epitome of a conquering soldier, he called out with pleasant assurance: "Tonight we will water our horses in the Tennessee River." Then he rode toward the front, leaving the depressed and ailing Beauregard in charge of operations two and a half miles to the rear of battle.

On that Sabbath morning of April 6, when General Sherman's men were leisurely stirring, some half dressed, some cooking breakfast, the Confederates attacked with vigor. Sherman should have been on his guard, for he had been warned by scouts of General Benjamin M. Prentiss that a full force was moving upon him. But he had refused to believe them. As Horace Greeley described the scene in his *Tribune,* "Neither officers nor men were aware of the approaching enemy until his magnificent lines of battle poured out of the woods in front of the camps and at double-quick time rushed in upon our bewildered, half-dressed, and not yet half-formed men, firing deadly volleys at close range, and then springing upon the coatless, musketless mob with the bayonets. Some fell as they ran, others as they emerged from the tents, or strove to buckle on their accoutrements; some tried to surrender, but the rebels could not stop then to take prisoners."

The battle was fierce and bloody. By ten o'clock, the struggle around Shiloh was over. Sherman's men had melted away. The Southern boys made a holiday of rushing into the abandoned tents, seizing spoils of war. Young Sam Houston, Jr., of Texas, who had all but broken his father's heart by putting on a Confederate uniform, scalded his hand snatching a succulent joint of beef from a boiling pot to share a good Yankee breakfast with his companions. General Johnston rebuked an officer for taking valuables from an enemy tent, and then, to make amends for hurting the man's feelings, he himself picked up a little tin drinking cup, saying, "I take this for my share of the spoils." Hooking a finger through the handle, he bore it like a miniature insigne as he directed the fight.

General Grant was eating breakfast at the Cherry Mansion in Savannah, nine miles down the river from Pittsburg Landing, when he heard what sounded strangely like a battle. Boarding a gunboat, he set off to see what was going on. He stopped at Crump's Landing, where Brigadier General Lew Wallace, the future author of *Ben Hur,* was stationed with 7,000 men. Grant gave him instructions in person about moving his troops,[3] and arrived at Pittsburg about half past nine.

Ten thousand Union soldiers, who had fled the field, cowered in the protection of the high riverbank as the Confederates pressed upon them. Grant could do little but hope for the arrival of General Buell's 20,000 men. He sent an urgent note to Buell, who had already reached Savannah and was awaiting his troops. The dispatch was delivered in mid-river as Buell was proceeding by boat to Pittsburg.

[3] Wallace got lost and did not cover the six miles to Pittsburg until almost six o'clock in the afternoon.

"About halfway up," as Buell later wrote, he "met a stream of fugitives that poured in constantly swelling current along the west bank of the river. The mouth of Snake Creek was full of them swimming across." Reaching the landing at one o'clock, Buell found the bluff "crowded with stragglers from the battle." "At the top of the bluff all was confusion. Men mounted and on foot, and wagons with their teams and excited drivers, all struggling to force their way closer to the river."

One of Grant's lieutenants, Brigadier General Prentiss, was the Federal hero of Shiloh. This Virginia-born businessman from Illinois got his men into a sunken road (later called the Hornet's Nest), which served as an excellent natural entrenchment, and retarded the Southern advance with great loss to the Confederates, who charged again and again in vain. Though Prentiss was finally forced to surrender with 2,000 men, he had saved the men at the landing from slaughter.[4]

General Johnston had been in the saddle since half past five in the morning, first in one part of the field, then in another. According to his lieutenants, the battle was fought as Johnston planned. But his personal presence and direction were needed to inspire the men on the field. He held brief conferences with general officers, and, at critical moments when the Confederates were hard-pressed, his appearance was essential to encourage the raw recruits.

His surgeon, Dr. David W. Yandell, had accompanied him throughout the morning. But on seeing a large group of helpless wounded, Federals mingled with Confederates, Johnston ordered Yandell to minister to them. To no avail the doctor remonstrated about leaving him. Then he asked what he should do about the wounded Federals. "These men," Johnston said, "were our enemies a moment ago; they are our prisoners now. Take care of them." With misgivings, Yandell left him; no one disobeyed Sidney Johnston.

In the early afternoon, at one spot where the firing continued for nearly an hour, Johnston said to Tennessee's Governor Harris, one of his aides: "They are offering stubborn resistance here. I shall have to put the bayonet to them." Then he rode up to a frightened regiment that was refusing to charge. Slowly proceeding down the line on Fire-eater, with hat off and his sword resting in its scabbard, Johnston

[4] Otto Eisenschiml, a leading figure of Chicago's Civil War Round Table, attacked Grant in his *The Story of Shiloh* for his "lack of generosity" which "prompted him in later years to describe Prentiss's gallant stand in such a manner that it appeared instead as a tactical error. 'In one of the backward moves,' Grant wrote, '. . . Prentiss did not fall back with the others. This left his flanks exposed, and enabled the enemy to capture him.'"

waved the little tin cup he had picked up in Sherman's camp. With his compelling, persuasive voice and a strange, selfless light in his gray eyes, he invited the untrained youths to taste death. Here and there he lightly touched the tips of their bayonets with the tin cup. "Men, they are stubborn," he said. "We must use the bayonet." When he reached the center, he cried, "I will lead you," and started forward. Thrilling to the force of his magnetism and example, the men rushed forward with defiant yells. Met by a burst of Federal flame and lead shot, many Confederates dropped wounded or dead. But those on their feet charged up the rise.

Fire-eater was hurt in four places. The sole of the General's boot was almost ripped off by a Minié ball; his clothing was pierced by flying missiles. But he himself was apparently uninjured. With relief and satisfaction, he watched the backs of the Federals as they retired upon their supports. Sending Governor Harris on a mission, Sidney Johnston sat there on his quivering horse alone on the field, while pink petals from a flowering peach orchard drifted down upon the groaning wounded and the silent dead.

As the Federals retreated, they turned to discharge desultory shots. Suddenly, the General felt a piercing pain in his leg. A chance Minié ball had struck his lower thigh and severed an artery, but he did not realize it. He did know that the resistant arc of the enemy had been crushed, and he believed the victory won. He expected to defeat Buell's army next day, if Buell brought his men across the river; if not, he would pursue and drive the Union forces out of Tennessee and Kentucky across the Ohio.

Governor Harris, returning from his mission, reined up sharply, aghast to see his commander pale as death and swaying in the saddle. "General, are you hurt?" he asked in dismay and rode up close to his side. "Yes," Johnston replied deliberately, "and, I fear, seriously." He reeled in the saddle toward Harris and never spoke again. The Governor walked the horses back a short distance to some protection, supporting the half-fainting man with his body and his left arm. Dismounting as gently as possible, he began to ease the General down between the horses, and then, with newly arrived help, laid him on the ground. At first no one could locate the wound. Then his boot was found to be filled with blood. Almost immediately, Colonel William Preston arrived. Lifting his brother-in-law's head in his hands, in a passion of grief and despair, he begged him to speak. A faint smile played on the General's lips, but no word came. The eyelids closed softly. The great heart ceased to beat.

Dazed and horrified, the men kneeling about their prostrate leader realized the awful truth and the ghastly irony: a simple tourniquet could have saved him. His innate chivalry had caused his death: first, his dismissal of his surgeon to tend wounded privates, and, second, his cavalier disregard for his own hurt. But he had fallen in sight of victory. The hour and the event he had planned had come. His fame was vindicated, and with his dying eyes he thought he beheld the turning of the tide for the Confederate cause.

To Jefferson Davis, at his home, late Sunday dispatches brought great news. The Confederates were "advancing victoriously." Davis was elated. He had expected victory, convinced that Sidney Johnston would do "all that military skill, foresight, energy, and strategy could accomplish." The President began composing a brief message to be read in Congress when it met at noon on Monday: "From official telegraphic dispatches, received from official sources, I am able to announce to you, with entire confidence, that it has pleased Almighty God to crown the Confederate arms with a glorious and decisive victory over our enemies."

He was interrupted by a shocking telegram from Colonel William Preston:

General Johnston fell yesterday at half-past two while leading a successful charge, turning the enemy's right, and gaining a brilliant victory. A Minié-ball cut the artery of his leg, but he rode on until, from loss of blood, he fell exhausted, and died without pain in a few moments. His body has been entrusted to me by General Beauregard, to be taken to New Orleans, and remain until instructions are received from his family.

Davis was stunned with grief as well as shock. He had lost his dearest friend. The memory of their school days together flashed through his mind. As a Transylvania student, he had instinctively taken Sidney Johnston, five years his senior, as his idol of young manhood; their friendship had ripened at West Point; they had risked death together in the Northwest among the Sioux, and at Monterrey in Mexico. In all his life, he had known no man so completely worthy of admiration as Sidney Johnston. He regarded him as the Confederacy's prime soldier, and he knew well from history that often in the annals of war the fate of an army depended upon one man. Davis's grief was doubly heavy; it was not only personal, but he suffered for the nation's loss. He did what he could to comfort the General's son, his aide. It was a relief to his own heart-struck dejection when Varina wept bitterly over the awful news.

When the President returned to his desk, he inserted Colonel Preston's dispatch verbatim in his message to Congress. Then he wrote on: "My long and close friendship with this departed chieftain and patriot forbids me to trust myself in giving vent to the feelings which this intelligence evokes. Without doing injustice to the living it may be safely said our loss is irreparable. Among the shining hosts of the great and good who now cluster around the banner of our country, there exists no purer spirit, no more heroic soul than the illustrious man whose death I join you in lamenting."

He paused, and, envisioning the battlefield, he wrote a final paragraph. "In his death he illustrated the character for which through life he was conspicuous—that of singleness of purpose and devotion to duty with his whole energies. Bent on obtaining victory, which he deemed essential to his country's cause, he rode on to the accomplishment of his object, forgetful of self, while his very life blood was ebbing away fast. His last breath cheered his comrades on to victory. The last sound he heard was the shout of victory. His last thought was his country, and long and deeply will his country mourn his loss."

Jefferson Davis sent the message to be read to the House. With sharply mixed emotions, the members rejoiced at the news of victory and bemoaned the loss of General Johnston. As a spontaneous spokesman for those ashamed Congressmen from Tennessee and Kentucky who had asked for Johnston's removal from command, Mr. Moore of Kentucky rose to remark that until the recent reverses at Donelson, no cloud had ever "obscured the bright sunshine of his matchless military fame." "He has fallen at the head of his army," Moore declared, "in the midst of the conflict, in the full tide of a glorious and brilliant victory. This crowning act of devotion . . . has dissipated every cloud which momentarily marred the splendor of his glorious name, and his memory passes into history, unclouded by any shadow of reproach."

Resolutions were passed. Then, in respect for Johnston's memory, the House adjourned. At the very hour of adjournment, the second Battle of Shiloh was turning so against the Confederates that Beauregard was ready to order withdrawal. That Monday evening, the consternating news reached President Davis that Beauregard was in retreat. Fortune in its reversals had never seemed more malignant.

From the various reports President Davis received later through the War Department, he was convinced that when Johnston fell, the Confederate Army was so fully victorious that if the attack had been vigorously pressed, General Grant and his men would have been fugitives or prisoners. Then the Confederates might have defeated Buell's forces as they successively came up, if they should have ventured to cross the river.

When Beauregard, who had maintained headquarters about two miles in the rear of the battle, was informed of Johnston's death, he, as the new commander, let things go on for a while as planned. In mid-afternoon, a dispatch reached him from Colonel Ben Hardin Helm, Confederate brother-in-law of President Lincoln, saying, mistakenly, that Buell's plans were changed and that he was moving toward Decatur, Alabama. Beauregard saw no reason to doubt the information. As a matter of fact, however, Buell's regiments were approaching Pittsburg Landing; the first troops were being ferried across the river. Seeing only the backwash of battle, the wounded and the exhausted, hungry stragglers, Beauregard decided, about half-past five, to bring the Confederates out of battle, to restore order, and to launch a fresh attack in the morning.

Bragg and Polk were both making ready for a last rush against Grant's shattered forces before dark. Although the Southerners were low on ammunition, they were full of the fight that goes with victory. In his own words, Bragg was "in the midst of a movement commenced with every prospect of success" when a messenger from Beauregard arrived in hot haste with a cease-fire order.

That night, Confederates occupied the abandoned Federal encampments and celebrated their success. Beauregard slept in the Shiloh Meeting House. Bragg occupied Sherman's tent. Grant spent the night in the open, sitting under a tree by the river. But no soldier's sleep was peaceful. Another heavy rain came, and, to disturb the Confederates' rest, Union gunboats sent shells at quarter-hour intervals bursting above their positions. In the morning, the Southerners were in poor form to oppose Grant with his fresh reinforcements: Lew Wallace's 5,000 and Buell's 20,000, which had been coming in all through the night.

Next morning the Federals attacked early. The Confederates fought hard. But after almost eight hours of fighting against heavy odds, Beauregard ordered retreat at two o'clock. The army that had been victorious only twenty-four hours before now began a painful march back to Corinth over the miserable roads. Beauregard made an orderly retrograde movement; he even carried away caissons loaded down with rifles and muskets picked up on the field. Grant made only a mild effort to pursue.

The Union's casualties amounted to 13,047; the Confederates' to 10,709.[5] Never before had a battle of such magnitude been fought in the Western Hemisphere.

Davis and a million others believed that if Johnston had lived, Shiloh might conceivably have proved decisive for the Confederate cause. Perhaps Lieutenant L. D. Young, who had helped effect Prentiss's surrender, best voiced the opinion of the soldiers, when he lamented:[6] "Why, oh why, did Beauregard not allow us to finish the day's work so gloriously begun by Johnston? Beauregard did not answer this question satisfactorily to the soldiers who were engaged, whatever the opinion of the world. What, but the spirit of envy and jealousy and an overweening ambition to divide the honor of victory with Johnston . . . which he hoped and expected to win on the morrow, could have controlled his course? The evening of the fateful sixth came, and with it the arrival of Buell, who turned the tide and sealed the fate of the Cause—the golden opportunity lost, lost forever!"

An effort had been made at Shiloh to keep the news of Johnston's death from the men. On April 10, after they reached Corinth, Beauregard officially informed them that General Johnston had been killed. When Jefferson Davis read his brief tribute to Sidney Johnston spoken to the soldiers, he reflected that Beauregard had chosen three correct adjectives to describe him: "reproachless," "fearless," "sagacious." And with fitting brevity Beauregard had concluded, "His courage was sublime." However culpable he might be for the loss of Shiloh, Beauregard had the grace to praise fittingly his dead Commanding General.

Some of the men demanded to see Johnston's body, but it had been taken on to New Orleans by Colonel Preston and a guard of honor. The soldiers could look, however, at the house of William Inge where their General had made his headquarters and where he had been

---

[5] These are the figures Rhodes accepts as the nearest to being correct.

[6] Young's *Reminiscences of a Soldier of the Orphan Brigade* contains one of the most vivid recountals of the action at Shiloh.

brought from the battlefield wrapped in a muddy blanket. Young Mrs. Inge herself had prepared the body for burial and with her own hands wrapped a Confederate flag about him. From what the returned soldiers told her, she believed always that Beauregard threw away the victory. "It was Beauregard's vanity and selfish ambition that cost us the battle," she maintained to her dying day. "Johnston's plan would have won it, but Beauregard wanted the victory to be his, and his alone. Therefore it was not to be won on the first day, which was Johnston's day, but on the second, which was Beauregard's alone." [7]

It was impossible for Jefferson Davis not to blame Beauregard in his heart for the bitter reversal of Confederate fortune at Shiloh. He read Northern papers, which piled abuse high upon General Grant. He studied the reports of the Confederate Generals engaged. "Concurring testimony, especially that of prisoners on both sides . . ." wrote Braxton Bragg, "left no doubt but that a persistent, energetic assault would have been crowned by a general yielding of his whole force." General Hardee said the "advance divisions were within a few hundred yards of Pittsburg, where the enemy huddled in confusion, when the order to withdraw was received." Polk reported: "We had one hour or more of daylight still left . . . and nothing seemed wanting to complete the most brilliant victory of the war but to press forward and make a vigorous assault on the demoralized remnant of his forces." When the Confederate troops approached the river, the Federal gunboats were ineffective because of the elevation required to fire over the high bank. While their fire must have seemed deadly to Beauregard, two miles in the rear, General Polk described the troops in advance as quite safe from it. Generals Breckinridge, Jeremy Gilmer, Randall Gibson, and virtually all the others confirmed these opinions.

General Buell, who was on the scene most of the afternoon, testified that at nightfall Grant's army for the most part was "scattered in inextricable and hopeless confusion for miles along the banks of the river." Buell's advance troops had reached Pittsburg a little before six. With them was Ambrose Bierce (later to win fame as a story writer), who declared that his Indiana comrades had to use rifle butts on the panicky stragglers before they could get off their transports. And the Union's Major General William Nelson described Grant's forces as "cowering under the river-banks . . . frantic with fright

[7] Otto Eisenschiml interviewed old Mrs. Inge in 1925 and used the incident and the quotations in his vivid monograph *The Story of Shiloh*.

and utterly demoralized." According to the belief of high officers and privates on both sides, the Confederates had complete victory in their grasp when Beauregard threw it away.[8]

The double blow of Sidney Johnston's death and the bitter second day's defeat were hard enough for Jefferson Davis to bear, but, coincidentally, on that black second day of Shiloh, General John Pope in conjunction with Federal gunboats captured the Confederate stronghold Island Number 10 in the Mississippi River and took more than 6,000 prisoners. This loss exposed Memphis and the Mississippi Delta down to Vicksburg.

Disgusted with Beauregard's pretense that the return to Corinth was a planned strategic maneuver,[9] Davis had to help him immediately to save his army, for the Union armies would be moving against him soon. On April 10, the President sent identical telegrams to the Governors of Mississippi, Louisiana, Alabama, and Georgia:

> General Beauregard must have reinforcements to meet the vast accumulation of the enemy before him. The necessity is imminent; the cause of vital importance; send forward to Corinth all the armed men you can furnish.

The next day, in answer to a dispatch from Governor Joseph E. Brown of Georgia, he telegraphed again: "Pikes and knives will be acceptable. Please send them to Chattanooga."

General Halleck arrived at Pittsburg Landing on the eleventh and took command of both Grant's and Buell's armies. With Pope's men released from Island Number 10 and with other reinforcements, he soon had 120,000 effective troops ready to march on Corinth. Now Davis saw the whole Mississippi Valley threatened with disaster.

[8] Right or wrong, that was what the majority thought then, and think now. After making an objective examination of the records, Federal General Morris Schaff wrote in *Jefferson Davis, His Life and Personality* (p. 171), published in 1922: "The weight of testimony seems to be that Beauregard threw away the victory."

[9] Only the most ardent Beauregard admirers were fooled. One newspaper rhymster wrote mockingly:

> "Here's to Toussaint Beauregard,
> Who for the truth has no regard.
> In Satan's clutches he will cry,
> 'I've got old Satan, Victori.'"

CHAPTER XX

THE PRESIDENT MAKES
TWO IMPORTANT DECISIONS

BEAUREGARD, in Mississippi, was only one of the President's worries. McClellan with 100,000 men was besieging Yorktown, opposed by Joseph Johnston with only 57,000. A fleet of Federal warships was on its way to attack New Orleans, the South's most valuable seaport.

The Confederate situation was critical on all fronts from lack of manpower. A majority of the 148 regiments of twelve-month men were now near the end of the agreed service. Davis was relieved to see reluctant Congressmen realizing after Shiloh that if the Confederacy was to succeed, short-term enlistments would have to be supplanted by three-year commitments. When he presented to Congress his request for conscription, the anti-Administration *Examiner* stoutly supported him, even advocating the passage of a conscript law "sufficiently potent to put 750,000 in the army."

On April 16, 1862, a year and three days after Sumter's fall, Congress passed a law drafting able-bodied men between eighteen and thirty-five for three years, or for the duration of the war if less than that term. Planters who owned as many as twenty slaves were exempted to keep up agricultural production, and to act as a disciplinary force. Foundry workers and essential railroad employees were exempted. The Secretary of War was given authority to exempt operatives in woolen and cotton factories. To prevent unpatriotic men who were fit for service from hiding behind desk jobs, the Chief Executive requested all government and state officials to choose their employees from those not subject to the draft.

Though the conscription law was fair and absolutely imperative to enable the Confederacy to oppose the augmenting armies of the North, loud complaints rose from the extreme State Rights men, who caused discontent among the people. Many smaller Southern planters, who deemed their own presence needful on the plantations, resented what they regarded as a denial of their constitutional rights. Senator William Yancey felt impelled to defend himself in Alabama for having voted for the bill, saying he had done so reluctantly "in face of a perilous military situation; the enemy being almost at the gates of the capital." Protests came from various localities; but the most vociferous were from Georgia, led by Robert Toombs, Vice-President Stephens, and Governor Brown. That triumvirate of anti-Davis men denounced the law as unconstitutional. To circumvent the success of conscription in his state, Governor Brown began creating several thousand superfluous state positions to be filled by voters reluctant to fight.

The conscript law raised an opposition to President Davis that was to continue to the end of the war, and this opposition, as Dr. Dodd declared, was "a most important, if not the greatest, cause of the final collapse of the Confederacy."

In numerous other instances, the President had to contend with the jealousy of individual states of their constitutional rights. North Carolina objected to the building of forty miles of new railroad connecting Danville, Virginia, and Greensboro, North Carolina. For war security, the President deemed this project essential. Finally, ignoring the obstructions of North Carolina politicians, he signed a bill and urged Congress to begin construction immediately "under the war powers of the Confederate Government." Again the President was supported by the *Examiner,* as well as by the other Richmond papers, and Congress ordered the line constructed. It was over this very stretch of railway that Mr. Davis and his Cabinet were to escape after the surrender at Appomattox.

The intense individualistic attitude of Southerners, often hiding under the doctrine of State Rights, continued to cost Jefferson Davis a draining toll of vital energy, and he had to waste precious hours in trying to make opponents see the logic, justice, and necessity of the Administration's moves.

Under the pressure of military reverses, mounting tensions, and Congressional wrangling, Mr. Davis had little time to give thought to his own Delta plantation. But he had written his white overseer,

Barnes, to reduce the cotton acreage.[1] He received the briefest reply from him under the date of April 13.

I am only Plantin 300 acres in cotton—I will have anuf meat to last untill June.

From his old brother Joseph, he learned more about Davis Bend affairs. The river was rising ominously—that perennial menace of Delta plantations. He was struck by a casual comment on General Beauregard: "The loss of Gen. Johnston at Shiloh was felt in the disorder that followed his fall. Beauregard may possess courage and he has engineering skill, but he wants character to command respect." [2]

On April 18, the day before the President received Joseph's letter, he learned that Federal men-of-war were trying to force their way up the river to New Orleans. The battleships were commanded by Tennessee-born Commodore David Glasgow Farragut, and a fleet of mortar boats, by David D. Porter, who had bought camels for Jefferson Davis when Davis was Secretary of War. The previous autumn, the President had put Maryland-born General Mansfield Lovell, whose home was New York, in charge of the New Orleans defenses. By December 5, 1861, Lovell had regarded his preparations as strong enough to repel any attack. The permanent forts, Jackson and St. Philip, seventy-five miles downriver, had been formidably strengthened. Gunboats blocked the way above the forts. Recently, obstructions had been sunk in the river at the narrowest points and heavy chains stretched across. Fire rafts were ready, but, unfortunately, the two ironclads, the *Mississippi* and the *Louisiana,* under construction in the New Orleans shipyards, were not finished.

The President was gratified to hear that five days of terrific bombardment of Fort St. Philip and Fort Jackson had proved futile. But the doughty Farragut determined to try to run by them. In the early morning of April 24, he got past with a large portion of his fleet. Then he attacked the poorly constructed Confederate gunboats, destroying all of them. After that, it was more or less easy sailing to the great port itself.

General Lovell lamented that the city defenses were manned by nothing better than "heterogeneous militia, armed mostly with shot-

---

[1] In March, 1862, Congress passed a joint resolution that the cotton crop should be curtailed.

[2] The letters quoted above are in the private collection of Jefferson Davis's grandson, Jefferson Hayes-Davis, at Colorado Springs, Colorado.

guns; against 9- and 11-inch Dahlgrens." Knowing that bombardment by Farragut's warships would demolish the city, Lovell decided not to offer resistance. Bales of cotton worth millions of dollars were hauled from the warehouses to the river banks and set afire to prevent their falling into the enemy's hands. On April 28, Lovell sent most of the movable public property and the ordnance stores out of the city to safety. Then he withdrew his troops.

As Farragut's warships docked, resentful citizens, almost suffocated by smoke from the burning cotton and hogsheads of molasses, stood on the shore shouting insults at the Yankees. In a little while, flags of the United States replaced the Stars and Bars on public buildings, and ladies wept bitterly behind their shuttered windows.

The fall of New Orleans was a major disaster for the Confederacy. It caused not only general lamentation, but considerable indignation. Secretary of the Navy Mallory came in for a share of the condemnation. President Davis was criticized for having placed a "Northerner" in command of the city's defense. Davis had not believed New Orleans would fall. From his long years in Washington, he knew the care and expense taken in building "impregnable" forts down river for the city's protection. On Lovell's conduct, he reserved his opinion. But he believed that the General had withdrawn the militia to prevent ruinous bombardment and to spare the women and children, whose "natural protectors" were in the armies at Corinth and before Richmond. At least, much of the public property and ordnance stores that Lovell had saved could be used in the defense of Vicksburg, the last important fortified town on the Mississippi.

On May Day, Farragut turned the captured city over to General Benjamin Butler, who had been sent with 18,000 men. Davis recalled that this same Butler had wanted him President of the United States, and, as a Massachusetts delegate, had voted fifty-seven times for him in the Democratic Convention of 1860. But from Butler's ugly actions in Maryland and the Fortress Monroe region, he was apprehensive of what he might do in the lower Delta.

Varina was almost frantic for news of her father and mother and sister Jenny, who lived in New Orleans, and Margaret, who was paying the family a visit at the time. Her husband tried to reassure her, but he, too, feared that Butler might make it very disagreeable for the in-laws of the Confederacy's President.

A few days later, the Davises learned that on the morning New Orleans fell, Margaret was in a dentist's office having the nerve of one of her teeth deadened. Suddenly there was great commotion in the streets, as the bell in Christ Church began to ring violently, warning the people that the city had fallen. In his excitement, and eager to get to the window, the dentist jerked his instrument out of Margaret's mouth and severely cut her lip. In pain and dismay, she rushed from the dentist's office and reached home, in the suburb called Algiers, as best she could. Just as she arrived, a message came from her father to join him at his office immediately, bringing Jenny and a few necessaries for travel. Mrs. Howell was visiting her sister up the river and was expected to return home that night. But they dared not wait. The father and daughters boarded a pig boat, which had been hurriedly prepared for them, and started upriver.

In the night, the steamboat on which Mrs. Howell was returning home passed their pig boat. It was hailed, and she was inquired for; but it refused to stop for fear of Yankee trickery. Reaching New Orleans, Mrs. Howell found the city in the wildest confusion, her family gone, her house looted. After much difficulty, and with one small bag, she managed to join her refugee family in Montgomery.

The relief of the Davises over the escape of the Howells made it easier to face the fact that war was pressing close upon their plantation home, Brierfield, below Vicksburg. The President had a more serious personal worry: the safety of his brother Joseph, Joseph's semi-invalid wife and granddaughter Lise, at adjoining Hurricane, and his eldest sister, Anna Smith, at St. Francisville, Louisiana.

Among the few personal friends Jefferson Davis saw often in the depressing weeks after Shiloh was the Reverend Doctor Charles Frederick Ernest Minnegerode. The German-born Rector of St. Paul's interested Davis as a personality as well as a man of faith and spiritual inspiration. Minnegerode was as loyal to the South as if his ancestors had landed at Jamestown.[3] His sympathy with the Confederacy's fight for independence was a common bond between him and Davis. In his youth, while a law student at Giessen, Germany, Minnegerode had belonged to a revolutionary secret society. Arrested by the Hessian authorities, he had been confined to a dungeon for eighteen months. After his health gave way completely, he was permitted to reside at his father's home, constantly guarded by four soldiers. When his case was dismissed five years after his arrest, he came to Philadelphia, at

[3] This comment on Minnegerode was made by General George Pickett in a letter to his sweetheart on July 18, 1862, published in *Soldier of the South*.

the age of twenty-three, with no assets but a distinguished profile, a thorough knowledge of the Bible, and a portmanteau filled with Greek and Latin classics. Eventually, he taught modern languages at William and Mary College, married one of Virginia's Carters, and entered the Episcopal ministry. But he never completely lost his German accent, and Davis could not but smile inwardly sometimes when, in inviting the congregation to prayer, the Minister would say, "Let us bray."

Ever since he had been chosen President, Jefferson Davis had considered joining a church. He had had his first religious stirrings as a little boy at St. Thomas's Academy in Kentucky when he had offered to profess Catholicism. At West Point he had come somewhat under the influence of the beloved Episcopal Chaplain, Charles McIlvaine, to whom Leonidas Polk made his first profession of faith. But Davis, who had married two Episcopalians and regularly attended services, had never felt impelled to become a church member. Though his father was a Baptist, the family did not stress orthodoxy. His mother had passed eighty before she was confirmed as an Episcopalian (by Bishop Polk). His brother Joseph kept a resident Episcopal minister on the Hurricane plantation for his family and the Negroes, but he himself had never been affiliated with a church.

During their courtship and early marriage, Varina had been surprised to discover that Jefferson had not only a deep religious feeling, but a steadfast faith. His intensely self-reliant personality hardly seemed to accord with a letter she received from him while he was fighting in Mexico. On August 16, 1846—when he was thirty-eight and she only twenty—he had written her from the mouth of the Rio Grande: "I have remembered your request on the subject of profanity and have improved. Have you remembered mine on the subject of prayer, and a steady reliance on the justice of one who sees through the veil of conduct to the motives of the heart? Be pious, be calm, be useful and charitable and temperate in all things." [4]

He did not yet capitalize the One representing Deity. But his admonitions to his girl wife, which sound somewhat priggish, were not amiss, for, off guard, the temperamental young Varina could be headstrong, sarcastic, and deceitful, and create scenes with his relatives if she did not get her way.

As the war progressed, Varina often found her husband at prayer, seeking guidance. Privately, she told Dr. Minnegerode that she be-

---

[4] On the back of the sheet, which is in the Confederate Museum, Richmond, Mrs. Davis has written "Letter from my own dearest Jeff."

lieved the President was wrestling with the thought of allying himself with "the visible church." When the Minister called and broached the subject, Davis met him more than halfway. Before becoming the leader of a people, he had felt he "was his own man"; now perhaps he should become "God's man." Yet he had doubts of his worthiness to become a communicant. From their talk, Dr. Minnegerode judged him "ready and most humble," and said he believed a burden would be lifted from the President's heart in this critical time if he were received into the church at once.

As McClellan's advance toward Richmond became obvious, Davis realized it might be expedient to send his wife and children away. And Varina was eager to see her husband received into the church before she left.

In the first week of May, Helen Keary, the sympathetic niece who was staying with the Davises, wrote to her mother lamenting the fall of New Orleans. In the letter she spoke of the family concern for the President's health and the hope that he would be confirmed. "Oh, Mother, Uncle Jeff is miserable. He tries to be cheerful and to bear up against such a combination of troubles; but oh, I fear he cannot live long, if he does not get some rest and quiet. Our reverses distress him so much, it makes my heart ache to look at him. He knows that he ought to send his wife and children away, and yet he cannot bear to part with them, and we all dread to leave him too. Varina and I had a hard cry about it today. There was confirmation in the church today, and we all hoped so much that he would go forward for confirmation. But he did not. . . ."

A postscript, added on May 9, announced: "Uncle Jeff was confirmed last Tuesday, in St. Paul's Church, by Bishop Johns. He was baptised at home in the morning before church."

Jefferson Davis had made his decision. Since he was not sure whether he had been baptized as a child, Dr. Minnegerode baptized him in a home ceremony. And then, in a special service at St. Paul's, Bishop Johns administered the rights of confirmation to the President and to his friends Josiah Gorgas, Chief of Ordnance, and his wife, Amelia, daughter of Alabama's Governor John Gayle.

After the ceremony, Varina remarked that "a peace which passed understanding" seemed to settle in her husband's heart.[5] Jefferson

[5] "From that day," said Dr. Minnegerode in a tribute to Jefferson Davis in 1889 (J. William Jones, *The Davis Memorial Volume*, pp. 415-424), " 'he never looked back.' He never ceased trying to come up to his baptismal vow and lead a Christian life. . . . His real nature was gentle, and conscience ruled him supreme."

Davis's religious faith was almost as sustaining to him as was Robert E. Lee's. Without the solace of religion, he could hardly have endured what was to come to the South.

On May 1, the day Ben Butler began his harsh rule of New Orleans, General Johnston announced to Richmond his decision to give up Yorktown immediately. In answer, President Davis, deeply disturbed, telegraphed him:

Accepting your conclusion that you must soon retire, arrangements are commenced for the abandonment of the navy-yard and removal of public property both from Norfolk and the Peninsula. Your announcement today that you would withdraw tomorrow night takes us by surprise and must involve enormous losses including unfinished gunboats. Will the safety of your army allow more time?

Davis and Lee could discern no necessity for such precipitate removal. Nor does there seem to have been, for, on that very same day, President Lincoln sent McClellan a telegram bespeaking his exasperation at the General's slowness.

Your call for Parrott guns alarms me—chiefly because it argues indefinite procrastination. Is anything to be done?

In his impatience at Little Mac's continued call for reinforcements, Lincoln got a big laugh by complaining that sending troops to McClellan was like "shovelling fleas across a barnyard: only half seemed to arrive."

Not content with Johnston's decision, which recalled his hasty departure from the Manassas line in March, President Davis sent Secretary of War Randolph and Secretary of the Navy Mallory to Norfolk and Yorktown to see if evacuation could be postponed. On May 2, while they were conferring with General Huger in Norfolk, an officer from General Johnston arrived with an order for immediate evacuation. Considering the enormity of the losses in stores and munitions involved, Randolph took the responsibility of countermanding Johnston's dispatch by ordering Huger to delay evacuation until he could remove such goods and arms as could be carried off by trains and wagons. To the commandant of the Navy Yard, Mallory gave similar instructions. The evacuation of Norfolk was delayed by a week, and thus irreplaceable matériel was saved, which Johnston would needlessly have abandoned.

In the early morning of May 4, the rear guard of D. H. Hill's brigade loosed a final round from the Yorktown batteries, spiked the heaviest guns, and took the muddy road to Williamsburg.

Davis, who deplored Johnston's further abandonment of guns and supplies, was moved by the courage and endurance of the Southern soldiers at Yorktown. The men had served almost without relief from April 3 to May 3. It had rained nearly every day. The trenches had run with water, and the weather was unseasonably chilly. Fires could not be kindled because of the watchful enemy. Often the Army had had to subsist upon nothing but salt pork and uncooked flour. Federal artillery and sharpshooters played on the Confederates day and night. Yet the men complained little of their grueling discomfort.

The President learned that General McClellan had moved his head-quarters to the White House on the Pamunkey, the splendid estate Rooney Lee had inherited from his mother's father. It was there that George Washington had courted Martha Custis and where he had lived when first married. Mrs. Robert E. Lee, who had been staying at White House with her daughter-in-law Charlotte, had left only a day or two before McClellan's arrival. As she departed, she pinned a hand-written plea to the front door:

Northern soldiers who profess to reverence Washington forbear to dese-crate the home of his first married life, the property of his wife, now owned by her descendants.

A Grand-daughter of Mrs. Washington

McClellan gave orders that the house was to be occupied by no one but himself and the grounds were to be in no way molested. And, like the gentleman he was, he put protective guards around the estate of President Tyler's widow on the James. He tried to exercise vigilance that his men did no looting, and acted with decency to all the district's inhabitants and their properties. Because of his civilized considera-tion, some Republican Congressmen and one or two members of Lincoln's Cabinet began whispering that he must be secretly in sym-pathy with the South.

For days, McClellan was severely impeded by wet weather and the execrable roads. His well-trained troops, though splendidly equipped, had to endure hardships in marching across boggy streams and through treacherous swamps. Forty-eight hours were required to move two divisions, with their trains, five miles. But slowly, steadily, Little Mac began advancing on Richmond.

When McClellan's army reached Williamsburg on May 5, Davis

knew that the fall of Richmond was a dire probability. The government archives were put in order and packed in case of flight. As officials began sending their wives and children to points south, the President decided it best for his family to leave, too. Reluctantly, Mrs. Davis began packing some luggage, in the event of their departure.

On the evening of May 9, while the Davises were giving a scheduled reception, a courier arrived and demanded to see the President in private. As Mr. Davis returned to the drawing room, he said, *sotto voce*, in answer to his wife's questioning look, "The enemy's gunboats are ascending the river." The reception went on; some of the guests stayed quite late. When the last had left, the President told Varina that he hoped the obstructions in the river would halt the gunboats, but he preferred that she and the children leave for Raleigh next morning. Varina remonstrated, but her husband quietly insisted.

The next morning, Jefferson Davis saw his family depart on a train filled with refugees. That day Norfolk was surrendered by its mayor to the Federals. In the night following, the *Virginia* (*Merrimac*), on which the Confederacy had banked so mightily, was blown up by her crew to prevent her falling into enemy hands. Her commander had tried hard to save her. To lighten her, some of the iron sheeting was torn away, and her coal was dumped overboard. But her draft was so great that she could not pass the bar at the mouth of the James. In her defenseless position, there was no alternative but to destroy her.

As McClellan approached Richmond with more than 100,000 men, the North could rejoice in a succession of Union victories: Roanoke Island, Fort Henry and Fort Donelson, the occupation of Nashville, Island Number 10, the capture of New Orleans. Washington was being protected by McDowell's army. Generals Frémont and Nathaniel Banks were in the Shenandoah Valley. Halleck, with Grant, Buell, and Pope, and 120,000 men, was creeping on Corinth. Opinion in the North ran that the war would end before the Fourth of July. The prospects for the Confederacy had never been so grim.

On the afternoon of May 12, the President rode to General Johnston's headquarters, about twenty-two miles from Richmond. The General was out when he arrived, so he stayed the night nearby and returned in the morning. Though the Army was reported to be in fine condition and spirits, Davis could not feel confident of Johnston's ability to defend the city. He wrote his wife the next day, "I know not what to expect when so many failures are to be remembered, yet will try to make a successful resistance."

Ending on an intimate note, Davis revealed his loneliness without his family.

I have no attraction to draw me from my office now and home is no longer a locality. Those who stay behind have double pain in parting from the loved of earth. To them everything brings remembrance of the loss. . . . Kiss my dear children, may God preserve you and them for happier days and lives of love for each other and usefulness to the country. . . . I am here interrupted and with a deep prayer for my own Winnie I close this hasty scrawl,

Your Husband.

At a special Cabinet meeting, in which Lee's advice was sought, the question was put as to what line to the south Johnston's army should take if Richmond were evacuated. Someone suggested Staunton, a hundred miles northwest. Davis saw tears rise in Lee's eyes. "But Richmond must not be given up!" the General protested with an unwonted display of passion. "It shall not be given up!" Lee's resolution accorded with Davis's own fighting spirit. When various municipal committees waited on the President to ask if he purposed to hold the city, he assured them positively that he did.

But early in the morning of the fifteenth, Richmond was in a state of high alarm. News reached the President that the *Monitor,* the new ironclad *Galena,* and three other Federal ships were attacking the unfinished fortifications of Drewry's Bluff on the James. Davis called for his horse and rode rapidly down to observe the firing. He never saw Southern gunners fight more effectively. He watched sharpshooters along the banks picking off Union sailors when they came above deck. He saw a lucky shot from the Drewry batteries rake through the *Galena* from stem to stern, making a frightful slaughter of men, and disabling the ship. After three hours' hard fighting, he watched the Federal ships turn and steam back down the river. Before the relieved President got back to Richmond, news of the enemy's repulse had preceded him, and the anxious townsfolk were again breathing freely.

The next day, after attending Sunday services at St. Paul's, Davis rode through rain and mud again to Drewry's Bluff. The soldiers cheered him loudly. He found the working parties doing their jobs on the fortifications with redoubled energy. That night he wrote Varina:

"The panic here has subsided, and with increasing confidence there has arisen a desire to see the city destroyed rather than surrender."

But Davis realized that the citizens had no conception of the horrible scenes that would follow the battering of rows of brick houses. He would endeavor to beat the enemy on either flank, but in no case would he consent to the Confederate Army being penned up in Richmond. "Be of good cheer," he wrote on, "and continue to hope that God will in due time deliver us from the hands of our enemies." Feeling his fighting blood rise, he added, "As the clouds grow darker, and when, one after another, those whom we trusted are detected in secret hostilities, I feel like mustering clans were in me, and that cramping fetters had fallen from my limbs."

Then, measuring a fault in himself against the sagacious behavior of his seven-year-old daughter in an incident her mother had related, he wrote: "Maggie is a wise child. I wish I could learn just to let people alone who snap at me; in forbearance and charity to turn away from the cats as well as the snakes." He knew this flaw in his nature, this inability to ignore completely unjust or malicious criticism. Try as he would to refrain from answering back, he would too often endeavor to make his attacker understand the true facts, and sometimes he would reveal his indignation.

He was indeed sincere when he wrote Varina: "I have no political wish beyond the success of our cause, no personal desire but to be relieved from further connection with office; opposition in any form can only disturb me insomuch as it may endanger the public welfare."

Later, on that same date, May 16, on a single sheet of thin blue paper, the tired man sent Varina another note and ended with a tinge of melancholy: "Good night, dear wife, may every consolation be yours until it shall be our fortune again to be united. Ever affectionately remembered when waking, sleep brings you to me in such reality that it would be happier to sleep on." [6]

The President sent a cheering letter to Joseph Johnston by Custis Lee, describing the repulse of the gunboats and the progress on the Drewry's Bluff works. As a gentle reminder, he added, "To you it is needless to say that the defense must be made outside the city." Touching on the various advantages of where and how the defense

---

[6] Many of the letters of Jefferson Davis to his wife in May and June, 1862, which may be read in the Confederate Museum, Richmond, are quoted by Mrs. Davis in her *Memoir,* and by Rowland, but the tender, intimate endings are generally omitted.

might be made, he ended tactfully: "As on all former occasions, my design is to suggest, not to direct, relying confidently as well as on your ability as your zeal, it is my wish to leave you with the fullest powers to exercise your judgment." [7]

But, in reality, Johnston seemed unsure what to do. From that early April day following his first Peninsula inspection, he had apparently wanted to bring his troops into Richmond. Only General Lee and the President had prevented him. On May 19, two days after writing Johnston that the defense *must* be made outside the city, Davis and virtually everybody else in Richmond felt a sense of outrage when Johnston brought his entire army to the gates of the capital. "I have but a moment to say that I am well as usual and busier than heretofore," the President wrote his wife briefly. "General Johnston has brought his army back to the suburbs of Richmond, and I have been waiting all day for him to communicate his plans. The enemy . . . have found out his movements while concealing their own. We are uncertain of everything except that a battle is near at hand."

The President was anything but satisfied with Johnston's movements. His forces had been withdrawn so dangerously close to Richmond that if the Confederate line failed to hold against a Federal attack, the foe might be in the main streets within two hours. Yet Johnston had given no sign that he intended to attack.

Davis and Lee rode out to Johnston's headquarters to ascertain his plans. They found him reticent and evasive. Though they talked so late into the night that they slept in camp, they could not discover that Johnston had any plans except to await "a more favorable opportunity to attack."

After their return to Richmond, Lee wrote Johnston, in the President's name, requesting a conference. Johnston did not reply. On May 21, Lee again suggested that Johnston communicate with the President. Next day, Davis and Lee went to Johnston's headquarters near the village of Mechanicsville, six miles northeast of the city. They were both disquieted to find "a depressing lack of organization." But Johnston would tell them nothing definite, and so made it extremely difficult for them to help him in the defense. Two days later, the Feder-

[7] Dunbar Rowland notes in his *Jefferson Davis, Constitutionalist* that the stock criticisms of the President that "he was continually overruling the plans of military commanders in the field, are not founded on a knowledge of the facts." They are, Rowland declares, "merely the idly repeated charges of Davis's enemies."

als occupied Mechanicsville, from which they could see Richmond's church spires.[8]

The President was so obviously disturbed about Johnston's strange silence that Lee went again to talk with him. He returned with the news that on Thursday Johnston expected to attack that part of McClellan's army that lay north of the Chickahominy. A. P. Hill was to move on the right flank and rear of McClellan's force. Gustavus Smith was to cross the Chickahominy at Meadow Bridge and, in conjunction with Hill, "double up the enemy." Then Longstreet was to attack him in front by way of Mechanicsville Bridge.

Davis brightened: at last an offensive would be initiated. But he could not help but anticipate the agonies and personal griefs that were bound to attend the fight. To his wife he wrote: "We are steadily developing for a great battle, and under God's favor I trust for a decisive victory. The enemy are preparing to concentrate in advance by regular approaches; we must attack him in motion, and trust to the valor of our troops for our success. It saddens me to feel how many a mother, wife and child will be made to grieve in bitterness, but what is there worse than submission to such brutal tyranny as now holds sway over New Orleans?"

A messenger arrived at the office of Adjutant General Cooper with a heartening dispatch from Stonewall Jackson in the Shenandoah Valley. He officially reported "brilliant success" for the three days from May 23 to May 26. The Federals had been routed at Front Royal; many prisoners had been captured. A large quantity of "medical, ordnance and other stores have fallen into our hands." On the twenty-fourth and twenty-fifth, General Banks's main column had been pierced and routed. After a stinging defeat at Winchester, Nathaniel Banks, onetime Speaker of the House, had fled across the Potomac at Williamsport.

Davis was both elated and gratified. While Johnston, Jackson's immediate superior, had his attention centered on retreating before McClellan in the Peninsula, the President had backed General Lee in suggesting to Stonewall that he strike at the enemy in northern Virginia after Ewell's forces were joined with his. In a second letter, approved by the President, Lee had written: "Whatever movement you

[8] While Davis was anything but content with Johnston's course of action, he had tried to believe that the General was fully in accord with his purpose to hold Richmond. But in Lieutenant General John B. Hood's *Advance and Retreat*, published after the war, there is evidence that Johnston told his volunteer aide, McFarland, on the retreat from Yorktown, that he expected to give up Richmond.

make, do it quickly, and create the impression, as far as possible, that you design threatening the Washington line." But before Jackson could strike, Joe Johnston ordered Ewell to leave the Valley. Jackson appealed directly to Lee, who got the President's sanction for him to go ahead with his aggressive plans. Without Davis's full support, none of Lee's preparations for Jackson's Valley operations would have been possible. Audacity had paid off well.

With 16,000 men, Jackson had been making spectacular marches, and attacking first one Federal army, then another. Swiftness and secrecy were potent agents in his success. His hardy soldiers moved with such celerity that they became known as the Confederacy's "foot cavalry." Not even Jackson's own officers knew where he was going to strike next. And when Federal commanders arrived where he was supposed to be, Jackson would be gone. After making a demonstration as if to cross the Potomac at Harpers Ferry, Jackson began his retreat toward Richmond. Frémont was ordered from the west to intercept him, and McDowell was ordered to send twenty thousand of his men from the east. McDowell, with most of his 40,000 men, had been preparing to join McClellan on the twenty-sixth. Now President Lincoln ordered McDowell not to join McClellan, but to keep 20,000 men at Fredericksburg for the protection of Washington and to send 20,000 to help capture Jackson. McDowell protested against the orders, and then obeyed "with heavy heart." McClellan had been promised that McDowell's well-trained First Corps would be sent to him at the strategic hour he called for it. Little Mac was so undone that he became ill.

Jackson, with wagon trains of priceless booty, slipped through open country before he could be halted. After he had secured the captured supplies, he turned back to make unpredictable forced marches against the Federals, leaving them defeated and baffled. President Davis received reports that Washington was gripped with fright. Secretary of War Stanton was telegraphing Northern governors that the enemy "in great force" was marching on the capital and urged them to send all available militia immediately.

These recent weeks had brought into full play Jackson's military genius. Davis admired his rapid marches and his vigor of attack. He noted with special pleasure the eagle-like swoop with which Jackson descended upon each enemy army. It was Jackson, far off in the Shenandoah, who had so far done the most to save Richmond, chiefly by preventing McDowell's union with McClellan.

On Thursday morning, May 28, as soon as he had dispatched pressing office business, President Davis rode out toward Meadow Bridge to observe the attack Johnston had told Lee he would make. On the road he came upon Gustavus Smith's division halted, the men dispersed about the woods. He could get no information, not even from young General Hood, who said he knew nothing except that they had been halted. Inquiring for General Smith, second in command, the President was informed that he had gone to a farmhouse in the rear, presumably ill. Riding to the top of a bluff, Davis could see through his field glasses two mounted sentinels across the river—nothing more. Colonel Joseph R. Anderson declared that he had not heard Hill's guns. Near Mechanicsville Bridge, Davis encountered Longstreet, walking up and down "in an impatient, fretful manner." His men, he said, had been under arms all day waiting for orders to advance. He did not know what was the matter. Later, Davis learned that General Smith had been informed by a countryman that Beaver Dam Creek, on the opposite side of the river, presented an impossible barrier. "Thus," Davis wrote his wife that night, "ended the offensive-defensive programme from which Lee expected so much, and of which I was hopeful."

The disappointed President spent the whole next day, May 29, in his office. He dictated a carefully worded reply to Governor Brown of Georgia, who was denouncing the conscript law as unconstitutional. Needing Brown's co-operation, Davis endeavored in a 4,000-word letter to convince him of both the constitutionality of the act and its absolute necessity.

On May 30, news reached the President's desk that the cautious Halleck, and his 120,000 men had finally occupied strategic Corinth. At a snail's pace, it had taken him a month and a half to cover the few miles from Shiloh; for, at each day's halt, he had insisted upon strong entrenchments being made. Beauregard had escaped with his army and all his supplies and was headed for Tupelo, fifty miles south. The loss of Corinth, one of the most important railway centers in the West, was a severe blow. It was a surprise, because Beauregard's defensive line was strong. Some Cabinet members had just been complaining that although the Government had increased Beauregard's forces to 100,000, he had "done nothing to recover the territory lost in the West." But by the General's reckoning, his effective strength numbered only some 52,000. Another 18,000 men were on the sick list, due to an outbreak of typhoid, because Beauregard had not provided for proper water.[9]

Davis had little time to bemoan Corinth's loss, for McClellan's troops, within the sound of Richmond's church bells, might storm the Confederate lines at any hour.

With the aid of his secretary, Burton Harrison, the President packed some valuable books, his sword, the pistols he had used at Buena Vista, and his dressing case. He wrote Varina that the articles were being sent to her in Raleigh that day. He said that "they might have a value to the boys in after time, and to you now." Then he added: "Thank you for congratulations on success of Jackson. Had the movement been made when I first proposed it, the effect would have been more important. In that night's long conference, it was regarded impossible. . . . Gen. Lee rises with the occasion . . . and seems to be equal to the conception. I hope others will develop capacity in execution."

By way of stilling her apprehension, he closed on a hopeful note: "If we fight and are victorious, we can all soon meet. If the enemy retreat to protect Washington . . . I can probably visit you."

All through the afternoon and night of May 30, a storm raged, with thunder, lightning, and monstrous rain. The sluggish Chickahominy turned into a tempestuous torrent and endangered its bridges. Two of McClellan's five corps were on the south side of the river; so his army lay astride the swollen stream. General McClellan was reported seriously ill. The President might have been expected to rejoice over his adversary's misfortune at this stage of the campaign, but he could not help but feel sympathy for his onetime young friend. McClellan still had some devoted Southern admirers, none more so than Virginia's Colonel George E. Pickett, who was to be immortalized by his charge at Gettysburg. From Mechanicsville Turnpike, Colonel Pickett wrote in romantic strain to his fiancée: "I have heard that my dear old friend, McClellan, is lying ill about ten miles from here. May some loving, soothing hand minister to him. He was, he is, he always will be, even were his pistol pointed at my heart, my dear, loved friend. . . . You, my darling, may not be in sympathy with this feeling, for I know you see 'no good in Nazareth.' "

At last, taking advantage of the swollen river and McClellan's re-

[9] The figure 52,000 is given in *Official Records*. The Federals dug deep wells for drinking water, and were quite healthy at Corinth.

ported illness, Johnston decided to strike. Shortly after noon on Saturday, May 31, the Confederates moved on the Federal positions south of the Chickahominy near a little railway station called Fair Oaks and a settlement known as Seven Pines.

As soon as the President learned that a fight was in progress, he called for General Lee. Together they rode out and arrived "in time to see the battle mismanaged." The Confederate staff work was woefully inefficient, and the attack was not going as Johnston had planned it. Davis and Lee could not resist the impulse to ride nearer to the sound of firing. Proceeding farther down the road for almost a mile, they came upon a heavy timbered wood with a field of green oats in a clearing. Suddenly they were under fire from concealed Federal batteries. In a smoke-filled scene of confusion, Postmaster General Reagan galloped up and chided the President about exposing himself so recklessly. But with the smell of battle in his nostrils, Davis was reluctant to leave. Dusk was descending when an excited messenger on horseback informed the President that General Johnston had been severely wounded. Davis turned his horse and soon came upon Johnston, being borne on a litter, conscious, but in considerable pain.

Just as the General was about to be lifted into an ambulance, Davis dismounted to speak to him. Johnston opened his eyes, smiled, gave the President his hand. In answer to a solicitous question, he said he did not know how seriously he was hurt, but feared a fragment of a shell had injured his spine. All the former tension and coolness between the two momentarily dissolved. With consoling warmth, Davis expressed his sincere regret and said he hoped the General would mend quickly and take the field again.

The President found General Gustavus Smith and asked him if he had made any plans for the morrow, which might mean desperate fighting. Nervously fatigued by the strain of the day, Smith said he had not yet formulated plans but must wait until he heard how the battle had gone with Longstreet and D. H. Hill. He thought he might have to withdraw his lines nearer Richmond. The President expressed the hope that he would be able to remain where he was, and pointed out that the Federals themselves might fall back and then the Confederates would have at least "the moral effect of victory." Bidding good night to Smith, whose lack of effective decision struck him forcibly, Davis turned his horse onto the shortest road to Richmond. General Lee on Traveller fell in beside him.

In the darkness, they passed between reserves already asleep on their arms in the woods to be fresh for the next day's conflict. This day's battle, of which Davis and Lee had been so hopeful, had ended with no decisive result. Unaccountable delays in bringing some of the Confederate troops into action had prevented a real victory. The dogged Longstreet had apparently bungled matters. Misunderstandings between him and Huger had halted advance. Four of Longstreet's brigades and three of Huger's had not been brought into action.

After some talk on the probabilities of the morrow, the two rode on in silence. Davis was deep in thought. Turning his head slightly toward his companion, he said, "General Lee, I am assigning you to the command of the army. When we get to Richmond, I shall send you the official order."

Jefferson Davis's decision, announced quietly on the dark road, marked a climactic moment in the war's history. It gave Robert E. Lee his chance to prove himself unsurpassed as a general in the Western Hemisphere.

Later that night, in Richmond, the President called on the wounded Johnston, who had been taken to the Crenshaw home on Church Hill. He found him free of fever and seemingly "unshaken in his nervous system," though his breathing was labored. Touched by Lydia Johnston's anxiety, Mr. Davis offered to share the Executive Mansion with the Johnstons. But the General's staff had just obtained an entire furnished house, which better suited their convenience. When he got home, the President wrote out an executive order naming Lee Commander of the Army of Northern Virginia.

That night, agitated citizens lay on their beds dressed, to nap, but hardly to sleep. And early in the morning the whole town seemed to be on the street. On his way to his office, the President saw litters, farm wagons, ambulances bearing the maimed and bloodstained. Some of the wounded who could limp or walk with sticks were so smutty with gunpowder that they looked like escapees from a mine disaster. Anxious women with fear-white faces and strained eyes rushed about in silent appeal searching for loved ones. Warehouses were turned into hospitals, and guest rooms of private homes filled with wounded strangers. At the surgeons' call for more beds, some churches sacrificed velvet pew cushions, which the members of altar guilds rapidly sewed together to make comfortable pallets. To give comfort to the dying, gentlemen went down into their cellars for their best port and Madeira. And ladies, accompanied by white-coated Negro butlers bearing white damask-covered trays of soups, chicken, beaten biscuits, fruit, jams and jellies, fed the mutilated sitting against trunks of shade trees, as they awaited a few feet of space in an improvised hospital.

About noon, in the withering heat of June 1, the President started out on horseback to the battlefield through street scenes of suffering and grief, compassion and loving kindness. Aware of Lee's modesty and Smith's self-esteem, Davis wanted to save them both embarrassment by telling Smith personally that he had placed the Virginian in command.

As the President approached the position where he had left General Smith the night before, he was hailed by General J. S. Whiting, who excitedly ran toward the road to stop him. "Sir," he called, "you are riding into the position of the enemy." Pointing, he said, *"There* is a battery, which I am surprised has not fired on you." Davis did not know that in the night Smith had withdrawn almost a mile toward Richmond and that the enemy had moved up. When he reached the new headquarters, the President tactfully softened the blow for Smith as well as he could, but he half realized that he had made an implacable enemy.

It was almost one o'clock of June 1, 1862, when Lee, having wound up imperative business, set out for the battlefield. As Commanding General, he rode forth into high fame with as much humility as resolution. To his daughter-in-law Charlotte, he wrote that he wished Joseph Johnston's mantle "had fallen upon an abler man." Lee did not have the confidence in his own genius that Jefferson Davis had.

When Lee arrived at Smith's headquarters, the three immediately went into conference, then set out to survey the field. The battle around the Seven Pines settlement had been going on for hours, but the Confederates, though fighting furiously, were having a difficult time in gaining advantage. In the battleground mud, the President's horse mired to his knees.

The fight around Seven Pines ended indecisively. It was accounted a Confederate victory, though the Southerners sustained more casualties than the Federals. Lee ordered the Army to return to the positions it had held before the attack, and in the late afternoon he set up his headquarters in the house of a widow named Mary Dabbs, about a mile and a half from the suburbs of Richmond. Here he issued his first address to his army, which began: "In pursuance of the orders of the President, General R. E. Lee assumes command."

The troops, who liked Joe Johnston, received the news politely, with mild cheering. Johnston's top officers, who, under his influence, were critical of the Davis Administration, revealed no pleasure at all in having a "staff officer" made their commander in the field. Longstreet went only so far as to express relief that the halting Smith was not given the command. The *Examiner* coolly stated that it hoped Lee would prove himself a "competent" successor to General Johnston, whom it lauded lavishly as the "most remarkable military character in America."

Apparently no one in the Confederacy agreed with Jefferson Davis on Lee's superb potentialities or discerned his organizational gifts, which were as marked as those of McClellan. Few except Colonel Ives and Davis, who was of a like disposition himself, dreamed that the gentle-mannered Lee was a gambler who would take most daring chances. The world at large thought Jefferson Davis was extremely audacious to put Lee in command.

CHAPTER XXI

RICHMOND IMPERILED

ON JUNE 2 when the President visited the Army, he found Lee in consultation with most of his general officers.[1] The tone of their conversation was quite despondent, as if they had all been infected with Joe Johnston's pessimism. One officer could see absolutely no probability of stopping the enemy's advance. In marked terms, Jefferson Davis expressed his disappointment at hearing such negative views. Lee remarked that before the President came in he had said much the same thing.

Davis withdrew shortly and rode slowly toward the front. He was soon joined by General Lee, who asked him what, under the circumstances, it was most advisable to do. Davis said he knew of nothing better than the plan Lee had previously explained and which Johnston had been unable to execute. There was one modification: at the best opportunity, General Jackson should be brought from the Shenandoah, where he was now engaged with superior forces. But before he could be withdrawn, the enemy had to be driven from the Valley. For this purpose, as well as to mask the design of joining Jackson's forces with Lee's, a division under General Whiting should be detached and ostentatiously sent by rail to reinforce Jackson and mystify McClellan. As soon as the Federals in the Valley were in full retreat, Jackson would move down rapidly with his entire force and strike the right rear flank of McClellan north of the Chickahominy.

General Lee was in complete agreement.[2] With the enemy at Rich-

---

[1] The day after Lee assumed command, the ambitious General Smith retired with some obscure nervous ailment, said to have been induced by lack of sleep.

[2] James Ford Rhodes wrote in his eminent *History of the United States* (Vol. IV, p. 30), "The harmony between Davis and Lee was complete."

mond's gates, the Commander in Chief and the Commanding General were willing to risk the strategy of reinforcing Jackson, a hundred miles away.

In the meantime, the Confederates before Richmond were without entrenchment. Though hampered by a deficiency of tools, Lee ordered immediate construction of a formidable line of works. By strong entrenchments, Lee felt he would be able to make Richmond safe enough for him to attack McClellan. And attack soon he must, for with McClellan's larger army possessing guns of superior range, the city could not be held indefinitely.

Lee's entrenching, however, brought fresh jibes from the press. Some romantics regarded it as "cowardly" for Confederates to resort to trenches. Blustering Robert Toombs complained disgustedly that West Point men, for whom he affected utter contempt, "were holding the army from battle, digging and throwing up sand." Like Lee, Davis was a confirmed believer in earthworks. "Politicians, newspapers and uneducated officers," he wrote Varina, "have created such a prejudice in our Army against labor that it will be difficult until taught by sad experience to induce our troops to work efficiently. The greatest generals of ancient and modern times have won their renown by labor. Caesar, who revolutionized the military system of his age, never slept in a camp without intrenching it."

On June 3, President Davis celebrated his fifty-fourth birthday by relaxing in the confidence that Lee would save Richmond, if it could be saved. That afternoon, he wrote his wife, who was impatient for news by wire. "I cannot telegraph to you of our military operations for fear of attracting attention and exciting speculation. . . . The events of the last few days have not varied our condition in any decisive manner, and you have seen enough of rumor to teach you to reject babbling."

Davis had been disturbed to discover the inferior work of Johnston's scouts. "The Federals," he wrote, "had been eight or ten days fortifying their position, and the first intimation I had that they had slept on the near side of the Chickahominy was on Saturday when I rode into an encampment from which they had been driven. . . . It is hard to see incompetence losing opportunity and wasting hardgotten means, but harder still to bear, is the knowledge that there is no available remedy. I cultivate hope and patience, and trust to the blunders of our enemy and the gallantry of our troops for ultimate success."

The next day, the President sent General Jackson a formal letter of congratulation on "the brilliant campaign you have conducted against the enemy in the valley of Virginia." The officer in charge at Staunton, he wrote, had been directed to gather all aid he could and move down the Valley to join him. "But it is on your skill and daring that reliance is to be placed. The army under your command encourages us to hope for all which men can achieve."

That night, Jefferson Davis visited a lady in her sitting room at the Ballard Hotel. His call was not publicized, for the lady, who had arrived that day, was Rose Greenhow, the famous Southern spy. The Washington authorities had been glad to get rid of her disconcerting and dangerous presence in prison. General John Adam Dix, on his way to take command at Fort Monroe, was her escort out of the Union. A cordon of guards with bayonets had been stationed about the boat to keep back Mrs. Greenhow's throng of admirers. At Fort Monroe, she signed a pledge that she would not return north of the Potomac during "the present hostilities." The officers on the ship treated her with most agreeable consideration, and the Captain provided a farewell luncheon with champagne. When Rose raised her glass, she looked lovingly in the direction of the Confederate capital and drank a toast to Jefferson Davis.

At first sight of her, the President was shocked to see the change in the beauty's appearance. Her once-lustrous brown hair was streaked with gray; her face had unwonted lines, and she looked very tired about the eyes. She had, he wrote his wife, "the air of one whose nerves are shaken by mental torture." With graceful courtesy, Mr. Davis bowed over her hand, held it for a moment in affectionate gratitude. "But for you," he said, "there would have been no Battle of Bull Run." Rose Greenhow was both touched and elated. Her former radiance lighted up her face. Later, she wrote, "I shall ever remember that as the proudest moment of my whole life, to have received the tribute of praise from him who stands as the apostle of our country's liberty in the eyes of the civilized world."

Alert little Rose Adele,[3] her daughter, who had helped with the spying, as a lookout, and who had shared her mother's prison cell, "inquired very affectionately for Maggie." She amused Mr. Davis by asking if there were any Yankees where Maggie was.

[3] The *Daily Enquirer* of June 16 reported that little Rose had spotted one of McClellan's officers disguised in a Confederate uniform at dinner in the American Hotel. The man had noted the child's suspicious glances and ducked before he was caught.

The President had Secretary of State Benjamin, an old friend of Mrs. Greenhow, send her a check for $2,500 as "an acknowledgement of the valuable and patriotic service rendered by you to our cause."

After the Battle of Seven Pines, there was no real engagement near Richmond until late June, but during the interim Davis had little surcease from anxiety. The Federals were preparing a formidable attack against Charleston, one of the vital ports to which blockade-runners could bring arms from Europe. The President sent Major General John Clifford Pemberton to command. South Carolinians were none too pleased, because Pemberton was a Northerner. A telegram from Governor Pickens on June 12 to the President begged also for Braxton Bragg:

Send Gen. Bragg if possible for three weeks or longer. He is best, and can perhaps be spared as Beauregard has fallen back and it will take him that time to put his army in position. Bragg will give new life and confidence. To save Charleston at this time is all important.

Davis wired Pickens:

Beauregard has stated his own health not being strong, he cannot spare Bragg, who has much of the administration duty of the army to perform.

He offered him Beauregard to take charge of the whole Department of South Carolina and Georgia. Though Pickens countered that "General Bragg was the proper man to be sent for a few weeks to Charleston," he invited Beauregard, who declined the transfer.

"If Mississippi troops lying in camp, when not retreating under Beauregard, were at home," the President wrote his wife with asperity, "they would probably keep a section of the river free for our use and closed against Yankee transports."

Letters came to the Executive Office from people of eastern Louisiana and southern Mississippi, who were in a panic about burning cotton. Fires blazed all along the river from New Orleans to Memphis; "white gold," they said, "going up in black smoke." Since the end of 1861, much of the cotton had been kept inland on plantations for fear bales stored in ports might draw enemy attack. Wherever there was imminent danger of Federal penetration, cotton was burned. On March 17, 1862, Congress had enacted a law providing for the destruction of all cotton and tobacco when in danger of falling into the hands of the enemy. But many patriotic adherents of the King Cotton theory were burning cotton whether the enemy approached or not. With English and French millworkers on half time and charity, they believed this destruction would force recognition, if not intervention. But President Davis, knowing that cotton was needed to send back to Europe in the blockade-runners that brought arms, was concerned over too wanton a destruction. So he wrote General Van Dorn, cautioning him against "unnecessary" sabotage.

The Confederate President was stirred to the bone marrow over what was occurring in New Orleans. A fortnight after assuming command, General Ben Butler had issued an order that aroused indignation on both sides of the Atlantic. Because a New Orleans woman spat in the face of an annoying Union officer, Butler angrily released a proclamation, Number 28. "Hereafter when any female shall by word, gesture, or movement insult or show contempt for any officer or soldier of the United States, she shall be regarded and held liable to be treated as a woman of the town plying her avocation." The outrage of the South, which claimed to hold ladies in sacrosanct respect, was hardly surpassed by that expressed in the House of Commons and in the British press. Prime Minister Palmerston said in Parliament: "It is a proclamation to which I do not scruple to attach the epithet infamous! Any Englishman must blush to think that such an act has been committed by one belonging to the Anglo-Saxon race." That more cautious diplomat Lord Russell, the Foreign Minister, went so far as to say that the character of the United States was at stake in repudiating the "brutal and insulting" order.

One of the most violent protests appeared in the *Saturday Review* of June 14, 1862. "Unless the author of this infamous proclamation is promptly recalled let us hear no more of the 'ties which bind us to our transatlantic kinsmen.' No Englishman ought to own as kinsmen men who attempt to protect themselves from a handful of women by official and authoritative threats of rape. . . . The most loathsome Yahoo of fiction could do nothing filthier."

The bitterness of New Orleans ladies of French blood motivated strong remonstrances from Mercier, France's Minister at Washington. The affair soon became such a national scandal that Seward secretly began planning for Butler's removal. Nothing in the war, before Sherman's hellish march to the sea, created such hatred for "Yankees" as "Beast" Butler's rule in New Orleans, in which his alleged "thievery" and extortion equaled his harshness.

With his attention demanded by all sections of the Confederacy, Jefferson Davis was under a constant strain. And he was gravely anxious about his septuagenarian brother Joseph, who had fled from his plantation home, but now had returned to Hurricane, coming thirty miles down the river from Vicksburg in an open boat. Jefferson feared such hazardous exposure in the blistering heat; it was from this very cause that his father, of sound constitution, had died in his early sixties. Joseph telegraphed that he had taken fifteen Negroes from Hurricane and twelve from Brierfield to Jackson, Mississippi. He would have taken more from Brierfield, he said, but an epidemic of measles prevented it. With no one to look after them properly, the President was concerned, too, about the welfare of his "people."

In the midst of his anxieties for the nation, word came from North Carolina that his infant son, Billy, was dangerously ill. His "heart sank within him," and immediately he dispatched his surgeon, Dr. Garnett, with what the physician regarded as a "specific remedy." The thought of his child's life in danger made the weary Davis realize more acutely how much his family meant to him. He wrote Varina, "My ease, my health, my property, my life I can give to the cause of my country. The heroism which could lay my wife and children on any sacrificial altar is not mine."

But Davis's resilience and strength of will kept him going for sixteen or eighteen hours a day. As soon as he could dispatch essential office work, he would be off daily in the muggy midsummer heat to visit the Army. He was almost always in close proximity of the field and in continual consultation with Lee. He noted with gratification that Lee seemed to have a keen understanding of the various officers' temperaments, as well as of the condition and morale of his troops. Officers came to feel that Lee was sympathetic with their problems and valued their opinions. Every day the Commanding General rode along the lines encouraging the efforts of working parties. More than often, the President was by his side, in fair weather or foul.

"I am in my usual health though the weather has been very inclement," Davis wrote Varina on June 11. "The roads to the different positions of the Army could not be worse and remain passable. The long boots presented me by Captain Keary protect me from mud but the poor horse suffers on every ride. . . ."

He told her of a little boy he had met in the street, wading in the gutter, with his trousers rolled up. "He looked something like Jeff, and when I persuaded him to get out of the water, he raised his sunny face and laughed, but denied my conclusion."

"We are reinforcing Gen. Jackson and hope to crown his successes with complete victory over all the enemy in the Valley. . . ."

The daring that was native to Jefferson Davis fired him with the hope of a crushing defeat of McClellan. He expressed his optimism to his wife: "I will endeavor by movements which are not without great hazard to countervail the enemy's policy. If we succeed in rendering his works useless to him and compel him to meet us on the field, I have much confidence in our ability to give him a complete defeat, and then it may be possible to teach him the pains of invasion and feed our Army on his territory."

On June 11, the President saw Whiting's selected eight regiments move openly, for the benefit of Federal spies, through Richmond to the railway station and take northbound trains. When Washington heard of it, the authorities there would be still more alarmed for their capital's safety.

The President's high hopes were given a further edge by a spectacular movement of James Ewell Brown Stuart, that dashing cavalryman whom he made a Brigadier General at twenty-nine. Davis had noted Jeb Stuart's daring, his hardihood, and his inspiring leadership; and though he questioned the young man's complete reliability and discretion, no one seemed to have a better "hound-dog nose for smelling out the enemy's position." This heavy-built extrovert, with handsome large features and a ruddy beard, was an odd combination of romantic show-off and intrepid soldier. His uniform was the most eye-catching in the Confederacy, set off by a flowing cape lined with crimson and a plumed hat caught up at a rakish angle with a dazzling buckle.

At two o'clock in the morning of June 12, on Lee's instructions, Jeb Stuart had set out with 1,200 selected horsemen to discover McClellan's weakest points. Among his officers were Lee's own tall, hefty son Rooney, his nephew Fitz, John S. Mosby, Heros von Borcke, an exuberant giant of a Prussian officer on leave, and Lieutenant Colonel Will Martin, who headed the Jeff Davis Legion, which was made up of three companies from Mississippi, two from Alabama, and one from Georgia. In less than three days, Stuart's cavalry managed to ride completely around McClellan's army, capturing prisoners here and there and bringing back spoils of war. Lee got more information than he had expected. McClellan's right flank, north of the Chickahominy, under the admirable and able General Fitz-John Porter, was exposed. McClellan's supply wagons were moving slowly away from Rooney's White House on the Pamunkey.

Lee conferred with Davis. They agreed that the Confederates would have to strike soon. The rains had ceased; the roads were beginning to dry. McClellan's plan was to take Richmond by advancing by slow stages until his siege guns were close enough to demolish the Confederate works. Vainly waiting for more reinforcements, McClellan still had his army astride the Chickahominy, a position Davis regarded as somewhat critical, though the enemy had an effective force of 105,000 men in front of Richmond. McClellan had been led to believe, through the misguided reckoning of the detective Allan Pinkerton, that Lee had twice his strength in numbers. Though thinking himself outnumbered, Little Mac counted on his superior artillery to win. He expected the now-entrenched Confederates to await his attack. But Lee determined to strike first, and at McClellan's exposed right flank, north of the river. The President and the Commanding General were, as usual, in complete accord.

Lee, who lacked effective artillery and had more than 15,000 less men than his enemy, was going to take a big gamble by withdrawing over half of his force from before Richmond to fall on McClellan's right. The entrenchments, at which editors had scoffed, might be held by a third of Lee's army, while he launched an attack with the major portion. On the eve of the approaching conflict, however, Davis knew that civilian critics of Lee were still to be found on every street corner.

When the President addressed the troops defending Richmond from McClellan's besieging army, he said, "You are fighting for all that is dear to man, and though opposed to a foe who disregards many of the usages of civilized war, your humanity to the wounded and the prisoners is a fit and crowning glory of your valour." The cynical Richmond *Examiner* commented that "the chivalry and humanity of Jefferson Davis will inevitably ruin the Confederacy."

Events had continued to go brilliantly with the Confederates in the Valley. With a strength of some 16,000 men, Jackson was keeping almost 60,000 Federals engaged. As Jackson started back up the Valley toward Richmond, Frémont, from the west, and McDowell's advance guard under James Shields, from the east, were converging to annihilate him. With amazing celerity, Stonewall slipped between them. Then on June 8 he had turned and given Frémont a stinging setback at Cross Keys. Next day he whipped McDowell's forces at Port Republic. By feints, forced marches, and the habit of appearing at unexpected places and striking hard, Jackson baffled his enemies and mauled them, one after another. Old Jack's hardy men joked about the

Spartan treatment their commander gave them: "three fights a day and one meal a week." Before Whiting's reinforcements joined him, Jackson had completely demoralized the Federals, and he was ready to confer with General Lee.[4]

The President's irritation with Beauregard was mounting; he could get no satisfactory answers to his questions. "There are those," he wrote Varina, "who can only walk alone when it is near the ground, and I fear he [Beauregard] had been placed too high for his mental strength, as he does not exhibit the ability manifested on smaller fields."

By telegram, the General had announced to the War Office "a most brilliant and successful retreat," and insisted that his "constant occupation" prevented his replying as to why he had abandoned the all-important Memphis and Charleston Railroad. For the public benefit, Beauregard wrote a long letter to the Mobile *Register*. "The retreat," he proclaimed, "must be looked upon, in every respect, by the country as equivalent to a brilliant victory." Though Davis understood that it was a remarkably successful retreat, he was repelled by Beauregard's efforts to hoodwink the people.

By June 13, the President's patience had come to an end. So he sent his aide, Colonel William Preston Johnston, with a list of specific interrogations concerning what General Josiah Gorgas called Beauregard's "inexplicable" movements. Why had he abandoned the strategic railway center? Davis wanted to know. What means had he employed after the loss of Island Number 10 to prevent the descent of Federal gunboats down the Mississippi? What had been the cause of so much sickness at Corinth? Why had he not cut the Federal line of communication and retaken Nashville? What were his future plans?

But before Johnston arrived, Beauregard had left for Bladon Springs, an Alabama watering resort above Mobile. He had got "a certificate of ill-health" from his physician on June 14, and turned his forces over to Braxton Bragg. The President was unprepared for such extraordinary behavior from the commander of the largest army in the

---

[4] In praising Jackson's magnificent soldiership in that spring of 1862, Davis was to write in his *Rise and Fall of the Confederate Government*: "In all these operations there conspicuously appears the self-abnegation of a devoted patriot. He was not seeking by great victories to acquire fame for himself; always alive to the necessities and dangers elsewhere, he heroically strove to do what was possible for the general benefit of the cause he maintained. His whole heart was his country's and his whole country's heart was his."

West, who had abruptly left his command without securing official approval or even informing the Government of his reason.

When Bragg telegraphed Richmond announcing Beauregard's departure and asking for instructions, the President called a Cabinet meeting. The members were astounded to learn that Beauregard had left his post when his troops were demoralized and "the territory was threatened with conquest." With the sanction of his Cabinet, on June 20, President Davis assigned General Bragg permanently to the command of the army. Beauregard was in Mobile when he received the news from the War Department announcing Bragg's appointment. Stung, he realized he had gone too far. He promptly forwarded his medical certificate to the Adjutant General, along with the brief statement that he would be ready to resume active duty whenever ordered.

Davis was all the more eager for a smashing defeat of McClellan, because if the Confederacy could be relieved in the East, concentrated attention might be turned to making a "desperate effort to regain what Beauregard has abandoned in the West." He wrote encouragingly to Governor Pettus of Mississippi, "The heroic determination of my neighbors gives assurance that you will use effectively all the means you possess. I would they were larger and earnestly wish it were consistent for me to be with you in the struggle."

To General Martin Luther Smith, New York-born West Pointer, who had resigned from the United States Army to fight with the Confederacy and who planned the chief works at Vicksburg, Davis telegraphed: "What is the condition of your defenses at Vicksburg? Can we do anything to aid you? I hope and expect much from you." Then he reassured Mississippi and eastern Louisiana somewhat by sending them the daring cavalryman General Earl Van Dorn.

With the mounting tension in Virginia, Jefferson Davis wrote his wife on June 21: "We are preparing and taking positions for the struggle which must be near at hand. The stake is too high to permit the pulse to keep its even beat, but our troops are in improved condition and are as confident as I am hopeful of success."

He did not tell her that Lee had secretly sent for Jackson. But that same Saturday night of the twenty-first, Stonewall took the train at Gordonsville, where he left his army. He rode in a closed car, and, fifty miles before the train reached Richmond, he slipped off at Frederick's Hill Station. Then throughout Sunday he stayed secluded in the house of friends. At midnight, he set out on horseback for Richmond. After hard riding, with changes of horses, Jackson appeared at Lee's headquarters near noon "with the dust and caked mud of three Virginia counties on him."

After summoning Longstreet and the two Hills, Lee disclosed his plans for attacking McClellan. He would secretly mass a concentration of almost three-fourths of his army north of Chickahominy and destroy the Federals on that side of the river. Jackson was to bring his army immediately to Ashland, sixteen miles north of Richmond, and then move on the enemy at three o'clock on the morning of the twenty-sixth. All the preparations were predicated on Jackson's keeping his time schedule.

The President could not be present at the all-important conference. The crushing pressure of national and family anxieties had finally made him ill, and his physician had put him to bed. But General Lee informed him fully of the meeting, and he had clear in his mind the plans for the imminent battle. That night, following the afternoon conference, Davis sent his wife some lines of cheer. "I am nearly well again," he wrote. "Be not disturbed; we are better prepared now than we were at the first of the month, and with God's blessing will beat the enemy as soon as we can get at him."

His mind turned on the disappointing Gustavus Smith, whose services were specially needed now. "Gen. G. W. Smith," he wrote with a touch of sarcasm, "after the manner of Beauregard has taken a surgeon's certificate and is about to retire for a season to recruit his health." He spoke of Joseph Johnston's condition: the General was "steadily and rapidly improving." And quite as aware of Johnston's soldierly qualities as of his deficiencies, Davis wished he were able to take the field. "Despite the critics who know military affairs by instinct, he is a good soldier . . . and could, at this time, render most valuable service."

The twenty-fourth and twenty-fifth, the President spent answering telegrams and urgent letters. He endeavored to cheer the Governors of South Carolina, Mississippi, and Louisiana, who were each calling on him for some special aid. With the military situation at Richmond approaching a tremendous climax, Davis had to give attention to Confederate affairs hundreds of miles away. He promised the Mississippi Governor some long-range rifles for sharpshooters and hoped buckshot might be got from Columbus. To Governor Moore of Louisiana he explained that in all parts of the country there was "a scarcity of arms," but he would do everything he could. He ended his telegrams and letters with encouraging phrases like "in your heroic determination" and "until we shall be able to drive the invader altogether from the soil."

In the afternoon of June 25, the President saw McClellan's yellow observation balloons hanging like pale oranges in the clear aerial blue above the city. Through powerful field glasses, from the top of the Executive Mansion he could faintly trace the army of McClellan hovering on the northern and eastern skirts of Richmond. General Lee had conferred with him that morning and issued the last orders to his lieutenants. Tomorrow, June 26, would mark Lee's big gamble. In the evening, the Reverend Dr. Minnegerode called on the President, who was grateful to have his spiritual support in the hour of impending crisis.

That night, with the fate of the capital highly uncertain, Davis wrote to Varina, letting his mind turn first to family matters, then to problems in far-off Mississippi, and back to his loved ones. He was grieved that their infant boy, Billy, was now suffering from a painful affliction of carbuncles. He continued:

Van Dorn is at Vicksburg and preparing to make a desperate defense. The citizens are of one mind as to preferring the destruction to the pollution of their homes by a Yankee garrison.

Bragg may effect something since Halleck has divided his force, and I hope will try, but there is reason to fear that his army has been woefully demoralized. Butler, properly surnamed the Beast, has added to his claim for infamous notoriety by his recent orders, and report charges him with wholesale peculation and daily selling licenses for private gain. For instance, two respectable gentlemen assured me that he sold permits for the export of salt at the rate of five dollars per sack. How much better it would have been had the city been left a pile of ashes, than that it should shelter such thieves and brutes in human form. . . .

Kiss my dear children, tell them how much their father loves them and wishes to be with them.

Farewell, dear Wife. May God preserve and sustain you in the midst of the sea of troubles which surround us. . . .

Once more farewell
Your Husband

A note of foreboding had crept into the letter, as if Davis faced the awful possibility of Richmond's destruction. The desperate chance that Lee and he had agreed upon seemed the only hope for saving it. But if McDowell should arrive, or if McClellan attacked the city while Lee had most of his troops across the river, what then?

"This is the day of battle," War Clerk Jones recorded in his diary on June 26. "Early in the morning a letter from Lee arrived for the Secretary of War stating that he would be at his headquarters at the Dabbs's house or beyond that *point,* whence carriers might find him if the Secretary had 'anything of importance to communicate to him.' I suppose," continued Jones, italicizing certain words, "Mr. Randolph had been previously advised of General Lee's intention to fight today; but do not *know* it. I know some of the brigadier-generals in the army do not know it; although they have been ordered to their commands. . . . It *is* characteristic of Lee's secretiveness to keep *all* of his officers in profound ignorance of his intentions, except those he means to be engaged. The *enemy* cannot possibly have any intention of his purpose, because the spies here have no intelligence."

Acting on a suggestion of President Davis, those in the official departments, including clerks and pages, voluntarily formed "a military organization for the defense of the city and especially of the archives," which had all been put back in their proper places after Lee had superseded Joseph Johnston in command. "In the fluctuations of a great battle, almost in the suburbs," Jones commented, "a squadron of the enemy's horse might penetrate even to the office of the Chief Executive, when a few hundred musket, in the hands of old men and boys, might preserve the papers."

CHAPTER XXII

THE FURY AND FRUSTRATION
OF SEVEN DAYS

THE CHOSEN DAY of June 26, 1862, was one of peculiarly oppressive heat. Throughout the forenoon, the President, engrossed in state business, continued to keep an ear turned to the open windows for the sound of Jackson's guns. But he could distinguish nothing beyond the customary street noises of Richmond.

After the midday meal, activities in most offices ceased. Officials joined with citizens on the hill north of the Jewish cemetery to observe and listen. The President rode out on the Mechanicsville Road with Burton Harrison and some others, including the Secretary of War. Lee's plan of advance was clear in his mind: General L. O. Branch, commanding the extreme left of the Confederate line, was to cross the river immediately on hearing Jackson's signal guns. A. P. Hill, with five brigades, was to cross at Meadow Bridge and drive the Federals from the village of Mechanicsville. Longstreet was to follow in his support. Then D. H. Hill was to proceed and join up with Jackson. Altogether, the four divisions were to push the enemy southeastward down the river.

With the swift-moving Jackson already twelve hours late, at three o'clock A. P. Hill boldly advanced unsupported. As the Confederates moved into the village of Mechanicsville, a heavy Federal artillery fire assailed them. Davis, who had crossed the river before Lee, saw men dropping everywhere among the scattered houses and in the open field. When Lee arrived and began giving orders, to his dismay he discovered the President, with some of his aides, the Secretary of War, and a group of riders who had fallen in behind. Fearful for Davis's safety, Lee turned to the small cavalcade, saluted his chief, and coolly demanded, "Who are all this army of people, and what are they doing here?" All eyes turned on the President, who looked about and said deprecatingly, "It is not my army, General."

"It is certainly not my army, Mr. President," Lee replied firmly, "and this is no place for it."

"Well, General," Davis said with the smile of one in the wrong, "if I withdraw, perhaps they will follow." With a military salute, he turned his horse about. The others followed. When out of Lee's range of vision, the President reined in his horse and remained at the edge of the battlefield.

As the fighting got too hot, the Federal commander, Fitz-John Porter, who was outnumbered, gave up the village and fell back upon his stout earthworks at Beaver Dam Creek. Then Davis saw the Confederates charge in the old brave way of battle, with banners aloft and fifes tootling, while Porter's gunners and well-trained infantry blasted them. Because D. H. Hill's brigade was moving too slowly in crossing the river, the President, among others, sent him an urgent message to hurry. All through the late afternoon, Davis kept thinking, "Will Jackson never come?"

Finally, D. H. Hill got his men into the conflict in support of A. P. Hill. The sickening, futile fight went on valorously, while Porter's artillery took a frightful toll of the Confederates and made the early dusk hideous with black, billowing smoke and earsplitting detonations. It was after nine before the clamor of battle ceased. Some 1,400 Southerners lay dead or wounded, while the Federal losses were comparatively small. Jackson had not arrived. When the sun set, he and his troops were still five miles from where they had been expected before dawn. But he had sent no report of his progress to Lee or to the Generals whose movements were contingent on his presence. Lee had been able to get into action only some 15,000 of his 56,000 men north of the Chickahominy.

As a kind of mocking stillness came over the gruesome scene, the President sadly headed his horse toward Richmond. While he rode through the starlit night, the sight of the mangled dead haunted his brain and the semistifled cries of men in agony still echoed in his ears. The day's unexpected debacle weighed like lead on his heart. And he knew that Lee's critics would be busy wagging their heads and recalling his autumn failures in the mountains of western Virginia. But his own faith in Lee's abilities was not a jot shaken.

When he got home, the President was cheered to hear of the fine performance of General John Magruder before Richmond while Lee was fighting Porter across the river. That ardent amateur actor had put on such a deceptive demonstration, with drum rolls and bugle calls, marching men, feints, and occasional blasts from his batteries that McClellan was deceived into believing a major Confederate attack might be launched at any hour against his main army. Magruder had fooled McClellan as cleverly as he had in the long siege of Yorktown; and he had also deceived Generals Edwin Sumner, Joseph Hooker, and William Franklin by sporadically attacking their pickets. But for Magruder's bemusing pageantry, McClellan might have been tempted to strike at the capital while the majority of its defenders were across the river.

Though the day ended with a Union victory, at two the next morning, McClellan, expecting Jackson to fall on Porter's rear, ordered that successful General to withdraw his troops to previously selected ground five miles to the east. Near Gaines' Mill, Porter took up a strong position on rising ground that resembled a ragged semicircle. He got his artillery skillfully placed and 9,000 reinforcing troops in position before the Confederates arrived.

Jefferson Davis, on the field again,[1] saw Southerners mowed down in charge after charge. From across the river, Federal siege guns got the Confederate range, and their heavy shells caused havoc in the gray ranks. It was almost eleven before Jackson arrived, late by twenty-four hours plus another full morning. Jackson's iron strength had faltered; having had only a few hours' sleep in four days, he was not thinking clearly. His doughty fighters, who had flourished in the bracing air of the highland counties, were listless after their march over sticky roads in the debilitating heat. Lee asked for no explanations, but sat on a stump and ran over, as best he could, the present battle situation. Jackson was to march toward Cold Harbor and turn the enemy out of his strong north-south position.

Misunderstanding the directions of a local guide, Jackson got lost again and had to retrace his steps through swampy bottom land. Some hours later, when Lee met him again on the road, looking very weary and sucking a lemon, Lee said with consummate tact, "Ah, General, I am glad to see you. I had hoped to be with you before now."

[1] John H. Worsham in *One of Jackson's Foot Cavalry* (pp. 99-100) says that Davis was on the field with Lee when Jackson's troops went into action. Rhodes (Vol. IV, p. 40) writes, "Lee was in immediate command and Jefferson Davis was on the battlefield."

Late in the afternoon, when Longstreet's and A. P. Hill's men were almost despairing, they heard a rousing yell from Jackson's men as they began driving the Federals out of their works. Soon Jackson himself appeared in all his disheveled fury, directing the battle with the half-sucked lemon in his hand. Amid the shrieking din, both sides fought valiantly. Later, participants declared they had never known more furious fighting than that around Gaines' Mill. Near dusk, Lee ordered a general assault. The blue lines finally broke. Porter fell back toward the woods by the river, leaving fourteen smoking cannon. "Long lines of dead and wounded," Davis wrote, "marked each stand made by the enemy in his stubborn resistance, and the field over which he retreated was strewn with the slain." As darkness fell, more Federal reinforcements reached Porter, but too late. He had already gone back to the Chickahominy flats.

Lee had won his first victory. He had won it with forces superior in number to the enemy engaged. But never again throughout the war was he to have such an advantage. Thereafter, he would be consistently outnumbered and would win chiefly on his daring and his superior strategy.

On the morning of the twenty-eighth, the President was informed that none of the enemy remained north of the Chickahominy. Pressure had been taken off the capital. Davis could respond feelingly to Lee's first official message of victory, beginning with the characteristic expression "Profoundly grateful to God." Yet he was saddened because the cost in Southern youth had been so great.

In the midst of the relief at the capital's safety, it pained Burton Harrison to lay a telegram from Vicksburg on his Chief's desk. The message had been dispatched on June 26, delayed in transit, and reached Richmond only on the twenty-eighth. Mr. Davis, seeing the look of solicitous sympathy on his young secretary's face, took up the half-sheet hesitantly. He read the telegraph operator's scrawl:

Well-authenticated rumour comes that enemy burned yours and your brothers houses and quarters night before last, light seen from this place, enemy advancing slowly.

M. L. Smith

When the first newspaper reports appeared, Davis wrote his wife philosophically: "You will have seen a notice of the destruction of our home.[2] If our cause succeeds we shall not mourn over any personal dep-

---

[2] Brierfield, however, was not destroyed, though Hurricane was burned to the ground.

rivation; if it should not, why, 'the deluge.' I hope I shall be able to provide for the comfort of the old negroes."

On June 27, the very day of Lee's victory at Gaines' Mill, President Lincoln issued an order creating the Army of Virginia, to consist of three departments, one of which was McDowell's army at Fredericksburg. Any reinforcements for McClellan from McDowell now seemed out of the question. That night, McClellan decided to make a full retreat, which he preferred to call "a change of base." He would slip away to Harrison's Landing on the James, where he would have the protection of Federal gunboats. It was a colossal undertaking: he had to move down between the Chickahominy and White Oak Swamp and then across the swamp with 100,000 men, 4,000 supply wagons, 350 big guns, and 2,500 beef cattle on the hoof. McClellan planned his retreat with expedition and remarkable skill.

During the lull of the twenty-eighth, Lee was compelled to wait until McClellan's purpose was revealed. In the meantime, he dispatched Stuart's cavalry and Ewell's infantry to cut the York River Railroad, which brought McClellan's supplies from the base at the White House on the Pamunkey. That night, President Davis visited several commands along the entrenchments on the south side of the Chickahominy. The enemy were still behind their works, but the next morning at sunrise it was discovered through field glasses that they were gone. McClellan was retreating toward the James. General Lee went over to the south side of the river to direct pursuit movements. Magruder was sent forward. He found the whole line of Federal works deserted and quantities of military stores abandoned or destroyed. Behind the enemy's fortifications, the terrain was so densely wooded and so intersected by swamps that reconnaissance was all but impossible. The regular roads were strongly guarded. Around three o'clock in the afternoon, near Savage's Station, Magruder attacked the Federal rear guard and inflicted considerable damage. McClellan abandoned over 2,000 sick and wounded in hospitals, after destroying the medical supplies that might have cured them or alleviated pain. As the Federals plunged into the dismal White Oak Swamp, Davis knew that a full retreat was under way.

At Savage's Station, Little Mac had paused in giving orders to send a bitter dispatch to Secretary of War Stanton: "I have lost this battle because my force was too small. . . . I have seen too many dead and wounded comrades to feel otherwise than that the Government has not sustained this army. If you do not do so now, the game is lost. If I save this army now, I tell you plainly that I owe no thanks to you or to any other persons in Washington. You have done your best to sacrifice this army."

The morning of Sunday, June 30, dawned "cloudless and calm," but it was an exciting awakening for Jefferson Davis. On this day, General Lee expected to destroy the retreating, grandly equipped Army of the Potomac. Then European recognition and an early end to this horror of slaughter would come.

Davis knew that Lee had made dispositions to enable Jackson, A. P. Hill, Longstreet, Huger, Magruder, and Holmes to converge on the Federals' moving army and cut it to pieces. Deaf old General Theophilus Holmes was ordered to bring his men from the south side of the James and occupy the heights of Malvern, toward which McClellan was moving. Huger was sent down the Charles City Road with his artillery to flank the Federals. Longstreet was routed down by the Darbytown Road. Jackson was ordered to cross the Chickahominy by the Grapevine Bridge, to proceed a short way along the river, cross White Oak Swamp from the north and be ready to join Magruder's troops on the south end or strike quickly wherever there was most need.

On Sunday afternoon, near Frayser's Farm and not far from the hamlet of Glendale, Longstreet and A. P. Hill initiated a stubborn battle against the Federal rear guard, expecting Jackson to appear and Huger's artillery to open up and cover the infantry's advance. When President Davis arrived at the battlefield about half past two, the Federal artillery fire was making a terrific uproar. Finding General Lee in an exposed field of brown sedge, he was much upset. "Why, General, what are you doing here?" he demanded solicitously. "You are in too dangerous a position for the commander of the army."

Lee replied that he was trying to find out something about "the movements and plans of those people." He always spoke of the Northern invaders as "those people." Then, with an odd smile, he countered, "But you must excuse me, Mr. President, for asking what *you* are doing here, and for suggesting that this is no proper place for the Commander-in-Chief of all our armies."

"Oh," Davis answered amiably, "I am here on the same mission that you are."

Waiting for the sound of Huger's answering guns, each restrained his sense of frustration. Neither yet knew that Huger's road was obstructed by felled trees and that he did not have sufficient axes to clear the way.

Suddenly, Federal shells began to burst very close. A. P. Hill, riding up, was amazed to see the President and General Lee calmly chatting. "This is no place for either of you," he said sharply. "As commander in this part of the field, I order you both to the rear."

Davis smiled and said pointedly, "*We* will obey your orders." He did not intend for Lee to stay behind in danger. When he rode off, Lee followed. After a few paces, Davis halted, not yet out of range. Hill again admonished them. "Did I not tell you to go away from here, and did you not promise to obey?" He made a pointing gesture. "Why, one shot from that battery over yonder may presently deprive the Confederacy of its President and the Army of Northern Virginia of its commander."

Bowing slightly, Davis and Lee rode off out of range, as the artillery fire grew more brisk. Just after three, Lee received a report that the enemy was now swiftly moving south toward Malvern Hill, an estate that had once belonged to his grandfather. This was bad news, because Malvern Hill was within gunshot of the Federal armored boats on the James. Neither Jackson nor Huger had yet arrived; McClellan might escape. Lee decided he must make a reconnaissance in person. Finding the report true, he sent orders for General Holmes to bring up his entire division and open fire on the retreating columns. But General Holmes had gone a roundabout way to occupy Malvern Hill and now he was too late. He was caught in a cross fire between McClellan's artillery and the gunboats on the river. Magruder with 18,000 men was ordered to his rescue.

Davis, tormented by the delays, saw the golden opportunity of crushing McClellan slipping away fast. On hearing of the new situation near the river, he galloped down and came upon General Lee returning. Once more the President admonished the General for exposing himself rashly. Lee again excused himself by saying that he could get accurate facts in no other way. The association of Lee and Davis on those battlefields, as Rhodes has pointed out, cemented a friendship already close: "each had affectionate concern for the other's safety." And Davis, with his own impetuous nature, could silently commiserate with Lee as frustration followed frustration.

After numerous unforeseeable delays, the main Confederate advance near Frayser's Farm began around five o'clock. The small num-

ber of Confederates engaged fought with determined fury. In impetuous charges, the infantry defied the Union grape, canister, and
shrapnel tearing into their ranks. Men charged with bayonets to silence the Federal batteries, and used musket butts to bash in enemy
skulls. As dusk came on, J. R. Anderson's brigade, yelling like Co-
manches, moved up and delivered a deadly volley at close range.
The Federals, believing that fresh reserves had entered the fray,
turned and fled, leaving guns, muskets, knapsacks, and jackets behind
them.

Everything in the way of captured equipment that President Davis
looked upon was immeasurably superior to that of his Confederates.
In abandoned Federal camps, there was an air of comfort and abundance. The Southern harness was so old and sun-dried that it
could scarcely hold together. Most of the rickety army wagons belonged to a former generation. The grimy Confederate uniforms were of
varied colors: gray, brown, and blue taken from fallen foes. The clothes
of some soldiers were little more than pieced rags. If only, the President thought in vain, he could give his men equipment half comparable to that of the enemy and food as plentiful as theirs!

Neither Jackson nor Huger arrived in time to take any part in the
Battle of Frayser's Farm, which ended in a minor Confederate victory.
If they had, Davis was convinced that McClellan's army "would have
been riven, beaten in detail, and could never, as an organized body,
have reached the James River."

In his official report, Jackson stated that "the marshy character
of the soil, the destruction of the bridge over the marsh and creek, and
the strong position of the enemy for defending the passage prevented
my advancing." But no satisfactory explanation was ever given to
General Lee or anyone as to why the usually swift Jackson failed to
get into action that fateful Sunday of McClellan's escape. The pious
General had fought, though against his will, on other Sabbaths. It had
taken him until noon to rebuild the Grapevine Bridge across the
Chickahominy because a Federal rear guard "obstinately resisted" the
action. Then, when he got to White Oak Swamp, where he found other
bridges destroyed, he did not reconnoiter, but merely sat down, silent
and apart. While McClellan's columns were marching to safety just on
the other side of the swamp, Jackson was writing a letter to his wife,
mentioning his loss of sleep and giving her instructions about church
contributions; she was to keep an account, for he was a confirmed believer in tithing.

General Wade Hampton, who had made an exploration of the swamp and found a comparatively easy way to cross it, eagerly reported the good news to Jackson, who was at the time sitting moodily on a fallen tree. Jackson inquired if he could build a bridge at the spot. "Yes, one strong enough for the infantry," Hampton replied. "Build it," Jackson ordered. When Hampton returned and said the job was done, Jackson regarded him with disinterest. After a painful silence, he got to his feet and stalked away.[3] At the supper table, the commander fell asleep with a bite of biscuit between his teeth. Major Robert L. Dabney, Stonewall's chief of staff and admiring biographer, could explain the General's behavior only by thinking that sleeplessness and physical exhaustion had caused his genius to suffer a temporary eclipse. Most expert commentators believe, as Davis did, that if Jackson had acted with his usual dispatch and vigor, he would have wrought McClellan's utter ruin.

President Davis was sickeningly aware that Jackson's failure, whatever the reason, to get to the battle around Frayser's Farm resulted in the loss of a climactic and momentous opportunity for the Confederacy. He saw that Lee's plans, by which Jackson, Longstreet, the Hills, Magruder, and Holmes were to converge on the enemy and hem him in for destruction, had failed woefully. Some 50,000 of the Confederates had not got into action, though the majority of them were close enough to hear the cannon's roar. It was clear to Davis that Lee's magnificent strategy had been foiled by the mismanagement or poor judgment of trusted lieutenants and by a general lack of knowledge of the terrain. Lee "bore grandly his terrible disappointment," and made no allusion to it. Davis uttered no word in criticism.

The next day, July 1, when Lee approached Malvern Hill, McClellan's artillery was posted in such a strategic way that it could blast the oncoming Confederates from any direction. The cool Fitz-John Porter had taken a position that appeared impregnable. One hundred death-dealing guns stood menacingly in tiers, some of them hub to hub. D. H. Hill, pugnacious by nature, advised Lee against attack. But Longstreet pooh-poohed hesitation. "Now that we have them on the run," he said, "is no time to get scared."

While belated troops were marching toward the base of Malvern,

[3] The incident is related in Charles Marshall's *An Aide-de-Camp of Lee*, pp. 111-112. Another version of the story says that Jackson merely pulled his old fatigue cap down over his eyes as a signal of dismissal. Frank Vandiver believes that Jackson's delay at Grapevine Bridge was caused not by listlessness, but by some order from army headquarters.

General Jubal Early rode up to Lee and ventured to remark that he feared the enemy would escape. The frustrated Lee, who had been holding in his wrath, glared at him and replied, "Yes, he will get away because I cannot have my orders carried out."

Though he realized that it was a desperate position on which to make a frontal attack, Lee ordered an advance. In the hot afternoon, the Southerners moved across a wide exposed meadow. When the Federal guns began playing upon them, a few turned and fled. The rest went doggedly on up the slope under a murderous fire, forced back the Federal infantry, and compelled some batteries to retreat to prevent capture. The Confederates charged, in Lee's opinion, with "a heroism seldom equalled." The sloping ground became thickly strewn with Confederate dead. Along the edges lay hundreds of large trees felled by the terrible Federal guns.

Around six o'clock in the evening, Magruder got into the fray with his 18,000 men. After having his orders to aid Holmes countermanded, he had got lost in the woods and, acting on earlier orders, which had also been countermanded—though in the confusion he was not informed of it—the dashing Prince John attacked McClellan's strongest position, the left flank. Boldly, he thrust his men forward up through thick underbrush to be blasted to bits by exploding shells, while other Generals looked on in horror. Finally, about nine o'clock, firing ceased. By an informal truce, lanterns appeared from both sides, and litter bearers began to carry off the maimed and mangled.

That night, General Lee, with nerves on the ragged edge, sent for Magruder. "Why did you attack?" he demanded coolly.

Magruder, stung at the implied rebuke, answered steadily, "In obedience to your orders, twice repeated." Lee said nothing further.

Tension was manifest throughout the camps. Brigadier General Toombs challenged his superior, D. H. Hill, to a duel. At one point during the furious artillery fire that day, Toombs had found his brigade unsupported and beginning to straggle. So he had ordered his men to double-quick obliquely to the left and lie along a rail fence in the high weeds. In this dubious, protective position, Hill had discovered him. The stern West Pointer from North Carolina upbraided the proud Georgian and ordered him to resume the advance immediately. Boiling with rage, embarrassment, and a sense of injustice, Toombs did so. But as soon as the day's fight was ended, putting his personal grievance foremost, he sought out the busy Hill and demanded satisfaction. Hill declined to apologize or to accept the challenge. Smarting and sulking, Toombs managed to transfer the blame for his humiliating experience to Jefferson Davis and West Pointers. A few days later, he was to write that other arch-malcontent Vice-President Stephens that Davis and the regular army men were conspiring to destroy all who did not bend to their will.[3] When personal woes came, though brought on entirely by the individuals themselves, many Southerners became adept at laying the blame on their President.

Ironically, as after Manassas in July of 1861, the morning of July 2, 1862, dawned with a heavy downpour, adding to the misery of the suffering wounded. When General Lee prepared to resume conflict, he was incredulous to find that the enemy's position was entirely deserted, except for their stiffened dead and some of their wounded who had been left for dead. Still under the misapprehension that Lee outnumbered him, McClellan had ordered Porter to withdraw; in the darkness, the Union troops had silently slipped away to Harrison's Landing. The drenched and exhausted Southerners, who had been soundly beaten the day before, had little will to pursue a superior force that had several hours' start on them.

But, finally, a minor pursuit was begun, with Jeb Stuart and his cavalry in advance. Stuart had just returned from further reconnaissance at the White House on the Pamunkey, McClellan's former headquarters. Hundreds of thousands of dollars' worth of Federal supplies were burning, by McClellan's order, but Stuart's men had put out the fires and salvaged much booty. The house on the historic dwelling site, however, was only a smoldering ruin; "not a vestige left," said Stuart, "except what told of desolation and vandalism." McClellan, in retreat, had not been able to stop his men's depredations.

Lee ordered Longstreet and Jackson to go in pursuit, but the torrential rainstorm impeded their progress. With minor harassment, the Federals reached the region of beautiful estates and the protection of the formidable gunboats.

While the North celebrated Independence Day with dampened ardor, War Clerk Jones wrote rejoicingly that a fatal blow had been dealt the Army of the Potomac. "The serpent has been killed, though

[3] Years later, as footnote to his unhappy experience at Malvern Hill, when the blustering Toombs mocked Georgia's handsome General John B. Gordon for stroking the battle scar on his cheek in a political campaign, Gordon sent word that if Toombs had a scar to stroke, it would certainly not be on the cheek of his *face*. At Antietam, however, Toombs did receive a wound, when his left hand was shattered by a rifle ball.

its tail still exhibits spasmodic motions. It will die, so far as the Peninsula is concerned, after sunset, when it thunders." But after he had surveyed the enemy's position on July 4, Lee wrote the President, "As far as I can now see, there is no way to attack to advantage; nor do I wish to expose the men to the destructive missiles of his gunboats."

Davis was constrained to agree with Lee's decision, though he suffered, in the words of Freeman, "much inward distress that a *coup de grâce* could not be administered to the foe." In truth, he was bitterly disappointed that McClellan's grand army had not been destroyed. The President replied to General Lee: "It is hard necessity to be compelled to allow him [the enemy] to recover from his discomfiture and to receive reinforcements, but . . . I fully concur with you as to the impropriety of exposing our brave and battle-thinned troops to the fire of the gunboats."

Davis, however, could not quite accept the fact that McClellan had reached a completely "safe" position. He hoped that damage could yet be done the disconcerted Federal force. In the same letter of concurrence, he offered to send Lee "two guns on traveling carriages to open fire on their batteries," and said he would direct Colonel Gorgas to send "some burning shells with the hope that you can use them against the enemy's encampments and perhaps his boats, or in the event of night operations they may serve to guide as well as to conceal your advance." Clearly, he was inviting the Commanding General to consider further harassment, if not all-out attack.

After offering his personal attention to the execution of anything Lee should ask for, he closed his letter by renewing his caution against "personal exposure either in battle or reconnaissance." With affectionate concern, he emphasized, "It is the duty to the cause we serve for the sake of which I reiterate this warning."

That same day, July 5, Jefferson Davis sent an address to the Army. As President, he tendered the thanks of the entire country "whose just cause you have so skillfully and heroically saved." "Ten days ago," he said, "an invading army, vastly superior to yours in numbers and the material of war closely beleaguered your Capital and vauntingly proclaimed our speedy conquest. . . . With well-directed movements and death-defying valor you charged upon him in his strong positions, drove him from field to field . . . compelled him to seek safety under cover of his gunboats. . . . A grateful people will not fail to bear you in loved remembrance." Then he ended with a strong reminder that the men were not to rest on their laurels. "But duty to a suffering country and to the cause of constitutional liberty claims from you yet further effort. Let it be your pride to relax in nothing that can promote your future efficiency; your one great object being to drive the invader from your soil, and, carrying your standards beyond the outer borders of the Confederacy, to wring from an unscrupulous foe the recognition of your birthright and independence."

This was the first public hint he had given of carrying the war into enemy territory, an idea that he and Lee had been considering and for which Jackson had been itching since the Bull Run rout almost a year before. At last, enough armaments were arriving from Europe and production at home had so increased as to enable the Confederate Government to consider invasion.

While never much given to "if onlys" after an event, Davis must have thought dismally of Jackson's sitting on one side of White Oak Swamp while McClellan pursued his orderly retreat within a few miles of Stonewall's seasoned warriors. And, with his military training, he may have considered, as did many less understanding men, that Lee's direct attack on Malvern Hill, where so many Confederates were sacrificed in the open, was something like a tactical error. "Nearly all the observers and writers," Rhodes later concluded, "agree that Lee's generalship at Malvern Hill was clearly defective. The attack is condemned and the execution of it is censured." But it was Lee's bold defiance, Davis knew, that had made McClellan the more convinced that the Confederates outnumbered him and had caused him to give up his powerful position on the heights of Malvern.

Though the last battle had been extremely costly to the Confederates—half of their losses at Malvern were from artillery—the result was that McClellan had left the field to his opponents. The sum of Confederate casualties during these days was appalling: 3,200 dead, 16,000 wounded, and almost 1,000 missing; in round figures, a total of 20,000. Federal casualties, at first thought to be greater, proved to be less: 15,700 in all. But Lee had captured fifty-two pieces of artillery, 35,000 much-needed muskets, and other small arms and supplies, and about 5,000 prisoners, including two generals, George A. McCall and John F. Reynolds.

Jefferson Davis was inexpressibly relieved that Lee had pushed McClellan's mighty army twenty miles farther from the capital. And he was convinced that Robert E. Lee was the only soldier in the Confederacy who could have saved Richmond. The psychological effect of the capital's loss would have been disastrous to the spirits of the people. Now, from a bold and menacing attitude, the enemy had been reduced to one characterized by McClellan himself as "safe" under the protection of Union gunboats. The North's high expectation for a quick possession of Richmond had vanished. Lee's success had given the stamp of prestige to Southern valor. Official Washington was in irate despair.

The joy of the Richmond citizens at their deliverance from the hands of the enemy was greater than any they had known since the Federal rout at Bull Run. But this time, in the words of an eyewitness, Prussian Major von Borcke, the people accepted their good fortune "with very becoming composure. No powder was wasted in salutes over the victory, no bonfires blazed, no windows were illuminated." With some, the feeling of relief was too deep for outward demonstration. Others had remained relatively calm throughout the siege, because their President had resolutely assured several delegations that the capital would not be evacuated. Relief in general was tempered by anxiety for what was yet to come. Lincoln's immediate call for 300,000 new men for three years' service increased apprehension.

But Confederate conscription was bearing fruit. On July 5, Jones wrote: "General Lee is bringing forward conscript regiments with rapidity; and so large are his powers that the Secretary of War has little to do. . . . The correspondence is mostly referred to the different bureaus for action, whose experienced heads know what should be done much better than Mr. Randolph could tell them."

Lee was no more content with the total result of the Seven Days' Battles than was the President. In his report he wrote: "Under ordinary circumstances, the Federal army should have been destroyed." He did not refer to Jackson's wrecking tardiness, nor did he lay blame on other subordinates who had failed to carry out his instructions.

In a letter of July 6 to his wife, Davis endeavored not to let the extent of his own disappointment show through. "Had all Lee's orders been well and promptly executed," he said dispassionately, "there would have been a general dispersion of McClellan's army. . . . Our success has been so remarkable that we ought to be grateful."

Davis was as much aware as McClellan that a few thousand more Federal soldiers might have given the latter a victory. By withholding McDowell's men from reinforcing McClellan, Secretary of War Stanton had failed to get Richmond, but he had damaged the effulgent reputation of the nation's most popular Democrat, who was already being mentioned as a Presidential candidate. In one sense, Davis could feel sorry for Little Mac in his struggle against Republican politicians. And he could appreciate the masterful organization of his retreat and the skill with which he had checked the advance of the Confederates. But with such a superbly disciplined, superbly equipped, and almost fanatically loyal army as McClellan possessed, Davis could not see why Little Mac had given up the siege. "The mustering clans" of his own fighting temperament would, under the circumstances, never have called retreat. "McClellan certainly showed capacity in his retreat," Davis wrote to his wife, "but there is little cause to laud a general who is driven out of his entrenchments by a smaller and worse-armed force than his own and compelled to abandon a campaign in the preparation of which he had spent many months and many millions of dollars and seek safety by flying to other troops for cover, burning his depots of provisions and marking his route by scattered arms, ammunition, and wagons."

Now that the peril had been removed, Jefferson Davis felt the incubus of fatigue heavy upon him. Every day he had been in proximity to the battlefields and in continual consultation with Lee. Some mornings he had risen at half past four and had not reached home until near midnight. Often he had covered forty miles on horseback, in rain or in suffocating dust. His sensitive, compassionate nature had been oppressed by the agony of the wounded, the sight and sound of rattling death wagons, the loss of personal friends. He was in extreme need of release from the tension caused by the strain and the horror.

But there was yet no surcease for him. Reports arrived indicating that all the Federal forces available were to be sent to the James River and one tremendous effort made to defeat the Confederates at Richmond. In the face of more impending trouble, he could write his wife reassuringly, "I am in my usual health." While confessing to her that the Army was "greatly reduced," he could hope recruits would be "promptly sent forward from most of the States." With sanguine assurance, he declared, "There are many causes which will interfere with the execution of the enemy's plans, and some things they have not dreamed which we may do. If our ranks were full we could end this war in a few weeks. There is reason to believe that the Yankees have gained from England and France as the last extension, this month, and expect foreign intervention if we hold them at bay on the first of August. . . . Our troubles have not ended but our chances have improved so that I repeat 'Be of good cheer.'"

Though the *Examiner* grumbled that Lee had let McClellan slip through his fingers, and the disgruntled Toombs wrote Stephens that Lee was "far below the occasion," Jefferson Davis was gratified that the people at large looked upon Lee as their deliverer. "The result of Lee's first month of command," wrote Frank Alfriend, "made evident to the world the wisdom of the President in that choice, which was at first declared the undeserved reward of an incompetent favorite." And on July 18, the Richmond *Whig* declared: "Lee has amazed and confounded his detractors by the brilliancy of his genius, the fertility of his resource, his energy and daring. He has established his reputation forever." The *Whig* editorial set the pattern for posterity's judgment. Lee had proved that he had the high qualities on which Jefferson Davis had staked his judgment of men.

While the South breathed easier, panic assailed Wall Street. President Lincoln, sunk in gloom, was bitterly criticized by the Radicals, who began demanding that he take a public stand against slavery, which McClellan sternly admonished him not to do. Now for the first time, as Burton Harrison, his young secretary, wrote, Jefferson Davis felt sure that, even against the insuperable odds, the South would win its independence.

CHAPTER XXIII

HIGH HOPE AT HOME AND ABROAD

AT LENGTH, the President received family letters giving details of the vandalism on Davis Bend. Though he expected bad feeling in the Union Army against anything connected with the name of Davis, he thought Hurricane would be spared because his aged brother had taken no part in the war. But it had been demolished with savage celebration. The books from Joseph's detached Greek-temple library had been removed and made into bonfires about the lawn. For some unexplained reason, the denuded building was left standing. The sets of china and glass had been taken out of the main house, dumped on the grass, and shivered with muskets. The paintings were slashed with bayonets.[1] Finally, the mansion itself was burned to the ground. While the President believed that the Joseph Davises were safe in Vicksburg, he grieved for the loss of their home, for his brother was seventy-five now and Eliza was a confirmed invalid.

Brierfield, Davis learned, had suffered a somewhat different fate. It was first ransacked; souvenirs were appropriated by individual soldiers. Among the items taken was a gold-headed cane, a prized gift from President Pierce. The furniture was then destroyed. Over the house's portico in huge painted letters the Federals mocked: "This is the house that Jeff built." Then some astounded Negro "contrabands" brought from other plantations were ordered to move into Jeff's house and live there. It seemed a good way of showing contempt for the Confederate President.

Jefferson Davis was particularly indignant at the treatment of Uncle

[1] Details of the vengeance wreaked on Hurricane and Brierfield are taken from Lise Mitchell's manuscript "Journal" and from conversation with Lise's daughter, Mary Lucy O'Kelley of Pass Christian, Mississippi.

Bob and Aunt Rinah. The aged Negroes were robbed of the stack of blankets he had bought for them before his departure for Montgomery. Ben Butler's boys accused the protesting couple of stealing, because they deemed the blankets far too good for slaves. To Bob and Rinah, "Yankees" were an incredible new kind of "white folks."

In contrast to the shameful news from Mississippi came good reports of the seemly behavior of McClellan's men in the rich region of plantation homes around Harrison's Landing. On July 7, from his camp, McClellan had written President Lincoln a kind of lecture. The war should be "conducted upon the highest principles known to Christian civilization. It should not be at all a war upon population, but against armed forces and political organizations. Neither confiscation of property, political executions of persons . . . or forcible abolition of slavery should be contemplated for a moment. In prosecuting the war all private property and unarmed persons should be strictly protected. . . . All private property taken for the military use should be paid or receipted for; pillage and waste should be treated as high crime; all unnecessary trespass sternly prohibited and offensive demeanor by the military towards citizens promptly rebuked." McClellan had scrupulously attempted to abide by his own high ethics.

On July 8, Jefferson Davis learned that the Confederate Army had abandoned its position in the region of Malvern Hill and was returning to the vicinity of Richmond. Lee took up his old headquarters, a mile and a half from the suburbs, and was in daily consultation with the President. President Lincoln brought Major General Henry Wager Halleck from Mississippi and made him General in Chief of the Federal armies. While the bookish, methodical Halleck was getting oriented in his new position, Lee repaired the ravages made by the Seven Days' Battles and reorganized his forces as a regular army. It was no easy task to co-ordinate the individualistic Southerners, either the gentlemen or the hillbillies. Davis did all in his power to strengthen Lee and to fill the gaps in the ranks and the officer lists. To ease the strained relations between Lee and Magruder, the President sent Prince John to command the District of Texas. General Huger, who had made such a poor showing in the Seven Days' Battles, was relieved of active duty and named Inspector of Artillery and Ordnance. Lee dispatched the energetic D. H. Hill to Petersburg, thirty miles south of Richmond, to begin construction of fortifications there.

Since the Battle of Manassas, a year before, Jefferson Davis, under staggering difficulties and despite glaring deficiencies, had created something beginning to resemble a compact engine of war. Out of seeming nothing, he had set up foundries and rolling mills at Selma, Atlanta, and Macon, a chemical laboratory at Charlotte, smelting works at Petersburg, a superior powder mill, with artificial niter beds at six scattered cities to supply the mill. Iron and lead mines had been opened; manufactories for the production of nitric and sulphuric acid were put in operation.

Inspired by Lee's victory, volunteers all over the Confederacy were joining up for three years. The response to conscription received a new impetus, despite the monotonous croaking of Vice-President Stephens, down in Georgia. "There is nothing," Stephens wrote, "that has given me half so much concern lately as these military orders and usurpations. Not even the fall of New Orleans. . . . Better in my judgement that Richmond should fall . . . than that our people should submissively yield obedience." [2]

In the midst of the difficult army reorganization, Jefferson Davis was disquieted to see the Richmond *Examiner* stirring up jealousies among Confederate generals. The paper extravagantly praised A. P. Hill, gave him the chief credit for victory, and ignored Longstreet, his direct superior. The indignant Longstreet defended himself in print and pointed out the editor's errors. Hill became infuriated at "Old Pete," and asked to be transferred to another command. When Hill refused to speak to one of Longstreet's staff officers, who had come on official business, Longstreet put him under arrest. A rumor of an impending duel ran through the camps.

But a new Federal menace was looming to the north. General John Pope, who had been given command of the three scattered armies in northern Virginia, was planning a direct offensive on Richmond. In an ill-advised, bombastic first order, Pope professed utter contempt for Southern soldiers and irritated the Union forces under him. "I have come to you from the West," he announced belligerently, "where we have always seen the backs of our enemies." Shortly, he issued a series of orders which served to make war on the noncombatant population.

Jefferson Davis was deeply shaken by the change Pope advocated from civilized to uncivilized warfare.

In four general orders between July 18 and July 23, Pope announced

---

[2] Allen Tate, in his *Jefferson Davis* (p. 134), condemned Stephens as "the bitterest enemy of his own administration." "He and the Governor of Georgia," wrote Tate, "did everything that disgruntled ingenuity could devise to cripple the war power of the Confederacy."

that the Army would as far as possible "subsist upon the country."
The cavalry would employ no supply or baggage trains of any description, but be given cooked rations for two days, and then lay all
the villages and neighborhoods through which they passed "under
contribution." Citizens living along the line of march would be punished for any injuries to track or road by bands of unknown guer-
rillas. Men who refused to take the oath of allegiance to the United
States would be banished from their homes, and if found anywhere
within Federal lines, or at any point in the rear, they would be considered as spies and "subjected to the extreme rigor of military law."
A person within the lines who communicated with the enemy was liable to the death penalty. Thus, a mother who sent her son a letter could
be regarded as a spy.

Davis was soon informed that Pope's soldiers had ransacked private homes and shot grazing cattle in the field. Some of his lieutenants
had sought to augment the horrors of civil war by arming slaves. Brigadier General Adolph von Steinwehr had seized upon innocent and
peaceful inhabitants, who were held as hostages, "to the end that they
may be murdered in cold blood," if any of his soldiers were killed by
some unknown persons whom he designated as "bushwhackers." Mc-
Clellan himself did not hesitate to denounce Pope as an "upstart
braggart," a mere political tool of the Radical Republicans, and a man
who mistook brutality in warfare for power.

President Davis addressed a strong letter to General Lee: "We find
ourselves driven by our enemies in their steady progress towards a
practise we abhor, and which we are vainly struggling to avoid. Some
of the military authorities of the United States seem to suppose that
better success will attend a savage war in which no quarter is to be
given and no sex to be spared. For the present we renounce our right
of retaliation on the innocent and shall continue to treat the private
enlisted soldiers of General Pope's army as prisoners of war; but if,
after notice to the Government at Washington . . . these savage
practices are continued, we shall reluctantly be forced to the last resort of accepting war on the terms chosen by our foes, until the outraged voice of a common humanity forces a respect for the recognized
rules of war. . . .

"You are therefore instructed to communicate to the commander-
in-chief of the armies of the United States the contents of this letter
. . . to the end that he may be notified of our intention not to con-

sider any officers hereafter captured from General Pope's army as prisoners of war."

In no sense did President Davis intend to allow the Confederate Army's actions to approximate those promulgated by Pope, unless his protests should fail. But, as when he stopped President Lincoln from shooting captured Confederate seamen as pirates, Davis had to take a stand, however revolting to his nature, firm enough to impress Pope and Stanton.

Lee was completely in accord with the President's order to notify the United States War Department that he would be forced to retaliate if Pope's stern orders were enforced. When Lee spoke of Pope in one of his dispatches and in private letters as the "miscreant" Pope, he used the term with Webster's definition: "destitute of conscience; unscrupulous, villainous." Lee could forgive his nephew Louis Marshall for fighting with the North, Freeman said, but not for joining Pope, for whom he had intense personal dislike as well as contempt.

General Halleck refused to accept Lee's letter because he said it contained insults to the United States Government. But the letter had good results. Pope's orders were considerably modified on August 14, and Steinwehr was reprimanded for the conduct of his troops.

When the cocky Pope advanced down to the town of Culpeper, General Lee and the President began to plan their strategy with the double purpose of destroying Pope and drawing McClellan from his James River base to protect Washington. On July 12, Jackson, who appealed directly to the President in his eagerness for an invasion of the North, had been ordered up to Gordonsville, thirty miles south of Culpeper, to keep an eye on Pope. Within a fortnight, when there was no indication that McClellan was going to make a demonstration, A. P. Hill, with 12,000 men, was sent to strengthen Stonewall.

McClellan, who reported 101,000 men present for duty on July 20, still believed himself outnumbered and was vainly waiting for reinforcements before again attempting to capture Richmond. His men, who continued to adore him, were beginning to believe with Little Mac that President Lincoln had sacrificed him to the clamor of a political faction.

When the news of McClellan's retreat reached London, it had such a stimulating effect on sympathy for the Confederacy that on July 18 the United States Minister, Charles Francis Adams, wrote his son,

"This reverse called out at once all the latent hostility here. . . . I shut myself up, went to no parties and avoided contact with everyone except friends."

President Davis received encouraging reports from the Confederate commissioners abroad, who had been most active since their arrival. In England, James Murray Mason, who possessed rare personal charm, had his social calendar filled with invitations from British gentry. Even if he did persist in chewing tobacco, everywhere he went he won friends for the South. The propaganda machine headed by Henry Hotz, editor of the *Index,* was doing effective work in convincing Europe that the Confederacy had the determination and strength to maintain itself. The *Index* continually attacked the Lincoln Government's policy of arbitrary arrests and imprisonments, its high tariff, its violations of freedom of the press, and pointed up, in contrast, the Confederacy's respect for personal liberty and its leaning to free trade.

At heart, England wanted the South to win, not only because her natural sympathies were with the Southern people, but because she was not at all averse to a weakened U.S.A. Though Lincoln had a superlative ambassador in the cultured Charles Francis Adams, many of the American agents abroad were hurting the Northern cause by their strident R-rolling speech and aggressive manners. Britain was still outraged by Butler's reported barbarity and thieving in New Orleans, particularly his notorious Order Number 28, which rendered any lady the prey of unrestrained drunken soldiers.

On July 20, many members of Parliament, friendly to the South, crowded Mason's headquarters and talked of bringing the matter of intervention before Parliament again. "England is seriously moved," Mason wrote his wife that same day; "and I shall look now speedily for intervention in some form."

Davis knew that public sentiment in France was divided because of the slavery question. But the French Government, which had ambitions in Mexico and needed cotton, wanted the South to win. John Slidell, Confederate commissioner, had been received with special courtesy in Paris, and was far more intimate at the court than was the American Minister. On July 16, Slidell had a most encouraging interview with the Emperor, which lasted an hour and ten minutes. When he left the Emperor, Slidell understood that Napoleon wanted to intervene for the South and was only waiting for England to join him.

After McClellan's defeat, Henri Mercier, the French Minister in Washington, sounded out Seward. "Be assured," Seward said menacingly, "that the Emperor can commit no graver error than to mix himself in our affairs." He gave Mercier the impression that the United States would immediately declare war on France if there should be any kind of intervention.

But Mercier was not convinced by Seward's bluster. On his own initiative, he had visited Richmond in mid-April to consult with his old friend Judah P. Benjamin and others, because Seward kept insisting that the majority of nonslaveowners longed for the opportunity to return to the Union. Though Mercier's visit had occurred just after Shiloh, following the loss of the Tennessee forts, when the Confederacy's prospects looked grimmest, he had left Richmond with the ingrained idea that the South was set on winning independence. Benjamin had admitted that it was quite possible that all the seaports and cities might be captured, but, he declared, the enemy would find only women and children, for the fighting men would have gone to the mountains to "wage ceaseless warfare until the northern armies had withdrawn from the South." Mercier had talked also with Lee, Wigfall, Clement Clay, and various private citizens. He had returned to Washington convinced that if necessary the South would fight until its population was exterminated. Now with Lee's recent victory, Mercier's belief in the Confederacy's strength was confirmed. He took care that his ideas should be known in Europe.

The night of July 16, while London newsboys were crying out falsely that McClellan and his whole army had been captured, William S. Lindsay, the shipbuilder, made a motion in Parliament demanding mediation. Lindsay pointed out that intervention would not mean taking sides with slavery, because slavery had "long since ceased to be considered the cause of the war." Protective tariffs and desire for power and markets were the motives of the North, he maintained, while the South sought only self-government. He felt that, in its just cause, the South was destined to win ultimately without intervention, but the war would be long drawn out, and, if for no other than selfish reasons, England should intervene to stop the war because of the impending ruin of the cotton industry in Lancashire. England had less than 200,000 bales of cotton, he said, as compared to 1,200,000 at the same time in 1861. Operatives completely out of work already numbered 80,000; some 370,000 others were on half time, and unemployment was increasing alarmingly. He insisted that an insurrection of laborers stared England in the face unless cotton could be obtained by intervening and stopping the war.

Though nothing definite was done about mediation, on July 25, United States Consul Thomas Dudley in Liverpool wrote sadly to Seward: "The current is against us and strong; and threatens to carry everything with it. . . . They are all against us and would rejoice in our downfall. . . . I think at this time we are more in danger of intervention than we have been at any previous period . . . if we are not successful in some decisive battle within a short period this government will be forced to acknowledge the Confederacy or else be driven from power."

While President Davis, of course, had no knowledge of Dudley's letter, it accorded with impressions of European opinion he was receiving from numerous sources. And a letter from the realistic Slidell, written that same July 25, lifted his spirits high. "I am more hopeful," he said, "than I have been at any moment since my arrival in Europe."

July, 1862, was, altogether, a month of rallying hope for the Confederacy. Cheering news came to President Davis from the western theater of war. Between the fourth and the twenty-eighth, that bold Confederate cavalryman Colonel John Hunt Morgan made four successful small raids on Union forces in Kentucky and Tennessee. Nathan Bedford Forrest, now an independent commander, captured Murfreesboro, Tennessee, and its Union garrison on July 13. On the fifteenth, the Confederate ram *Arkansas* steamed out of the Yazoo River into the Mississippi just above Vicksburg to win special fame.

Davis was particularly elated by the incredible exploit of the *Arkansas*, a homemade ironclad that had been floated down the river from Memphis in a half-finished stage, and run up into the swamp-bordered Yazoo. In late June, Farragut's fleet had managed to pass Vicksburg's batteries and join the Union fleet from up the river. Thirty-seven enemy sloops and other ships converged to break down the resistance of, to use Van Dorn's phrase, "the beautiful and devoted city." Under the command of a middle-aged Kentuckian and onetime U.S. Naval Lieutenant, Isaac Newton Brown, the *Arkansas* had been pieced together with railroad iron and a variety of makeshift materials, which had to be transported from a railroad twenty-odd miles away. Without regular shipwrights, and using farm hands and infantry for sailors, Brown got his rust-colored monster moving on July 14. The next day, singlehanded, the *Arkansas* battled thirty-seven warships of the combined fleets of Farragut and Flag Officer Charles H. Davis.

After furious firing for days, the *Arkansas*, with a crew reduced to twenty, routed both Federal fleets. Before the month ended, Farragut turned his battered ships and headed south, while the flotilla from the north steamed back toward Memphis.

The naval siege of Vicksburg had been foiled. "The most disreputable naval affair of the war," wrote the seething Gideon Welles, "was the descent of the steam ram *Arkansas* through both squadrons." President Davis received a telegram from Van Dorn: "Glorious for the navy, and glorious for her heroic commander"; and another a week later: "The failure was so complete that it was almost ridiculous." Brown was everywhere praised as a master of ingenuity, as well as for his gallantry.[3]

Yankee ingenuity had long been a byword, but the ingenuity of the easygoing Southerners in war astounded the Northerners and surprised the Southerners themselves. Davis was pleased with his people's resourcefulness, as shown by the building of a formidable, if crazy, ironclad in a swamp. From home-industry foundries, which sprang up all around the Confederacy, serviceable small arms were now being manufactured. Opium poppies were cultivated to get desperately needed painkillers. Nitrogen was extracted from urine for gunpowder. Patriotic ladies carefully saved the contents of their night jars, wherefrom, in the words of James Street, many a good Northerner "hit the dust."

At the end of July, on the twenty-ninth, the Confederate cruiser *Alabama,* which had been constructed semisecretly, slipped out of Liverpool Harbor, to be manned and commissioned at sea near the Azores with the brilliant Captain Raphael Semmes in command. The President expected great success for Semmes.

A Cincinnati paper of July 30 used for the first time in print the term "Copperhead" in reference to Southern sympathizers in Ohio and Indiana. In the so-called Copperheads, with their vocal and *sub-rosa* opposition to the war, Davis saw another sign to brighten the Confederacy's chances. In August, as Lee prepared his advance against General Pope, Jefferson Davis had sound reasons to be sanguine.

In the Federal armies, there was conflict of demands. Pope wanted McClellan's men to reinforce him, while McClellan continued to demand reinforcements from Pope's forces. On August 3, General Hal-

[3] On August 5, while Brown was recuperating from a wound and fever, the *Arkansas* pushed her unpredictable engines too furiously on being ordered to Baton Rouge to help General Breckinridge in a land attack. When her engines failed completely, she was abandoned and her powder magazines exploded to save her from enemy capture. Her dazzling career had lasted just twenty-three days.

leck settled the matter by ordering McClellan to abandon his James River base and send his troops by water transport to the vicinity of Washington. McClellan was astounded to be reduced to an inferior command.

While he had not yet taken Richmond, he had by no means given up his object. His army was in prime condition and he was planning an attack on Richmond by way of Petersburg (Grant's ultimate way in 1865). In Professor Randall's opinion, Lincoln, "having withheld from his chief General the full use of the armies in the East, now submitted to the Radical clamor for his removal." "The promotion of Pope to the high command," Randall declared, "was one of those measures of amateurish experimentation in which the authorities at Washington so often indulged."

McClellan protested that his own withdrawal from the James would be "disastrous." But Stanton ignored his protest and was soon to deny him any command of active duty. On August 9, as McClellan prepared to move, Jackson fought Banks at the foot of Cedar Mountain, drove him back with heavy loss, and then quickly slipped away across the Rapidan.

On August 15, President Davis said farewell to Lee as the Commanding General left Richmond by train. Resolute in spirit, Lee purposed to move fast now to ruin Pope before McClellan's huge force could join him. With Longstreet's corps, Lee followed Jackson up the valley. President Davis expected the best.

An infectious optimism that ran through the South caught War Clerk Jones. "We have also news from Missouri of indications of an uprising which will certainly clear the state of the few Federal troops remaining there," he wrote on August 17. "The *draft* will accelerate the movement. And then if we get Kentucky, as I think we must, we shall add a hundred thousand to our army!"

The next day's entry in his diary was tinged with increased excitement: "From Texas, West Louisiana, and Arkansas, we shall soon have tidings. The clans are gathering, and 20,000 more, half-mounted on hardy horses, will soon be marching for the prairie country of the enemy. Glorious Lee! and glorious Jackson! They are destined to roll back the dark clouds from the horizon."

That day, August 18, in an atmosphere of table-turned optimism, the Confederate Congress convened. On the twenty-first, President Davis gave his message to Congress. "The vast army which threatened the capital of the Confederacy," he announced, "has been defeated and driven from the lines of investment, and the enemy, repeatedly foiled, is now seeking to raise new armies on such a scale as modern history does not record, to the subjugation of the South. . . . The perfidy which disregarded rights sacred by compact . . . has been intensified by the malignity engendered by defeat."

On August 23, the second major campaign in the region of Bull Run began. Out of Thoroughfare Gap, Jackson, stealthy as a tiger, having rounded Pope's right flank, fell savagely on his rear. Davis knew that the intrepid Stonewall was again fighting according to his chosen maxim: "Attack at once and furiously." At Manassas Junction and at Bristoe, the Confederates celebrated with monumental bonfires, as they destroyed Pope's supplies and feasted on captured delicacies.

When the infuriated Pope turned north to flay Jackson, he found that he had vanished from Manassas. By the time he did meet him, Lee and Longstreet, with reinforcements, were ready to assail the Federals, who were now reinforced with McClellan's troops.

The second great battle of Manassas on August 30 ended in a whopping Confederate victory and another Federal rout resembling Bull Run. On September 1, a final conflict at Ox Hill sent Pope scurrying to the entrenchments of Washington. General Lee established headquarters at Leesburg, a few miles from the Potomac. Never had Jefferson Davis's hopes for the South been so high.

Varina was with him to share his happiness. During the second Battle of Manassas, Mrs. Davis had returned from Raleigh for a brief visit to Richmond, bringing with her the second boy, three-year-old Joe, for minor medical attention. She had left the three other children in care of Mr. Davis's niece Helen Keary and a nurse. In having some of his family with him, the President could let down somewhat from the battle tension he was under. He never failed to be interested in the childish doings of his offspring. And now he enjoyed a letter from his eldest and favorite, seven-year-old Maggie, often called "Polly."

Raleigh
Aug. 28, 1862

My dear Father:

We are all well. Jeffie and I have been sick, but we are well now. Billy is so sweet, he is growing fast and laughs so loud. Jeffie and I say our lessons everyday and nearly always get 9. This ink that I am writing with, I made myself with red paint.

Please, Father, let me come home. We love to be with you.

Kiss our dear Mother and sweet little Joe for me. Cousin Helen and Jeff join me in love to all. Your daughter,

Polly

In the two months following Lee's seven days' drive against Mc-Clellan, the change of fortune in the Confederacy had been almost magical. The entire Federal campaign in Virginia had been thrown into dismay and confusion. The foe had been driven back to Washington. The Shenandoah Valley, with its late summer harvest, was again in Confederate possession. Union forces had been withdrawn hastily from the Carolina coasts. In Tennessee and Kentucky, Southern troops were reclaiming lost towns and territory. On August 12, Colonel John H. Morgan had captured the Union garrison at Gallatin, Tennessee. And, on the twenty-eighth, Braxton Bragg had set out from Chattanooga on his Kentucky campaign: destination, Ohio. On August 30, Kirby Smith won a battle at Richmond, Kentucky.

A pall had fallen over the North. Washington was gripped by fear. Pope's demoralized men were in no mood or condition to make an effectual resistance. In the grim extremity, President Lincoln acted, completely contrary to the desires of Stanton and Salmon Chase and a host of Radical Republicans. He turned to the one man who could save Washington. Calling on McClellan at his home during breakfast, he humbly pressed him to assume again full command of the Army of the Potomac. While Stanton fumed and Chase declared he would rather lose Washington than return the command to McClellan, Lincoln sagely ignored his advisers and pinned his hope on Little Mac, who alone had the dynamic appeal to rally the disheartened troops. Never, it was reported, was cheering among soldiers for an adored commander more heart-deep or vociferous than when McClellan was restored to them.

According to George Kimball of the Twelfth Massachusetts, "From extreme sadness we passed in a twinkling to a delirium of delight. . . . Whenever General McClellan appeared, men threw their caps high into the air and danced and frolicked like schoolboys. The most extravagant demonstrations were indulged in. Hundreds even hugged the horses' legs. It was like a great scene in a play with the roar of guns for accompaniment."

CHAPTER XXIV

ANTIETAM AND A STRANGE
PROCLAMATION

AFTER Second Manassas, Davis knew that Lee had to make some prompt movement, either withdraw or go forward. Information was received that the Federals were expecting 60,000 replacement troops at Washington, besides the vast army already there. The harvests of western Maryland were said to be bounteous. The green corn was ripe; the apples, red. If other supplies failed, the men could subsist on stewed fruit and roasting ears. And if the Federals could be drawn out of their Washington defenses, Richmond would not be molested.

On September 3, 1862, Lee decided to cross into Maryland. That day, Davis received a dispatch from him that he would do so unless the President objected. "As long as the army of the enemy are employed on this frontier," Lee said reassuringly, "I have no fears for the safety of Richmond." He added that, if results justified, he purposed to carry the war into Pennsylvania.

President Davis had more or less pledged himself to an invasion across the Potomac "whenever it should prove practical." Heretofore, the might of the enemy and the lack of arms had prevented this. Now was perhaps the psychological time, since he had Lee to lead the Army of Northern Virginia. So he gave his Commanding General carte blanche.

Jefferson Davis was keyed up in anticipation. The stakes were sky high. If Lee won one decisive victory beyond the Potomac, Marylanders would doubtless rise and throw off the Federal tyranny that had held them under martial law for more than a year. The peace party in the North would cry aloud for war's cessation. European recognition would inevitably follow, and the Confederacy would be an independent nation.

Davis already believed that when the complete news of the Federal defeat at Second Manassas reached England, recognition might follow. He did not know that on September 2, Mercier, the French Minister, had advised his Government that, owing to the crushing defeats of Northern armies, the time was near when the North might accept mediation.

But Davis was not easy in his mind when he considered the numerical disparity between Lee's forces and the enemy army in the vicinity of Washington. He knew that Lee's forces were tragically under strength and markedly inadequate in equipment. Lee, too, was fully aware of the hazardous risk he was taking. "The army is not properly equipped for an invasion," he wrote the President. "It lacks much of the material of war, is feeble in transportation, the animals being much reduced, and the men poorly provided with clothes and in thousands of instances are destitute of shoes. . . . What concerns me most is the fear of getting out of ammunition."

A more deterrent factor, which neither the President nor Lee had allowed for, was wholesale straggling. When Lee's army approached the Potomac, a great many of the tired soldiers balked. Thousands began to lose themselves in the woods. They felt they had done enough in chasing Yankees out of Virginia. They wanted to go home now and attend to their farms or businesses, or to have a rest before they fought again, if they ever had to. After a fortnight of constant movement and fighting, some of them were just too frazzled to march farther. Others limped painfully on bleeding bare feet. Even Lee's magical influence failed to hold his men, and the cavalry had to be employed to round them up.

A perturbed Lee wrote the President: "Our great embarrassment is the reduction of our ranks by straggling, which it seems impossible to prevent. . . . Our ranks are very much diminished—I fear from a third to one-half of our original numbers." In that first week of September, when he desperately needed every available man, Lee lost between 10,000 and 20,000, many having claimed they were morally opposed to invasion.

Yet, resolutely, Lee marched into Union territory. During the two days' crossing of the Potomac at White's Ford, from both shores ragtag regimental bands persistently played "My Maryland!" As they waded the stream, the tattered troops lustily sang the rousing words "The despot's heel is on thy shore, Maryland! My Maryland!"

On September 6, the President received word that Lee's army had crossed the river without opposition. Lee's next dispatch to him was dated "Headquarters, Frederick City, Maryland, September 7."

As Lee approached Maryland, Davis had written him: "It is deemed proper that you should, in accordance with established usage, announce by proclamation, to the people of Maryland, the motives and purposes of your presence among them at the head of an invading army." He then proceeded to give suggestions of certain points to touch upon.

Lee issued a proclamation on September 8, in which he said: "The government of your chief city has been usurped by armed strangers; your legislature has been dissolved by the unlawful arrest of its members; freedom of the press and of speech has been suppressed; words have been declared offences by the arbitrary decree of the Federal Executive, and citizens ordered to be tried by a military commission for what they may dare to speak. . . . Our army has come among you, and is prepared to assist you with the power of its arms in regaining the rights of which you have been despoiled. . . . It is for you to decide your destiny, freely and without restraint. This army will respect your choice, whatever it may be; and while the Southern people will rejoice to welcome you to your natural position among them, they will only welcome you when you come of your own free will."

The President had the hope that if Lee won a victory, Maryland, at this late hour, might yet secede, which event would spark recruitment in Kentucky, where the Confederates were currently winning victories. Because so many ardent Southerners from Maryland were already fighting with Confederate troops, Davis had reason to expect a more demonstrative reaction from the citizens than was forthcoming. But it was the blue-blooded Eastern Shore counties that so favored the Confederacy. These western Marylanders, with a large German-blooded population, were on the whole pro-Union.

Many persons, however, received Lee rapturously. Others were afraid to show their colors for fear of neighbor spies and reprisals. But for policy's sake, even loyal Federals set out tables of piled food for the hungry soldiers, who gorged themselves on white bread and country butter, real coffee, cakes, and pies, and succulent apple dumplings. For two days, the soldiers shopped in the local stores, buying items they had not seen in a year, and paying for them with Confederate currency.

The Southern boys did not make an altogether happy impression on the scrubbed and prosperous citizens of Frederick. One youth in particular, Leighton Parks, looked with amazement on the ill-kempt, ragged army that had whipped the Yankees in Virginia. Later, he set down his impressions for *Century Magazine*. "They were the dirtiest men I ever saw, a most ragged, lean and hungry set of wolves. Yet there was a dash about them that the Northern men lacked. They rode like circus riders."

The day Lee delivered his proclamation, he wrote to President Davis suggesting that the Confederacy should make a proposal of ending the war, based on recognition of its independence. "Being made when it is in our power to inflict injury upon our adversary, would show conclusively to the world that our sole object is the establishment of our independence and the attainment of an honorable peace." If Lee's army was successful, Davis was to join him, and, at the head of his victorious troops, the President of the Confederacy would offer peace to the North. With this coming just before the approaching Congressional elections, if the Republican Administration refused mediation, Northern voters might be likely to return the peace-party Democrats to power with such a Congressional majority that President Lincoln would have to accede to Southern independence. Davis awaited the event.

On September 9, believing from his knowledge of McClellan that he would make no sudden rush on the Confederates, Lee sent Jackson back across the Potomac to capture Harpers Ferry, with its Federal garrison of 12,000 and its valuable concentration of ordnance and supplies. That same day, in Richmond, War Clerk Jones wrote gleefully in his diary, "Lord, what a scare they are having in the North! They are calling everybody to arms for the defense of Philadelphia, and they are removing specie from Harrisburg and all intervening towns." The whole Confederacy was keyed up with high expectations, while the North shuddered in contemplating another possible Seven Days or Second Manassas.

In the meantime, in an effort to halt future straggling, Lee requested the President to create a permanent court-martial invested with authority to decree the death penalty. He also asked for extension of the conscription law to include able-bodied men up to forty-five years of age.

When the President promptly recommended to Congress the passage of the measures, a terrific uproar and debate ensued. Alabama's Senator William Yancey, who had become increasingly anti-Administration, proposed a return to the old volunteer system as a solution to the problem. Finally, the eloquent rabble-rouser went so far as to declare on the Senate floor that he preferred conquest by the enemy to the despotism of Jefferson Davis. Congress continued the debate while Lee pushed on in Maryland.

While Lee was moving from Frederick to Hagerstown, from which he might more easily march on Harrisburg, Pennsylvania, Benjamin brought the President a discouraging letter from Slidell. Dated August 24, it had been written just before the triumphant engagements around Manassas began. Slidell had lost hope of England's joining France in intervention, because he cynically believed that England desired "an indefinite prolongation of the war, until the North shall be entirely exhausted and broken down." Nothing would help the Confederacy now, he declared, but "a strong and continued current of important successes."

Well, Davis reflected, that is what the Confederacy had recently scored. And now Lee in Maryland was expecting a victory on Union soil. Davis and his Secretary of State believed the action of Europe hung on Lee's success. But they did not know how rosy for Confederate hopes the current climate of British opinion really was.

Top British statesmen were feeling that the situation in America justified an offer of mediation to the warring sections. On September 14, with apparent relish, Palmerston, the Prime Minister, wrote the Foreign Secretary, Lord Russell, about the "very complete smashing" the Federals had received from the Confederates on August 29 and 30. "It seems not unlikely," he said, "that still greater disasters await them, and that even Washington and Baltimore may fall into the hands of the Confederates." If that should happen, Palmerston asked if Russell did not think England and France might "recommend an arrangement upon the basis of separation."

Three days later—while shrieking shells were whizzing across Antietam Creek—Russell replied: "Whether the Federal army is destroyed or not, it is clear that it is driven back to Washington, and has made no progress in subduing the insurgent States. . . . I agree with you that the time is come for offering mediation to the United States Government, with a view to the recognition of the independence of the Confederates."

At this most golden hour, however, the future of the Confederacy was blighted by the loss of two sheets of paper. On the morning of September 12, Sergeant John M. Bloss and Private B. W. Mitchell of Company E, Twenty-seventh Indiana, lay down to rest in the grass on the recent Confederate campsite near Frederick. One of them spied a long envelope, which contained three cigars wrapped in two sheets of official-looking paper.[1] Together, they read incredulously a copy of General Lee's Special Order 191. Addressed to Major General D. H. Hill, it was signed by Colonel C. H. Chilton, Assistant Adjutant General. Eight paragraphs revealed Lee's full plans for the next four days, the dispositions of his forces, and their positions at the hour. The excited soldiers ran with the document to their colonel, who rushed it to McClellan.

At first McClellan suspected it to be a ruse, but a staff officer who coincidentally had known Chilton in happier days recognized his handwriting. Making the most of such fantastic good luck, the careful, slow McClellan, with unaccustomed celerity, decided to move on Lee immediately, while the Confederate forces were divided. Within an hour, staff officers were dashing off in various directions, giving orders that put the vast Union Army in forward motion.

The mystery of how such a vitally important document could be lost has never been solved. In the 1870's, Jefferson Davis was still trying to get more enlightenment on the subject from Colonel C. H. Chilton, who had made out and dispatched the order. D. H. Hill was able to produce a copy, which had been sent to him by his brother-in-law, Stonewall Jackson, who presumably did not know that Hill had been given an independent command when the Confederates had crossed the river. This copy was in Jackson's handwriting. The copy Lee had sent directly to Hill was the one that fell into McClellan's hands. Did one of Hill's staff officers keep it as a souvenir and then inadvertently lose it? Dr. Dodd declared simply, "It was lost by the carelessness of D. H. Hill." Whether Hill or a subordinate lost the order, the circumstance should have been reported immediately. Longstreet had taken care to

---

[1] According to his testimony in *Antietam and the Lost Dispatch*, it was Bloss who found the envelope, which contained *two* cigars. In *Battles and Leaders* (Vol. II, p. 603), Colonel Silas Colgrove of the Twenty-seventh Indiana stated that Private Mitchell found the order wrapped around three cigars.

chew his order to bits. In any case, the failure of the Maryland campaign was due in large part to the lost dispatch.

Lee had reached Hagerstown on the eleventh and was eagerly awaiting word announcing Jackson's capture of Harpers Ferry. But unexpected and disquieting news reached him that McClellan had his plans and was already marching over Catoctin Mountain. Before daylight of the fourteenth, Lee quickly left Hagerstown and retraced his steps. A small battle was fought on South Mountain that day, and on the fifteenth, Lee took a position behind Antietam Creek, a half mile in front of the little town called Sharpsburg.

On September 15, President Davis received good news. At eight o'clock that morning, the Federals had surrendered Harpers Ferry and the "impregnable" position of Maryland Heights. The capitulation included the Union garrison of 12,000, seventy pieces of artillery, and 13,000 small arms. Leaving A. P. Hill, with 4,000 men, in charge of the prisoners and the booty, Jackson was preparing to join Lee at Sharpsburg.

While Lee was struggling desperately to pull his divided army together before McClellan struck, a messenger in hot haste brought him the word of Jackson's complete success at Harpers Ferry. "Let the news be announced to the troops!" the elated Lee cried. Orderlies dashed off along the lines announcing Jackson's great haul. The soldiers cheered and cheered and cheered. But it was the Confederates' last cheering for weeks to come. As McClellan's 87,000 men marched on cautiously but relentlessly, it was no longer Pennsylvania's cities that were endangered; it was Lee's under-strength army that was in peril.

The fighting Major von Borcke, aide to Jeb Stuart, questioned Lee's sagacity in accepting battle at Sharpsburg. He had it from Lee's own lips that the Commanding General had less than 40,000 men, including Jackson's, for the impending conflict, which was to stretch four miles along Antietam Creek. As he and General Stuart passed the "thin lines of our ragged, weather-beaten soldiers, many of them without shoes," the Prussian said he did not think the Confederates equal to the impending contest.

When Jackson arrived from Harpers Ferry on the sixteenth, he was incredulous on learning that McClellan had moved so swiftly. In Richmond, all that day, the President tensely awaited battle dispatches. But, fortunately, McClellan was not ready until the morrow.

In the chilly dawn of September 17, Federal General Hooker led the onset of battle that became known as "the bloodiest day of the war." Men on both sides fought as if the destiny of their homeland and their posterity depended on its outcome. Young men heroically gave up their lives in cornfields and orchards, beside country churches and along the creek bank. The carnage was more frightful than any veteran had ever seen.

Around four o'clock, when Lee's central position was almost in the grasp of assaulting Federals, A. P. Hill's division arrived from Harpers Ferry, dressed in new blue uniforms captured with the arsenal. Only when they began to fire at close range did the Federals recognize them as Rebels. McClellan's advance was checked. The fierce Battle of Antietam was over; it had ended in a draw.[2] Lee still held his battle-ground. But his invasion of the North had been halted. McClellan had saved Washington, and perhaps, as it turned out, the Union.

All the next day, the eighteenth, Lee's depleted army waited to be attacked. Though Lee himself strongly considered attack, he could not do so against the arrayed Northern might. Reinforcements greater than McClellan's losses were said to be arriving to swell the opposition. The Confederates lacked the manpower for a countermove. There was little to be gained by remaining longer north of the Potomac. That night, on Jackson's and Longstreet's advice, Lee, with heavy heart, decided to withdraw. Orders went out. The retreat got smoothly into motion. Lee saved his army and all his supplies, leaving nothing for the enemy but three hundred men so severely wounded that they could not be transported.

Shortly after sunrise, the entire Confederate Army had safely crossed the river into Virginia. Lee sat on his horse in the stream, watching the passage of men, artillery, wagon trains. When the last of the wagons bearing the wounded came in sight, General John W. Walker heard Lee murmur, "Thank God!" A bone-weary soldier, who paused for a last backward look as he stepped out of the water onto Virginia soil, cried disgustedly, "Damn My Maryland!"

When Lee crossed the Potomac back into Virginia on that September 19, 1862, the curve in the Confederacy's fortunes turned decisively

[2] According to Rhodes (Vol. IV, p. 153), the Union loss at Antietam was 12,410; the Confederate, 11,172. Freeman (Vol. II, p. 408) says that Lee sustained 13,609 casualties in killed, wounded, or captured in the whole Maryland campaign, while Federal casualties, including the loss of Harpers Ferry garrison, amounted to 27,767. Freeman comments: "A commander who disposes in thirteen days of enemy forces exceeding 50 per cent of his entire army is not usually charged with failure."

downward. Never again was President Davis to know such golden prospects for independence.

For his own purposes, President Lincoln chose to regard the drawn Battle of Antietam as a Federal victory. With a sense of history upon him, he reached into a pigeonhole and drew out an Emancipation Proclamation, which he had devised two months before and laid by on Seward's warning that a time of Federal defeat was not propitious for announcing it. Calling his Cabinet, Mr. Lincoln informed them amiably that he was not seeking their counsel, but merely telling them what he was going to do: release the document to the press.

Lee's failure to win the Battle of Antietam was as cutting a disappointment to Jefferson Davis as it was to the General himself. And if Lee had been victorious, the Emancipation Proclamation would certainly have been postponed and probably never have been issued.

Scrupulously careful not to let Lee get a hint of his discontent, Davis sent Custis to his father to console him, but ostensibly to communicate ideas not prudent to put in writing. Then he dispatched a long letter reviewing military affairs in various sectors. An important bit of good news was that Congress had acceded to the wishes of Lee and Davis and raised the conscript age limit to forty-five. The President hoped that the supply of shoes that the Quartermaster General had been directed to send to Winchester had reached him and "relieved our barefoot soldiers." Davis closed on a warm note of reassurance: "I am alike happy in the confidence felt in your ability and in your superiority to outside clamor, when the uninformed assume to direct the movements in the field. . . . In the name of the Confederacy I thank you and the brave men of your Army for the deeds which covered our flag with imperishable fame."

Lee was touched by the President's moral support. "I wish," he replied, "I felt that I deserve the confidence you express in me. I am only conscious of an earnest desire to advance the interests of the country and my inability to accomplish my wishes."

In commenting on military affairs, the President did not mention the new annoyance created by Beauregard. He left it to Custis to tell his father what he would of the vexing problem. During his six weeks' stay at Bladon Springs and Mobile, Beauregard had whiled away the time by corresponding with certain anti-Davis editors. He conducted a little press campaign to counteract newspaper charges that he had made serious errors in the West. He prepared a glowing article, extolling himself for his conduct at Shiloh, and his faithful aide, Colonel Jordan, sent it to the Savannah *Republican,* under Jordan's name, as that of "a staff officer on the scene." Davis had read the piece with much resentment, for Beauregard attempted to belittle Sidney Johnston.

On August 25, Beauregard had again informed the War Department that he was ready to report for duty. At the same time, he had written to his Congressman brother-in-law, Charles Villeré, that he desired the Western command. On August 29, however, orders were drawn in the War Office appointing Beauregard to head the Department of South Carolina and Georgia, with headquarters in Charleston. Davis regarded it as a highly important post, for which "the hero of Sumter" was eminently fitted. Outraged at not getting a field command, Beauregard pressed his brother-in-law to stir up friends to demand that the President return him to the Western command. In the meantime, he prepared another grand, but impractical, plan for an offensive, and sent copies to both Bragg and Cooper.

On September 13, while Davis's attention was riveted on Lee in Maryland, two Congressmen from Louisiana presented a petition on Beauregard's behalf. The President read the entire document aloud in their presence, including the fifty-odd signatures at the end. Calling for the official correspondence that bore on Beauregard's removal, he read that aloud, too. He reminded the petitioners that Beauregard had left his army without permission. Though the General was doubtless in need of rest, he was not seriously ill, for the newspapers reported that he was wined and dined by Augusta Evans, the popular novelist, and others in Mobile, where he played the social lion, however unwilling. "The General should have stayed at his post," Davis declared emphatically, "even if he had to be carried about in a litter."

A vision of himself lying seriously wounded the morning after the Battle of Buena Vista may have risen before Davis. He had been waiting for an ambulance to take him back onto the battlefield to rally his troops when word came from Zachary Taylor that his presence would not be required because the enemy had retreated during the night. In any case, for the sake of the Confederacy, the President would not reappoint a general to a command that he had previously bungled. "If the whole world," he flatly told the committee, "were to ask me to restore General Beauregard to the command which I have already given to General Bragg, I would refuse it."

In bad temper, Beauregard went to Charleston, while his admirers stored up new rancor against the President.

On September 22, Abraham Lincoln issued his proclamation of emancipation. To Davis, it seemed hardly a proclamation at all, but a warning that the President of the United States would declare free all slaves in the Confederacy unless the rebellious states returned to their allegiance by January 1, 1863. He noted particularly that slaves were to be free only in those states where Federal law was a nullity. The border states of Maryland, Kentucky, and Missouri, so divided in sympathies, were excluded, and also the Union state of Delaware, which had slaves.

Davis had heard rumors that Lincoln might make a gesture of freeing the slaves, as Seward had hinted in interviews with foreign ministers in which mediation was suggested. Seward had darkly implied to France's Mercier that the blacks would rise in bloody revolt, and that, in consequence, the whole economic and social system of the Southern whites would be destroyed, along with cotton, the coveted commodity.

Though of course Davis did not know it, Sumner had told Lincoln on July 4, 1862, in the gloom of McClellan's defeat before Richmond, that he needed not only more men at the North, but "at the South, in the rear of the Rebels." In other words, he should make use of the slaves to fight the Confederacy. Lincoln had replied—according to Sumner's account of the interview[3]—that he would issue the edict of emancipation if he were not afraid half of his officers would fling down their arms and three more states secede.

On July 13, Lincoln had taken a long carriage ride with Seward and Welles to sound them out on emancipation. In his diary, Welles reported: "He . . . said he had about come to the conclusion that it was a military necessity . . . for the salvation of the Union." At a Cabinet meeting on July 22, President Lincoln had read aloud a draft of his proposed edict. Seward counseled postponement. At a time when the public mind was depressed by the recent reverses of the Seven Days' Battles, he declared, "it would be considered a last *shriek* on the retreat." Seward thought the measure should be presented to the country only if supported by a military success. Lincoln temporarily laid the document aside.

[3] The story is told in Sumner, *Works,* Vol. VI, p. 31, in his letter of August 5, 1862, to John Bright in London.

In the tense days of early September, when Washington feared Confederate seizure, President Lincoln had received a religious delegation from Chicago who petitioned him to decree national emancipation. The President's attitude was negative. "I do not want to issue a document," he said wryly, "that the whole world will see must be inoperative like the Pope's bull against the comet." And, practically, he asked, if multitudes of Negroes did throw themselves upon the North, "what should we do with them, how could we feed them?"

However, at a Cabinet meeting on the Monday following the doubtful battle at Antietam, Montgomery Blair had been the only Secretary to offer substantial objections to issuing a proclamation; he feared the effect on the approaching Congressional elections and adverse reactions in the Border States.

Lincoln, the realist, knew perfectly well that he had no way of enforcing his law. But he believed it might do the Confederate war effort harm by stirring up unrest among the slaves, in effect, making the Negroes allies of the North. And he had his mind on England and France, as well as on the disaffected Abolitionists in his party.

Not in 1862, or ever, did Mr. Lincoln pretend that the Emancipation Proclamation was anything but a war measure. To the goading Horace Greeley, he was perfectly frank in stating that expediency guided his policy. Lincoln, in truth, had little concern with the Negro per se. He directly blamed their presence in Anglo-Saxon America for the terrible war that was going on. He could foresee no bright destiny for Negroes in the United States, and, by his own testimony, he wanted them out of the country. His views and attitudes were clearly stated in a little speech he made to a delegation of prominent free men of color on August 4, 1862, only a few weeks before the release of his proclamation. The speech and circumstance were printed in the New York *Tribune* of August 15, 1862.[4] Mr. Davis, who, like General Lee, assiduously read Northern papers to get special information and to gauge the temper and climate, had read with some surprise Mr. Lincoln's explicit and frank sentiments about Negroes in the *Tribune*.

For some time, President Lincoln had cherished a phenomenal plan of getting Negroes out of the country by colonization. A Congressional act providing $100,000 for the colonization of former slaves of the District of Columbia had become law on April 16, 1862. And

---

[4] The speech is included in *The Collected Works of Abraham Lincoln,* Vol. V, pp. 370-375, edited by Lincoln authority Roy P. Basler.

on July 16, an act had been approved by which slaves in the hands of the Federal Army were freed and $500,000 was granted for their deportation. Since October, 1861, Mr. Lincoln had been interested in the "Chiriqui Project," whereby Negroes might be settled in Central America. On the afternoon of August 14, when the President gave audience to the committee of colored men, who wanted to know his opinion of their future in America, he came quickly to the point. He said that a sum of money had been appropriated by Congress and placed at his disposition to aid the colonization of persons of African descent, and he confessed it was "his duty, as it had for a long time been his inclination, to favor the cause."

"Why should people of your race leave this country?" he asked kindly, and answered his own question with remarkable candor: "You and we are different races. We have between us a broader difference than exists between almost any other races. . . . This physical difference is a great disadvantage to us both, as I think your race suffers very greatly, many of them, by living among us, while ours suffer from your presence. In a word, we suffer on each side." He deplored the great wrong that had been inflicted on the Negroes by bringing them to America. "But even when you cease to be slaves," he said with painful frankness, "you are yet far removed from being placed on an equality with the white race. . . . On this broad continent, not a single man of your race is made the equal of a single man of ours."

When one of the visitors made a movement as if to protest, Mr. Lincoln quickly said, "I do not propose to discuss this, but to present it as a fact with which we have to deal. I cannot alter it, if I would. . . . I need not recount to you the effects upon white men growing out of the institution of Slavery . . . see our present condition—the country engaged in war!—our white men cutting one another's throats, none knowing how far it will extend. . . . But for your race among us there could not be war, although many men engaged on either side do not care for you one way or the other. It is better for us both, therefore, to be separated. . . . There is an unwillingness on the part of our people, harsh as it may be, for you free colored people to remain with us."

The President urged the amazed committee to permit themselves to be colonized, as a help to those less fortunate and less intelligent than themselves. He told them that the particular place he had in mind was in Central America, "where the climate was similar to their own native land." He mentioned valuable coal lands, where they could find immediate employment digging coal until "they got ready to settle permanently in their homes."

While Mr. Lincoln admitted that political affairs in Central America were not as satisfactory as he wished, he assured the Negroes that all factions there welcomed colonization and "are more generous than we are here." "To your colored race," he declared, "they have no objections. Besides, I would endeavor to have you made equals. . . .[5] I ask you then," he continued, in his peculiarly appealing way, "to consider seriously not pertaining to yourselves merely, nor for your race, and ours, for the present time, but as one of the things, if successfully managed, for the good of mankind—not confined to the present time, but . . . 'Into eternity'."

The President rose. The audience was over. The *Tribune* ended its account with the flat statement: "The delegation then withdrew." It made no comment on the colored men's reaction. But later, as Davis heard, the Negroes confessed disheartenment at President Lincoln's dim prospect for their future in the United States.

Jefferson Davis had been somewhat puzzled when he read the account in the Republican party's top official organ. Could Mr. Lincoln mean all that he stated so forthrightly? Or was he using his persuasive powers to stir the Negro leaders to accept colonization? Could he be fearing the future political power of the Negro? It had been reported in the Montgomery *Daily Advertiser,* as early as March 26, 1861, that President Lincoln was being pestered by Negro applicants for Government appointments. Certainly, Davis understood clearly, Lincoln had no devotion to the Negro's "cause," as did some New England Abolitionists. And Lincoln's own state was to reveal its attitude toward the dark-skinned race the following November, when a majority of 100,000 voted for a new article in the Illinois Constitution prohibiting any Negro, free or slave, from immigrating into the state.

The Emancipation Proclamation, as Davis saw at once, was calculated not only to create trouble in the South, but, more significantly, to prevent European intervention by shifting the issue of war from Union to freedom of slaves. Had Lincoln shrewdly turned the war for Southern independence into something many British statesmen would fear to touch, lest they appear to take the side of slavery? With some ap-

---

[5] Mr. Lincoln was mistaken in his surmise, for when an expedition of Negro colonists was readied, the Central Americans refused to accept them and even threatened war if the United States persisted in the venture.

prehension, the Confederate President waited for the reaction from England, where recognition had been so nearly won.

Whatever Lincoln's intentions, the effect of the proclamation on the South was electrical and spine-stiffening. In high indignation, the Richmond *Whig* stigmatized Mr. Lincoln's edict as "a dash of the pen to destroy four thousand millions of our property." The disruption of the social and economic structure of the region was called a significant calculation. But the darker purpose, as the South interpreted it, was to loose a flood of nightmarish evils, surpassing the loss of property and laborers. The Richmond *Enquirer* accused the North of desiring the ghastly excesses of the 1831 Nat Turner Insurrection in Virginia, which led to the end of Southern manumission societies.

Senator James Phelan of Mississippi voiced the indignation of multitudes when he blasted the proclamation in oratorical periods. "Infuriated by continual defeat, maddened by revengeful passion and exasperated by despair of effecting our subjugation through the modes of civilized warfare," he declared, "our brutal foes at length seek to light in our land the baneful fires of servile war, by emancipation among us of four million of negro slaves, with the design of effecting an indiscriminate slaughter, of all ages, sexes, and conditions of our people. A scheme so atrocious and infernal is unparalleled in the blackest and bloodiest page of savage strife. . . ." [6]

Despite the Northern press's general approbation, in certain quarters the proclamation was condemned with almost as much vehemence as in the South. In New York, the Democratic supporters of Horatio Seymour's campaign for governor denounced Lincoln's measure as foreshadowing "the butchery of women and children." General McClellan was rumored to consider the edict "as outrageous as it was unsound," but his officers advised him not to denounce it openly, for fear he would be relieved of his command.

Although the Abolitionists were jubilant, Mr. Lincoln found no real "heartiness" in the general response. Six days after its appearance, he wrote Vice-President Hannibal Hamlin: "The stocks have declined and troops come forward more slowly than ever. . . . The North responds to the proclamation . . . in breath; but breath alone kills no rebels."

Many leading Republicans openly frowned on the document. The

[6] Phelan's resolution, which well expressed the sentiment of outraged Southerners, is quoted in full in *Southern Historical Society Papers*, Vol. XLVII (1930), p. 29.

powerful editor-politico Francis Blair, Sr., who had urged Lincoln to send the Sumter relief expedition that launched the war, saw dark mischief in the measure and declared that the President "had ruined himself by his proclamations." Thurlow Weed, Seward's devoted friend and backer, claimed that "it has strengthened the South and weakened the North." That President Lincoln lost many friends in the North was soon to be evidenced in the adverse verdict on his Administration expressed in the fall elections.

Jefferson Davis was gratified to note that the first reaction abroad was one of incredulous shock. Europeans, though by and large antislavery in sentiment, were horrified at the proclamation, which seemed a prelude to black insurrection, "with arson, the slaughter of innocents, and a host of unmentionable horrors." The London *Times* led all the rest in condemning Lincoln's unconstitutional act.[7]

In a memorandum to the British Cabinet, cool Earl Russell wrote: "There is surely a total want of consistency in this measure. . . . If it were a measure of Emancipation it should be extended to all the States of the Union. Emancipation is not granted to the claims of humanity but inflicted as a punishment." The confidential opinion of the English Foreign Secretary was much the same as that of the Confederate President, who knew that the edict was inspired by no humanitarian motive, but was purely a war measure.

In the South, there was no longer any lingering love for the old Union. Apparently, according to editorials, telegrams, and letters that poured into Richmond, the proclamation had aroused the people to a stiffer determination "to resist to the death a power that had no respect for property rights or constitutional guarantees."

---

[7] An excellent summary of British press opinion is to be found in J. B. McMaster's *Lincoln's Administration*, p. 292.

CHAPTER XXV

BRAGG INVADES KENTUCKY AND GLADSTONE SPEAKS AT NEWCASTLE

WHILE the entire nation was stirred by Lee's invasion of Maryland, exciting things had been happening in the West. Jefferson Davis was almost as interested in Kentucky as in Maryland, and the stake was about as high. Major General E. Kirby Smith, of Bragg's command, had marched from Knoxville into Kentucky, pushed an opposing Union force out of his way, and occupied Lexington, where Davis had attended Transylvania College. The loss of Lexington was deplored in the North as "the loss of the heart of Kentucky." Cincinnati, Ohio, was in danger; on September 15, a detachment of Smith's men advanced to within a few miles of the city. The citizens were consternated. Martial law was declared; all saloons were closed; horsecars stopped service; citizens drilled in the streets, with some over-age ministers and judges in the ranks. Laborers were taken from their employment to dig trenches. Frantic pleas for help went to Washington, as women excitedly prepared bandages for the aftermath of battle.

But the coolheaded Smith had no intention of attacking Cincinnati unless Bragg could make juncture with him. Bragg and Buell had begun a race for Louisville. Three of the state's distinguished pro-Union citizens telegraphed Halleck: "The fate of Kentucky is hanging in the balance, and the army of Buell is in imminent peril." Smith urged Bragg to join him in attacking Louisville, saying he believed that together they could destroy the force already there without difficulty. Along his northward way, Bragg captured the Union garrison at Munfordville, but lost valuable time in doing so. Since he had only three days' rations left, he turned off the direct road to Louisville and entered Bardstown, while Buell pushed on to Louisville.

"Some thirty-five miles southeast of Louisville," reported an Alabama youth, "in the heart of the famous blue-grass region, our regiment went into camp at Bardstown, and remained about two weeks, and lived on the 'fat of the land,' drilling part of every day. . . . It was a land of fat beef, fat mutton, 'milk and honey,' Bourbon whiskey, and pretty women, as well as fine horses and brave men. It was the home of many of our Confederate soldiers who were in what went by the name of the 'orphans' brigade.' "[1] In the daytime Kentuckians constantly visited the camp. Sympathetic ladies sent delicious food to load the soldiers' tables. But, because Union troops were piling into Louisville and preparing to drive Bragg from the state, young Maxwell understood the citizens "could not *safely* be very public in their kind greetings of Confederates."

Davis learned that Buell had occupied Louisville on September 25. While detachments from Bragg's forces made threats against both Louisville and Cincinnati, the Confederates were busy sending out commissary stores, horses, and cattle. The owners were paid for all supplies in Confederate money, which Southerners then believed would be as good as any nation's at war's end.

Both Davis and Bragg had expected Kentucky volunteers to flock to Southern banners, but only one brigade had yet been recruited. The President received a discouraging letter from Bragg, in which he declared that the Kentuckians hesitated to risk the loss of their property by joining the Confederacy. Bragg said he needed 50,000 more men to complete his mission in the state; but, alas, Davis had none to send him.

The President had other troubles on his mind in early October. When Colonel Gorgas, Chief of Ordnance, called on him one balmy evening, he found Davis sorely depressed by bad news from Corinth. On the third and fourth of the month, Generals Van Dorn and Price, with greatly inferior forces, had attacked the entrenched army of General Rosecrans and been severely repulsed. The courageous "Buck" Van Dorn had apparently allowed himself to be drawn into a trap, where his forces were slaughtered. The Confederates had lost men, arms, and artillery that they could ill afford to spare. Davis understood Van Dorn's good motive in attacking: to keep Rosecrans from sending aid to halt Bragg's invasion of Kentucky. But the Mississip-

---

[1] From *Autobiography of James Robert Maxwell of Tuskaloosa, Alabama,* which gives a spirited account of war from a private's viewpoint. Maxwell was a cadet at the University of Alabama when he volunteered to help train and drill raw conscripts.

pian had been too daring. "We were out-generaled," the President lamented to Gorgas.

The correspondents believed the fault to be entirely the rash Van Dorn's. And soldiers on the spot bore them out. "Van Dorn deserves the bitterest condemnation of our whole country," wrote another young Alabamian to his bride. "General Price was seriously opposed to attacking Corinth, but Van Dorn would go and make Price take his little army. The result is that Van Dorn is badly whipped and our army seriously worsted. . . . Our army blames Van Dorn, but no one utters a syllable of censure for Price." [2] There were so many allegations against Van Dorn that he himself demanded a court of inquiry. The result was that the court declared unanimously that all the charges were disproved.

While the Confederates were meeting disaster at Corinth, General Bragg had stopped at Frankfort, the Kentucky capital, on October 4, and assisted in the inauguration of Richard Hawes as Provisional Confederate Governor. It was a short-lived triumph, however, for Union guns began dropping shells in the outskirts of the city before Hawes had finished his inaugural address. With Louisville secure, Buell turned with 55,000 men to fight Bragg. The two armies clashed at Perryville on October 8. Major General William Joseph Hardee, who had written the standard book on tactics used by both armies, was aghast when Bragg ordered Polk to attack with part of his force. He sent his superior a pleading dispatch: "Do not scatter your forces. There is one rule in our profession which should never be forgotten; it is to throw the masses of your troops on the fractions of the enemy."

But Bragg scattered his forces. Though greatly outnumbered,[3] the Confederates pushed the enemy from his positions and drove him back almost two miles before night set in. "We had whipped them to a frazzle," wrote young Jim Maxwell. The Union dead numbered 335 more than the Confederate. But hearing that fresh enemy masses were accumulating, Bragg withdrew in good order. Both Generals claimed victory at Perryville.

Bragg started for Tennessee in a storm of dissension with his own subordinates. The disconsolate General felt that he had abandoned "the garden spot of Kentucky to its cupidity." "The love of ease and

[2] The letter of John Y. Kilpatrick to his bride is one in an unpublished collection owned by Dr. Emmett Kilpatrick of Camden, Alabama, son of the Confederate soldier by a later marriage.

[3] Buell had 55,000 soldiers in one column and 22,000 in the other. The first was larger than the forces of Bragg and Smith if they had combined.

fear of pecuniary loss," he wrote the President, "are the fruitful sources of this evil." Kirby Smith, his best lieutenant, was not at all content with Bragg's conduct of the campaign. He and Hardee had good reason to criticize Bragg for dividing his forces.

When Bragg passed through the Cumberland Gap into Tennessee, on October 26, the invasion of Kentucky was over. Jefferson Davis gave up his native state as lost to the Confederacy. As he wrote to General Holmes in Arkansas: "The expectation that the Kentuckians would rise en masse with the coming of a force which would enable them to do so, alone justified an advance into that State while the enemy in force remained in Tennessee. That expectation has been sadly disappointed, and the future is to be viewed by the light of late experiences."

General Gorgas, never quick to praise, wrote in his private journal: "The battle of Perryville closed the brilliant successes of the Kentucky campaign, by a drawn fight in which we captured artillery, and inflicted heavy loss on the enemy. Bragg, however, effected the object he had in view, the withdrawal of the supplies he had captured. The military results of this campaign were the capture of 10,000 prisoners, eight or ten thousand small arms, several batteries of artillery. . . ."

Near the end of October, leaving his army at Knoxville, General Bragg went to Richmond to report in person to the President. He could say that, though opposed by superior numbers, he had yet succeeded in getting away with the largest supply of provisions any army had collected. He had brought out 15,000 horses and mules, 8,000 head of cattle, 50,000 barrels of pork, droves of hogs on foot, and an estimated million yards of Kentucky-made cloth. Exaggerated estimates ran that his wagon trains stretched for forty miles. However, because the Kentuckians had not actively allied themselves with the Confederacy, many Southern noncombatants severely scored Bragg. Most of his subordinates, too, criticized his conduct, but Davis, like Gorgas, thought he had done well under the circumstances. Andrew Johnson, Military Governor of Tennessee, used his influence with Washington to secure Buell's removal for not opposing Bragg more effectively.

President Davis rewarded Kirby Smith for his excellent soldiership by making him a Lieutenant General. In a long personal letter to the Floridian, Davis, caught in the brambles of officers' wranglings and dislikes, tried to restore harmony and persuade Smith to stay in Bragg's command. He wrote that General Bragg "spoke of you in the most complimentary terms and does not seem to imagine your dissatis-

faction." Although another commander might "excite more enthusiasm" than Bragg, Davis felt that he would probably not be
"equally useful." "General Bragg cannot move into Middle Tenn.
with prospect of success without your cooperation. You are now second in rank and possess to an eminent degree the confidence of the
country. Your own corps could not be useful led by another commander. How then can I withdraw you or withhold your troops? . . .
When you wrote me, your wounds were fresh, your lame and exhausted troops were before you. I hope time may have mollified your
pain and that future operations may restore the confidence essential to
cheerfulness and security in campaign." Davis's appeal to Smith's
patriotism was effective. Neither Kirby Smith nor any member of his
staff uttered another recorded word of criticism of Bragg's Kentucky
campaign for the duration of the war.

Few people could know how close England had come to intervention. Had Lee been successful at Antietam, undoubtedly European
recognition would have followed. Prime Minister Palmerston had felt
confident of Lee's success, and secretly predicated his support of recognition upon it. Now after Antietam he became hesitant and reluctant.

William Gladstone, Chancellor of the Exchequer, however, had no
such reservations. He firmly believed in the Confederacy's cause; he
grieved over the distress of the cotton-factory workers; and he feared
a revolution if they were not relieved. When the Campaign of Second
Manassas was beginning, on July 26, 1862, as quoted in E. D. Adams's
Great Britain and the American Civil War, Gladstone had written
Colonel Neville that the South had won its independence. Now, just
after the news of the Emancipation Proclamation reached England,
on October 9, Gladstone made a speech at Newcastle that stirred all
Britain and the literate world.

"We may have our own opinions about slavery," the Liberal leader
said; "we may be for or against the South. But there is no doubt that
Jefferson Davis and the other leaders of the South have made an army;
they are making, it appears, a navy; and they have made what is more
than either—they have made a nation. We may anticipate with certainty the success of the Southern States as far as their separation
from the North is concerned."

Gladstone's strong words were immensely gratifying to Jefferson
Davis, for Gladstone had enormous prestige with his followers, and
was recognized as a man of such incorruptible courage that he would

"be willing to break up his party rather than deny his conscience." Such forthright expression coming from a prominent member of the British Cabinet indubitably seemed to presage official recognition. A small uproar, however, resulted in England. Although Foreign Secretary Russell was secretly in favor of the Confederacy,[4] he mildly rebuked Gladstone.

Clearly, the general tenor of the British press favored some movement on England's part to halt the carnage. The *Economist* of October 18 heartily supported Gladstone. His Newcastle speech "echoes the general sentiment of the country," the weekly claimed, "and probably the real opinion of most members of the Government." *Blackwood's Magazine* declared: "Not only does international law justify our recognition of the Southern Confederacy, but humanity demands that we would take measures to put an end to such horrible war."

Though Davis could not know what was going on behind the scenes in Britain's Cabinet, Lord Russell was writing confidentially to a colleague that he believed the United States would accept a proposal of mediation. If nothing resulted, he said, "I shall then be for recognizing the South. The Democratic Party may by that time have got the ascendancy. I heartily wish them success." [5] Three days later, the French Emperor, believing England ready to intervene, let it be known officially that he would invite a joint offer of mediation.

Despite Britain's insistence on consulting Russia, the Confederate lobby had reason to be confident that England would join France. Mason reported the cotton famine "looming up in fearful proportions"; the public mind "very much agitated and disturbed at the fearful prospect for winter."

In the South, breasts swelled with hope. President Davis, General Lee, Benjamin, and the rest of the public figures, great and minor, eagerly awaited the meeting of the British Cabinet. They looked for a decision that might end the pain and horror.

The President, relieved that McClellan had not begun his advance on Richmond a month after Antietam, could give more attention to other problems in the Confederacy. By the end of September, he had already sent Major General John C. Pemberton to command the De-

---

[4] Since April, 1861, the observant young Henry Adams had looked upon Russell as showing the "clearest determination to break up the Union."

[5] From *The Later Correspondence of Lord John Russell*, edited by G. P. Gooch, which is most revealing.

partment of Mississippi. Partly because a New Yorker, General Lovell, had been in command of New Orleans when it fell, Mississippians were not pleased that a Philadelphian was put in charge at Vicksburg, though Pemberton had married a Virginian and believed in the justice of the Southern cause. A West Point graduate, he had joined the Confederacy at the very outbreak of the war. Even in his undergraduate days, he had been known as a devout adherent of State Rights. Davis knew him to be completely loyal, and he had confidence in his military abilities. To Governor Pettus, he commended him as "an officer of great merit."

Earlier in September, the President had sent identical letters to the Governors of the four Confederate States west of the Mississippi: F. E. Lubbock of Texas, T. O. Moore of Louisiana, H. M. Rector of Arkansas, and C. F. Jackson of Missouri. Cogently, he explained the delays in arrangements for the Trans-Mississippi Department: Virginia was pressed "by the whole force of the United States Government" and Richmond was closely invested by "the largest and best-commanded army of the enemy."

Then Davis assigned old Major General Holmes to command the Department, with Major Generals Richard Taylor, T. C. Hindman, and Sterling Price in the districts of Louisiana, Arkansas, and Missouri respectively. Holmes, who had had long service in the old Army, was by no means an ideal man for the job. Approaching sixty, he seemed much older. He was not particularly aggressive, and he was handicapped by deafness. But Davis had no other high-ranking man to offer. He hoped that the qualities of Holmes's three top lieutenants would make up in considerable measure for their chief's deficiencies.

In writing General Holmes a detailed military letter on October 21, the President suggested earnest consideration of a conjoint movement with Pemberton and Bragg to drive the enemy from Tennessee and Arkansas "while the rivers are low."

North Carolina also received special attention from the President, who had been told that Zebulon Vance, the new Governor, might prove difficult because he was "mighty interested" in his own political future. Vance had first made his reputation as an opponent of State Rights, and had run against the Administration candidate. Then, as soon as he was in authority, he became a determined State Rights advocate. Vance wrote that he was mortified "to find brigades of North Carolina soldiers in the field commanded by strangers, and in many cases our own brave and war-worn colonels are made to give place to colonels from distant states." The well-publicized fact that General Lee advocated putting soldiers where they could be most useful to the common cause did not affect Vance's public utterances. Davis's attitude toward Vance was conciliatory, for he knew that only by a united resistance could the Confederacy hope to succeed.

In reply to letters marked by veiled hints of recalcitrance, the President attempted to make Governor Vance see the light of the over-all picture.

I feel grateful to you for the cordial manner in which you have sustained every proposition connected with the public defense and trust that there will always be such co-intelligence and accordance as will enable us to cooperate for the public good.

The Conscript Act has not been popular anywhere out of the army. There, as you are aware, it served to check the discontent which resulted from retaining the 12 mos. men beyond the term of their original engagement, and was fairly regarded as a measure equitably to distribute the burden of public defense, but the State authorities have nowhere offered any opposition to its execution, or withheld their aid except in the State of Georgia. . . .

Like yourself I have hoped that the party distinctions which existed at a former time would be buried in the graves of the gallant men who have fallen in the defence of their birthright, and that we should all as a band of brothers strike for the inheritance our fathers left us.

Governor Brown of Georgia was far more troublesome than Vance. After the Conscript Act was passed in September, Brown had coolly informed the President that he would not allow its enforcement in his state until the Legislature convened in November. Though at the end of October Lee was falling back to Fredericksburg and the armies of Bragg and Van Dorn were confronted by superior Federal forces, Brown held the law in suspension. When the Georgia Legislature did meet, he demanded, in his prim, self-righteous twang, to know whether the Confederacy "should continue to have States or have a consolidated military despotism."

"Nothing could be more unfortunate," Davis wrote his loyal friend Senator Benjamin H. Hill in Georgia, "not only for the success of our cause, but also for the future reputation of the great State of Georgia, than any conflict between the authorities of that State and the Confederate Government on this question."

The President was reassured by Hill that public opinion in Georgia was favorable to the Conscript Act, despite Governor Brown's shrill criticism and the vehement opposition of Linton Stephens, the Vice-President's brother, who was determined that the State Supreme Court would deny its constitutionality.

Not only did Jefferson Davis have to soothe politicians, but he was continually faced with heartbroken appeals from wives and mothers. Some of the letters he felt constrained to answer himself, as he did one from Mrs. Mary Wilkinson of Vicksburg.

Your letter, informing me of the death in battle of Col. Wilkinson and asking my advice in reference to your son, has been received.

I sympathize with your bereavement, my dear Madam, and realize your anxiety. It would give me pleasure to be able to assist the son of a father who fell so nobly for his country, and who has himself fought so well that country's battles. And I regret that I cannot now point out some path on which duty and safety might go together. . . .

Though we cannot yet see the termination of the present war, it may, under God's pleasure, be near at hand. If it be otherwise, I shall be happy to give your son any aid or counsel in my power.

The President was accused by the press of being too tenderhearted, of too frequently remitting the execution of a deserter condemned by a military court. But how could one not, he argued, sympathize with husbands who answered pathetic pleas of despairing wives to come home and help get something to eat for the children? The pay of a soldier was only eleven dollars a month; with the current inflation, that amount would hardly provide a week's coarse food for a family. "The poorest use that can be made of a soldier," Davis often said, "is to shoot him."

Davis felt sorry, too, for young boys who had adventurously volunteered to fight and then found warfare too terrifying. Though his aides tried to keep private tales of woe from him, he heard a touching story about a lad of sixteen who had volunteered without his parents' consent. For cowardice in battle, the youth had been sentenced to wear the galling ball and chain for six months, and he had already served three months. The President at once remitted the rest of the sentence.

Adding to the pressure of manifold vexing problems in the early fall, citizens were urging the President to bring back a portion of Lee's army to protect Richmond on the south. But Lee said he doubted the wisdom of detaching troops, because it might make him too weak to meet the advance of McClellan. He wrote Davis that he did not apprehend an immediate movement of the Federal Army. The General was staying close to the Potomac, he said, "subsisting his army on what, if he retreated, would subsist the enemy."

On October 14, the day after the Confederate Congress adjourned, Davis received a cheering communication from General Lee at Winchester. "The cavalry expedition to Pennsylvania has returned safe. . . . It had crossed the Potomac at Williamsport and recrossed at White's Ford, making the entire circuit, cutting the enemy's communications, destroying arms, and obtaining many recruits." Jeb Stuart had taken 1,800 horsemen and gone into Pennsylvania, pushing up as far as Chambersburg. Then he had made another spectacular swing around the enemy's army. The only private property he took was horses, for which he paid in Confederate currency. Davis glowed with pleasure, and even the Northern press paid tribute to the gallant Stuart's boldness. Albert Richardson of the New York *Tribune* wrote: "The cavalry raid of the Rebel General Stuart around our entire army . . . is the one theme of conversation. It was audacious and brilliant." [6]

In late October, the President was happy to have Margaret Howell, Varina's sister, back in the Richmond household after a prolonged stay with her parents in Montgomery, where her father had a position with the Commissary. He looked upon Maggie more as a daughter than a sister-in-law, for she had lived with the Davises since she was a little girl of eight. When she was fourteen, she had begun reading aloud to "Brother Jeff" in the evenings to save his eyes, and he had taught her to be careful of her diction. In the crisp fall weather, Maggie rode horseback with him for an hour before sunset. They made a striking couple on their way to the military camps or over the autumn-tinted hills: the fifty-four-year-old President in Confederate gray on his white Arabian and the twenty-year-old girl on a handsome black horse named "Oliver Cromwell."

On special occasions, Maggie donned a smartly tailored broadcloth habit trimmed with jet and a black velvet hat trailing a white ostrich plume. She wore white gloves and carried a gold-handled riding crop, a present from Richmond's Mayor. Oliver had a white saddle and white reins, gifts from another admiring friend. Maggie wore her gala outfit when Company F, Second Regiment, Florida Infantry, chose to

[6] Albert D. Richardson's *The Field, the Dungeon, and the Escape* is one of the more sprightly books of war memoirs, written from a confessedly biased Abolitionist viewpoint.

be called the "Howell Guards" in her honor, and the President presented them with a knot of green-and-gray silk colors.[7]

Despite the loss of her parents' New Orleans home, Maggie kept her spirits high. Her native wit and sense of the ridiculous amused the President. But Mr. Davis sometimes winced at her impulsive, caustic comment; and he cautioned her, as he did Varina, to curb her irrepressible cleverness in society. His wife already had enemies, chiefly in the circle of Lydia Johnston and Charlotte Wigfall, but she had made some staunch friends in Richmond and she was really enjoying her role as First Lady.

Another bright event for Davis was the return of the James Chesnuts from South Carolina; there was no couple with whom he felt more completely at ease. Colonel Chesnut had answered the President's call to serve on his staff. He was sound and dependable, and his loyalty was heart-warming. Davis perhaps preferred Mrs. Chesnut's company to that of any lady in the Confederacy except his wife's. She had such sparkling distinction that when hosts did not take her in to dinner themselves, they almost invariably designated her as partner to the guest of honor. But she was more than an ornament to society; her sparkle was backed by cultivated intelligence and good common sense.

Mary Chesnut herself was overjoyed to be back in the capital. "Mr. and Mrs. Davis," she wrote in her diary, "received us with warmth and cordiality. . . . Mrs. Davis has been so kind to me that I can never be grateful enough, yet even without that I should like her. She is so clever, so brilliant, so warm-hearted and considerate to all around her. After being accustomed to the spice and spirit of her conversation, when one is away from her, things seem flat and tame for awhile."

Though there was nothing in the way of a furnished house to be found in Richmond now, Mrs. Davis had mentally earmarked for the Chesnuts the lower floor of a Mrs. Lyon's house at the corner of Tenth and Clay, which had recently been vacated by Colonel W. M. Browne, another Presidential aide. She took Mrs. Chesnut to inspect the apartment, and the landlady's young daughter, Emma Lyon, later recorded the event: "Mrs. Davis was always exceedingly genial and pleasant without any airs of superiority and walked in upon my mother who was arranging the dining table and upon invitation partook of the

---

[7] The details are taken from an unpublished biographical manuscript furnished the author by a great-great niece of Jefferson Davis, Mrs. Richard W. Graves of Little Rock, Arkansas.

viands, as she and Mrs. Chesnut were going upon a tiresome shopping excursion."

Mrs. Chesnut moved in promptly with two South Carolina servants, and was immediately caught up in a round of private theatricals for charity, dinners, breakfasts. She and Mrs. Davis saw each other often; they shopped together or drove out on fair afternoons in Varina's elegant *calèche,* sometimes with the merry and undisciplined Davis children tumbling over them. In the mornings, Emma Lyon frequently saw Mrs. Davis driving "to the hospitals to cheer the sick or wounded soldiers with dainties carried in a large basket." [8]

The President would occasionally dine *en famille* with the Chesnuts, and he would be fed on turkey, ham, and partridges sent from Mulberry, the South Carolina plantation. In this household, he could find much the same sympathetic understanding and relaxation that President Pierce had enjoyed at the Davis home in Washington.

In her memoirs, Constance Cary set down her impressions of the Davis household. Burton Harrison, who was courting the popular Constance, had moved into the White House and occupied a third-floor bedroom above the President's own room.

We were all interested in what Burton Harrison had to say of the Davises. Every one knew the traditions of Mrs. Jefferson Davis, as handed down from her career as a Senator's wife in Washington, in the administrations of Pierce and Buchanan. She was declared to be a woman of warm heart and impetuous tongue, witty and caustic, with a sensitive nature underlying all; a devoted wife and mother, and most gracious mistress of a salon. Miss Margaret Howell, the exceedingly clever sister of Mrs. Davis . . . was the young lady of the Richmond White House; and it is safe to say that no wittier talk was ever bandied over the teacups in any land than passed daily between the several bright spirits thus assembled at the President's table.

Concerning the affairs, big or little, of "The Chief," Mr. Harrison was wont to preserve continual discreet silence. He would say only that the President had the happiest relations with his family, by whom he was revered, incidentally remarking that to accompany the chief on horseback, always his duty, together with some of the aides, was to sit in the saddle indefinitely, in good or bad weather alike, never knowing when they were to bring up at home again, and keeping Mrs. Davis in continual uncertainty as to her dinner-hour, to say nothing of her husband's fate.

[8] "Family Reminiscences of Emma Lyon Bryan," in the Walter Fleming Collection of Jefferson Davis Papers (Box 5, Folder 2) in the New York Public Library, is full of intimate glimpses of the Davises, who were neighbors.

In early November, the attention of Richmond was again focused sharply on the battle front. The President received word from Lee: "McClellan is moving more rapidly than usual, and it looks like an advance." After Antietam, McClellan had remained north of the Potomac, but on October 26, his army, 116,000 strong, began to cross the river; six days later, the last division was over. Then he pushed down to Warrenton. According to Rufus Ingalls's report in *Official Records,* "The march from the Potomac at Berlin to Warrenton was a magnificent spectacle of celerity and skill." Lee had remained at Winchester until McClellan's mighty force started across the river; then he quickly brought his own army south behind the Rapidan, between Richmond and the enemy.

As a new chorus of "On to Richmond" swelled in the North, Jefferson Davis heard strange news, which he discredited: Lincoln had relieved McClellan and ordered Ambrose Burnside to take command of the Army of the Potomac. But the report turned out to be true.

At a late hour on the night of November 6, while writing a letter to his wife in his tent near Warrenton, McClellan received an officer who had come from Washington by special train in a snowstorm. The man bore a letter from President Lincoln, dated November 5. McClellan suppressed any show of feeling as he read that he was removed from command. General Burnside, however, who had accompanied the messenger to his tent, was visibly moved.

In the morning, when the astounding news spread, black gloom fell upon the troops. Men came to him, singly and in delegations, urging him to refuse to obey the order. He found it hard to calm them.

Next day, McClellan prepared a brief farewell to his army. After expressing the love and gratitude he bore the men, he said: "In you I have never found doubt or coldness. . . . The glory you have achieved, our mutual perils and fatigues, the graves of our comrades fallen in battle and by disease, the broken forms of those whom wounds and sickness have disabled . . . unite us still in an indissoluble tie."

Burnside, who admired his friend McClellan, was reluctant to take the command, for he felt that he lacked the ability. At his entreaty, the cashiered General stayed on a couple of days to acquaint him with the work. Burnside had told President Lincoln and the Secretary of War "over and over again that he was not competent to command so large an army and that McClellan was the best general for the place."

The troops were mystified as to why Lincoln had designated Burnside, who had blundered disastrously at Antietam and whose only small success had been in North Carolina, where he had had everything in his favor. To drown their discontent, several officers drank heavily and muttered around campfires that the Government at Washington should be put out and McClellan be made head of civil, as well as military, affairs.

On November 10, when, by way of saying farewell, little McClellan passed through the camps on his huge black horse, miles of soldiers broke into frantic yelling. Thousands of hardy veterans shed tears like little boys. "Send him back!" they howled. "Send him back!" Some regiments threw down their weapons, swearing vainly that they would no longer fight.

When McClellan reached the turnpike to Centreville, where he was to board the train, he passed between Fitz-John Porter's corps and that of the venerable Edwin V. Sumner. The men stood at attention, presenting arms smartly; but as emotion overcame them, their rifles wavered, and, calling out good-bys, they blubbered unabashed. When the General reached the station, an honor guard 2,000 strong was ranged for the last salute. As he boarded the one-car train sent hopefully to take him out of history and out of the Republican party's way, the men discarded discipline, swarmed about his coach, defiantly uncoupled it, and swore they would not let him go. In the howling din, Little Mac stepped out on the rear platform and quietly raised his hand. There was instant silence. In one imploring sentence, he urged them to stand by General Burnside. Then he retired, not trusting his emotions or the soldiers' temper to allow him to say more. The car was recoupled. The train began to move. Cannon boomed a heavy farewell. McClellan's military career was over. He sat alone, choked up, but glowing with that incomparable feeling of a leader who has received a mighty demonstration of an army's devotion.

Jefferson Davis, who had known McClellan intimately in happier days, found the accounts of his departure affecting. He could feel both with the cashiered commander and with the disconsolate men. Like Lee, though less emphatically, Davis believed that McClellan was basically the ablest commander in the Union Army.[9] But, he reflected,

---

[9] The majority of historians devoted to Lincoln minimize McClellan, but one of the foremost, J. G. Randall, an ardent Lincoln admirer and biographer, champions McClellan as the best of the Union generals. Five years after Appomattox, when Lee was asked which Union general whom he had opposed during the war was the ablest, without hesitation, he said: "McClellan by all means."

McClellan was a Democrat, and had already been mentioned as the logical candidate to oppose Lincoln in the next Presidential election. Had not the Democrats in the time of President James K. Polk tried to hamper Davis's Whig father-in-law, Zachary Taylor, in Mexico, and take the luster off his military campaign because he was too popular? Now McClellan had evidently done enough for glory; to do more might seriously endanger Republican prospects in 1864.

Lincoln's immediate excuse for his rash act seemed to be the fact that McClellan had permitted Lee to thrust Longstreet's corps between Richmond and the Federals. Whatever the reason, Davis felt that small gratitude had been rendered McClellan, who had saved Washington, sent Lee back to Virginia after Antietam, and made it possible for Lincoln to issue his Emancipation Proclamation.

Later, Mr. Lincoln explained to Albert Richardson, correspondent of the *Tribune*, that it was after the Battle of Antietam that he "gave up" McClellan. According to Richardson, Lincoln said: "I directed McClellan peremptorily to move on Richmond. It was eleven days before he crossed his first man over the Potomac; it was eleven more days before he crossed the last man. Thus he was twenty-two days in passing the river at a much easier and more practicable ford than that where Lee crossed his entire army between one dark night and daylight the next morning." [10] While Mr. Lincoln's view of McClellan's crossing into Virginia does not agree with statements in the *Official Records*, he indirectly paid high tribute to General Lee.

As Davis saw it, Lincoln could hardly have done the Confederacy a better turn than to substitute a second-rate commander for a first-rate one. The change would help to offset Lee's inferiority in numbers and equipment. Though the Army of the Potomac was still by far the finest the North possessed, its shining star was gone. To the historian Rhodes, the substitution was "indefensible."

[10] *The Field, the Dungeon, and the Escape,* p. 324.

CHAPTER XXVI

THE PRESIDENT GOES WEST

ON NOVEMBER 15, President Davis was informed that the Federals were again on the march. But Burnside had changed McClellan's plans. Instead of proceeding down the railroad, McDowell's way to Richmond, he was angling southeast along the Rappahannock toward Fredericksburg. Lee quickly rearranged his own defensive plans. By the time Burnside reached the heights of Falmouth, north of the river, Lee, with Longstreet, had occupied the opposite hills, south of Fredericksburg, and was throwing up fortifications, although the natural defenses were capital in themselves. Jackson was alerted to be ready to join him.

Burnside's strength was reckoned at 106,000. In a few weeks, President Davis had built up Lee's depleted forces to something over 72,000. As winter set in, the two armies faced each other, with the river between. The Army of the Potomac was ranged behind 147 modern guns, which commanded the town. Lee had such inferior artillery that he deemed it useless to attempt to silence those guns. So he awaited attack.[1]

Both Davis and Lee deeply regretted the almost certain ruination of the fine old Colonial town, where the mother of George Washington had lived on Charles Street. All Richmond knew that a battle must soon be waged, but the citizens were not unduly alarmed. They expected Lee to hold the enemy. And many looked to a smashing Confederate victory that would bring peace. The President had a sanguine letter from General Lee suggesting that a complete triumph would probably end the war. But Lee wrote to his wife, "I tremble for my

---

[1] According to Rhodes, in the last week of November, when his pontoons for bridging the river arrived, Burnside's forces amounted to 113,000, and Lee's to 78,000.

country, when I hear of the confidence expressed in me. I know too well my weakness, and that our only hope is God." Davis had confidence in Lee as the instrument of God.

The first trains loaded with Fredericksburg refugees—women, children, Negroes—clanked into Richmond on November 22. While Lee was expecting battle, the harassed President received from south and west appeals for more men. General Whiting said that he thought Wilmington might be attacked immediately, and that if he did not receive 10,000 reinforcements, he could not save the city. General Magruder wrote that Pemberton had only 20,000 men in Mississippi; if he did not have 50,000 more at once, the Valley would be lost. A few days before Burnside began marching toward Fredericksburg, Grant had started from Corinth in the direction of Vicksburg, and now occupied the aristocratic old town of Holly Springs.

The insuperable problem of Davis and the Confederacy was always lack of manpower. To make the situation worse, the Federals now began arming blacks to fight the Southerners. Union officers in South Carolina officially created the first Negro regiment, recruited from slaves belonging to ravaged plantations along the coast. As Professor Randall wrote, the use of Negroes as Union soldiers was "a natural accompaniment of emancipation." However, as early as April 12, 1862, General David Hunter, who commanded the Federal Department of the South, on his own initiative, had organized a regiment of captured slaves. According to T. W. Higginson, in *Army Life in a Black Regiment*, they had been "driven like cattle, kept for several months in camp, and then turned off without a shilling, by order of the War Department."

A large majority of Northerners could not stomach the idea of arming blacks to kill Southern whites. But with the Emancipation Proclamation and its resultant propaganda came a gradual change in sentiment; in November, Captain Higginson of Massachusetts was elevated to a colonelcy to take command of the black "First Regiment of South Carolina Volunteers." Higginson used them for raiding purposes, and was charmed with their alacrity in thieving and burning the fine old coastal plantations. "I had been an Abolitionist too long," he wrote fervently, "and had known and loved John Brown too well, not to feel a thrill of joy at last on finding myself in the position where he only wished to be."

On November 26, President Davis, gravely apprehensive at this manifestation of black evil, sent identical letters to each of the Confederate Governors, in which he warned them that the Federal Government was planning to enlist and arm such slaves as they could wrest from their owners, and "thus to inflict on the noncombatant population the horrors of a servile war." He recommended such legislation as would empower the Governors to command slave labor for the prosecution of public defense works. Even if he had desired to make soldiers of Negro slaves, under the State Rights doctrine, he had no such power.

The day after McClellan said farewell to his army, President Davis was amazed to read a copy of an important letter Secretary of War Randolph had sent to General Holmes more than a fortnight before without his knowledge. Randolph had assumed an authority his office did not possess, and which might cause serious mischief. Davis, much disturbed, wrote him:

> I regret to notice that in your letter to Genl. Holmes of October 27th, a copy of which is before me, that you suggest the propriety of his crossing the Mississippi and assuming command on the East side of the river.
>
> His presence on the west side is not less necessary now than heretofore, and will probably soon be more so. . . .
>
> The withdrawal of the commander from the trans-Mississippi Dept. for temporary duty elsewhere would have a disastrous effect and was not contemplated by me. . . .

Davis was not opposed to the transfer of troops; he approved of it and had had General Cooper suggest it to Holmes that same week. But he was opposed to the suggestion that Holmes himself cross the river with them to the east bank, which would have left the Trans-Mississippi without a commander and would have put Pemberton, who was familiar with the terrain and its problems, in a subordinate position. In the opinion of Shelby Foote, Randolph's action was indefensible, and Davis "bent and bent before he stiffened." [2]

As Rembert Patrick stated in his excellent study of Jefferson Davis's Cabinet, the President himself would not have been so rash as to order such an important change in military plans without first consulting his Cabinet or his army advisers. War Clerk Jones wrote in his diary: "The President has rebuked the Secretary of War in round terms for ordering Gen. Holmes to assume command on *this* side of the Mississippi. . . . This is the first thing I have ever known

[2] Douglas Freeman told the author and told Rembert Patrick in 1952 that he had been too favorable to Randolph, that further study had convinced him that Davis was right in the controversy.

him to do without previously obtaining the President's sanction—and it must be confessed it was a matter of some gravity. Of course it will be countermanded. . . . He has not been to see the President—and that may be significant as this is his usual day."

Randolph did not come to see the President; but, on the morning of the fourteenth, he wrote that he had modified his instructions to Holmes by transmitting a copy of the President's letter. Again Randolph had erred. "Confusion and embarrassment," Davis wrote him, "will inevitably result unless all orders, and directions in relation to movements and stations of troops and officers, be sent through the established channel, the Bureau of orders and correspondence.[3] In these matters and in all cases of selection of persons to be appointed commissioned officers I have to request a reference before action is taken."

In less than an hour, Randolph replied that the President's meaning was not clear. Davis answered immediately:

My letter of this date of the meaning of which you are in doubt had reference to the general arrangements of the army. The removal of an Army, the transfer of a Genl. from the Dept. he had been selected to command, the assignment of Genl. officers, and the highest officers of the supplying and disbursing Departments of the staff, are material to the public defence; and such like cases would all suggest the propriety of reference.

The usage has been free conference, and its advantages are apparent.

The appointment of commissioned officers is a constitutional function, which I have neither power nor will to delegate, and much which is disagreeable will be avoided by consultation in the first stage of selection.

Under the circumstances, the Chief Executive felt that he had to make his meaning emphatically clear as to both law and propriety. Now he considered the matter settled, and turned his attention to an important matter on which they had agreed.

On that same day, the President gave the Secretary of War sanction to send the first agent into Texas to purchase or impress cotton for the Government. By early fall, Confederate agents abroad had spent millions of dollars and paid enormous bonuses to blockade-runners. Now, with letters of credit and bills of exchange exhausted, it was imperative to use cotton as a medium of exchange, however much it undercut

[3] Randolph's nephew-in-law, R. G. H. Kean, had been appointed Chief of the War Bureau, a position he held throughout the war. He became a subtle enemy of the President, and in his private journal he often scored Mr. Davis in a clever, satirical style. His diary, which was published in 1957, shows Kean as a captious young man, who seemed to admire no one but his uncle and the Assistant Secretary of War, Judge John A. Campbell.

the King Cotton theory. Cotton, hauled in wagons out of Texas into Mexico, was shipped from Matamoros in exchange for powder, lead, copper, blankets, sugar, coffee. Fleets of ships gathered off Matamoros to exchange supplies for cotton. The Government, willy-nilly, had to have a lion's share of the trade and keep the route open.

That afternoon of November 14, into Randolph's office walked Joseph E. Johnston. The General had reported two days before that he was recuperated from his wound and would welcome active service. Now he had come to discuss his next assignment. In the course of conversation, he suggested the advisability of General Holmes sending a part of his forces east of the Mississippi. Randolph, very pleased, showed him a copy of his October 27 letter to Holmes. After a pause, he said that the President had countermanded the move; but he did not explain why. Exactly what Johnston replied and the tone and manner he used are not revealed in his *Narrative,* but from his resentment of Davis, his attitude may be surmised.

That night, War Clerk Jones recorded in his diary: "It seems that after acting some eight months merely in the humble capacity of clerk, Mr. Randolph has all at once essayed to act as PRESIDENT. The Secretary of War did not go to the President's closet today. This is the third day he has absented himself. . . . It is a critical time and the Secretary of War should confer freely with the President."

Randolph was never to confer with the President again on any subject. On the fifteenth, his curt resignation was laid on the President's desk. Davis was completely taken by surprise. He was hurt because Randolph had not had the courtesy to call and discuss the matter. Perhaps if they could have talked things over—but instead of waiting an hour or so to cool down, Davis impulsively recorded his indignation.

Sir:

I have this moment received yours of this date, notifying me that you resign the office of Secretary of War, and leave the Asst. Secretary in charge of the office. As you have thus without notice and in terms excluding inquiry retired from the post of a constitutional adviser of the Executive of the Confederacy, nothing remains but to give you this formal notice of the acceptance of your resignation.

Very respectfully your obt. svt.

Jeffn. Davis.

Randolph had not given the President an hour in which to choose a successor. He left his desk strewn with papers of half-finished business. "A profound sensation has been produced in the outside world by the resignation of Mr. Randolph," Jones wrote, "and most of the people and the press seem inclined to denounce the President, for they know not what. In this matter the President is not to blame; but the Secretary has acted either a very foolish or a very desperate part. . . . Randolph's friends would make it appear that he resigned in consequence of his being restricted in his action; but he knows very well that the latitude allowed him became less and less circumscribed. . . ."

The President's friends believed that Randolph had been stirred up by the Administration's foes. Many said he was tired of the office and glad to make excuse to return to private life. The newspapers did not dilate on his accomplishments as Secretary of War, but seized the occasion to criticize the President. Some implied that Randolph had been sacrificed to a mere whim of Jefferson Davis's.

Randolph had not made a bad Secretary of War; but he had certainly not made an outstanding one. Though he performed his routine duties well, during his eight months' incumbency the President's chief adviser on military policy was Robert E. Lee.

Some later commentators have credited Randolph with getting the President's attention focused on the western theater. But Mississippi was never far from Davis's mind, for his heart and home were in the Delta. Immediately after the critical Seven Days' Battles, he was in correspondence about the defense of the West with Governor Lubbock of Texas. Only in the autumn had sufficient arms come in to supply the Trans-Mississippi. Davis, like Randolph, was in favor of the co-ordination of western forces, so far as it was feasible. But to bring Holmes's force east of the Mississippi would have wrought havoc in the morale of Missouri, Arkansas, and Louisiana.

Being left without a day's grace in which to find a successor, the President appointed as ad interim Secretary the only General then available in Richmond—Gustavus W. Smith, who was said to have "no liking for Davis and no respect for Lee." Some thought Davis appointed Johnston's most ardent military partisan as a conciliatory gesture of good will. In any case, the position was purely temporary, and Smith held office for only four days.

Jefferson Davis was exceedingly tired from the emotions of the Randolph trouble. He had made another enemy who had powerful social and political connections. Again, for the sake of the national welfare, he had to endure in silence heaped-up criticism.

The President's choice for a new Secretary of War was an intimate friend, James Alexander Seddon, a successful, well-to-do Richmond lawyer, who, as a follower of John C. Calhoun, had served in the United States Congress. Never robust, he was one of those semi-invalids who by resolution and application often accomplish more than men with ox-like constitutions. Seddon was esteemed for his practical ability to think, reason, plan; and he had used his persuasive powers to help put Virginia into the Confederacy. He possessed moral and physical courage in strong degree. Reed-thin, Seddon was slenderer than the very slender President; wags said his bones rattled audibly when he descended stairs. At forty-seven, he wore a black skullcap to protect his head from drafts. With his prominent nose, sallow complexion, great dark eyes, and long black hair curling over his ears, he looked more like an orthodox rabbi than a member of an F.F.V., and nothing like a Secretary of War.

Everyone recognized Seddon's abilities, and his appointment had the enthusiastic backing of the two strongest anti-Administration papers: the Richmond *Examiner* and the Charleston *Mercury*.

On the day of the announcement, Wigfall bitterly denounced the President in the Senate. Davis called Reagan and asked him what the matter was with his fellow Texan. Reagan had no idea. Davis then told him that perhaps he himself knew. When Wigfall had called the day before and urged the appointment of Seddon, the President had not confided in him that the appointment had already been made. Since he had charged the members of the Cabinet not to speak of it, he did not feel at liberty to do so himself. He asked Reagan to say that his silence had not meant withdrawal of confidence in Wigfall, that this was no time for friends to quarrel, and that he certainly meant no disrespect.

Reagan sought Wigfall and gave Davis's explanations and apologies. The Senator expressed gratification, saying he would call on Reagan at his home that evening. Reagan immediately told Davis that all was well. But Wigfall did not go to see Reagan, and the next day he made another attack on the President in the Senate. The implacable Wigfall was not to cease his denunciation of his onetime good friend until the Confederacy collapsed. He found relief in deriding Davis, while continually extolling Joseph Johnston. Nothing was ever Johnston's fault, but always the President's. Eventually, Wigfall sought to alienate Seddon from Davis; when he failed, he wrote sneeringly to Clement Clay that Seddon was "subjugated" and had lost his manhood "if he ever had any." [4]

Seddon took over his new position with a will and obvious efficiency. The first problem he had to face was a demand from General Holmes for $24,000,000 for the needs of his Trans-Mississippi Department. Next, was a matter of moment in which Seddon immediately revealed his influence with the President. With the West so far from the seat of Government, Seddon thought that, for better co-ordination, the armies in Tennessee and Mississippi should be under one commander with a centralization of authority. Davis agreed with the idea. Seddon said that only an able tactician and daring leader could hope for success. Davis wondered where he would find that combination. Seddon recommended Joseph E. Johnston.

The idea of Johnston as a daring leader surprised Davis. Though the country at large seemed to have strange confidence in him, Davis himself had not discerned any manifestation of his daring. He thought him a good soldier and personally brave, but he had found him over-cautious and fussy. Would Johnston ever find conditions "just right" for risking his reputation in a fight? Though his confidence in Johnston had been severely shaken, it had not been destroyed. So the President put the matter to his Cabinet. Seddon made a forceful and eloquent presentation of his case for Johnston. The astute Benjamin, who as former Secretary of War had found the General excessively querulous and almost "criminally wasteful," expressed vehement opposition. It would prove ruinous, he warned. Seddon finally won the support of all Cabinet members except Benjamin. On November 24, 1862, by Special Order No. 225, President Davis appointed Joseph E. Johnston to the important command.

Johnston was given "full power to direct the entire Western campaign." He was empowered, at his discretion, to assume personal command of any of the armies in Tennessee and Mississippi. Seddon made it very clear in writing that he had complete authority, and the President wrote him to the same effect. As Eckenrode has pointed out, Johnston's "position was now more powerful than Lee's," for Lee was a departmental commander with only one army to command. Johnston's department embraced Tennessee, Alabama, Mississippi, eastern

[4] The many comments on the subject by War Clerk Jones are interesting. Wigfall had to pass through Jones's office to reach the Secretary of War. The correspondence of Wigfall to Clay, in the Clay Papers at Duke University, is most revealing.

Louisiana, western Georgia, western North Carolina, and the several armies therein. Here was Johnston's rich opportunity to play a decisive part in the war.

Just as the matter of Johnston's command in the West was settled, the President got disheartening news from Europe. After two days of heated discussion, the British Cabinet had decided against joining France in intervention. Lord Russell was constrained to give as reasons Russia's refusal to be a direct party to the plan, and the belief that the United States would reject the proposed armistice and declare war. A better reason was Lee's failure at Antietam. It was later to be learned that Gladstone had offered the strongest arguments in favor of the Emperor's proposal, and that Russell had secretly urged acceptance.

The disappointed South was bitter at England's decision. But Benjamin almost immediately brought the President reports of fresh hope from Slidell, who was convinced the Emperor would execute his plans without England. Even John Bigelow, the United States Consul General, believed Napoleon would "compel us to make peace or fight him . . . before he takes any steps backward." Benjamin's bland confidence persuaded the President yet to hold hope for France's intervention.

Davis took cheer from the final results of the fall elections in the North. Lincoln lost the support of his own state, Illinois, and also the important western states of Ohio, Indiana, and Wisconsin. In the East, the Democrats won powerful New York and Pennsylvania, as well as New Jersey. Some Northern journals declared frankly that the returns expressed "a want of confidence" in the President of the United States. To Davis, the results reflected a strong resentment against Lincoln's political expediency of changing a war for union to a crusade for the Negro. Of course, in Lincoln's view, this new move concerning the Negro problem was a means of attaining restoration of the Union.

In the North that early winter of 1862, the public's depression was at its lowest point as dark dissatisfaction spread among the Federal troops. Letters home from Union soldiers bespoke resentment, disillusion, even hate. A young soldier from New England named John W. Chase wrote bitterly to his parents: "I don't feel as much like fighting as I used to for it looks to me as if fighting for the Union and Constitution is played out and that now we are fighting for the Abolition of

Slavery. Speaking of Abe, I have gone clean back on him. He may be a good rail splitter but rather a poor President, I reckon. . . . Let the nigger go to hell for all of me."

Northern papers were finding fault with Grant because his recent attempts in Mississippi had ended in failure. More was being written about the napping Grant of Shiloh than the victorious Grant of Fort Donelson. The New York *Times* complained that Grant remained "stuck in the mud of Northern Mississippi, his army of no use to him or anybody else." Soldiers wrote home of Grant's extraordinary intemperance. His second in command, Major General John Alexander McClernand, an ambitious Illinois politician, who had been criticizing Grant ever since Shiloh, was intriguing to have him removed.

After the November elections had gone so against the Republican Administration, Jefferson Davis was eager to know what new tack Lincoln would take in his December 1 message to the convening Congress. The message turned out to be nearly 50,000 words long, but to Davis the important thing in it was a plea for compensated emancipation. Mr. Lincoln had apparently grown melancholy over the prolongation of the war, which he had expected to be quickly resolved. As he had written Greeley: "My paramount object in this struggle is to save the Union. . . . If I could save the Union without freeing any slave I would do it." [5]

Compensated emancipation, he now said to Congress, was the only way of ending the war "without convulsion." By his plan—almost a bow to State Rights—each state would decide when to act on the matter, "now, or at the end of the century, or at any intermediary time." The Federal Government's part would merely be to bear the expense by issuing long-term bonds in payment to loyal masters for the slaves. It would be expensive, yes, but cost nothing in blood, and even less money in the long run than continued costly war. Ready cash was not involved. And full emancipation, Lincoln said, "would probably not come before the end of thirty-seven years." He asked for this gradual emancipation for the sake of the Negroes as well as their owners, and pointed up "the vagrant destitution" that would attend immediate emancipation in localities with large Negro populations.

Congressmen listened politely, and many were moved by Mr. Lincoln's "earnestness," though he did not deliver his message in person. But most of them seemed bemused or apathetic. The Republicans were disappointed by the message's "singular reticence" in regard to

[5] The famous letter appears in *The Collected Works of Abraham Lincoln,* Vol. V, p. 388.

the pursuit of war. The Representatives of border states, where many owned slaves, showed no enthusiasm for the plan. When Lincoln's close friend Senator Orville Browning from Illinois returned home after hearing the message, he wrote in his diary that he was surprised "by the hallucination the President seems to be laboring under that Congress can suppress the rebellion by adopting his plan of compensated emancipation." To many a Radical, the idea of paying the South for property that might be confiscated was ridiculous. The response of the Northern public was not at all encouraging.

Davis took note that the United States Congress made no effort to put President Lincoln's scheme into practice. Some of his advisers regarded the Lincoln gesture as a move to create divisions in the South. But it would look well for Lincoln in the historical record; he had said in his message: "Fellow citizens, we cannot escape history."

Davis wondered if Lincoln suffered pangs of remorse for calling out troops and starting a war without the advice or consent of Congress. Did he not sometimes remember his words in the House of Representatives when he castigated President Polk, the Democrat, for the war with Mexico: "He feels the blood of this war, like the blood of Abel is crying to Heaven against him . . . originally having some strong motive . . . to involve the countries in war . . . he plunged into it, and has swept on and on till disappointed in his calculation he now finds himself he knows not where." [6]

Whatever pricks of conscience may have stung Mr. Lincoln in early December of 1862, when Congress ignored his plans for compensated, gradual emancipation, he determined to unleash on the first of January his revised proclamation for immediate emancipation regardless of any "violent convulsions."

In the week before Joseph Johnston's departure for the West, a breakfast was given at Tom Griffin's restaurant on Main Street by Majors Alfred Barbour and Blue Moore, who had been reappointed to their old posts as, respectively, Johnston's Quartermaster and Assistant Quartermaster. The party, though really in honor of Johnston's return to command, was purported to commemorate a reconciliation of Representative Henry S. Foote and Senator William L. Yancey, who had been estranged. These two enthusiastic partisans of General Johnston were among the President's most troublesome opponents.

[6] Lincoln's friend William Herndon quotes this in the biography *Herndon's Lincoln*, Vol. II, p. 278.

Foote and Yancey sat at the right and left of Major Barbour; Johnston sat by Major Moore, and next to him was John Daniel, the *Examiner*'s black-bearded young editor, a devoted admirer of Johnston and relentless foe of both Davis and Lee. Daniel's other chief enthusiasm, General John B. Floyd, whom Davis had removed from command for his dubious behavior at Fort Donelson, was another guest. And so was General Gustavus W. Smith, who had never forgiven the President for giving Lee command of the Army of Northern Virginia instead of giving it to him.

Of this celebrating group, Yancey and Foote were the life of the party, which lasted from ten to twelve. According to a guest, James Louis Clark of the Maryland Cavalry, Johnston was in a strangely taciturn mood and scarcely spoke. Daniel, at his side, was likewise glum and untalkative. But the rest were in festive mood. As the breakfast was breaking up, Mr. Yancey called for fresh glasses and more champagne. Then, rising, he looked significantly at Johnston, and said, "This toast is to be drunk standing." When all had risen except the General, Yancey lifted his glass and called out in his magnificent, oratorical voice, "Gentlemen, let us drink to the health of the only man who can save the Confederacy—General Joseph E. Johnston!" The glasses were emptied, and the standing men clapped their hands. The General, who had been willing to evacuate Richmond in May, looked grave. Slowly, he got up and raised his glass. "Mr. Yancey," he said solemnly, "the man you describe is now in the field—in the person of Robert E. Lee. I will drink to his health." This he proceeded to do, with what mixture of admiration and jealousy only the man himself knew.

The day before the Johnstons were to leave for Chattanooga, Mrs. Davis called to say good-by. Despite the cooling off of friendship after the President ranked Lee one notch above Johnston, Varina had endeavored faithfully to keep a semblance of the old warm relationship. The couple received her cordially enough, but instead of being happy, Johnston was "sad and dispirited." He was loath to leave Virginia. Varina divined that he coveted Lee's command.

Johnston postponed his departure as long as possible. Then a railroad accident delayed him, so he did not reach Chattanooga, his new headquarters, until December 4. On that very day, with apt timing, the Richmond *Examiner,* which Professor Dodd termed "a sort of Johnston organ," declared there was no chance for Johnston's success in the West. It pointedly claimed that it was he who had organized the army of Lee and Jackson, with the implication that he should have superseded Lee at Fredericksburg. The *Examiner* editorial, preparing the nation in case of Johnston's failure, seemed an ironic follow-up to Yancey's refulgent toast to "the only man who can save the Confederacy."

The night of December 6 was bitter cold in Richmond. Ice formed in washstand pitchers even in rooms where fires burned. President Davis, who had been unwell for a fortnight, was wakeful. He could not help but suffer for the ill-clad, ill-sheltered soldiers enduring the freezing weather at Fredericksburg. Since Randolph's upsetting resignation, he had had much to trouble his mind. Before the superior forces of Grant and Sherman, Pemberton was falling back toward Vicksburg, which was also endangered by enemy gunboats pushing nearer and nearer, both downriver and upriver. General Johnston's melancholy attitude at departure had been anything but reassuring. Despite his fatigue, Davis felt impelled to go west to answer imploring calls from his own state to come and bolster morale. Anxious citizens in Mississippi, as well as soldiers, were complaining. Although Johnston's appointment was decidedly popular in the West, some Mississippians were clamoring for Jefferson Davis himself to take personal command of the troops.[7]

After Johnston's arrival at Chattanooga had been heralded, Senator James Phelan wrote Mississippi's Governor Pettus: "I am filled with the conviction that if Pres. Davis will come to Miss. and assume command of the Army the whole face of affairs will be changed. The step will attract the country. Its effect will be electrical—and the spirit of our people now so deeply depressed will rebound with energy and hope. The army will awaken to newness of life and activity. I believe the whole people will respond to his call, to form beneath his banner. . . . I know and feel Davis' presence in this state at this crisis is the great, the important move."[8]

Besides letters from prominent men on the critical state of military affairs, bitter recountals of Federal raids on private estates reached the President. From Brandon, Mississippi, Gustavus Adolphus Henry wrote him of the wanton destruction at his Arkansas plantation,

[7] On December 22, Jones wrote in his diary: "It is said our President will command in Mississippi himself—the army having no confidence in Pemberton, because he is a Yankee."

[8] This letter from Senator Phelan, in the State Archives, Jackson, Mississippi, one of many calling for Jefferson Davis's presence, is much like appeals after the fall of Fort Donelson.

twenty miles above the mouth of the White River. When a gunboat had convoyed enemy transports down the Mississippi on Tuesday, November 18, some Federal soldiers had stopped to invade his place, and had taken away horses and mules. "On Wednesday," he said, "they turned loose upon me a band of drunken and malignant robbers. Killed at least a 100 head of fine cattle, a very large number of pork and stock hogs, enough to have supported a place of 100 negroes. Took off 14 mules and even robbed my negroes of their blankets and money, and did other things which would be improper for me to write or for you to hear. The next day they burnt a vast amount of fodder, 5,000 bushels of corn and my fine steam ginhouse, a corn-mill, and sawmill. . . . Other neighbors shared, in a less degree, the same fate."

Stories of spiteful depredations caused Jefferson Davis acute distress, while the demoralization and robbery of the slaves made him tremble inwardly with indignation. But what could he do, except try to console? His brother Joseph, he himself, and numerous relatives had also suffered from vandals.

Before Davis had read the Phelan and Henry letters, he had already determined to go west, though he dreaded to leave Richmond when Burnside's superior force was facing Lee and there were few reserves to protect the capital. On December 8, the President wrote Lee a long, detailed letter on military affairs and informed him of his proposed trip west:

. . . Entirely concurring in your views as to the propriety of concentrating all disposable force for the impending struggle on the North and South side of Richmond, I regret that I find so little to be drawn on for that purpose.

In Tennessee and Mississippi the disparity between our armies and those of the enemy is so great as to fill me with apprehension, and I have called on Genl Holmes to ask him, if it can be safely done, to send reinforcements to Genl Pemberton. . . . Genl. J. E. Johnston has been sent to command the Western Department, composed of Tennessee, Alabama, Mississippi, and the Eastern part of Louisiana. It was believed necessary to have greater co-operation among those armies, and it was sought in this mode to obtain it.

I propose to go out there immediately with the hope that something may be done to bring out men not heretofore in service, and to arouse all classes to united and desperate resistance. . . .

I have been very anxious to visit you, but constant labor has caused me to delay until necessity hurries me in an opposite direction. . . .

During the period of my absence I shall feel an increasing anxiety to know the events in this quarter, and to have your views in relation to them.

You can send me dispatches to be forwarded from this place. Col. Lee will accompany me. Col. W. P. Johnston will remain at the office.

I hope to return by New Year. May God bless and preserve you.

As ever, your friend

Jeffn. Davis

The President's staff urged him to leave Richmond in secret, so that his absence would create no alarm. Taking two aides, Custis Lee and his nephew Joseph R. Davis, the President went by special train via Petersburg and Lynchburg. The trip was without incident, and the party reached Chattanooga on the eleventh, the very day the Federals threw their pontoon bridges across the Rappahannock at Fredericksburg.

The following morning Davis proceeded to Murfreesboro, Tennessee, where he was warmly received by Bragg. That night, he was serenaded by an enthusiastic crowd. He made a speech, urging the Tennesseeans to defend their soil to the end. He assured them that he had no anxiety about Richmond and that if the people would sustain the struggle a while longer, European intervention would come and end the war.

Next day, the President inspected the troops and talked with officers; he was gratified to find the men "in fine spirits and well-supplied." Everything seemed satisfactory with Bragg, who was rich in captured Federal stores. Davis agreed that Nashville was too strongly fortified and garrisoned for attack. "Much confidence, however," he wrote his wife, "was expressed in our ability to beat them if *they* advance."

On his return to Chattanooga, Davis found telegrams announcing a battle at Fredericksburg. He considered returning to Virginia at once. But reassuring dispatches soon arrived. The President learned that General Lee had been attacked at 9 A.M. on December 13 in a fog. The fight raged all day and until after darkness fell. Lee repulsed the Federals at every point, inflicting severe punishment. One dispatch said that when some Confederate officers had been wounded, their men, in a fury, ran desperately into enemy ranks and slaughtered the foe with knives and bayonets. Apparently it was the Federals' most disastrous defeat yet.

Full of relief and gratitude, the President sat down in his hotel room and wrote Varina a newsy "family" letter about his visit to Bragg's camp. He told her that Lydia Johnston was "not quite pleased with her location" and that General Johnston would go directly to Mississippi and reinforce General Pemberton.

It is raining this morning and unreasonably warm. I have traveled constantly since starting and feel somewhat the want of rest, but otherwise am better than before the journey. . . . Many of the officers inquired for Col. [Preston] Johnston and felt, as I did, regret at his absence.

Kiss the children for their loving Father. They can little realize how much I miss them. Every sound is the voice of my child and every child renews the memory of a loved one's appearance, but none can equal their charms, nor can any compare with my own long-worshipped Winnie.

> She is na my ain lassie
> Though fair the lassie be
> For well ken I my ain lassie
> By the kind love in her eye.

Give my love to Helen and Billy, and to Col. Johnston.

Ever affectionately,
Your husband.

Davis was obviously feeling good, for he rarely indulged in quoting poetry in his most intimate letters, though he was a devotee of Robert Burns.

In reading a series of cheering dispatches from Fredericksburg, the President learned that the Union forces had made six charges across the plain between Fredericksburg and the hills where the Confederates lay entrenched, and that they had been mowed down with deadly effect. Seeing the battle in his mind's eye, the President admired the gallantry with which the Northerners had attacked and met death. He was very proud of Lee's men, who had halted a Federal advance of 106,000. Enemy casualties were double the Confederates';[9] and Lee had captured 11,000 stands of arms. The Southerners had also acquired quantities of clothing, some by a means that shocked many warmly clad noncombatants. Lee had something of a shock himself when he came out of his tent in the morning and beheld a phenomenal sight. The dead Federals lying piled between the lines were no longer blue, but mottled white. Peering fixedly into his field glasses, Lee saw that they were naked. In the night, chilled Confederates had crept forward and relieved the dead men of overcoats, jackets, shirts, boots, and long underwear.[10]

[9] Rhodes wrote: "The Confederate loss was 5,377; the Union 12,653 of the flower of the army."

[10] Richard Lewis wrote some grisly details of the stripping to his mother on December 19, 1862 (*Camp Life of a Confederate Boy*, p. 27).

The audacious valor of an Alabama horse artillerist named John Pelham singled him out for special commendation. Davis remembered the handsome young man who had resigned from West Point just before his graduation in 1861. In Montgomery, he had commissioned Pelham a lieutenant and sent him to Virginia. The planter's son had proved his mettle in numerous engagements. He had advanced rapidly in rank until he was known as "The Boy Major."

At Fredericksburg, he was credited with holding an entire brigade of General George G. Meade's at bay with a single gun for almost an hour, firing up the road into the blue masses with devastating effect. Whenever the Federals got his range, he would change his position so swiftly that the confused bluecoats thought he had a full battery. When Lee gazed across the plain at Pelham's "one gun fighting an army," he exclaimed, "It is glorious to see such courage in one so young." Stonewall Jackson, who had formed a high opinion of Pelham at Gaines' Mill, asked him to direct the fortification of his line for the second day's battle at Fredericksburg. By daylight, when he saw the stout defenses, arisen as if by magic, the marveling Stonewall said to Jeb Stuart, "If you have another Pelham, I wish you would give him to me." Davis knew that the young Alabamian was idolized not only by his men, but by his chief. And now it seemed that the South had a new hero.

On the sixteenth, Burnside was gone somewhere toward the Potomac. Lee would have pursued him if he had divined that the Federals were giving up after one big effort. "The contest will now have to be renewed," he wrote regretfully to Mrs. Lee, "but on what field I cannot say." Davis was disappointed that Burnside's army had not been sufficiently destroyed to make the victory more decisive, so that Lee could have sent reinforcements to Pemberton.

Richmond, so the papers said, received the news of Lee's victory complacently, as something fully expected. But on December 16, Jones wrote in his diary: "Today the city is exalted to the skies." Lee had "saved the capital." Before the enemy could approach Richmond "from some other place," Lee would be between him and the city; "if he can beat him on the Rappahannock he can beat him anywhere." Joseph Johnston, who was in Chattanooga with the President, seemed to think differently. The news of Lee's great victory did not stir Johnston to ardent praise of his compatriot. In a letter to Louis Wigfall, he exclaimed: "What luck some people have! Nobody will ever come to attack me in such a place." He did not use the word "luck" to the President, but it seemed that Lee's success held its drop of wormwood for Johnston.

After another brief, encouraging visit to Bragg's camp, the President suggested that Johnston order the transfer of a few thousand troops to Pemberton's relief.

While President Davis was in Murfreesboro, General Grant issued from Holly Springs, Mississippi, an extraordinary command expelling all Jews from his Department of Tennessee. Speculators had been following—at a respectful distance—the Federal Army in conquered regions to buy cotton and send it North. Grant was already indignant about flagrant violations of the Treasury's specie regulations, "mostly by Jews and other unprincipled traders," as he wrote Assistant Secretary of War C. P. Wolcott. He had instructed his commanding officer at Columbus, Kentucky, to refuse all permits to Jews to come South.[11]

Grant's father, Jesse, an Ohio leather merchant, presumably seeking a little profit out of the war, came for a visit, sponsoring some Jewish dealers who wanted to dicker for cotton. General Grant sent his father and his mercenary friends packing. Then in cold fury he issued General Order 11 from Holly Springs on December 17, 1862.

"The Jews, as a class violating every regulation of trade established by the Treasury Department and also department orders, are hereby expelled from the department within twenty-four hours from the receipt of their order.

"Post commanders will see that all this class of people be furnished passes and required to leave, and anyone returning after such notification will be arrested and held in confinement until an opportunity occurs of sending them out as prisoners."

Grant's drastic order caused a deep sensation in the land. Editorials bespeaking outrage appeared. In one day, cotton in Memphis dropped fifteen cents a pound. President Lincoln was called upon to intervene. But he was to revoke the order only on January 4, 1864, after many innocent and highly respected Southern Jews had been embarrassed and inconvenienced.

Jefferson Davis thought that Grant's assumption that Jews alone were responsible for illicit cotton trading was as ridiculous as it was unfair. He was reminded how often he had been urged to take action

[11] In *Official Records,* Series I, Vol. XVII, Part 2, pp. 421-422, Grant expresses himself fully on the Jewish traders who managed to slip through the lines "with their carpet sacks" and "with pockets full of gold."

against Jewish speculators in the Confederacy, who seemed able to get passports and permits when no one else could.[12] While he keenly deplored profiteering, he steadfastly refused to have Jews singled out as special offenders.

From Chattanooga on December 15, Davis telegraphed the Secretary of War:

Returned to this place from Murfreesboro last night. Found the troops there in good condition and fine spirits. Enemy is kept close in to Nashville and indicates only defensive purposes. Cavalry expeditions are projected to break up railroad communications between Louisville and Nashville, and between Memphis and Grant's army.

General Johnston will go immediately to Mississippi, and will, with the least delay, reinforce Pemberton by sending a division, say 8,000 men, from the troops in this quarter.

I will proceed in the train of today. . . .

The President invited Johnston to accompany him to Jackson, Mississippi. Just as they were leaving Chattanooga, Davis received discouraging news. The Emperor of France would not pursue alone his proposal of a six months' armistice, with temporary suspension of the blockade, which would have opened Southern ports to foreign commerce. The drive for recognition on which Benjamin, Mason, and Slidell had worked so diligently had come to nought. So Davis's return to his home state for the first time since he had left for his inauguration in February of 1861 was somewhat marred by the unexpected intelligence from abroad. Following so closely upon the Fredericksburg success, it emphasized the fateful pattern of the Confederacy's up-and-down fortune.

The route of the President and General Johnston was roundabout, by way of Montgomery and Mobile. They reached Jackson on the morning of the nineteenth and left that same evening with six staff officers for Vicksburg, fifty miles due west. They conferred with General Martin L. Smith and inspected the fortifications. Three days later they went to see General Pemberton at Grenada, where he was constructing entrenchments to stop the Federals from crossing the Yalobusha River. Johnston was not pleased with the work. He did not like

---

[12] War Clerk Jones's diary bristled with resentment of Jewish traders and the passports they wangled. After resigning as Secretary of War, Randolph allied himself with a Jewish attorney and made considerable money in getting passports and special privileges for Jewish speculators.

Pemberton, and, as he wrote, the two "differed widely as to the mode of warfare best adapted to our circumstances." [13]

On Christmas Day, the President was back in Jackson to enjoy dinner at the home of his niece Mrs. Ellen Anderson. Relatives came from all around to greet him. At least for a few hours, warmed by the affection of devoted kin, he could forget the hateful business of war.

In Richmond, though Varina was not indulging in any special entertaining during his absence, but was making the season largely a children's festival, gay parties were planned for soldiers on leave and for distinguished foreign visitors. Among the latter was the Marquess of Hartington, the future eighth Duke of Devonshire, who was accompanied by Lord Edward St. Maur. Since the President was leaving for the West when they arrived, he had asked Colonel and Mrs. Ives to be their hosts.

In a letter written home on Christmas Day, Hartington commented on the "crowdedness" of Richmond, the high prices, the shabbiness of people's clothes. "However," he declared, "they are in good spirits, though they do not think very much of the Fredericksburg victory, as they never had any doubt whatever about it." While he himself was convinced that the Northern Democrats really wanted peace, he said that the Southerners did not expect peace for some time and were ready to go on for any length of time. "I believe," the young nobleman wrote, "many of them think the longer the better, because it will widen the breach between them and the Yankees, against whom their hatred is more intense than you can possibly conceive. . . . They say that the way in which the Federals have carried on the war, the ascendancy of the Abolition party . . . have entirely destroyed every vestige of Union feeling and I believe that it is so."

The day after Christmas, with General Johnston in the assembly, the President addressed the Mississippi Legislature. He spoke frankly of his sore disappointment at lack of recognition by European powers. "Put not your faith in Princes," he said, "and rest not your hopes on foreign nations. This war is ours; we must fight it out ourselves."

With much tenderness, Davis alluded to his attachment to his state.

---

[13] On January 5, 1863, however, General Johnston telegraphed General Cooper that the enemy had made several attacks upon the line between Vicksburg and Snyder's Hill and was "repulsed with a loss of 1,100; ours 150." "Lieutenant-General Pemberton," he declared, "deserves high credit." *Official Records,* Series I, Vol. XVII, Part 2, p. 826.

He said that though as President he had determined to make no distinction between the various parts of the country, yet his heart always beat more warmly for Mississippi, and he "looked on Mississippi soldiers with a pride and an emotion, such as no others inspired." Davis presented a forthright, dignified defense of his Administration. Among other things, he made clear the necessity of the conscription law. With the damaging recalcitrance of Georgia's Governor Brown in mind, he said fervently, "I hope no conflict will arise between the States and the common cause. If any State chooses to inflict such a blow by making conflicting military laws, I hope Mississippi will be the last to join such a suicidal policy."

He explained the proviso in the conscription law that exempted men who owned twenty or more slaves. Its object, he said, was not to draw any distinction of classes but "simply to provide a force, in the nature of a police force, sufficient to keep our Negroes in control. The poor do, indeed, fight the battles of the country," he declared. "It is the poor who save nations and make revolutions. . . . But look through the army; cast your eyes upon the maimed heroes of the war whom you meet in your streets and in the hospitals; remember the martyrs of the conflict; and you will find among them more than a fair proportion drawn from men of property. . . . Men of the largest fortune in Mississippi are now serving in the ranks."

The President was eloquent in recommending that the Legislature take measures for assisting the families of absent soldiers. "Let this provision," he said, "be made for the objects of his affection and his solicitude, and the soldier, engaged in fighting the battles of his country, will no longer be disturbed by dreams of an unprotected and neglected family at home."

In conclusion, he enjoined the Legislators to prepare for a desperate contest against "a power armed for conquest and subjugation." "The South," he declared, "could never, never reunite with the North." And in the hearing of Joseph Johnston, he said with ringing emphasis, "Vicksburg must not fall."

When the applause had died away, he presented General Johnston, who was most enthusiastically received. The Virginian spoke only two sentences. First, he regretted that he had done so little to merit such a greeting. "I promise you, however," he said, "that hereafter I shall be watchful, energetic, and indefatigable in your defense." A few months later, when he did not go to Pemberton's aid in besieged Vicksburg, Mississippians were to recall Johnston's vain promise.

The next few days, the President spent in and around Jackson, visiting nearby towns and plantations, talking with people, high and low, and endeavoring to cheer their spirits. With Custis Lee, he went to visit his brother Joseph on the newly bought plantation, Fleetwood, near Bolton, between Vicksburg and Jackson. It pained him to see the old man struggling to make a worn-out plantation agreeable for his family and his Negroes. Joseph had already half built some twenty new cabins on the place, and was planning to erect more. He said he could not bear to have "his people" uncomfortable, nor could he abide miserable, ramshackle cabins on any place.

The President rode to the farm that Joseph had bought for him about three miles from Fleetwood. In sore need of repairs and improvements, it did not look promising. But it would provide refuge and food for his uprooted slaves, who greeted him with touching affection. The soil of both places was so poor and worked-out, that to Joseph, accustomed to opulent Delta earth, it seemed almost a waste of labor to cultivate it; but he had to try because of the troop of Negroes depending upon him to feed them.[14]

The President called on the Coxes in Hinds County. These kind friends had taken in the Joseph Davises when they had fled Vicksburg after fleeing Hurricane. Mr. Cox had also secured the Jefferson Davises' parlor furniture for safekeeping just before the Federals wrecked Brierfield. And he had hidden in the loft of a cabin some of the President's most valuable books and a prized box of family letters written to Davis when he was at school in Kentucky and West Point, together with his and Knox Taylor's love letters.

Wherever Davis went in Mississippi, he heard distressing stories of unjustified enemy depredations. Near Grenada, a poor widow had been plundered of her only cow and everything of value in her home. The Federals offered to furnish her with rations if she would take an oath of allegiance to the United States. She refused, and was forced to live on parched corn.

Far more gruesome tales came from New Orleans, where Ben Butler, puffed with power, had once called himself "Christ's Vice-Regent." A prominent druggist named Moore, who had many Mississippi friends, had been condemned to months of hard labor with ball and chain for sending a few ounces of quinine into the Confederacy. But Moore was only one of hundreds who had felt "The Beast's" cruelty.

[14] Details of the visit are related in Lise Mitchell's "Journal."

Butler's notorious treatment of Mrs. Philip Phillips, wife of the former United States Congressman, was the most talked of and the most condemned. Jefferson Davis, who had the usual chivalric Southern attitude to womankind, was appalled at the ghastly details of Eugenia Phillips's ordeal.

Butler was furious with Mrs. Phillips for collecting money for the widow of William Mumford, whom he had hanged for helping to haul down a United States flag from the mint five days before he took command of New Orleans. In June, he had arrested her for allegedly laughing at a Federal officer's funeral procession that passed under her balcony "with twenty empty carriages in the procession."

When Eugenia Phillips was brought to him, Butler wasted no time with amenities, but glanced at a placard that he kept in his office to remind himself that "The venom of the she-adder is as dangerous as the he-adder." "I do not call you a vulgar woman of the town," he shouted at her, "but an uncommonly vulgar one." When she would not humble herself and beg clemency, but showed contempt and disgust at his railing, he sentenced her, to break her spirit, to an indefinite stay on Ship Island, that narrow strip of barren sand guarding the pass between New Orleans and Biloxi. The lady was put in an open boat with "rude, drunken soldiers" and made to endure a twelve-hour journey in burning summer sun with "not a drop of water to relieve the horror." Her prison, set in the sand, was, as she saw it, a "huge box with a small door hung on leather straps. An iron ring was the only furniture," she wrote. "Not a seat, bed, table, comfort of any kind was there to receive a woman tenderly cared for all her life." As mosquitoes and sand flies in swarms began to attack her and she thought she would go wild, a kindhearted young Union captain, horrified at her plight, exclaimed, "My God, can such things be!" and got a piece of netting, which he hung over a nail. Mrs. Phillips crouched under the netting, thanking God she was saved. "Thus—" she wrote "on the ground I passed a wretched night, no one coming near me, not one particle of food." [15]

When a doctor at the hospital sent her some tea and toast the next morning, General Neal Dow, the commander, arrived in time to dash the contents of the tray to the ground and kick down the soldier-waiter. When she attempted to write the good doctor a note of thanks, General

---

[15] The details of Eugenia Phillips's imprisonment are taken from her unpublished manuscript, "A Southern Woman's Story of Her Imprisonment During the War of 1861 and 1862," in the Library of Congress.

She was shortly supplied with some rude pieces of furniture.

Dow swore at her, declaring that if she ever communicated with any-one outside her prison, he would "hang her up by the legs."

For three months, the delicately brought-up Eugenia was fed cold tea and pieces of "rancid, stale bread, yellow with saleratus; nothing else, never a warm mouthful." When storms came, rain poured in on her, and she would creep under the table to avoid the wet. The heat was almost unbearable. She was allowed no exercise, and no candle at night. Daily, she "witnessed the best men of New Orleans, with ball and chain, breaking stones for the fort"; one was the druggist, Mr. Moore. After a month, Mrs. Phillips suffered from brain fever. But when she begged for ice, "though hogsheads of ice were melting nearby," she was refused a drop, on the grounds that "Butler denied her all comfort."

All the while, Unionist friends of the Phillipses, like Maryland's Senator Reverdy Johnson, were entreating for her release. At first, But-ler declared that if Lincoln and the whole army requested it, he would refuse. Finally, however, in September, because so much pressure was put on him, Butler had released the prisoner on the pretense that she was going to have a baby, saying that he did not want "the wholly in-nocent to suffer." Arriving at her New Orleans home at sunup, Mrs. Phillips barely had strength to ring the bell. When her Negro man-servant unlocked the door and beheld the wraithe, he cried, "Oh, my God, my Mistress' corpse!," slammed the door, and fled. Upstairs, her husband, ill from protracted anxiety, believed her dead body had been brought home, became "like one turned to stone," and could not move. Painfully, Eugenia crawled up the stairs and fainted in trying to reach his bed. For weeks, she was desperately sick. Now, in Decem-ber, still sick, she refused to take a loyalty oath to the United States. So she and her husband were banished from New Orleans, and all their newly acquired property was confiscated.

Jefferson Davis's blood boiled at such inhuman treatment accorded any woman. And Eugenia Phillips was a lady who had sometimes sat next to him at dinner in the days of Pierce and Buchanan. In his ir-repressible outrage that such things could be, two days before Christ-mas he had issued a proclamation declaring Ben Butler beyond the pale of civilization and ordering any Confederate commander who captured him to hang him straightway as a felon. Though his proclama-tion made Confederates rejoice, Davis knew it might prove as inopera-tive as Lincoln's Emancipation in Southern states. Butler, who took superlative precautions for his life and was the most heavily guarded man in the land, had already been transferred back to Washington.

The increasing hatred between the two sections was a corroding thing that Jefferson Davis deplored. But the harsh actions of generals like Butler and Sherman were stirring the people to call upon him for retaliation.

A story of Sherman's ruthlessness came to Davis in Jackson fresh from Columbus, Mississippi. As military commander of Memphis, General Sherman had announced that he would banish the wives of ten Rebel officers if anyone fired on the Union gunboats in the river. When they were shot at, Sherman made a list of ten ladies, whom he ordered to leave Memphis within twenty-four hours. One of them, the wife of Major Minor Meriwether, whom Davis knew, was on the list. Since Elizabeth Meriwether, mother of two little boys, was expecting another baby within a few weeks, she begged General Sherman to let her stay in her home until her baby was born. But the General eyed her coldly. "I am not interested in Rebel wives or Rebel brats," he said. "If you are in Memphis after tomorrow you will be put in prison to stay until the rebellion is crushed."

Mrs. Meriwether, who had been considerately received by General Grant on some previous business, was at first incredulous. But she rushed home, threw a pile of clothes and blankets in the back seat of her "rockaway," put the two little boys, Avery and Rivers, aged five and three, on top of the pile, and started southeast, pulled by their mule, named Adrienne, which happily had not been confiscated. It was cold, and the roads were deep in slush. Frequent skirmishes between the enemy armies took place on either side of her. Finally, on Christmas Day, as she neared Columbus, her labor began. She stopped at a farmhouse and was taken in. In the night, assisted by an old Negress, she gave birth to a third boy, whom she named Lee for the General.[16]

On December 30, Jefferson Davis said good-by to his relatives and friends in Jackson and left for Mobile.

During the last half of December, while the President was in the West, things went extremely well with the Confederate forces. Nathan Bedford Forrest led a freshly recruited cavalry outfit, many with-

---

[16] The story is taken from Elizabeth Meriwether's *Recollections of 92 Years,* which was published by the Tennessee Historical Commission in 1958. Lee Meriwether was also destined for longevity. He was physically active and keenly alert at ninety-six, when the author was his house guest in St. Louis in November, 1958. Mrs. Meriwether took shelter in Tuscaloosa, Alabama, from 1863 to the war's end, and became an intimate friend of the President's brother Joseph Davis, also a refugee there in 1864.

out arms, up into Tennessee, grabbed a succession of Federal bases, got horses for all his men, and armed them with Union weapons. Then he cut up railroads and telegraph lines, and with little damage to his own force. At Cumberland Shoals, below Nashville, fiery little Joseph Wheeler attacked and destroyed several Federal transports loaded with supplies.

Best of all, on December 20, Buck Van Dorn made a bold attack at Holly Springs, captured 2,000 prisoners and destroyed some million dollars' worth of Grant's essential supplies, thus temporarily checking the planned Federal assault on Vicksburg and leaving Grant's troops in danger of starvation. Van Dorn's brilliant success, which offset his October repulse at Corinth, was like a fine Christmas gift to the President.

In Kentucky, the Confederate raider John Hunt Morgan continued his depredations on Union encampments; two days after Christmas, he was at Elizabethtown, just below Louisville. From Vicksburg, Pemberton reported, on December 27, that his lines had been attacked at four different points and that each attacking party had been "handsomely repulsed." From the twenty-seventh to the twenty-ninth, 30,000 troops under General Sherman, with sixty guns, attacked Brigadier General Stephen D. Lee at Chickasaw Bayou on the Yazoo above Vicksburg. The total Confederate strength by highest estimates was less than 14,000. This South Carolina Lee, who had gone with Chesnut to deliver Beauregard's ultimatum at Sumter, inflicted a stinging defeat on the enemy, who lost 1,776, while his own casualties amounted to a mere two hundred, of whom, sixty-three were killed. It is of interest to note that Sherman's repulse was accomplished, in large part, by two of the brigades from the divisions Davis had ordered detached from Bragg, over Johnston's objections.

Sherman, smarting under his setback, took his fleet of transports back to the Mississippi River, leaving all his entrenching tools behind. General Grant had already brought his army to the very northern border of the state, and apparently intended to operate from Memphis. With a minimum of losses, in December the Confederates had repulsed enemy brigades on various fields. When the President left for Mobile, the western theater was in a far, far better situation than when he arrived.

The appearance of Jefferson Davis on his home soil was indubitably beneficial in allaying popular mistrust, grounded in the supposition that Virginia engrossed his attention to the exclusion of concern for the Mississippi Valley. Those who had urged him to come to relieve the situation felt vindicated in their belief in his magnetic influence.

On the last day of 1862, the famous little *Monitor,* which had dramatically appeared to save the wooden Federal fleet from the iron-clad *Merrimac,* went down in a storm off North Carolina. The same day, like another footnote to history, the western part of Virginia that had withdrawn from Old Dominion allegiance was admitted to the Union as a new state.

The death of the *Monitor* and the birth of West Virginia were minor events compared to the battle between Bragg and Rosecrans, whose armies faced each other before Murfreesboro the night of December 30. Early the next morning, Bragg struck first, and threw back the Federal right. With difficulty, Rosecrans was able to hold the turnpike to Nashville. It was a bloody battle, in which the Federals, outnumbering the Confederates by 7,000, sustained the greater losses. The President was in Mobile when he received the relayed telegram from Bragg: "God has granted us a happy New Year."

All in all, 1862 was the Confederacy's big year. At the year's end, supplies were coming in, despite the vigilance of the blockade. The special event of New Year's Day was Prince John Magruder's remarkable capture of Galveston, which opened up a valuable port for blockade-runners. Magruder, who ever "had a penchant for desperate work," took down from Houston a ragtag force and some improvised gunboats armored with cotton bales. He routed the enemy, sank some Federal boats, and captured the warship *Harriet Lane.* It seemed a bright omen. And, according to diaries and press weather reports throughout the South, the sun of January 1, 1863, "shone in great splendor on a people radiant with smiles." As Jefferson Davis proceeded by train from Mobile to Augusta, his heart could echo the audible and the unuttered longing that ran through the South, "Oh that peace would return! But with independence."

CHAPTER XXVII

CONGRESS DILLYDALLIES

JEFFERSON DAVIS could greet the New Year of 1863 with a smile. Richmond was secure; the Federal Army, somewhere beyond the Rappahannock, was disorganized and sunk in gloom. Morale in Mississippi had been definitely stimulated by his visit. Since June, when he had put Lee in command, the Army of Northern Virginia had won a series of victories: Port Republic, Cross Keys, Gaines' Mill, Savage Station, Frayser's Farm, Cedar Mountain, Second Manassas, Harpers Ferry, Fredericksburg. And now, with Rosecrans's defeat by Bragg in Tennessee, the dawning year seemed singularly propitious.

But, as often before when the Confederacy's fortunes were lifted high, an unlooked-for disappointment followed. On January 2, Bragg had expected Rosecrans to be retreating toward Nashville; to his surprise, he found the stubborn Federal Army where he had left it New Year's Eve. In an effort to dislodge Rosecrans's left and center, victory-flushed Confederates under Breckinridge made a successful assault, but they did not stop where they were told to stop. Rushing on, they suddenly found themselves under terrific fire from fifty-odd guns. They were mowed down disastrously.

On January 3, the rival armies remained in watchful position, not knowing which side had won, only aware that their losses had been frightful: the Union forces of 44,000 had lost some 13,000; the Confederate forces of 37,000, some 10,000.

At 12:15 A.M. of January 3, Generals Benjamin F. Cheatham and J. M. Withers sent to Bragg, through Polk, a joint letter stating that "this army should be promptly put in retreat." Polk endorsed the letter, with the notation: "We could now, perhaps, get off with some safety

357

and some credit." Bragg did not agree until word came from Wheeler that reinforcements were joining Rosecrans. Then he gave the order to withdraw, partly to safeguard his enormous trains of captured supplies. His objective was Tullahoma, thirty-five miles southeast of Murfreesboro, a position that barred the Federal way to strategic Chattanooga. Rosecrans was too worn out to follow. Unharassed, Bragg moved expeditiously to new winter quarters in a fertile valley along the Duck River.

Jefferson Davis did not learn of Bragg's withdrawal until he neared Richmond. After brief visits in Augusta and Charlotte, he made his last overnight stop in Wilmington on January 4. Troops stationed in that North Carolina seaport turned out to serenade him at his hotel. Citizens gathered. The President appeared on the hotel balcony and addressed the crowd for an hour. One who heard him wrote, twenty-seven years later, to the editor of the *Virginian,* that his "fervid eloquence" and "purity of diction" would never be forgotten by his hearers. Davis's admonition to the soldiers "left an impression that time will not efface." "Soldiers," the President said, re-echoing former words, "I charge you always to be kind to prisoners. Fight the enemy with all the power God has given you, but when he shall surrender remember that you are Southern gentlemen and treat him with courtesy and kindness." Then he repeated a sentiment he had expressed on the Spotswood balcony after his return from Manassas in July of 1861: "Never be humble to the haughty, and never be haughty to the humble!"

The next day, the President, with his two aides, left for Richmond. After three weeks of constant traveling, covering 2,750 roundabout miles, inspecting, counseling, making speeches, and having just heard of Bragg's retreat, he arrived thoroughly exhausted. When his wife saw how fatigued he was, she begged him to retire immediately. But a crowd had gathered at the White House to serenade him, and he felt he must greet them. He told of his trip to the West and spoke briefly of depredations by Union troops on defenseless civilians. "Our enemies," he said, "have come to disturb your social organization on the plea that it is a military necessity. For what are they waging war? They say to preserve the Union. . . . Do they hope to reconstruct the Union by striking at everything which is dear to men?"

He spoke of his regret at having so little opportunity for social intercourse with the citizens. He explained that the constant duties and anxieties of office left him scarcely a moment for repose. He hoped that the time might come when he "could participate in quiet enjoyments with them." "Whilst a man's sympathy is attracted by the sufferings of fellow creatures," he said, "whilst every thought is directed to the dangers of his country, there is little time for the cultivation of the social enjoyments that pertain to a time of peace. I can only give this as my excuse for my seldom appearance among you."

He closed, as was his custom, on a spirit-lifting note. "One year ago many were depressed and some despondent. Now deep resolve is seen in every eye, an unconquerable spirit nerves every arm. And gentle woman, too—who can estimate the value of her services in this struggle? . . . With such noble women at home, and such heroic soldiers in the field, we are invincible." [1]

The next morning, the President was ill. His physician insisted that he must have some days of absolute rest. But with Congress convening on the twelfth, there was little time; he had to prepare his message. On the sixth, he stayed in bed, but on the seventh he held a Cabinet meeting at his home.

While the President, in his weakened condition, was collecting his thoughts to compose the Congressional message, Burton Harrison reluctantly brought him two letters from Joseph Johnston in Jackson. A long one was dated January 2 and a shorter one of two pages was dated January 3. The first was full of details of troop movements, provisions, Grant on the Tallahatchie, hope in Van Dorn. Johnston asked for 20,000 more men. Would the victory at Fredericksburg enable General Lee to spare a part of his force? Despite the series of successes in Mississippi since Van Dorn's brilliant feat at Holly Springs, Johnston revealed a deep-seated anxiety. "Should the enemy's forces be respectably handled," he wrote despondently, "the task you have set me will be above my ability. But the hand of Almighty God has delivered us in times of as great danger. Believing that He is with us I will not lose hope." [2]

Davis was perturbed by Johnston's tone. Commanding Generals should show resolution, for troops could sense their officers' apprehensions. But the second letter was even more disturbing. Though John-

---

[1] The speech was quoted in the daily Richmond *Enquirer* of Wednesday, January 7, 1863.

[2] The letter, which gives something of a summary of the Mississippi situation, appears on page 823 of *Official Records*, Series I, Vol. XVII, Part 2. Johnston's dispatches and letters that precede and follow page 823 are highly revealing and show that Johnston as Commander of the Department moved troops about at will.

ston had another small victory to report, he asked for another command.

Mr. President,

You were so beset while in Jackson that I had no opportunity to speak to you fully of my Military position.

The distance between the theatres of operation & the different objects of the armies in my command, make it impossible for me to exercise any general control. I must either take the immediate direction of one of the armies—thus superseding its proper commander,—or be idle except on the rare occasions when it might be expedient to transfer troops from one department to another. . . . In the second [contingency], I should, generally, be idle & a distant spectator of the efforts & services of my comrades—a position which would inevitably disgrace me. I have already lost much time from service—& therefore can ill afford to be inactive at any time during the remainder of the war. I am anxious to earn by labour at least, some part of the confidence you & the people of Mississippi have given me.

With these views I respectfully & earnestly beg some other position which may give me better opportunity to render such service as I may be capable of.

Lieut. Genl. Pemberton certainly conducted operations at Vicksburg with skill & vigor. The enemy was repulsed with eight times our loss. . . .

Most respectfully
Your obt sert
J. E. Johnston

Davis read the second letter with a sigh. Could Johnston never be satisfied? He had been given what was in reality the largest command in the Confederate Army. The purpose of the command, as Secretary of War Seddon had planned it, was to co-ordinate the Army of Tennessee and the Army of the Mississippi Valley. Johnston had accepted the position with this understanding. Now he seemed to dread the responsibility. It was rather a pathetic letter, too, for the man seemed so painfully concerned with his reputation.

The President now had neither the strength nor the time to soothe the Commanding General. On January 8, he merely sent him a brief telegram: "To hold Mississippi is vital. The difficulty arising from the separation of troops of your command is realized but cannot be avoided."

Though far from well, Davis took up again the reins of government. His penetrating mind surveyed the whole realm of military, political, and diplomatic affairs. The general situation was promising. The closing in of winter made an attack on Lee's army improbable. With Congress again in session, he hoped to get through some important legislation. Secretary of State Benjamin came to see him, exuding cheer over the Confederacy's improved outlook. The blockade had been broken at Charleston. At Galveston, not only had the *Harriet Lane* been captured, but the *Westfield,* the Federal squadron's flagship, had been blown up. The enemy force at Sabine Pass had been seized, together with thirteen guns and "stores to the value of one million dollars." Benjamin had apprised the foreign consuls of the opening of these two additional ports, Galveston and Sabine Pass.

Benjamin maintained that all was not lost in regard to foreign recognition. In late November, 1862, when the President learned that the drive of the Confederate commissioners, agents, and lobbyists for recognition had failed, he had felt that the best chance for recognition had passed. The only real weapon the Confederacy had to force England's hand against Seward's constant threat of war was the withholding of cotton. And cotton could no longer be entirely withheld. Confederate credit in England had run out. The South was now forced to ship cotton through the blockade in order to get money to buy armaments.

But Benjamin had had news from Mason in London that the cotton famine was extending itself and that there was misery among the millhands. Some two million Englishmen were reduced to semistarvation; life savings of factory workers had melted away. Families had sold their furniture, bedding, clothing, even kitchen utensils, until they had nothing left but "barren floors and walls and a roof." They were months in arrears on rent; some daughters supported their parents by prostitution. "Events are maturing which must lead to some change in attitude of England," Mason wrote hopefully.

In France, too, the cotton operatives had suffered severely, living largely on bran and water, while their "half-naked children roamed the countryside begging food." While the President was in the West, Slidell had written: "I feel very sanguine that not many months, perhaps not many weeks, will elapse without some decided action on Napoleon's part." It did the President good to find his Secretary of State so optimistic, even if he could not fully share his optimism.

Davis had been concerned about the effect of Lincoln's revised Emancipation Proclamation, issued on January 1, 1863. But in the first fortnight, it had no effect whatever in the South except to stir up a deeper resentment of the meddlesome North. On January 7, War Clerk Jones noted: "A large body of slaves passed through the city today, singing happily. They had been working on fortifications north of the city and go to work on them south of it. They have no faith in the efficiency of Lincoln's Emancipation."

Jefferson Davis read with some disdain the passage in the printed proclamation that said slaves "are, and henceforth shall be, free," and that "the Executive Government . . . will recognize and maintain the freedom of such persons." It was obvious that few of Lincoln's troops could get near enough to the slaves to set them free, let alone maintain their freedom.

But Davis was gravely disturbed at two passages in the text. One read: "The Executive Government of the United States, including the military and naval authority thereof . . . will do no act or acts to repress such persons, or any of them in any efforts they may need for their actual freedom." This seemed a direct invitation for the slaves to revolt against their masters. Another admonished: "And I hereby enjoin upon the people to be declared free to abstain from all violence, unless in necessary self-defense." The words *unless in necessary self-defense* were as if underscored in blood. And Mr. Lincoln promised that "such persons will be received into the armed service of the United States."

The Richmond *Examiner,* on January 7, blasted the proclamation as the "most startling political crime in American history." This statement, by the foremost anti-Davis paper, the President found to be the general opinion of his people.

By no means did all Northern papers express jubilation. The New York *Herald* of January 3 wrote off the proclamation as "practically a dead letter," and declared that it was "unwise and ill-timed, impracticable, and outside of the Constitution." Confiscation of private property, without appeal or compensation, with no judicial sanction or the approval of Congress, was patently illegal.

In the new proclamation, revised from the September one, Davis noted that the Confederate State of Tennessee was exempted from the edict as well as Maryland, Kentucky and Missouri. So slavery was quite acceptable among friends, but evil for enemies. In England, Foreign Secretary Russell also remarked on the fact that the edict made slavery "at once legal and illegal" and lacked altogether a "declaration of a principle adverse to slavery."

"It is a little less than a mockery," said London's *Quarterly Review* with high scorn, "to ask us to believe that Northerners are fighting solely to extinguish, and the Southerners solely to perpetuate, slavery. There is, however, a small, and we believe diminishing set of English-men and women who are enthusiastic about Mr. Charles Sumner and Mrs. Beecher Stowe, as being enlightened apostles and beneficent philanthropists. We might ask the admirers of this gifted pair in what philanthropy consists. Does it include self-denial: If so, what sacri-fices has either made for the negro? How will their record read by the side of Stonewall Jackson's or Robert Lee's? The cause of the Federal Government is not a crusade . . . but the unholy dream of universal empire revived in the West."

On January 12, 1863, when President Davis sent his message to the convened congress, he naturally referred to the Emancipation Proc-lamation with indignation: "We may well leave it to the instincts of common humanity," he said, "to pass judgment on a measure by which millions of human beings of an inferior race, peaceful and contented laborers in their sphere . . . are encouraged to a general assassination of their masters by the insidious recommendation 'to abstain from violence unless in necessary self-defense.' "

As if avouching the cordial relations between master and slave, a letter reached Jefferson Davis two days later from the faithful colored overseer, Ben Montgomery, who had stayed on to guard the Brierfield and Hurricane plantations as much as possible from Federal depreda-tions and to keep food crops in cultivation. Though most of "the peo-ple" had departed for the new Davis plantations in Hinds County, some had stayed to help Ben with the farming. It was particularly heartwarming at this time to have tactful reassurances from the in-telligent Ben, who was managing the disrupted plantation affairs with discretion.

Hurricane, January 11th, 1863

Dear Master,

Though there are but few here comparatively, I think a knowledge of how we are getting along may be of some interest to yourself and mistress. We are about as well as usual.

. . . Since getting the corn over, which was near 300 bushels, the cart has been principally engaged hauling wood. And Warren has been attending the stock which had become much scattered. . . . The crop of clover—from present appearance—will be tolerable good. And the Fescue grass seems to be coming up very well on the ridge between the hospital and quarter.

I find that the present number of people here and Brierfield will require about 15 bushels meal weekly for bread, besides some will be necessary for some of the stock & some little to the hogs that are here to prevent them from straying off. So I think of getting more while it is to be had. . . .

To avoid exhausting my little means I am devoting some time to shoe-making for some of the neighbors that desire. The tanning will be continued. I am having bark gathered for the purpose, having lost all by the preparation made sometime since to move. . . .

Your servant
Ben

On the same day that Davis heard from Ben Montgomery, Congress-man Clement L. Vallandigham from Ohio spoke bitterly in the Federal House of Representatives against the war as well as Lincoln's procla-mation: "You have not conquered the South. You never will," he de-clared passionately. "The war for the Union is, in your hands, a most bloody and costly failure. The President confessed it on September 22. . . . War for the Union was abandoned; war for the negro begun, and with stronger battalions than before. With what success? Let the dead at Fredericksburg and Vicksburg answer. . . . But ought this war to continue? I answer no—not a day, not an hour."

That was bold, courageous talk, Davis thought. Radical Republi-cans regarded it as treasonous. From this hour, Vallandigham, who was for union with compromises, was regarded as the leading Copper-head in the West, though the opprobrious term came to be used for all Democrats and any person who advocated peace.

On January 16, at the request of the President, General Lee came to Richmond from Fredericksburg for a conference. Lee was discouraged about the lack of provisions and the poor railway transportation, which brought supplies to the Rappahannock by a single-track road. There was little forage for the horses. In this unusually bleak and frigid January, many of the men still lacked proper shoes and suf-ficient blankets. But Lee said the soldiers had made themselves rea-sonably comfortable by building huts with mud-and-stick chimneys. Some had tents with stoves. Altogether, they kept remarkably cheer-ful with snow battles, amateur theatricals, music, and religious meet-ings, as well as drilling. Davis promised to do everything he could to relieve Lee's men, and to urge Commissary General Northrop to cut the red tape.

The two old soldiers talked of the December victory and of young John Pelham, whose praise was on everybody's lips. In his official re-port of the Battle of Fredericksburg, Lee had singled Pelham out for special honor, calling him "the Gallant Pelham." [3] Davis always felt a thrill to hear of youthful valor; a soldier who had just ceased being a boy had so many more years to risk losing than an older man.

While Lee was still in Richmond, a report came that the Army of the Potomac was on the march and approaching the Rappahannock. He hurried back to his army. Nothing, however, came of the Federal advance. Burnside, wrangling with his Generals all the way, pushed through mud and sleet, attempting to find a better crossing on the upper Rappahannock. He shortly gave up in disgust and rushed to Washington.

Davis heard that Burnside's discontented men, wanting McClellan, were at the point of mutiny. Burnside recommended the removal of Stanton and Halleck, who, he believed, had lost the nation's esteem. Instead, President Lincoln removed Burnside. He put in command Major General Joseph Hooker, a hard-drinking, boastful, handsome fighter, who bore the soubriquet of "Fighting Joe." This fifth successive commander to be appointed to lead a march on Richmond proved efficient at organization and in checking demoralization in his army, but he would have to wait until spring to blast the Confederates out of his path.

Jefferson Davis again faced the problem of Braxton Bragg. Secretary of War Seddon, who had little confidence in the North Carolinian, urged the President to remove him. Davis, however, like Gorgas, thought that, despite some fumbling, Bragg had done well. But he knew there was still much resentment and discontent among his lieutenants. Bragg was a good soldier and a first-rate trainer of men, but he inspired none of the affection that McClellan or Lee did. He was prickly, brusque, and seemingly lacking in sympathy. His discipline was unusually stern. He had held down desertions by having deserters shot, but this had made him feared rather than admired by his soldiers.

After the withdrawal from Murfreesboro, Bragg had asked his corps and division commanders to commit to writing "what had transpired between them and him in regard to his retreat from Murfreesboro." The officers deliberately misinterpreted Bragg's circular as a request for a vote of confidence. They were in virtual agreement that Bragg did not possess the confidence of the army "in that degree necessary to insure success." Hardee, while declaring his highest regard for

[3] Decades later, the Illinois poet Edgar Lee Masters was to write that the young cannoneer stood by his guns at Fredericksburg with "the fiery spirit of the archangel Michael."

Bragg's "purity of motives, his energy and personal character," was compelled to say that the general officers were "unanimous in the opinion that a change in the command of the army is necessary."

Polk forwarded copies of the whole correspondence to President Davis, along with the opinion that Bragg should be transferred. He suggested that the disliked General might serve Davis well in Richmond. "His capacity for organization and discipline, which has not been equalled among us, could be used by you at headquarters."

Davis was much perturbed by the criticisms. He knew Bragg had many personal enemies, who distrusted as well as hated him. But, before removing or transferring Bragg, he felt he should have the Commanding General of the Department, Joseph Johnston, make a personal inspection and express his opinion.

On January 22, Davis wrote Johnston, asking him to visit Bragg's army and report on morale. "As that army is a part of your command . . . you have a right to direct its operations, and do whatever else belongs to the General Commanding."

Johnston repaired immediately to Tullahoma. His first reports were surprisingly reassuring. And to Senator Wigfall, who had become more of a confidant since his denunciations of the President in November, Johnston wrote privately on January 26: "Bragg has done wonders, I think—no body of troops had done more in proportion to numbers in the same time. At Murfreesboro he killed, wounded and took 17,000 and within the three weeks preceding, 7,500. His own loss in all that time about 9,000." This superlative, exaggerated, estimate of Bragg's accomplishments, almost suggested that Johnston would like to rank him above both Lee and Jackson.

In the same letter, Johnston referred to something that gnawed at his consciousness: Lee's world-renowned successes with the Army of Northern Virginia. "After commanding our most important, and I may add, best army for a year," he lamented to Wigfall, "it is hard to lose that command for wounds in battle and to receive a nominal one. I must confess I cannot help repining at this situation. The President, however, intends that I shall hold a high position and an important one, but I think he mistakes the relation between Tennessee and Mississippi."

Following three weeks of observation and interview in Bragg's camp, Johnston sent another good report to the War Office; and on February 14 he wrote to Wigfall from Knoxville, repeating his high commendation of the controversial General. "Bragg has commanded admirably in Tennessee," he said authoritatively, "and made the best use of his troops of all arms. . . ." He heaped up praise of Bragg: "More effective fighting is not to be found in the history of modern battles. . . . My object now is to persuade that in the neighborhood of Murfreesboro it [the army] was well commanded and fought most gallantly, inflicting upon the enemy more harm in proportion to its numbers, if my memory is not at fault, than any army of modern times." [4]

Seddon was astounded and the President pleased to find the critical Joseph Johnston so heartily approving of Braxton Bragg. On February 19, in writing Johnston, Davis touched on the unprepossessing personality of Bragg. "It is not given to all men of ability," he said in sympathetic understanding, "to excite enthusiasm and to win the affection of their troops, and it is only the few who are thus endowed who can overcome the distrust and alienation of their principal officers." Davis hoped that Bragg's abilities would in time overcome the dislike of his subordinates. Naturally, with Johnston's extremely favorable estimate before him, he could not remove Bragg.

In his message to Congress on January 12, the President had urged the legislators to devise adequate tax laws. He was fully aware of the tremendous difficulties the South faced in its efforts to finance the war. It lacked specie, and it was anything but plentifully supplied with banking houses. The Confederacy's hundred-million-dollar loan of August 19, 1861, had been taken up chiefly by the large planters and paid for partly in paper and partly in produce. Cotton and other commodities had been turned over to Treasury agents in return for bonds. But the result had not proved satisfactory. Davis did not believe the fault was that of Secretary of the Treasury Memminger, who was made the butt of cartoons for alleged incompetency. He had been continually thwarted by Congress's inertia in the matter of taxation. The states had met their war-financing quotas, not by raising the amount of taxation, but by issuing bonds or paper money.

Two-thirds of the South's wealth was in land and slaves. Direct taxation was now a difficult problem, because large portions of some Confederate states were dominated by Union troops. It was ob-

---

[4] The letters of Johnston to Wigfall about Bragg are quoted in full in *A Southern Girl in '61*, the wartime memoirs of Wigfall's daughter, Mrs. D. Giraud Wright. The first letter from which quotation is made is found on pages 121-123; the second on page 125.

viously unjust that the planters in uninvaded areas should make up the differences in their state's quotas. And under the Constitution it was difficult, if not impossible, for Congress to levy a direct tax except by apportioning it according to population.

After doing what he could to stir up Congress, Davis left the subject of finances largely to Memminger and other members of his Cabinet, particularly Benjamin, who was an astute businessman.

In late January, Benjamin presented to Congress the plan for a loan proposed by John Slidell in Paris. Erlanger and Company, a powerful French banking firm, had suggested to Slidell that a foreign loan be offered to the bond-buying public throughout Europe. The sum of 75,000,000 francs was to be borrowed by the Confederacy through the issuance of seven-per-cent bonds, secured by cotton and payable after twenty years. But the Erlangers asked a twenty-three-per-cent commission and various extra concessions for handling the bonds. Benjamin almost said no to such usury. In the end, he wrote Mason in England that the contract would have been declined "but for the political considerations indicated by Mr. Slidell, in whose judgement in such matters we are disposed to place great confidence." Benjamin and Slidell had been dickering over this loan since December, and the latter had indicated that Erlanger had great influence over the French Emperor, who looked "with favor upon the scheme."

Because the Confederacy was so desperate for money, the President concurred with his Secretary of State. On January 29, Congress agreed. The bonds were put on the market on March 19. At first they looked like a good buy to European investors and speculators, for they were secured by cotton at the low price of sixpence a pound, whereas the current Liverpool market price was four times that amount. In London, the bonds were bought enthusiastically. On March 20, Mason congratulated Benjamin on the "triumphant success of our infant credit; it shows malgré all detraction and calumny that cotton is King at last."

Mason was far too optimistic. The bonds had been put on the market too high, at ninety per cent of their face value, and by April they had already sagged. Investors soon realized that the cotton that secured the bonds was still across the ocean in the South; and if the Confederacy failed to gain its independence, the bonds would be worthless. But Erlanger got a lot of cash from the financing, and the Confederacy had at least $2,500,000 in hand for its purchasing agents to spend immediately on armaments abroad. In the end, the bondholders were to lose. The firm of Erlanger was to be severely criticized for extortion, and when Slidell's daughter married an Erlanger son, many fingers pointed accusingly at the Confederate commissioner in Paris.[5]

In the meantime, Congress wrangled over direct taxes.

When Congress was in session, the President always had his most strenuous time. He had to handle that turbulent body with the utmost skill. At the end of January, matters almost got out of hand when a bill was introduced to create a Confederate Supreme Court. Two of Davis's friends, Senators Benjamin Hill of Georgia and James Phelan of Mississippi, were among the bill's staunch advocates. Yancey and Wigfall, intense State Rights men, led the embattled opposition. One reason for the passion of their disapproval was the fear that President Davis would appoint Assistant Secretary of War John Campbell as Chief Justice, for Campbell was distrusted as a pro-Union man. On January 30, Yancey spoke eloquently against the organization of any court with appellate jurisdiction over the State Supreme Courts.

Five days later, in debating the bill, Senator Hill made some bitter remarks objecting to Yancey's disparagement of his arguments. Yancey replied insultingly to Hill, and abused him at length. Robert Barnwell, feeling that Yancey had given Hill good cause for offense, rose twice to persuade Yancey to apologize. Twice Yancey declined. Then, his anger mounting, he declared that instead of retracting anything, he wished he had used "language of greater severity." Hill rose and called out, "You had better, then, do so now." Yancey replied loftily, "I have said all in that way that is consistent with my character as a gentleman."

As he stooped to sit, with his hands upon the arms of his chair, he felt a violent blow on his right cheek just below his eye and temple. Hill had hurled a glass inkwell with a metal top. Senators saw blood spilling on Yancey's collar, neck, and shirt bosom. As he turned to face Hill, Yancey ducked another missile, a heavy glass tumbler, which shattered on a window ledge. In the hubbub, Yancey started for his opponent through twelve feet of intervening desks. Nearby Senators grabbed him, and the President of the Senate shouted for the sergeant at arms to remove both men.[6]

[5] One of the best expositions of the Erlanger loan and its consequences may be found in Frank Owsley's convincing *King Cotton Diplomacy*.

[6] A dramatic account of the disturbance, as related by Yancey, in connection with his protest to the Senate asking for removal of censure, is in the Appendix to John Witherspoon Dubose's *Life and Times of William Yancey*.

The row in the Confederate Senate was a most unfortunate occurrence. Since Hill was a recognized admirer and supporter of the President, it gave the latter's enemies a fresh opportunity to condemn the Administration. After the fracas, Yancey became quite cool to Davis. The debating continued, wasting much of Congress's time. Yancey, speaking against the bill for three hours one February day, devoted the last hour and a half to further invective against Hill. In the end, the bill failed to pass, partly because of the fear that it would curtail the rights of the states. The Confederacy was to end its days without creating a Supreme Court.

General Lee, as well as the President, watched the proceedings of Congress with apprehension. In February, Lee renewed his urgent appeal for the completion of the Richmond defenses, which he had begun in June of 1862. Davis liked the untypical heat and vigor of Lee's language in letters to the Secretary of War and to his son Custis. Utterly disgusted with Congressional dillydallying, Lee lamented to Seddon: "More than once have most promising opportunities been lost for want of men to take advantage of them, and victory itself has been made to put on the appearance of defeat because our diminished and exhausted troops have been unable to renew a successful struggle against fresh numbers. . . ."

The failure of Congress to do something constructive stirred Lee to anger. It relieved the President's own sense of frustration to see the General's strong sentiments in a letter to Custis. "Our salvation will depend on the next four months," he wrote on February 12, "and yet I cannot get even regular promotions made to fill vacancies in regiments, while Congress seems to be laboring to pass laws to get easy places for some favorites or constituents, or get others out of service. I shall feel very much obliged if they will pass a law relieving me from all duty and legislating some one in my place, better able to do it." Again, on February 28, Lee wrote bitterly to his son: "What has our Congress done to meet the exigency, I may say extremity, in which we are placed? As far as I know, concocted bills to excuse a certain class of men from service, and to transfer another class in service, *out* of service, where they hope never to see service."

Though Lee had been "disciplined from boyhood to respect civil authority," as Dr. Freeman has stated, the failure of Congress to act aroused him to perhaps the highest indignation he had known. But Lee knew Congress's deficiencies only in regard to military affairs. Davis had to suffer over Congress's ineptitude in countless civil matters, and to hear himself denounced continually by enemies like Foote and Wigfall.

The weary President saw Congress still doing little that was worth doing, except to work on a necessary tax bill; but he noted that certain members were ever quick to find objections to any measures he himself advocated. At a time when there was a crucial lack of essential manpower in the Army, Congress and State Governors, like Brown of Georgia, seemed bent on diminishing what the Confederacy had. Were Southern politicians to defeat the Confederacy by their self-interest, stupidity, and plain cussedness? How could he and Lee win against the big odds when a fight was, in effect, waged against them by their own remiss compatriots?

In such a critical situation, it might have been a temptation to an executive to take matters in his own hands, dissolve Congress, and become a dictator. Many of the President's admirers believed that this was what he should do. But dictatorship was against every principle that Jefferson Davis held sacred. It was opposed to the very cause of Constitutional rights and self-government for which the South was fighting.

CHAPTER XXVIII

RICHMOND ENTERTAINS
WHILE GRANT IS STYMIED
IN THE WEST

AFTER Murfreesboro, little of great military importance occurred on any front in January. On February 8, the President put Major General E. Kirby Smith in command of the Trans-Mississippi. The aging Holmes did not regret being relieved of arduous administrative duties. His army was depleted by sickness and desertions. The Arkansas citizens were restless and dissatisfied. Civil government was fast disappearing. Holmes still held Little Rock, but the northwestern mountain region was lost, and in the east Federal gunboats pushed far up the Mississippi's tributaries.

In late January and throughout February, Grant and Sherman battled the Mississippi River itself, endeavoring to change the stream's course by cutting a canal a mile and a quarter long near Vicksburg where the great river made a hairpin turn. If they succeeded, the town would be isolated high above a drying river bed. Jefferson Davis was interested to see what Grant could do in attacking the willful river, on the banks of which he had spent so much of his life.

Nature favored the Confederates, and for all the Federals' prodigious digging, the Mississippi would not bend to Yankee will, but continued to lave the feet of Vicksburg. Finally, after seven weeks, Grant gave up canal-cutting in disgust. His problem now was to reach the high east bank of the river and attack Vicksburg's left flank and rear. In a roundabout way, he moved his troops to Milliken Bend, about twenty miles northwest of Vicksburg. In the swamps opposite Vicksburg, Grant's army was spread out for forty miles. As he wrote, "Troops could scarcely find dry ground on which to pitch their tents."

Malaria, measles, and smallpox broke out among the men. The Western newspapers found grievous fault with Grant. Some declared he was utterly incompetent and accused him of gross misconduct and drunkenness. One influential journalist, in a letter to Secretary of the Treasury Chase, demanded that he be removed from command. But Lincoln wisely stuck by him.

At New Orleans, Federal Major General Nathaniel P. Banks, with 25,000 men, was preparing to move up the river in an attempt to capture Port Hudson, Louisiana. While Grant waited for the Federal fleet to run the Vicksburg batteries, he began a slow march south.

Davis was relieved that the first half of March was quiet in the fighting field, except for the activities of the two noted Confederate raiders whose names began with M. Lieutenant John S. Mosby attacked the Federals at Fairfax Court House and captured Brigadier General Edwin H. Stoughton in bed, for which he was made a Major. The other, John Hunt Morgan, who had been named Brigadier General in December, dashed into Kentucky with his "terrible men" and harassed the Federal forces with slashing surprise attacks.

Lincoln and Stanton were so worried about the widespread fault-finding with Grant that they sent Charles Dana to his army to observe and resolve their minds about his abilities. Almost simultaneously, because of the continuing discontent among Bragg's officers, Secretary of War Seddon persuaded Davis, on March 9, to let him send to Joseph Johnston the following dispatch: "Order General Bragg to report to the War Department here for conference; assume yourself direct charge of the army in Middle Tennessee."

The telegram reached Johnston in Mobile, where he was inspecting the defenses. Johnston had no desire to take over the responsibility of Bragg's army, but he returned to Tullahoma on the eighteenth. In Johnston's words, "There, without the publication of a formal order on the subject, I assumed the duties of commander of the army." But because Mrs. Bragg was critically ill and her husband was devoting himself to her care, Johnston postponed sending him to Richmond.

A new and different kind of trouble loomed up with the resignation of Brigadier General Robert Toombs from the Army. He was angered at not being made a Major General. After his slight wound at Sharpsburg, where he had fought well, he had retired to his home in Washington, Georgia, to await a promotion. Jones recorded on March 12, that General Toombs's resignation was making "some sensation in certain circles . . . it is probable he will cause some disturbance." It was rumored that Toombs would run for governor of Georgia in the fall. "There were intimations," Jones wrote, "that Georgia might make peace with the United States. This would be death to the Government —and destruction to Toombs. . . . He cannot have any such design. . . . Still it behooves the President to be on his guard. He has enemies in the South, who hate him much."

The President had no enemy more bitter just then than Robert Toombs, who felt that Davis alone was responsible for his lack of higher rank. As a personal friend of Davis, Reagan had gone twice to him to urge Toombs's advancement. "But the President," wrote Reagan, "while speaking kindly of General Toombs, said he had in no case made a promotion against the objection of superior officers; adding that both General Lee and General Magruder objected to his advancement." Reagan felt he could not explain to Toombs, for that would have betrayed the confidence of the Generals and "transferred Toombs's quarrel to them."

Davis regretted Toombs's discontent and feared he would cause trouble in Georgia. Mrs. Chesnut had written in her diary in June of 1862, "Toombs is ready for another revolution, and curses freely everything Confederate from the President down to a horse boy." Now, in his disappointment at not shining in the Army, he nursed his grievance and seemed determined to undermine confidence in the Administration.

At the President's bidding, General Lee came down to Richmond on March 10 for another conference. It always did Davis good to talk with Lee. He could speak heart to heart with him almost as intimately as he had with the late Sidney Johnston. Lee quietly exuded that reassuring confidence which Joseph Johnston so palpably lacked. And, like Sidney Johnston, he was apparently blessed with rugged health. Despite hardships and poor food, Lee had not known a day's sickness since the war began.

But Lee still encountered considerable difficulty in securing proper rations for the Army. He told the President that he had urged his soldiers to scour the woods for sassafras buds and wild onions to prevent scurvy. He was considering sending two divisions far down in southeast Virginia near Suffolk for forage and supplies and to recover the productive counties along the Chowan River in North Carolina. Provisions were plentiful in eastern North Carolina, including stores of bacon, which could only be collected by army wagons. If the blustery, chilling weather continued, he expected no aggression from Hooker, though Union observation balloons continued to rise above the Federal camp. Lee said he kept his men in a state of preparation to resist attack.

On March 14, while Lee was in Richmond, the House of Representatives was deadlocked on the revenue bill. Kean commented acidly in his diary: "This is a fresh instance of the *smallness* of this Congress. Certainly no deliberative body ever met in this state with less statesmanship in it."

Sleet on March 16 made the inclement weather more disagreeable, yet it brought a kind of dispensation. Jones noted that "the movements of the armies must perforce be stayed. But the season of slaughter is approaching."

A harbinger of wholesale death came almost immediately. Early in the morning of March 18, President Davis received intelligence that a portion of the Federal Army had crossed the Rappahannock. General Lee bade him a quick farewell and left by special train for the front. In the afternoon, a dispatch arrived from General Jeb Stuart: the cavalry had beaten back the enemy at Kelly's Ford near Culpeper and forced him to recross the river.

A few hours later came the blight of malice that often mocked Confederate victories, large and small. The boy major, John Pelham, had been mortally wounded. He had been on a visit to friends in Culpeper when the cavalry clash occurred. Riding out over the snow-covered fields as an observer with no official duties to perform, he had sat on his horse chatting with companions. But at one point near the front his impetuous bravery carried him away. He rose in his stirrups and cried, "Forward boys! Forward to victory and glory." A few minutes later, a Union shell burst above his head, fractured his skull, and knocked him from his mount.

Without waiting for an ambulance or stretcher, men laid him, unconscious and bleeding profusely, across his horse, his legs hanging down one side, his head and arms down the other. He was taken to the home of his hosts, the Schaklefords, where he died. Jeb Stuart gazed in despair at the pale handsome face of the young man "who had been his right arm in many pressing dangers." With tears streaming, he leaned down and kissed the sculptured brow. Then he telegraphed Richmond: "The noble, chivalric, the gallant Pelham is no more. . . ."

Jefferson Davis mourned with Stuart. Young Pelham, like Sidney Johnston, was unsurpassed as a representative of his breed. Reputed to have "every manly virtue," he was idolized by his men and admired and loved by his superior officers. Davis could hardly bear to reflect on the tragic waste. Could the South ever recover from the loss of Pelham and those young men like him? Could American culture afford to sacrifice such men of quality, so promising for leadership? And now, as soon as the weather cleared, thousands more of the fine brave men on both sides would give up their lives and their future usefulness. But not just yet. Nine inches of snow fell in Richmond on the night of March 21 and further postponed the hour of slaughter.

Davis was relieved that the situation in Mississippi had not reached the critical stage. In mid-March, Pemberton reported that the enemy's dredge boats were only halfway through the canal at Vicksburg. But Pemberton needed horsemen. He begged Joseph Johnston to return Van Dorn and his 4,000 cavalrymen, which Johnston had borrowed to strengthen the Army of Tennessee as soon as he had taken temporary command of Bragg's forces. But Johnston replied coolly: "General Van Dorn's cavalry is much more needed in this department than in that of Mississippi and East Louisiana."

Davis thought Van Dorn's cavalry should be aiding Pemberton in keeping Grant from reaching Vicksburg. But he and Seddon hesitated to intervene, not knowing Johnston's plans. Seddon was rather embarrassed that Johnston had seemingly accomplished nothing since accepting the whole command of the West. The only direct move he had made was to bring Van Dorn's cavalry from Mississippi to Tennessee; to many, this looked as if Johnston's motive was chiefly to protect himself.

On March 22, Robert Kean, Chief of the War Bureau, recorded: "General Johnston has written another of his brief, unsatisfactory, almost captious letters, protesting against Bragg's removal, against any detachment to meet the movement of the enemy towards Corinth."

The War Department was soon irritated by "another sharp, captious letter" from General Johnston, quarreling about a matter of no great importance. Kean was so annoyed that he impulsively set down one of the harshest opinions of Johnston ever recorded. "The letter in manner and spirit," he wrote acidly, "is of a piece with his jejune and ice-tempered character of correspondence. He treats the Department as an enemy with whom he holds no communication which he can avoid and against which he only complains and finds fault. He is *a very little man,* has achieved nothing, is full of himself, above all other things, eaten up with morbid jealousy of Lee. . . . I apprehend the gravest disasters from his command in the Western Department."

The Secretary of War was becoming apprehensive, too, and wondering if he had not made a grave error in urging the President to give Johnston such a powerful position.

Johnston was never to obey Seddon's order to send Bragg to Richmond. When Bragg's wife recovered, Johnston quickly gave him back the command. Finally, on April 10, the President was to receive a letter from him expressing his "inability to serve in the field," and declaring, "General Bragg is therefore necessary here."

In mid-March Mrs. Davis was called to the sickbed of her father in Montgomery. On the nineteenth, the President was notified of Mr. Howell's death. He felt a surge of grief, for he was sincerely fond of his amiable, New Jersey-born father-in-law, whom he had generously assisted with cash and influence ever since he had been in the family. Putting aside official business, he wrote a tender letter of condolence to Mrs. Howell, whom he affectionately called "Ma," though she was only a few years older than himself.

After expressions of sympathy and some words of praise for the endearing ne'er-do-well, he said, "When you are sufficiently composed to think of future arrangements you will tell me how I can serve you, and surely will not hesitate to believe that my best efforts are always at your command. Varina is with you and will act for me under the circumstances, which prevent me from going to you. . . ." He spoke of his hope of being with her again, and signed himself "Affectionately, Your Son, Jeffn Davis." [1]

After her father's burial in Montgomery, Mrs. Davis stayed on for some weeks to be a comfort to her mother, who became ill herself. Friends of the days when she had presided as First Lady in the first capital of the Confederacy called. Among them was Mrs. Robert Tyler, the onetime New York stage star Priscilla Cooper, now living in the country near Montgomery. She wrote to President Tyler's widow in Virginia: "I went to see Mrs. Pres't Davis while in town. She was extraordinarily gracious, affectionate, and you should have heard her speak of your own sweet self, or, as she called you, 'My beautiful step-

---

[1] This letter, in the Jefferson Hayes-Davis collection, is one of the many heretofore unpublished ones that reveal the family solicitude of Jefferson Davis.

mother,' so fresh, agreeable, graceful. . . . I really thought her one of the most charmingly entertaining persons I ever met with." [2]

In the first three months of 1863, stimulated by the December victory at Fredericksburg, Richmond indulged in unstinted entertainment. The ladies did their best to make soldiers on leave forget the discomforts of camp. The President himself relaxed to a degree, and occasionally he and his wife would go to a concert or a private theatrical or a charade party in which their little daughter was a talented performer. Sometimes he enjoyed diversion at the few homes in which he felt most comfortable, with the Semmeses, the Iveses, and with Judah Benjamin, who, despite the blockade, was still incredibly well-stocked with gourmet delicacies, French wines, and superlative Havanas. Now and again, the President spent an afternoon at Judge James Lyons's country place, a mile and a half from Richmond. But most of all, he liked being with the James Chesnuts, though their Clay Street apartment would sometimes be spontaneously crowded.

"We received there," Mrs. Chesnut wrote, "all that the Confederacy had of good and great from Mr. President Davis and the Lees down to the humblest private—who was often our nearest friend or relative." Once a month, a man came up from Mulberry, the South Carolina plantation, bringing "wine, rice, potatoes, hams, eggs, butter and pickles" for the Chesnuts' open-house entertaining. And Lawrence, their colored manservant, proved resourceful at working miracles. His simple formula was "You give me the money, and I'll find everything you want." So his mistress would hand him a roll of bills; he would return loaded with "unattainable" goodies, and she would ask no questions. Molly, Mrs. Chesnut's maid, was also a splendid cook, who took pride in her culinary skill, especially in roasting turkeys. Mary Chesnut had a genius for hospitality, whether she entertained privates at a taffy-pulling or the President at a small seated dinner.

One evening while his wife was in Montgomery, Mr. Davis went alone to the Chesnuts'. The hostess was at the far end of the drawing room when L. Q. Washington gestured to her in alarm. She saw that the President had come in and was standing before the seated Wigfalls. To her dismay, they did not rise, but "turned their backs on him." Passing rapidly to where he stood, in her most gracious manner,

---

[2] This lively praise from the glamorous Priscilla Cooper appears in a private letter quoted in Elizabeth Tyler Coleman's biography of her great-grandmother.

Mary Chesnut made her "obeisance before him," as did the rest of the guests. "I was proud," she wrote, "to receive him in my house as himself, Jeff Davis; the others stood up to receive the head of the Confederacy as well." If the President noticed the intended Wigfall snub he gave no indication.

Mrs. Chesnut had as houseguests this season the Preston girls from South Carolina, Mary and Sally Buchanan. The latter, called "Buck," was considered "the most enchanting creature" in Richmond, except for the fabulous Cary cousins, Hettie and Constance. Buck had "the knack of being fallen in love with at sight and of never being fallen out of love with," and in the string of men who wanted to marry her was the gallant General John Hood. Jefferson Davis, himself, was quite taken with Buck, whose father, General John S. Preston, was to become head of the Conscription Bureau. To honor the Chesnuts' guests, he gave a breakfast at the White House, where the Preston girls and Mrs. Chesnut were the only ladies present among his several aides. The President thoroughly enjoyed being host. Throwing off cares of state, he became the attractive self of his youth. "He was so kind and so amiable and so agreeable," wrote Mrs. Chesnut, "we were all charmed." Buck Preston came away "in a very ecstasy of loyalty." When she got back to the Chesnut house, "she hurrahed for Jeff Davis and professed her willingness to fight for him to the death."

It was not yet impossible for those who had accessible plantations to get foodstuffs and even luxuries. But poor families and those of moderate means were suffering from lacks in basic supplies, as were the soldiers in camp.

The President was seriously concerned about the inflationary prices. On March 25, 1863, gold was quoted at nearly five to one, and the price of foodstuffs was in proportion. A barrel of flour now cost $30 in Richmond. Butter was $3 a pound. Eggs cost $2 a dozen; beef, $1.50 a pound. It took five times more money for a Southerner to live in the spring of 1863 than in 1860.

Amid the general hardships, some private fortunes were being accumulated. Davis heard the current talk that the Charleston firm of John Frazer had already made nine million dollars in the import business. In Richmond, the Crenshaws were reputedly making hundreds of thousands monthly from their woolen factories and their flour contracts. While the President grieved that men would profit grossly from their country's woes, it was difficult for his advisers to think of proper democratic or legal processes to stop abuses. But he again urged Congress to devise means to curtail inflation.

In the last week of March, the President had a new worry: Lee fell ill. After his return to camp following the fight at Kelly's Ford, Lee contracted a serious throat infection, which settled into inflammation of the pericardium, that thin membranous sac that encloses the heart. His chest, back, and arms were wracked by paroxysms of pain. Jefferson Davis was seriously alarmed. Without an active Lee, how long could the Confederacy stand?

Though disturbed over Lee's condition, the President's major activities were directed to the West. After an interview in which Davis gave his Chief of Ordnance instructions about sending munitions to Mississippi, Gorgas wrote in his diary: "He is at present evidently wholly devoted to the defense of Mississippi and thinks and talks of little else."

Davis had been receiving expressions of dissatisfaction with General Pemberton, not only from anxious Mississippians, but from men like Judge William Brooks, former President of the Alabama Convention.

On April 2, he wrote Brooks a long letter, in which he stoutly stood up for the Philadelphian. "I selected General Pemberton," he said, "for the very important command from a conviction that he was the best qualified officer for that post then available, and I have since found no reason to change the opinion I then entertained of him." He pointed out the numerous victories that the General had achieved against superior forces, "at Vicksburg, Port Hudson, on the Tallahatchie, and at Deer Creek." Thus far Pemberton had foiled the enemy's every attempt to get full possession of the Mississippi. "If success is an evidence of qualifications, I am surprised that General Pemberton's merits should be doubted.

"With reference to the fact that General Pemberton was born at the North," he continued, "being alleged as a justification of distrust in his fidelity to our cause, I can imagine nothing more unjust and ungenerous. . . . In addition to other proofs which he has afforded of his devotion to the cause of the Confederate States, I may add that by coming South he forfeited a considerable fortune." [3]

Davis hoped that the influential Brooks would make widely known

---

[3] Pemberton's mother disinherited him when he resigned his commission in the United States Army and offered his services to Virginia. The President did not foresee the embarrassing penury Pemberton was to undergo after the war, along with recriminations.

his high regard for Pemberton. It distressed him to note the suspicions so many Confederates had of the Northern-born men who had come to their aid. He had no patience with that narrow kind of Southern prejudice. Two of the men he still held most dearly in his affections were Northerners: Franklin Pierce of New Hampshire and General George W. Jones of Iowa.

While the President was writing to Brooks, a few hundred women and some teen-age boys gathered purposefully in Capitol Square. Led by a pistol-toting amazon named Minerva Meredith, who wore a stiff white feather rampant in her shoddy hat, the mob said it was hungry and must have food. Small groups of men, mostly foreign residents "with exemptions in their pockets," joined them. The crowd swelled in number until there were perhaps a thousand. It left the square by the west gate, proceeded down Ninth Street, passed the War Department, and turned into Main Street. Along the march, the mob increased; a few persons half-sheepishly carried hatchets and knives. War Clerk Jones asked a pale-faced boy where the crowd was going. An emaciated young woman answered pleasantly that they were going to find something to eat. Jones, who abominated the war profiteers, wished her luck, saying she would find plenty "in the hands of the extortioners."

"Bread! Bread!" the crowd began to chant. "Give us bread for our children." A few shouted, "Our children are starving while the rich roll in wealth." One yelled, "Down with the aristocrats!" Some onlookers scented a hint of the French Revolution in the air. On Cary Street, the women rushed into the various stores of speculators and proceeded to clean them out. Having impressed drays and carts along the way, they loaded them with white flour and corn meal, slabs of meat, shoes, and whatever they took a fancy to. When the doors were barred against the mob, glass windows were smashed as well as the doors. An eyewitness saw a youth rush out of a shop with a hat chockfull of Confederate bank notes. Not satisfied with necessities, some raiders started in on the jewelry shops. Mayor Mayo called for fire brigades and ordered the hoses to be turned on the mob. The drenched citizens fled from one street to join up with another mob coming down another street. Governor Letcher called out a company of militia and had the Mayor read the riot act. When Mayo threatened to fire, a few timid women slunk away. The rest, loaded with spoils, stood their ground defiantly.

When the President learned the cause of the commotion, he immediately determined to go to the scene of anarchy. His aides, failing to restrain him, sent an armed guard to accompany him. In the midst of the tense excitement, Jefferson Davis mounted a dray. (Emma Lyon Bryan said it was "a goods box.") At first, some bold youths threw crusts of bread at him. But "he held them with his magic eloquence," Mrs. Bryan wrote, "explaining to them the stress of the situation." He reminded the citizens that they had taken "jewelry and finery" as well as food. Persuasively, he urged them to return to their homes so that "the bayonets now menacing them might be sent against the common enemy." He explained that such unlawful acts might actually bring famine, for country people and shop owners would hesitate to bring food to the city. He "would gladly share his last loaf with people in need," he said, and he trusted everyone to bear current privations with fortitude and remain united against the Northern invaders, "the authors of all our sufferings." The crowd, impressed by his fearlessness, his sincerity, and the melodious quality of his voice, listened in awed silence. But when he paused, a low muttering growl of defiance came from the rear. Sunlight glinted on a butcher knife.

The President's manner changed. Signaling to his military escort, he commanded in a clear, cool voice: "Make ready." Rifles were aimed and cocked. Turning back to the people, he said with incisive determination: "My friends, I will give you five minutes to disperse. If at the expiration of that time you remain here, I will order this command to fire on you."

Davis drew out his watch and held it deliberately where all might see. Surveying the crowd steadily, he looked directly into any eyes he could catch. Finally, glancing at his watch, he called out: "My friends, you have one minute more." Some started backing away. Others began to run. When the President returned the watch to his pocket, the crowd had dispersed. He descended from the dray, told the police to arrest the ringleaders, and walked back to his office.[4]

After the President had quelled the riot, he calmly spent an hour with General Gorgas. They talked of many things, "especially the establishment of furnaces and a foundry on Trinity River in Texas." Gorgas observed in his diary that he was much impressed by Davis's

[4] There are numerous lively reports of "The Bread Riot" besides that of Mrs. Bryan; among them, the Richmond *Examiner* of May 4, 1863, Varina Davis's second-hand version, and that of War Clerk Jones. Most of the newspapers suppressed the story or made light of it.

"understanding of the geography and resources of the country." The President spoke regretfully of the inflationary prices. As large as his own salary appeared, he lived no better than he had as a Senator in Washington, and it took his entire income to defray expenses.

The day after the Bread Riot, some "local women, Maryland refugees, and foreigners" stood on street corners demanding food. The Government issued rations. Though a report was circulated that the riot had been stimulated by Northern agents, the disturbance had some good effect on the profiteers, for prices declined appreciably within a fortnight. The *Dispatch* of April 21 reported that hog-round had dropped to $1.25 a pound, butter to $2.25, beans to $20 a bushel, corn meal to $7, dried apples to $10. Coffee fell to $4 a pound, and French brandy to $65 a gallon. Best of all, as Gorgas noted, "beef returned to one dollar."

Two days after the Bread Riot, Congress passed significant resolutions. It warned the people against assuming that the war would end within the present year, and stressed the importance of producing food "to meet every contingency."

Six days later, the President issued a stirring proclamation on the subject. "We have reached the close of the second year of the war," he said, "and may point with just pride to the history of our young Confederacy. Alone, unaided, we have met and overthrown the most formidable combination of naval and military armaments that the lust of conquest ever gathered together for the subjugation of a free people. We began this struggle without a single gun afloat while the resources of our enemy enabled them to gather fleets which, according to their official list published in August last, consisted of 427 vessels, measuring 340,036 tons and carrying 3,628 guns.[5] Yet we have captured, sunk, or destroyed a number of these vessels . . . while four of their captured steam gunboats are now in our possession, adding to the strength of our little Navy, which is rapidly gaining in numbers and efficiency. To oppose invading forces composed of levies which have already exceeded 1,300,000 men, we had no resources, but the unconquerable valor of a people determined to be free. . . ."

He then came to his specific exhortation: "Your country, therefore, appeals to you to lay aside all thought of gain, and to devote yourselves to securing your liberties, without which those gains would be valueless. . . . Let fields be devoted exclusively to the production of corn, oats, beans, peas, potatoes, and other food for man and beast; let corn

[5] By April of 1863, the Union's naval strength was considerably greater.

be sown broadcast for fodder in immediate proximity to railroads, rivers, and canals, and let all your efforts be directed to the prompt supply of these articles in the districts where our armies are operating. . . ."

To move the selfish, he asked, "Is it not a bitter and humiliating reflection that those who remain at home, secure from hardship and protected from danger, should be in the enjoyment of abundance, and that their slaves also should have a full supply of food, while their sons, brothers, husbands, and fathers are stinted in the rations on which their health and efficiency depend?"

Closing with a patriotic call to fealty, he said, "Let us all unite in the performance of our duty, each in his sphere, and with concerted, persistent, and well-directed effort . . . we shall maintain the sovereignty and independence of these Confederate States, and transmit to our posterity the heritage bequeathed to us by our fathers."

The proclamation, dated April 10, was sent broadcast across the land. Perhaps the majority heeded the President's appeal. A few reacted like the defiant Robert Toombs, who responded by letting it be known that he was increasing his cotton acreage.

Good news had arrived from Charleston. Beauregard had made a brilliant defense in repulsing a fleet of monitors under Admiral Samuel F. DuPont on April 7. That clear April morning with a smooth sea, the formidable Federal vessels had steamed up the main channel, past the Morris Island batteries, and launched a terrific bombardment on Fort Sumter. Beauregard's well-trained gunners had shown themselves superb marksmen in landing direct hits on the Union warships. His new installations and arrangements were put to the test and proved his skill in engineering and artillery. One monitor was sunk and two hopelessly disabled. Admiral DuPont on his flagship *Ironsides* was relieved to escape the Confederate fire with no more damage than he sustained. Charleston again exulted and Beauregard was once more a hero. Davis's wisdom in sending him to defend strategic Charleston was verified. Though Beauregard had been disgusted with the assignment, looking upon it as punishment when he yearned for a field command, Davis had judged his abilities aright. Beauregard had confounded the Federal attackers and brought gloom to Washington.

By the middle of April, to the President's inexpressible relief, General Lee wrote that he was well again, except for occasional twinges, which were attributed to rheumatism. But now Davis, overwhelmed with work and anxieties, was sick. His physician feared that his remaining good eye was failing. "Total blindness would incapacitate him for the executive office," wrote Jones in distress. "A fearful thing to contemplate!" On the twenty-second, the papers said Davis was "dangerously ill" with inflammation of the throat.

The operations in Mississippi were a large part of Davis's worries. From mid-March until April 5, Union gunboats had attempted to get soldiers to the east of Vicksburg by way of the Yazoo River. The Confederates had felled trees into the Yazoo *behind* the Federal ships as well as before, and sharpshooters picked off the enemy on deck or in the process of dragging trees out of their way. The North was very impatient with Grant and Sherman, who had been employing desperate tactics to get at Vicksburg since November. Grant had become so frustrated that, according to Sylvanus Cadwallader of the Chicago *Times,* he went on the wildest drunk of his life and almost ended his career in disgrace. Finally, to Davis's relief, the Yazoo expedition was given up as a lost maneuver.

Though confined to his room, Jefferson Davis would devise defensive measures for Pemberton's consideration. In a cipher telegram of April 22 he asked: "Have you tried the use of fire rafts, to be set adrift from the Cove at upper batteries of Vicksburg when boats are attempting to pass? Covered with pine or dry cypress, they would be dangerous to passing vessels and at least would serve by lighting the river to aid gunners in their aim. Have you tried anchoring fire rafts in the river on dark nights?"

While, in the last half of April, Union gunboats were making daring attempts at running by Vicksburg's batteries, Colonel Benjamin H. Grierson, one of the boldest of the Union cavalrymen, went on a rampaging raid, zigzagging through Mississippi to Baton Rouge, tearing up tracks, burning railway depots, plundering, and terrifying the citizens. This flaming former schoolteacher was softening resistance to Grant, who was slowly moving down the Louisiana shore looking for a crossing. Pemberton was helpless to halt Grierson because Joseph Johnston had removed his cavalry to Tennessee.

While Western papers still expressed violent indignation at Grant's slowness and the waste of Western lives in the fever-ridden swamps of Louisiana, the East was elated at the thought of a speedy conquest in Virginia. It was generally believed that the mighty Army of the Potomac would shortly overwhelm the poorly equipped Lee. The North knew that the Confederates were still deficient in almost everything except pluck and leadership. The Federal forces had never been so numerous or so well provided with tools to make a successful war.

Senator Charles Sumner wrote the Duchess of Argyll on April 26 that there were then 800,000 Union soldiers under arms, "better clothed and better fed than any soldiers ever before." "The North," he told Her Grace, "had sufficient powder and saltpetre for three years, 500,000 unused muskets in our arsenals" and "the best armorers in the world producing them at the rate of 50,000 a month." [6] The implication was that the South could never win against such powerful opposition.

Davis was painfully aware of the odds against Lee as Hooker moved to attack. The Army of the Potomac, which Hooker proclaimed "the finest army on the planet," was said to be in prime condition, with morale again high. According to estimates, the Federals had more than double the Confederates' number: 130,000 to 60,000.[7]

The President could not help being apprehensive about Lee. Longstreet, with the main part of his corps, including Hood and Pickett, was far away besieging Suffolk, down near Norfolk. On April 12, Longstreet, with his 12,000 men, had crossed the Blackwater near Franklin, Virginia, going farther and farther away from Lee's army. His purpose was to drive the Union forces out of the region and to collect foodstuffs. Food was important, but Lee needed fighting men. By the detachment of two whole divisions, including Generals Hood and Pickett, Lee's strength had been dangerously reduced. Lee hoped that Longstreet could finish his work quickly and return before Hooker began a major offensive. But on April 22, when the Union forces made a raid on Port Royal, eighteen miles below Fredericksburg, it looked to Davis like the prologue of the big drive. Not until April 27, however, did Lee "inquire how soon" before Longstreet could join him. Though Longstreet held Hood and Pickett near the railroad, so they could be returned on necessity, he seemed too absorbed in his work in southern Virginia to give a satisfactory answer. As Freeman frankly

[6] The letters of Sumner to both the Duchess of Argyll and John Bright, as quoted in Volume IV of Edward L. Pierce's *Memoirs and Letters of Charles Sumner,* reveal Northern optimism in the spring of 1863.

[7] The figures are Randall's and Rhodes's and those in *Battles and Leaders.* Freeman estimates 138,000 for Hooker, 62,500 for Lee. Walter Taylor in *Four Years with General Lee* gives the strength of the Confederate commands that actually participated at Chancellorsville as only 41,358. On April 29, Hooker's officers compiled the number ready for duty as 138,378 (*Official Records*).

confesses, "A careful reading of the correspondence between Lee and Longstreet raises the suspicion that he permitted Longstreet to browbeat him."

Though confined to his room and urged to be quiet, the President was eager to join Lee. His physician convinced him that such a trip was impossible. So he lay feverishly awaiting dispatches from Fredericksburg and reports on the tax issue in Congress.

It was not until late April, after weeks of debate, that Congress finally enacted a comprehensive tax law, which combined "the features of an income tax, a license tax, and a general internal revenue measure." [8]

No direct tax was levied on acres or slaves, but an ad valorem tax of eight per cent was imposed on all products of field and forest and a one-per-cent tax on all money held on July 1, 1863. An almost interminable series of license and occupational taxes were imposed, "ranging from $500 a year for bankers to $40 for bowling alleys." Retail liquor dealers were assessed ten per cent of their gross sales. Salaries were taxed from one per cent on $1,000 up to fifteen per cent for an income of more than $10,000. To curtail speculators, a ten-per-cent levy was laid upon wholesale profits on foodstuffs and clothing.

Earnings from farm products were not taxed in money; but a new "tax in kind" was levied, whereby one-tenth of all cotton, corn, wheat, hog meat, hay, molasses, tobacco, and other products was to be apportioned directly to the Government. By this unique tax, the farmer was required to deliver his tenth in containers or sacks furnished by the Government to collection depots within eight miles of his farm.

To the Quartermaster General service was assigned the duty of collecting the food products and transporting them to army supply stations. The tithes of cotton, wool, and tobacco were to be sent to the Secretary of the Treasury, who would determine whether the produce was to be sold, exported, or held to secure Confederate bonds. Farmers were allowed certain generous exemptions in corn, potatoes, beans, and other commodities for family use before the tenth was taken. Products of incapacitated soldiers were exempted, and, later, those of farmers who owned no slaves.

The tax in kind had mixed values: it could not always be collected;

---

[8] A clear summary of the ingenious tax act may be found in E. Merton Coulter's invaluable *The Confederate States of America,* pp. 176-182. His entire Chapter VIII, Money, Bonds, and Taxes, is a fine exposition of the intricate problems involved.

many small farmers were bitter about giving up one-tenth of their sweat-earned produce. The host of agents employed to collect the tax were to be derided as slackers, and often accused of cheating.

While varied howls of displeasure rose, the Richmond *Examiner* was to declare that "no one who has two grains of common sense can fail to see that the only chance of the Confederate currency rests on these taxes." When Judge Lyons, who opposed the "impressment," asked the President why he did not veto the bill, Davis said simply, "General Lee has asked for it. Congress has passed it. How then can I veto it?" Despite injustices and some bitter feelings, this radical method of securing foodstuffs staved off starvation among the soldiers.

CHAPTER XXIX

A MOCKING FATE FELLS
STONEWALL JACKSON

PRESIDENT DAVIS was keyed up in anticipation of the Union offensive about to strike at any hour. Hooker decided not to risk another frontal attack on Lee, like Burnside's, but to move around the Confederate left. As a prelude to crossing the Rappahannock, on April 27 he dispatched cavalryman George Stoneman with 2,000 men to raid southern Virginia. Then he divided his huge army into two wings. During the next two days, he put his largest force over the river some twenty miles above Fredericksburg, into a dismal stretch of scrub land known as the Wilderness. To deceive Lee, he sent the other troops under Major General John Sedgwick across the river below Fredericksburg. This maneuver put Lee's inadequate troops between the two Federal armies.

By the afternoon of April 30, Lee divined that Hooker's first object was to turn the Confederate left. So, after a cracker-barrel conference with Jackson, he determined on an audacious move and divided his own small forces. He sent Stonewall with his crack troops to make a flanking movement on the Federal's right. Hooker's main army was concentrated at Chancellorsville, a crossroads with one large dwelling and numerous outbuildings belonging to a Mr. Chancellor. After a forced march Jackson, by three o'clock in the afternoon of May 2, was west of the Union position. He formed his troops in battle line, and a little after five gave the order to advance.

On this same pleasant afternoon, the Union's Eleventh Corps was relaxing. Some of the men were already cooking their supper. A few were stretched out idle. Others indulged in camp pastimes. Suddenly, out of the thickets came wildly scurrying rabbits and a rush of deer.

Then with a high-pitched, spine-shivering yell, the boys in gray burst upon the foe, "front, flank, and rear." Taken completely by surprise, the Federals offered brief opposition, and ran for their lives.

Isolated groups resisted doggedly for a while, and then they, too, joined the panicky mass that fled through the underbrush of trackless woods. Some ran for a mile, and some, for two. At dusk, when Federal reinforcements appeared, the Eleventh Corps paused to offer resistance. But night thickened. Jackson now ordered the rear division, under A. P. Hill, to pass to the front, while he himself, on a sorrel horse, rode with some of his staff far out beyond the Confederate front to make personal reconnaissance. Fired on by Union soldiers, Jackson's party turned back as pale moonlight lighted their way.

When Hill's advance troops saw a party of horsemen galloping toward them, they fired two volleys. Jackson felt a shattering wound in his upper left arm, while his right hand was pierced by a ball. His terrified horse bolted. Tree branches slashed Stonewall's face and tore off his cap. With a useless arm and a wounded hand, he could not stop his horse. But soldiers finally seized the sorrel's bridle. Half fainting and a mess of blood, Jackson was lifted from the saddle. A tourniquet was applied to stop the hemorrhage. But the Federals were now coming nearer, and Jackson had to be got to the rear of the Confederate lines. He insisted that with support he could walk. A man on either side held him up, and he stumbled on until litter-bearers appeared. The General was lifted to their shoulders. As the men moved toward safety, the road was suddenly raked by enemy shrapnel. One of the bearers was shot in both arms. Someone caught the released handle before Jackson was dropped. The General was laid flat on the moon-silvered road, while missiles flew above him. When the artillery paused, other litter-bearers were commandeered, and Jackson was hoisted again. His agony was severe; but morphine would soon be in reach.

The men proceeded with their precious burden out of the enemy's reach. But lying in ambush in the path was a treacherous root. Or was it a clod or a creeper? Whatever material substance, the trifling thing held diabolical power to harm the Confederate cause. It caught the foremost bearer's foot and tripped him. As the man plunged headlong to the ground, the litter sagged precipitously. Jackson tumbled off, his weight landing heavily on the mangled arm. One agonized groan escaped him. Aghast, Captain James Smith rushed to his side. "Are you much hurt, General?" For a moment Jackson could not speak; the breath was knocked out of him. He himself wondered if he were dying. But he said, "No, Mr. Smith; don't trouble yourself about me."

Finally the party reached the haven of a rude ambulance silhouetted in the moonlight. And then came another gruelling ordeal for Jackson, as the vehicle jolted laboriously over the rutted road. Along the way, passing men were begged for whisky, but not a drop was to be had. Dr. Hunter Maguire, Jackson's personal physician, who had been sent for, appeared out of the night. To his anxious question, Jackson gave a frank answer: "I fear I am dying."

After first aid was given, the ambulance was started again. It reached the field hospital shortly before midnight. Between one and two on the morning of May 3, Jackson's left arm was amputated about two inches from the shoulder.

While the battle at Chancellorsville was still in progress, President Davis was told that General George Stoneman's raiders were approaching unguarded Richmond. They had struck the central road at Louisa Court House and torn up the track. At Ashland, they had captured a trainload of sick and wounded soldiers, removed the sufferers, and burned the cars and the depot. Then they had started down the Brook Turnpike toward Richmond.

In ill-concealed perturbation, Colonel Chesnut went home to midday dinner and then rode off without telling his wife anything disturbing except that the President was quite ill. Sensing unknown danger, Mrs. Chesnut called on a neighbor, whose husband was an army officer; she was told that Stoneman was "only forty miles away." The two ladies, protected by three Negro menservants, went together to Capitol Square. Looking through the iron railings, they saw men of all classes, including Senators, falling into ranks and being mustered into companies.

Then Mrs. Chesnut went to the President's mansion, where she found the family was at supper. As she sat down on the white marble steps of the entrance to wait, General Elzey came out and said that danger was really imminent. Men spurred to and from the door "as fast as they could ride," bringing and carrying messages. After a while, Mrs. Davis came out and embraced her silently. "It is dreadful!" Mrs. Chesnut said. "The enemy is within forty miles of Richmond." "Who told you that tale?" Mrs. Davis asked scornfully. "They are within *three* miles."

Mrs. Chesnut "went down on her knees like a stone." "Be quiet," Mrs. Davis cautioned her. "The President is ill. Women and children must not add to the trouble." Then she begged her friend to spend the night with her, which she was thankful to do. Most of the night the ladies sat up, serving refreshments from a side table to officers who constantly came and went.

Early the next morning, Mary Chesnut was amazed to see Mr. Davis come downstairs accompanied by his physician. He was very pale and weak. Her husband and Custis Lee loaded his pistols for him. She watched the President ride off in Dr. Garnett's carriage, with his two aides on horseback alongside. The tocsin was brazenly sounding the alarm, adding to the city's consternation, as old men and young boys, shouldering heavy muskets, marched out to the city's defenses.[1]

The excitement did not abate until word came that the enemy was flying down the Peninsula before General Wise and Rooney Lee. The President learned that the enemy had indeed come within a mile and a half of James Lyons's country place, which was a mile and a half from the city.

A courier, arriving in hot haste, delivered a dispatch from General Lee. It was dated Milford, May 3. At one swift glance, Davis saw victory. Then he read carefully: "Yesterday Gen. Jackson, with three of his divisions, penetrated to the rear of the enemy, and drove him from his positions, from the Wilderness to within one mile of Chancellorsville. . . . This morning the battle was renewed. He was dislodged from all his positions around Chancellorsville and driven back towards the Rappahannock, over which he is now retreating. Many prisoners were taken, and the enemy's loss, in killed and wounded, large. We have again to thank Almighty God for a great victory. I regret to state that Gen. Paxton was killed, Gen. Jackson severely, and Generals Heth and A. P. Hill slightly, wounded."

Davis, troubled about the severity of Jackson's wound, passed the victory dispatch among his aides. Then he dictated a message for Lee: "I reverently unite with you in giving praise to God for the success with which He has crowned our arms. In the name of the people I offer my cordial thanks to yourself and the troops under your command for this addition to the unprecedented series of great victories which your army had achieved. The universal rejoicing will be mingled with the general regret for the good and the brave who are numbered among the killed and the wounded." Concealing his concern about Jackson, the President was persuaded to drive about with a couple of

---

[1] A lively account of the citizens' alarm at the Federals' approach is to be found in the Richmond *Examiner*, May 5, 1863.

aides in an open carriage. People on the streets rejoiced to see their leader "exhibiting the finest spirits."

All day Sunday, May 3, the battle had continued in the vicinity of Chancellorsville. Because of A. P. Hill's wound, Jeb Stuart had taken command of Jackson's corps. At 3 A.M., Lee began sending Stuart word to "prosecute with the utmost vigor, to give the enemy no time to rally, and to press to the right in order that we can unite both wings of the army." At dawn, Stuart sent Stonewall's corps charging forward with the battle cry "Remember Jackson!" The troops under Lee's direct command supported it. The Federals at first resisted the onslaught, but finally the Confederates pushed them back with vengeance.

In midmorning, General Hooker, confounded, was leaning against a porch pillar at Chancellor House, observing the losing fight, when a cannon ball rent the pillar asunder and knocked him senseless. Before he was borne away, the Confederates had virtually won the battle. By ten o'clock, Lee could report that the Confederates were "in full possession of the field."

On Monday, leaving Stuart with 22,000 men to stall off 80,000 Federals, Lee turned to combat Sedgwick near Fredericksburg. That night, May 4, Sedgwick retreated. Hooker, in deep depression at not proving his boast of outgeneraling Lee, held a council of war and decided to withdraw all his forces across the river. Lee had won another victory against an army double his strength. "Superb in Southern strategy, superb in tactics—and superbly fought" was the tribute to be paid by the Northern historical collaborators Ralph Newman and E. B. Long. When the news of Hooker's defeat reached Washington, Mr. Lincoln, in anguished dismay, cried out: "My God, my God! What *will* the country say?"

By May 6, the enemy was completely gone. Lee had won his greatest victory. Davis was very proud, and yet, like Lee, he was disappointed. If his whole army had been with him, Lee might have demolished Hooker. It had been a grave error not to have had Longstreet's 12,000 at his side. Lee's failure to recall Longstreet, as Freeman wrote in *R. E. Lee*, "must be written down as one of the great mistakes of his military career." But Lee himself was not blamed by the public for the error. Davis's War Department was.

Chancellorsville had been a costly victory. Though Hooker's casualties passed 17,000, Lee's were more than 12,000, and thus greater in proportion. Jefferson Davis regarded Jackson's serious wound as a disaster in itself. Of the number Lee lost, he remarked, there "was one, a host in himself."

Lee had sent an order to have Jackson carried out of danger to Guiney's Station. There, at the Chandler farm, an outbuilding had been readied for him. Mary Anna Jackson, with their child, arrived, and was shocked to find her husband in such a serious condition.

Although still confined to his house and in much discomfort, the President worked strenuously that drizzly sixth of May. And, according to Jones, he returned to the War Department that day fifty-five letters which had been written to him on various subjects. "He had read them all; and in his own hand had endorsed on many what he wished done." Jones noted with relief that the President had evidently not lost his sight.

Jefferson Davis was rent with anxiety over the critical affairs in Mississippi, where Grant's army was said to be moving toward Jackson, the capital. On the very day Hooker set up headquarters on the near bank of the Rappahannock, General Grant had successfully crossed the Mississippi with an initial 20,000 men at Bruinsburg, halfway between Natchez and Vicksburg. Pushing inland with remarkable celerity, he had taken Port Gibson; and, on May 3, he had forced the Confederates to evacuate the fort at Grand Gulf. Now a discouraging letter from Joseph E. Johnston at Tullahoma arrived, reporting that he was not well enough to take the field in Mississippi, as Secretary of War Seddon expected him to do.

On April 30, the day Grant crossed the river, Davis had wired Johnston: "General Pemberton telegraphs that unless he has more cavalry the approaches to North Mississippi are unprotected, and that he cannot prevent cavalry raids." Pemberton had informed Johnston on May 1 that a furious battle was raging at Port Gibson, where Grant's forces outnumbered the Confederates threefold. "I should have large reinforcements," he pleaded. Johnston had merely transmitted Pemberton's urgent call to the War Department, with the curt notation: "They cannot be sent from here without giving up Tennessee."

Johnston did not return Van Dorn or release a single man to Pemberton's aid. The President ordered Beauregard to forward troops from Charleston. He urged Mississippi's Governor Pettus to furnish for short service "militia or persons exempt from military service, who may be temporarily organized to repel the invasion," and he ordered arms and munitions for them to be sent to Jackson.

Deeply worried about his aging brother as well as the Mississippi Valley, the President wrote Joseph on May 7 an intimate letter that bared his thinking on many things.

"You can realize how deeply solicitous I am for your safety," he said. "The dispatches leave me in doubt as to the force of the enemy and the efficiency of the measures taken to meet him. As he [Grant] must be deficient in transportation, great embarrassment must necessarily attend any movement into the interior, and if our cavalry are equal to the task of cutting his line of communication and destroying his trains, he must soon be compelled to return to the river, if not beaten in battle." Since Pemberton had held the Federals at bay for five months, Davis did not anticipate the sudden swiftness of Grant's drive. Nor did he surmise that the Union General could feed his army by pillaging the countryside.

Concerning the combat around Chancellorsville, he wrote: "The battle recently fought on the Rappahannock was certainly a great victory, in view of the thorough preparation of the enemy and his superiority of numbers, not less than two to one. He is however, reinforcing heavily, and our railroads are so poor and badly administered that my efforts to reinforce first do not promise well. . . ."

Then, being careful not to criticize Joe Johnston by name, he revealed a desperate need. "The withdrawal of Van Dorn from North Mississippi was one of those blunders for which it is difficult to compensate. A General in the full sense of the word is a rare product, scarcely more than one can be expected in a generation, but in this mighty war in which we are engaged, there is need for half a dozen. . . ."

He wrote on, to make his brother know that he was doing what he could for Pemberton. "I have sent all the force at command, and arms for the militia, and though I cannot but be apprehensive, am hopeful that General Pemberton will repel the invader. I hope, however, to give him further reinforcements in a very short time."

At the end, he turned to family matters.

It is sad to me to know that you and Sister Eliza in your old age are denied the repose required, and to feel powerless to give you the personal assistance, which in the order of nature, is due from me. . . .

My health is not good, but has improved so much with the last few days that it may be reasonably expected that the recent attack is at an end. It commenced with fever, and was followed by bronchitis. The cough only remains and my present debility is no doubt due to confinement and anxiety. My official duties have not been suspended at any time, except in the matter of personal interviews, which inability to talk rendered necessary to suspend.

I am interrupted, and with love to Sister Eliza, Lise, and others of the family with you,

I am ever affectionately,
Your brother
Jefferson Davis

The President had been interrupted by the distressing report that Stonewall Jackson had contracted pneumonia and was critically ill. He would have been the more alarmed if he had known that in the night, while his physician napped, Jackson, to relieve the pain in his side, had insisted on an attendant putting cold, wet towels on his stomach. A pneumonia specialist from Richmond was promptly sent up to Guiney's. All that evening, as Mrs. Davis wrote in her *Memoir,* the President, unable to think of anything but the possible calamity, "sat silent until past midnight." He kept a servant at the telegraph office to rush the latest bulletin to him.

The next day, Davis received a pressing letter from Lee written on May 7, before the General learned of Jackson's pneumonia. Lee urged him to procure more cavalry from somewhere "as speedily as practicable" to meet the much larger cavalry force of the enemy. "The disparity between our infantry force and that of the enemy," he wrote, "is too large to reasonably expect success. The strength of the enemy seems to be greater than I had estimated, as from various sources, it is stated that they crossed the Rappahannock with 120,000 men. Our effective strength with which we marched to meet him, according to the last returns, did not reach 40,000." He ended with a plea for the President to come and confer with him. "There are many things about which I would like to consult Your Excellency, and I should be delighted if your health and convenience suited, if you could visit the army. I could get you a comfortable room in the vicinity of my headquarters, and I know you would be content with our camp fare. Should this, however, be inconvenient, I will endeavor to go to Richmond, though I feel my presence here is now essential."

Davis would have liked nothing better than to go to his friend; he felt the need of Lee's counsel as much as Lee longed for his. But Dr. Garnett insisted that he was not sufficiently recuperated even to go to his office on Capitol Square. And with Grant's army rolling up through

Mississippi, the President was compelled to be close to his Secretary of War and the Richmond telegraph office.

On Saturday, news came that Jackson was sinking. Davis shut himself in his room, as Stonewall's troops, General Lee, and the whole believing South prayed. At Guiney's Station, the heartbroken Anna Jackson, at her husband's bedside, summoned strength to sing hymns to soothe him. Over and over she crooned his favorite spiritual, "Show Pity, Lord."

That same tense Saturday of May 9, Seddon, almost in despair over Joseph Johnston's do-nothingness about Mississippi, came to the President. So far, Johnston's help to Pemberton had consisted only of telegraphic admonitions like this one: "If General Grant's army lands on this side of the river, the safety of the Mississippi depends on beating it. For that object you should unite your whole force." It looked to Seddon as if Johnston was ducking responsibility and malingering. He had not mentioned any specific ailment; he merely claimed he was not well.

After consultation with Davis, Seddon sent Johnston a peremptory, though tactfully phrased, order: "Proceed at once to Mississippi and take chief command of the forces there, giving to those in the field, as far as practicable, the encouragement and benefit of your personal direction. . . ." Johnston was instructed to take 3,000 good troops from Bragg's army. "You will find reinforcements from General Beauregard to General Pemberton, and more may be expected. Acknowledge receipt."

The military tone of Seddon's order somewhat revitalized Johnston. "I shall go immediately," he replied, "though unfit for field-service." He took the train at Chattanooga; but, because of railway difficulties, necessitating a roundabout journey, he was not to reach Jackson, Mississippi, until four days later.

The tenth of May was such a balmy, beautiful day in Richmond that Jefferson Davis felt a surge of hope for Jackson's life. But at Guiney's, before noon, the physicians thought that Anna should inform her husband his end was near. Bravely, she told the General that before the day ended he would be in heaven. Was he willing to go? she asked. "Yes," he said calmly. "I prefer it." It was Sunday, and he had always hoped to die on the Sabbath. In the early afternoon, to relieve the distressing terminal breathing, Dr. Maguire offered the sufferer brandy in water. He declined. "It will only delay my departure, and do no good." Shortly after three, Jackson roused to give a battle order.

Then, as he breathed his last, his mind turned to a peaceful haven. He did not babble of green fields like Falstaff, but said softly in a clear voice, "Let us cross over the river and rest in the shade of the trees."

That evening, President Davis was handed a telegram from General Lee. "It becomes my melancholy duty to announce to you the death of General Jackson. He expired at 3:15 P.M. today." It was the most dismal dispatch Jefferson Davis had received since that sickening one from Shiloh announcing Sidney Johnston's death. Could Lee manage without his foremost lieutenant? No other of Jackson's caliber or peculiar genius existed. Davis looked upon Jackson somewhat as "the complement of Lee." So he wrote later, adding, "united, they had achieved such results that the public felt secure under their shield." The President had set his recent hopes of the Confederacy's success on these two: Lee and Jackson. Only three days before, when Jackson's recovery was expected, Davis had written his brother Joseph of his need for six great generals. Of the Confederacy's three most outstanding ones, Lee, Jackson, and Sidney Johnston, Lee alone remained.

The splendid victory against big odds at Chancellorsville, following that of Fredericksburg, had lifted Davis's heart high for a day or so. But again Fate had mocked the Southern cause with peculiar malignancy, just as, in another hour of victory, Sidney Johnston had bled to death because he had chivalrously sent his surgeon to attend other men's wounds. The ironic twist was somewhat the same: the irreplaceable Stonewall had been shot by his own men and his litter-bearer had stumbled disastrously over a tree root. It was hard to accept the tragedy as God's will, as the dying Jackson had done.

The President asked for the handsomest Confederate flag in the capital to be sent down to cover the warrior's body, which was to be brought by train to Richmond. The next day, while all the city's flags hung mournfully at half-mast, Davis, awaiting the arrival of Jackson's body, received more unexpected bad news. Major General Earl Van Dorn, who had completely ruined Grant's first plans for taking Vicksburg by destroying his supply base in December, had been killed. But not in battle. An irate, jealous husband, Dr. George B. Peters, had walked into his headquarters in Spring Hill, Tennessee, and shot him in the back as he sat writing at his desk.

Jefferson Davis experienced profound regret over the dashing Van Dorn. Though he had been unpredictable, often undependable, and sometimes defeated, Van Dorn had been an excellent cavalryman. His death was a sharp loss to the Confederacy, and right now his services were critically needed.

If Johnston had only acceded to Pemberton's plea for the return of Van Dorn at the end of March, Davis reflected, he would be alive to help stop the swift-moving Grant, who was about to take the town of Raymond.[2]

At eleven o'clock, Jackson's body arrived at the station and was taken first to the Governor's Mansion. The President, with his wife, went there to take a last look at the dead hero; in Varina's words, "at the patriot saint." "His countenance," she thought, "still bore the marks of the anguish he had suffered." As her husband bent over the fallen chieftain, she saw a tear drop on the death-still face. When they returned home and a man came to talk of business, Davis remained dazed and silent. "You must excuse me," he said at length. "I am staggering from a dreadful blow. I cannot think."

In the funeral procession to the capitol next day, the President followed the hearse in a carriage. He had insisted on walking, but, the morning being unseasonably hot, his aides had persuaded him to ride. Behind the President came the Cabinet and heads of departments on foot, two and two, Benjamin and Seddon in the lead. Watchers on the street saw that Davis was "very thin and frail, and gaunt with grief"; quite different from his appearance a few days before, just after he had received the victorious news of Chancellorsville.

Before being taken to Lexington for burial, Stonewall Jackson lay in state in the capitol. A procession of mourners streamed past until late in the night. As sorrowing women passed the bier, they each dropped a white blossom onto the flag the President had sent to cover him. "Jackson's whole heart was his country's," as Jefferson Davis was later to write; "and his whole country's heart was his." But few, if any, in the concourse of mourners could realize so acutely the magnitude of the loss as did the Confederacy's President. In his telegram of condolence to Lee, he began: "A great national calamity has befallen us."

[2] In his official report months later, in referring to the advance of the enemy from Bruinsburg, Pemberton made this statement: "With a moderate cavalry force at my disposal, I am firmly convinced that the Federal army under General Grant would have been unable to maintain its communications with the Mississippi River, and that the attempt to reach Jackson and Vicksburg would have been signally defeated in May, 1863."

CHAPTER XXX

THE CLIMACTIC DECISION

AFTER Chancellorsville, many patriotic Northerners gave up the hope that the South could be conquered. Some industrialists and businessmen who had begun to make big money out of the war feared it would stop. Though the national debt was mounting alarmingly, huge private fortunes were being made. Partly because wages had skyrocketed, there was little enthusiasm for enlisting. The Federal Government, individual states, municipalities, and even city wards offered attractive bounties to those who would take up arms. With still more generous bait, President Lincoln tempted Europeans to emigrate to help swell the Union armies.

When the news of Lee's victory reached England, the British were convinced that the Confederates would triumph. Even before Chancellorsville, English leaders believed that the South would eventually win its independence. On the very day of the battle, May 2, 1863, a lead editorial in the London *Times* advised the North that the Union was "irreparably divided." Referring to the American Revolution, the editor said, "We have all come to the conclusion that they had a right to be independent, and it was best they should be. Nor can we escape from the inference that the Federals will one day come to the same conclusion with regard to the Southern States."

Whatever the ultimate outcome of the war, Varina Davis was now almost beside herself with worry. She did not see how her husband could bear up under the strain. The pressure from the last day of April until General Jackson's funeral had been more intense than any he had undergone. Though wracked by a persistent cough, the President held

conferences at home, and with sharp lucidity dictated numerous letters and telegrams. He was continually pestered by little things. General Longstreet accused Northern-born Major General Samuel Gibbs
French of some alleged misconduct at Suffolk, and Seddon proposed
that French be relieved and questioned by a court of inquiry. Davis
promptly and sharply vetoed the move. He declared such courts were
nuisances, and he could not have General French molested at such a
critical time.

Much worse was to come. The President had hardly recovered from
his emotion over Stonewall Jackson's death when he received word
from Mississippi that Grant had defeated the Confederates at Raymond on the twelfth and was marching on the state capital. Joseph
Johnston, who had assumed direct command of Mississippi operations
on the ninth, did not reach Jackson until the thirteenth. His first telegram to the Secretary of War was like a presage of doom: "I arrived
this evening, finding the enemy's force between this place and General
Pemberton, cutting off communication. I am too late."

Johnston, in his own opinion, had arrived just in time to retreat. But
next day, he instructed Pemberton as follows: "If practicable, come
up in his [the enemy's] rear at once. To beat such a detachment would
be of immense value. Troops here could cooperate. All the troops you
can quickly assemble should be brought. Time is all important."

The tardy General Johnston, having urged speed and concentration,
promptly abandoned Jackson, withdrew all his forces to the northeast,
and sent orders to the incoming reinforcements to halt until further
orders. The brigades of John Gregg and W. H. T. Walker had arrived
in Jackson from southern Mississippi just before Johnston came. He
took them all with him. By his own report, Johnston retreated six and
a half miles from Jackson the first day, and ten and a half miles farther the next. He wound up at Calhoun Station, seven miles south of
Canton. Though Pemberton informed him by courier that he would
march to meet Grant on the fifteenth, Johnston did not move.

Colonel S. H. Lockett, Chief Engineer of the Vicksburg defenses,
later wrote: "Pemberton moved out from Edward's Depot in obedience to General Johnston, ordering him to attack in the rear a force
he supposed General Johnston was going to engage in front. Instead
of this, he encountered Grant's victorious army returning, exultant
from the capture of Jackson." Pemberton was naturally expecting
Johnston to attack the Federals from one side while he assailed them
from the other. But Johnston, having moved farther away from any

possible conflict, opened a prolonged correspondence with Pemberton, "from which," in the later words of Davis, "a confusion with consequent disaster resulted."

On May 16, Johnston sent a detailed dispatch to Richmond from his retreat seventeen miles above Jackson. He ended with unintentional irony: "My object is to unite all the troops." As Davis read the report, his jaw tightened. Seizing his pen, he endorsed on the back: "Do not perceive why a junction was not attempted, which would have made our force nearly equal to the estimated strength of the enemy, and might have resulted in his total defeat." [1]

On May 15, after sleeping in the room that Johnston had occupied on the night of the thirteenth, Grant ordered Sherman to destroy Jackson "as a railroad center and manufacturing city of military supplies." Then he turned west toward Vicksburg and Pemberton's intervening force.

In two battles in the next two days, the unsupported Pemberton was beaten back, first at Champion's Hill and then at the Big Black River Bridge. On May 18, he took cover within the Vicksburg fortifications. Grant moved up to storm the works. Johnston, sixty-seven miles away from Vicksburg, wrote letters counseling the War Department to do something.

In a journal entry of May 17, Robert Kean wrote sarcastically: "J. E. Johnston . . . telegraphed he was *too late*. . . . Johnston had retired towards Canton. His 'strategy' seems of the kind Yankee correspondents ascribe to all their commanders—retreat and sacrifice is always 'strategical'. I have little confidence in the General who came near losing Richmond and who thinks so much of himself. Grant is now in a position where a man of daring energy like the lamented 'Stonewall Jackson' would destroy him."

On the day Johnston abandoned Jackson, and while the President was considering the urgent advisability of sending some of Lee's troops to save Vicksburg, General Lee himself arrived in Richmond. A few days before, Secretary of War Seddon had desired General Lee to send to Mississippi Major General George Pickett's division from the Army of Northern Virginia. But Lee had responded that that would be a dangerous and doubtful expedient. He had something else in his mind.

[1] The endorsement on the back of Johnston's letter appears in *Official Records,* Series I, Vol. XXIV, p. 216.

Jefferson Davis was delighted to see his friend and top General. Lee looked somewhat thinner, he thought, and a little pale, though as handsome as ever. After some talk, Lee came to the special point of his visit: to persuade the President to let him invade Pennsylvania.

Having repulsed a foe more than twice his size, Lee looked to new laurels and greener pastures, literally. Virginia was low on foodstuffs and fodder; the land north of the Potomac waxed fat. He stressed the fact that while the four-to-one Northern manpower was constantly increased by immigrant mercenaries, in the Confederacy the lack of manpower grew steadily worse. Some daring strategy was essential. Though he had just buried his most valuable lieutenant, Lee wanted the President to let him take a colossal gamble. The Secretary of War was summoned for conference. Then at an informal meeting with the Cabinet, Lee set forth his arguments for a campaign in enemy land.

For the three days that Lee was in Richmond, the President was severely tested. He had hoped that General Lee would consent to send a portion of his victorious troops to join Pemberton and Johnston in defeating Grant's army now closing on Vicksburg. To Davis, the necessity of holding Vicksburg and Port Hudson and the two hundred miles of curling river between them was of prime importance. Letters from military men and civilians were continually arriving urging Pemberton's reinforcement by a part of Lee's command. A delegation of influential citizens from Columbus, Mississippi, including Bishop Paine and former Governor Whitfield, had just been in Richmond conferring with the President about the state's defense.

Davis found Lee strongly disinclined to weaken his own forces by a single regiment. Hooker's army, though defeated and discouraged, was still powerful, having more than 100,000 men, and being continually reinforced. Lee proposed to draw Hooker out of Virginia by invading the North, where the Confederates could get food for men and horses, and stimulate the activities of the increasing Northern peace party, which was becoming vitally active. The triumphant Lee, Davis observed, was in a fighting mood. Even Northern papers were using that magic word "invincible" when they wrote of him. Davis considered well. A sweeping victory on Northern soil would encourage England to grant recognition. If Lee were successful in Pennsylvania, the end of the war would be accelerated. It was a worthwhile, if hazardous, gamble. But keeping a portion of the Mississippi River open was absolutely essential to Confederate interests. Supplies coming in from

Texas ports had to be got across the river. Already, there was grumbling talk of secession in Arkansas. In a completely isolated Trans-Mississippi, morale might hopelessly disintegrate.

Jefferson Davis found it hard to oppose Lee in anything, and he was not sure what was best to do. He called his Cabinet to meet early Saturday morning on the second-floor council room of his home. Everyone recognized the supreme gravity of the conference. The fate of the Confederacy might hang on the issue.

The President read aloud letters from the Governor of Mississippi and others pressing for assistance from Lee's army to drive away the besieging Grant. Each Secretary spoke his mind freely. Only one, Postmaster General Reagan, came out in vigorous opposition to Lee's plan. The Texan felt that General Lee was so absorbed in defending Virginia that he did not realize the full import of the West and the Trans-Mississippi. Reagan emphasized the vital necessity of holding intact the communications with the territory beyond the Mississippi. He passionately advocated the destruction of Grant's army as of prime importance. He favored a plan of allowing General Lee to *threaten* invasion across the Potomac, without executing it. In the meantime, he said, the defenses of Richmond should be strengthened and supplies collected for a siege. Some 25,000 or 30,000 of Lee's troops should be dispatched to crush Grant. Reagan argued cogently that this victorious army could then be turned against the Federal forces in Tennessee and either defeat them or drive them across the Ohio. Some who disagreed with Reagan believed that if Lee threatened Washington and Baltimore, the Federals would withdraw from Vicksburg. But Reagan scoffed at the idea; Grant had gone too far, he said, and was determined to take Vicksburg if his army was not destroyed.

With fixed attention and the utmost respect, the President listened to Reagan's plan. Impressed by the Texan's lucidity and fervency, he was inclined to agree that the Confederacy should play the safer game with Vicksburg. And he had as much heart interest in the Mississippi region as Lee did in Virginia. He knew that his sisters and brother and his Mississippi neighbors, who had sent their sons to Virginia, were looking to him for salvation. But naturally he could not let the claims of friendship and family sway him.

The Cabinet talked through the afternoon, anxiously considering everything involved in the two campaigns. Several times Mrs. Davis sent up refreshments. Finally, at nightfall, the President called for an informal vote. All except Reagan voted for Lee's plan to make war in

Pennsylvania. Though not convinced that they had come to the better decision, Davis would not go against Lee and the will of his Cabinet. He saw Reagan depart with an air of prophetic gloom.

"In giving way to Lee," wrote the Virginia historian Eckenrode, "the President displayed a patriotism so lofty that it deserves no word of comment." And in Eckenrode's opinion, "the one occasion of the war when Lee asserted himself strongly . . . was the one occasion when he happened to be wrong." Davis, he wrote, "has been blamed for preferring his own judgment to that of his generals, but in this case when he went against his judgment he made the mistake that decided the outcome of the war."

Lee was made happy by the Cabinet's decision and its confidence in him. That evening he called to pay his respects to Constance Cary's mother, who had done outstanding service in nursing the wounded. The fascinating Constance, now being ardently courted by President Davis's secretary, Burton Harrison, wrote: "It was broad moonlight and I recall the superb figure of our hero standing in the little porch without, saying a last few words, as he swung his military cape around his shoulders. It did not need my fervid imagination to think him the most noble looking mortal I had ever seen. We felt, as he left us and walked off up the quiet leafy street in the moonlight, that we had been honored by more than royalty."

For Jefferson Davis, sleep was more difficult that night than usual. Very early the next morning (Sunday), an urgent note was brought to his bed. It was from Reagan, who had gone home a most disquieted man, believing that a fatal mistake was being made. He had remained restless until midnight, and then, after getting to bed, he could not sleep at all. Finally, in intense perturbation, he rose before daylight and wrote Mr. Davis that he felt strongly that they were doing wrong. Strategic considerations cried out for the immediate relief of Vicksburg. He begged the President to convene the Cabinet again to reconsider the question.

It was an extraordinary request after the Chief Executive had made a decision backed almost unanimously by his Cabinet. But Davis respected Reagan as a man of absolute sincerity, of solid convictions and no self-interest. He believed in the good man's loyalty to himself, though Reagan had openly disagreed with him more often than any other Cabinet member. Once, Reagan had even offered to resign, fearing his disagreements caused the President embarrassment. But Davis

had assured him that he always welcomed honest opposition; he said
he had been a member of a Cabinet himself, and "if the Cabinet should
accept without question the opinions of the President, he did not well
see what their use could be as advisers." Now, because of his own
doubts, he wrote Reagan that he would call the Cabinet to reconsider.[2]

Before the summons had gone out, however, most of the members
had gathered in the President's office. In unofficial discussion, Reagan,
as well as the President, saw that reconsideration was useless. The
Cabinet was still backing the plan of General Lee, "whose fame now
filled the world."

On May 18, after Lee had left Richmond, the President telegraphed
Johnston about new accessions of state militia available to him, and
urged him to unite with Pemberton "and attack the enemy in his retrograde movement to the river." Every effort would be made to aid
him, Davis said, and he desired to know fully his wishes. Hopefully,
to animate the Commanding General, he added, "Your presence will
effect much to inspire confidence and activity."

Though the people of Mississippi had confidence in Johnston,
Davis's carefully chosen word "activity" had no effect. For on that
same day, Johnston wrote General Cooper that he had met "a Mr.
Shelton," who had come from General Pemberton's headquarters and
told him the army had fallen back to Vicksburg. "I was preparing to
join General Pemberton personally when this information came. It is
now impracticable and would be useless. I shall endeavor," he wrote,
as if nothing more vigorous was expected of him, "after collecting all
available troops, to hold as much of the country as possible." He reckoned Pemberton's forces at 28,000, with provisions for sixty days.
"Whatever efforts the Government may propose to make," he admonished, "must therefore be carried into immediate effect." Johnston
gave no indication whatever of hazarding his own forces in attacking
Grant.

Instead, without informing the War Department, he sent, on that
same day, a courier to Pemberton with an extraordinary communication. "If it is not too late, evacuate Vicksburg and its dependencies, and
march to the northeast."

[2] In his *Memoirs*, John Reagan wrote in two places of the Cabinet meeting that
considered Lee's invasion of Pennsylvania. On pages 120-122 he told the story to point
out the error of those who supposed Jefferson Davis to have been arbitrary. On pages
150-153 he gave more details and humbly invited the verdict of careful military critics
on his plan as opposed to that of General Lee and the Cabinet.

Knowing that the surrender of the river would mean the severance of the Confederate States, Pemberton called a council of war. "The opinion was unanimously expressed," he wrote Johnston, "that it was impossible to withdraw the army from their position with such *morale* and material as to be of further service to the Confederacy." He announced his decision to hold Vicksburg as long as possible: "I still conceive it to be the most important point in the Confederacy." Before Pemberton finished his dispatch to Johnston, Union guns opened up on the fortifications. The siege had begun.

On Monday, May 18, Colonel Arthur Lyon Fremantle of the Coldstream Guards, who had entered Texas in April as a military observer from England, arrived at Jackson to find smoldering ruins. The four railroads that met there had been destroyed in each direction for three to five miles. He recorded in his diary: "All the numerous factories have been burnt down by the enemy, who were of course justified in doing so; but during the short space of thirty-six hours, in which General Grant occupied the city, his troops had wantonly pillaged nearly all the private houses. They had gutted all the stores and destroyed what they could not carry away. All this must have been done under the very eyes of General Grant, whose name was in the book of the Bowman House. . . . I saw the ruins of the Roman Catholic church, the priest's house, and the principal hotel, which were still smoking, together with many other buildings which could in no way be identified with the Confederate Government."

Four days later, Grant ordered an assault in force at Vicksburg and was repulsed with more than 3,000 casualties. When Johnston still made no move to attack Grant's rear, the President telegraphed Bragg at Tullahoma: "The vital issue of holding the Mississippi at Vicksburg is dependent on the success of Genl. Johnston in an attack on the investing force. The intelligence from there is discouraging. Can you aid him? If so, and you are without orders from Genl. Johnston, act on your judgement." Bragg replied next day: "Sent thirty five hundred with the General: three batteries of artillery and two thousand cavalry since; will dispatch six thousand more immediately."

Davis had submitted the question to Bragg's judgment, having, as he later wrote, "full reliance in the large-hearted and comprehensive view which his self-denying nature would take of the case." "Your answer is in the spirit of patriotism heretofore manifested by you," he replied to Bragg. "The need is sore, but you must not forget your own necessities."

How different, Davis reflected, was Bragg's attitude from that of
Joseph Johnston, who, hardly a fortnight before, had been disinclined
to loose a single soldier from the Army of Tennessee for Vicksburg's
defense.

"I have made every effort to reinforce you promptly, which I am ag-
grieved has not been successful," Davis telegraphed Pemberton on
May 23. "Hope that General Johnston will soon join you with enough
force to break up the investment and defeat the enemy."

Then by telegram he reminded Johnston, who was returning cautiously to burnt-out Jackson, that the disparity of numbers between
Pemberton and Grant rendered prolonged defense dangerous.[3] "I hope
you will soon be able to break the investment," Davis said, "make a
junction and carry in munitions. . . . If my strength permitted I
would go to you."

Some of his advisers believed that the President's appearance in his
home state would fire the Mississippi heart, as it had in December.
And some felt that the mere thought of Davis's coming might spark
action in Johnston. But with Lee mobilizing for departure to Pennsylvania, it was not prudent for the President to leave Virginia.

After Lee's return to his camp, there was a heavy exchange of letters
between him and the President. In preparing for his Northern campaign, Lee reorganized his entire army into three corps and submitted
to Davis details of the arrangements. Longstreet, who had returned
from Suffolk, commanded the First Corps; Ewell had Jackson's old
Second Corps; A. P. Hill, the new Third. Captain Justus Scheibert of
the Prussian Engineers, who had been sent by his chief, Prince von
Raziwell, as an observer and was now with Lee's forces, wrote: "Here
in this camp was now spun the thread of one of the greatest invasive
marches, only slightly suspected in the army and directed solely by
the hands of the President, of General Lee, and of the three corps commanders."

In a letter of May 26, Davis wrote the busily occupied Lee in a vein
more cheerful than the Western situation warranted: "Our intelligence from Miss. is, on the whole encouraging. Pemberton is
stoutly defending the entrenchments at Vicksburg, and Johnston has
an army outside, which I suppose will be able to raise a siege, and combined with Pemberton's forces may win a victory. . . . General
Bragg had bravely and patriotically detached strong reinforcements

[3] By May 25, Grant had an effective force of 50,000.

to Genl. Johnston, so much so that I have had to warn him to be mindful of his own necessities."

In the next five days, however, as the Mississippi situation worsened, the President found the inactivity of Johnston exasperating in the extreme. Grant, on the other hand, though cut off from his supplies, had been operating brilliantly in enemy country. He had marched 180 miles, had fought five battles, and was now besieging Vicksburg. Johnston would not even hazard the slightest harassment of Grant's rear. But he used much energy in sending copious telegrams and letters, while Vicksburg became a pluperfect hell, with bursting shells dropping in the town night and day.

On May 31, the President again wrote Lee, merely hinting at his troubles. "Genl. Johnston did not, as you thought advisable, attack Grant promptly, and I fear the result is that which you anticipated if time was given. The last intelligence indicates that Grant is concentrating on the Yazoo, where he connects with his gunboats and river transportation, and threatens the line of communications between Jackson and Vicksburg. The position, naturally strong, may soon be intrenched. . . . It is useless to look back, and it would be unkind to annoy you in the midst of your many cares with the reflections which I have not been able to avoid. All accounts we have of Pemberton's conduct fully sustain the good opinion heretofore entertained of him."

It was not difficult for Lee to imagine Davis's dark reflections on Johnston's inactivity, while day by day Grant grew stronger and Halleck ordered fresh troops from Missouri and Kentucky to reinforce him. The President gave the sympathetic Lee no inkling of his personal worry over his old brother Joseph. He had already heard of Joseph's encounter with the foe. A detachment of Union troops had appeared at Fleetwood, Joseph's plantation, with orders from General Peter J. Osterhaus "to leave no board unburned," in the phrase of Lise Mitchell, Joseph's granddaughter.

"Dr. Emanuel, who was there," Lise wrote in her *Journal*, "tendered the family all the aid he could in taking the furniture out of the house. The ladies watched them [Union soldiers] break open trunks and rob them of silver, jewels, and other valuables. At length the torch was brought, when one of the servants called out, 'There comes Marse Joe,' and looking up they saw my brother, Captain Mitchell, entering the house. Supposing he had a company with him, they ran for their horses, and rode away as fast as they could. My brother was alone . . . and did not know Yankees were there." The invalid Eliza and another female relative were sent away to safety, and young Lise stayed on to minister to her grandfather.

The anxious President pressed his brother Joseph to leave everything and come to Richmond.

. . . It has been to me a constant source of deep anxiety to know that you were exposed to the malignant outrages of the cruel foe with whom we are at war.

No effort was spared by me to prevent an invasion such as had occurred. . . .

My information is too vague to justify an opinion as to the practicability of executing my purpose,—an attack on Grant when in the interior, by combined forces of Johnston and Pemberton. Thus alone was a complete victory to be expected. Now the enemy has reached the river, made a junction of his forces and got to his river transportation. He has had time to intrench his position, and the chances are less favorable for his overthrow.

Please make such arrangements as are advisable, and come here. I will try to make you and Sister Eliza comfortable. Lise half belongs to me, and will, I hope, be contented to share with me. I asked General J.R.D. [their nephew Joseph R. Davis] to see you about the negroes. The faithful ones deserve to be saved from the fate to which the Yankees would consign them.

God help and preserve you. Would that my arm were with you, to strike though it were its last blow for one to whom I am most of all indebted.[4]

---

[4] The above letter was lent to the author by Mrs. Mary Lucy O'Kelley, daughter of Lise Mitchell Hamer and great-granddaughter of Joseph Davis.

CHAPTER XXXI

JOE JOHNSTON MADDENS THE WAR DEPARTMENT

TOWARD the end of May, despite the unrelieved tensions, Davis's usual vigor had returned and he relaxed by riding horseback in the late afternoons. Sometimes his aide Preston Johnston accompanied him and sometimes Custis Lee. Burton Harrison generally went, too. Occasionally, John Reagan rode with him. Davis's cavalier appearance on the streets on his white Arabian delighted the populace. "The President," wrote Jones on June 2, in an outburst of romantic admiration, "rides out every afternoon and sits as an English king could do four centuries ago."

Once when Reagan was riding with the President along the line below Richmond, they passed a small lad in a soldier's uniform. "My boy," the President asked, "are you a soldier?"

"I am, sir." "How old are you?" "Fourteen," the lad replied truthfully.

Davis inquired what his command was and sought out his captain. To the officer, the President said kindly but firmly, "I think you should send that boy home; we should not destroy the seed corn."

On June 3, Jefferson Davis reached the age of fifty-five. He looked remarkably well as he now basked in the affectionate attentions of his family. On his previous birthday, Varina and the children had been in Raleigh, because McClellan was closing in on Richmond. Lee had had command of the Army of Northern Virginia for a year and a day. And just a year ago, Davis was composing a laudatory letter of congratulation to Stonewall Jackson for his brilliant successes in the Shenandoah. Jackson, alas, was in his grave, and Lee's need for him had never been so pressing. Coincidentally, on the President's birth-

411

day, Lee began to move toward his new objective beyond the Potomac. He ordered Ewell in the van to drive the Federals from Winchester and Martinsburg.

By special messenger, Lee sent to Richmond seven flags "of those captured from the enemy in the recent engagements on the Rappahannock." They were ticketed to show what troops had taken them.[1] The President could consider them a birthday gift as well as a bright omen of future victory.

Though feeling apprehension because of Jackson's absence and the Confederacy's inferior numbers, Davis knew that the morale of Lee's men was excellent and that the people's confidence in Lee as a General had never been equaled in American history. Longstreet later wrote that Lee's own belief in victory was so supreme that his corps commanders, fearing his audacity, tried to get him to promise that he would not fight the enemy except on grounds of his own choosing.

On June 3, an incident occurred in Chicago that aroused Northern indignation against the Federal Administration. At three o'clock in the morning, mounted soldiers, on orders from General Burnside, galloped up to the Chicago *Times* building, followed shortly by two infantry companies. The military took possession, stopped the press, and confiscated the papers already printed. Angry citizens, Republicans as well as Democrats, held a meeting, denounced Burnside's highhanded action, and demanded that President Lincoln rescind the order. Lincoln, who had already lost friends by allowing Burnside to prohibit the circulation of the New York *World* in Ohio, Indiana, and Illinois, finally yielded to the pressure.

A more serious blunder had been made in the Vallandigham case. As the peace party grew in Ohio, General Burnside had issued a drastic order on April 13 declaring that all persons found within the Federal lines who committed acts for the benefit of the enemy would "be tried as spies and traitors." "The habit of declaring sympathies for the enemy," he proclaimed, "will no longer be tolerated in this department."

At a picnic on May 1, Clement Laird Vallandigham, United States Congressman and Ohio's leading Democrat, commented with strong disapproval on "such a tyrannical order." Three days later, a body of soldiers violently broke into his house before daylight and hustled him

---

[1] Lee's note accompanying the trophies of victory is the last communication from him recorded in *Official Records*, Series I, Vol. XXV, Part 2, p. 853.

to the train for Cincinnati, where he was locked in a military prison. At his trial before a Military Commission, Congressman Vallandigham was sentenced to imprisonment for the duration of the war.

"Nothing like this," wrote the Chief of the Confederate War Bureau in his secret diary, "has occurred in two centuries in any country save in Russia and France during the madness of the Reign of Terror. . . . Lincoln has been guilty as usual of a great blunder." The historian Rhodes was to write decades later, "The arrest and punishment of Vallandigham were not only contrary to the Constitution and statutes, but were likewise bad policy."

Here and there throughout the North, similar night arrests had been made. A person holding political views opposite to those of the Administration might be arrested on an affidavit of an unfriendly neighbor that he had spoken disloyal words. As Jefferson Davis saw it, the United States Government held the keys to the prisons, arrested citizens at its pleasure, and generally usurped the sovereignty that belonged to the states.

Davis read of the terrific stir over Vallandigham created in the North. James Brooks, an avid Peace Democrat, soon to be a United States Representative from New York, offered "to lead an army to put down such tyranny." The hubbub caused President Lincoln to change the Congressman's sentence to banishment within the Confederacy.

Before Davis had had time to decide what to do with Vallandigham, the exile was thrust across the border into Confederate territory. He made his way to Bragg's camp. Polk and Hardee showed him special courtesies at Shelbyville. There the British Colonel Fremantle met him and found him most agreeable.

At last, Vallandigham was notified by Richmond that if he held himself a loyal citizen of the United States, he could not reside in the Confederacy, but that he would be furnished with a safe conduct to some seaport. Bragg informed President Davis that the banished citizen desired to leave for Bermuda by way of Wilmington. So Davis sent Robert Ould, commissioner for the exchange of prisoners, to meet Vallandigham at Lynchburg and conduct him to Wilmington. "His departure for a neutral port," the President wrote, "will be facilitated by all the courtesy and kindness due to his condition."

In the memorandum of Vallandigham's conversation with Ould, which was brought back to the President, Davis took special note of the Copperhead's opinion that if the Confederates "can only hold out this year," the peace party of the North "would sweep the Lincoln dynasty out of political existence."

But Vallandigham could not approve of Lee's invasion; he believed it might unite all parties in the North. Eventually, he hoped for amicable reconstruction of the old Union under a Democratic regime; but if reconstruction were utterly impossible, he was in favor of recognizing the South's independence. From Bermuda, Vallandigham purposed to go to Canada, to plan and conduct in exile his fall campaign for governor of Ohio.

In the meantime, instead of making any move to relieve Pemberton, Joseph Johnston continued to bombard Richmond with vague and discouraging dispatches. On June 5, Seddon telegraphed General Johnston that he regretted his inability to promise more troops; he had drained the Confederacy's resources even to danger on several points. But he urged Johnston to speedy action. "With the facilities and resources of the enemy time works against us," he emphasized. In another dispatch, Seddon reminded Johnston that, despite his own underestimate of his strength, by the records he had a force of 32,000. With Pemberton's approximate force of 31,000 facing Grant, Richmond could not understand why Johnston did not use the two armies to try to crush Grant between them.

General Johnston seemed much concerned over petty matters. On June 11, he was upset because Major General Samuel Gibbs French, who had arrived to strengthen him, was Northern-born. Davis answered with controlled irritation: "Those who suggest that the arrival of Genl. French will produce discontent because of his Northern birth are probably not aware that he is a citizen of Missi., was a wealthy planter until the Yankees robbed him, and before the Confederate States had an army was the Chief of Ordnance and artillery in the force Missi. raised to maintain her right of secession. . . . If malignity should undermine him as it has another, you are authorized to notify him of the fact and to relieve him."

On June 12, Seddon received a dispatch from Johnston questioning the extent of his command. To settle forever the matter of his full authority as Commanding General, the President himself replied with laconic emphasis: "The order to go to Missi. did not diminish your authority in Tennessee, both being in the country placed under your command in original assignment."

In his dealings with the hesitant, indecisive Johnston, Davis felt he had exercised extreme patience. He ever tried to base his attitude to his Generals on reflection and calm consideration of all the factors, military and political, in a situation.

But instead of the action the Administration expected from him, Johnston announced flatly on June 15 that he considered saving Vicksburg hopeless. The astounded Seddon came to consult with the President. To abandon the stronghold without a struggle on Johnston's part would be ruinous to civilian morale. Davis knew that the whole war effort was largely dependent on the spirit of the people. Together he and Seddon phrased a stiff reply, which was sent in the Secretary of War's name.

> Your telegram grieves and alarms us. Vicksburg must not be lost without a struggle. The interest and honor of the Confederacy forbid it. I rely on you to avert this loss. If better resources do not offer, you must hazard attack. It may be made in concert with the garrison, if practicable, but otherwise without. By day or night, as you think best.

In contrast to the worsening condition in Mississippi, the news of Lee's advance was cheering. Ewell captured Winchester on June 14. Next day, he began crossing the Potomac. General Robert Edward Rodes of Ewell's division occupied Martinsburg, as the Federal garrison fled before him into Maryland. Soon the President was reading an official report that Albert Jenkins, with his Confederate cavalry, had reached Chambersburg in Pennsylvania.

On Wednesday evening, June 17, Secretary of State Benjamin brought Colonel Arthur Lyon Fremantle to call on the President. Tea was served; "uncommonly good tea, too," the Englishman remarked— the first good tea he had tasted in the Confederacy. Mr. Davis, wearing a linen coat and gray trousers, looked older than his fifty-five years, Fremantle thought. He was extremely thin and his face was emaciated. But "his features are good, especially the eye which is very bright, and full of life and humour. He looked what he evidently is, a well-bred gentleman."

The day before, while Fremantle was in Wilmington, he had seen, he said, "the river quite full of blockade runners." He had counted "eight large steamers, all handsome leaden-colored vessels which ply their trade with the greatest regularity." He regarded this blockade-running "as an extraordinary instance of British energy and enterprise." In the course of talk, the President agreed with Benjamin that the United States had no intention of going to war with England if Her Majesty's Government recognized the Confederacy.

The Colonel spoke of the wretched scenes of depredation he had witnessed in Mississippi and declared his admiration for the "quiet, calm, uncomplaining manner in which the women bore their suffering and grief." Davis said with feeling that he "always considered *silent despair* the most painful of misery to witness, in the same way that he thought *mute insanity* the most awful form of madness."

The President was touched by an affecting story General Polk had told Fremantle at Bragg's headquarters on May 29. A poor widow in most humble circumstances had lost three sons in battle, one after another, and had only one left, a boy of sixteen. So distressing was her case that Polk himself went to see her. "She looked steadily at him, and replied to his condolences with one sentence: 'As soon as I can get a few things together, General, you shall have Harry, too.'" With tears in his eyes, the fighting Bishop had asked the Britisher: "How can you subdue such a nation as this?"

Fremantle had been moved by the spirit with which wounded men returned to the front, even though their wounds were not perfectly healed. In the same car with him in Alabama had been "several quite young boys of fifteen or sixteen who were badly wounded, and one or two who were minus arms and legs." He had been surprised to learn that a Southern soldier when wounded was not given his discharge, but was employed at small work he was competent to perform. The women took care to get the slightly wounded cured as quickly as possible and returned to their fighting outfits. The Colonel said he had observed in Polk's camp "a fine-looking man with both his hands blown off at the wrists." With a curry comb and brush fitted onto his stumps, he had acquired considerable skill in grooming artillery horses.

After an hour or so of talk and more tea, Colonel Fremantle left, most favorably impressed by the Confederate President. "Nothing can exceed the charm of his manner," he declared, "which is simple, easy, and most fascinating." In summing up his qualities, the Britisher wrote: "His services as a statesman pointed him out as the only man who, by his unflinching determination and administrative talent, was able to control the popular will."

On the walk home, Benjamin told Fremantle that to prepare a

treaty for peace it would only be necessary to write the word "self-government" on a blank piece of paper. "Let the Yankees accord that," he said, "and they might fill up the paper in any manner they choose. . . . Each State should decide fairly upon its own destiny. All we are struggling for is to be let alone."

As Fremantle prepared to leave Richmond on June 19, to catch up with General Lee, who was nearing the Potomac, he wrote in his diary, "I hear every one complaining dreadfully of General Johnston's inactivity in Mississippi, and all now despair of saving Vicksburg."

In the midst of the June tensions, another welcome visitor to the White House was Mary Elizabeth Stamps, with her two little girls. Mary was the wife of Captain Isaac Davis Stamps, son of the President's second sister, Lucinda, by her second marriage. She had come from Woodville, Mississippi, for a long-promised visit and in the fleeting hope of saying good-by to her husband before he left with the Army of Northern Virginia for Pennsylvania. Though no blood relative, Jefferson Davis admired his nephew's wife above all his other nieces.

Mary was a beautiful young woman of twenty-six. Setting off her delicate features, rich white complexion, and dark brown hair with copper lights, she had memorable sea-blue eyes, clear and fearless. Her carriage was superb; as a growing girl she had had a board strapped to her back and been made to walk up and down stairs balancing books on her head. A skilled horsewoman, she was also a bluestocking. Brought up in wealth, with a liking for agronomy, she was framed to be the mistress of a plantation. But she had married Jefferson Davis's amiable, handsome, impecunious nephew, who was reading law. To encourage her unaggressive husband, she had studied with him and had perhaps become more fascinated by legal science than he.

Jefferson Davis was proud of Mary's distinction and natural elegance, for he was a refined and somewhat fastidious man. Though her beauty was feminine, her appeal was more to the mind, to the imagination rather than to the senses. She had a mental directness that gave an edge to her woman's vision. She also possessed much of that unworldly spiritual endowment of the Davises, which was foreign to Varina's nature. The President found his nephew's wife harmonious and stimulating. She, in turn, regarded him not merely as a venerated older kinsman of the family she had married into, but as a man whose inflexible principle, pride, and courage lifted her heart to near hero worship. But neither of them dreamed that their mutual sympathies would flower into such an attraction of mind and spirit as emerged in the next decade.

Varina, too, greatly enjoyed Mary's company in the house, for she liked women of brains and character. And she was delighted to have the well-behaved little girls among her own less-restrained brood. Varina was extremely good for Mary, as she always was for persons worried or distressed. Mary had unhappy forebodings about her husband's going north to battle and longed to say good-by to him. Spurred on by the warmhearted Varina, the President hesitantly inquired if Captain Stamps could possibly be spared from his command for a three days' leave. Isaac came down to Richmond, had a blessed reunion with his wife and children, and was back with his men before they crossed the Potomac.

Varina insisted that Mary stay on at the White House until the Northern campaign was over. Not only was Mary's husband with the Army of Northern Virginia, but also her father, Brigadier General Benjamin Grubb Humphreys, later to become Governor of Mississippi, and her husband's half brother, Brigadier General Joseph R. Davis, who, until recently, had been a Presidential aide. Joe Davis had insisted on getting into actual fighting, just as Isaac had insisted on not getting promoted lest his uncle be further charged with nepotism. Mary remained, and was a joy to the household, and particularly to the President, who felt it would be a mighty relief to his own feelings if he himself were in the fight.

Being extremely anxious, and doubting Johnston's abilities in crises, the President, urged by others, considered taking command in Mississippi. As Commander in Chief of the Confederate Army and Navy, he had the clear "right" to do so. He did not hesitate because he was unwilling to pawn his own high prestige in such a daring move. What stopped him perhaps was the lack of the proper person to carry on his executive duties, as it had been in the spring of 1862, when Johnston was retreating to Richmond.

In a letter of June 4, 1878, to the Reverend Mr. Frank Stringfellow, the noted Confederate scout, Davis wrote: "It might have been better, as you suggest, if I had taken the field. It was contemplated when Johnston retreated from Yorktown, but the duties of the Executive Office were many and important, and to whom could they have been entrusted? The vagaries on Military matters of the Vice-President, and the lethargy and timidity of the President of the Senate [R. M. T. Hunter], rendered each unfit for the duty. At a late period of the war both were so despondent as to be willing to abandon the effort for independence, and then I could not conscientiously have entrusted them with the powers of negotiation." [2]

Grant's strength continually increased, while Johnston demurred and wrote letters. On June 21, Seddon, near despair, telegraphed Johnston "to follow the most desperate course the occasion may demand. Rely upon it," he exhorted the Commanding General, "the eyes and hopes of the whole Confederacy are upon you, with the full confidence that you will act, and with the sentiment that it were better to fail nobly daring, than through prudence even to be inactive. I rely on you for all possible to save Vicksburg."

The President, watching the mails anxiously for news from his brother, received a note from his friend Cox saying that the Yankees had burned all his corn which was to feed his Negroes. They had been dissuaded, however, from burning the Cox residence, and, so far, the special books, the boxes of Jefferson Davis's personal letters, and his parlor furniture were safe.[3]

In the meantime, Joseph Davis had called several times on General Johnston, who received him most civilly. Though Johnston made himself charming to the President's brother, Joseph could not get any real cheer from his interviews. From "General Johnston's Headquarters, Jackson, June 23, 1863," he wrote his brother in Richmond that he did not know where to take his family. Joseph had not accepted the President's invitation to come to Richmond, because he could not abandon his "people." He expressed himself in the brief, disjointed paragraphs of a confused and anxious old man.

I do not know where to go with the few negroes that remain at home.

I have had frequent confidential conversations with General Johnston.

Eliza is still feeble, but was up this morning. This is one of our troubles and difficulties of moving—

If V.B. can be held we shall raise corn sufficient for our wants of the few that remain—

[2] This revealing letter is among the interesting Frank Stringfellow papers in the University of Virginia Library.

[3] Cox's letter, dated June 14, is among the many relating to the tense days of the Vicksburg siege in the Jefferson Hayes-Davis collection. Another is the June 23 letter of Joseph Davis.

Stamps says the enemy robbed Sister Anna[4] of most of her property—
I feel your loss as more serious than mine.

It particularly grieved Jefferson Davis not to be able to give protection to the dearly loved relatives Joseph and Anna, both old enough
to be his parents. And there was the dread that worse might come:
Union soldiers could heap indignities upon the President's brother.
The Yankees, however, did not return to Fleetwood for three or four
weeks. "It was said they feared an ambush," Lise wrote, "as they
could not understand how an old man and a young girl would remain
alone unless they felt well protected."

Jefferson Davis suffered, too, for the noncombatants bottled up in
Vicksburg. Many were friends whom he had known since he settled at
Brierfield thirty years before. Some battle-shocked soldiers who had
deserted told frightful tales that reached Richmond. By night and day,
Federal gunboats on Vicksburg's western water front and Grant's
army to the east hurled bombs into the town. The explosions of shrapnel shells were often accompanied by the shrieks of terrified women
and children. On hearing the descent of a shell, dogs in the street
"would dart aside—then as it exploded, sit down and howl in the most
pitiful manner." Wailings over the slaughter of loved ones added to
the horror.

In the hills and in the high banks bordering roads, men dug out
caves for temporary homes. Some brave women risked their lives in
the iron hail to bind up the wounds of the fallen. A citizen named Edward S. Gregory saw ladies "walk quietly along the streets while shells
burst above them, their heads protected only by parasols held between
them and the sun." Gnawing hunger added to the general woe. Mule
meat became a luxury. Cats disappeared into stews. Caught rats were
dressed for broiling. In lieu of bread, people ate ground-up dried peas,
supplemented by shoots of young cane. On diminished army rations,
Pemberton's men grew weaker and weaker. To relieve hunger pains,
Pemberton impressed the city's entire store of chewing tobacco for
his men.

As Grant systematically dug, coming closer and closer to the Confederate works, mines and countermines exploded with lethal horror.
Pemberton became so shorthanded that "no man within the lines was

---

[4] Anna Smith, the eldest Davis sister, lived in St. Francisville, Louisiana, where the
President's first wife, Sarah Knox, was buried. William Stamps was the husband of
Jefferson Davis's second sister, Lucinda, and father of Captain Isaac Davis Stamps and
stepfather of Brigadier General Joseph R. Davis.

ever off duty more than a small part of each day." At the end of June, the troops were cut to quarter-rations. Officers reported their men so physically exhausted that none had the strength for any duty except to stand in the trenches and fire. On June 28, Pemberton received a moving "appeal for help," composed by some desperate men in the trenches. "Our rations," they wrote, "have been cut down to one biscuit and a small bit of bacon per day, not enough to stand the hardships we are called upon to stand. . . . If you can't feed us, you had better surrender us, horrible as the idea is, than suffer this noble army to disgrace themselves by desertion. . . . Men are not going to lie here and perish even if they love their country dearly. . . . Hunger will compel a man to do almost anything."

The harassed Pemberton sent urgent appeals to Johnston by men who risked their lives to reach him. Returning couriers from Johnston had to resort to singular ways of entering the city. One took a skiff on the Yazoo and proceeded to its confluence with the Mississippi, where he tied it up. At dark, he removed his clothes, placed his dispatches securely within them, bound the bundle firmly to a large plank, and then, holding on to the plank, floated through the enemy fleet to Vicksburg.

Though Johnston was fully informed of the pitiable state of the besieged, he still hesitated even to create a diversion to halt the punishment inflicted on the town. Yet the starving people in Vicksburg held on to the hope that Johnston would come to their rescue. They had not forgotten his promise to the Mississippi Legislature in December: "I shall be watchful, energetic, and indefatigable in your defense."

General Gorgas, in his diary on July 1, 1863 (his forty-fourth birthday), noted: "Everyone is looking anxiously to see what Johnston will do." No one was so anxious as the President, who knew that after weeks of proddings from the War Department, Johnston had at last begun to move. "Field transportation and other supplies having been obtained," Johnston later reported, "the army marched toward the Big Black, and on the evening of July 1st encamped between Brownsville and the river." But the second and the third of July were spent in reconnaissance. On the third, he sent a messenger to Pemberton saying that an attack on the enemy would be made "about the seventh," to create a diversion which might enable the Confederates to cut their way out. The messenger never arrived; Grant captured him.

CHAPTER XXXII

"AN UNWONTED EXPRESSION
OF SADNESS"

IN RICHMOND tensions tightened. Anxiously, President Davis
awaited dispatches from Lee and kept an eye on signs in the North.
Longstreet had followed Ewell up the east side of the Blue Ridge.
A. P. Hill had lingered at Fredericksburg to see what move Hooker
would make. Davis wondered if Hooker would attempt to cross the
Rappahannock and advance on Richmond. This was just what Fighting Joe wanted to do; but Lincoln opposed the idea, warning Hooker,
in a memorably graphic figure, "not to get caught like an ox jumped
half over the fence, unable to gore one way or kick the other."

After the march northward was advanced, Davis was surprised to
get a request from Lee that Beauregard and most of his force be
brought from Charleston to northern Virginia. By thus threatening
Washington, Lee felt pressure on his army would be relieved. Though
on June 7 Lee had vaguely suggested using Beauregard, he had not
mentioned such a plan as this. The President knew that Charleston was
being pressed dangerously from the sea. Still, wanting to do anything
Lee requested that was possible, Davis was reluctantly willing to send
Beauregard. But Beauregard himself turned down the idea.

So the President, in time, wrote Lee of the impossibility of using
Beauregard or any of his command, which had been reduced to
strengthen Johnston in Mississippi. He sent the dispatch by courier,
but the man was presumably captured by Federals at Chambersburg.

Davis, already apprehensive about the scope of Lee's gamble, was
made more anxious by Lee's letter saying, "I have not sufficient troops
to maintain my communications, and, therefore have to abandon
them." Lee now risked feeding his army on enemy country, and was

transporting just about enough artillery ammunition for one major battle. He hoped, if things went well, to "bring up more ammunition by cavalry escort." His plan was audacious in the extreme; but on he marched with exalted confidence.

In his mind's eye, aided by dispatches, Davis followed Lee's movements north to make the supreme effort for independence. On June 25, while bands played "Dixie" and summer rain fell gently, Lee rode Traveller across the shallow Potomac.

Hooker had followed Lee's progress in a somewhat parallel line to keep between the Confederate Army and Washington. On the twenty-seventh, Hooker completed his own crossing of the Potomac. Davis noted that Lee had already accomplished his first objective: to draw the Army of the Potomac from Virginia.

The next day, June 28, Hooker established headquarters at Frederick, Maryland, where the famous dispatch had been lost that caused Lee to fail at Antietam. Hooker now engaged in a hot telegraphic controversy with General in Chief Halleck, and in anger asked to be relieved. Lincoln was pleased to accommodate. To replace him, he chose the able, scholarly Major General George G. Meade. With resolution, the surprised Meade took command, and presently began pushing divisions toward the Pennsylvania border. He had to find Lee and fight him while yet protecting both Washington and Baltimore.

Davis learned that Dick Ewell, far in advance of the other Confederate divisions, had taken everything in his way. First, he had driven the hated Milroy from Winchester and captured rich supplies. He had occupied Sharpsburg, Maryland, full of sad memories of Antietam. Despite having had a leg amputated, which necessitated his being strapped to the saddle, he had pushed swiftly up to Chambersburg. By June 27 he was at Carlisle, Pennsylvania, only a few miles from Harrisburg, the state capital.

From Carlisle, Ewell dispatched General Jubal Early to seize York. Without opposition, Early accomplished his mission, put the town "under contribution," and collected 1,200 pairs of shoes, 1,000 hats, three days' generous rations, and $28,000 in money. In the meantime, Ewell destroyed the Northern Central Railroad that ran between Baltimore and Harrisburg. All Pennsylvania was aroused. Even Pittsburgh expected attack; its factories shut down; its laborers were mobilized.

The Councilmen of New York City, Republicans and Democrats alike, begged Lincoln for McClellan's recall. When Governor Andrew

G. Curtin made a patriotic speech in Philadelphia, his audience howled, "Give us McClellan!" The French Minister, Count Mercier, believing Washington to be vulnerable, had a French war vessel alerted to bear him away. When Ewell got within three miles of Harrisburg, and cannonading was heard in the city, it was thought that the Rebels would continue their march on to Philadelphia.

President Davis heard the rumor running through Richmond that Harrisburg had been destroyed. Pennsylvania-born Josiah Gorgas wrote confidently in his diary, "If not true now, I presume it soon will be." He noted that already a thousand fat beeves "derived" from above the Potomac had been sent into Virginia.

The United States correspondent of the London *Times*, who had formed the opinion that the Northern people were sick of war, wrote his paper that a Lee victory would be welcomed in New York. He envisioned General Lee and Jefferson Davis riding "in triumph up Broadway amid the acclamations of a more enthusiastic multitude than ever assembled on the Continent." [1]

Lee, on reaching Pennsylvania, had requested the various subsidiary commands back in Virginia to move northward and to occupy the vacated Confederate positions. D. H. Hill, commanding Petersburg and the James River, was mightily opposed to Lee's request; he feared a sudden attack by the enemy from Fort Monroe. General Whiting, in eastern North Carolina, was also strongly averse. The President agreed with Hill's and Whiting's well-reasoned views and would not compel them to accede to Lee's wishes. And soon Richmond was to be in serious danger.

With approbation, Davis read a copy of Lee's General Order No. 73, dated "June 27, 1863, Chambersburg, Pennsylvania." After complimenting the troops on their behavior during the past ten days, Lee reminded them that they had in their keeping "the yet unsullied reputation of the army." He said that the duties exacted of them by civilization and Christianity were no less obligatory in the enemy's country than in their own. In emphatic language, he warned: "The Commanding General considers that no greater disgrace could befall the army . . . than the performance of the barbarous outrages upon the innocent and defenseless, and the wanton destruction of private property that have marked the course of the enemy in our own country. Such proceedings not only disgrace the perpetrators . . . but are sub-

[1] Ironically, the wishful prognostication appeared in the *Times* on July 9, when Lee's men were huddled on the banks of the flooded Potomac, preparing to meet an attack from pursuing Federals.

versive of the discipline and efficiency of the army, and destructive to our present movement."

Both Davis and Lee had the hope that a civilized deportment of Southern troops in enemy territory might have a salutary effect on certain unconscionable Northern commanders, whom the Administration in Washington made no effort to curb.

Because it was believed that Lee's appearance in the Susquehanna Valley would be tremendously stimulating to the peace party in the North, Lee wrote Davis that he thought the South should encourage the idea that peace might bring a restoration of the Union. Though the President himself would say nothing on the restoration theme, the Richmond papers stopped hammering on the impossibility of reunion.

When, on June 28, Lee had had no word from Jeb Stuart, the General became uneasy. Stuart had been left in Virginia to guard the Blue Ridge passes and screen the movement of Longstreet until he was across the Potomac. Then he was to join Ewell at Carlisle, Pennsylvania. Lee did not know where the enemy was, and he feared to be completely cut off from the Potomac. However, he ordered Ewell to move upon Harrisburg and alerted Longstreet and Hill to follow the next day.

After Stuart had crossed the Potomac according to schedule and was resting near Rockville, he saw, in the distance on the road to Washington, a Union supply train of some 150 wagons. The temptation lured him to give chase. By the time the last wagon driver surrendered, Colonel William Blackford, Stuart's aide and future biographer, found himself on a hill in full view of the capital. Stuart, having lost valuable time, finally passed with his captured wagons east of the Federal Army and headed for Ewell's corps. All the while, eyes and ears in Lee's camp were strained for the approach of a courier from Stuart with news of the enemy's whereabouts.

On the night of the twenty-eighth, a Confederate scout named Harrison, in civilian dress, was brought to Lee's tent outside Chambersburg. He reported that all the Federals had crossed the Potomac and that General Meade was approaching Pennsylvania. The surprised Lee quickly determined on a new course of action. He called his various divisions to gather about Cashtown, a village on the turnpike between Chambersburg and Gettysburg. The seizure of Harrisburg was countermanded. Ewell was ordered back from Carlisle, where Jeb Stuart was trying to join him. Seriously embarrassed by the lack of Stuart's "eyes" to tell him of the enemy's position, Lee was more worried than anyone had ever seen him. Most of all, he feared some dread mishap to his fearless cavalryman.

While the Army of Northern Virginia was moving up through Pennsylvania, reports came to President Davis that some 30,000 Federal troops at Yorktown were starting to march on Richmond. He called Governor Letcher in conference. About three o'clock on Saturday afternoon, the twenty-seventh, Davis and Letcher issued a joint proclamation calling upon citizens to organize themselves into companies, battalions, and regiments. "No time is to be lost, the danger is great."

In a separate proclamation, Mayor Mayo of Richmond warned the people to "avoid the fate of New Orleans." He said the advancing enemy might assail the city before Monday morning. The President had Custis Lee order the various Department companies to parade, "armed and equipped." Some 3,500 convalescents in the hospitals at Camp Lee put themselves in readiness to fight in the city's defense.

In the midst of the excitement, the diarist Jones noted, on June 29, that Judge Campbell, Assistant Secretary of War, was urging the President to go to Mississippi, but that R. M. T. Hunter opposed the idea. "Mr. H. is willing to trust Johnston, has not lost confidence in him," Jones wrote. "And he tells the Secretary [Campbell] to inform the President how much he esteems him." It could hardly have occurred to Davis that the ambitious Hunter, who aspired to be the next President of the Confederacy, did not want him to acquire more honor by appearing on the Mississippi scene as a savior.

With Richmond threatened and two big battles imminent, Mrs. Davis found her husband "a prey to the acutest anxiety." At the same time, he felt those "mustering clans" stirring within him. Though the President's presence was essential in Richmond, he was torn between two desires: to be in Mississippi and to be with Lee in Pennsylvania. "If I could take one wing and Lee the other," Varina heard him say, "I think we could between us wrest a victory from those people."

As Lee's forces were converging at Cashtown, Major General Harry Heth, in the vanguard, ordered "a shopping tour" at the market town of Gettysburg, nine miles away. His footsore Confederates needed shoes. In the afternoon of June 30, when J. J. Pettigrew's brigade went to get the shoes, it found the town occupied by a Union advance force. By chance, with no definite idea of each other's intentions or whereabouts, the opposing armies had made contact.

Returning swiftly after an unavoidable small clash, Pettigrew reported to Lee. Still missing Stuart's intelligence, Lee moved forward early the next morning. He felt it prudent to meet the enemy on the eastern side of the Alleghenies. On July 1, 1863, there began, unplanned, the greatest battle ever fought in the Western Hemisphere.

Jubal Early's veterans from Ewell's army swept the Federals from Gettysburg and took 4,000 bewildered prisoners, who reported that the entire Union Army was moving toward the town. General Meade had not reached the scene when his second in command, John F. Reynolds, received a mortal bullet in his brain. The routed Federals sought refuge on the heights to the east and south, known as Cemetery Ridge because of the community burying ground there. It was to prove a remarkably fortunate and strong position.

Lee decided Ewell must undertake pursuit. He sent Ewell discretionary orders. He suggested that, "if practicable," he "push those people off the hill, without committing the whole army to battle."

Lee's discretionary orders threw Ewell off balance. He had been accustomed to Stonewall Jackson's explicit instructions. Though Jubal Early was eager to go on, Ewell hesitated, saying he did not know "what he would find up there."

The first battle had ended in a near rout of the Union forces. Major General Winfield Scott Hancock was the savior of the Federals at Gettysburg that day. With clearheaded, vigorous organizational ability, he gave "cool, concise, positive directions," which halted the panic. He proceeded to fortify the position Lee had intended that Ewell should take.

About five o'clock in the afternoon of July 1, Longstreet joined Lee. Together they surveyed the terrain before them from a long rise west of the town called Seminary Ridge because of the Lutheran college on its top. A mile and a half across the valley rose Cemetery Ridge, stretching three miles long and rising at its southern end to a height of almost nine hundred feet. This hill was known as Big Round Top. An intervening smaller hill was called Little Round Top. At the foot of Little Round Top lay a wilderness of boulders, tangled underbrush, and stunted trees known as Devil's Den. The road from Emmitsburg, Maryland, ran on a bias between the two ridges. In one place a peach orchard flourished east of the road, while wheat fields lay on either side.

Before Lee had spoken, Longstreet, according to his later statements, had formed his own plan. "We should throw the army around to their left," he said, "and interpose between the enemy and Washington." He wanted to force the Federals to do the attacking. But Lee felt that to lead his army around the Union left into the unknown would be unwise. The best chance of victory in his opinion was to attack the two corps immediately in front. "If the enemy is there tomorrow," he told Longstreet, "we must attack."

Longstreet proceeded to argue with his chief. But Lee urged him to bring up his men as soon as possible. Complaining that one of his divisions was six miles away, Longstreet grew indefinite, and then sulky. He hoped Lee might change his mind about a frontal attack.

Meanwhile, Ewell, who held the town of Gettysburg, could not make up his mind to advance further, though exuberant younger officers were eager to get at the bluecoats before they entrenched themselves on the heights. Reportedly, one older officer in disgust threw down his sword and swore he would never again serve under such a general. But Lee had not said positively: "Occupy Cemetery Ridge."

Afternoon became evening, and then night came on. The Confederates' splendid opportunity passed. According to Union officers, no one could have "stopped a Southern onslaught on the night of July 1." One of Ewell's artillerymen later said sadly, "The tide which might have led on to overwhelming victory had ebbed forever."

That night, Lee went to Ewell's headquarters to discuss operations for the next day. Jubal Early, who had been so eager to attack in the afternoon, was now dubious about the morrow—"the approaches are difficult." Lee gave some orders, but left dissatisfied. He decided that if he attacked from the right, Longstreet would have to make the chief offensive. But Old Pete, as he was nicknamed, though a good fighting man, was so *slow*.

In the meantime, the bulk of the Federal Army with General Meade had arrived, and, after a midnight reconnaissance, began throwing up fortifications and placing batteries strategically.

The next morning, the Federals braced themselves to meet an offensive. Lee was up early. Longstreet took his own sweet time. Stonewall Jackson, some said, would have occupied the Big and Little Round Tops before Longstreet crawled from his cot. When Hood arrived with a message from Lee urging Longstreet to speed up, Old Pete complained that he did not want to do so until Pickett came up from Chambersburg. Though Ewell gained some small advantage on Culp's Hill to the northeast, there was no concerted action at all. Longstreet was not ready to begin his attack until the afternoon was well advanced. By that time the Union's Sixth Corps, the last of Meade's

95,000 men—not including the first day's dead and wounded—were on the spot. Longstreet's "terrible obstinacy" had caused Lee great embarrassment.

Returning scouts reported that the Round Tops were not occupied and that the level ground behind them was filled only with unguarded hospital trains. General Hood sent word to Longstreet that Meade's left flank and rear were open, and suggested the direction of attack be changed, and that the Round Tops be occupied along with the ground in the rear. But Longstreet would not use his discretionary powers, and ordered the battle to be made along the Emmitsburg Road, as Lee had planned.

At last, at two o'clock, Lee confidently expected the fight to begin. Colonel Fremantle, who had been with Lee's forces for several days, climbed an oak tree for observation. He had as companion the bearded young Prussian Captain Justus Scheibert.[2] Scheibert had been sitting there since five o'clock in the morning. The Englishman and the German were joined on their perches by Francis Lawley,[3] correspondent of the London *Times*, who amused the professional soldiers by asking unmilitary questions.

For two and a half hours, they waited for action. "Until four-thirty p.m.," Fremantle wrote, "all was profoundly still." He began to doubt if a battle were coming off that day at all. Then Longstreet's cannon opened up. His men struck at the Federals' right, while Ewell again attacked their left. A. P. Hill was held in the center in readiness to prevent the enemy's rushing reinforcements to either sector that might give way. Now that he had been forced into the battle he deplored, Longstreet fought with his best energy. As long tongues of flame spurted from the rival batteries, he hurled his divisions against the exposed Union position at the base of the Round Tops. Union General Daniel Sickles had brought his Third Corps down into the open wheat field and peach orchard, whereupon the Confederates began to tear the Third Corps to pieces with flashing sheets of musket fire amid roars of what the Yankees called "Rebel wolf cries." The Union troops broke, abandoning guns and caissons. Violent combat with bayonets took place in Devil's Den. The slaughter on both sides was frightful.

[2] Only in 1958 was Scheibert's valuable *Seven Months in the Rebel States During the American War, 1863* translated, by Joseph C. Hayes and edited with an introduction by William Stanley Hoole. The Prussian officer's observations are among the most interesting by foreign commentators.

[3] Lawley's descriptions of the Gettysburg battle appeared in the London *Times* in August, 1863.

Toward sunset, while the fighting was still at its height, Federals and Confederates both seemed struck simultaneously with the importance of the Round Tops, and each tried to occupy them before the other did. The Union forces got to Little Round Top a few minutes before the Southerners. Taking cover behind boulders and piled rock, they poured a deadly fire on the Confederates. The gallant Twentieth Maine, commanded by Colonel Joshua L. Chamberlain, won the position for the Union, then lost it. Five times the Federals rallied, once almost pressing against Confederate bayonets. Finally, the Southerners found their stand untenable and retreated.

In writing of how near he came to winning this all-important position, Little Round Top, Confederate Colonel William Oates said: "If I had had one more regiment, we would have completely turned the flank and won Little Round Top, which would have forced Meade's whole left wing to retire. . . . Had General Longstreet seen the necessity of protecting my flank, I would, with the 600 veterans I had, easily have captured that place." At the end, though the Southerners possessed the open field, Little Round Top was secure in Federal hands.

If Longstreet had not been hours late in starting, the Confederates might well have taken the hill. His obstinacy and slowness had perhaps cost Lee the victory. But in his official report, Lee, with extraordinary restraint, merely stated: "Longstreet's dispositions were not completed as early as were expected."

The meeting of the officers in Meade's camp that bloody night of July 2 was "one of gloom." By Meade's report, the Union casualties in the two afternoons of fighting were already 20,000.

The second day's battle was comparable to Chancellorsville and Second Manassas. Meade considered retiring to Pipe Creek, across the Maryland line, where he had hoped the engagement would take place. But the officers voted to stay where they were and fight it out, instead of retreating before Lee, as Pope, Burnside, and Hooker had done. According to the New York *Times,* dispatches from Davis to Lee, dated June 28, were intercepted at Hagerstown on July 2.[4] They were presumed to be "of greatest importance" and would have great bearing on "coming events." One of these dispatches was supposed to inform Lee that Beauregard could not come to northern Virginia to make a threat against Washington. The information that Washington

---

[4] Near Hagerstown, during his retreat, Lee read the New York *Times* report of the intercepted dispatch, and, in a postscript to a letter to Davis of July 8, "thought proper to mention this, that you may know if it is so."

was safe supposedly influenced Meade's decision not to withdraw.

Meade further strengthened his lines with earthworks the night of July 2 and vigilantly awaited Lee's move. The Federal Commander, in his strong position, had no notion of taking the offensive.

Lee, however, determined to attack once more, though Longstreet, who had fought furiously, was still sullen. After the battle, he had not gone to see Lee, but had merely sent a verbal report. He deemed the afternoon conflict "the best three hours' fighting by any troops on any battlefield."

After hard riding from Carlisle, Stuart and his tired men arrived at last, ready for any assignment of duty.

Jefferson Davis knew nothing of what was going on in Pennsylvania. He had not been able to hear from Lee for three days. While no news might be good, there was something ominous about the silence. His anxiety increased. His physician, Dr. Garnett, was "seriously alarmed" about his health. Gorgas observed in his diary, "The death of the President would indeed be the most serious calamity that could befall us."

The President, however, was actively concerned about the defense of Richmond. He sent word to Gorgas to inspect the works personally. The town's militia was occupying the roads, while the few regular troops held the field. The clerks and Government employees, numbering some 2,000 were ordered out under arms to the outer lines of the earthworks, in support of D. H. Hill's command, which had come up from Petersburg. Reports reached Davis that 25,000 men under General Dix were advancing from Rooney Lee's plantation on the York. It was hard for Dr. Garnett to keep his patient in his room.

This same July 2, Davis sent Alexander Stephens on a mission to Washington. After an absence of almost a year in Georgia, except for a brief visit in April, the Vice-President had come to Richmond at the President's summons. Stephens had suggested a meeting with Union authorities on the exchange of prisoners. He had offered to be the negotiator and had asked to be empowered to discuss "*any* point in relation to the conduct of the war." Davis, who had good reason to distrust Stephens because of his open criticism and his attempts to curtail the Administration's power, had no intention of allowing him authority beyond that concerning the treatment of prisoners.

He gave Stephens a letter for President Lincoln that covered the subject of disputes arising over the cartel already in force. Adding a devout plea for the exercise of humanity in warfare, he reminded the Union President that he himself had refused to seek redress by retaliation for the cruel abuses of some Union commanders. Retaliation, he said, might "obviously tend to lead to a war of indiscriminate massacre on both sides." It would be "a spectacle so shocking to humanity and so disgraceful to the age in which we live and the religion we profess that I cannot contemplate it without a feeling of horror that I am disinclined to doubt you would share."

Davis's special letter of instruction to Stephens was specific: "Your mission is one of humanity, and has no political aspects."

When Stephens learned that the last of Lee's army was actually in Pennsylvania, he balked at going. But the President and Cabinet insisted that he proceed because of the likelihood of Vicksburg's fall. Besides, Davis knew that the facts might be twisted so that it would appear he had refused to allow the Vice-President to go. Stephens made his plans to sail down the James on the morrow with Robert Ould, Confederate agent for the exchange of prisoners.

Mrs. Davis and Mary Stamps, along with Burton Harrison and Dr. Garnett, marveled at the official business the President would attend to while ill. Finally, the President closed his weighted eyes in a sleep of nervous exhaustion, not dreaming that the next day, July 3, 1863, would be chronicled by some facile historians as the date on which his nation's fate was sealed.

On the morning of July 3, at eight o'clock, Virginia's thirty-eight-year-old Major General George Pickett rode with the shining Lee and the somber Longstreet along the line of Pickett's prostrate infantry. The men "had been told to lie down to prevent attracting attention"; so the widowed Pickett wrote his young sweetheart that morning. "And though they had been forbidden to cheer they arose and lifted in reverential adoration their caps to our beloved commander. . . . Well, my darling, their fate and that of our beloved Southland will be settled ere your glorious brown eyes rest on these scraps of penciled paper—your soldier's last, perhaps."

All the morning, Longstreet delayed, hoping that Lee would change his mind. Four agonizing hours later, Pickett scrawled on another bit of paper: "Our detachments have been thrown forward to support our artillery which stretches over a mile along the crests of Seminary Ridge. The men are lying in the rear, my darling, and the hot July sun pours its scorching rays almost vertically down upon them. The suffering and waiting are almost unbearable. . . ."

Then the artillery, under Porter Alexander, let loose, and Pickett penciled a few more lines: "Well, my sweetheart, at one o'clock the awful silence was broken by a cannon-shot, and then another and then more than a hundred guns shook the hills from crest to base, answered by more than another hundred—the whole world a blazing volcano—the whole of heaven a thunderbolt—thus darkness and absolute silence—then the grim and gruesome low spoken command—then the forming of the attacking columns. My brave Virginians are to attack in the front. Oh, God in mercy help me as He never helped me before!"

Alexander sent a message to Pickett: "If you are coming at all you must come at once, or I cannot give you proper support; but the enemy's guns are still firing from the cemetery itself."

Pickett rode up to report to Longstreet. Before handing him the letter to send to his beloved Sallie, he added a few more words: "And a package to give you if—Oh, my darling, do you feel the love of my heart, the prayer, as I write that fatal word 'if'."

Longstreet knew the order for Pickett's charge, but the hardened old war horse could not bring himself to give it. "Alexander has my instructions," he said. "He will give you the order."

As the Federal fire slackened, Alexander saw through glasses that three enemy batteries had pulled back; dead horses, mangled men, and the debris of fractured gun carriages lay strewn about. He sent Pickett another hastily written note. "For God's sake, come quick . . . or my ammunition won't let me support you."

When the courier dashed up, Pickett read the note and handed it to Longstreet. "Shall I obey it and go forward?" Longstreet gave him a long look, then slowly grasped his hand. Clasping his other hand over Pickett's, without speaking, he "bowed his head upon his breast." Pickett saw tears glistening on Old Pete's cheeks and beard.

He took his letter back and dashed off an ending:

Now I go . . . now and forever I am yours—all yours, my beloved. It is almost three o'clock. I'll keep up a brave heart for Virginia and for you, my darling.

> Your
> Soldier.

Gettysburg, July 3, 1863

Longstreet pocketed the letter, and then rode fast to Alexander. He found that the ammunition was really running out. "Stop Pickett," he

ordered, "and replenish your ammunition." "There is no more ammunition with which to replenish," Alexander said. "And, besides, if
we wait for that we will lose all the effect of our previous fire."

At that moment, Longstreet saw Pickett at the head of 5,000 Virginians and 10,000 from other commands riding gracefully over the
crest of Seminary Ridge to begin his descent down the slope. "With
his jaunty cap raked well over his right ear, and his long auburn locks,
nicely dressed, hanging almost to his shoulders," wrote Old Pete, "he
seemed a holiday soldier."

The men, as well as their General, knew the odds against
them. Though Private John Dooley admitted that "the enthusiasm of
ardent breasts in many cases *ain't there,*" the majority stepped forward as if quite prepared to lay down their lives on the altar of patriotism.

Up on Cemetery Ridge, the waiting Union forces stared in wonder.
They had seen an army forming in line of battle under their very eyes,
and now with symmetrical precision this army was marching proudly,
following tipped banners, like warriors in some age of chivalry. As the
Southerners crossed the mile of open ground, through fields of trem-
bling wheat, over stretches of bronzed stubble and green meadow, they
looked as though they were maneuvering on dress parade.

The Union batteries let loose a withering fire with short-range ammunition. Down went a thousand men in gray. With deadly aim, the
Union guns began decimating the Southern ranks. "Directly in front
of us," wrote Private Dooley, "breathing flame in our very faces, the
long range of guns which must be taken, thunder on our quivering,
melting ranks. . . ." But the Confederates pushed on until they were
within musket range. "Volley after volley of crushing musket balls
sweeps through the line and mows us down like wheat before the
scythe." Wide-mouthed Napoleons spewed canister upon the men
struggling up the breast of the hill. The carnage was frightful. Blasted
men leapt in the air and then dropped dead. Some toppled over like
quail shot on the ground. The Confederates would kneel and pause for
a volley, then rush on up the slope. A sublime heroism pervaded the
scene; even the naturally timid felt the contagion of courage. One
young man in gray jumped up, and yelled to his faltering comrades,
"Come on! You want to live forever?"

For some minutes, the Union soldiers were wonder-struck. As Federal Lieutenant Frank Haskell reported vividly: "An ocean of armed
men sweeping upon us! More than half a mile their front extends; more

than a thousand yards the dull gray masses deploy . . . barrel and bayonet gleam in the sun, a sloping forest of flashing steel. Right on they move . . . through orchard and meadow and cornfield, magnificent, grim, invincible. . . . Then the thunders of our guns as the range grows shorter and shorter . . . without wavering or halt, and hardy lines of the enemy continue to move on. The Rebel guns make no reply to ours, and no charging shout rings out . . . but the courage of these silent men amid our shots seems not to need the stimulus of other noise."

The Confederate artillery, which had fired steadily since one o'clock, had ceased firing just as Pickett's men charged up the hill. The big guns remained mute during the slaughter. Where were the 8,000 other men Pickett was expecting? Two of his brigadiers were already down. But Brigadier General Lewis Armistead was still alive and leading an assault near the fortified hilltop. Beside him, boys held high their battle flags.

"Along each hostile front," wrote Haskell, "the volleys blaze and roll; as thick the sound as when a summer hail storm pelts the city roofs." Then in dismay he noted, "The larger part of Webb's brigade —my God, it was true—there by the group of trees and angles of the wall, was breaking from the cover of their works, and, without orders or reason, with no hand lifted to check them, was falling back, a fear-stricken flock of confusion! The fate of Gettysburg hung upon a spider's single thread." Young Haskell, with drawn sword, rushed to halt "the tide of these rabbits" and drive them back to the fray, while "the damned red flags of rebellion began to flaunt and thicken along the wall they had just deserted."

Huzzahs suddenly rent the air. For a moment, the Southerners, both those upright and those groveling in agony, thought Pickett's supports had arrived. But the cheers were from the enemy; fresh Union troops had come up.

Armistead, in the Confederate lead, sprang up on a stone wall, lifted high his sword with hat run through the tip, and cried, "Give them the cold steel, boys!" A few score men with him pierced the Federals' position on the crest. Forty yards within the wall, Armistead laid his left hand on a smoking Union gun by way of claiming capture. Then a bullet felled him. He died in a moment of triumph, for at least a hundred gray uniforms were swarming about him and Stars and Bars were flying beside enemy cannon.

But the Union men rallied and converged from all sides. The Confederates jabbed with bayonets and shot with pistols. One color sergeant used the butt of his staff as a lance. Finally, a soldier whose musket was struck from his grasp lifted his hands in surrender. When no support came, Pickett, in anguish, saw his brave soldiers begin to stumble back down the slope.

As the wavering men were being mowed down, "a young beardless Confederate color-bearer," in advance of the line, looked to the right and the left, and, seeing his comrades reeling and dropping, deliberately raised the colors high in the air and jabbed the staff into the ground. Within 150 feet of the Union line, he stepped back, "straightened himself like an adjutant on parade," folded his arms, as if to say, "I might as well die here." Colonel P. P. Brown of the 157th New York, watching in amazed admiration, yelled above the din: "Don't fire on that boy! Don't kill that boy!" The hero's look of mingled despair and exalted resignation gave place to a radiant smile. He put his hand to his cap to salute the Yankee chivalry. The Union soldiers cheered. The youth took up his colors, wheeled, then slowly followed his fellows. Lieutenant James Page of Michigan wrote, "Not a solitary one of Pickett's heroes was behind him except the dead and the dying."[5]

Down the hill, across the flats, the bleeding remnants staggered, while vengeful musket balls whizzed about them. Moving faster, the men in gray stepped carefully among the still-warm dead. One soldier stopped to drag off a fellow whose feet had been shot away. Another, lamed, used two rifles for crutches and hobbled on his own power.

As the men passed the heartbroken Pickett, who had been directing the advance from below, they saw he was almost frantic with grief. General Lee rode out to meet them, saying soothingly over and over, "It is all my fault." When Colonel Fremantle, who had watched the whole conflict from his tree, climbed down, he observed Lee closely. "His face did not show signs of the slightest disappointment, care or annoyance, and he was addressing to every soldier he met a few words of encouragement, such as 'All this will come right in the end: we'll talk it over afterwards, but in the meantime all good men must rally.' "

With superhuman self-composure, Lee, in the emergency of expected counterattack, exhorted the slightly wounded "to bind up their hurts and take up a musket." Fremantle saw desperately wounded men take off their hats and cheer the commander. He remarked Lee's skill in

[5] The incident is taken from James Madison Page's *The True Story of Andersonville, A Defense of Major Henry Wirz,* almost in the eyewitness's exact language.

handling a distraught and tearful officer who came to report the shattered state of his brigade. Lee grasped the man's hand, saying, "Never mind, General, *all this has been my fault*. It is *I* who have lost this fight, and *you* must help me out of it in the best way you can."

But it was not all Lee's fault by any means, as everyone knew. From the beginning, delaying officers had not carried out his plans. Lee's orders, according to his aide, Walter Taylor, required that 23,000 men, instead of 15,000, should have made the assault with Pickett.

When Lee rode up to the sorrowing Pickett, he told him to place his division where he could be ready to repel the advance of the enemy should they follow up their advantage. "I have no division now," Pickett said in abject despair. "Armistead is down. Garnett is down, and Kemper is mortally wounded." "Upon my shoulders rests the blame," Lee reiterated. "The men and officers of your command have written the name of Virginia as high today as it has ever been written before."

That night, Pickett wrote his sweetheart how faithfully his men had kept their word to follow him "on—on—on to their death, and I, believing in the promised support, led them—on—on—Oh, God!" Inconsolable over his slaughtered men, he ended his last letter from Gettysburg: "Your Soldier lives and mourns and, but for you, my darling, he would rather a million times rather be back there with his dead, to sleep for all time in an unknown grave."

Night fell, and the counterattack did not come. A pale moon rose on the blood-soaked field and gently laved the patriotic dead in a bath of silver light. By the flickering flames of lanterns, the Confederates gathered up their helpless wounded.

General Lee rode Traveller over to Powell Hill's headquarters to discuss plans for the Third Corps to lead the retreat next day if the Federals did not attack. There seemed no other course open to him; the artillery was almost out of ammunition. His wounded must be saved before the Federals possessed the mountain gaps.

Near one o'clock in the morning of the Fourth of July, Lee rode slowly back to his tent. He had never felt such fatigue or known such a load of lead in his heart. An officer who saw the moon's illumination upon his handsome face was shocked at the unwonted expression of sadness.

CHAPTER XXXIII

VICKSBURG FALLS AND
LEE RETREATS

AS WILD, conflicting rumors about a fight in Pennsylvania reached Richmond, Varina heard her husband exclaim, "With Jackson, Lee would be on his feet!" But still no word came from the General.

With Vicksburg communications cut, the President was as much in the dark about the besieged Pemberton as about Lee. Though he did not suspect that the Union advance forces at Vicksburg were within a minute of the Confederate defenses, he feared that Pemberton's army was on the verge of collapse from starvation. He believed that Johnston, after delaying for forty-odd days, was at last moving forward to help him. Would he get there in time to be of use?

On July 2, Pemberton, not having received any word from Johnston, and despairing of relief, realized that he had to make some drastic decision. Yet the Vicksburg *Daily Citizen* of that date, printed on small squares of wallpaper, tried to laugh at the desperate situation. With flippant defiance it wrote:

On Dit.—That the great Ulysses—the Yankee Generalissimo, surnamed Grant—has expressed his intention of dining in Vicksburg on Sunday next, and celebrating the 4th of July by a grand dinner and so forth. . . . Ulysses must get into the city before he dines in it. The way to cook a rabbit is "first to catch the rabbit." . . .

At eight o'clock on the morning of the third, a flag of truce was being passed out of the Confederate lines in Vicksburg. All firing ceased, pending negotiations on capitulation. The strangest silence fell upon the town. When the rival commanders conferred under a stunted oak, Pemberton quickly squelched Grant's old "unconditional surrender" theme, so publicized after Fort Donelson. In the end, Grant offered to

permit the Confederate troops to stack their arms and go
to their homes under parole. He did not want the trouble and expense
of shipping some 31,000 men to distant Northern prison camps, and
he hoped most of them would be too disheartened to join up again
after they were officially exchanged. The officers were to be exchanged
at once and each allowed to keep his horse, his arms, and all personal
property.

The terms were generous. After his seven months of hard struggle
to take Vicksburg, Grant, recalling his near disgrace at Shiloh, was
glad to have the coveted stronghold capitulate on almost any conditions.[1] Besides, having intercepted Johnston's last dispatch, he knew
that Johnston's forces were on his rear and could cause him serious
trouble, while Bragg might yet abandon Tennessee and move his whole
force against him. The situation was risky. Grant had conducted a brilliant campaign, and he wanted to clinch a victory.

On his return to headquarters, Pemberton called a council of war.
His General officers considered. Though Vicksburg and the river and
the guns and muskets would be lost, 31,000 starving men would be
allowed to return to their homes. Pemberton put the alternatives: surrender and save whole skins or sell lives dearly in a rather hopeless effort to cut their way through the Federal lines. All but South Carolina's
Stephen D. Lee and one other voted for surrender. Lee's opinion, as
recorded in *Official Records,* read: "I do not think it is time to surrender this garrison and this post yet. Nor do I think it practicable to
cut our way out. . . . I still have hope of Johnston relieving the garrison."

Since there was no evidence of any forthcoming aid from Johnston,
Pemberton finally agreed to follow the almost unanimous decision. He
said that he himself would prefer to die at the head of his army, his
only hope of saving himself from shame and disgrace.

That evening of July 3, Roger Pryor, who was in Richmond serving
on a court-martial, called at the Executive Mansion. Mrs. Davis was
glad to see him, but regretted that the President was not receiving.
Despite the oppressive sultriness, at Mrs. Davis's urging, the young
Brigadier stayed on chatting. After some time, to their surprise, the
President himself came in, "weary, silent, and depressed." Davis could
hardly ever bear to stay in bed. He would generally remain in his room

---

[1] Halleck, however, was to reprove Grant sharply for loosing 31,000 men back into
the man-short Confederacy.

on doctor's orders, but often he would sit up with his clothes on. Rest-less tonight and imbued with intimations of disaster, he had come down to greet Pryor. He knew that the ambitious politician, who had no great talent for soldiering, had pulled every possible wire to get a high command in the field. But Davis could not risk the lives of sol-diers to prevent making a personal enemy. Though the *Examiner* openly named Pryor in the ranks of the President's enemies, Davis wanted him to know he bore him not the slightest ill will. He was, how-ever, too worried to pretend to be optimistic.

"Presently," wrote Mrs. Pryor in her *Recollections,* "dear little Joe entered in his night robe, and kneeling beside his father's knee repeated his usual evening prayer and asked for God's blessing on the country. The President laid his hand on the boy's head and fervently responded, 'Amen.'" It was a nightly custom in the household. Joe was never abashed to say his prayers before company, nor was the President in the least self-conscious at the act of childish faith. The na-tion for which the boy asked Heaven's blessing was this night in its ultimate need.

Shortly, Pryor took his leave. Davis knew he would be unable to sleep, and he did not want to lie down. Encompassed by national cares, he was also a prey to personal anxieties. For days, he had been unable to hear from his brother Joseph, whose temporary home lay in the path of the contending armies. Mary Stamps could not sleep either. Though she bravely tried to conceal her dread, her uncle was acutely aware of it. He saw her sea-blue eyes clouded with anxiety and her proud head held strangely in a rapt, listening attitude. Finally, she confided to him that her husband was trying to get some message to her. Of course, she did not know of the battle that had ended disastrously at Gettysburg; but all day she had thought Isaac was try-ing to tell her something. Since Mary was a woman of such common sense and intelligence, Davis could not help wondering at her extra-sensory perception. He remembered that Isaac had had a premonition when he bade his wife and children good-by that he would never see them again. Mary now told him that Isaac had got her to promise that if he were killed, she would see that he was eventually buried in the plantation cemetery at Woodville. The President tried to soothe away her apprehensions and urged her to get some rest. Then he himself went to bed, but his mind turned again and again to Mississippi and his old brother.

In the middle of that night between July 3 and 4, Lise Mitchell was roused by voices in the yard of her grandfather's house near Bolton, Mississippi. Taking her revolver, the girl called through the front door to ask who was there. A man replied that he was a courier from General Johnston with a message for Mr. Joseph Davis. Fearing it might be a trick of the enemy, she aroused the old gentleman, who was handed a letter from Johnston warning him to leave at once, because Vicksburg would be surrendered the next day. Joseph Davis was taken by surprise; he had thought that with Johnston's help the garrison would surely hold, and he had made no preparations for sudden flight. But since the attempt to burn his house, "his people" had been busy "rounding up such oxen as had escaped capture, and mending old wagons considered worthless by the enemy." Now the Negroes were alerted for the exodus in the morning.

"Early next morning," Lise wrote later, "our sad and dispirited army had begun to pass." The yard was soon filled with Johnston's soldiers, who stopped for water. They had not got within sight of Grant's army. At length General Johnston himself arrived and had a private consultation with her grandfather. His staff and many other officers waited for Lise to give them breakfast, the last meal ever served at Fleetwood. "In the rear of that worn and broken army," Lise wrote, "in the clouds of dust and the heat of a July sun, my grandfather and I in a carriage, followed by the roughly mended old wagons full of negroes with their clothes and bedding and with the few necessities we were able to gather for ourselves, began what proved to be a long and weary journey."

On July 4, instead of the Stars and Bars, white flags flew from the Confederate forts at Vicksburg. The astounded townspeople, who had endured so much, turned pale in an agony of grief when the Yankees entered the town, "their banners flying and their hateful tunes sounding." The citizens had confidently expected Joe Johnston to come to their rescue. "Oh, how desperately we had awaited him!" one bewailed. Now Southern soldiers unabashedly let the tears stream down their faces. Some privates greeted the promulgation of the surrender order with "fearful outbursts of rage and indignation," venting their sorrow in loud curses. Sergeant Osborn H. Oldroyd saw wrathful men of the Third Louisiana Infantry break their rifles against trees and scatter their last ammunition on the ground. Regimental flags were torn into fragments and sentimentally distributed among the men "as a sacred memento that they were no party to the surrender." A few die-hards wrapped their battle flags about their bodies in defiance of surrendering them. In impotent fury, several hundred soldiers swore they would not sign their paroles.

Grant did take his Fourth of July dinner in Vicksburg after all, and the next day he issued to the famished Confederates five days' rations of bacon, hominy, peas, coffee, sugar, salt, and crackers. Over the food, the Southerners relaxed somewhat and began to swap yarns of the siege with Northern boys. One bluecoat, seeing S. H. Lockett, Chief Engineer of the Defenses, on the white pony which he had ridden every day along the lines, called out jovially, "See here, Mister—you on the little white horse! Danged if you ain't the hardest feller to hit I ever saw; I've shot at you more'n a hundred times."

Almost as soon as he had finished his first meal in Vicksburg, Grant sent Sherman to lead the advance against Joseph Johnston. As they moved east, the Federals were amazed to see four-foot corn flourishing in plowed rows where the bloody Battle of Champion's Hill had been fought in May. On either side of the roads, the advance Federals fired the dwellings, the outhouses, the cotton gins, and often the fences. Marching to banners of flame and spirals of smoke, they expressed little sympathy for the burned-out civilians. One Ohio Colonel, was said (in the *History of the 53rd Regiment Ohio Volunteers Infantry*) to take peculiar satisfaction in seeing "chimneys standing there without any house."

On the morning of July 4, President Davis impatiently asked about messages from Mississippi and Pennsylvania, but nothing from either state had come to the War Office. There was, however, one item of good news. After four nights of sleeping on the ground, the volunteer defenders of Richmond were allowed to return to their homes. General D. H. Hill reported that the enemy had retreated down the Peninsula.

While Vicksburg was being surrendered at the other end of the Confederacy, Lee in Pennsylvania was bracing himself for retreat. At Gettysburg, the national holiday had broken sunny and tranquil. In Lee's camp came the anguish of roll calls, with grim, pregnant silences punctuating the "Here's" of the vocal. Nothing along Cemetery Ridge, however, suggested that Meade was preparing a hostile move. In the romantic conception of Thomas Nelson Page, "the two armies lay facing each other like spent lions nursing their wounds."

All through the morning, Lee awaited attack and rather longed for it. At noon, he gave orders to start moving south. As the first ambulances were being loaded, a violent summer squall burst menacingly. While the torrents washed the red grass green again, Lee wrote a cautious dispatch to President Davis. Because the wires had been cut between Chambersburg, Pennsylvania, and Martinsburg, Virginia, the message had to be sent by courier on horseback to the telegraph station at Martinsburg.

It was laborious work to pack some 12,000 wounded men into the few ambulances and the long lines of old springless wagons. Around four o'clock, in deluging rain, the advance cavalcade got under way. Lying on the rough boards, in their blood-stiffened uniforms, which rasped the inflamed wounds, the men endured a purgatory worse than any battlefield. The miserable procession gradually stretched for seventeen miles. Orders ran to keep straight on to the Potomac, despite the pounding rain; if any wagon had a mishap, it was to pull to the side and not halt the exodus. The sleepless Lee was anticipating pursuit and a terrible fight.

As the wagons jolted over the rocky roads, the night became a horror of suppressed groans, curses between clenched teeth, and sudden stabbing screams of pain. "For four hours," wrote General John Imboden, "I hurried forward on my way to the front, and in all that time I was never out of hearing of the groans and cries of the wounded and dying." Scarcely one man in a hundred had received adequate surgical aid, and few of the wagons had even a thin layer of straw. Many had been without a mouthful of food for thirty-six hours, and there was no time to fill a canteen for a dying man begging for water. All through the black night, the driving storm continued. "During this one night," Imboden wrote, "I realized more of the horrors of war than I had in two preceding years."

On July 5, Jefferson Davis again tensely awaited dispatches, which did not come. In the dread uncertainty, the President did not wish to see anyone officially, and Dr. Garnett was able to keep him in his room. But he fixed his attention on the door where Burton Harrison might appear at any moment with a telegram. In the afternoon, he learned that a flag-of-truce boat had brought to Richmond "intelligence of a great battle at Gettysburg, Pennsylvania." Sailors said the Yankee papers claimed a victory.

That night, Lee's dispatch of July 4 was brought to the President. He noted that it was sent from "Hd. Qrs. A.N. Va. near Gettysburg, Pa." He read it through hurriedly and then again slowly.

Lee briefly sketched his movements from the time the rear of the army had crossed the Potomac and Ewell had pushed on to Carlisle and York. He spoke of concentrating at Gettysburg, and driving the enemy from the town. "On the second day," he said, "we attempted to dislodge the enemy, and though we gained some ground, we were unable to get possession of his position. The next day a more extensive attack was made." But the enemies' numbers were so great that the Southern troops were "compelled to relinquish their advantage and retire." "It is believed," he wrote, "that the enemy suffered severely in these operations, but our own loss has not been light." He mentioned by name nine Generals who had been wounded, and one, killed. He signed himself "Very respectfully, Your Obt. servt." [2]

Davis was puzzled. What did it mean? Was it much worse than Lee implied? Was he trying to break bad news gently? He had not used the word "retreat." But certainly there was no hint that Lee's invincibility had been further demonstrated.

Davis's nephew, Brigadier Joseph R. Davis, must be all right, for Lee had not included him among the general officers who had sustained injuries. What of his other nephew, Captain Isaac Stamps? The President tucked the dispatch away. The press should not know until something more definite was revealed.

All this time, while expectations blew hot and cold in Richmond, the hospital trains of the Army of Northern Virginia kept up their slow, steady pace through the driving rains and the ever-deepening mud. On the sixth, the first contingent of ambulances reached Williamsport, near Falling Water, where Lee had left pontoon bridges. The Potomac was heavily swollen with the prodigious rains. Most of the pontoons had been previously destroyed by Federal raiders. The river was unfordable, uncrossable. Escape was cut off.

Davis, of course, knew nothing of this unexpected cataclysm General Lee had to face. In the forenoon of the seventh, there was still no further news from Lee; at two-thirty, Custis Lee told War Clerk Jones that nothing had been received from his father.

That afternoon, Alexander Stephens returned baffled and crestfallen from his attempt to confer with President Lincoln. His mission could not possibly have been worse timed. He had arrived at Hampton Roads on the fourth, when the North was learning of the two decisive victories. His request to proceed to Washington had been answered by Secretary of War Stanton, who ordered the Admiral in charge of

---

[2] The text of this cautious message (*Official Records*, Vol. XVII, Part 1, p. 298) is omitted in Freeman's *R. E. Lee*, though mentioned as being sent.

the Roads to hold no communication with him. The Confederate Vice-President had not even been permitted to land. While Lincoln and his Cabinet supposedly took his request under consideration, Stephens wilted in the torrid July heat on the motionless *Torpedo*.

Isolated, virtually a prisoner on his own truce boat, Stephens knew nothing of Lee's retreat or Vicksburg's fall. So he was dumfounded by a curt official reply on July 6: "The request is inadmissible. The customary agents and channels are adequate for all needful military communications and conference between the United States forces and the insurgents." In the words of Dr. von Abele, "Lincoln could afford to be rude."

On that same afternoon of Stephens's return, the first report of Vicksburg's capitulation reached the Confederate War Department by *press* telegram. The Secretary of War had to telegraph the Commanding General and ask for the facts.

At last, in the evening of the seventh, three days after the surrender, a casual confirmatory dispatch arrived from Johnston, who had retreated back to Jackson. Seddon brought it to the President:

Vicksburg capitulated on the 4 inst. The garrison was paroled and are to be returned to our lines, the officers retaining their side-arms and personal baggage.

This intelligence was brought by an officer who left the place on Sunday, the 5th.

The news of Vicksburg's fall was hard for Jefferson Davis to take. A mortal blow had severed the Confederacy, and Johnston had not risked a finger to prevent it. Gorgas, to whom the announcement of the capitulation appeared incredible, wrote in his diary that the President was "bitter against Johnston." When he observed to the President that Vicksburg apparently had fallen from want of provisions, Davis replied: "Yes, from want of provisions inside and a General outside who wouldn't fight."

The next day, the President heard again from his General who had fought. In a letter dated Hagerstown, Maryland, July 7, Lee calmly announced: "Finding the position too strong to be carried . . . I determined to withdraw to the west side of the mountains. This has been accomplished with great labor. One of the reasons," he said, "for moving in this direction after crossing the mountains was to protect our trains with the sick and wounded which had been sent back to Williamsport, and which were threatened by the enemy's cavalry." He spoke of his 6,000 Federal prisoners, 1,500 of whom he had paroled.

His wounded were waiting to be ferried over the flooded Potomac, while the enemy's harassing cavalry was being fought off by Stuart.

Though Lee did not tell that he had had to leave 2,500 Confederate dead unburied in Pennsylvania, the situation was darker than Davis had surmised. Lee was not only in full retreat, he was in serious danger.

With superb self-composure, however, Lee was urging diligence in relieving the perilous plight at the river. The few ferryboats that had not been destroyed by the enemy were employed in ceaseless transportation of the wounded. Old warehouses were dismantled, and their timbers utilized for a makeshift bridge. Much of the material had to be floated downstream five and three-quarter miles. The engineering training of the Prussian Captain Scheibert was used to advantage. But, as Scheibert wrote, "there was such a shortage of tools that a squad had to be content with an ax, a saw, and a chisel." Rain poured all the time.

During the bridge-building, Lee arranged his defenses at Hagerstown to meet Meade's attack. He ordered eight miles of entrenchments dug. His outward calmness was the more admirable, for, besides his distress at the campaign's failure, he had an acute personal sorrow to bear. He learned that on June 29 his bedridden, wounded son Rooney had been seized in a private home, Hickory Hill, and whisked away to Fortress Monroe as a hostage. "The Northern Government threatened to hang him at the slightest dissatisfaction with the South's behavior."

Yet, on July 8, in a desire to spare the harrowed President undue apprehension, Lee sent him a remarkable message. "I hope that Your Excellency will understand that I am not in the least discouraged, nor that my faith in the protection of our All Merciful Providence, or in the fortitude of this army is at all shaken; but though conscious that the enemy have been much shattered in the recent battle I am aware that he can be easily reinforced, while no addition can be made to our numbers."

How characteristic of Lee, Davis thought, to send such reassuring words from his imperiled situation. He knew now that the exposed Army of Northern Virginia, with a raging river at its back, was in danger of destruction by Meade's augmented forces. The President in Richmond was as impatient for the subsidence of the flood as was the halted Lee; and, like Lincoln, he wondered why Meade did not strike.

Davis ordered 3,000 infantry and two artillery batteries to proceed to Winchester to cover Lee's communications. As detailed dispatches from the General arrived almost every day now, Davis lived Lee's ordeal as acutely as if he himself were standing ankle-deep in Maryland mud, surveying the bridge-making.

At 5:30 A.M., July 10, Lee sent an urgent message to Jeb Stuart: "We must prepare for a vigorous battle and trust in the mercy of God and the valor of our troops." A dispatch later in the day told the President that the Potomac continued "past fording," and that, owing to the rapidity of the stream and the limited ferry facilities, all the wounded and the prisoners were not yet over. "It would appear to be the intention of the enemy to deliver battle," Lee wrote. "I trust that the courage and fortitude will be sufficient to relieve us from embarrassment caused by the unlooked-for natural difficulty of our situation." Although Lee kept a firm grip on himself, Colonel Alexander later wrote that the General never appeared so deeply anxious as on that day.

On the morning of July 10, when Vicksburg's fall was officially confirmed, Davis received unexpected bad news from another quarter: the enemy had caught Beauregard napping and landed on Morris Island off Charleston. Though they had not captured Fort Wagner at the other end, they had a secure foothold. The Confederacy's prime seaport was in danger. Seddon sent a stiff reprimand to Beauregard, demanding to know how he had let the Federals establish themselves on the island. The possible fall of Charleston, in addition to Vicksburg's loss and Lee's imminent danger, put an additional strain on the President's frayed nerves. But Davis rose above his sorrow and his worries with remarkable resiliency. The next day, he received Mrs. Rose Greenhow and sent her on a secret mission to Europe. Two days later, Jones recorded: "The President is quite amiable now. The newspaper editors can find easy access and he welcomes them with a smile."

As the van of Meade's pursuing force came nearer, Lee sent Davis another confidence-inspiring dispatch on the twelfth. "So far everything goes well. The army is in good condition." Then, with the old spirit of invincibility, he added, "But for the power the enemy possesses of accumulating troops, I should be willing to await attack, excepting that in our restricted limits the means are becoming precarious. The river has now fallen to four feet, and a bridge, which is being constructed, I hope will be passable by to-morrow." On the morning of the thirteenth, Captain Scheibert found General Lee lively and even pleased by the thought that the Federals would attack him, "which he seemed most ardently to desire." "Captain," Lee said cheerfully, "for once we can receive the enemy here behind defensive work." But in a letter to his wife, the General revealed something of his apprehension: "I trust that a merciful God, our only hope and refuge, will not desert us in this hour of need and will deliver us by His power, and all hearts be lifted up in adoration and praise His unbounded lovingkindness."

The President had hardly finished reading his last letter from Lee when a report came that Meade's army, strengthened by 11,000 fresh reinforcements under Sedgwick, was going to attack. With a swift river at his back, Lee might need Elijah's faith in a heavenly host to withstand the Union onslaught.

Moving cautiously, the long way round, Meade, constantly prodded by President Lincoln, had finally decided to attack on July 13. Imbued with the Lee legend and feeling the tremendous weight of responsibility, he called his corps commanders in council. Five of the seven opposed attack. Their adverse opinion caused Meade to delay one more day for further reconnaissance. Then he determined to strike on the fourteenth with everything he had.

On the thirteenth, the Potomac, though still almost breast-high, was fordable for infantry, and the hastily put-together bridge was declared ready. Lee ordered Ewell's divisions to start fording the river; the supply trains and the rest of the army would cross by the bridge. In the afternoon, as if to prevent the deliverance, the heavens opened up again. As much water seemed to be in the air above, men said, as in the river below. The soaked regiments crowded the banks, miserably waiting for the mud-impeded wagons to get on. The march, which Lee had hoped would go swiftly, became snarled. The army had a herculean fight with mire. Strained nerves all but snapped. Some officers voiced their disgust and despair in such loud voices that Lee rebuked them for upsetting the soldiers. Men were so exhausted that they dropped to the puddled ground and slept, while the wagon trains swayed dangerously over the "crazy" bridge.

All through the night, as torches sputtered in the rain, the fantastic crossing proceeded. A. P. Hill, whose corps was the last to go over, was ordered to keep straight on the bridge and not to halt unless absolutely compelled to. When he was within a half-mile of the bridge, a cannon's discharge echoed along the river gorge. The attack Lee had been expecting for seven days had begun.

Hill's men plodded doggedly on, and were soon tramping over the bridge's roughened planks. General Henry Heth, with a few artillerists in the extreme rear, struck back at the enemy, then turned to the bridge and safety, leaving two guns stuck hopelessly in the mud.

When the last man was over, the bridge was destroyed. Lee, nearly dropping with exhaustion, gratefully accepted a steaming cup of coffee from Jeb Stuart. He was filled with an immeasurable relief. His army was intact on Virginia soil. He had brought through safely all his wounded and 4,000 Union prisoners, besides his equipment. When Meade arrived, he found nothing to shoot at. The escape did seem miraculous, like something related in the Old Testament.

To Jefferson Davis, painfully disappointed in the outcome of Gettysburg, Lee's successful crossing under cataclysmic stress was a triumph in itself. But as Winston Churchill was to write with startling succinctness, nine decades later: "Lee had lost only two guns and the war." There was, however, no despair in the mind of the Confederacy's President.

CHAPTER XXXIV

"MISFORTUNES DEVELOP
SECRET FOES"

THE PRESIDENT, feeling acutely the sorrow of his people for their dead, was faced with personal grief in his home. His nephew Isaac Stamps had been killed. When the official report of her husband's death was received, Mary, who had kept up a brave front despite her premonition of fatality, fainted. For days, she lay very ill. The President was peculiarly distressed at her leaden grief, for, as he had told Fremantle, "silent despair is the most painful of misery to witness." He was touched to see how Varina nursed Mary with most tender solicitude. Her sensitive and loving thought for the little girls in their bewilderment and grief were never to be forgotten by six-year-old Lucy Stamps.[1] Nor did Mary ever forget the attentions of the sympathetic and affectionate Davis children. "I think without flattery," she later wrote Varina, "that you have the noblest children, the finest natures that I ever saw— Their gentle looks and words and tears for my sufferings are treasured up and valued."

As soon as Mary Stamps had enough strength, she asked to be taken to the hospitals to talk with wounded companions of her husband. She learned that Isaac, who had suffered agonies from wounds in the bowels, had stayed all night on the field in the open air from preference, and "was attended there in the moonlight by several friends who never left him." Her father, General Humphreys, had spent several hours with his son-in-law. Next morning, Isaac was carried in an ambulance to the rear and laid down to rest, just where he had lain the day before awaiting orders to charge. At two o'clock, as Pickett's

---

[1] Details were related to the author by Anna Farrar Goldsborough, daughter of Lucy Stamps Farrar. Contemporary letters were lent to the author by Mrs. Stamps Farrar of New Orleans.

men ranged themselves to prepare for their fatal charge, Isaac died, murmuring, "My poor wife! God help her to bear it."

Isaac had told the surgeon, Dr. Peets, to send his wife his sword, the gift of his Uncle Jeff, to keep for his children, and the penknife, which she had given him, to keep for herself. Mary, who now had them both, made only one request of her uncle. As soon as practicable, she wanted a pass and safe conduct through the lines to Gettysburg to secure her husband's body for burial in Woodville, Mississippi. The President promised her to do his best.

While sorrow pervaded the President's home in Richmond, there was no real joy in the Washington White House. According to John Hay's diary, Mr. Lincoln was irritated in the extreme at Lee's escape. "We had only to stretch forth our hands and they would have been ours," he declared repeatedly. "Nothing I could say or do could make the army move." On July 7, Lincoln had written Halleck: "If General Meade can complete his work . . . by the literal or substantial destruction of Lee's army, the rebellion will be over." On July 14, just as his Cabinet assembled, Lincoln got a whispered message that Lee had safely crossed the Potomac. He was so upset that he promptly canceled the meeting. As Secretary of the Navy Welles walked slowly away, the President overtook him. "He said," Welles wrote, "that he had dreaded, yet expected this; that there had seemed to him a determination that Lee, though we had him in our hands, should escape with his force and plunder. 'There is bad faith somewhere!' he exclaimed. 'What does it mean, Mr. Welles? Great God! What does it mean?'"

In his gnawing frustration, Lincoln, who had now grown very sick of the war, impulsively dashed off a censorious letter to Meade. "And yet you stood there," he wrote in sharp reprimand, "and let the flood run down, bridges be built and the enemy move away at his leisure without attacking him. . . . If you could not safely attack Lee last Monday, how can you possibly do so south of the river . . . with very few more than two-thirds of the force you then had in hand? . . . Your golden opportunity is lost, and I am distressed immeasurably because of it."

Happily, having relieved himself of some bitterness by the writing, President Lincoln did not send the letter; but his secretaries, Nicolay and Hay, preserved it and quoted it (Volume VII, page 280) in their biography. Halleck sent Meade a more moderate telegram: "The escape of Lee's army without another battle has created great dissatisfaction in the mind of the President." Meade promptly asked to be relieved of his command, but his request was not granted.

Jefferson Davis had no thought of criticizing Lee for the Confederate blunders at Gettysburg. He felt that if Lee's orders had been properly and promptly obeyed, the outcome might have been successful.

Military critics seem to agree that the Confederates would have won at Gettysburg had they occupied Little Round Top on the evening of the first day. But perhaps, in reality, the Battle of Gettysburg had been lost weeks before at Guiney's Station, when death overtook Stonewall Jackson. Because of Jackson's absence, Davis had never felt assurance about the Pennsylvania push. And Lee later told his nephew Fitzhugh: "Had I Stonewall Jackson I would have won a great victory." Davis always so believed.

Davis knew that everybody in the South had varied opinions about what went wrong at Gettysburg. Soldiers on the spot and later historians severely criticized Longstreet's stubbornness; his self-will, close to insubordination; his "slowness" on both the second and third days, though he had fought magnificently on the second. Most commentators believe that Dick Ewell should have pressed on to take Cemetery Ridge before Meade arrived. And somehow Ewell had been unable to do anything right the second day. Little A. P. Hill, through no fault of his own, was unwell and lacked his usual fighting fury. Many put heavy blame on Jeb Stuart. The "ifs" chiefly concerned Longstreet, Ewell, and Stuart. If each, or even one, of these Generals had given top or accustomed performances, or had obeyed Lee with more discretion, the result at Gettysburg might well have been different.

But Lee was not considered entirely blameless. He should have been more specific in his orders. He had fallen into his old weakness—first exhibited in the western Virginia campaign—of allowing too much freedom of decision to his corps commanders.

Lee, who deplored self-justification, was scrupulously careful in his reports not to censure anyone for the failure. But in the 1890's, two decades after the great soldier's death, Longstreet, in his book, ascribed the Gettysburg failure to Lee's mistakes, against which he claimed he had remonstrated in vain. Richard Taylor answered tellingly in *Destruction and Reconstruction:* "That any subject involving the possession and exercise of intellect should be clear to Longstreet and concealed from Lee is a startling proposition to those having knowledge of the two men."

In his *Rise and Fall*, Jefferson Davis was to reveal some of his thinking on Gettysburg. "Had there been a concentrated attack at sunrise on the second day, with the same gallantry and skill which were exhibited in partial assaults, it may reasonably be assumed that the enemy would have been routed. This, from the best evidence we have, was the plan and the expectation of General Lee. These having failed, from whatsoever cause, and Meade having occupied in force the commanding position of Round Top, it must be conceded that it would have been better to withdraw than to renew the attack on the third day. The high morale and discipline of our army, together with the unqualified confidence of the men in their commanding general excluded the supposition that they would be demoralized by retreat."

Considering the fact that Confederate losses at Gettysburg were fewer than those of the Union[2] and that the Army of the Potomac was farther away from Richmond than it had been when McDowell assumed command in 1861, Davis felt that the general strategy of Lee's Northern campaign had been justified.

Despite Mr. Lincoln's disappointment in Lee's escape, the Battle of Gettysburg revived the drooping spirits of the North, temporarily hushed the pleas of the peace party, made British statesmen lean farther away from recognition, and caused Confederate malcontents to heap fresh abuse on their President, whom they represented as sacrificing the Mississippi Valley for Virginia. Though Lee took full responsibility for the initiation, as well as the prosecution, of the Pennsylvania campaign, some contemporary papers, as well as future careless historians, blamed Jefferson Davis for *sending* Lee to invade the North.

When Lee recrossed the Potomac, hope of independence flickered low in the breasts of many Southerners who had sacrificed so cheerfully. With Vicksburg in the hands of the enemy, with Lee repulsed at Gettysburg, with strategic Chattanooga imperiled, and Charleston in great danger, it seemed as if the war's end might be very soon. And most likely it would have been except for the indomitable will and courage of Jefferson Davis. While the South was in deep depression, President Davis gave no indication that he had lost hope. "Adversity

---

[2] Rhodes gives the Union loss in killed, wounded, and missing in the three days' battles as slightly larger in each category than the Confederates, with 23,000 total casualties for the North, as against 20,451 for the South.

only stiffened his power of resistance," wrote Landon Knight, his Ohio biographer, "and added to his strength of character, which was to win the respect of his enemies and the admiration of the rest of the world."

Davis's patience and powers of endurance, however, were tested to the limit in dealing with Joseph E. Johnston.

In trying to duck the blame that would be laid on him, Johnston now telegraphed the War Department: "I considered my assignment to the immediate command in Mississippi as giving me a new position and limiting my authority." His defensive statement was so obviously oblique that the President sent for the entire correspondence with Johnston and Bragg on the subject of Pemberton's relief.

On the eighth, in a complex of emotions over Johnston's inexplicable behavior, the President telegraphed him.

Your dispatch of 7th to Sec. of War announcing the disastrous termination of the siege of Vicksburg received same day. Painfully anxious as to the result I have remained without information from you as to any plans proposed or attempted to raise the siege. Equally uninformed as to your plans in relation to Port Hudson, I have to request such information in relation thereto as the Government has a right to expect from one of its commanding generals in the field.

On that very day Port Hudson's garrison capitulated after withstanding a grueling six weeks' siege. On the eleventh, Davis was still vainly trying to get some positive word from Johnston.

But far from giving up all hope in the Trans-Mississippi, the President issued moving proclamations and began writing letters to revive civilian morale. Arkansas was threatening to separate from the Confederacy. To that state's apprehensive Senator, R. W. Johnston, Davis wrote on July 14:

"Your letter found me in the depths of gloom in which the disasters of the Missi. River have shrouded our cause. Though it was well for me to know the worst, it pained me to observe how your confidence was shaken, and your criticism severe on men who I think deserve to be trusted.

"In proportion as our difficulties increase, so must we all cling together, judge charitably of each other and strive to bear and forbear, however great may be the sacrifice and bitter the trial. . . . Our people have not generally realized the magnitude of the struggle in which we are engaged."

Coming to specific practical matters, he said: "I have long seen the importance of establishing manufactures of all munitions of war in the trans-Missi Dept." He was directing skilled workmen to be sent over. "A foundry and rolling mill should be located where iron is cheapest, and where the works are least likely to be interrupted by hostile invasion." Davis hoped that tanneries and shoe factories could be well dispersed. He pointed up emphatically that it would be mad or suicidal for any state of the Confederacy to seek safety by separation from the rest. What could be expected, he asked, but such degradation as to a freeman would be worse than torture at the stake? "Proud, honorable men may have opposed the Act of Secession, but can anyone not fit to be slave and ready to become one, think of passing under the yoke of such as the Yankees have shown themselves to be by their conduct in this war?" He ended with a patriotic appeal: "The sacrifices of our people have been very heavy both of blood and of treasure, many like myself have been robbed of all which the toil of many years had gathered, but the prize for which we strive, freedom and independence, is worth whatever it may cost."

On the same day, July 14, the President sent morale-boosting letters to Governor Reynolds of Missouri and Governor Lubbock of Texas, as well as to several general officers, among them, Joseph E. Johnston, J. C. Pemberton, and Kirby Smith. He reminded Smith that with the Mississippi River lost, his difficulties as Commanding General would be materially aggravated. "You now have not merely a military, but also a political problem involved in your command. The endurance of our people is to be severely tested," he said, "and nothing will serve more to encourage and sustain them than a zealous application of their industry to the task of producing within themselves whatever is necessary for their comfortable existence."

He closed on a warm, personal note: "We are now in the darkest hour of our political existence. I am happy in the confidence I feel in your ability, zeal and discretion. The responsibility with which you are charged is heavy indeed. . . . It grieves me to have enumerated so many and such difficult objects for your attention when I can give you so little aid in their achievement. May God guide you and grant us a future in which we may congratulate each other on the achievement of the independence and peace of our country."

Far from giving up, on the day Lee completed his retreat across the Potomac, Jefferson Davis was spreading the hope of ultimate freedom. At the same time, Joseph Johnston's newspaper friends were busily promulgating the idea that Vicksburg had been lost because Davis had "interfered." The General persisted in declaring that he had not been given proper authority. So, in a voluminous letter of July 15, the President reviewed the entire case for him, proving that in order after order, dispatch upon dispatch, there was not one hint of evidence that Johnston's authority had been limited. After marshaling all the facts and quoting from telegrams and dispatches, in one strong statement Davis wrote conclusively: "In no manner, by no act, by no language, either of myself or of the Sec. of War, has your authority to draw troops from one portion of your Dept. to another been withdrawn, restricted or modified."

At first, the Mississippians were furious with Johnston for not going to Vicksburg's aid. But Johnston's friends were adroit at placing the blame on the President and the Northern-born Pemberton, whom they charged with insubordination. At the little town of Brandon, there was a clamoring to hang Pemberton. Sharp-tongued Lydia Johnston gave out everywhere that her poor husband was "the victim of the President's persecution."

United States General Morris Schaff understood something of what President Davis had to put up with in Joseph Johnston. In 1922, after making a study of the Johnston dispatches in *Official Records,* he wrote: "Johnston may have been—what many of his friends claimed, a great soldier—but if there be in all his military correspondence a line or a word breathing confidence and hope I have yet to see it."

There was one such letter General Schaff may not have known. Burton Harrison recalled a communication from Johnston to the President written from Bunker Hill, near Martinsburg, Virginia, in June, 1861, shortly before the First Battle of Manassas. It impressed Harrison "as being a curious commentary upon his subsequent career as a Commander of Armies." Johnston, noting that General Patterson was in position and wishing him to attack, wrote, "If Patterson does not soon attack me, I shall attack him—for in battle there is always a chance of success, whereas a retreat, before an organized Army, is, in its effect even upon disciplined troops, generally equivalent to a defeat!" The exclamation point is Harrison's. Well might he exclaim, for, ironically, after First Manassas Johnston's entire strategy was that of retreat. But for the notable exception of Seven Pines, when he was prodded to action by Davis, he never sought a single battle, but restricted himself entirely to retrogressive movements.

On July 21, after Johnston had given up Jackson a second time without risking a shot, Davis wrote Lee: "Genl. Johnston is retreating on the East side of Pearl River, and I can only learn from him of such vague purposes as were unfolded when he held his army before Richmond." A week later, he wrote Lee again: "Genl. Johnston, after evacuating Jackson, retreated to the east, to the pinewoods of Mississippi, and if he has any other plan than that of watching the enemy it has not been communicated."

And then Davis hinted at some other depressing worries. "You know how rare a quality is that which is esteemed administrative capacity and how much it was needed in our condition." He spoke of the evils in the Quartermaster's Department, the worsening conditions of railroads, the irreplaceable loss in the southwest of locomotives and machinery.

With a kind of prescience, he went on: "War can only be successfully prosecuted while we have the cordial support of the people. . . . Misfortunes often develop secret foes and oftener still make men complain. It is comfortable to hold some one responsible for one's discomfort. In various quarters there are mutterings of discontent, and threats of alienation are said to exist with preparation for organized opposition. . . . Others, who faithful but dissatisfied, find an appropriate remedy in the removal of officers who have not succeeded. They do not count the cost of following their advice. Their remedy to be good should furnish substitutes who would be better than the officers displaced." Davis ended his intimate letter on a patriotic note that yet revealed his heart-seated weariness at the unjust blame put upon him. "If a victim would secure the success of our cause I would freely offer myself."

While dark clouds hung over the Confederacy in mid-July, Northern skies were none too bright despite the recent success of Federal arms. In New York City, where a strong strain of sympathy for the South had persisted since the formation of the Confederacy, two newspapers, the *World* and the *Journal of Commerce,* continued to voice criticism of President Lincoln and his Government. Both Mayor Fernando Wood and Governor Horatio Seymour were frank in their antiwar sentiments. The Republicans were accused of conscripting Democrats heavily, while going light on registered Republicans. They were also charged with manipulating Negro suffrage for party benefit.

On July 13 and 14, while Lee was bringing his army over the Potomac, antidraft riots broke out in New York. Citizens seized rifles and ammunition at the Second Avenue Armory, overpowered police and militia. The armed mob went on a demented rampage. President Davis read shocking reports, which at first he discounted.

Colonel Fremantle, who had bidden farewell to General Lee along the Potomac on the ninth, arrived in New York on the thirteenth.

The Englishman was struck immediately by the "well-dressed people" and the number of "men capable of bearing arms but having no intention of doing so." He found the streets covered with placards inviting enlistments: "bounties of $550 were offered." Huge pictures hung across the streets depicted terrified Southern "graybacks" being chased by well-armed Federals. But shopkeepers were closing their doors. Blocks of buildings were burning; citizens prevented the firemen from playing water on them. Soldiers marching up thoroughfares were hooted at by small boys. Negroes were fleeing to the refuge of the military, pursued by angry men shouting, "Down with the bloody nigger! Kill all niggers!" When the astonished Englishman inquired what the Negroes had done to invite killing, a bystander replied, "Oh, sir, they hate them here; they are the innocent cause of all these troubles."

Fremantle was told that men who could not pay four hundred dollars for exemption "naturally hated being forced to fight in order to liberate the very race they are most anxious should be kept slaves." The reasons given him for the mob frenzy in New York were much like the explanations given him a few weeks before at Monroe, Louisiana, by some forty deserters from Grant's army. The Yankees claimed they deserted because they had been betrayed; they had "enlisted to fight for Union and found they were risking all to free the negroes."

On July 14, the terror in New York increased. Streetcars stopped running; telegraph lines were cut; railroad tracks were torn up. No persons of color were visible on any street; but they were not safe in their homes. Some were captured in restaurants at their work and dragged off to be bludgeoned to death. Innocent Negroes were hanged on lampposts and their bodies set afire.

For four days, terror reigned, marked by a series of grisly lynchings. A mob even swarmed onto a British ship in the harbor, and, despite the Captain's protests, cruelly beat up the foreign Negroes among the crew. The police were barely able to save the *Tribune* Building from total destruction. Men searched the city for the *Tribune*'s editor, singing, "We'll hang Horace Greeley to a sour apple-tree." A Negro orphanage on Fifth Avenue was burned to the ground. Looters had a field day, among them screeching women who opposed conscription.

Troops were rushed back from Gettysburg; cadets from West Point came to aid the police; the entire naval force in the region was called upon to help quell the disturbance. Finally, in desperation, the military raked the streets with cannon fire.

But what really stopped the rioting was a posted notice: "The draft has been suspended in New York City and Brooklyn." The newspapers carried the word in huge print. Order was finally restored. According to the *Tribune* of July 25, some 350 persons had been killed; but other estimates went much higher. Casualties, including the injured, amounted to 1,000, and private property damage was estimated at $1,500,000.

Republican papers claimed the outbreak had been sparked by Confederate agents. But Democratic party feeling and a sincere desire for peace were mingled with race prejudice and resentment against what the anti-Lincoln papers called the "incompetence" of the Administration. Men resented fighting against their convictions and were indignant at governmental "frauds and profiteering." Apparently, from the magnitude of the outbreak, the London *Times* correspondent had not been far wrong in predicting that if the South won in Pennsylvania, Jefferson Davis and General Robert E. Lee would receive a rousing welcome along Broadway. All in all, as Davis read various dispatches and comments from the Northern press, he had reason to believe that the riots were symptomatic of a deep dissatisfaction that might prove helpful to the Southern cause.

Soon after the tumult subsided, the Democratic City Council of New York voted that the exemption money of four hundred dollars for impecunious draftees would be paid from the city treasury. To meet Governor Seymour's charge that the conscription as practiced was "unequal, fraudulent, and a disgrace," President Lincoln reduced the New York quotas. When the draft was resumed a month later, he took the precaution of sending 10,000 infantrymen and three artillery batteries from the Army of the Potomac to see that the business went off quietly.

During New York's bloody pandemonium, Fremantle had been surprised to hear everyone talking of the "total demoralization of the Rebels." To him it sounded absurd, since only a few days previously, he had left Lee's army "as full of fight as ever," much stronger and more efficient from every military point of view than when it had crossed the Potomac to invade Maryland the previous September. In the Colonel's opinion, Lee's army had "not lost any of its prestige at the battle of Gettysburg, in which it had most gallantly stormed strong intrenchments defended by the whole Army of the Potomac."

Fremantle took ship for England and completed his book of observations at sea. "The mass of respectable Northerners," he wrote, "though they may be willing to pay, do not very naturally feel themselves called upon to give their blood in a war of aggression, ambition and conquest. . . . The more I think of all I have seen in the Confederate States of the devotion of the whole population, the more I feel inclined to say with General Polk—'How can you subjugate such a people as this?' and even supposing that their extermination were a feasible plan, as some Northerners have suggested, I never can believe that in the nineteenth century the civilized world will be condemned to witness the destruction of such a gallant race."

As soon as it could be got into print, Fremantle's *Three Months in the Southern States, April-June, 1863* was published in England. And not long afterward, in Mobile was printed a separate edition bound in wallpaper, which Jefferson Davis was to read with gratification for the sympathetic understanding of the South's cause and struggle.

On an evening in late July, another foreign visitor, Captain Justus Scheibert, called to pay his respects and make his adieux to President Davis before returning to Europe. The Prussian officer was received "with great propriety" by the butler, "a negro of refined manners, in frock coat and white tie." Since he heard voices in the drawing room, Scheibert asked to be granted a brief private audience. But almost immediately, as he reported, "the head of the Confederacy stood before me, extended both hands, and greeted me warmly and cordially as a friend of General Lee." He escorted the foreign guest into the drawing room and introduced him to the group. Scheibert found the President "a gentleman in whose company one feels at ease after the first moment and whose conversation was that of an important man."

Davis questioned him in detail about the Pennsylvania expedition, and "expressed himself in quite measured terms" about Vicksburg's campaign and fall. He listened attentively to Scheibert's opinion of Lee's troops. The President, wrote the Prussian, "showed himself in society, as well as in private conversation, to be an energetic man, full of humanitarianism and a true Christian." When the conversation became more general, a lady expressed indignation at the damage to the Davis estates in Mississippi and the removal and destruction of the President's and his brother's library. But Davis merely replied that some sacrifice in property or blood was demanded of even the lowliest Confederate, and no word was to be wasted on such trifles. Yet he confessed that he pitied his poor Negroes, who had been driven off by Federal troops and abandoned to misery or ruin.

The conversation turned to two captured Federal captains who had been drawn by lot for execution as payment for two Confederate captains who had been unjustly hanged. In spite of the pressure of public opinion, when the time came for the execution, the President had always postponed it from month to month. He said it was his endeavor, so far as possible, to keep this war within the limits of humanity, since war was "by nature barbaric." Whether the President discussed war or politics, Scheibert found his manner "just as calm and unimpassioned as statesmanlike."

In 1868, five years later, when his account of seven months in the Confederacy was published in Europe, and Jefferson Davis was being made the scapegoat of the South's misfortunes, Scheibert wrote: "The fact that an uncritical, partisan madness now besmirches his character . . . cannot rob him of the place in history, which will be given him when calm reason stands in judgment over blind confusion."

At the end of July, death removed two of Jefferson Davis's opponents from the political arena. First, bitter Sam Houston, who was vainly trying to maneuver Texas into seceding from the Confederacy. Second, the turbulent William Yancey, who died at his plantation near Montgomery of an acute kidney ailment. Some papers implied that he died of a broken heart. The *Examiner* of July 30 took occasion, in praising Yancey, to assault the President, saying that Davis had unfortunately been "inflicted" on the Confederacy at Montgomery, and then had denied participation in governmental affairs to the great men who were the authors of secession. Of course, the South knew that Davis had offered Yancey a post in the first Cabinet, and, when he declined that, had sent him to Europe as chief commissioner.

Though relieved of a potent troublemaker in Congress, the President was grieved that Yancey had not been reconciled to him. He was touched to learn that his onetime friend, who had presented him to Montgomery in the memorable phrase "The man and the hour have met," had remembered him in his will. Yancey bequeathed him a treasured spyglass that had once belonged to George Washington. When the glass was delivered, the President wrote Mrs. Yancey: "In receiving this bequest, precious from the associations connected with the object and from the very gratifying sentiment which is manifested by the bequest . . . I assure you that the treasure committed to my care derives greatly enhanced value from the proof which it affords of the kind feelings of my former associate and friend, the distinguished patriot and statesman whose loss is deplored by his country."

CHAPTER XXXV

"FORGIVE ME FOR LEANING . . .
UPON YOUR GREAT HEART"

AFTER Joseph Johnston, at his own request, had been removed from further command of the Department of Tennessee on July 22 and had been given control only of the forces in Mississippi, he turned his energies to self-justification. It is true that Johnston was outnumbered and had his difficulties, as did every Southern commander; but he had not used his troops with any vigor. As Davis wrote on March 1, 1865, "Not once during the campaign did he act on the maxim of attacking the foe in detail—a rule peculiarly applicable when an army is contending against an enemy superior in numbers." Unfortunately for Davis, Johnston was an able and subtle personal antagonist. As a Virginia gentleman who had married a spirited Maryland blue-blood he had great influence. As a general he took exceptionally good care of his men and won their affection. He possessed definite magnetism, and he had the power to make those around him believe in the infallibility of his opinions.

President Davis read with indignation a copy of a lengthy letter from Dr. D. W. Yandell of Johnston's staff, which was being passed around in Richmond. It was obviously calculated to extol Johnston and lay the entire blame for the loss of Vicksburg on Pemberton and the Richmond Government. The "letter," almost 6,000 words in length, was written to Dr. John M. Johnson, surgeon to General Hardee, and embraced a period of thirty-two days' activity, from May 13 to June 13.[1]

Since an army doctor does not write a "merely friendly" letter of such weight and magnitude, replete with exact quotations from official

[1] A copy of the Yandell letter is in Confederate Memorial Hall, New Orleans. It may be read more conveniently in Rowland, Vol. VI, pp. 2-13.

correspondence, Davis was convinced that it was intended for ultimate publication.

Yandell pointed up the fright and demoralization of the Mississippians on Johnston's arrival in Jackson and "the gloom that oppressed all—except Johnston," upon whom he bestowed the highest possible praise by comparing him to Albert Sidney Johnston "as he rode down upon the ensanguined field of Shiloh." Davis noted that Yandell did not remark that Sidney Johnston was leading his men *into* battle rather than away from it. "I never saw a brain . . ." the staff officer declared, "which exhibited a finer sweep or more striking power. Amidst the depressing surroundings," he continued glowingly, "Johnston preserved the elastic step and the glowing brow of a genuine hero."

The surgeon pictured the General's health as good, his strength as "quite sufficient," and blamed the Government for *sending* him "too late." Davis knew too well that Johnston had refused to go when first ordered, claiming he was ill, and that he had gone at last only when peremptorily ordered to by the Secretary of War.

In the following pages, Yandell quoted secret dispatches from the War Office and repeated official communications of Johnston ordering Pemberton to attack or "hold out," while he himself retreated. Toward the end of his "article-letter"—after Johnston had returned in June to abandoned, burned-out Jackson and sat there while Pemberton pleaded for help—Yandell penned his most naïvely ironic line: "I never saw such comprehensive energy, and untiring industry as Gen. Johnston has exhibited."

When Davis read articles based on extracts from the letter in the Atlanta *Appeal* and the Charleston *Mercury,* he wrote Pemberton, calling his attention to the "internal evidence of its origin," and indicated some points that the General should notice in his official report. On August 9, he wrote Pemberton more specifically on the tack Johnston was taking: "The statements in relation to operations connected with the battle of Bakers Creek sufficiently warn you of an attempt to place on you the responsibility for all which preceded and followed that event, and indicate the points to be covered.

"To some men," he said, "it is given to be commended for what they are expected to do, and to be sheltered when they fail by a transfer of the blame which may attach; to others it is decreed that their success shall be denied or treated as a necessary result; and their failures imputed to incapacity or crime."

Then he spoke of "the popular delusion so readily created by un-scrupulous men who resort to the newspapers to disseminate false-hood and forestall the public judgment." By way of consolation, he wrote, "I am no stranger to the misrepresentation of which malignity is capable, or to the generation of such feeling by the conscientious discharge of duty." He assured Pemberton that his confidence in both him and General Lee had not been diminished "because 'letter-writers' have not sent forth your praise on the wings of the press."

Never had Davis known a more flagrant case of public ingratitude than the South's clamor against Pemberton, who had held Grant at bay from early December to July.

As Davis saw it, Pemberton rightly preferred to risk his army "rather than to surrender the objects of the whole campaign without an effort." During the harrowing forty-seven days, the General had shown extraordinary fortitude, while his engineering skill and his "fertility of expedients" had been conspicuously displayed. In the end, though the river port and the guns were lost, 31,000 of Pember-ton's men were saved. Yet by many critics, Davis's appointment of the Northern Pemberton to the command of Vicksburg was persistently regarded as a major blunder.

Pemberton now had charge of the paroled Vicksburg soldiers in en-campments in Mississippi and Alabama, and was sending them home on furloughs until they could be exchanged. As critical abuse poured in against Pemberton, whom many now regarded as a designing traitor, Davis regretfully realized that his capacity for usefulness as a com-mander in Mississippi was over. When this current service with pa-roled men was done, the President would call him to Richmond and see if he could find him some other command.

Anti-Administration papers continued to take their cue from parts of Yandell's letter to extol Johnston, denounce Pemberton, and cast a cloud on the President. Davis was especially troubled that Johnston seemingly had no care how much the "disclosures" damaged the mo-rale of a people already depressed. Unquestionably, the doctor had had access to his General's confidential files.

The President finally sent Johnston a newspaper cutting with a significant comment: "It is needless to say that you are not considered capable of giving countenance to such efforts at laudation of yourself and detraction of others, and the paper is sent to you with the confi-dence that you will take the proper action in the premises."

Johnston replied in a vague, roundabout manner, forwarding copies of communications from both surgeons, which claimed in effect that although a copy of Yandell's "strictly private and confidential" letter had been "lent" to a newspaper editor, permission to print portions had not been granted. On August 24, Davis wrote him bluntly that he could not accept his explanation. Because it was obvious to Johnston that the President saw through his indirect efforts to discredit his superior and protect himself, his animosity increased. As Mrs. Chesnut wrote, Johnston's "hatred of Jeff Davis became a religion with him."

While the President was concerned about the repercussions of Yandell's letter, he had sent Lee a cutting from the Charleston *Mercury* full of aspersions on the Gettysburg failure and spouting special abuse of Major General Heth. Davis wanted some facts to answer the accusations. From his camp at Culpeper, Lee replied with calm wisdom:

> I regret much its general censure upon the operations of the army, as it is calculated to do us no good either at home or abroad. But I am prepared for similar criticism and as far as I am concerned the remarks fall harmless. I am particularly sorry . . . that occasion should be taken to asperse your conduct, who of all others are most free of blame. I do not fear that your position in the confidence of the people can be injured by such attacks, and I hope the official reports will protect the reputation of every officer. . . .
>
> In the meantime, as you state, much falsehood may be promulgated. But truth is mighty and will eventually prevail. . . . To take notice of such attacks would, I think, do more harm than good, and would be much what is desired. . . . No blame can be attached to the army for its failure to accomplish what was projected by me nor should it be censured for the unreasonable expectations of the public—I am alone to blame, in expecting too much of its prowess and valour.

After Lee's sage and magnanimous letter, Davis decided not to reply to the *Mercury*.

In answer to Lee's question about the propriety of resuming his former position in the rear of Fredericksburg, Davis agreed that it would be best to draw the enemy by strategy to attack the Confederates in an entrenched position. Then, in the intimacy of their friendship, he gave another hint of his own anxieties: "I need your counsel, but must strive to meet the requirements of the hour without distracting your attention. . . ."

Both men were excessively weary, not only of the burdens heaped upon them, but of the snipings and broadsides aimed at them by newspapers and politicians. The criticisms had wounded Lee more deeply than he would admit, and he was disturbed over the censure that his failure had brought upon the President. On August 8, he came to a momentous decision, and requested to be relieved of his command.

When Jefferson Davis read the General's letter, the beginning was so disarming, so characteristic of Lee, that he little dreamed he was holding one of the most unnerving letters he would ever receive.

I am extremely obliged to you for the attention given to the wants of this army, and the efforts made to supply them. Our absentees are returning, and I hope the earnest and beautiful appeal made to the country in your proclamation may stir up the whole people, and that they may see their duty and perform it. Nothing is wanted but that their fortitude should equal their bravery, to insure the success of our cause. . . .

I know how prone we are to censure, and how ready to blame others for the non-fulfilment of our expectations. This is unbecoming in a generous people, and I grieve to see its expression. The general remedy for the want of success in a military commander is his removal. This is natural, and in many instances proper. . . .

Davis noted the echo of Sidney Johnston's noble letter after Donelson. But he was unprepared for the shock of what followed:

I have been prompted by these reflections more than once since my return from Pennsylvania to propose to Your Excellency the propriety of selecting another commander for this army. I have seen and heard of expressions of discontent in the public journals at the result of the expedition. . . . I, therefore, in all sincerity, request Your Excellency to take measures to supply my place. I do this with the more earnestness because no one is more aware than myself of my inability for the duties of my position. . . . In addition, I sensibly feel the growing failure of my bodily strength. I have not yet recovered from the attack I experienced the past spring. . . . Everything, therefore, points to the advantages to be derived from a new commander, and I the more anxiously urge the matter upon Your Excellency from my belief that a younger and abler man than myself can readily be obtained. . . .

I have no complaints to make of any one but myself. I have received nothing but kindness from those above me, and the most considerate attention from my comrades and companions in arms. To Your Excellency, I am specially indebted for uniform kindness and consideration. You have done everything in your power to aid me in the work committed to my charge, without omitting anything to promote the general welfare. I pray that your efforts may at length be crowned with success, and that you may long live to enjoy the thanks of a grateful people.

Davis laid down the letter appalled. But he did not fail to remark the modesty, magnanimity, and unselfish patriotism, as well as the loyal friendship for himself, reflected in and between the lines. Of course he could not give Lee up; it would be calamitous.

On August 11, Davis composed his reply with loving care.

It well became Sidney Johnston when overwhelmed by a senseless clamor to admit the rule that success is the test of merit, and yet there has been nothing which I have found to require a greater effort of patience than to bear the criticisms of the ignorant, who pronounce everything a failure which does not equal their expectations or desires. . . . Expressions of discontent in the public journals furnish but little evidence of the sentiment of an army. . . . I wish I could feel that the public journals were not generally partisan nor venal.

Then, with Joseph Johnston in mind, he wrote:

Were you capable of stooping to it, you could easily surround yourself with those who would fill the press with your laudations, and seek to exalt you for what you had not done rather than detract from the achievements which will make you and your army the subject of history and object of the world's admiration for generations to come.

Coming to the core of the matter, Davis said:

But, suppose, my dear friend, that I were to admit . . . the points which you present, where am I to find that new commander who is to possess the greater ability which you believe to be required?

My sight is not sufficiently penetrating to discover such hidden merit if it exists. . . . I have impressed upon you the propriety of avoiding all unnecessary exposure to danger because I felt our country could not bear to lose you. To ask me to substitute you by some one in my judgment more fit to command, or who would possess more of the confidence of the army or of the reflecting men in the country is to demand of me an impossibility.

It only remains for me to hope that you will take all possible care of yourself, that your health and strength may be entirely restored, and that the Lord will preserve you for the important duties devolved upon you in the struggle of our suffering country, for the independence which we have engaged in war to maintain.

So it was concluded. Satisfied that he still had his Chief's full confidence and that there really was no one else to take his place, Lee would stay at his post. Had it not been for Jefferson Davis's will and his inspired wording in refusing to accept the resignation, Lee's additional nobleness in the record would not have been earned in 1864 and his fame today would be less glorious.

In the midst of his anxiety over Lee's proffered resignation, Davis received a surprising, comforting letter from Georgia's Herschel V. Johnson, who had stood for Vice-President of the United States on the ticket with Stephen A. Douglas in 1860, when the Democratic party disastrously split. From his plantation, Sandy Grove, near Barton, Johnson wrote:

It cannot be otherwise than acceptable to receive assurance from friends, of their deep sympathy with you in your great public responsibilities & their unshaken confidence in your ability and patriotism. I am too humble for such assurances from me to be worth much but I confess that I am too selfish to forego the pleasure of their expression. You have my entire confidence and poor prayers to God, that He will sustain you, under trial & vouchsafe to you wisdom to guide you in your arduous and perilous path of duty. Our recent worries produced gloom for a time, but I see the reactions, and very soon the people will rally to a higher and better heroism.

Your proclamations thrill the popular heart. The time has arrived which will test the patriotism of the home-staying people—those who have not yet borne arms or shared the hardships of the war. Have they those public virtues—patience, fortitude, courage, self-abnegations, living and vital, which alone can make them equal to the emergency? I trust and believe they have; and if they have, then the tide of battle, under the blessing of God, will soon turn in our favour.[2]

Jefferson Davis, who was always appreciative of the least kindness, was deeply touched by Johnson's warm expression of confidence. Heretofore, he had had no particular reason to look upon the Georgian as a friend. And now, out of a clear sky, as if sensing his present intense need for moral support, when too much was being demanded of him, Johnson had assured him that he could still "thrill the popular heart" and had given him hope that the home-staying people could meet the trials confronting them.

In that same climactic week in which the President persuaded General Lee to retain command, he received a long letter from Mary Stamps at Fincastle, Virginia, beginning, "My beloved Uncle." She had been seriously ill with some undiagnosed disease, which caused swelling and made breathing painful. Letters had come to her from numerous comrades of her husband, describing his death place at Gettysburg, "a soft spot in a wheatfield under a medium-sized oak," and relaying loving farewell messages to her and the children. "I wish very much, dear, gentle, sympathizing Uncle," Mary wrote, "that you could read them." Captain Isaac had said to his Lieutenant that he "had rather die on the battlefield in defense of his wife and children and country than to live and see it subjugated." "He then asked," Mary continued, "how the battle went, and when they told him that he was

---

[2] This letter from Johnson, which has not been printed before, is in the large collection of letters to Davis at Duke University.

dying in the greatest victory of the war, (for then they believed so) he exclaimed, 'Thank God! I die contented.' "

Jefferson Davis read on, noting details of his nephew's end and communing with Mary in her grief. He recalled how, strangely, she had said on July 3 that her husband was trying to send her some word. "Uncle, did I not tell you," she asked, "that if I could only hear it, there were messages for me? I knew it and I have them, and my soul is yearning and famishing still for some word that might have escaped all their memories."

"Were it not, my dear Uncle," she continued, "that I knew you wanted to hear all about 'the dear boy' it would be sufficient apology to say that it comforts me to write to you about it—I often wish during the day that night would come when, the company all gone, I might see my dear Uncle's face and live over part of Isaac's life in tender recollection. As day after day passes with no more to do for him and no more to hear, I find myself bowing before the reality of my lonely lot.

"Dear Uncle, you will forgive me for leaning, along with my country and as a part of it, upon your great heart. It is not that I would oppress it, but that it rests me. Yours can lean only upon its God, and through Him, our common Father, I hope to repay a part of your tenderness to me."

Jefferson Davis read that last paragraph over again. He was profoundly moved. Mary, young as she was, seemed to be saying in prose something unsayable, as good poetry does. "Forgive me for leaning, along with my country . . . upon your great heart . . . it rests me." And, spontaneously, she had, as it were, turned a mystical light on his aloneness: "Yours can lean only upon its God."

Mary's perceptive understanding strangely comforted him, and brought her spiritually very close. Though as a widow Mary Stamps was to have many ardent suitors, she never gave her devotion to any man except her husband and her husband's uncle.

CHAPTER XXXVI

SEPTEMBER SHADOWS AND
A VICTORY

IN SEPTEMBER, affairs were going badly for the Confederacy. On the sixth, word reached President Davis that Fort Wagner, on Morris Island in South Carolina, had been lost, and that Charleston was in serious danger. The authorities in Mobile were expecting an attack by General Banks. Congressman E. S. Dargan wrote that Alabama was "almost exhausted and the people were fast losing hope of independence." Governor Vance disobeyed orders to burn cotton in the vicinity of enemy forces, and demanded more troops to guard certain points in North Carolina. The Raleigh *Standard* had been treasonably exciting the people to resistance against the Confederate Government and even urging co-operation with the enemy.[1]

In Georgia, Vice-President Stephens was craftily fostering dissatisfaction with the Administration. The blustering Toombs, who had resigned from the Army, was running for the Senate, eager to defy Davis in Richmond. Governor Brown was reported to "lie awake o'nights thinking up projects to embarrass the President." "What would they have," cried the historian Eckenrode, decades later, "those critics of a man who sought to save his country in the only possible way?"

Relations with England worsened. In August, President Davis had had Benjamin write officially to Mason that, in light of the recent Parliamentary debates, he was convinced that England would not recognize the Confederacy and that Mason might consider his mission at an end and leave London. But in a private letter, sent under separate cover, Benjamin told him to use his discretion in carrying out the order. In the third week of September, Mason informed Lord Russell

[1] An infuriated mob finally wrecked the *Standard* office in September.

that he was terminating his mission. He left London with some sadness, because he had made many warm friends there. He went to Paris, where Slidell, in contrast to Mason's reception by the British Cabinet, had been receiving flattering attention from the Emperor and Empress and France's foremost ministers.

Not only had Britain failed to recognize the Confederacy or receive its commissioner officially, but, as a neutral, England's concessions of belligerent rights to the North had been greater than to the South. Northern money was being lavishly spent for British woolens as well as war material; and England needed American wheat. The angry Richmond *Whig* accused Great Britain of wishing to see the two sections virtually destroy each other before peace was made, "thus relieving her of a powerful rival, of whom she lived in continual dread."

The South was especially indignant just then about the British consuls. Since the Confederacy was not recognized as a nation, these officials, in effect, were accredited to President Lincoln. After the spring of 1863, the resentment against the consuls had been growing more intense. Two had recently been expelled, and when England announced that British conscripts could not fight in the Confederate Army, a public clamor arose to send all the consuls away. President Davis had withstood this pressure in an effort to keep relations with England as friendly as possible, but by the end of September, he was ready to agree with his Secretary of State that the British consuls should go.

An unexpected and climactic difficulty arose in England over the ironclad rams being built by the Lairds at Birkenhead. Bulloch had successfully transferred the ownership of the Laird rams to the French Bravay Company, which made new contracts with the Lairds to complete the ships for them as agents of the Pasha of Egypt. While it was ostensibly a bona fide sale, the United States was convinced the rams were to be resold to the Confederacy as soon as they put to sea.[2]

On September 1, Lord Russell wrote the protesting United States Minister that his Government could not in any way interfere with these ships. Adams was so deeply affected that he lamented in his

[2] In the late spring of 1863, contracts had been signed for the construction of four wooden cruisers at Bordeaux and Nantes. On June 18, when Slidell was conferring with the Emperor, he also begged permission to have some ironclads built. Though in the fall of 1862 Napoleon had suggested that the Confederates build ironclads in France, he now became cautious. But, acting on Napoleon's former invitation, Bulloch had already closed a secret contract with the firm of Arman to construct two ironclads in France.

diary, "The prospect is dark for poor America." To Russell, however, he sent a stiff dispatch, beginning: "At this moment, when one of the ironclad vessels is on the point of departure from this kingdom on its hostile errand against the United States." He said he would consider it as a first step toward the bombardment of New York and Boston and Portland, and toward breaking the Union's blockade. He added a telling line that became famous: "It would be superfluous in me to point out to your lordship that this is war."

While in 1862 the British Cabinet had upheld the right to sell an unarmed vessel like the *Alabama,* regardless of its destination, it now reversed its stand. For Seward had darkly threatened that the launching in England of a Confederate war vessel might involve a war, "which would endanger Canada" and expose British commerce to United States raiders. He had shrewdly added, "and break up the war profits reaped by England." These war profits were now bringing renewed prosperity to Britain.

Russell, somewhat staggered by the threat of annexing Canada, announced that the Laird vessels would be prevented from leaving Liverpool on a trial trip until satisfactory evidence could be given as to their ultimate destination. So, to the frustration of Bulloch, Secretary of the Navy Mallory, and President Davis, the ironclads were "detained." Mallory, however, told the President that since the rams were privately owned, he felt reasonably assured that through legal procedure they would ultimately be released. But Davis was doubtful.

Because of waste and confusion among numerous purchasing agents abroad, the President, on September 18, ordered C. J. McRae in Paris to assume the duty of supervising all the Confederacy's monetary matters in Europe. Every contract would now go through McRae's hands, and all department agents would be instructed to report to him. It was a wise action; McRae turned out to be as able and provident as Davis had deemed he would.

On that same September 18, the President accepted the resignation of his tall, genial Attorney General, Thomas Hill Watts, who had been elected Governor of Alabama in late August "without any canvass or scramble for office." Though some Administration enemies claimed he had resigned because he disliked Davis, his relations with the President had always been most cordial.[3] Watts was an excellent choice as

---

[3] Watts stayed on in office until October 1. His service in wartime is ably presented by Rembert W. Patrick in *Jefferson Davis and His Cabinet.* President Davis waited until the end of the year to fill the post, and then selected George Davis, another onetime Whig, from troublesome North Carolina.

Governor to calm unrest in Alabama, and would really be more useful there than in Richmond. Though a Whig and pro-Union before 1861, he was now vehemently opposed to any "reconstruction" with the States dominated by Mr. Lincoln. "If I had the power," he declared extravagantly after his election in September, "I would build a wall of fire between Yankeedom and the Confederate States, there to burn for ages, as a monument to the folly, wickedness and vandalism" of the radical North. He was to pay enthusiastic tribute to Davis in speeches in Alabama in October and November, declaring him "the right man for the right place," and one whose ability to administer the Government was not surpassed by any other man. He said that after close association with the President since March of 1862, he had a far higher appreciation of his virtues than when he had entered the Cabinet.

In the late summer, as prices in the Confederacy soared to absurd heights, a group in Enterprise, Mississippi, attempted to form societies of citizens throughout the South to engage in selling and buying only at reduced prices. In thanking one of the founders of the so-called "Confederate Society" for his efforts, the President wrote feelingly on September 17: "The passion for speculation has become a gigantic evil. It has . . . seduced citizens of all classes from a determined prosecution of the war to a sordid effort to make money. It destroys enthusiasm and weakens public confidence. It injures the efficiency of every measure which demands the zealous co-operation of the people in repelling the enemy, and threatens to bring upon us every calamity which can befall free men struggling for independence."

In thanking the writer for the comforting tone of his patriotic letter, Davis summed up his own ordeal and casually identified one of the chief causes of the Confederacy's ultimate failure: "It is a relief to receive such a communication at this time when I am burdened by the complaining and despondent letters of many who have stood all the day idle and now blame anybody but themselves for reverses which have come and dangers which threaten."

A warm letter from his boyhood friend Howell Hinds echoed what Davis had written the "Confederate Society" in Enterprise. Howell, as a little boy, had been the companion of seven-year-old Jefferson for hundreds of miles on pony back to St. Thomas's School in Kentucky. Now on his Mississippi plantation, he was recuperating from a wound and on parole, waiting to hear of his exchange.

"You have been one of the best abused men in the Confederacy," he told his old friend, "and it is what you had a right to expect from non-combatant croakers and speculators—a race of men who have done more to injure our cause than all else. I hope to see them exterminated; at least they should not be allowed to live in this country. They have been the cause of thousands of good men leaving their posts and going home to look after their families for fear of their being in destitution in consequence of starvation prices."

Howell Hinds was so right, Davis reflected. Speculators and extortioners were the cause of thousands of desertions, and they deserved hanging more than the deserters who worried about their loved ones.

The military situation in the West was approaching another serious climax. Because of reinforcements from the Army of Tennessee sent to Johnston, who made no use of them, Bragg had been too weak to attack the Federals. In fact, during the last days of the Vicksburg siege, Rosecrans had flanked Bragg in his Tullahoma position and caused him to fall back to Chattanooga on July 7. President Davis had had the peril of Bragg's army to add to his anxieties in that grueling first week of July. But Bragg had held on to Chattanooga until Rosecrans was sufficiently reinforced to push him out. Extricating his army from a perilous position, on September 9, Bragg had made a skillful retreat across the Tennessee border to Chickamauga Creek in Georgia. That same day, the Confederate garrison at Cumberland Gap capitulated. The next day, the Southern forces relinquished Little Rock, Arkansas.

In mid-September, when it seemed that Rosecrans was set to swoop down on Bragg's Army of Tennessee, the President appealed to Lee to transfer part of the Army of Northern Virginia to aid Bragg. Lee agreed to send Longstreet and his entire corps, including E. P. Alexander and his artillery unit. Longstreet was eager to go, to make a name for himself apart from Lee; the widespread censure for his lateness at Gettysburg still rankled.

Davis now called in Brigadier General A. R. Lawton, who had been acting as Quartermaster General since Colonel Abram Myers' removal. He explained that Longstreet's 11,000 men had to be sent all the way from the Rapidan to the shadow of Lookout Mountain. Everything, he said, turned on the question of transportation and supply, and had to be decided and performed with telegraphic haste. Lawton, who had served under Stonewall Jackson, was to make a quick, searching study and say exactly when Longstreet's corps could be delivered in the vicinity of Chickamauga. The President turned the matter over entirely to his new Quartermaster General, who agreed that speed was all-important, and made his calculations.

The first detachment from the Rapidan region arrived in Richmond the day after the interview. With excitement, the townsfolk watched detachment after detachment pass through the city and fill every available train. Longstreet's first troops, under Hood, joined Bragg about the hour the Federals fired the first gun. Hood arrived with his horse ready to leap from the train and an arm still in a sling from the wound at Gettysburg. Considering the sorry state of the tracks and rolling stock, the achievement in moving so many men with such celerity and delivering them at the psychological moment was a remarkable feat.

"Never before," wrote General Moxley Sorrel, "were so many troops moved over such worn-out railways. Never before were such crazy cars—passenger, mail, coal, box, platform, all and every sort, wobbling on the jumping scrap-iron—used for hauling soldiers. But we got there." Making use of sixteen different railroads, and traveling almost nine hundred miles, the troops went by way of Petersburg to Wilmington, on the Atlantic Coast, and thence west to Atlanta and Ringgold, near the battlefield.[4] Davis now felt he had found the right man for Quartermaster General in Lawton. His aides recalled the President's perfect timing of Joseph Johnston's departure to join Beauregard at First Manassas.

On September 19, the rival armies clashed along the Chickamauga. The Confederates fought with irresistible fury. In a daring charge, Hood was so severely wounded that, to save his life, his leg was amputated on the battlefield. The hard day's battle ended in a wild rout of Federal forces. Stanton's Assistant Secretary of War, Charles Dana, who was on the scene as an observer, was swept back into Chattanooga by the "panic-stricken rabble," along with Generals Rosecrans, Thomas L. Crittenden, Alexander McCook, and Philip H. Sheridan. He began his wailing dispatch to Stanton: "Chickamauga is as fatal a name in our history as Bull Run." Longstreet, who had arrived with his last troops after dark on the nineteenth, aroused Bragg from sleep before midnight. In an hour's conference, Bragg changed some plan of the next day's battle and gave Longstreet command of the left. He also

---

[4] Alexander's artillerymen, however, leaving Petersburg on the seventeenth, did not arrive at Ringgold, the terminus near Chickamauga, until the twenty-fifth, five days after the battle was over.

handed him a map to study, for Longstreet was utterly unfamiliar with the region. The next day, despite confusions of orders, costly delays, recriminations, and disappointments, the Confederates finally drove the last bluecoat back into Chattanooga. Longstreet was principally responsible for making the second day's battle decisive.

One imperturbable Union officer, however, had held long enough to make his fame: Major General George H. Thomas, a Virginian, and the only Southerner of importance who fought in the Federal Army.[5] The first day, Thomas doggedly maintained Snodgrass Hill against the Confederate assaults, and won from a newspaper the epithet "Rock of Chickamauga." Next day, Thomas retired into Chattanooga, where Rosecrans and the Federal forces were shortly cut off with scant provisions.

Altogether, it was one of the Confederacy's most brilliant, if most sanguinary, victories, won by sheer valor, and in spite of inexcusable delays. Jefferson Davis had reason to feel gratified and to be grateful to Bragg. It was the Confederacy's first real success since Stonewall Jackson's death in May.

"The effect of this great victory will be electrical," wrote Jones at the War Office. "The whole South will be filled again with patriotic fervor, and in the North there will be a corresponding depression. . . . Surely the Government of the United States must see the impossibility of subjugating the Southern people, spread over such a vast extent of territory. . . ."

The elated South, as well as the President, expectantly awaited still more thrilling news announcing the destruction or surrender of the Union forces.

But Bragg did not follow up his victory, and this failure was to be severely criticized as a flaw in his generalship. Forrest and some of the others were champing to press on while the Federals were demoralized. Forrest had climbed a tree on Missionary Ridge, and, with a captured pair of Yankee field glasses, made sweeping observations. He rushed a penciled note by way of Polk to Bragg: "The enemy trains are leaving, going around the point of Lookout Mountain. . . . I think they are evacuating as hard as they can go. . . . I think we ought to press forward as rapidly as possible."

Thirty-three years later, Longstreet wrote that it was "that dispatch which fixed the fate of the Confederacy." The Commanding General

[5] Thomas's family never forgave him for fighting against the South. His sisters kept his portrait turned to the wall.

considered that if the enemy was evacuating Chattanooga, that strategic town might be occupied without further bloodshed. He did not know that Forrest was partially mistaken. At the time, Bragg, nervously exhausted, contended that he lacked supplies and that his men were "too fought out" to pursue immediately. His losses in killed and wounded were appalling: some 2,000 dead and 14,000 hurt. The fighting Hood was near death, and Bragg's Surgeon General, Ben Hardin Helm, Mrs. Lincoln's brother-in-law, was dead. The sluggish Chickamauga ran pink with diluted blood. Battle-hardened veterans were nauseated at beholding beneath a hospital's windows a pile of human arms and legs stacked like cordwood, "twenty feet long and twelve feet high."

Bragg had no reserves to replace his weary troops. Nearly half of his army consisted of reinforcements received shortly before or during the battle. Longstreet's forces had come "without a wagon or an artillery horse," and almost a third of the Confederate artillery horses on the field had been lost. Alexander and his batteries were still en route. Pursuit was difficult because the retreating Federals had destroyed bridges. Jefferson Davis took all these factors under consideration in weighing Bragg's merits and demerits.

After a two-day breather, Bragg moved up and invested the town, which the enemy had not evacuated, as Forrest had anticipated. In the meantime, he began reckoning the errors of his lieutenants. He blamed several Generals for not making the battle more decisive. Upbraiding officers right and left, he put Polk and Hindman under arrest and sent them to Atlanta. D. H. Hill was bitingly censured. Hill had been ordered to attack at dawn. At five, a courier, dispatched by Polk to urge haste, had returned with the disconcerting news that he could not even find Hill. Finally, Bragg himself had dashed to seek him, found him in his tent, and demanded to know why he was not in battle. Hill replied coolly that he was still issuing breakfast rations, and could not move "for an hour or more." Bragg, all but exploding with anger, laid the chief blame on Hill's superior, Polk. The first day's attack, which should have been made at dawn, had been delayed until almost eleven.

For the time, Bragg seemed more interested in disciplining subordinates than in finishing off the enemy. In truth, some of his positive orders had been disobeyed and his plan of battle deranged by officers' mistakes. On the other hand, they claimed that his orders had been confusing and contradictory.

Along with detailed reports of the victory, the President received the disconcerting dispatch concerning the arrest of General Polk. Davis, who had been fond of Polk since their West Point days, knew how much the fighting Bishop was loved by his men. In an effort to stop any disrupting court-martial, he telegraphed Bragg: "From the statement of the case I think it was unfortunate that the evil resulting from delay had not been pointed out to the Lt. Genl. to prevent its recurrence, and confidence preserved by abstaining from further action. It is now believed to be better that the order in his case should be countermanded." Privately, Davis let Polk know that he considered Bragg's summary action "a great blunder."

On the twenty-ninth, Bragg made a formidable enemy of Forrest by temporarily assigning all the cavalry in the Army of Tennessee to General Joseph Wheeler, a diminutive Alabamian of terrific energy. Forrest had fought his way to within thirty miles of Knoxville, and was halfway back to Chattanooga when the order reached him. In furious indignation, he relinquished most of his horsemen to Wheeler, galloped to headquarters, tongue-lashed Bragg, and reputedly threatened to kill him if their paths again crossed. Then he took leave to visit his wife in La Grange.[6]

During the days following, Davis learned that the friction between Bragg and his lieutenants was becoming alarming. A petition to oust Bragg as Commander, supposedly sparked by D. H. Hill, came to the Executive's desk. In answering a letter from Bragg complaining of the numerous failures of his subordinates to carry out his orders, the President framed a careful reply. "I can well appreciate," he said, "the disappointment resulting from the delays and disobediences of orders to which you refer, but I sincerely regret the consequences." But he virtually commanded that Lieutenant General Polk be released from arrest, and reminded Bragg that controversy might entail further harm. "To change the commander involves the necessity of an investigation with all the crimination and recrimination to be thus produced."

Then he wrote frankly and somewhat sternly: "The opposition to you both in the army and out of it has been a public calamity in so far that it impairs your capacity for usefulness, and I had hoped the great victory which you have recently achieved would tend to harmonize

[6] On October 3, Wheeler made a spectacular raid on a Union supply train of eight hundred "six-mule-wagons" that extended ten miles. He burned the loaded wagons, killed the mules, and brought away prisoners.

the army." He pointed out that to expose the many errors and faults that occurred in any battle "diminishes the credit due, impairs the public confidence, undermines the morale of the Army, and works evil to the cause for which brave men have died, and for which others have the same sacrifice to make."

Suggesting the wiser course of letting unhappy matters drop, he said, "It not infrequently happens that in a state of excitement one believes himself impelled to do that which a calm observer would regard differently. I fervently pray that you may judge correctly, as I am well assured you will act purely for the public welfare."

While Bragg took the President's reproaches and advice in good part, the situation between him and his officers became so explosive that Davis considered going to Chattanooga to try to restore harmony. When Longstreet wrote that "with such a commander as Bragg nothing but the hand of God can save us," Davis ordered a private train to be made ready.

Though it was impolitic, the President invited the disconsolate Pemberton to accompany him and his staff, in the hope of finding the General a new command with the Army of Tennessee. The President's party left Richmond on October 6. Going by way of Augusta, they reached Atlanta the night of the eighth. At the station they were met by the smirking Governor Brown, who, desiring the President's support for re-election, exuded cordiality when he presented Davis to the people. Now accompanying the Presidential party were Generals Longstreet and Breckinridge and Howell Cobb as well as Pemberton. As the train passed Marietta on its way to Bragg's nearby headquarters, Jefferson Davis "was greeted by loud cheers."

At Bragg's headquarters on Missionary Ridge, the President listened attentively and impartially while the black-browed Commander unburdened himself of his resentments and laid heavy condemnation on subordinates. Davis could see that Bragg was justified in feeling that some officers had caused losses by not carrying out his orders, and his understanding of men's frailties made him tolerant of Bragg's inability to win men. He put the General in a conciliatory mood, and at the end of the conference Bragg offered to resign. But Davis was faced with the difficulty of finding another officer capable of commanding the army. Though he had failed to follow up, Bragg had won a heartening victory at Chickamauga; and rarely in the annals of war had a victorious general been removed.

The President called Longstreet, Hill, Buckner, and Cheatham, who had been temporarily given Polk's command, to meet him at Bragg's headquarters. He asked for their views on the military condition and future operations. As Davis later wrote, "after a discussion of various programmes, mingled with retrospective remarks on the battle of Chickamauga," he inquired if there were any other suggestions. Then Longstreet unexpectedly announced that he thought the Commanding General "could be of greater service elsewhere than at the head of the Army of Tennessee." An ominous silence followed. The President inquired how the others felt. In general, they sustained Longstreet's opinion.[7] It was a painfully embarrassing experience for them all.

Surly D. H. Hill was peculiarly severe in his criticism of his fellow North Carolinian. On the thirteenth, while at headquarters, the President received a formal application in writing from Bragg asking that Hill be removed from his command. Realizing that there was no reconciliation possible between these two extremely difficult personalities, Davis replied officially and tactfully: "Regretting that the expectations which induced the assignment of that gallant officer to this army have not been realized you are authorized to relieve Lt. Genl. D. H. Hill from further duty with your command." The President asked Hill to return to duty in his own state of North Carolina. Hill was indignant at the outcome, and thereafter had little liking for Davis.

Because of earlier dissatisfaction felt by Bragg's officers, the President had twice before considered removing him, but Joseph Johnston had objected and praised his achievements so highly that Davis had given up the idea. If he had had the right general for the top command, Davis might have removed Bragg now. His old friend Leonidas Polk was too ponderous for such a job. Forrest had a certain genius as a cavalry officer, but his training was not for the highest command; besides, he had a sulphurous temper and was deficient in education. Hood was daring and loved by his men, but he had just had a leg amputated. While Longstreet was undoubtedly a tough fighter, he had been an important cause of Lee's failure at Gettysburg. Hardee was an admirable, able man, whom the President liked and trusted, but Hardee did not want large responsibility. Beauregard had his hands full protecting Charleston from the Federal ironclads and Fort Wag-

---

[7] The above version, by Davis, written a few weeks after the conference, is an endorsement on the back of a letter concerning Cheatham's command. The letter is in the possession of Stanley Horn of Nashville. Longstreet, who is notoriously unreliable, indicates in his book, written in 1896, seven years after Davis's death, that the President "made known the object of the call, and asked each General in turn their opinion of the Commanding General."

ner, which had recently fallen into enemy hands. As the President had written his brother Joseph in May, he had compelling need of a great general in the West. If only Albert Sidney Johnston were alive!

Many who agreed with Davis in thinking Bragg an abler soldier than others then available believed that he should be ousted as a matter of policy because the public condemned him.[8] Though Davis had often written to various Generals that success depended in great measure on public opinion, he could never bring himself to be unjust to a victorious officer to please the populace and boost his own popularity. And he knew that both Lee and Beauregard, the other two field officers, besides Joe Johnston, who ranked him, were friendly to Bragg.

In the end, for want of a better alternative, Davis decided to leave Bragg in command. He made his decision known on the thirteenth.

The next day, the President addressed the soldiers, "a fine-looking lot—strong, lean, long-bodied fighters." After praising them for "the glorious victory on the field of Chickamauga," he pointed out that the hopes of the Confederate cause now depended largely on them. He stressed "devotion, sacrifice, and harmony." Speaking largely for the benefit of Bragg's discontented lieutenants, for Bragg himself, and for the distant Joseph E. Johnston, he said significantly:

When the war shall have ended, the highest meed of praise will be due to him who has claimed the less for himself in proportion to the service he has rendered. The bitterest self-reproach which may hereafter haunt the memory of anyone will be to him who has allowed selfish aspiration to prevail over a desire for the public good.

Then he touched on a concept that held within itself the power to wreck the Confederacy: "He who sows the seeds of discontent and distrust prepares for a harvest of slaughter and defeat." It was a negative thing that Davis had to combat more than ever in a variety of instances, political, civil, military. The warning might have served well as a handwriting-on-the-wall motto in the tents of disgruntled officers and over the desks of those politicians and editors whose jabs at the Administration put doubts in the minds of the soldiers and their folks back home.

The President closed his brief address with a comprehensive ex-

---

[8] As a contrary opinion, in a brochure by A. S. Abrams called *President Davis and His Administration,* published in Atlanta in 1864, the author declared: "The President never displayed greater ability and firmness than when he refused to relieve General Bragg from command; for not only are the military abilities of General Bragg appreciated by a large majority of his army, and the people, but by General Johnston—a military authority, we think, of some importance" (p. 7).

hortation: "To zeal you have added gallantry; to gallantry, energy; to energy, fortitude. Crown these with harmony, due subordination, and cheerful support of lawful authority that the measure of your duty may be full."

Jefferson Davis stayed at headquarters for three more days, inspecting the fortified positions, reviewing troops, offering advice, and pouring oil on troubled waters. Then he began trying to settle some of the differences by reorganization. He quashed the charges against Polk, and decided to give him Hardee's command in Mississippi and to give Hardee Polk's corps in the Army of Tennessee. Since the fuming Forrest absolutely refused to serve further under Bragg, the President courteously invited the cavalryman to meet him in Montgomery some days thereafter to confer about a new command. Davis had no intention of losing the peculiarly valuable services of Bedford Forrest. But when he asked if General Pemberton would be acceptable to the soldiers as a corps commander, he learned that he definitely would not be.

Militarily, the President saw that the Confederate situation at Chattanooga was good. On inspections, he noted that Bragg had made excellent disposition of his forces on the heights and in the valley surrounding the town. The Union forces were ringed from Lookout Mountain on the west to Missionary Ridge on the east. The Federals commanded only the difficult terrain north of the Tennessee River. Bragg held all the good roads south of the town. Except for one hazardous, winding, sixty-mile mountain detour from Bridgeport, there was no way of getting a crate of food to the pocketed Federals. Starvation into submission was the core of Bragg's strategy, and it seemed entirely practicable. As Bragg himself saw it, his strategic dispositions, faithfully sustained, would insure the enemy's surrender or speedy evacuation for want of food and forage. "Possessed of the shortest road to his depot and the one by which reinforcements must reach him," he wrote later, "we held him at our mercy, and his destruction was only a question of time." So it seemed. But the end was to be quite different.

CHAPTER XXXVII

DISASTER FOLLOWS HIGH
EXPECTATIONS

ON OCTOBER 13, while Jefferson Davis was still at Bragg's headquarters, the exciting and portentous Ohio elections took place. In the
gubernatorial race, the worried Union party maintained that a vote
for Vallandigham was a vote for Davis. The New York *Tribune* of
October 3 had declared that the people of England, as well as those
of both loyal and disloyal states, felt that the fate of the Union
depended on Ohio's election returns of the second Tuesday in October.
The Ohio Democrats claimed that their cause was that of civil liberty,
that they opposed the despotism of Mr. Lincoln, that they were ac-
tivated by the spirit of their candidate, who stood for freedom of
speech and press.

After Gettysburg, even according to a partisan like Rhodes, Mr.
Lincoln had "assumed the power of a dictator." The Boston *Courier*
quoted Joel Parker, prominent Professor in the Harvard Law School,
as asking the public, "Do you not perceive that the President is not
only a monarch, but that his is an absolute, irresponsible uncontrollable government; a perfect military despotism?"

Jefferson Davis had heard the story, continually reiterated, that
Seward boasted to Lord Lyons that he could ring a bell on his right
hand and order the arrest of any citizen of Ohio; he could ring a bell
on his left hand and cause the imprisonment of a citizen of New York,
and no power on earth except that of the President could release them.
"Can the Queen of England do so much?" he inquired blandly. While
the story was never authenticated, Davis thought it sounded like his
former friend. If Seward did not actually say just that much to the
British Minister, it was well known that both he and Stanton brought

about arrests by mere telegrams. And now the banished Vallandigham, in Canada, was forced to conduct his campaign on foreign soil. Davis, knowing what a stimulus to peace a Democratic victory in Ohio would be, was keenly eager to hear the result.

More than 185,000 persons voted for the exiled candidate and a bid for peace. But by a majority of 61,920, the Ohioans voted Republican and for war's continuance. Davis took some comfort in the fact that such a goodly proportion of Ohioans had expressed a desire for peace. And New Jersey, by ballot, definitely denounced the Republican Administration.

Lincoln had astutely deferred a fresh call for troops until after the Ohio election. Four days later, on October 17, 1863, he asked for 300,-000 fresh volunteers "for three years or the war, but no more than three years." The United States Government, the states, the counties, and "other political divisions" were lavishly liberal with inducements of bounty.[1] Davis reflected ruefully on the bare Confederate Treasury, which could afford no bounty and only eleven paper dollars a month for a Southern soldier. How eager "those people" were to conquer the South!

Shut up in Chattanooga, the bluecoats were soon getting a taste of what Pemberton's men had endured in Vicksburg. They were cut to half-rations, then to quarter-rations. As hungry soldiers managed to steal from the meager three ears of corn a day allotted the horses, the famished beasts, in their misery, chewed up saplings and gnawed wagons into uselessness. Eventually, more than 10,000 horses and mules died. Charles Dana was writing Stanton that it was not possible to hold out another week without a new line of supplies. The alarmed Federal Government held heated midnight arguments about the means of relief.

When President Davis left for Selma on October 17, Bragg and his officers seemed full of confidence, though mutual admiration could hardly be said to prevail. But Davis warned Bragg against letting the Federals bring in heavy reinforcements. He "must not allow time to Mr. Lincoln," else he would lose the great opportunity of beating Rosecrans. Hooker, with 12,000 men, had some time since been sent West to help break the investiture of Chattanooga, and he was now

---

[1] In an advertisement of the New York County Volunteer Committee in the New York *Tribune*, *World*, and *Times* of February 13, 1864, bounties of $677 for new recruits and $777 for veterans were offered.

encamped at Bridgeport, Alabama, seeking a reasonable way to reach Chattanooga. Also on October 17, Secretary of War Stanton, in great perturbation, met General Grant in Indianapolis, and they traveled together to Louisville formulating plans.

A few days later, Davis learned that General Grant had been put in charge of a newly created military Division of Mississippi, which included top command of the Federal armies of Tennessee, Ohio, and Cumberland—in fact, everything west of the Alleghenies except Banks's forces in Louisiana. Rosecrans was removed from command, and George Thomas, who had been Bragg's lieutenant at Buena Vista, replaced him. Thomas declared laconically that he would hold Chattanooga until starved. Grant began planning furiously to draw troops and top officers from all over the land and to get food and supplies into Chattanooga.

When the Confederate President arrived in Selma, he "was welcomed by the citizens en masse." In addressing the crowd from his hotel balcony, he said that if the nonconscripts would gather their guns, go to the rescue and relieve regular soldiers from guarding various points, the enemy at Chattanooga would be dealt a blow from which he might not recover. A little more sacrifice upon the part of the people, he urged, "and spring would see the invader driven from our borders." The President visited the cannon factory and other manufactories of Selma, and then went by way of Demopolis to Meridian.

In Mississippi, the President received a letter from Varina that both cheered him and saddened him. She said their children talked of him constantly and that when little Joe came into their bedroom in the morning, he peeped into every corner looking for his father.

"I have been engaged in a woeful billing since you left," she wrote, "house cleaning, sewing, mending . . . organization of our winter forces." Then, as if against her will, negative emotions bubbled to the top, and she cried out, "Dear husband, I do hate the battle of life so, and am not sure eternity would not be more charming to me if we laid still, instead of progressing—the 'wild desire to know' has gone out of me." Those friends and foes who saw Varina only in her buoyant or aggressive moods little dreamed how often her husband had to cheer his wife's spirits.

At Lauderdale Springs, near Meridian, the President visited Joseph and Eliza. His gentle sister-in-law was dying in a delapidated makeshift house. Eliza had seemingly summoned her ebbing strength to have one more glimpse of "Brother Jeff," whom she had loved tenderly since the day she first saw him. The Episcopal Bishop of Mississippi, William Green, came to give her last communion.

From Lise, his great-niece, the President got melancholy details of their refugee existence. The family had escaped from Jackson just before Sherman again took over the town on July 16. For three weeks, her old grandfather had traveled on, encumbered by some sixty of his "people." A few of the Negroes had stayed behind to take their chances with the Yankees, but the others had followed Marse Joe, looking to him for food and protection. Occasionally, the wanderers had found an abandoned cabin to shelter the older members of the party, "while the rest camped in the wildwoods."

The stock had become so exhausted, Lise said, that they had to have a long rest; so the Davis tents had been pitched on the west bank of the Tombigbee River in Choctaw County, Alabama, where there was pasturage. Joseph and Eliza had found rude board at a little farmhouse, and the rest of the white party lived in a deserted three-room cabin. Mr. Cox and Eliza's nephew, Joe Nicholson, had returned to Fleetwood to see what could be salvaged for use. But the enemy had burned the house and persuaded one of the trusted female servants, who had been left behind to look after things, to reveal where the best silver and some jewelry had been buried. After three weeks in Choctaw County, Joseph had moved up to Lauderdale Springs, a kind of rural health resort, with an officers' hospital nearby. The abler Negroes were hired out to the hospital, and the family took possession of the old house in which they now were.

The disruptions and hardships of the last months had sealed Eliza's fate; she had scarcely left her bed since arriving at Lauderdale Springs. The bafflement and distress of Joseph at not being able to furnish his wife with a more comfortable deathbed gave Jefferson inexpressible pain. The sorrow of his own great helplessness struck him forcibly. In the fall of Joseph, who had been one of the state's richest planters and most honored citizens, the President saw in microcosm the South's degradation if the North won the last battle. It grieved him immeasurably that he could do nothing to help his beloved relatives except speak words of comfort. Saddened and unquiet, Jefferson said his good-bys and left for Meridian on his way to Mobile.

In Meridian, on October 23, Davis sent the official telegrams that changed the respective positions of Polk and Hardee. That same night, General Grant arrived in Chattanooga, "wet, dirty, and well," according to Dana, but on crutches, the result of a fall he had had in New Orleans. He had had a terrible journey over sixty miles of execrable mountain roads, which he found "strewn with the debris of broken wagons and the carcasses of thousands of starved mules and horses."

While the Confederate President was en route to Mobile, Eliza passed away. Her body was placed in a friend's vault until the day came when she could be removed to the family graveyard at Hurricane.[2]

After inspecting the defenses of Mobile, the President reviewed the troops on Government Street. According to the Mobile *Daily Tribune* of Sunday, October 25, his countenance and his warm salutations to officers showed his gratification. As the whole cortege was about to move off, a voice proposed "Three cheers for our President!" Shout on shout rent the air and "was gathered up by each company along the whole line." Civilians joined lustily in the "most hearty welcome."

The crowd followed the President to the Battle House Hotel where he was "accorded a serenade." Then he made an impromptu speech. He complimented the valor and good conduct of the troops. He urged the people to constant effort. "Those who remain at home not less than those in arms," he said, "have duties to perform. There is no sphere wherein something may not be done by everyone. Everyone can rid himself completely of the self, of narrow interests. The men using opportunities given by the war to make fortunes," he declared, "will be detested by their posterity."

The paper praised the President's remarkably clear enunciation. "Although speaking without the slightest apparent effort, his words penetrated far down the street and were distinctly heard by most of the vast crowd gathered on the occasion."

Leaving Mobile's citizens and soldiers in an animated state of mind, Davis proceeded to Montgomery, where he had requested Forrest to meet him. He granted the cavalry officer's request to transfer from Bragg's command to the North Mississippi, and recommended him for a major generalship. But Davis had no available army to give the doughty fighter, who would have to scrape up most of his own forces.

Forrest traveled with the President from Montgomery to Atlanta,

---

[2] A few days after Eliza's death, Lise and her grandfather returned to Hinds County hoping to recover some of Joseph's property. They found only desolation. Every box of Jefferson Davis's valuable books and papers hidden in a loft on Mr. Cox's place had been discovered by Federal soldiers, who had carried off what books and letters they wanted and burned the rest. One of the house servants, however, had managed to save Lise's much-loved set of Audubon's *Birds and Beasts of North America*.

and had full opportunity to express his grievances and to dilate on his hopes. He asked for certain sections of his old organization, amounting to about three hundred men, to form a nucleus for the new command. When they reached Atlanta, Davis wrote Bragg to give Forrest what he wanted.

In Atlanta, on the twenty-ninth, as the President prepared for the last stage of his trip—Macon, Savannah and Charleston—he wrote two other letters to Bragg. In one, he again urged harmonious cooperation and forbearance in personal antipathies. In the other, he expressed regret that the rains had interfered with projected offensive operations. "It is reported that the enemy are crossing at Bridgeport," he wrote. "If so, it may give you the opportunity to beat the detachment moving up to reinforce Rosecrans, as was contemplated." Again he nudged Bragg: "The period most favorable for actual operations is rapidly passing away, and the consideration of supplies presses upon you the necessity to recover as much as you can of the country before you."

In one last warning plea, in answer to some telegraphed complaints from Bragg, Davis said:

"The removal of officers of high rank or important changes in organization usually work evil, if done in the presence of the enemy. My recollections of my military life do not enable me to regard as necessary that there should be kind personal relations between officers to secure their effective cooperation in all that is official, and the present surely much more than any circumstances within my experience should lift men above all personal considerations and devote them wholly to their country's cause.

"With this hope, which I prayerfully trust may be realized, I prefer to postpone the consideration of any further removal of general officers from their commands, and relying upon the self-sacrificing spirit which you have so often exhibited, must leave you to combat the difficulties arising from the disappointment or the discontent of officers by such gentle means as may turn them aside."

What more could a Commander in Chief have said to soften a burredged personality? As General Morris Schaff later wrote, it is difficult to see how rebuke could have been made less offensive or appeal more impressive.

After his efforts to create harmony among Bragg's squabbling officers, some of whom were now charging each other with misconduct, the President braced himself to rally the public spirit at Savannah and at Charleston, where General Beauregard and Robert Rhett vied for first place as his chief detractor.

Just before he boarded the train for Macon, Davis wrote a last hopeful and inspiriting note to General Hardee, who was one of the few officers he addressed without an honorific:

My dear Hardee:

I regret very much not having seen you before leaving. . . . The information from the army at Chattanooga painfully impresses me with the fact that there is a want there of that harmony, among the highest officers, which is essential to success. I rely greatly upon you for the restoration of a proper feeling, and know that you will realize the comparative insignificance of personal considerations when weighed against the duty of imparting to the Army all the efficiency of which it is capable.

With my earnest prayers for your welfare, I am

Very truly your friend

Jeffn. Davis

At Macon, from the balcony of the Lanier Hotel, the President addressed a "wildly enthusiastic crowd." Savannah responded to his appearance with an exuberant torchlight procession. But this display of patriotic good will pleased him no more than a gracious letter from Bragg saying: "General Forrest's requests are all granted and he has left for his new field, apparently well satisfied." Davis was relieved. While he was in the West, Bragg had certainly striven to be co-operative. Perhaps all would yet be well.

In her diary on that Hallowe'en night of Davis's arrival, Josephine Clay Habersham recorded meeting him.

I was writing to Joseph Clay [her brother with Bragg] when Neyle [her husband] came in, said he had seen the President, and I had better go to the Masonic Hall to the "Shaking of hands." We did so—were much pleased with the affability of the President. He has a good, mild, pleasant face . . . and, altogether, looks like a President of our struggling country *should* look—care worn and thoughtful, and firm, and quiet.

On November 1, in Savannah, the President heard from Bragg that Longstreet had failed to check Grant in opening a new line of communication to relieve the besieged Federals. Five days after Grant arrived in Chattanooga, he boldly secured communication by setting pontoon bridges across the Tennessee. Longstreet, who had charge of holding the route against the Federals, was unsuccessful in defeating Grant's maneuver. At nearby Wauhatchie in the last week in October, a bungling of orders caused the Confederate attack to end in fail-

ure. Longstreet's planning was bad and his execution worse. Jealousy
between two of his brigadiers, Albert Jenkins and Evander Law,
caused trouble. The Union wagon mules, excited by the midnight
fighting, broke loose and stampeded toward the Confederates, "trace
chains rattling and whipple-trees snapping over the stumps of trees."
The Southerners retired in confusion. Longstreet admitted that the
failure was due to "an oversight" of his. Stanley Horn more accurately
charged him with "culpable carelessness."

Bragg was sour with condemnation. Davis telegraphed him: "The
result is a bitter disappointment, as my expectations were sanguine
that the enemy, by throwing across the Tennessee his force at Bridgeport, had insured the success of the operations suggested by General
Longstreet, and confided to his execution. Such disobedience of orders
and disastrous failure as you describe cannot be consistently overlooked. I suppose you have received the explanation due the Government and I shall be pleased if one satisfactory has been given." Davis
had fully expected Bragg and Longstreet to prevent Grant from bringing in supplies. Now he dispatched Colonel Chesnut to Bragg's camp
to inform him of the whole situation.

Longstreet, having failed, did not want to serve longer in proximity
to Bragg. So Bragg sent him and his force up to Knoxville to destroy
Burnside. It was not bad strategy, for Grant was disturbed, fearing
that Knoxville and the control of East Tennessee might fall to the
Confederates. But while Grant was consolidating, and gathering 60,-
000 troops to meet Bragg, the latter reduced his own force by almost
one-third. To make sure of Longstreet's success, Bragg sent Alexander
with his artillery and Wheeler with his cavalry. In the meantime,
Bragg's position on Missionary Ridge seemed impregnable.

At one o'clock on the afternoon of November 2, when his private
train was approaching Charleston, Jefferson Davis heard the booming
salute fired in his honor. When the train stopped at the platform, it
was boarded by several dignitaries. The President stood up to be
greeted by General Beauregard, Colonel Jordan, his aide, and Colonel
Rhett in the lead. Davis wondered how the visit would turn out when
the first three hands raised to salute him belonged to three enemies.
Did it mean some change of heart or was it merely official formality?
Beauregard rode beside the President in the first carriage of the procession that moved slowly to the city hall. According to the *Daily
Courier* of November 3, 1863, "The streets were thronged with people
anxious to get a look at the President. The men cheered and the ladies

waved their handkerchiefs." The President noted the festive flags on the façades of public buildings and private houses. From the city hall to the courthouse stretched garlands of laurel, from which depended a huge banner bespeaking "Welcome."

It was the first time Jefferson Davis had seen Charleston since 1851, when he had accompanied the remains of John C. Calhoun from Washington. Then he had been the most admired Southerner among the living, and South Carolina had helped to drape the mantle of her illustrious son about his shoulders. For the last two trying years, however, venomous antagonism to him had smeared the pages of the Charleston *Mercury*. Davis was not unmindful of his South Carolina enemies or that the man sitting beside him loved him no better than did Robert Rhett or Joseph E. Johnston. But outwardly he gave no indication that he knew he was not as well liked as when he had walked in Calhoun's funeral procession. With his beautiful smile and his gracious dignity, he charmed the crowds lining his way.

From the portico of the city hall, the President made an address. Although Charleston's coastal defenses had been under bombardment for weeks, he told the citizens reassuringly that he did not believe their seaport city would ever be taken. But if it should be otherwise, he trusted theirs would be "the glory he had desired for his county-town Vicksburg, and the whole left one mass of rubble. Look at New Orleans," he reminded them sadly. "Who possesses property there? It is only a question whether you will leave it a heap of ruins or a prey for Yankee spoils."

Glancing toward Beauregard, he said: "Let us trust to our Commanding General—to those having the charge and responsibilities of our affairs." Then he declared earnestly, "It is by united effort, by fraternal feeling, by harmonious cooperation, by casting away all personal consideration and looking forward with an eye devoted singly to the salvation of our country, that our success can be achieved." Finally, in this city of Robert Rhett, he aimed a direct blow at the croakers throughout the Confederacy. "He who would seek to drag down him who is struggling, if not a traitor, is first cousin to one." Then he charged significantly: "He who would attempt to promote his own personal ends; he who is not willing to take a musket and fight in the ranks, is not worthy of the Confederate liberty for which we are fighting."

After the applause, the President retired to the council chamber, "where a large number of officers, distinguished citizens, and their

ladies were presented to him." Then he was conducted to the home
of former Governor William Aiken, whose house guest he was. Aiken,
who had arranged a dinner party that evening for military and civil
leaders to meet the President, had been astounded to receive a curt
note of regret from Beauregard on October 31: "Candor requires me
to inform you that my relations with the President being strictly official, I cannot participate in any act of politeness which might make
him suppose otherwise."

Though the host was greatly embarrassed at this insult to the Chief
Executive, Davis did not let the General's rudeness spoil his enjoyment of Charlestonian hospitality. Mrs. Chesnut wrote in her journal
that he "had an enthusiastic reception, Beauregard, Rhetts, Jordan to
the contrary notwithstanding. Mr. Aiken's perfect old Carolina style
of living delighted him; those grey-haired darkies and their automatic
noiseless perfection of training."

While Davis had no intention of giving offense to Beauregard, the
General's proud emotions were roiled. He had been infuriated by the
President's address. Although Davis had said, "Let us trust to our
Commanding General," he had not eulogized him or mentioned him
by name, and Beauregard took it all as a grievous slight. Furthermore,
Beauregard may have regarded the President's allusion to detractors
as a personal slur. In a letter to Augusta Evans, the Mobile novelist,
the General bemoaned his hurt feelings. Davis, he charged melodra-
matically, "had done more than if he had thrust a fratricidal dagger
into my heart! he has *killed* my *enthusiasm* in our holy cause! . . .
May God forgive him—I fear I shall not have charity enough to pardon him."

After several pleasant days in Charleston, during which he inspected the defenses, Davis returned to Richmond on November 9 as
the season's first snow fell lightly. Jones noted in his diary that the
President had everywhere been "received with cheers. His austerity
and inflexibility have been relaxed, and he has made popular speeches
wherever he has gone. . . . The press, a portion rather, praises the
President for his carefulness in making a tour of the armies and forts
south of us; but as he retained Bragg in command, how soon the tune
would change if Bragg should meet with disaster!"

The words were prophetic, though Bragg at the moment seemed to
be holding well, and the Federals were worried. In an effort to force
the recall of Longstreet from his purposed assault on Burnside, Grant

had ordered Thomas on November 7 to attack the Confederate right. But Thomas reminded him that the horses were dead from starvation; he "could not move one artillery piece." So Grant was constrained to watch and wait until he had gathered the last detachment of 60,000 men and an abundance of supplies.

Davis was gratified to have a long, reassuring letter from Howell Cobb in Atlanta. The General had just returned from a visit to Bragg's army at Chattanooga and reported a better feeling among the officers for General Bragg, who was "regaining their confidence."

While the President was feeling happy that his Western trip had been fruitful, he got cataclysmic news from Secretary of the Navy Mallory. England had ordered "the seizure" of the ironclads being built at Birkenhead. The Confederacy's most potent weapons for winning independence had been snatched from her. If the ironclad rams had got to sea, they could most likely have broken the blockade at Wilmington and Charleston and the Gulf ports, and then have cut off sea communications of the North with New Orleans. The North had feared that Boston, New York, and Philadelphia would be put under contribution. Bulloch had had the dream, as he wrote Mallory on July 8, not only of "sweeping the blockading fleet from the sea front of every harbor," but "of ascending the Potomac and rendering Washington untenable." Now his splendid work abroad seemed to have come to nothing.

Depressed as Davis was with disappointment, he did not fail to note Seward's acute sagacity in handling the British Cabinet. But he had something like contempt for mighty England's acquiescence in Seward's demands when the press sentiment was so strongly pro-Confederate. While Mallory still had hope for the rams as long as their ownership remained in litigation, Davis knew that fear of losing Canada was potent in keeping England on the side of might.

One of Davis's first acts after his return was to have Custis Lee send Bragg a reminder of the kind he had sent numerous times to Johnston during the Vicksburg campaign. The President felt assured, Colonel Lee wrote, that General Bragg "would not allow the enemy to get up all his reinforcements before striking him, if it can be avoided." The President did not deem it necessary to call the General's attention "to the importance of doing whatever is to be done before the enemy can collect his forces, as the longer the time given him for this purpose, the greater will be the disparity in numbers between your and his troops."

But Bragg, believing his own position to be absolutely secure, let Sherman and his Western rowdies join the Army of the Cumberland and form a strong north and left wing.

While in the West, Davis had been kept informed about the situation in Virginia, where nothing of considerable consequence had happened. But he longed to talk with General Lee.

Lee and Meade had frequently changed their positions, but no significant battle had taken place on Virginia soil since Second Manassas. After Longstreet went to Chickamauga, Meade had advanced, and Lee had withdrawn south of the Rapidan. After Hooker went west with two Union corps to help Rosecrans, Lee had made a flanking maneuver and swung northwest over the Rapidan. Meade backed quickly away from Culpeper, and, on October 14, reached Centreville, while Lee halted close to the hallowed fields of Manassas. They were in just about the relative positions of the opponents in July, 1861. President Lincoln was said to be in a melancholy state of frustration.

Meade later pushed Lee south again, and then the Southerners built comfortable huts for winter quarters near the Rappahannock. With only 44,000 men, Lee could make no frontal attack on the mighty Army of the Potomac. On the day of the President's return, a sudden mass attack on some of Lee's brigades at Rappahannock Bridge had resulted in the capture of 1,200 Confederates.

Now, since Lee could not come to Richmond, on November 21 the President went to his headquarters near Orange Court House. Davis found both officers and men still chagrined because they had been thrown back from the Rappahannock. "There was no earthly excuse for it," declared Colonel Walter Taylor of Lee's staff. And young Sandie Pendleton, son of the noted clergyman artillerist, said it was "absolutely sickening." The Confederates had had to give up their agreeable huts and were now building new ones south of the Rapidan.

But despite the humiliating setback, Davis found the morale excellent. For three days, he remained at Lee's headquarters, getting detailed accounts of operations in Virginia and talking over the Western situation. The General had hoped to have the President review the troops, but rains prevented. The inclement weather, however, gave the two old friends much time to sit about the fire and enjoy each other's company. Davis was relieved that Lee's rheumatism was much better. It had been so bad in October, Lee confessed, that for a brief time he had had "to be hauled about in a wagon." Davis promised to do all he could to supply deficiencies in blankets, overcoats, and shoes for the ill-equipped army.

Longstreet, the "old war horse," had been a disappointment to them both. After failing to prevent Grant from establishing a new supply line, he had failed to make any impression whatever on Burnside, entrenched at Knoxville. Davis could not help being apprehensive about Chattanooga, for Bragg had allowed Grant to bring in all the food he needed as well as thousands of reinforcements, the very thing he had warned him to prevent. On the twenty-third, the day before Davis left Orange Court House, Grant was beginning the Battle of Chattanooga.

When the President reached Richmond, he was handed an ominous dispatch from Bragg. "We have had a prolonged struggle for Lookout Mountain today and sustained considerable loss in one division." It was a prelude to unexpected disaster.

By the twenty-second, when the Federals had recovered from their near-starvation and were full of beans and freshly clothed, Grant was ready to strike. Bragg now faced an army of 60,000 that outnumbered him more than three to two, and boasted five top Union officers: Grant, Hooker, Thomas, Sherman, and Sheridan. The next day, Thomas occupied Orchard Knob, a rise on the plain before Missionary Ridge. At noon on November 24, in heavy mist and drizzle, Hooker began the Battle of Lookout Mountain, euphemistically called the "Battle Above the Clouds." Hooker's climbing Federals outnumbered the Confederates in the Lookout sector by five to one. On the morning of the twenty-fifth, the Stars and Stripes flew on Point Lookout. But Pat Cleburne gave Sherman such a rough time on the north end of Missionary Ridge that the aggressive Ohioan had to call for help.

Missionary Ridge, across the valley, rose a steep five hundred feet above its base, and looked impregnable. Thomas ordered his men to take the positions along the lower edges, which they did. Grant, standing with Thomas on Orchard Knob, was amazed to see the soldiers push beyond the place they were told to halt and then start clambering up the steep face. In anger, he demanded to know who gave such an order. Thomas said that he certainly had not. General Gordon Granger declared that the men had started up on their own without orders.

The flabbergasted Confederates, who had not believed such a feat possible and who might easily have stopped the winded Federals as they reached the crest, were seized with panic. They could plainly see the swarm of climbing bluecoats covering the side of the mountain and occasionally taking cover in the crevices; but because of the scalloped topography of the ridge, they could see but a few of their fellow defenders, and they were afraid to shoot for fear of killing their own men. As the Federals poured over the top, the Southerners broke and ran. The contagion of fear was partly caused by lack of inspiring leadership. Bragg was to write Davis—probably in gross exaggeration— that General Breckinridge, the commander of the left center, "was totally unfit for any duty from the 23rd to the 27th—during all our trials—from drunkenness."

The Confederate right, however, which Hardee and Cleburne commanded, vigorously repulsed Sherman's attacks and prevented the retreat of the left center from turning the whole into a Bull Run rout. But a gap two miles wide had been made in the Confederate line, and Bragg had no recourse but to withdraw. During the night, the disrupted army moved southeast down into Georgia.

Pat Cleburne, with 4,000 men, gallantly and furiously beat back the pursuing Hooker's Federals at the railroad junction of Ringgold, twenty miles southeast of Chattanooga, giving Bragg's artillery and wagon trains and the shamed infantry time to pass on down toward Dalton. Cleburne's angry men fought the last of the Federals off with musket butts, pistols, and rocks. Hooker did not press beyond Ringgold. Grant rushed Sherman off to Knoxville to the relief of Burnside.

The suddenness of the victory of Missionary Ridge was as incredible to the Union officers as to the Confederate. When General Granger reached the triumphant men after they had won the battle, he rode along the lines, jestingly declaring, "I am going to have you all courtmartialed. . . . You disobeyed orders." The men on impulse, with no order from officers, had heroically carried the day and won for Grant one of the decisive battles of the war.

In the night of the twenty-fifth, a dispatch from Bragg at Chickamauga Station announced the defeat to Richmond:

After several unsuccessful assaults on our lines today, the enemy carried the left center. . . . The whole left soon gave way in considerable disorder. The right maintained its ground, repelling every assault. I am withdrawing all to this point.

President Davis promptly telegraphed rallying advice:

You must draw forward all available troops, local defense and others as rapidly as possible. The reinforcements sent you by Johnston should be near at hand, and I hope Longstreet is in condition to cooperate. Your minute knowledge of the ground will enable you to choose advantageous positions.

Bragg's defeat was all but incomprehensible to Davis. In the three days' fight, comparatively little blood had been shed. Only 361 Confederates had been killed, while the victorious Federals had lost 752, a little over twice that number. The 2,170 wounded Confederates were less than half the 4,722 wounded enemy. Had there ever been such a signal setback with so small a loss of life?

Now Bragg prepared to set up winter quarters at Dalton, a little railway junction fifteen miles farther southeast. Fearing that the triumphant Union forces would fall upon the broken Army of Tennessee, the President telegraphed Bragg on the twenty-seventh: "Are you in communication with General Longstreet? Have the reinforcements from General Johnston arrived? . . . You need to concentrate rapidly."

The answers were negative. Johnston's reinforcements had not arrived. On the twenty-fourth, Longstreet had launched another desperate attack against Burnside's fortifications at Knoxville and been severely repulsed. Many said he did exactly what he had criticized Lee for doing at Gettysburg. Before he could attack again, word came ordering him to Dalton. Just as he was ready to start, communications were cut. Then Sherman's army barred his way.

As the President saw it, the Federal forces in Chattanooga should have been destroyed or forced by starvation to surrender. Neither had happened. In the Battle of Missionary Ridge, as Davis wrote, some of the Confederates "inexplicably abandoned positions of great strength, and by a disorderly retreat compelled the commander to withdraw the forces elsewhere successful." But Bragg had fought without one of his top Generals of Chickamauga to sustain him: Polk, D. H. Hill, Forrest, and Longstreet were all somewhere else, largely because of Bragg's unfortunate, prickly disposition. And Hood was incapacitated. As it turned out, perhaps it had been an error to send Longstreet to Knoxville. Yet if Longstreet had defeated Burnside, it would have proved ruinous to the Federal campaign in Tennessee.

The President knew that Bragg's services as a field commander were over. On November 29, Bragg spared the President the painful necessity of dismissing him by asking to be relieved of command. The request came at the end of a military dispatch to Adjutant General Cooper: "I deem it due to the cause and to myself to ask relief from command." Davis promptly acceded to his request, and ordered the command of the army to be given to General Hardee.

On December 1, in "shameful discomfiture," Bragg penciled a draft of a private letter to the President. "The disaster admits of no palliation, and is justly disparaging to me as a commander of trust. However, you may find upon full investigation that the fault is not entirely mine." Then, with wry humility, he added, "I fear we both erred in the conclusion for me to retain command here after the clamor raised against me." [3] He sent a fair copy to the President by a special aide.

In time, the War Department received a candid official report from Bragg, bespeaking profound chagrin.

No satisfactory excuse can possibly be given for the shameful conduct of the troops on the left in allowing their line to be penetrated. . . . Had all parts of our line been maintained with equal gallantry and persistence no enemy could have dislodged us. But one possible reason presents itself to my mind in explanation of the bad conduct of veteran troops who had never before failed in any duty assigned them, however difficult and hazardous. They had for two days confronted the enemy marshalling his immense forces in plain view, and exhibiting to their sight such a superiority of numbers as may have intimidated weakminded and untried soldiers; but our veterans had so often encountered similar hosts when the strength of position was against us, and with perfect success, that not a doubt crossed my mind.

The Confederates had held the commanding positions about Chattanooga for so many weeks that they had come to regard the Federals as their prisoners, and the conquering Grant, years later, remarked with a grin that Missionary Ridge *was* "impregnable."

The President was surprised to receive a strange second letter from a rejuvenated Bragg, quite different in tone from the one delivered by his aide. It surged with extravagant new hope. "The whole responsibility for the disaster rests on my humble head," Bragg said. "But we can redeem the past. Let us concentrate all our available men, unite them with this gallant little army, still full of zeal and burning to redeem its lost character and prestige, and with our greatest and best leader at its head, yourself if practicable, hurl the whole upon the enemy and crush him in his power and glory. I believe it practicable, and trust that I may be allowed to participate in the struggle."

The report of the men's renewed zeal was encouraging. But the President had no notion of letting Bragg remain with the Army of Tennessee, and, in his reply, he ignored the personal flattery. In time, he might need to utilize Bragg's organizational skill, but for the present it would be best for the unhappy General to fade into private life.

[3] The penciled draft is owned by the Western Reserve Historical Society, Cleveland, Ohio.

CHAPTER XXXVIII

THE CONFEDERACY'S
GREATEST NEED

ON NOVEMBER 30, 1863, Mrs. Chesnut pithily summed up the military situation: "Anxiety prevades. Lee is fighting Meade, Bragg is falling back before Grant, Longstreet—the soldiers call him Peter the Slow—sitting down before Knoxville." After another costly repulse, Longstreet gave up the siege of Knoxville on December 4, marched along the valley into upper East Tennessee, and settled in winter quarters in the most pro-Union section of the South. He was to wait there until April of 1864, when Lee needed his help against the Army of the Potomac under its new commander, Ulysses S. Grant.

To Jefferson Davis, the loss of Chattanooga, so important to Confederate communications, was almost as disappointing as the fall of Vicksburg and Lee's failure at Gettysburg. Men were Davis's greatest want. He had become increasingly worried about the South's crucial lack when the North began obstructing the exchange of prisoners after Gettysburg. The Southern need of manpower was all the more conspicuous in comparison with the North, because the Lincoln Administration was steadily drawing upon the able-bodied paupers of Europe to swell the Federal armies. The more Northerners showed reluctance to be drafted, the more energetically did Union agents abroad round up emigrants. By withholding Southern prisoners and increasing foreign mercenaries, the Union was hurting the South in its most vulnerable spot.

As early as the summer of 1862, the Federal Government had realized that only overwhelming numbers could conquer the South. On August 8, 1862, by way of acquiring more men to fight "the insurgents," Seward had sent to United States embassies and consulates a circular known in the Confederacy as "the notorious No. 19." Published throughout Europe, it glowingly advertised the land of opportunity to underpaid European laborers, and barely hinted at service in the Army. Enthusiastic William Dayton, Minister to France, had written Seward on September 9, 1862, that he felt sure widespread emigration would result from "the inducements there held out to laborers, and the temptation of our military service with its pay and bounties." Though the Union already possessed four times the white population of the South, Dayton believed that "the exhaustive character of the struggle" called for "some such remedy to supply the depletion."

Consul General John Bigelow in Paris took upon himself the responsibility of "this advertising for soldiers in disguise." All of Europe was covered, as he later confessed in his *Retrospections*[1]—with a network of emigration agencies to toll men to America. The offer of free land in the Homestead Act of 1862 was a glittering lure. Seward, in writing Bigelow, expressed the opinion that "the immigration of a large mass from Europe would decide it [the war]." And this foreign influx explained what Bigelow called "the mysterious repletion of our army during the four years of war."

President Davis had sent an Irish-born priest and a Catholic army officer to Ireland to try to dissuade men from emigrating to the United States in wartime. These Confederate emissaries had found Federal agents circulating vigorously among the depressed districts of Ireland, recruiting able-bodied men, ostensibly as laborers. In the fall of 1863, Davis noted that, in contrast to Horace Greeley's 1860 dictum expressing horror at the thought of pinning one part of the Union to the other with bayonets, the Lincoln Administration was beguiling all the aliens it could to assist in the South's pinning.[2]

The New York *Herald* estimated the number of European immigrants in the year 1863 as "almost 200,000" and believed that "at least 150,000 have joined the army." The Union's Admiral Porter was of the opinion that a majority of the 80,000 naval seamen were aliens. The London *Economist* estimated that up to 1864, some 100,000 from Catholic Southern Germany had been mustered into the Union Army.

[1] In this book, John Bigelow is frankly illuminating on the subject of emigration for service in the Federal Army, particularly on page 563 of Volume I.

[2] London's *Economist* of June 25, 1864, was to report that 30,000 Irishmen emigrated to the United States in 1861; 40,000 in 1862; 110,000 in 1863; and estimated that 100,000 of these enlisted in the Union Army. And the *Index* was to report that in 1864, 100,000 male emigrants to America sailed from Liverpool alone.

Other Central and South European countries contributed a share, and Dudley Mann declared that their jails and poorhouses were scoured by the North's recruiting agents. Dr. Frank Owsley, who made a detailed investigation of the matter, came to the conclusion, in *King Cotton Diplomacy*, that "between 400,000 and 500,000 mercenary troops . . . were by force of bounties and trickery induced into the American army."

In an effort to diminish the waxing odds against the Confederacy, Jefferson Davis turned to Pope Pius IX. If His Holiness were aware of what lay behind the alluring inducements to emigration, he might prevent many Catholics from swelling the Federal forces. The President commissioned Dudley Mann in Brussels to seek audience with the Pope. Pius had already publicly deplored the fratricidal war; as early as October 18, 1862, he had enjoined the Cardinals in New York and in New Orleans to use their influence to bring about peace.

On November 11, Mann presented a letter to the Papal Secretary, Cardinal Antonelli, together with a manifesto that the President had prepared for the Pope. Davis's early years in a Catholic boys' school in Kentucky had given him a profound respect for the Roman Catholic Church, and his regard shone through in the document. Addressing the Pope as "Very Venerable Sovereign Pontiff," Davis thanked him for his peace exhortation to the Catholic clergy in America. He assured His Holiness that the Southern people, "threatened even on their own hearths with the most cruel oppression and terrible carnage," fought "merely to resist devastation of our country . . . and to force them to let us live in peace under the protection of our own institutions and under our laws."

To Cardinal Antonelli, Mann disclosed the real purpose of his visit. "But for the European recruits received by the North," he said, "the Lincoln Administration, in all likelihood would have been compelled some time before to retire from the contest." The continued destruction of life, he suggested, was the result of beguiling Catholic Irishmen and South Germans from their homes "to take up arms against citizens who had never harmed or wronged them in the slightest degree."

Cardinal Antonelli spoke of Mann's "most Honorable President," and said that the sentiments expressed in his letter were "entirely in accordance with the disposition and character of the august head of the Catholic Church."

Two days later, Mann was received in private audience by the Pope, and presented President Davis's letter. According to Mann, Pius was "visibly moved by it." The diplomat suggested that the Pope try to stop the emigration of good Catholics, who on reaching America were immediately tempted by the high bounties to enter the Union Army, where they were "put in exposed positions to be slaughtered." Shocked by such revelations, the Pope promised to write a personal letter to President Davis "of such a character that it may be published for general perusal." On December 3, 1863, in his own handwriting, Pius IX addressed himself to "The Illustrious and Honorable Jefferson Davis, President of the Confederate States of America."

"It has been very gratifying to us to recognize, illustrious and honourable sir," said the Pope, "that you and your people are animated by the same desire for peace and tranquility." Of the North, he wrote: "Oh, that the other people also of the States and their rulers . . . would receive and embrace the counsels of peace and tranquility."

Mann felt that he had achieved a diplomatic coup in getting in writing the Pope's words "President of the Confederate States of America." To him, it was clearly the mark of recognition. While Davis was deeply grateful for the Pope's expressions of sympathy and great good will toward the Confederacy, he could not share Mann's rapture.

Secretary of State Benjamin, in reply to Mann, revealed his own estimate of the letter, as well as Mr. Davis's. "The President," he wrote, "has been much gratified at learning the cordial reception which you received from the Pope and the publication of the correspondence here has had a good effect." Then soberly he pointed out to Mann, "As a recognition of the Confederate States we cannot attach to it the same value that you do, a mere inferential recognition. . . . Nothing will end this war but the utter exhaustion of the belligerents, unless by the action of some of the leading powers of Europe in entering into formal relations with us the United States are made to perceive that we are in the eyes of the world a separate nation."

As it was to prove, while there was only a slight decrease in foreign enlistments because of the Pope's injunction against emigration, there might well have been a considerable increase if His Holiness had not intervened.

The President was now faced with a critical situation near at hand: Hardee did not want even the temporary command of the Army of Tennessee. Davis sent Preston Johnston posthaste to reason with him at

Dalton, not allowing Johnston time "to tell his wife good-by or to put a clean shirt in his travelling bag." A discouraging report came back: Hardee could not be persuaded to keep the command.

In his extremity, Davis telegraphed General Lee on December 6: "Can you go to Dalton, as heretofore explained?" Lee had recently been in Richmond, where the President had discussed with him the probable advisability of his taking command of the Tennessee army. "Can go if ordered," Lee replied. "Have written by mail."

The President eagerly awaited the detailed reply. "I can, if desired," the General wrote, "but of the expediency of the measure you can judge better than I can." He thought no good would be accomplished unless it was intended for him to take permanent command. He feared he would not receive cordial co-operation. And he felt that General Ewell was in too indifferent health to assume command of the Army of Northern Virginia. Then, with his sublime tact, Lee said: "I hope Your Excellency will not suppose that I am offering any obstacles to any measure you may think necessary. I only seek to give you the opportunity to form your opinion after a full consideration of the subject. I have not that confidence either in my strength or ability as could lead me of my own option to undertake the command in question."

Davis feared he would have to leave Lee where he was. But what was he to do for a successor to Bragg? His mind was racked with worry. He asked Lee to come to Richmond as soon as it was convenient.

As December 7, the day of Congress's convocation, approached, enemies of the President loaded their political guns with the pleasurable anticipation of deer hunters. Some did not disguise their vindictive intentions. On the night of December 4, Wigfall, calling on the Chesnuts, began his conversation "by wanting to hang Jeff Davis." He talked a lot of "virulent nonsense," Mrs. Chesnut wrote. But her husband managed him beautifully, and he calmed down to his "usual strong common sense."

The anti-Administration papers busied themselves sowing seeds of discontent. "Again," Mrs. Chesnut noted, "the *Examiner* publishes the story of Mr. Davis's cotton remaining unburned. This was settled last year. Mr. Davis's cotton was burnt, and all the world knows it; but the *Examiner* knows that the everlasting harping on this sort of thing must annoy Mr. Davis, so it persists." While the *Examiner*'s innuendoes and falsifications were galling to Davis, when Congress met, he had really staggering problems to face. "Gloom and unspoken despondency," Mrs. Chesnut wrote on the seventh, "hang like a pall everywhere."

In his address to Congress, which was read on the eighth, the President manifested no false cheer. He did not minimize the grave defeats at Gettysburg and Vicksburg. He explained Bragg's failure on Missionary Ridge by confessing that a division of the army had shown unwonted cowardice. He accused England of unfairness and of deception in a neutrality that gave every advantage to the United States. "The partiality of Her Majesty's Government," he said, "in favor of our enemies has been further evinced in the marked difference of its conduct on the subject of the purchase of supplies by the two belligerents." He held out no further hope of Britain's recognition, though he hinted that the Confederacy would not frown on France's establishment of Archduke Maximilian on a throne in Mexico.

Davis was strongly insistent that new conscript laws should bring into service those who had formerly sent substitutes. He explained that the want of laborers and of seamen seriously affected the operations of the Navy Department, though foundries and workshops had been improved for the construction of vessels at Richmond, Wilmington, Charleston, Savannah, Mobile, and Selma. "The skill, courage, and activity of our cruisers at sea," he said proudly, "cannot be too highly commended. They have inflicted heavy losses on the enemy without suffering a single disaster, and have seriously damaged the shipping interests of the United States by compelling their foreign commerce to seek the protection of neutral flags." He took some satisfaction from the success of various coast defenses from Norfolk and Charleston to Galveston.

The President urged Congress to take strong action to halt inflation, and recommended compulsory funding and a large tax action as a means of diminishing the currency.

In one department he could report that financial affairs were in excellent condition: for the last fiscal year, the Post Office had an excess on receipts amounting to $675,048.34.

In regard to prisoners of war, he spoke with both sadness and indignation: "I regret to inform you that the enemy has returned to the barbarous policy with which they inaugurated the war, and that the exchange of prisoners has been for some time suspended. In July last the fortune of war again favored the enemy, and they were enabled to exchange for duty the men previously delivered to them against those captured and paroled at Vicksburg and Port Hudson. The prisoners taken at Gettysburg, however, remained in their hands. . . . With a disregard of honorable obligations almost unexampled, the enemy did not hesitate, in addition to retaining the prisoners captured by them, to declare null the paroles given by the prisoners captured by us. . . . They have since openly insisted on treating the paroles given by their own soldiers as invalid, and those of our soldiers, given under precisely similar circumstances, as binding."

Pointing up the humane treatment the Confederates accorded captured Federals, Davis said, "By an indulgence, perhaps unprecedented, we have even allowed the prisoners in our hands to be supplied by their friends at home with comforts not enjoyed by the men who captured them in battle. In contrast to this treatment the most revolting inhumanity has characterized the conduct of the United States toward prisoners held by them. One prominent fact, which admits no denial or palliation, must suffice as a test. The officers of our Army, natives of southern and semi-tropical climates, and unprepared for the cold of a northern winter, have been conveyed for imprisonment during the rigors of the present season to the most northern and exposed situation that could be selected by the enemy. There, beyond the reach of comforts, and often even of news from home and family, exposed to the piercing cold of the northern lakes, they are held by men who cannot be ignorant of, even if they do not design, the probable result."

Toward the end of his message, he said, "The frontier of our country bears witness to the alacrity and efficiency with which the general orders of the enemy have been executed in the devastation of farms, the destruction of the agricultural implements, the burning of the houses, and the plunder of everything movable."

How differently had the Confederates behaved on Northern soil, he avowed. In pointing up the psychology of the North's attitude, he declared bitterly, "These considerations have been powerless to allay the unchristian hate of those who, long accustomed to draw large profits from a union with us, cannot control the rage excited by the conviction that they have by their own folly destroyed the richest sources of their prosperity. They refuse even to listen to proposals for the only peace possible between us. . . . We now know that the only reliable hope for peace is in the vigor of our resistance."

At the close, touching on a fact noted by the world at large, he said, "God has blessed us with success disproportionate to our means."

The next day, Henry Foote rose in the House of Representatives to denounce the Chief Executive. One of the gabbiest of Legislators, he declared he could not restrain himself in silence when his adopted state of Tennessee "was bleeding." He attributed Confederate disasters to the President, "who kept unworthy and incompetent men in command." The following day, Foote again belabored Jefferson Davis as the cause of the recent calamities, and included Commissary General Northrop in the indictment as "a monster" and "thoroughly incompetent." Davis was by now used to both Foote's and Wigfall's denunciations, but he regretted that their inimical tirades avouched disharmony to the enemy.

CHAPTER XXXIX

THE PRESIDENT RIDES ALONE—
UNDAUNTED

ON DECEMBER 10, after a pleasant luncheon party, as Mrs. Chesnut and Mrs. Lyons walked home with Mrs. Davis, they met Mr. Davis alone on horseback, without an aide. "Surely that is wrong," Mary Chesnut wrote anxiously. "It must be unsafe for him when there are so many traitors, not to speak of bribed Negroes. But Burton Harrison says he prefers to go alone, and there is none to gainsay him." Young as he was, Burton Harrison divined his Chief's profound desire now for solitude to work out not only questions of state but personal problems that could be solved only by what the President regarded as Grace.

The life of every man holds some need of the mystery of solitude and communion, and particularly that of a man placed in the glare of high public service. With a house full of exuberant young children, with a vivacious wife who had a rare talent for sprightly conversation, with messengers and emissaries and politicians streaming in and out, it was well-nigh impossible for Jefferson Davis to enjoy an hour of seclusion at home.

Dr. Minnegerode, his minister since the spring of 1861, also understood his need of being alone at times. For two years, the clergyman had been aware of "the struggle, the hope, the fears of Davis's inner life," and had sounded his heart, which he "opened to his pastor unreservedly." He had watched the President's "conquest of himself amidst the indignities he had to bear." "Of course he had his faults," wrote Minnegerode; "he would not have been human without them. But it was just in the conflict with his failings . . . that he was preserved from self-deception or spiritual pride." Those lonely rides were, in the Rector's opinion, "not only filled with anxious thoughts about his country and plans for the guidance and defense of his people," but often "the time of humble, prayerful intercourse with his Heavenly Father."

Jefferson Davis seems to have felt that in his most severe trials a spiritual power was sustaining him. Though since Gettysburg Mrs. Davis had not once heard her husband sing about the house, sometimes in the night she would hear him in the next room repeating old-fashioned country hymns.

Since Davis had had no vacation in the three years of his Presidency, he would have welcomed the respite of an ocean voyage. He had felt the healing balm of pathless water when he had gone to Havana after Sarah Knox's death, and again on the ocean voyage to Maine in the summer of 1855. Acutely responsive to the sea's clarification, he could easily subscribe to Keats' exhortation:

> O ye who have your eyeballs vext and tir'd
> Feast them upon the wildness of the sea.

But since he could not sail on salt water, on land he could best relax and listen for direction during a solitary horseback ride.

When he rode through Richmond in the December near-dusk, sitting his Arabian with consummate ease and grace, people would sometimes get the impression that he was plunged in sorrow. A few perceptive ones may have guessed that he was purging his consciousness of the day's annoyance or yesterday's grief, but only Minnegerode suspected that he was trying to give up a sense of self. To give up a sense of self, even for a saint, brings a kind of spiritual sorrow.

Ever since he returned from his Western trip, the President had been riding out in the late afternoons. But on the particular tenth of December that Mrs. Chesnut recorded her anxiety, he had uncommon problems on his mind. Because of the severe treatment of Southern prisoners in the icy Northern concentration camps, in which the men were not allowed sufficient clothing or blankets or even allowed visits from friends, the President with sad reluctance was about to decide that no more packages of comforts for Union prisoners could be permitted. His "humanity" and "chivalry" to the enemy had been so often derided by the press and the public that he could no longer refrain from making some token gesture at retaliation.

And having so many vindictive antagonists in the new Congress, he also was considering resigning. He was quite willing to relinquish his office, he had told Judge Lyons, but only if the Vice-President would also resign, for "he could never surrender the Government to one who would immediately surrender it to the enemy, as he was sure Mr. Stephens would." [1]

And on this December 10, Davis had to wrestle with a very special conflict within himself. Lee had arrived in Richmond that day to beg off from going West. Their old friend Leonidas Polk was urging Joseph E. Johnston for the command of the Army of Tennessee. Colonel Chesnut had just reported that, despite Vicksburg, Johnston would be a popular choice with both the Army and the people. The President seemed to confront the inevitable. Would he have to bend his will and give the command to a General in whom he had lost confidence and to a man who hated him? Whatever chanced, he would humbly try to rise above the discords of human experience.

On his return home about first dark, Mrs. Davis saw that her husband's square military shoulders were somewhat relaxed, and she knew that he had attained some inner quietude. So, though her heart was never at ease while he was out alone, she would not protest against his rides, but let him get a little peace—even at the risk of his life.

In Congress, Henry Foote was loud in championing General Johnston's cause. In a perverse effort to elevate Johnston and annoy the President, Foote reverted to the disputed Vicksburg campaign and introduced a resolution in the House calling for all official correspondence between the Government and Johnston for May, June, and July, 1863. Though Johnston was upset,[2] Davis was not at all displeased to have the facts brought into the open.

The irresponsible Foote then introduced a resolution that the President be requested to remove all commanders who did not possess the confidence of the Army and the populace. What a tangling disruption would have resulted if his proposal had been acted upon! Foote next pointedly demanded to know why General Johnston was not immediately appointed to command the Army of Tennessee; with unconscious irony, he shouted: "The country is tired of delay."

[1] In a letter to W. T. Walthall on July 31, 1878 (Rowland, Vol. VIII, p. 213), James Lyons wrote that the President had more than one conversation with him on the subject of resigning.

[2] When the correspondence was published in early February, 1864, the unhappy Johnston wrote his brother Beverly complainingly. He begged him to see several Senators to try to have *all* the material given out. He said, "I don't perceive that our cause will be benefitted by my being thought worse than I am." This letter of February 14, 1864, is among the J. E. Johnston papers in the Huntington Library.

His fellow Congressman from Tennessee, William G. Swann, rose to defend the Administration, and read into the record the explicit order given Johnston to assume full command in the West, and he quoted from Johnston's letters the extravagant praise of Bragg that had had much influence on the President's decision to retain the controversial General.

At a Cabinet meeting, Seddon, though confessing his disappointment at Johnston's "absence of enterprise," formally suggested that General Joe be given another chance with the command of the Army of Tennessee. Benjamin snorted with disapproval and disgust. He had an even lower opinion of Johnston's abilities now than he had had in 1861-62, and he spoke specifically of his early "tendencies to defensive strategy and a lack of knowledge of the environment."

The President agreed with Benjamin about Johnston's deficiencies in regard to offensive warfare, but what available General had the proper qualifications? Hardee, the best of the lot, simply would not have the place, and something had to be done immediately.

On the fifteenth, General Lee rode with the President to inspect the Richmond defenses, and that night he dined with the Davises. They must have discussed the matter of Johnston. How much weight Lee wielded in this case is not known. But, finally, when a majority of the Cabinet agreed on Johnston, "the President," as Seddon wrote, "after doubt and with misgiving to the end, chose him, and not as with exaltation on this score, but as the best on the whole to be obtained."

On December 16, President Davis telegraphed General Johnston: "You will turn over the immediate command of the Army of Mississippi to Lt. General Polk and proceed to Dalton and assume command of the Army of Tennessee." Never had he sent an order with less enthusiasm. Instead of being self-willed and uncompromising, as his enemies charged, Jefferson Davis, against his better judgment, had again yielded to Seddon and Lee, as well as to a large section of public opinion.

While Seddon gave Lee no specific credit for influencing the President, Mrs. Chesnut recorded with dramatic succinctness, "General Lee has done this." And Wigfall wrote Johnston: "You owe your appointment to Genl. Lee and doubtless will appreciate his kindness."

It must have been rasping to Joseph Johnston to learn that he owed his command to his magnanimous rival, of whom he was so jealous. But acid Lydia Johnston rejoiced that her husband's "punishment" was over, that his friends had "untied his hands." Johnston, piqued because Hardee had been Davis's first choice for the place, entrained for Atlanta on December 22, with still another chip on his sore shoulder.

On Sunday, December 20, General Gorgas noted in his diary: "Johnston doubtless has taken command of Bragg's army; unless Bragg remains as his Chief of Staff I do not hope good from the change." "Certainly," wrote Mrs. Chesnut on the twenty-first, "Jeff Davis did hate to put Joe Johnston at the head." Then, as other alternatives crossed her mind, she made a sharp comment: "Detached from General Lee, what a horrible failure, what a slow old humbug is Longstreet." Like a cry from the heart, she added: "Oh, for a day of Albert Sidney Johnston out West! And Stonewall could he come back to us here! ! !"

As Christmas grew near, the soldiers in Virginia who could get leave went to their homes or to Richmond for a little fun and frolic. The Davises received many who came to pay their respects, "some without arms, some without legs," and the ebullient Colonel Heros von Borcke without a voice. Because of a throat wound, he could only whistle. John Hood, affectionately known as "Sam," came with one leg missing and an arm virtually useless.

Everyone made a fuss over the tall Kentuckian turned Texan, who was still without an artificial leg; a very fine one, with duplicates, had been ordered from England. He was carried into houses by orderlies and set on drawing-room couches à la Madame Récamier, but covered with a light blanket to hide his disfigurement. Nothing was too good for Hood. Ladies cut up oranges for him, though oranges cost five dollars apiece. Mary Chesnut prepared rice puddings with her own hands; it was the dessert the hero craved above all others. Davis had already made him a Lieutenant General for gallantry at Chickamauga. Now when he attended services at St. Paul's, "Sam" leaned upon the President's arm.

On Christmas Day itself, the Davises were moderately quiet except for the children's racket. They had kinsfolk for dinner, and made it largely the children's day. There is no record of the President's Christmas menu. But at a Christmas Eve dinner at the John Prestons, where three Kentucky Generals were among the guests, Mrs. Chesnut dined on "oyster soup—*soup a la reine;* besides boiled mutton, ham, boned turkey, wild duck, partridge, plum pudding, sauterne, burgundy, sherry, and Madeira." So much for having connections with abundant South Carolina plantations and old wine cellars not yet depleted. Mary

Chesnut had not the faintest suspicion that within a year her own alliance with a great plantation could not prevent her reduction to a diet of cornpone and molasses.

While some officials entertained soldiers, others took the holiday as a complete rest. "Christmas," wrote General Gorgas, whose wife was ill, "was not a merry one to me, and I passed it very quietly, almost sadly, at home." "It is a sad, cold Christmas, and threatening snow," J. B. Jones recorded. "The children have a Christmas tree, but it is not burdened. Candy is held at $8 per pound. . . . I shall have no turkey today, but do not covet one. It is no time for feasting. . . . No merriment this Christmas. Occasionally an *exempt,* who has speculated, may be seen drunk. But a somber heaviness is in the countenances of men as well as in the sky above."

Except for his satisfaction in being surrounded by his family, Jefferson Davis felt that the Christmas of 1863 was the saddest he had known since 1835, when he had just lost his bride Sarah Knox.

The Lees, Davis reflected sympathetically, were having a mournful holiday season. The General had dutifully returned to his bare winter quarters to spend Christmas with his homesick men. Rooney was still imprisoned in damp Fortress Monroe. Charlotte, his lovely wife, was dying, and her husband was not permitted to visit her. On December 27, she died, and also one of her children the same day.

In a diary entry of December 29, apropos to the Confederacy's dark situation, Mrs. Chesnut quoted from a letter she had written Mrs. Davis in September. "There is another party, politicians and men with no stomach for fighting, who find it easier to cuss Jeff Davis and stay at home than to go to the front with a musket. They are the kind who came out almost as soon as they went into the war, dissatisfied with the way things were managed. Joe Johnston is their polar star, the redeemer!"

The President was relieved on December 30 when the Senate passed an act "to put an end to the exemption from military service of those who have heretofore furnished substitutes." Only two dissenting votes were cast; Wigfall was "strangely indisposed." The speculators were consternated. Many would have to leave their ill-gotten gains and shoulder a musket. Though the President might be excoriated by personal enemies, in the main he was still getting his way with Congress.

On the last morning of 1863, from his second-floor study, Jefferson Davis watched the rain pouring outside. Downstairs, Varina and several ladies busied themselves with preparations for the Presidential reception the next day.

At the end of the year, no one knew so well as the President that the fortunes of the Confederacy were at an appallingly low ebb. The South had lost much territory. Finances were in a state of collapse. The North, which had taken new hope after the Chattanooga victory, was receiving boatloads of immigrants to swell the Federal ranks. The Union blockade had tightened its strangle hold. The South needed everything: from pencils and calico to horseshoes and railroad engines. Faithful soldiers in winter camps were belly-pinched with hunger; many a heroic youth was without overcoat or shoes. The North was relentlessly enforcing its proclamation declaring all medicines contraband, so that the sufferings in camp and home were magnified.

In enemy land, General Grant was being hailed as the savior of the Union. But while Grant was being idolized, the realist himself recalled how hard he had had to fight for his victories; he would never forget how many months it had taken him to capture Vicksburg. Grant knew the war was far from over.

According to Secretary of the Navy Welles, Seward was now largely directing matters in Washington. While Lincoln undoubtedly adopted Seward's best policies, as President of the United States, he was far more sagacious and adroit than the public realized. In a shrewd gesture, to sow dissension and rupture the Confederacy, President Lincoln issued a proclamation promising full pardon to all Confederates who would take an oath of allegiance. He proposed to restore "loyal" governments in seceded states where a tenth of the voters of 1860 would take a prescribed oath.

Disaffection did break out. In Arkansas, secession talk rumbled. In Georgia and North Carolina, revolt against both impressment of supplies and conscription of men threatened. Discouragement and fear had entered the wrangling Congress like a devil's wedge. The malignant newspapers continued to try to undermine public confidence in the President.

When the midnight bells proclaimed the end of the Confederacy's painful year of 1863, Jefferson Davis had an incubus of burdensome thoughts to plague his hours of sleep. Instead of looking to some surcease of trouble in 1864, he faced amplified problems. But he still had faith that, despite the crying need of manpower, if the Southern people would support him for one more year, independence might be won.

Thoughtless critics then, and nine decades later, said that Davis's hope evinced his lack of a sense of reality. Regardless of denigrators, Jefferson Davis had a very sound sense of reality. Though the United States was growing stronger materially, he knew that the Northern peace party was also augmenting. In the coming presidential election year of 1864, if a Democrat were elected, the war might cease. Millions in the North were revolted by what some Union soldiers were doing to the South. Northern conscripts became more reluctant to serve; more substitutes were being paid to fight. Food in the South was sufficient if the people could be persuaded to relinquish it to impressment agents and if transportation troubles could be remedied. Even though railroads were in a precarious condition, they were still functioning, in their fashion. Wilmington was still a thriving port for blockade-runners. Texas, while cut off, was yet a part of the Confederacy, and flourishing. Tightly organized under Kirby Smith, that state was doing a tremendous business in cotton hauled by oxcart over the plains to the ports in exchange for supplies.

While England's blocking of the rams' sailing had been a severe blow to the Confederacy, the matter was not final. Napoleon was about to establish a monarchy in Mexico. It was not impracticable to expect some indirect help from France; for only by the Confederacy's independence could the French venture be sure of success. Besides, there was no reason to believe that the vessels being built in France might not be released in the coming year.

In the meantime, though the North was gathering a mighty army to crush Johnston in the West and a mightier one to force Lee off the road to Richmond, the Confederacy's only ally, lowly mud, had effectively closed combat operations on almost all fields.

Realizing completely the odds against him, Davis manifested no hint of giving up. He was convinced, if his people were not, that the Northern radicals meant only one thing: the humiliation of complete subjugation.

In an article in the October *Atlantic Monthly*, Charles Sumner, with cool arrogance, discussed how to treat the rebel states after their conquest. He advocated eleven military governors, "all receiving their authority from one source, ruling a population amounting to upward of nine millions. And this imperial dominion, indefinite in extent," he said, "will also be indefinite in duration . . . the whole region which they are called to sway will be a military empire, with all powers, executive, legislative, and even judicial, derived from one man in Washington." The principles of State Rights and the consent of the governed on which the United States was founded were summarily swept into the rubbish heap. Sumner himself freely admitted that "in undertaking to create military Governors of states, we reverse the policy of the Republic as solemnly declared by Jefferson, and subject the civil to the military authority."

Everything the Senator from Massachusetts said was anathema to Jefferson Davis, the strict constitutionalist. He would call up every man available to combat to the death the evil intentions of the Radical Republicans. The Confederate President was fighting for principle, the rights of states and individuals that had been inherent in the minds of the Founding Fathers. His spirit would not quail.

On January 1, 1864, Jefferson Davis woke to a morning bright with sun. Though there was an invigorating wind, it was not cold. His children were shouting with joy as they rushed in to get their father's New Year's kiss. With the change in the weather, the depressed Richmond mood suddenly shifted to one of determined gaiety.

A tremendous throng came to the President's reception. Mrs. Davis, still in mourning for her father, looked unusually handsome in black. Ladies wore their most elegant prewar frocks "with their finest diamonds." Colonel Ives and Colonel Browne received at the door, as gentlemen ushers, in full-dress regalia with sashes and swords. Colonel Chesnut, in civilian dress, stood attentively behind the sparkling Mrs. Davis and, having no real responsibility, greatly enjoyed himself, relishing the First Lady's *sotto voce* wit. The popular young L. Q. C. Lamar was there, just returned from Europe; his appointment as emissary to Russia had not been confirmed by the Senate, because the Czar, who trembled at revolutionaries, was not inclined to receive him. But at the Davises' he was lionized almost as much as General Hood.

The President received his guests with more than his usual urbanity; he was charming, and radiated cordiality. When old friends appeared in the line, he was "as warm and free as a boy" with them. Besides politicians, Mrs. Chesnut watched "the daredevils and the dandies come, the fellows who dance and fight with light heads; who take fire and famine, nakedness, mud, snow, frost, gunpowder and all, as it comes." And when he gave each soldier a firm handclasp, Davis, who admired young men's mettle, had appreciation in his eye, as if he held a hero's hand.

The guests left under the spell of the President's dauntless assurance, which seemed to say to his Southern enemies as well as to the radical North: "You have not half that power to do me harm as I have to be hurt."

When the party was over, the President's arm was stiff with the New Year's handshaking, and Mrs. Davis's hand was tender to the touch. Seeing that social contact meant so much to people, the President would try to please them by holding more receptions.

While many loyal Southerners on New Year's Day felt that the fate of the Confederacy had been unhappily sealed at Chattanooga, Davis reflected on his armies in the field, organized, ready to face 1864, however bloody. Again and again they had demonstrated how much they could do with so little. Though his spirit would often be fevered by tribulation, though he would be continually plagued by "fresh swarms of flies" and obstructed by Congress and even renounced by some of his friends, Jefferson Davis would keep his vision on principle. Because he was no self-deluder, he was to become more valiant; his behavior, the nobler. As Ohio's Landon Knight wrote, "Our admiration for the man vastly increases as we see him steering, wisely now, his foundering nation into that dark year 1864, destined to reveal to us a great man, growing greater, better and more lovable under the heavy accumulation of terrible misfortune." While in the immediate years to come, the President's fame would in no sense accord with his dessert, he could recall Lee's Biblical assurance, "But truth is mighty and will eventually prevail."

Acknowledgments
Sources and Notes on Sources
Index

ACKNOWLEDGMENTS

LET me first express my gratitude to Dr. O. C. Carmichael, recent President of the University of Alabama, for granting me an extensive leave of absence from professorial duties to write Volume II. I am deeply indebted to the Board of the David Warner Memorial Foundation, established by Mildred and Herbert Warner, for a grant that made it possible for me to retire for two and a half years to devote all my time to the biography; and I am especially grateful to Jack Warner, President of the Foundation and President of Gulf States Paper Corporation, and to Ernest G. Williams, member of the Board of Trustees of the University, for their stimulating interest in my project.

For the use of unpublished material I am profoundly grateful to Jefferson Davis's only living grandson, Jefferson Hayes-Davis, of Colorado Springs, who gave me exclusive right to make use of five large boxes of intimate family papers. Other direct descendants of Jefferson Davis who have been generous in their help are Mrs. Lucy Hayes Young, of Colorado, only living granddaughter, and Mrs. John W. Stewart, of Santa Barbara, California, eldest great-granddaughter. Among collateral relatives, I am especially indebted to Mrs. Anna Farrar Goldsborough of Newark, New York, who has written me voluminously on Davis family matters. Other great-grandnieces who have been graciously helpful are Mrs. Mary Lucy O'Kelley, of Pass Christian, and Mrs. Ralph Wood, of Biloxi, Mississippi; and Mrs. Crampton Harris of Birmingham. Isaac Farrar and Maude Ellen Farrar Kirkpatrick of New Orleans have given me access to valuable family letters inherited from their father, Stamps Farrar, great-nephew of President Davis. Mrs. Richard W. Graves, of Little Rock, great-granddaughter of Jefferson Davis, furnished me with a manuscript memoir of Margaret Howell, sister of Mrs. Jefferson Davis and "the young lady" of the Confederate White House.

I am grateful to Mrs. Jessie Palfrey Leake, granddaughter of General Josiah Gorgas, for the use of her ancestor's diary, and for unpublished letters of Jefferson Davis to both General and Mrs. Gorgas; to Francis H. Inge, for the gift of holograph letters from Admiral Buchanan, first Superintendent of the U.S. Naval Academy and first commander of the famous *Virginia-Merrimac*; to Dr. Emmet Kilpatrick, lifelong student of Jefferson Davis and the Confederacy, for a copy of his father's youthful war memoirs;

to Preston Haskell, for a copy of Colonel John Haskell's unpublished recollections of the war years.

Interested persons in twenty-three states have kindly sent me authentic material. I thank them all, though I cannot list all the names. However, I must express my especial gratitude to Dr. Allan Nevins for his uncommon generosity in letting me select from his private historical files many interesting Davis items which had escaped me, and for his further kindness in sending me other material. I am also uncommonly grateful to Dr. Archibald Henderson, distinguished biographer of Bernard Shaw, for original researches in sources hard to come by.

For hours of helpful talk and the exchange of letters, I am indebted to the late Frank Owsley, Professor of Southern History, University of Alabama; to Shelby Foote, author of *The Civil War*; to John W. Tilley, author of *Lincoln Takes Command* and *A Confederate Primer*; to Rucker Agee, founder of the Alabama Historical Association; to Dr. Holman Hamilton, Professor of History at the University of Kentucky; to J. Frederick Waring of Western Reserve Academy, Ohio; to Dr. Charles Summersell, Head of the History Department, University of Alabama. And I must repeat my expression of deep gratitude to the late Douglas Southall Freeman, who, before his untimely death, gave me most generous and helpful advice in his Richmond home and through correspondence.

For photostats of a large collection of holograph Davis letters inherited from his grandmother, Elizabeth Tillman Hooks, a foster daughter of the Davises, I am indebted to Matt Tom Green of New Orleans. To Lee Meriwether, ninety-six-year-old author and lawyer of St. Louis, who knew Jefferson Davis, I am indebted for two days of conferences, for personal reminiscences, for the use of his files, for out-of-print books.

For other letters from Jefferson Davis or his immediate family, I am indebted to Charles Abbot, Sr.; to the Reverend Mr. William Blackford; to Carl Haverlin, President of Broadcast Music. My special thanks to Mrs. H. E. Suits, of Kirkwood, Missouri, whose grandfather Judge Halyburton administered the oath to Jefferson Davis at his second inauguration, for a gift of holograph Davis letters and for photographs.

To Prewitt Semmes, Jr., of Michigan and California, I am very grateful for the gift of a first edition of Admiral Raphael Semmes's *Service Afloat* and for other material about his great-grandfather; and to Eva McSherry, of Greenbrier White Sulphur Springs, West Virginia, for the gift of a first edition of Jefferson Davis's two-volume *Rise and Fall of the Confederate Government*.

To Charles Dobbins, of Washington, D.C., I am indebted for the use of his complete files of three Montgomery newspapers for the period when Montgomery was the capital of the Confederacy; and to Monroe Cockrell, historical writer of Evanston, Illinois, I am grateful for a large map of the Vicksburg region and campaign.

To Senator Lister Hill of Alabama I am indebted for a color transparency of the portrait on the jacket and for the permission he secured from the

War Department for its use. My special thanks to Hilary Milton, who discovered the Davis portrait in the basement of the Pentagon, and who did special researches for me.

For assistance in research, I am grateful to Sarah Maude Leverty, of Richmond, Virginia; Thomas J. Rountree, of Southeastern Louisiana College; Iris Singh Wilkinson, native of India, for work at Duke University; and Ronald Giradeaux Crowe, of the University of Alabama.

For generous assistance in libraries and museums, I thank David C. Mearns, Chief, and Dr. C. P. Powell of the Manuscript Division of the Library of Congress; Dr. Dallas Irvine, of the National Archives, Washington; Robert W. Hill and Edward B. Morrison of the New York Public Library; India Thomas, Regent, and Eleanor Brockenbrough of the Confederate Museum, Richmond; Dora Pool of Confederate Memorial Hall, New Orleans; William Stanley Hoole, Director, and James Govan of the University of Alabama Library; John Cook Wyllie, Librarian of the University of Virginia; Francis L. Berkeley, Jr., Curator of Manuscripts of the University of Virginia; Mattie Russell of Duke University; James W. Patton of the University of North Carolina; Peter Brannon, Director of the Alabama State Archives of History; Ruth Rowell, Regent, First White House of the Confederacy, Montgomery; Marguerite Murphy, Regent, The Jefferson Davis Shrine, "Beauvoir," Biloxi, Mississippi; Dr. Chester Bradley, Curator of Jefferson Davis Casemate Museum at Fort Monroe, Virginia; Lucille Peacock of the Evans Memorial Library, Aberdeen, Mississippi.

I am grateful to Harriet Owsley for permission to quote from her husband's *King Cotton Diplomacy*; to Houghton Mifflin and Appleton-Century for quotations from their editions of Mary Boykin Chesnut's *A Diary from Dixie*, edited respectively by Ben Ames Williams and by Isabella D. Martin and Myra Lockett Avery; to John S. Tilley, author of *Lincoln Takes Command*; to William Stanley Hoole, editor, and Joseph C. Hayes, translator, of Justus Scheibert's *Der Bürgerkrieg in den Nordamerikanischen Staaten*, Number 9, in the Confederate Centennial Studies published at Tuscaloosa, Alabama.

For gifts of out-of-print books, I am grateful to Edward Jay, of Syracuse, New York; Mrs. John G. Lonsdale, of Hot Springs, Arkansas; Virginius Dabney, Editor of the Richmond *Times Dispatch*; Frank LaMotte, of Ponte Vedra, Florida; Mayor Walter Chandler, of Memphis, Tennessee; DeVane King Jones and Cecil Williams, of Tuscaloosa, and Anna Garber Webb, of Demopolis, Alabama.

For documentary material, letters, rare old newspapers, and photographs, I thank Brigadier General Donald Armstrong of Washington, D.C.; Dabney Lancaster, of Millboro Springs, Virginia, whose father and grandfather were fiscal advisors to the Confederate Government and personal friends of General Lee; Thomson King, Director of Maryland Academies of Sciences; Thomas M. Galey, of Owensboro, Kentucky; Thomas Waring, Editor of the Charleston *News and Courier*; Ralph McGill, Editor of the Atlanta *Constitution*; Walter Stauffer, of New Orleans, grandson of General Richard

Taylor; Mrs. Murray F. Wittichen, President General of the United Daughters of the Confederacy; Mrs. Elmer Deiss, Historian General, U.D.C.; Mrs. W. R. Shotwell, of Birdsboro, Pennsylvania; Ben W. Griffith, of Macon, Georgia; Dr. Thomas W. Martin, William Brantley, and Margaret Gage Bush, of Birmingham; Cyril Clemens, of St. Louis; Warren Jefferson Davis, of La Jolla, California; Mildred White Wells, of Lookout Mountain, Tennessee; Catherine O'Quinn, of New York; Jean Read, Virginia Bragg Tyson, and Judge Walter Jones, of Montgomery; Nicholas McGowin, Marshall Marriott, and E. J. Cleverdon, of Mobile; the Reverend Mr. Emmett Gribbin, Elizabeth Warner, Jean Shook, and Dean Paul Garner, of Tuscaloosa; J. S. Lyell, of Knoxville; Dr. H. Morton Mason, of Richmond; Frank E. Everett, Jr., of Vicksburg; Mrs. Percy Anderson, of Memphis; Nell Stephens Murfree, of Los Angeles.

I am much indebted to Frances Tillotson, great-grandniece of Major General John Porter McCown, C.S.A., and lifelong student of the War Between the States, for a critical reading of my manuscript. I thank John Temple Graves, widely known Southern columnist and lecturer, and his wife, Rose, for reading parts of the manuscript and offering helpful suggestions. My special gratitude to Dr. Johnstone Parr for preparing a bibliography of magazine articles of the war period and for gifts of out-of-print books, and to Jean Brown for diligent assistance in typing.

Others who have been of help in various ways are: Dr. Frank Rose, President of the University of Alabama; Dr. James H. Newman, Executive Vice-President; Dr. Harry Redman, Jr., of the Department of Romance Languages of the University of Alabama; Dr. Roland Abegg, Southeastern Louisiana College; Brigadier General James E. Morrisette, retired, and Major General Kelley Parsons, retired; Frank McCorkle Moody, President of the First National Bank of Tuscaloosa; Harry Mabry, newscaster of WBRC-TV, Birmingham; Lieutenant Colonel Forrest J. Pettigers, Chief of Legislative Liaison at the Pentagon; and the Reverend Mr. Churchill Gibson, of Fairfax, Virginia.

My warm thanks to Tom Green, Manager, for his countless courtesies while staying at Longfellow House, Pascagoula, Mississippi, where in a garden guest cottage overlooking the Gulf of Mexico I began Volume II at Christmas, 1955, and where I finished the book in 1959.

I am much indebted to Dr. Rembert W. Patrick, Head of the Department of History at the University of Florida and specialist in the period, for critical suggestions and for his careful reading of the galley proof; and to Shelby Foote, author of The Civil War and Shiloh, for the same most generous and painstaking service. To Naboth Hedin of West Dennis, Massachusetts, Swedish-born author and retired Director of the American-Swedish News Exchange, I am profoundly grateful for his critical reading of my manuscript, for editorial suggestions, and helpful queries.

Most of all, and equal to the sum of all other assistance, I thank my wife, Thérèse, for seven years of devoted labor in research, for her four typings of this manuscript, for critical appraisals, and unflagging patience and stimulation.

SOURCES AND
NOTES ON SOURCES

FOR the reader's ease and assurance, as in Volume I, I have made considerable use of "internal documentation," quoting my authority directly in the text. And because much of the material is controversial, I have felt constrained to employ some essential footnotes when the occasion seemed to demand them or to add pertinent information not justified in the text itself. The authorities mentioned in the body of the book will not always be repeated in the Sources. Because many readers find distracting the little numbers that point to sources in the back of a book, I have foregone them, as in *Jefferson Davis: American Patriot*.

At the conclusion of Volume III, a full bibliography will be listed: documents in manuscript, letters, monographs, newspapers, magazine articles, and books.

The material for Jefferson Davis's war years is far more voluminous than that of the period from his birth in 1808 to his inauguration as President of the Confederacy in February, 1861. Yet the same six paramount sources mentioned in Volume I are still of transcending value for *Jefferson Davis: Confederate President*: (1) the hitherto unpublished letters owned by his grandson Jefferson Hayes-Davis of Colorado Springs; (2) reminiscences of descendants and collateral relatives and holograph letters in their possession; (3) Mrs. Davis's two-volume *Memoir* of her husband; (4) Dunbar Rowland's ten-volume *Jefferson Davis: Constitutionalist*, a collection of letters by Davis and to him, together with many of his addresses; (5) the McElroy Collection in the New York Public Library, including the vast quantity of Walter Fleming papers; (6) Davis's own *The Rise and Fall of the Confederate Government* and his *Short History of the Confederate States*.

To the thirteen biographies of Jefferson Davis that preceded mine, listed chronologically in Volume I, and Eron Rowland's life of Mrs. Davis, must now be added Ishbel Ross's 1958 biography of the President's wife, *First Lady of the South*.

The series of books which have been indispensable in dealing with Davis's war years are the 128-volume *The War of the Rebellion, a Compilation of* the *Official Records of the Union and Confederate Armies* and the thirty-volume *Official Records of the Union and Confederate Navies*. Next in importance comes the monumental four-volume *Battles and Leaders,* edited by Robert Underwood Johnson and Clarence Clough Buel in 1887, with a new introduction by Dean Roy F. Nichols of the University of Pennsylvania in 1956. Frank Moore's eleven-volume *The Rebellion Record* has been frequently consulted, and so has James D. Richardson's *A Compilation of the Messages and Papers of the Confederacy* and *The Dictionary of American Biography.*

Senator John Daniel's *Life and Reminiscences of Jefferson Davis by Distinguished Men of His Times* and J. William Jones's *The Davis Memorial Volume,* have furnished me with much valuable information.

Among the outstanding general works on the subject and the period that I have found especially helpful are: James Ford Rhodes's *History of the United States,* Volumes III and IV; J. G. Randall's *The Civil War and Reconstruction;* E. Merton Coulter's *The Confederate States of America;* Frank Owsley's *King Cotton Diplomacy;* Rembert W. Patrick's *Jefferson Davis and His Cabinet;* and Edward Channing's *The War for Southern Independence,* Volume VI of his *History of the United States.*

Invaluable to my work are the holograph letters by Jefferson Davis in the Library of Congress, New York Public Library, Confederate Memorial Hall, New Orleans, Confederate Museum, Richmond, and in the libraries of the University of Virginia, the University of North Carolina, and Duke University. Peculiarly valuable are the Burton Harrison Papers in the Library of Congress; also useful are the Clement Clay Papers at Duke University and the Chesnut Papers at the University of North Carolina.

Diaries and journals of the period have proved of inestimable value. The two outstandingly helpful in providing intimate glimpses of Jefferson Davis in official and private life are the two-volume *A Rebel War Clerk's Diary* by John Beauchamp Jones and Mary Boykin Chesnut's *A Diary from Dixie.* Because Mrs. Chesnut was an unusually intelligent and perceptive woman, with clear-eyed judgment and refreshing wit, her diary is by all odds the best by any private citizen of the Confederacy. Other revealing memoirs by women are Mrs. Roger Pryor's *Reminiscences of Peace and War;* Virginia Clay-Clopton's *A Belle of the Fifties,* edited by Ada Sterling; Mrs. D. Giraud Wright's *A Southern Girl in '61;* and Constance Cary Harrison's *Recollections Grave and Gay.* Two books of reminiscences by T. C. De Leon which have furnished me sprightly material are *Four Years in Rebel Capitals* and *Belles, Beaux and Brains of the '60's.* Josiah Gorgas, Confederate Chief of Ordnance, kept a diary from 1857 to 1877, which has proved most serviceable; a portion of it has been edited by Frank Vandiver and published as *The Civil War Diary of General Josiah Gorgas.*

Easily the most illuminating of the books by men officially connected with the Confederate Government is John H. Reagan's *Memoirs.* Highly revealing is Gideon Welles's *Diary,* giving intimate glimpses of activities in Mr. Lincoln's Cabinet.

The prime reporting by a European correspondent appeared in the London *Times*. The correspondent, William R. Russell, also published *My Diary, North and South,* which is foremost in its field and which I have found richly contributive. Another revealing diary is that of Britain's Lieutenant Colonel Arthur James Lyon Fremantle, *Three Months in the Southern States, April-June, 1863.* A third most perceptive and entertaining journal is Catherine Cooper Hopley's *Life in the South: from the Commencement of the War, by a Blockaded British Subject.*

Among the notable reminiscences of Continental soldiers with the South are Heros von Borcke's *Memoirs of the Confederate War for Independence* (1866) and Captain Justus Scheibert's *Seven Months in the Rebel States During the North American War, 1863* (translated in 1958).

Unfortunately, no memoirs were left by the Confederacy's three great generals: Lee, Jackson, and Albert Sidney Johnston. But three ambitious generals, Longstreet, Beauregard, and Joseph E. Johnston, wrote controversial books about their parts in the conflict (Beauregard published his under the name of his friend Alfred Roman). Longstreet's vivid *Manassas to Appomattox* is almost as unreliable as it is readable.

Admiral Raphael Semmes's two-volume *Service Afloat* is one of the fascinating true adventure stories of the nineteenth century and also a splendid exposition of the Southern cause and rights.

James Dunwody Bulloch's *Secret Service of the Confederate States in Europe* is excellent for its information, as are Captain Robert E. Lee's *Recollections and Letters of General Robert E. Lee,* and *Lee's Dispatches,* edited by Douglas Southall Freeman and Grady McWhiney.

Among the best of the Confederate officers' reminiscences are General Richard Taylor's *Destruction and Reconstruction,* General John B. Gordon's *Reminiscences of the Civil War,* and General Jubal Anderson Early's *Autobiographical Sketch and Narrative of the War Between the States.* William Willis Blackford's *War Years With Jeb Stuart* is one of the bright books of its kind.

Of the biographies of Confederate Generals, Douglas Southall Freeman's *R. E. Lee* is indubitably foremost. Frank Vandiver is the American who has given the fullest and most scholarly life of Stonewall Jackson. Burke Davis has written most agreeable and admirable shorter biographies of both these pre-eminent soldiers, and of Jeb Stuart as well. *The Life of General Albert Sidney Johnston* by his son William Preston Johnston remains the best biography of that heroic personage. T. Harry Williams's biography of P. G. T. Beauregard seems the most accurate, if cutting, appraisal of the controversial Creole. *Another Kind of Valor* by G. E. Govan and J. W. Livingood presents a most kindly view of Joseph E. Johnston and may be read along with Bradley T. Johnson's *A Memoir of the Life and Service of J. E. Johnston.*

Rudolph von Abele's *Alexander H. Stephens* is by all odds the superior life of the Confederate Vice-President. Robert Douthat Meade's *Judah P. Benjamin* is the best biography of the much disputed Cabinet member. Lloyd

Lewis's *Sherman: Fighting Prophet* is one of the best-written biographies of this time. *The Personal Memoirs of Ulysses S. Grant*, edited by E. B. Long, has been frequently consulted. Warren W. Hassler's life of George Brinton McClellan should be read in connection with *McClellan's Own Story*.

I have made frequent use of Roy Basler's nine-volume compilation of Lincoln's *Collected Works*. *The Lincoln Papers*, well edited by David Mearns, throws new light on the great enigmatic figure. The same nine biographies of Abraham Lincoln listed as sources in *Jefferson Davis: American Patriot* have been frequently consulted. The most scholarly and most eminently judicial still seems to be the four-volume work of J. G. Randall, the last volume having been finished, after Professor Randall's death, by Richard N. Current. But I have studied the one-volume edition of Sandburg's extolling *Abraham Lincoln: The Prairie Years* and *The War Years* and Benjamin P. Thomas's *Lincoln* as contra Edgar Lee Masters's condemnatory *Lincoln, the Man*. Kenneth P. Williams's *Lincoln Finds a General* and T. Harry Williams's *Lincoln and His Generals* give special information on Union military affairs. The liveliest account of Washington in wartime is Margaret Leech's *Reveille in Washington*.

Shelby Foote's extremely well-written first volume of *The Civil War*, a projected three-volume narrative history, is of outstanding importance. Alexander H. Stephens's *A Constitutional View of the Late War Between the States* remains essential reading. Douglas Southall Freeman's three-volume *Lee's Lieutenants* is as valuable as his *R. E. Lee*.

Among the best books on the Southern struggle is Robert Self Henry's concise one-volume *The Story of the Confederacy*, which may be read profitably in connection with Jefferson Davis's *A Short History of the Confederate States*. For a rapid survey of historical events with thumbnail biographies of the leading actors in the drama, I recommend heartily Volume II, *The Civil War: The Picture Chronicle* by Ralph Newman and E. B. Long, a most fair and telling summary, with an introduction by Allan Nevins. *Facts the Historians Leave Out, A Youth's Confederate Primer* by John S. Tilley should be required for high-school and college students. Tilley's scrupulously documented *Lincoln Takes Command* is an excellent source for the beginning of the war.

A beautifully written book on the Northern side of the conflict is *This Hallowed Ground*, by Bruce Catton, whose three former works on the Army of the Potomac ending with *A Stillness at Appomattox* should also be essential reading.

Among the works of special merit dealing with particular theaters of the war are Stanley F. Horn's *The Army of Tennessee*, Earl Schenck Miers's *The Web of Victory: Grant at Vicksburg*, Franklin Haskell's *The Battle of Gettysburg*, Jay Monahan's *Civil War on the Western Border*.

Otto Eisenschiml's *Why the Civil War?* and W. A. Swanberg's *First Blood*, which deal with the inception of the war and the events dramatized at Fort Sumter, were published after the first half of *Jefferson Davis: Confederate President* had been finished and sent to the publishers. Though I cannot claim them as sources, I have now read them and recommend both.

A miscellany of other works I have profitably consulted includes: *The Correspondence of Robert Toombs, Alexander H. Stephens and Howell Cobb*, edited by Ulrich Phillips; Gustavus Vasa Fox's *Confidential Correspondence*; Allan Nevins's *The Statesmanship of the Civil War*; *Divided We Fought, a Pictorial History*, edited by Donald David and associates; Clement Eaton's *A History of the Southern Confederacy*; W. E. Woodward's *A New American History*; Clifford Dowdey's *The Land They Fought For*; Edward A. Pollard's *The Lost Cause*; Frederick Law Olmstead's *The Cotton Kingdom* (new edition, 1933), edited by Arthur M. Schlesinger; Frank Owsley's *State Rights in the Confederacy*; *The Diary of a Public Man*, anonymous; *Mystery of "A Public Man"* by Frank Maloy Anderson; Samuel W. Crawford's *The Genesis of the Civil War*; Avery Craven's *The Coming of the Civil War*; Charles W. Ramsdell's *Behind the Lines in the Southern Confederacy*; *The Living Lincoln*, edited by Paul M. Angle and Earl Schenck Miers; John Bigelow's *Recollections*; *Soldier of the South: General Pickett's War Letters to His Wife*, edited by Arthur Crew Inman.

Among other biographies which furnished me with material are *Charles Francis Adams* by Charles Francis Adams, Jr., *Life of William H. Seward* by Frederic Bancroft, *Franklin Pierce* by Roy Franklin Nichols, *General Edmund Kirby Smith* by Joseph Howard Parks, *Braxton Bragg* by Don C. Seitz, *Pemberton, Defender of Vicksburg* by John C. Pemberton III, *"First With the Most" Forrest* by Robert Self Henry, *Stephen R. Mallory* by Joseph T. Durkin, *Joseph E. Brown* by Louise B. Hill, *Salmon Portland Chase* by Albert Bushnell Hart, *The Gallant Pelham* by Philip Mercer, *Lucius Q. C. Lamar* by Wirt A. Cate.

For vivid side-glances on the war and the times, I recommend: Katharine M. Jones's *Heroines of Dixie*, Bell I. Wiley's *The Life of Johnny Reb* and *The Life of Billy Yank*, Harnett Kane's *Spies for the Blue and Gray*, James D. Horan's *Confederate Agent*, Ishbel Ross's *Rebel Rose*, Lee Meriwether's *My Yesteryears*, Elizabeth Meriwether's *Recollections of 92 Years*, and James Robert Maxwell's *Autobiography*. Two well-chosen large anthologies are *The American Iliad* by Otto Eisenschiml and Ralph Newman and *The Blue and Gray* by Henry Steele Commager. A shorter work, *The Confederate Reader* by Richard Harwell, contains fresh material; and Stark Young's *A Southern Treasury of Life and Literature* offers colorful items throwing light on the war years.

The list of monographs and special studies are too numerous to be recorded here, but of special interest must be mentioned William B. Hesseltine's *Civil War Prisons*, Henry Adams's *The Great Secession Winter of 1860-61*, Ella Lonn's *Desertion During the Civil War* and the several valuable studies by the admirable late Charles W. Ramsdell.

I have made use of the *Southern Historical Papers*, the *New-York Historical Society Collections*, *The Mississippi Valley Historical Review* and *The Kentucky Historical Society Papers*.

Newspapers have been of inestimable value in bearing witness to events right after they occurred and also for their editorial comments. Among the most useful have been the Montgomery *Advertiser* and the Montgomery *Daily Mail* for the first four months of the Confederacy. The files of four Richmond papers: *Enquirer, Dispatch, Examiner,* and *Whig,* have furnished material pro and con. Of other Southern papers, the most referred to have been Charleston's *Mercury* and *Daily Courier*; New Orleans' *Picayune* and *Times-Democrat*; Mobile's *Tribune* and *Register.*

Of the Northern papers, the New York *Herald, Tribune, Times, World,* and *Sunday World,* the Chicago *News,* Washington's *Post* and *Chronicle,* and the *National Intelligencer,* have been most frequently consulted. The London *Times* has been of special service.

Periodicals have yielded excellent source material ranging from *Blackwood's Edinburgh Magazine, The London Economist, The Index,* and *The London Illustrated News* to *The Confederate Veteran,* the last a veritable treasure trove of interesting items. Also useful have been *Southern Literary Messenger, De Bow's Review, Belford's Magazine, Century, Atlantic Monthly, North American Review, Harper's New Monthly Magazine* and *Harper's Weekly. The Southern Bivouac, Journal of Southern History, Journal of Mississippi History, Alabama Historical Review,* and *United Daughters of the Confederacy Magazine* have all provided material.

CHAPTER I

Reports and editorials in the New York *Times,* New York *Herald,* London *Times,* London *Economist,* Richmond *Examiner,* Richmond *Enquirer,* Baltimore *Sun,* Charleston *Mercury,* Charleston *Courier*; Montgomery *Daily Mail, Daily Advertiser, Weekly Advertiser,* and *Daily Constitution* for March and April, 1861

Sources of Mr. Lincoln's inauguration are from newspaper reports, the varied accounts by eight of his biographers, *The Diary of a Public Man,* and Margaret Leech's *Reveille in Washington*

Reminiscences of Southern women include Mrs. Roger Pryor's *Reminiscences of Peace and War,* Mrs. D. Giraud Wright's *A Southern Girl in '61,* and Mary Boykin Chesnut's *A Diary from Dixie*

Varina Davis, *Jefferson Davis: A Memoir by His Wife*

John R. Reagan, *Memoirs*

T. C. De Leon, *Four Years in Rebel Capitals*

H. J. Eckenrode, *Jefferson Davis: President of the South*

Rembert Patrick, *Jefferson Davis and His Cabinet*

Rudolph von Abele, *Alexander H. Stephens*

Henry D. Capers, *Memminger*

Frank Owsley, *King Cotton Diplomacy*

Dunbar Rowland, *Jefferson Davis, Constitutionalist,* Vol. V

Jefferson Davis, *The Rise and Fall of the Confederate Government*
Letters and Times of the Tylers
Official Records

CHAPTER II

E. Merton Coulter, *The Confederate States of America*
Lewry Dorman, *The Free Negro in Alabama,* 1819-1861
Clayton (Alabama) *Banner,* April 18, 1861
W. E. Woodward, *A New American History*
National Republican, March 9, 1861
Quarterly Review
Debow's Review
John Tilley, *Lincoln Takes Command*
Alfred Roman, *The Military Operations of General Beauregard*
Henry G. Connor, *John Archibald Campbell*
Thad Holt, Jr., *Justice John A. Campbell,* a monograph
Gideon Welles, *The Diary of Gideon Welles*
David C. Mearns, *The Lincoln Papers,* Vol. II
W. E. Smith, *The Blair Family*
J. G. Randall, *Lincoln, the President*
Carl Sandburg, *Abraham Lincoln, The War Years*
John G. Nicolay and John Hay, *Abraham Lincoln: a History*
Katharine M. Jones, *Heroines of Dixie*
James Ford Rhodes, *A History of the United States,* Vol. III
Pleasant A. Stovall, *Robert Toombs*
Ulrich B. Phillips, *The Life of Robert Toombs*

CHAPTER III

The most important sources are *Official Records;* Jefferson Davis's *Rise and
    Fall*; John Tilley's *Lincoln Takes Command*; the Montgomery, Charles-
    ton, and New York newspapers for April 5 to April 15, 1861
David C. Mearns, *The Lincoln Papers*
Eba Anderson Lawton, *Major Robert Anderson and Fort Sumter*
Avery Craven, *Edmund Ruffin, Southerner*
Montgomery C. Meigs, *Diary,* March-April, 1861
American Historical Review, Vol. XXVI
Kenneth M. Stampp, *And the War Came*
William Howard Russell, *My Diary, North and South*
Martin J. Crawford, letters in *Official Records*
Samuel W. Crawford, *Genesis of the Civil War*

The diary of Mrs. Chesnut and the reminiscences of Mrs. Pryor and Mrs.
  Wright are highly significant.
Rhodes, *History,* Vol. III
Randall, *Lincoln*
Abner Doubleday, *From Moultrie to Sumter*
Horace Greeley, *The American Conflict*
The Diary of a Public Man
Battles and Leaders
The National Intelligencer
Margaret Leech, *Reveille in Washington*
J. G. Randall, *The Civil War and Reconstruction*

CHAPTER IV

Official Records, Army; *Official Records, Navy*; Tilley, Randall, Davis,
  Nicolay and Hay, Sandburg, and Rhodes are basic sources here.
The Diary of Gustavus Vasa Fox
Montgomery C. Meigs, *Diary*
Martin J. Crawford letters, *Official Records*
Gideon Welles, *Diary*
Gideon Welles, *Lincoln and Seward*
E. Merton Coulter, *The Confederate States*
Robert McElroy, *Jefferson Davis, the Real and the Unreal*
Avery Craven, *The Coming of the Civil War*
Samuel W. Crawford, *Genesis of the Civil War*
William Howard Russell, *My Diary, North and South*
The London *Times*
The National Intelligencer, New York *Tribune,* New York *Herald*; the Mont-
  gomery newspapers of the period, and now including the Montgomery
  Evening Mail

CHAPTER V

William H. Russell, *My Diary, North and South*
Captain Robert E. Lee, *Recollections and Letters of General Robert E. Lee*
Rudolph von Abele, *Alexander H. Stephens*
Douglas Southall Freeman, *R. E. Lee*
Edward A. Pollard, *The Lost Cause*
Montgomery newspapers
George Fort Milton, *The Age of Hate*; *Andrew Johnson and the Radicals*
George Francis Robert Henderson, *Stonewall Jackson and the American
  Civil War*
Nicolay and Hay, *Abraham Lincoln*

The Baltimore *Sun,* New York *Tribune*
Official Records
Mrs. Pryor, *Reminiscences*
Rhodes, *History,* Vol. III

CHAPTER VI

Varina Davis, *Memoir*
Eron Rowland, *Varina Howell: Wife of Jefferson Davis*
Manuscript notes of Caroline Phelan Beale taken in 1906 in New York from
    Mrs. Jefferson Davis
Ishbel Ross, *First Lady of the South*
T. C. De Leon, *Four Years in Rebel Capitals*
William H. Russell, *Diary*
Mrs. Chesnut, *Diary*
Montgomery newspapers
Davis, *Rise and Fall*

CHAPTER VII

Frank Owsley, *King Cotton Diplomacy*
James Dunwody Bulloch, *Secret Service of the Confederate States in Europe*
Robert McElroy, *Jefferson Davis, the Real and the Unreal*
De Leon, *Four Years in Rebel Capitals*
Mrs. D. Giraud Wright, *A Southern Girl in '61*
Mrs. Chesnut, *Diary*
John Beauchamp Jones, *A Rebel War Clerk's Diary*
Joseph E. Johnston, *Narrative*
Gilbert E. Govan and James W. Livingood, *A Different Kind of Valor*
Rembert Patrick, *Jefferson Davis and His Cabinet*
Recollections and Letters of General Robert E. Lee
Charleston *Mercury*
Rowland, *Jefferson Davis, Constitutionalist,* Vol. V
Varina Davis to Clement C. Clay, Jr., May 10, 1861, (Duke University)

CHAPTER VIII

William E. Dodd, *Jefferson Davis*
Recollections and Letters of General Robert E. Lee
Rhodes, *History,* Vol. III
Frank Alfriend, *Jefferson Davis*
Raphael Semmes, *Service Afloat*

Unpublished holograph letter of W. T. Sherman, June 7, 1861, to D. H.
  Armstrong in possession of the latter's grandson, Brigadier General
  Donald Armstrong, Washington, D.C.
Joseph E. Johnston, *Narrative*
Frank Vandiver, *Mighty Stonewall*
Catherine Cooper Hopley, *Life in the South*
Mrs. Chesnut, *Diary*
Battles and Leaders
Robert Self Henry, *The Story of the Confederacy*
Frank Owsley, *State Rights in the Confederacy*
Robert McElroy, *Jefferson Davis, The Real and the Unreal*
Katharine M. Jones, *Heroines of Dixie*
Ishbel Ross, *Rebel Rose*
Official Records
James Richardson, *A Compilation of the Messages and Papers of the Con-
  federacy*

CHAPTER IX

John W. Daniel, *Life and Reminiscences of Jefferson Davis*
Journal of Mary Elizabeth (Lise) Mitchell, University of North Carolina
Jubal A. Early, *Autobiographical Sketch*
Unpublished memoirs of Colonel John Haskell
Shelby Foote, *The Civil War*
Lloyd Lewis, *Sherman, Fighting Prophet*
Henry, *The Story of the Confederacy*
Battles and Leaders
Rowland, *Jefferson Davis, Constitutionalist*, Vol. V
Diaries of William H. Russell and Mary Boykin Chesnut
Varina Davis, *Memoir*
Alfred Roman, *Beauregard*
Bradley T. Johnson, *A Memoir of the Life and Service of Joseph E. Johnston*
Joseph E. Johnston, *Narrative*
Official Records
Nicolay and Hay, *Abraham Lincoln*
William T. Sherman, *Memoirs*
New York *Times, Herald* and *Tribune*, July 22, 23, 24, 25, 1861
Richmond newspapers for the same dates

CHAPTER X

Davis, *Rise and Fall*
Thomas Jordan to General Beauregard, April 18, 1878, Confederate Memorial
  Hall, New Orleans

Alfred Roman, *Beauregard*

Joseph E. Johnston, *Narrative*

Charles Francis Adams to William Seward, Mss. State Department Archives

Sherman, *Memoirs*

Russell, *My Diary, North and South*

Joseph Mills Hanson, *Bull Run Remembers*

Bruce Catton, *This Hallowed Ground*

Henry Steele Commager, *The Blue and the Gray*

Battles and Leaders

The London, New York, and Richmond newspaper recountals of the rout

Leech, *Reveille in Washington*

Frank Alfriend, *Jefferson Davis*

Constance Cary Harrison, *Recollections Grave and Gay*

Varina Davis, *Memoir*

McClellan's Own Story

De Leon, *Four Years in Rebel Capitals*

J. G. Randall, *The Civil War and Reconstruction*

Rhodes, *History*, Vol. III

Unpublished letter from W. E. Winn in possession of William Brantley, Birmingham, Alabama

CHAPTER XI

Lise Mitchell, *Journal*

Mrs. Chesnut, *Diary*

Phillips, *Life of Robert Toombs*

Alfriend, *Jefferson Davis*

Caleb Huse to Jefferson Davis, July 19, 1889, Rowland, Vol. X

Hopley, *Life in the South*

Letters in Rowland, *Jefferson Davis, Constitutionalist*, Vol. V, concerning this period are highly significant

Burke Davis, *Gray Fox*

Burton H. Wise, *The Life of Henry A. Wise*

Ella Lonn, *Salt as a Factor in the Confederacy*

Freeman, *R. E. Lee*

Allan Nevins, *Frémont, Pathfinder of the West*

Benjamin P. Thomas, *Abraham Lincoln*

Joseph E. Johnston's *Narrative*

Davis, *Rise and Fall*

Letter of Eliza Davis, August 10, 1861, in possession of Mrs. Mary Lucy O'Kelley, Pass Christian, Mississippi

CHAPTER XII

William Preston Johnston, *The Life of General Albert Sidney Johnston*
Letters in Rowland, Vol. V
Official Records
Varina Davis, *Memoir*
Eugenia Phillips, unpublished *Memoir* in Manuscript Division, Library of Congress
George W. Bagby, *The Old Virginia Gentleman and Other Sketches*
Jefferson Davis to James Lyons, August, 30, 1878, Rowland, Vol. VIII

CHAPTER XIII

Pierce Butler, *Judah P. Benjamin*
Robert Douthat Meade, *Judah P. Benjamin*
Rembert Patrick, *Jefferson Davis and His Cabinet*
John Witherspoon DuBose, *Life and Times of William Yancey*
G. P. Gooch, editor, *The Later Correspondence of Lord John Russell*
C. F. Adams, *Charles Francis Adams*
Henry Adams, *The Education of Henry Adams*
Rudolph von Abele, *Alexander H. Stephens*
H. J. Eckenrode and Bryan Conrad, *George B. McClellan, The Man Who Saved the Union*
Davis, *Rise and Fall*
Jefferson Davis to his wife, October 2, 1861, Confederate Museum, Richmond
Mary Anna Jackson, *Life and Letters of General Thomas S. Jackson*
Jefferson Davis to Beauregard, October 16, 1861, in possession of Charles Dobbins, Washington, D.C.
T. Harry Williams, *P. G. T. Beauregard*

CHAPTER XIV

Bruce Catton, *Mr. Lincoln's Army*
T. Harry Williams, "Investigation 1862" in *American Heritage*, Vol. VI, No. 1
Eckenrode and Conrad, *George B. McClellan*
McClellan's Own Story
Russell, *My Diary, North and South*
Freeman, *R. E. Lee*
Richmond newspapers from September 1 to November 6, 1862
London *Times*, September 19 to October 16, 1862
Davis, *Rise and Fall*

CHAPTER XV

Official Records
Rowland, *Jefferson Davis: Constitutionalist,* Vol. V
Battles and Leaders
E. D. Adams, *Great Britain and the Civil War*
Frederic Bancroft, *The Life of William H. Seward*
Worthington C. Ford, *A Cycle of Adams Letters*
J. B. Moore, *Principles of American Diplomacy*
Abraham Lincoln, *Works,* Vol. II
Varina Davis, *Memoir*
Jones, *Diary*

CHAPTER XVI

Virginia Clay-Clopton, *A Belle of the Fifties*
T. C. De Leon, *Belles, Beaux and Brains of the '60's*
J. G. Randall, *The Civil War and Reconstruction*
Morris Schaff, *Jefferson Davis, His Life and Personality*
Frank Vandiver, *Mighty Stonewall*
G. F. R. Henderson, *Stonewall Jackson*
Robert Self Henry, *The Story of the Confederacy*
U. S. Grant, *Personal Memoirs*
Stanley Horn, *The Army of Tennessee*
Jones, *Diary*

CHAPTER XVII

Aris Sonis Focisque, The Harrisons of Skimino, edited by Fairfax Harrison
Burton Harrison Papers, Library of Congress
Shelby Foote, *The Civil War*
The correspondence of Thomas Reade Rootes Cobb, 1860-1862
De Leon, *Four Years in Rebel Capitals*
Jones, *Diary*
James Lyons to W. T. Walthall, July 31, 1878, Rowland, Vol. VIII
Jefferson Davis to W. M. Brooks, March 13, 1862, Rowland, Vol. V

CHAPTER XVIII

Joseph T. Durkin, *Stephen R. Mallory, Confederate War Chief*
Henry, *The Story of the Confederacy*

Shelby Foote, *The Civil War*
William Conant Church, *Life of John Ericsson*
Catton, *Mr. Lincoln's Army*
Richmond *Examiner*, February, March, and April, 1862
James Dunwody Bulloch, *Secret Service of the Confederate States in Europe*
Johnson, *A Memoir of the Life and Service of Joseph E. Johnston*
Govan and Livingood, *A Different Kind of Valor*
J. E. Johnston, *Narrative*
E. P. Alexander, *Military Memoirs of a Confederate*

CHAPTER XIX

Johnston, *The Life of General Albert Sidney Johnston*
McClellan's Own Story
Eckenrode and Conrad, *George B. McClellan*
Freeman, *R. E. Lee*
J. E. Johnston, *Narrative*
Davis, *Rise and Fall*
Accounts of the battle of Shiloh are voluminous. In *Battles and Leaders,* Vol. I, pp. 465-610 are some vivid articles, which have been considered in connection with the reports in *Official Records*.
Alexander Downing, *Downing's War Diary*
Otto Eisenschiml, *The Story of Shiloh*
Hamilton Basso, *Beauregard: The Great Creole*
Williams, *P. G. T. Beauregard*
Morris Schaff, *Jefferson Davis, His Life and Personality*
Lew Wallace, *An Autobiography*
The Sherman Letters, 1837-1891
Lieutenant L. D. Young, *Reminiscences of a Soldier of the Orphan Brigade*

CHAPTER XX

Davis family letters in Jefferson Hayes-Davis Collection
The accounts of the capture of Forts Jackson and St. Philip and of New Orleans in *Battles and Leaders* present varying viewpoints
Unpublished memoir of Margaret Howell (Mme. de Stöess)
Marietta Minnegerode Andrews, *Memoirs of a Poor Relation*
Catherine Cooper Hopley, *Life in the South*
Letter from Helen M. Keary, May 7, 1862, from the files of Allan Nevins
Jefferson Davis to the Reverend Mr. Frank Stringfellow, June 4, 1878, Manuscript Room, University of Virginia
J. E. Johnston, *Narrative*
McClellan's Own Story

Varina Davis, *Memoir*
Davis, *Rise and Fall*
Jefferson Davis's letters of June and July, 1862, Rowland, Vol. V

CHAPTER XXI

Richmond newspapers, June, 1862
Gamaliel Bradford, essay on Ben Butler in *Damaged Souls*
Benjamin F. Butler, *Autobiography*
James Parton, *General Butler at New Orleans*
London's *Saturday Review*, June 14, 1862
Ishbel Ross, *Rebel Rose*
Varina Davis, *Memoir*
Letters of Joseph E. Davis in Jefferson Hayes-Davis Collection
John W. Thomason, Jr., *J. E. B. Stuart*
Eckenrode and Conrad, *George B. McClellan*
Burke Davis, *Gray Fox*
Josiah Gorgas, *Diary*
Williams, *P. G. T. Beauregard*
Vandiver, *Mighty Stonewall*
Douglas Southall Freeman, *R. E. Lee* and *Lee's Lieutenants*
Jones, *Diary*
Most of the Davis letters quoted herein are in Rowland, Vol. V

CHAPTER XXII

Burton Harrison Papers, Library of Congress
Constance Cary Harrison, *Recollections Grave and Gay*
James Longstreet, *From Manassas to Appomattox*
Davis, *Rise and Fall*
Freeman, *Lee's Lieutenants* and *R. E. Lee*
Robert Stiles, *Four Years with Marse Robert*
William Starr Myers, *General George Brinton McClellan*
McClellan's Own Story
G. F. R. Henderson, *Stonewall Jackson*
Vandiver, *Mighty Stonewall*
John H. Worsham, *One of Jackson's Foot Cavalry*
Richard Taylor, *Destruction and Reconstruction*
Alexander, *Memoirs*
Catton, *Mr. Lincoln's Army*
Letters of Davis to Mrs. Davis in her *Memoir*
Heros von Borcke, *Memoirs of the Confederate War for Independence*
Nicolay and Hay, *Abraham Lincoln*, Vol. V

Gorgas, *Diary*
Alfriend, *Jefferson Davis*

CHAPTER XXIII

Lise Mitchell, *Journal*
Myers, *General George Brinton McClellan*
Allen Tate, *Jefferson Davis*
Varina Davis, *Memoir*
Pope's orders of July 1862, *Official Records*, Series 1, Vol. XII, Part 2
Jones, *Diary*
Rhodes, *History*, Vol. IV
Davis, *Rise and Fall*
Owsley, *King Cotton Diplomacy*
Foote, *The Civil War*
Admiral Raphael Semmes, *Service Afloat*
Freeman, *R. E. Lee*
Burke Davis, *Gray Fox*
Henderson, *Stonewall Jackson*
Letter from Maggie Davis, called Polly, August 28, 1862, in possession of
    Carl Haverlin, President of Broadcast Music, New York
General John Pope's lengthy account of the Second Battle of Bull Run in
    Battles and Leaders, Vol. II, is peculiarly interesting when compared
    with *Jackson's Raid Around Pope* by Major General W. B. Talliaferro,
    CSA, and Longstreet's story, which follow

CHAPTER XXIV

Davis, *Rise and Fall*
Freeman, *R. E. Lee*
George B. McClellan, *From the Peninsula to Antietam,* in *Battles and
    Leaders,* Vol. II
Lee's Dispatches to Jefferson Davis
Heros von Borcke, *Memoirs of the Confederate War for Independence*
McClellan's Own Story
R. H. Chilton to Jefferson Davis, December 7 and 8, 1874, Rowland, Vol. VII
Leighton Parks, *Century Magazine*, Vol. 70, No. 2
J. B. Hood, *Advance and Retreat*
Albert B. Hart, *Salmon Portland Chase*
Carl Sandburg, *Abraham Lincoln*
Lincoln's *Works*
Nicolay and Hay, *Lincoln*
Walter Taylor, *Four Years with General Lee*
Edward L. Pierce, *Memoirs and Letters of Charles Sumner,* Vol. IV

CHAPTER XXV

Joseph Howard Parks, *General Edmund Kirby Smith*
Autobiography of James Robert Maxwell of Tuskaloosa, Alabama
Unpublished collection of war letters of John Y. Kilpatrick in possession of
his son, Dr. Emmet Kilpatrick, Camden, Alabama
Jefferson Davis to T. H. Holmes, October 21, 1862, Rowland, Vol. V
Stanley Horn, *The Army of Tennessee*
Gorgas, *Diary*
Blackwood's Magazine and *The Economist*, October, 1862
Louise B. Hill, *Joseph E. Brown and the Confederacy*
Albert E. Richardson, *The Field, the Dungeon, and the Escape*
Mrs. Chesnut, *Diary*
Unpublished Family Reminiscences of Emma Lyon Bryan, New York Public
Library
Constance Cary Harrison, *Recollections*
Randall, *Lincoln*

CHAPTER XXVI

T. W. Higginson, *Army Life in a Black Regiment*
Recollections and Letters of General Robert E. Lee
Letter from Davis to the Governors, November 26, 1862, Rowland, Vol. V
Edward Younger, editor, *Inside the Confederate Government, the Diary of
Robert Garlick Hill Kean*
J. E. Johnston, *Narrative*
Frank Vandiver, *Rebel Brass*
Letters of Davis to Randolph, Rowland, Vol. V
Reagan, *Memoirs*
Clement Clay Papers, Duke University
Owsley, *King Cotton Diplomacy*
De Leon, *Belles, Beaux and Brains of the '60's*
Randall, *Lincoln*
Herndon's Lincoln, edited by Paul Angle
Davis letters in Jefferson Hayes-Davis Collection
Philip Mercer, *The Gallant Pelham*
Address of Jefferson Davis to Mississippi Legislature, Mississippi State
Archives, Jackson
Earl Schenck Miers, *The Web of Victory*
Lise Mitchell, *Journal*
Eugenia Phillips, unpublished *Memoir* in Manuscript Division, Library of
Congress
Elizabeth Meriwether, *Recollections of 92 Years*

CHAPTER XXVII

New York and Richmond newspapers, January 1 to January 13, 1863
Ben Montgomery to President Davis, January 12, 1863, Alabama State
    Archives, Montgomery
James L. Vallandigham, *A Life of Clement L. Vallandigham*
Mercer, *The Gallant Pelham*
Don C. Seitz, *Braxton Bragg*
Mrs. D. Giraud Wright, *A Southern Girl in '61*
Coulter, *The Confederate States*
Horn, *The Army of Tennessee*
Freeman, *R. E. Lee*

CHAPTER XXVIII

The Memoirs of Colonel John S. Mosby
Virgil Carrington Jones, *Ranger Mosby*
R. G. H. Kean, *Diary*
Jefferson Davis to Mrs. Howell, March 19, Jefferson Hayes-Davis Collection
Elizabeth Coleman, *Priscilla Cooper Tyler*
Mercer, *The Gallant Pelham*
Mrs. Chesnut, *Diary*
John C. Pemberton, III, *Pemberton, Defender of Vicksburg*
Jefferson Davis to William M. Brooks, April 2, 1863, Rowland, Vol. V
President's Proclamation, April 10, Rowland, Vol. V
Manuscript of Emma Lyon Bryan, New York Public Library

CHAPTER XXIX

Burke Davis, *They Called Him Stonewall*
Vandiver, *Mighty Stonewall*
Mary Anna Jackson, *Life and Letters of General Thomas J. Jackson*
Frans C. Bengtsson, "Stonewall Jackson," an essay in *A Walk to Ant Hill*
Mrs. Chesnut, *Diary*
John Esten Cooke, *A Life of Gen. Robert E. Lee*
Freeman, *Lee's Lieutenants*
Jones, *Diary*
Family letters in Jefferson Hayes-Davis Collection
Jefferson Davis to Joseph E. Davis, May 7, 1863, in possession of Mrs.
    Mary Lucy O'Kelley, Pass Christian, Mississippi

CHAPTER XXX

After *Official Records,* Series 1, Vol. XXIV, Rowland, Vol. V, Freeman, *R. E. Lee,* and Davis, *Rise and Fall,* the most important source for this chapter is John Reagan's *Memoirs*

Constance Cary Harrison, *Recollections*

Eckenrode, *Jefferson Davis*

Lieutenant Colonel Arthur James Lyon Fremantle, *Three Months in the Southern States, April-June, 1863*

CHAPTER XXXI

John Reagan, *Memoirs*

Randall, *The Civil War* (orders suspending Chicago *Times,* and the Vallandigham case)

Fremantle, *Three Months in the Southern States*

Reminiscences of Mary Elizabeth Stamps and Captain Isaac Davis Stamps by Anna Farrar Goldsborough, their granddaughter, in letters and conversations with the author

Family letters in Jefferson Hayes-Davis Collection

John Fiske, *The Mississippi Valley in the Civil War*

Earl Schenck Miers, *The Web of Victory*

Edward W. Gregory, *Vicksburg During the Siege in Annals of the War*

S. H. Lockett, *Century War Book*

Mrs. James M. Loughborough, *My Cave Life in Vicksburg*

Osborn H. Oldroyd, *A Soldier's Story of the Siege of Vicksburg*

Southern Historical Society Papers, Vol. XI

Johnston, *Narrative*

Gorgas, *Diary*

Grant, *Personal Memoirs*

John C. Pemberton, III, *Pemberton, Defender of Vicksburg*

Articles on the siege of Vicksburg in *Battles and Leaders* are particularly vivid

CHAPTER XXXII

Official Records; Battles and Leaders; Freeman, *R. E. Lee;* and Davis, *Rise and Fall* are the basic sources used

Varina Davis, *Memoir*

Jones, *Diary*

Longstreet, *From Manassas to Appomattox*

Jubal Early, *Autobiographical Sketch*

Justus Scheibert, *Seven Months in the Rebel States During the North American War, 1863*

Fremantle, *Three Months in the Southern States*

Von Abele, *Alexander H. Stephens*

Soldier of the South: General Pickett's War Letters to His Wife, edited by Arthur Crew Inman

Franklin Aretas Haskell, *The Battle of Gettysburg*

John Haskell, unpublished *Memoirs*

Colonel George Meade, *The Life and Letters of General Gordon Meade*

James Madison Page, *The True Story of Andersonville*

CHAPTER XXXIII

The same sources as used for the Vicksburg campaign in Chapter XXXI

Mrs. Pryor, *Reminiscences*

Reminiscences about Mary Stamps given to the author by Anna Farrar Goldsborough

Lise Mitchell, *Journal*

History of the 53rd Regiment Ohio Volunteers Infantry

Freeman, *R. E. Lee*

John Imboden's story of the retreat from Gettysburg and the crossing of the Potomac in *Battles and Leaders*, Vol. III

Walter H. Taylor, *Four Years with General Lee*

Fremantle, *Three Months in the Southern States*

Von Abele, *Alexander H. Stephens*

Morris Schaff, *Jefferson Davis, His Life and Personality*

Nicolay and Hay, *Abraham Lincoln*

Randall, *Lincoln*

CHAPTER XXXIV

Letters of Mary Stamps in possession of Mrs. Stamps Farrar, New Orleans

Nicolay and Hay, *Abraham Lincoln*

Randall, *Lincoln*

Rhodes, *History*, Vol. IV

Richard Taylor, *Destruction and Reconstruction*

John Haskell, unpublished *Memoirs*

Landon Knight, *The Real Jefferson Davis*

Jefferson Davis to Senator R. W. Johnston, July 14, 1863 and to the governors and general officers the same day, Rowland, Vol. V

Schaff, *Jefferson Davis, His Life and Personality*

Fremantle, *Three Months in the Southern States*

New York newspapers for July 14 to July 25, 1863

Scheibert, *Seven Months in the Rebel States*
Jefferson Davis to Mrs. William Yancey, December 16, 1863, Rowland, Vol. VI

CHAPTER XXXV

Letter of Dr. D. W. Yandell to Dr. John M. Johnson, June 17, 1863, Rowland, Vol. VI
Letters of Lee to Davis, August 8, 1863 and Davis to Lee, August 11, 1863, Rowland, Vol. V
Herschel V. Johnson to Jefferson Davis, August, 1863, Duke University
Letter of Mary Stamps to Jefferson Davis from Fincastle in the collection of the Stamps Farrar family, New Orleans

CHAPTER XXXVI

Coulter, *The Confederate States*
Owsley, *King Cotton Diplomacy*
Patrick, *Jefferson Davis and His Cabinet*
Howell Hines to Jefferson Davis, October 11, 1863, Rowland, Vol. VI
Horn, *The Army of Tennessee*
Reminiscences of A. R. Lawton in *Life and Reminiscences of Jefferson Davis,* edited by John W. Daniel
Henry, *The Story of the Confederacy*
Henry, *"First with the Most" Forrest*
John A. Wyeth, *Life of General Nathan Bedford Forrest*
Seitz, *Braxton Bragg*
Arndt M. Sickles, *Simon Bolivar Buckner, Borderland Knight*
A. S. Abrams, *President Davis and His Administration*
Grant, *Personal Memoirs*
President's address to Bragg's soldiers, October 14, 1863, Rowland, Vol VI

CHAPTER XXXVII

New York *Tribune,* October 3, 1863
Mobile *Daily Tribune,* October 25, 1863
Rhodes, *History,* Vol. IV
Randall, *Lincoln*
Letter of Varina Davis to her husband in Jefferson Hayes-Davis Collection
Lise Mitchell, *Journal*
Telegrams sent from Meridian, October 23, 1863, are in Rowland, Vol. V, as well as in *Official Records*

Ebb Tide, As Seen Through the Diary of Josephine Clay Habersham, 1863, edited by Spencer B. King Jr., 1958, University of Georgia Press

Williams, *P. G. T. Beauregard*

Charleston *Daily Courier,* November 2, 3, 4, 1863

Roman, *Beauregard*

Mrs. Chesnut, *Diary*

Horn, *The Army of Tennessee*

Bulloch, *Secret Service*

There are several vivid accounts of the battles of Chickamauga and Missionary Ridge in *The Confederate Veteran,* besides those in *Battles and Leaders*

Sherman, *Memoirs* and Grant, *Personal Memoirs*

The account of President Davis's visit to Charleston and his speech of November 2, as reported in the Charleston *Daily Courier,* November 3, 1863, is reproduced in Rowland, Vol. VI, pp. 73-78.

General Beauregard's note of October 31, 1863, declining to dine with the President, is in the National Archives (War Department Collection of Confederate Records)

CHAPTER XXXVIII

Rhodes, *History,* Vol. IV

John Bigelow, *Retrospections,* Vol. I

Economist, June 25, 1864

Owsley, *King Cotton Diplomacy*

Coulter, *The Confederate States*

Mrs. Chesnut, *Diary*

Davis, *Rise and Fall*

President's Message to Congress, December 8, 1863, Rowland, Vol. VI

CHAPTER XXXIX

Marietta Minnegerode Andrews, *Memoirs of a Poor Relation*

Varina Davis, *Memoir*

Mrs. Chesnut, *Diary*

Gorgas, *Diary*

Jones, *Diary*

Official Records

James M. Matthews, editor, *Public Laws of the Confederate States of America . . . Third Session of the First Congress, 1863, and Fourth Session of the First Congress,* 1863-64

Welles, *Diary*

Atlantic Monthly, October, 1863

Landon Knight, *The Real Jefferson Davis*

INDEX